THE PAINE WEBBER HANDBOOK OF STOCK AND BOND ANALYSIS

THE PAINE WEBBER HANDBOOK OF STOCK AND BOND ANALYSIS

KIRIL SOKOLOFF
EDITOR IN CHIEF

McGRAW-HILL BOOK COMPANY

NEW YORK   ST. LOUIS   SAN FRANCISCO   AUCKLAND   BOGOTÁ   DÜSSELDORF
JOHANNESBURG   LONDON   MADRID   MEXICO   MONTREAL   NEW DELHI   PANAMA
PARIS   SÃO PAULO   SINGAPORE   SYDNEY   TOKYO   TORONTO

Library of Congress Cataloging in Publication Data

Main entry under title:

The Paine Webber handbook of stock and bond analysis.
    Includes index.
    1. Stocks—United States.   2.   Bonds—United
States.   3.   Investment analysis.   4.   United States
—Industries.   I.   Sokoloff, Kiril.   II.   Paine
Webber Inc.
HG4921.P3   332.6'7   79-11401
ISBN 0-07-059576-3

 234567890   DODO   786543210

The editors for this book were W. Hodson Mogan and Joan Zseleczky, the designer was
Scott Chelius, and the production supervisor was Sally Fliess. It was set in Melior by
University Graphics, Inc.

Printed and bound by R. R. Donnelley & Sons Company.

TO CHARLES L. GRIMES

CONTENTS

PART ONE / EQUITY ANALYSIS

Contents

PART TWO: / FIXED-INCOME ANALYSIS

Contents

BOARD OF EDITORIAL ADVISORS AND CONTRIBUTORS

KIRIL SOKOLOFF *Editor in Chief*

Equity and fixed-income research analysts of Paine, Webber, Jackson & Curtis Incorporated and Paine Webber Mitchell Hutchins Inc. are as follows:

EQUITY ANALYSTS

MARGO N. ALEXANDER, *Vice-President*
CHARLES A. BENORE, *First Vice-President*
ROBERT G. BRUCE, *Vice-President*
PETER E. BUTLER, *First Vice-President*
NED W. DAVIS, *Vice-President*
LOUIS J. GANZ, *Vice-President*
SANFORD J. GARRETT, *Vice-President*
J. PETER GASKINS, *Vice-President*
RONALD A. GLANTZ, *First Vice-President*
LEE S. ISGUR, *Vice-President*
MICHAEL J. JOHNSTON, *President*
EDWARD A. JONES, *First Vice-President*
CHARLES M. KELSO, JR., *Vice-President*
BERT S. KRAMER, *Assistant Vice-President*
JOSEPH E. LAIRD, JR., *Vice-President*
BRUCE E. LAZIER, *Vice-President*
HAROLD M. LEVINE, *Vice-President**
ELI S. LUSTGARTEN, *Vice-President*
DAVID H. MacCALLUM, *Vice-President*
THOMAS H. MACK, *Vice-President*
WILLIAM P. MALONEY, *Vice-President*
RONALD I. MANDLE, *Vice-President*
PETER F. MARCUS, *First Vice-President*
J. KENDRICK NOBLE, JR., *Vice-President*
BRADFORD L. PEERY, *Vice-President*
JOHN V. PINCAVAGE, *Vice-President*

*Effective February 1, 1979, joined Merrill Lynch.

PREFACE

It is better to know some of the questions than all of the answers.
JAMES THURBER

If you aren't confused, it's because you haven't studied all the facts.
ANTHONY GAUBIS

There are few who would disagree that being able to ask the right questions is the key to investment success. Too often, investors are victims of "a little knowledge," a situation which could easily be avoided if further background information or a checklist of questions to ask were available. The goal of this book is to provide that information.

National surveys of institutional investors have repeatedly placed the equity analysts of Paine Webber Mitchell Hutchins at the top of the equity analyst fraternity. For instance, a poll conducted among hundreds of institutional investors in 1978 by *Financial World* found Paine Webber to be first in terms of research. (Paine Webber also placed first in a similar poll taken in 1977.) *Institutional Investor Magazine* also took a poll of institutional money managers in 1978, as it has done for the last seven years. Some of the conclusions are summarized below:

- Only four analysts have led their groups for seven years in succession, and three of them were from Paine Webber (Ronald A. Glantz, autos; J. Kendrick Noble, Jr., book and magazine publishing; and Charles A. Benore, utilities)
- Beverages—C. James Walker was one of five runners-up
- Broadcasting—Ellen Berland Sachar was one of four runners-up
- Chemicals—Peter E. Butler was one of five runners-up
- Containers—H. Edward Schollmeyer placed first
- Cosmetics—Edward A. Jones was one of five runners-up
- Drugs—J. Peter Gaskins was one of five runners-up
- Electrical Equipment—Robert T. Cornell was first, as he has been since the category was added to the poll in 1974

- Electronics—Thomas H. Mack was one of five runners-up
- Food—Roger W. Spencer shared a three-way tie for third place
- Hospital Supply—Robert G. Bruce was third
- Household Products—Edward A. Jones was one of two runners-up
- Leisure Time—Lee S. Isgur was first
- Machinery—Eli S. Lustgarten was one of seven runners-up
- Oil Services & Equipment—John B. Walker was third
- Paper & Forest Products—Lawrence A. Ross tied for third place
- Photography—William A. Relyea placed second
- Railroads—John V. Pincavage was one of four runners-up
- Retailing—Stuart M. Robbins placed third
- Steel—Peter F. Marcus was second

Paine Webber also has one of the largest fixed-income research staffs of any brokerage firm in the country. Now that we have seen so many downgradings of previously sacrosanct bond issues and concern is growing about high levels of world wide indebtedness, fixed-income credit analysis is becoming more and more important to investor survival.

The combination of stock and bond analytical strength made Paine Webber the obvious choice for the assistance needed in putting this book together. For an idea of the resources and experience made available to you in this book, consider the following statistics concerning Paine Webber:

- The firm spends some $8 million a year on its research effort
- The 52 equity and fixed-income analysts of the firm have close to 600 years of experience in the investment business, most of it in specialized areas
- These 52 analysts have a combined total of 69 advanced or undergraduate degrees in finance or in their own specialties

Kiril Sokoloff

HOW TO USE THIS BOOK

This book should not be read from cover to cover; it is meant as a reference text only. When the time comes for you to consider any type of new security investment, be it fixed-income or equity, this book should prove useful to you.

The first step is to turn to the Contents or the Index and look for the category of investment which you are considering. As you can see, we have made the listing in the Index particularly detailed to provide you with quick access to the specific piece of information you require.

This book should be helpful to investors on all levels of experience. Some data contained herein may not be relevant to the layperson, but a vast amount will be. Such categories as Key to Analyzing the Industry, Most Common Investor Mistakes, When to Buy/Sell the Stocks, Unique Aspects of the Industry, Some Investment Considerations, and Questions to Ask Yourself before You Make an Investment are relevant to all investors, *particularly those who have only a cursory knowledge of the field*. We have also provided in-depth background for those who wish additional information.

The main purpose of the book is to provide investors with the key questions to ask about an investment. Whether you ask the questions of your broker, your investment advisor, or yourself, the answers will help you get to the core of the suitability of the investment. How many times have you looked back on an investment loss and said: "If only I'd known . . . !"

You may not be able to get all the answers to the questions presented herein; time or inaccessibility of information may prevent full satisfaction. But, in a way, knowing what questions to ask is a form of risk disclosure. If you go into an investment with your eyes open, with a full awareness of the risks, with an understanding of the basics, and with a knowledge of when to cut your losses, you will be way ahead of the game.

THE PAINE WEBBER HANDBOOK OF STOCK AND BOND ANALYSIS

PART ONE

EQUITY ANALYSIS

CHAPTER 1

THE AIRLINE INDUSTRY

John V. Pincavage

KEY TO ANALYZING THE INDUSTRY

Being able to correctly forecast airline traffic growth, which depends heavily on consumer spending, and therefore consumer psychology.

MOST COMMON INVESTOR MISTAKES

1. Failing to realize how volatile this group is.
2. Incorrectly judging the swings in this group.

SOME GENERAL POINTS TO REMEMBER ABOUT THE INDUSTRY

1. In evaluating traffic, one must differentiate between freight and people. A package doesn't go on vacation, it doesn't lose a job, and it doesn't worry about inflation. Consumers do worry about the outlook for the economy, and therefore consumer psychology is a key factor in evaluating trends for traffic growth.
2. Three critical factors determine airline profitability: (a) business travel, which is dependent on the economic outlook (corporate

profits may be used as a proxy); (b) government spending, especially the trend of spending on defense contracts and research and development; (c) the desire for pleasure travel, which depends on discretionary spending, which is a function of disposable income, which is dependent on inflation and the general economic health.

3. The degree of elasticity for airline prices is a matter of some debate. During 1975, airlines lowered prices, but volume did not expand significantly. However, the discount fares initiated in 1977 and 1978 attracted considerable new traffic.

4. The new market for this industry with some exciting potential is persons earning under $15,000 a year, who represent 65 percent of the population in the United States.

5. Weather can have a big effect on the outlook for airline companies. A very cold winter can increase the desire of consumers to fly to warmer climates, and a good snow season can increase interest in a skiing vacation out West. In fact, anything that motivates a person to do something can be a factor for this industry.

6. A year with very heavy auto sales will probably not be a good year for airline traffic.

7. With adequate traffic, nearly any airline can make money; without it, no airline can make money.

8. On the cost side of the equation, labor and fuel are the two most important factors. Labor accounts for 45 to 50 percent, and fuel for about 25 percent, of total costs. Thus, the two of these factors account for up to 75 percent of total expenses. The remaining expenses are accounted for in large part by travel agent commissions, depreciation, and landing fees. Therefore the trends in labor and fuel expenses are critical variables for this industry.

9. It's important for you to know where the airlines are in their equipment cycles. A company with a lot of older airplanes generally will have higher earnings because depreciation will be less. On the other hand, the airplanes may be inefficient and small and require more maintenance than a modern, up-to-date fleet. Of course, the newer fleet would have a greater depreciation, which would result in a drain on earnings. The typical pattern is that when airlines make money they add more planes, thus reducing industry profitability.

10. This industry is characterized by high financial and operating

leverage. After the break-even point is reached, 75 to 80 percent of revenues flow to operating income. Thus, two or three persons can make a difference between a profitable flight and an unprofitable one.

11. The airline industry is probably the most leveraged group in the entire stock market. It has very high operating leverage, as we explained above, combined with financial leverage. The airline industry is a very debt-heavy industry. Financial leverage accentuates the swings even more.

12. A key long-term factor to consider is the changing role of government regulation of the industry. For one thing, the distinction between charter and scheduled flights is breaking down. The government is encouraging price competition rather than service competition. To put it succinctly, the Civil Aeronautics Board, which regulates the industry, is at present in favor of competition.

   Even though the Civil Aeronautics Board has said that it thinks that a 12 percent return on investment is adequate for the industry, such a return has happened only once in the last 15 years.

   Because of the increased competition, there could be a shakeout in the industry in the years ahead, and although that would be bad on an intermediate-term basis, it could be very positive on a longer-term basis.

SOME INVESTMENT CONSIDERATIONS

1. This is a very volatile, highly speculative industry and is not the place for anyone who cannot afford to take a significant risk.

2. The most common mistake investors make in the industry is misjudging the swings. When the group looks ready to move, be sure that you consider these stocks only as short-term trade. When the rate of gain in traffic starts to slow or the industry begins to spend heavily for new equipment, you should sell these stocks.

3. Investors should determine which airlines offer the best long-term potential by analyzing (a) current competitive position relative to the industry and to direct competitors; (b) financial strength, using debt/equity ratio and cash flow; (c) equipment status, by looking at replacement and expansion needs; (d) the

impact of regulatory reform; and (e) the potential for market share gains.

4. Airline stock prices have tended to peak well in advance of earnings peaks. The airlines as a group have tended to reach a top in advance of market tops and have generally bottomed a bit after the market.

5. The airline industry's capital formation problems and the specter of regulatory reform have received much attention. However, investors may be overlooking the fact that some airlines stand to benefit from the industry's problems.

In fact, certain airlines should be able to show faster earnings growth because they are in extremely favorable positions to gain market share. They are in this position because in general they have historically been among the most profitable airlines and possess superior financial strength. This in turn has allowed continued investment in new aircraft, resulting in substantially lower average fleet ages and relatively minor replacement problems.

In the new, more competitive environment, it will be critical for an airline to control feed traffic into major hubs. The most competitive and thus the potentially less profitable routes should tend to be those between major cities or areas which have the highest density of passengers. There should be less competition between secondary areas and either major areas or other secondary areas, and thus higher prices and profits can be earned. So an airline which controls feed traffic can compete on the major routes and make money on the minor ones. Delta Airlines' use of Atlanta is a perfect example of this strategy.

Thus, such airlines will be able to turn their attention to meeting the needs of the expanding market and, because they have the ability to add new capacity faster than financially weaker competitors, should show substantial share gains. Regulatory reform should hasten market share gains, because such airlines have the ability to add capacity to expand into new markets and withstand extended price cutting longer than competition because of their higher margins and financial strength.

QUESTIONS TO ASK YOURSELF BEFORE MAKING AN INVESTMENT IN THE AIRLINE INDUSTRY

1. What is the outlook for inflation, discretionary income, and the economy?
2. What is happening to airline traffic?
3. What is happening to airline yields (airline ticket prices multiplied by traffic; revenue per passenger mile)?
4. What's happening on the cost side of the equation, particularly in terms of fuel price, labor? What is the trend in labor costs?
5. Where is the airline in the equipment cycle?
6. What is the financial position of the individual company you're interested in? (In a period when you are extremely optimistic about the industry, go with the most leveraged airlines, such as Pan Am and TWA. If you are only reasonably optimistic, or uncertain, stick with the more financially strong airlines, such as Delta and Northwest Airlines.)

CHAPTER 2

THE AUTOMOBILE INDUSTRY

Ronald A. Glantz

KEY TO ANALYZING THE INDUSTRY

Being able to accurately identify the current phase of the automobile sales cycle.

MOST COMMON INVESTOR MISTAKES

1. Not getting out early enough because you believe in the optimism of the industry leaders. (The down year, when it comes, is generally worse than expected.)
2. Not getting into the stocks early enough because of economic pessimism, deterioration in the industry's financial ratios, or a cut in dividends. (Earnings, dividends, and financial ratios improve very quickly during an up sales year.)

THE FACTORS WHICH AFFECT AUTOMOBILE AND TRUCK SALES

1. The outlook for the economy, especially the level and direction of real consumer disposable income.

2. Consumer confidence. Most vehicles must be paid off over the following 4-year period.
3. Availability of credit. Sixty percent of all cars are purchased on time and another 12 percent are leased.
4. The current and forecast price and availability of gasoline.
5. The rate of inflation, especially for food. This is a factor because a car purchase is basically postponable. The savings rate frequently increases in the United States when the rate of inflation increases, and the additional savings often come out of automobile-buying funds.
6. The level of new-car prices. This is usually unimportant, but buyers occasionally will buy in anticipation of higher prices, so that sales are "borrowed" from subsequent months.
7. New models and new features, both of which can help sales.
8. Styling used to be important, but recently has proven to be a negative influence, judging by the reception of American Motors' Pacer and the 1978 General Motors four-door intermediate cars. (For a detailed discussion on the automobile of the future, please turn to Appendix I, "Changes in the Automobile over the Next Decade.")
9. The stage of the cycle. Sales tend to peak every 4 years because of the 4-year trade-in cycle. Thus, sales peaked in 1965, 1969, and 1973. This cycle may be changing to 5 years, since consumers are keeping cars longer.
10. Manufacturing capacity can occasionally limit sales. This could happen because of a certain-size engine or a certain style (such as the 1977 Thunderbird or 1978 Chevette) which can't be produced at a high enough rate to satisfy demand.
11. The market penetration of imports, of course, has a major influence on Detroit's sales. The high degree of import share is basically a function of several factors. They are:

   a. Competitive models. Our small cars are old and few in number, while there are more than 100 small-sized imports.
   b. Unique features. For example: convertibles, which are produced only by foreign manufacturers; diesels; Wankel engines; and unusual handling or styling.
   c. Relative price.
   d. Image of durability.

Once imports have taken over 10 percent of the total market, price becomes the key factor in getting additional market penetration. (Five percent of the market will go to imports no matter what; another 5 percent will go to them for styling or unique features.)

THE FACTORS WHICH DETERMINE DETROIT'S PROFITS

1. Sales.
2. Market share.
3. Pricing, which in turn is influenced by import sales and by occasional government pressure in the form of jawboning or price controls.
4. Product mix. Large cars are more profitable than small cars; options are more profitable than the basic car; appearance options are more profitable than functional options.
5. Interest rates. Captive finance companies can be quite profitable when interest rates are low.
6. Costs, especially labor, indirect expenses (in the form of pension and medical benefits); and the price of steel. Note that costs typically increase the most during the first year of labor contracts, as contracts are usually front-end–loaded.
7. Productivity, which is generally the lowest in the first year of a model introduction.

Of the above factors, sales volume is the most important. The industry generally breaks even on the first shift, which covers overhead. While productivity is less on overtime or the second shift, net profits are greater, since overhead has already been paid for.

After volume, import share is second-most important: the last car sold is incrementally four times as profitable as the average car, and that incremental car may be competing with an import when import share is increasing. Also, when import share is increasing, Detroit must hold down prices or offer rebates on all competitive cars, not just the incremental units.

UNIQUE ASPECTS OF THIS INDUSTRY

1. Cars are a postponable purchase, and therefore the industry is more volatile than most.

2. Frequent inventory corrections mean that factory sales are more volatile than retail sales.

3. The industry is politically sensitive. Government can help or hurt sales through taxation policies (consumer, excise), import restrictions, legislation (safety, pollution, warranty), and general propaganda (profits too high, mileage too low, energy shortage, etc.).

4. International events can be important. The oil embargo, for example, hurt sales. Foreign countries can dump autos here. Wars can hurt sales (for example, following the wars in the Middle East, many private citizens made relief contributions to Israel and thus had less money for buying cars), but the ending of wars can help sales (soldiers typically buy a car within a few months of returning from the front).

5. Legislation can cause anticipatory buying (for example, to beat higher prices of catalytic converters) or cause a revolt (like that against the interlock on seat belts). In general, legislation raises prices, and the result is a minor negative impact on sales and earnings.

LONG-TERM STRUCTURAL CHANGES

1. At the present time, it is less expensive to manufacture in Japan than in the United States. However, it is cheaper to manufacture in the United States than in Germany. Stronger yen may lead to an improvement in competitive position versus Japan.

2. American Motors Corporation may drop out of the car business.

3. High capital expenditures that are necessary to improve fuel efficiency in order to meet mandated mileage standards may cause Chrysler to drop models, reducing its competitive position.

4. Volkswagen is now manufacturing in the United States. Volvo has an unused plant. Honda is planning to build in the United States. Other foreign manufacturers may open plants in the United States.

5. Russia (which exports the LADA to Canada), Korea, and Brazil may export to the United States.

HOW TO DETERMINE WHERE YOU ARE IN THE SALES CYCLE

1. Follow final sales of cars and trucks as a percentage of final sales of goods. As you can see from Exhibit 2-1, there is a close correlation.

EXHIBIT 2-1

Final Sales of Cars and Trucks as a Percentage of Final Sales of Goods *(Paine Webber Mitchell Hutchins Inc.).*

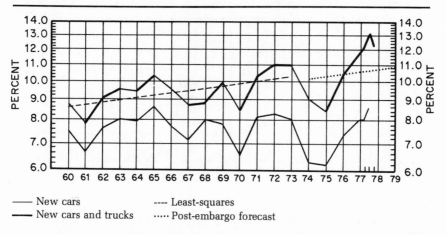

—— New cars   ---- Least-squares
—— New cars and trucks   ····· Post-embargo forecast

2. Follow the directions of used car prices. Generally they lead sales upwards or downwards by 2 to 6 months. (See Exhibit 2-2.)
3. Follow automobile consumer installment debt as a percentage of consumer disposable income. (See Exhibit 2-3.)
4. Observe the different opinions on industry sales outlook. A substantial public disagreement over the following year's sales level is an important indicator. When sales seem to be at bottom, believe the most optimistic sales forecast. When sales look excellent, believe the most pessimistic forecast.

EXHIBIT 2-2

Seasonally Adjusted Trade-in Relative Price Index *(Paine Webber Mitchell Hutchins Inc.).*

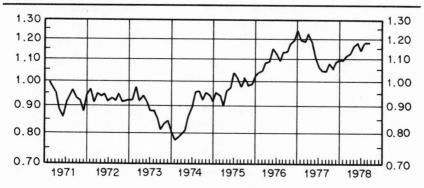

EXHIBIT 2-3
Automobile Consumer Installment Debt Outstanding as a Percentage of Consumer Disposable Income *(Paine Webber Mitchell Hutchins Inc.).*

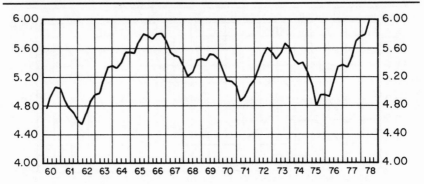

LEADING INDICATORS FOR BUYING OR SELLING THE AUTO STOCKS

1. Auto stocks tend to lead the sales cycle by 1 to 3 years.
2. The prices of the stocks are fundamentally determined by the yield of the stocks, so you must act when you expect interest rates to change.
3. Similarly, yields are a function of dividends, which are a function of earnings, which are a function of sales. So, in the final analysis, you must forecast auto sales and estimate where you are in the sales cycle.

FACTORS WHICH TYPICALLY MOTIVATE AUTO STOCKS

1. For 1 week, sales for 1 quarter, earnings and changes in the dividend; for 6 months or more, anticipation of changes in rate of sales and earnings growth.
2. Occasional outside events, such as devaluation or the oil embargo.
3. Interest rates.

RECENT DEVELOPMENTS WHICH MAY HAVE AFFECTED THE OLD GROUND RULES

1. Deterioration in the value of the dollar is causing higher import prices, which eventually should lead to lower import market

share and remove some of the pressure on industry prices and profit margins.

2. Huge capital expenditures necessary to downsize autos will reduce historic dividend payout ratios (dividends paid as a percentage of earnings) and may affect market share.
3. Energy availability and cost.
4. Government restrictions, such as safety, pollution, and gas mileage legislation.
5. VW's decision to manufacture in the United States.
6. Mandated fuel economy improvements will make cars increasingly similar, with unequal effects on the various manufacturers.

QUESTIONS TO ASK YOURSELF BEFORE MAKING AN INVESTMENT IN THE AUTO INDUSTRY

1. Where are you in the auto sales cycle? What's happening to final sales of cars and trucks as a percent of final sales of goods? Are autos taking an unsustainably large share of the economy? What's happening to used car prices? What's happening to auto installment debt as a percent of consumer disposable income? What are the different opinions on the industry's sales outlook?
2. What is the trend in import penetration? Is it cheaper to manufacture autos in Germany or Japan than in the United States?
3. What's the outlook for interest rates?
4. What's happening to energy prices?
5. What's the trend in dividend payout ratios (dividends paid as a percent of earnings) for the industry? Are the huge capital expenditures being made to downsize autos likely to eat further into the payout ratios?

CHAPTER 3

THE BANKING INDUSTRY

Ronald I. Mandle

KEY TO ANALYZING THE INDUSTRY

1. Knowing the factors affecting asset (loan) growth and the factors affecting the interest rate spread between a bank's cost of funds and its effective loan rate.
2. There appears to be a close relationship between bank stock performance and changes in the demand for commercial and industrial (C&I) loans at certain points in the business cycle. A chart of percentage changes of C&I loans (seasonally adjusted) at annual rates and the absolute and relative price behavior of New York City bank stocks would indicate that the two major bank stock moves in the last 12 years, in 1967 and 1972, have accompanied major cyclical increases in the growth rate of C&I loans. (C&I loans correlate most closely with business spending for inventories and plant and equipment.)

MOST COMMON INVESTOR MISTAKE

Believing that banking is a growth industry which rates a premium valuation to the rest of the stock market.

GENERAL POINTS TO REMEMBER ABOUT THE INDUSTRY

1. Loan demand and the level of interest rates are the key determinants of the outlook for the banking industry.
2. Banks basically do better when interest rates are rising or when interest rates are stable at high levels.
3. The asset quality of banks is important. If a bank has made poor-quality loans, it will suffer even when times are good, and it will really hurt when times are bad.
4. To put it succinctly, the interrelationship between loan demand, interest rates, asset quality, and growth in deposits is what determines bank profitability and thus the performance of bank stocks.
5. A certain portion of the industry is multinational, and since a lot of profits come from overseas, the international outlook is an important factor to evaluate for this portion of the industry. Multinational banking operations do business mainly with large corporations and governments; the funds used to make loans to these entities are generally obtained from the open market, unlike those for domestic operations, which are funded in large part through deposits subject to interest rate ceilings. You will see that relying on market funds can have a significant effect on profitability.
6. There are two types of banks: retail; and wholesale, or "money-center." The retail banks are more consumer-oriented; most of their loans and deposits are, respectively, to and from individuals.
7. Most banks have more assets (i.e., loans) that respond to interest rate changes than liabilities (deposits). Typically, 70 percent of the assets of a money-center bank will be interest rate–sensitive, while 50 to 60 percent of its liabilities may be. The liabilities of retail banks, on the other hand, tend to be less interest rate–sensitive, because they are consumer deposits, which have a ceiling on the amount of interest that can be paid.

   Thus, the reason why rising interest rates may be good for certain kinds of banks is that the banks' assets may respond to rising interest rates while their liabilities or deposits do not.

   Retail banks generally tend to do well in the early stages of a rising interest rate trend. In other words, a bank's loans may be responding to higher interest rates while the cost of deposits stays constant at, say, 5 percent. Thus, as the spread rises between a bank's cost of funds and the amount of interest that it can charge on a loan, so will bank profitability. On the other hand, the effect of disintermediation must be considered. If interest rates rise too much, then personal banking deposits may be siphoned off to higher-yielding money market instruments. If that happens, then the retail bank may be strapped for funds. As a result, the banks will then have to go into the open market and acquire funds either in the form of certificates of deposit, commercial paper, or federal funds, which sometimes cost nearly as much as the interest rate at which the money can be loaned out. Also, the high rate of interest can hurt the customers of banks and force them into delinquency on loan or interest payments and endanger the viability of certain bank loans.

8. Retail banks tend to have more overhead than money-center banks. The reason for this is that most retail banks have a large number of offices and large staffs, both of which are necessary for the personal type of business which is their hallmark. This high overhead means a high volume of business is needed for retail banks to be profitable.

9. The basic factors which affect loan demand are the following: business capital spending, inventory requirements of business, the outlook for housing, consumer confidence, and the level of interest rates.

10. The major factors which affect consumer lending are: auto sales, consumer disposable income, consumer confidence, and housing starts. In estimating the future outlook for consumer loan demand, you should study these factors carefully.

11. This industry is highly regulated, and there exists a great competition among the various regulatory authorities to control the banking industry. Therefore, you must know what is happening on the regulatory front, as it might affect the future profitability of the industry.

12. Deposit growth is essentially related to the growth in the money supply.

13. Bank profitability tends to lag the business cycle. However, you don't want to hold onto a bank stock for too long. That's because quality of assets and loans will become a very important investor concern in an economic downturn; the whole banking industry often comes under some kind of cloud during such periods.

14. As interest rates rise, you sometimes have a lag in the prime rate or in a bank's effective loan rate. Although the cost of funds—federal funds, bank commercial paper, large certificates of deposit, etc.—may be increasing dramatically, the bank prime rate may lag by weeks or even months if political pressures are severe. In such circumstances, the spread between a bank's cost of marginal funds and the yield of its loans can shrink sharply.

15. Another important consideration is that overseas banking has become clouded over. At one point, international banking was viewed as one of the brightest stars in the banking firmament, but now that foreign economic growth has slowed and competition has mounted, this area has lost a lot of its attractiveness.

ANALYZING INDIVIDUAL BANK STOCKS

1. Be sure to learn about the different kinds of loan demand which your bank has—is it consumer-related, mortgage, commercial, or international?

2. When loan demand starts to increase, competition for funds will rise, interest rates will increase, and the cost of funds for banks will rise. Thus, bank profitability depends on the mix of assets and liabilities. Is loan demand taking place in the areas where the bank is strong? Is the bank able to obtain funds at an interest rate which is less than that which it can charge for its loans?

    In analyzing a bank, it is therefore important to prepare a pro forma income statement and a balance sheet set up by type of loan. This will enable you to determine what types of loans are being made and where the funds for those loans are being obtained. As part of your analysis, you'll want to find out what percentage of the bank's loans are tied to the prime rate, and what percentage are term loans, with a fixed rate. (Generally speaking, the more loans that are tied to current interest rates, the better.) You'll also want to know what percentage of the bank's investment portfolio is in liquid assets. (Banks invariably have a large amount of security investments, such as T-bills and U.S. government notes, so if loan demand increases, you'll want to know if the bank can raise additional funds by selling off its investment portfolio.) For these reasons, you should take an ad hoc approach when you analyze banks.

3. Retail banks tend to get hurt more than money-center banks in an economic downturn. That's because the cost of funds of retail banks will remain the same (the 5 percent or so that they pay for time deposits) while the interest rates they get on their loans will fall dramatically as the prime rate declines.

   Of course, the fate of retail banks depends on how well the bank's service area is doing. For example, in the 1974–75 recession, Texas banks didn't experience much of a recession because the Southwest, especially Texas, maintained strong economic growth. However, in the Southeast, banks were hit hard because of overbuilding in the real estate market of that region.

4. In analyzing money-center banks, you should look into the profitability of bond trading. In a period of falling interest rates, banks can make considerable profits on the bond investments which they hold. (As bond interest rates fall, bond prices rise, and these banks can thereby make considerable profits.)

5. Another important thing to study is the maturity of the assets of a bank versus the maturity of its liabilities. Ideally, you'd like the assets to be of a shorter maturity than the liabilities.

6. The basic factor which influences the profitability of money-center banks is commercial loan demand.

7. It's critical to know the amount of foreign loans that a bank has. For example, Citicorp derives slightly more than 80 percent of its earnings from outside the United States. (In fact, Citicorp disclosed in 1977 that it earned more from its banking operations in Brazil than it did in the entire United States.) Overseas lending may not be as attractive in the years ahead as it has been in the recent past, because economic growth overseas has slowed and competition has increased.

8. Loan loss reserves are an increasingly important aspect of analyzing a bank. Prior to 1974, loan loss reserves were based on a 5-year moving average of loan loss experience. But now, this formula has been abandoned. Banks built up loan loss reserves quite substantially from 1974 to 1976.

THE PERFORMANCE OF BANK STOCKS

The stock prices of banks both in New York City and outside of New York City move in a pattern that is at times out of phase with the overall stock market. The market as a whole and bank stocks as a group are typically in phase in absolute performance only in the final stages of a bear market.

For example, both bank groups tended to bottom in price at about the same time as the market in 1966, 1970, and 1974. In the past decade, however, the stocks' peaks have shifted in relation to those of the overall market. That is, in the 1962–66 cycle, bank equities peaked 15 to 16 months before the market top; they peaked approximately with the market in 1968; and they peaked 9 months after it in 1973.

This pattern of relative performance makes sense in terms of bank earnings and investor psychology. That is, in the final stages of a bear market, fear pervades the investment community; nowhere is this fear more focused than in the financial sector in general and banks in particular. This would account for their equities' bottoming with the market. Furthermore, bank stocks generally do quite well in the first few months after the bottom, because investor fears are easing. The next year or so, though, is often difficult for bank stocks and bank earnings; as loan losses begin to rise, loan demand weakens and interest rates fall. This would account for the lagging bottom of the stocks relative to the market in recent cycles. Then, as the fundamentals improve, the equities perform better. The fundamentals usually continue to improve well after the overall market tops as interest rates go on rising and loan demand surges. Thus, the stocks give good relative performance early in the bear market, before the fears that characterize the final stage emerge.

It is apparent that bank stocks achieve their highest multiples in the latter stages of the business cycle—e.g., in 1964–65, 1968–69, and 1973–74. The corresponding business cycles peaked in 1966, 1969, and 1973. In addition, in the first two of these cycles, the low relative multiple was reached more than a year after the overall market bottom.

This lagging behavior by bank equities makes sense because the industry's earnings typically look weakest, compared to total corporate profits, in the early stages of the business cycle, when interest rates are low, loan demand is weak, and industrial earnings are recovering strongly. As the economic rebound progresses, loan demand and short-term interest rates usually rise, causing a better comparison between bank and industrial profit growth.

If total bank credit growth lags behind gross national product increases, and commercial loan growth in particular is very modest, emphasize certain retail banks over the typical money-center organization. The keys to this view would be: (1) the typical retail bank services smaller corporate customers, who have fewer alternative sources of funds than does the average client of a money-center bank and are therefore more likely to borrow from their bank; (2) retail banks usually have a higher proportion of consumer and mortgage loans, expansion of which would probably continue at attractive rates; and (3) a moderate interest rate outlook, which would occur in a slow-growth economy, would enable banks with retail networks to fund the bulk of their asset expansion with consumer demand and savings deposits. This source of funds is typically more stable and lower in cost over the business cycle and is especially attractive when rates are rising.

The reasons why bank stocks are more volatile than they used to be are as follows:

1. The interest rate environment is increasingly volatile.
2. "Cost-free" loans (demand deposits and capital) are declining as a percentage of total assets, and thus banks are more frequently required to rely on purchased funds to fund their loans.
3. There's been a secular increase in leverage for banks.

WHEN TO BUY/SELL BANK STOCKS

You should consider buying a money-center bank stock when you notice that commercial and industrial loans are starting to pick up. There is a very close correlation between rising C&I loans, as they are called, and the performance of money center banks. (However, sometimes C&I loans can be misleading. The tax rate for banks in New York City can be as high as 63 percent, as against the normal corporate tax rate of 48 percent. Thus there's a big incentive for New York City banks to book a loan outside of New York City, thus effectively understating the actual volume of loan demand.)

The time to sell bank stocks is when interest rates have peaked. Interest rates tend to peak slightly ahead of loan demand, and generally several months ahead of a recession. You'll also notice that interest rates generally peak several weeks or months before C&I loans do. Since banks will be less attractive relative to other investments after an economic downturn, it is not wise to hold onto bank stocks during a period of economic weakness. Bank profits coming out of recession are relatively unattractive in relation to other industrial companies.

QUESTIONS TO ASK YOURSELF BEFORE MAKING AN INVESTMENT IN THE BANKING INDUSTRY

1. What's the level of loan demand?
2. Where is loan demand coming from?
3. Is the bank putting its money where its mouth is? In other words, if interest rates are expected to rise, are banks lending short-term and actively trying to acquire long-term deposits?
4. What's the bank's loan loss provision? Is it adequate? Be sure to look at the past experience of the bank and the present composition of its loans. What kind of loan loss experience has the bank had over the past few economic cycles?
5. What percentage of loans are nonperforming? This figure is required to be disclosed by the accountants and can therefore be easily obtained.
6. Has the bank acquired any real estate in lieu of foreclosure? This is a form of nonperforming assets.
7. What are the overhead costs of the bank? (For instance, Morgan Guaranty, with only a few offices, is the envy of most banks.) Compute the level of overhead costs as a percentage of loan costs. (Overhead costs are personnel, equipment, occupancy, and other expenses. You should adjust this figure to reflect a bank's trust department, which is basically a break-even operation.)
8. What is the bank's tax rate? (Many banks invest in municipal bonds, which is good up to a point. However, if by investing in municipal bonds a bank has reduced its effective tax rate to 20 percent, which is about as low as it should prudently go, it will not be able to continue to improve profits through lowering the tax rate. Thus, if you see that a bank has grown very rapidly over a period of time, and you notice that its effective tax rate has dropped sharply, in large part because of the purchase of municipal bonds, you should keep in mind that this trend may not continue. Also, if a bank's profits drop, the municipal bond holdings may be less attractive and the effective return from the municipals may drop from, say, 8 percent to 4 percent. This could affect the bottom line.)
9. Be sure to look at the balance sheet and prepare a pro forma asset and liability sheet to determine where the bank is making its loans and where it is obtaining its funds to make those loans.

After you have done that, you should be able to get an idea of how favorable the spread will be between the cost of funds and the rate at which those funds can be loaned out.

10. What's the spread between a bank's cost of funds and its effective loan rate? If it's currently favorable, what could happen to narrow the spread or make it negative? What is the possibility such an event could occur?

11. What is the amount of the bank's international loans? What is the quality of those loans?

12. Are you aware of the distinction between retail and money-center banks, and do you know what is the best economic climate for each one?

13. What is the likelihood that disintermediation will occur in the banking industry?

14. What is the outlook for loan demand, and for the particular areas which cause it? Business capital spending? Inventory requirements of business? Housing markets? Consumer confidence? The level and direction of interest rates?

15. Have you prepared a pro forma income statement and balance sheet delineating the bank's sources and uses of funds?

16. Are you aware that you shouldn't own bank stocks prior to a recession?

17. If you are interested in a regional bank, what is the long-term economic outlook for that area?

18. What is the outlook for commercial and industrial loans?

19. Are interest rates close to peaking? If so, shouldn't you consider selling your bank stocks?

CHAPTER 4

THE BEVERAGE INDUSTRY

C. James Walker

SOME GENERAL POINTS TO REMEMBER ABOUT THE INDUSTRY

1. Total beverage consumption in the United States probably hasn't changed much in the last 10 years. (Of course, no one knows how much pure water is consumed.) Although the total population has increased, this has been partially offset by air conditioning in the home and in the office, which has lessened thirst and thus consumption of soft drinks and beer.

2. A major factor affecting this industry is demographic trends, such as population growth and the average age of the population. For instance, the younger generation drinks more soft drinks, and therefore it is not surprising that the per capita consumption of soft drinks was increasing during the 1970s.

3. Another key consideration involved in the outlook for the industry is the relative value or price of one drink versus another. In 1978, for instance, beer was a better value relative to other beverages, a fact which helped increase beer demand.

4. Another factor which affects the outlook for the industry is new-product development. For example, low calorie beer has added

significantly to the potential for beer consumption, as it has attracted weight-conscious beer drinkers.

The Brewer Industry

KEY TO ANALYZING THE INDUSTRY

1. Having a good fix on market share trends for all the brewers.
2. Knowing when an increase in market share by one brewer is due to some factor other than price discounting.

MOST COMMON INVESTOR MISTAKES

1. Focusing only on the trends and results for one company. One must look at the entire industry and its market share and profitability trends. For instance, one brewer might do well for several quarterly reporting periods because it discounted prices in its major markets. But it's inevitable that increased competition and industry price cutting will follow, with a concomitant cut in profitability.
2. Paying too much attention to earnings. Basically, earnings don't matter much in predicting stock price movements for this industry. For instance, a brewer could be showing spectacular current earnings because of reduced or flat advertising expenditures. As a result, the brewer might soon lose market share, and today's earnings could turn into tomorrow's losses.

SOME GENERAL POINTS TO REMEMBER ABOUT THE INDUSTRY

1. There are forty-seven brewers nationwide, although the top five have 70 percent of the sales. This is a highly concentrated industry; only four of the top five producers are nationally distributed (Miller, Schlitz, Pabst, and Anheuser-Busch). These top five have been gaining market share at the expense of smaller brewers. Because of the entrance of Philip Morris into the beer business through the purchase of Miller, marketing of beer has become a more important factor than ever before in the industry. The key factor in marketing is image creation; i.e., what kind of person drinks what kind of beer?

2. The international potential for beer is very limited, at best. There is a close allegiance to local beer the world over, and a desire exists in each locality to protect the local brewer.
3. The capital costs of a new brewery are extremely large, and therefore entry into this industry is very difficult.
4. The attrition rate for small brewers has been relatively constant—2½ to 4 million barrels a year have been lost by the small brewers to the majors in recent years. In fact, the major brewers seem to be gaining market share at the expense of each other. This is an important area to watch.
5. Since 1959 there's been an increasing degree of vertical integration in the business. For example, in 1978 Schlitz produced internally some 80 percent of its beer can needs. (Note that regional brewers don't have the capital to build their own can plants and therefore are at a competitive disadvantage.)
6. At the present, the industry is dependent on aluminum prices. Thus, rising aluminum prices are bad for brewers.
7. Another factor to consider is whether Coors will build a plant in the East. If Coors does put up a plant, it could have annual production of as much as 10 million barrels. This is significant, since total industry production is currently 150 million barrels per year.
8. Government's main influence on the industry is via tax. For instance, the federal excise tax on a barrel of beer (31 gallons) is $9. (The federal tax on a hundred-proof gallon of whiskey is $10.50.)
9. Although this industry is recession-resistant, it is not recession-proof. In the recession year of 1975, for example, total beer consumption increased 1.2 percent; in 1977 it was up in excess of 4 percent.
10. The basic growth rate of beer consumption has been around 3½ percent a year.
11. The Federal Trade Commission has been investigating the beer industry since 1972 to determine if price cutting by the majors has hastened industry consolidation. If the FTC were able to make a substantive case, it could be troublesome for the industry.
12. The Schlitz indictment, which alleges that there are kickbacks at bars which push Schlitz beer, could also be a negative for certain brewers.

THE FACTORS WHICH DETERMINE INDUSTRY PROFITABILITY

The profitability of the industry is dependent on volume growth, capacity utilization, the product mix, the labor or productivity per barrel, and the degree of vertical integration. The importance of labor productivity can be seen in the fact that one worker can produce 2500 barrels per year in an old beer plant and 10,000 barrels in a new plant.

HOW TO ANALYZE THE INDUSTRY

The brewer industry should be analyzed on the basis of market share, on a state-by-state basis. For example, Pabst derives over 50 percent of its sales from seven states, while Coors derives 100 percent of its sales from eighteen states and 40 percent from one state. Therefore, a successful analysis of the industry depends on knowledge of what is happening to market share in certain states. (The alcoholic beverage control board in most states will provide market share data for various beers, although this information can be quite expensive. A better alternative is to subscribe to *Beer Marketer's Insights,* 55 Virginia Ave., West Nyack, N.Y. 10994, at a cost of approximately $60 a year.)

THE TIME TO BUY/SELL BREWER STOCKS

The time to sell a brewer stock is when you first see a price cut by a major brewer in a healthy economic environment. After a price cut, the share of market typically increases for the brewer, and in retaliation another brewer will cut prices to regain the market share it lost.

An earlier signal is the trend in market share positions for the big five brewers. If you notice one brewer is suddenly gaining market share in its major markets, you can bet that the competition will fight back, probably by means of a lower price.

Don't forget the importance of the Teamsters' contracts, which come up every 3 years. (Teamsters transport beer, and a highly inflationary wage settlement or a strike could hurt brewer profits.) Typically, 6 months before the contract is negotiated, brewer stocks enter a period of weakness.

The best time to buy a brewer stock is when: (1) you notice that vertical integration is rapidly taking place, with a concomitant reduction in costs and boost in profits; (2) the industry or a particular company is producing or marketing an innovation which you think will be successful; (3) there's an acceleration in total beer consumption.

To summarize, the two major factors which motivate brewer stocks are market share gains that occur without price discounting, and an improvement in industry growth trends.

QUESTIONS TO ASK YOURSELF BEFORE MAKING AN INVESTMENT IN A BREWER STOCK

1. Have you analyzed other brewers in relation to the company that you are interested in?
2. Have you looked at your company in the context of the entire beer industry?
3. Have you analyzed the direction of pricing versus cost?
4. Does your brewer have a wide variety of brands which are doing well?
5. What's the cash flow of the company? Can cash flow more-than-cover the company's dividend?
6. Have you analyzed the record of the company in good and bad times?
7. What are the market share trends for all brewers?
8. Has market share growth of your company been achieved by price discounting? What is the competition likely to do to regain market share? Is a price war in the cards at all?
9. Are you paying too much attention to the brewer's earnings, and not enough to the market share trends?
10. What is the likelihood that Coors will soon announce the building of a new plant in the East?
11. What is happening to vertical integration in the industry? What is your company's position in terms of vertical integration?
12. What is the status of the Schlitz indictment?
13. What is the status of the FTC inquiry into the industry?
14. What are volume growth trends? What's happening to labor productivity per barrel?
15. When is the next teamsters' contract due for renegotiation?

The Soft Drink Industry

KEY TO ANALYZING THE INDUSTRY

1. Being able to correctly assess the outlook for unit volume growth.
2. Being able to predict advertising costs as a percent of sales. These are the largest advertisers in the world; a marked increase or decrease in advertising expenditures can have a big impact on profits.
3. Predicting the price of sugar, which is one of the key ingredients of soft drinks. Eight hundred thirty-eight ounces of soft drinks come from 1 gallon of syrup, which uses 6 pounds of sugar.

MOST COMMON INVESTOR MISTAKE

Paying too high a price for the stocks.

SOME GENERAL POINTS TO REMEMBER ABOUT THE INDUSTRY

1. Think of the soft drink industry as twofold: domestic and foreign. Domestic industry sales can be categorized by drinks sold through food stores, those sold at soda fountains, and those sold through vending machines.
2. Soft drink companies have a low cost of goods, since the bottling of the drinks is done by regional bottlers, which are the ones stuck with the high capital requirements.
3. One of the things that adds to the uncertainty of analyzing this industry is the weather. Unusually hot or cold weather can significantly add to or subtract from final demand.
4. The soft drink industry in the United States is considered a mature industry.
5. The Federal Trade Commission is considering opening up the hitherto restricted domain of local bottlers to national competition. This would be bad for the industry because it might diminish the availability of the product in small, out-of-the-way markets. What's more, the soft drink companies would rather have a large number of local bottlers than three or four big ones that control the market.

HOW TO ANALYZE THE INDUSTRY

In analyzing the future of the soft drink industry, one must evaluate each of the three major markets: food stores, soda fountains, and vending machines. The food store aspect of soft drink sales is relatively mature. The one exception to this is the conversion to 64-ounce bottles from 6½ ounce bottles, which is accelerating. By the same token, it's highly improbable that bottles will get any larger than 64 ounces, so this area is unlikely to show a growth rate faster than that of the general economy.

The fountain area has been the key growth area for this industry in the past. In fact, 3 percent of all Coca-Cola sold in the United States is sold through McDonald's restaurants. But here again, the fast-food industry is slowing down and is, in fact, experiencing a declining growth rate in new outlets.

The vending side of the business is totally unpredictable. It is highly economy-sensitive. Layoffs at plants, for instance, have a major impact on the amount of soft drink consumption at vending machines.

Now that many gas stations have gone out of business, the total number of vending machines in the country has been reduced. However, the hotel/motel market is taking up some of the slack and offers some potential. Basically, however, the soft drink vending machine business should grow on a long term basis at a rate of only ½ percent a year.

In analyzing soft drink companies, ask yourself what the downside potential is for the stock in terms of its dividend yield. In other words, ask yourself how low the stock could go before the dividend yield would slow its decline.

QUESTIONS TO ASK YOURSELF BEFORE MAKING AN INVESTMENT IN A SOFT DRINK STOCK

1. What is happening to the price of sugar?
2. What is happening to total soft drink consumption?
3. What's the recent and 5-year record of earnings for the company you're interested in?
4. What's the international political sentiment towards your soft drink company? Is the company likely to be kicked out of any important markets?

5. What's the outlook for the company's dividends and earnings?
6. What's the outlook for the company's major costs?
7. Are the stocks cheap or expensive in relation to their historical range?
8. What is the outlook for the weather? Is any unseasonably hot or cold weather expected across the United States?
9. What is the possibility that high fructose could become a sugar substitute in soft drinks? (This could lower costs.)
10. Is the FTC nearer to opening up regional competition for bottlers?

The Liquor Industry

SOME GENERAL POINTS TO REMEMBER ABOUT THE INDUSTRY

1. Wine is taking an increasing percentage of the total liquor industry. The only aspect of the hard liquor business that's growing is the so-called white side of the business, which includes vodka and rum.
2. This is a high-risk business, since whiskey must be aged for 4 or 5 years and the producer has no way of knowing what demand will be like 4 or 5 years in the future.
3. The two major long-term trends in the industry are the increasing movement away from brown goods (whiskey, etc.) to white goods, and a switch to lower-proof liquor. This latter move is good for profits.
4. Industry profits are dependent on: (a) unit growth and (b) position in the industry. (For instance, some producers/distillers don't make any profits at all on certain lines.)
5. Be sure that the industry is growing, and not just the company. An increase in market share could be misleading and temporary; a price war could soon develop to regain market share, which would hurt profitability.
6. Earnings motivate liquor stocks.
7. The Schlitz indictment has important implications for the liquor industry, because kickbacks may also have taken place as a means of promoting sales of certain types of liquor.

QUESTIONS TO ASK YOURSELF BEFORE MAKING AN INVESTMENT IN A LIQUOR STOCK

1. What is the value (price/earnings ratio, historical price range, etc.) of the stock in relation to that of the overall stock market?
2. What are the company's brand representations?
3. What is the relative market share of each category of the company's products?
4. What is happening to unit sales growth for the industry and in the area where your company is strongest?
5. Does the Schlitz indictment present any potential problems to your company down the road?

CHAPTER 5

THE BOOK AND MAGAZINE PUBLISHING INDUSTRY

J. Kendrick Noble, Jr.

KEY TO ANALYZING THE INDUSTRY

1. Judging correctly the demographic trends, such as increased high school or college enrollments.
2. Evaluating the future impact of labor (60 percent of total expenses), paper, printing, and postage costs on profits.
3. Being right on the trend of advertising revenues.

MOST COMMON INVESTOR MISTAKES

1. Considering all publishing stocks to be alike. There are great differences in markets served and other factors which prove out over time. Consider track records.
2. Concentrating on earnings or book values alone. As stocks of small companies, publishing stocks may perform well in good markets and badly in bad markets regardless of earnings prospects, and consistently sell for less than book value or much more than book value.

3. Looking to federal government appropriations as the key to book publishers' earnings. What counts are local—and, increasingly, state—expenditures.

THE BEST WAY TO INVEST IN THE INDUSTRY

The publishing industry is highly diversified and is connected to almost every aspect of the economy. In theory, you should be able to shift from one publishing stock to another as the economic cycle favors one area of the economy and then another. The most practical method, however, is to find a particular sector of the economy about which you are optimistic and then find a publishing company which serves that market.

SOME GENERAL POINTS TO REMEMBER ABOUT THE INDUSTRY

1. There are certain major trends which investors must follow closely. For instance, advertising took an unusually large share of the economy in the 1920s, and again in the late 1950s and early 1960s. Then, things went in the other direction in the late 1960s and early 1970s; advertising, as well as textbook sales per capita, turned down considerably. (Needless to say, such events did not help publishing stocks.) As this is written, both these trends seem to be improving again in the late 1970s.
2. After price controls came off in 1974, magazines, then newspapers, and then book publishers became quite aggressive on pricing. This represented a significant change in the way the industry viewed itself; the industry discovered that its products were not quite as price-sensitive as it had originally thought. This could be the beginning of a major, long-term shift in the economics of publishing.
3. Starting in 1973, under price controls, the magazine industry changed some things which had been in effect since the 1940s. Basically, the industry had always tried to limit circulation price increases and, in effect, had subsidized readers in order to increase the readership base for the purpose of attracting more advertisers. But during the period of price controls, the only way the industry could raise prices to offset costs was to increase circulation prices. This strategy worked well, and

within 2 years after price controls were removed, the average magazine price doubled.

4. The continuing increase in postal rates could have a significant effect on the industry over the long term and must, therefore, be watched and monitored closely.

5. The trends in the price of both newsprint and coated papers are very important. In analyzing these trends, you should consider production capacity in both Canada and the United States. Canada provides more than half of United States newsprint needs. Part and parcel of evaluating trends in newsprint prices is the interrelationship between the Canadian and the U.S. dollar. Canadians typically sell newsprint for U.S. dollars, and so in a period when the Canadian dollar falls against the U.S. dollar, the Canadian producers are in effect getting a price increase.

    At any given time, the amount of productive capacity for paper is generally known, since it takes about 3 years to bring a new paper mill on stream. Thus, a shortage of newsprint capacity can often be predicted in advance.

6. The big-city newspaper operations carry a lot of national advertising and are, therefore, more subject to cyclical shifts in the economy than the small newspapers, which depend on the more stable local advertising.

7. Publishers get their revenues from two basic sources: the readers and those who wish to reach the readers. This last group includes everything from government, which purchases books, textbooks, and even magazines, to advertisers.

8. On the cost side of the equation the major factors are paper, printing, postage (especially for magazines), and in-house labor. On a longer-term basis, as mentioned previously, the availability and price of paper is a key area for investors to watch. On the other hand, printing costs in all aspects of publishing seem to be in a long-term decline as a percent of total costs. This is occurring because of the introduction of labor-saving equipment.

9. Basically, publishing is not a fast-growth sector of the economy, but is relatively quite stable, with the exception of advertising and government expenditures, which are cyclical. Thus, publishing is not hurt too much in a slow-growth economy, except in those sectors which are dependent on advertising.

10. One potential long-term trend in the industry is the evolution of the media company, which is involved in motion pictures, newspapers, broadcasting, and book publishing.

11. To a certain extent, any advertising-related investment offers some protection against inflation, since most advertisers figure their budgets as a percent of sales, which, in turn, should reflect inflation over a period of time.

12. Although not more than thirty-two companies have ever been included in industry tabulations of income data, some sixty companies or their equivalents have been continually engaged in schoolbook publishing for the past 20 years. Of these, the leading five have about 42 percent of industry revenues, the next five about 14 or 15 percent, the next ten another 14 or 15 percent, the next twenty another 14 or 15 percent, and the last twenty about 8 or 9 percent.

Historically, profit margins in schoolbook publishing have tended to vary according to size in this industry; selling expenses are the key difference, since both large and small publishers used to maintain comparable sales forces. Between 1969 and 1977, however, the margins of smaller companies tended to show an erratic rise while those of middle-sized publishers showed an erratic decline. In five of the six years between 1972 and 1977, the margins of the middle group reported by the Association of American Publishers were lower than those reported for the smallest tier. Larger-company groups have tended to show rising margins, and, indeed, in the poor industry sales year of 1976, the large-publisher group (its members have varied through the years) recorded pretax profit margins of 19.1 percent—the best year ever. These trends may reflect a "tiering" of the industry.

At the lower end, some companies reporting as entities may have become subsidiaries of others. Moreover, they tend to concentrate on specialty lines for industry markets, which are relatively small. At the higher end, companies appear to be concentrating on the efficient production of materials aimed at the largest, most profitable market sectors. In between, the middle-sized companies appear under pressure from the larger companies' market successes and from costly efforts to expand their product lines (marked by relatively high selling and administrative expenses). Assuming a continuation of these trends, larger school textbook publishers would be in a better position, and medium-sized ones in a worse position.

13. The high cash flow of the larger companies also suggests that they may be aggressive acquirers of other companies, augmenting their growth rates, while the middle-sized companies may be likely acquisitions, antitrust considerations permitting. Alternatively, the latter might refocus on the specialty markets of smaller publishers.

14. Historically, the driving forces behind school budgets have been the numbers of teachers and the average salaries paid teachers. An examination of the best available education statistics, the biennial government statistics series, shows that instructional staff costs accounted for about 92 to 94 percent of instructional costs from 1939 through the present.

Thus, when you're estimating future textbook expenditures, be sure to compare them with actual expenditures for teachers in the schools. From 1939 to 1968, domestic textbook dollar sales to public schools, on average, equalled 2.64 percent of the expenditures for teachers' salaries. This figure remained remarkably consistent for 29 years—war years, peace years, years of rising enrollments and years of falling enrollment—and it suggests a valuable tool for forecasting textbook dollar sales to schools.

15. This is a labor-intensive industry, although the only part of the industry that has any direct printing capacity is newspapers. (This is a wise policy, because most publishers have a wide variety of products, and therefore it is useful to have access to a wide variety of printers. As a result of this policy, some of the labor cost increases of the 1970s have been pushed onto others and have not had to be absorbed by the publishers.) Labor costs and outside printing generally run about 60 percent of total expenses. Publishing is basically a people business: the getting, massaging, and packaging of information.

16. One of the important structural changes taking place in the industry is the fact that the government is not willing to subsidize the dissemination of information any more. For this reason, second class postage rates have risen on average more than 20 percent a year since 1970. The government now feels that people must pay their own way, and this will have a significant effect on the industry in the future.

17. Medium-sized newspapers and the largest book publishers generally have the highest profit margins.

18. The magazine industry had deteriorating profit margins for many years. It was hit by changes in style and by inflation. From 1976 to 1978, magazines, for the first time in years, increased their share of advertising revenues. Whether they will be able to hold this share and increase it in the years ahead remains to be seen.

19. Business of publishing originates with the need for a certain type of information. The critical factor for success is to identify who needs information and what kind of information that is, to obtain the information or create it, to transform it into an acceptable form, and to market it at the right price. When a publication starts, there's a period of high revenue growth, followed by a saturation of the market, usually within 6 months to 5 years. After that, growth depends more or less on demographic changes.

20. Demographics are an important factor in analyzing the publishing industry. You have to have favorable demographics in order to be favorably disposed toward a broad group of stocks. One of the best ways of choosing among these companies is to look at a particular sector of the economy that you are favorably disposed towards and then find a publishing company which is serving that market. Let's say you wanted to capitalize on trends in retail sales. You could either buy some stocks in a small newspaper located in the South (which is growing faster than the rest of the country) or buy stock of a newspaper in the suburbs (which are growing faster than the urban areas). If at all possible, try to find a company with a good earnings record over a 10-year period.

21. On the other hand, publishing is a bad area to invest in if wage and price controls are put on. The industry consumes large amounts of paper and would be affected by a rise in paper costs (or a shortage in paper products).

22. It is worthwhile for an investor to use whatever knowledge of demographics he or she already has to help in this analysis. For example, if you are connected with a teacher's pension fund you can have a better idea of demographic trends in textbook publishing than most professional investors.

23. Long-term demographic trends are especially important. By the early 1980s, there may be another play in the schoolbook market

as publishers and educational institutions start to gear up for the growth in elementary, then high school, and possibly, still later, college textbooks which may come in the 1980s as a result of the jump in the birthrate that is expected to follow from the recent high marriage rate among young adults.

STOCK MARKET CONSIDERATIONS

1. Publishing stocks are defensive in nature, as publishers generally have stable earnings.
2. The industry stocks generally outperform the stock market during the first 6 months of a market recovery, when publishers are still showing good earnings gains in spite of a poor economic outlook. Then, in the second half of the first year after the economic recovery begins, the publishing stocks start to underperform the stock market, as other companies whose profit margins had been squeezed start to report unusually high earnings gains. Then, in the second half of the second year and in the third year, publishing stocks again start to outperform the rest of the market (the recovery in the education sector is taking place, advertising spending is accelerating, etc.). The fourth year of an economic recovery (if the recovery lasts that long) can be the best year in the entire cycle for publishing stocks. Thus, while the publishing stocks generally sell at a p/e (price/earnings) discount to the stock market, they may go to overvaluations in the latter stages of an economic recovery. However, even though these companies' earnings tend to do very well in the latter stages of an economic recovery, it does not pay to hold on to them too long. These stocks tend to take a real beating in a bear market, and the punishment gets worse as the bear market goes on. Most publishing stocks are of small companies, and these typically get hurt in a bear market.
3. Textbook publishing stocks and those of chains of small newspapers tend to hold up well in a recession. Investors generally perceive that the magazine and big-city newspaper stocks are more dependent on advertising revenues, and therefore might be more hurt by a cyclical downturn.
4. Book publishing stocks generally show some weakness as a group in late spring. One of the reasons for this is that first-quarter earnings for the industry are not usually good.
5. Publishing stocks have historically moved when earnings have

come through, usually not much in anticipation of them. Publishing stocks are a relatively inefficient area of the market, and therefore there's quite a lot of opportunity for investors to make money in this group.

6. These stocks often move as a group, and thus it can pay to buy a package of publishing stocks.

QUESTIONS TO ASK YOURSELF BEFORE MAKING AN INVESTMENT IN THE BOOK AND MAGAZINE PUBLISHING INDUSTRY

1. What's happening to the major trends? Is advertising increasing or decreasing in its share of the GNP? Are textbook sales per capita increasing or decreasing? What's happening to costs of postage, paper, printing, and labor? What's the outlook for paper and newsprint capacity?
2. How has the advent of the "media company" affected the profitability of the industry?
3. Are you considering the purchase of a medium-sized textbook publisher? Has its profit margin been under pressure? If so, should you be buying it?
4. If you're considering a textbook company, have you fully analyzed demographic trends, such as prospective enrollments and teacher salaries?
5. What is the government's latest ruling on the postage costs of the dissemination of information? What effect will that have on industry profits?
6. What's happening to the battle for market share of advertising dollars between magazines, newspapers, and broadcasting?
7. Have you checked out the demographic outlook for the market which your publishing company serves?
8. Is your company gaining, losing, or holding market share in the major areas where it competes?
9. Does your own personal knowledge of demographic trends lend itself towards a particular type of publisher?
10. Have you studied the relative performance of publishing stocks over the course of a stock market cycle? Are you investing with or against the cycle?

CHAPTER 6

THE BROADCASTING INDUSTRY

Ellen Berland Sachar

KEY TO ANALYZING THE INDUSTRY

The key to both investing in and understanding the broadcasting business is leverage. In this context, the term "leverage" is being used to describe the increased—or decreased—earnings power of a business where costs are largely fixed and revenue gains—or losses—can have a direct and immediate impact on its level of profitability. Thus, in times of strong advertiser demand, the broadcasting business can be extremely profitable, while in times of weak advertiser demand, significantly less so. It is for this reason that we cannot stress enough to investors or potential investors the importance of making some judgment on the advertising outlook *before* committing money to stocks in this area.

Another important element to understand about the broadcasting business is that it is a commodity business. Television's pricing structure, unlike that of any other mass advertising medium, is determined almost entirely by considerations of supply and demand. The reason is simple: television broadcasters have, as determined by the number of hours in the day as well as by industry practice, a fixed inventory of commercial time to sell. The size of this inventory varies by time of day and by type of programs shown. In prime time (8:00–11:00 P.M. Eastern time), for example, networks can sell 6 minutes per hour of straight programming and 7 minutes per hour of feature film or other "long-form" entertainment. In daytime, on the other hand, networks can sell 12 minutes per hour. Other day parts and station owners are governed by similar rules. Adding to the volatility of the business is the fact that television's basic unit of sale, time, is perishable. An unsold spot is potentially a dark one on a station's or a network's schedule. The schedule cannot be shortened to accommodate the loss, as can the length of a magazine or newspaper.

On the cost side, too, the broadcaster has less flexibility than his counterparts in the publishing world. Program commitments are made well in advance of the "selling season." While sales commissions will, of course, be reduced in slow times, staff reductions are harder for the broadcaster to effect, because his is to begin with not a very labor-intensive business. In sum, then, a weak advertising demand environment can seriously erode a broadcaster's level of profitability, given his relatively high level of fixed costs and his virtually unchanging volume of sales inventory.

In the television business, as in any media business, what is being sold to the advertiser is audience, not time or space as is commonly assumed. The greater the "reach" of a given program, newspaper, or magazine, i.e., the more people who read or watch, the higher the "cost per thousand," i.e., the unit price per thousand viewers or readers, that advertising vehicle can command. Herein lies the importance of "ratings." Ratings are, simply put, a measurement of the size of the audience for a given show. They are always expressed in percentages of the total number of households in the United States owning television sets. "Shares" are another measurement of audience size. They are expressed in percentages of the total audience watching television at any given time. A show, therefore, with a 20 rating and a 31 share is being watched in 20 percent of American television-owning households and in 31 percent of the total homes watching television at that time.

Ratings are determined in two ways. For the network numbers, the A. C. Nielsen Co. (hence the term "Nielsens" for ratings) has a scientifically selected sample of 1200 homes in which it installs "audimeters," devices which are directly connected to the television set and telephone in the sample home, thereby relaying directly to the Nielsen computer information on the amount of time the TV set is on in a given home and which shows are being watched. For the stations, the Nielsen Co. and Arbitron, a subsidiary of Control Data Corp., circulate diaries to a scientifically determined number of homes in a given television market for a month at a time at three or four specified times of the year (known as the "sweep" periods) and conclude from the responses which station or stations are being watched most frequently in any given time period. The Nielsen and Arbitron results are usually in agreement, but not always.

To both the networks and the stations, ratings mean more than households, however. They can translate to higher profits. The more homes a show reaches, the higher the cost per thousand an advertiser will pay for time on that show. Since the cost of higher-rated shows is not necessarily greater than that of low-rated or untried shows, the profit differential can be enormous (see the section "The Financial Impact of Ratings" in this chapter).

To sum up, then, the broadcasting business is a relatively high-fixed-cost business, with a rather volatile pricing structure and a very perishable inventory to sell. Consequently, profits can be very high in times of strong advertiser demand and very depressed in times of weak advertiser demand. Because of the way the business is organized, there are two ways to invest in it: through the networks and the group station owners.

THE NETWORKS
The Nature of the Networks' Business

The three television networks are, in essence, program suppliers. Basically, they use the advertising revenues they collect from national advertisers to pay for programming, some of which they produce themselves but most of which they buy from independent producers. In and of themselves, the networks are not government-regulated. However, each of the networks also owns five VHF television stations, the maximum number permitted any single owner, known in the trade as the "owned-and-operated" stations. It is as station owners that they, like any other group or individual owning one or more broadcast properties, are subject to the various FCC (Federal Communications Commission) rules and restrictions.

In addition to its "O&O's," each network has roughly 200 station affiliates around the country—one per market—which carry its program schedules. The network can thus sell the advertiser a national audience. In return for carrying the "network feed," the station receives "network compensation," i.e., a negotiated percentage of the revenues the network collects from the advertisers based on that station's size and competitive standing and other factors. This anachronistic practice, whereby a station *is paid* to carry programming instead of *paying for* it, dates back to the early days of broadcasting, when networks, in their eagerness to amass large national audiences, offered stations financial compensation as an inducement to sign on with them. The risks of signing on with a network have long since been discounted, but the practice still remains.

In effect then, television programming in the United States is determined by the advertisers, in that revenues received from them pay for network programming. This explains why the networks have traditionally fought so hard against over-the-air pay television (also known as subscription TV or STV), cable television (CATV), and more recently, pay cable television. Any splintering of the networks' audience would erode their revenue base. Without that base, they would be unable to pay for programs. Consequently, were any of these alternatives to conventional broadcasting to succeed to the extent envisioned by their promoters, the networks would surely be out of the broadcasting business as we currently know it (see Chapter 8 for further discussion of CATV).

Since the advertisers on network television are largely producers and suppliers of consumer goods and services of various kinds, investment in network stocks, in effect, represents a protected way to "play" consumer spending or a recovery from an economic recession. Over 80 percent of network television advertising revenues derives from the following ten categories: food and food products; toiletries and toilet goods; automotive products; proprietary medicines; soaps, cleansers and polishes; household equipment; beer and wine; confectionary items and soft drinks; entertainment and amusement; and pet foods and supplies. With both big- and small-ticket items represented, as well as consumer durables and consumer nondurables, a shortfall in advertising spending in one area, say automobiles, due to a downturn in the economy could easily be made up for by an increase in spending in another, say, confectionary items and soft drinks. The risk of disappointment, therefore, is spread among many different kinds of product categories. In buying the networks, therefore, the investor plays them all.

The network business, among all the media businesses, is unique in several respects. For one thing, no other single advertising medium in the United States today can offer the makers of these goods and services the giant reach that network television can. On a given evening, a prime-time show with a 20 rating, the minimum acceptable for survival on a network schedule, reaches 14.9 million homes. Few publications (actually only *TV Guide*, which in itself says a lot about how Americans spend their leisure time) and certainly no television alternative (be it on cable or over-the-air) can offer the advertiser comparable numbers. For the makers of these products, then, network television has become an accepted and even necessary marketing tool.

Secondly, with only three games in town, the networks form an oligopoly of sorts. If we assume a balanced-demand environment, price strength at one network will usually mean price strength for all. The advertiser, then, with few meaningful alternatives for the disposition of his advertising dollars, is left with little bargaining power. The inventory of available time, remember, is limited. The inventory of preferred available time is more limited yet. Hence, in times of strong advertising demand, the networks have the upper hand in all price negotiations. In times of weak advertising demand, of course, the tables are turned, and it is the advertisers who call the tune. This explains why we have repeatedly emphasized the importance of assessing the advertising demand outlook before making an investment in this area.

The Financial Impact of Ratings

It is in connection with network programming, especially prime-time programming, that ratings receive the most attention, both in the trade and out. The reason is simple: higher ratings can mean substantially higher profits for a network. Illustration: At recent prices, one hour of prime-time series entertainment would cost the network roughly $400,-000 in license fees. If the show were very successful, the commercial time on it could go for as much as $190,000 per minute. This would produce over $1.1 million in gross revenues per hour for the network. If the show were not very successful, the time could go for as little as $85,000 per minute, or $510,000 of gross revenues per hour to the network. In other words, with the high-rated show, the network would have a gross profit of over $700,000 per hour, with the lower-rated show, a gross profit of only $100,000 per hour. In view of such a potentially wide differential in profitability, one can easily see why the networks cancel and replace shows as often as they do. The lure of that maximum profit potential is very hard to resist.

The effect a ratings improvement can have on the profits of a network is best illustrated by the figures in Table 6-1. ABC, for many years the third-ranked network, began a sharp turnaround with the hiring of Fred Silverman in 1975, until then the head of programming for CBS. In just 2 years, ABC network profits rose from a low of $29 million to a record high for them of $165 million. Their revenue growth in the same

TABLE 6-1   TELEVISION NETWORKS

REVENUES (IN MILLIONS)			
	1975	1976	1977
ABC	$ 510.0	$ 708.0	$ 918.0
CBS	596.0	725.0	843.0
NBC	573.0	684.0	820.0
Total	$1,679.0	$2,117.0	$2,581.0
PRETAX INCOME (IN MILLIONS)			
	1975	1976	1977
ABC	$ 29.0	$ 83.0	$ 165.0
CBS	106.0	129.0	139.0
NBC	73.5	83.0	102.0
Total	$ 208.5	$ 295.0	$ 406.0

Source: *Television Digest*

period was substantial, but not nearly so dramatic as the profit increase. Clearly then, ratings can be important for investors as well as for advertisers. Hence the stir on Wall Street in January of 1978 when this same Fred Silverman left ABC for the then third-ranked network, NBC.

One word of caution: the broadcasting business is very much a "futures" business. Advertisers buy time on shows *before* they know how the shows will actually perform. If sold on a "guaranteed" basis, as prime-time shows on some networks are, the advertiser may have some recourse—a "make-good"—in the event of a ratings disappointment. If not sold that way, the advertiser is left with his disappointment and a bargaining tool in his next go-around with the network.

For the investor in these stocks, too, the most rewarding strategy is playing the future. Since a turnaround in the ratings can have such a dramatic effect on a network's earnings, an educated guess on the timing of a turnaround in a network's ratings can prove most profitable. Lacking such clairvoyance, however, most investors would do better simply to rely on advertising-demand—related indicators.

THE GROUP BROADCASTERS

Another way to invest in the broadcasting industry is to buy the stocks of the group broadcasting companies. According to FCC regulations, an individual or a group may own up to seven television stations—five VHF and two UHF—and fourteen radio stations—seven AM and seven FM. Many of the companies with such holdings are publicly held, e.g., Capital Cities Communications, Metromedia, Taft Broadcasting, Storer, Wometco, and Lin. Several of the publicly held newspaper chains now also have significant broadcast interests and might also be included in this discussion, e.g., Gannett Co., Knight-Ridder Newspapers, Harte-Hanks Communications, Lee Enterprises, Multimedia, and The Washington Post Co.

Sources of Revenue

Revenues in the group broadcasting business are derived from three sources: network compensation, i.e., the monies paid the stations by the networks in return for carrying network programming; national and regional advertisers (known in the trade as national "spot" advertising), i.e., the giant manufacturers of food, toiletries, automobiles, proprietary medicines, household products and equipment, and confectionary items and soft drinks, who also purchase the bulk of network television time; and local advertisers, i.e., food stores, department and discount stores, restaurants, banks, automobile dealers, etc., who have traditionally spent the bulk of their advertising dollars in newspapers.

Network Compensation For several years, network compensation did not grow significantly but, rather, actually declined as a percentage of a station's total revenues, so that it now accounts for only about 10 percent of the total. The reasons are simple: networks base their compensation on a complicated formula which takes into account the size of the market involved, the share of that market the affiliate can deliver, the competitive situation in the market, and other factors. Since these factors, by and large, have tended to vary little from year to year, the amount of compensation has remained relatively stable, too. Also, the station's other sources of revenues—spot and, more importantly, local advertising—have grown so tremendously in recent years that network compensation as a percentage of the total has necessarily declined. Since ABC's rise to the number one position in the prime-time ratings, however, this situation has changed somewhat, as ABC, in an effort to upgrade and enlarge its station lineup, has offered stations higher compensation as an inducement to switch affiliations. The other networks have, of necessity, been forced to pay up as well.

Spot Advertising In an effort to promote sales in a particular area of the country or to introduce or test-market a new product, large national advertisers (e.g., Procter & Gamble, General Motors, American Home Products) purchase national television time on a spot basis rather than on a network basis. Such buys are made according to market size, e.g., the top fifty or top twenty-five markets; or for a given region, e.g., the South Atlantic or New England; therefore, stations in the larger markets tend to attract more spot dollars than stations in smaller markets. For network affiliates in general, though, spot advertising accounts for about 50 percent of their revenues and local about 40 percent. On a cost-per-thousand basis, spot buys are usually more expensive than network buys, but since fewer thousands are being bought, the advertiser's actual dollar outlay tends to be lower than it would be for network time.

To buy station time, agency media buyers negotiate with television "rep" firms (television national sales representatives) for "availabilities" and prices, thereby vastly simplifying for them the process of buying time on the over 700 commercial television stations in the United States. Several of the larger group broadcasters own their own rep firms (e.g., Metromedia's and Washington Post's Post-Newsweek group), as do the network owned-and-operated stations. Other station groups and individual stations contract with independently owned national sales organizations.

Over the years, "spot" has undoubtedly been the most volatile factor in the television business, with huge increases some years and modest increases the next. The reasons are easily discernible: unlike network advertising, spot advertising requires a relatively short lead time.

Hence advertisers tend to buy spot on a last-minute basis. As a result, the pricing structure on spot can be less than stable. This is particularly true when network prices are weak. Since basically the same advertisers are the major purchasers of both network and spot time, a decline in network prices usually signals a major shift of dollars out of spot and into network on the grounds of increased cost efficiency. This leaves the individual station owner with little discretion over pricing structure in this area.

Local Advertising   Local advertising, according to the FCC, refers to "time purchased in behalf of retail or service establishments in a given market . . . even though the establishments may be a part of a national or regional chain." The distinction between local and spot advertising revenues, often a hazy one, is, according to the FCC, "based on the type of advertiser to whom the time is sold rather than how or by whom it is sold."

Since reps are not involved in the sale of time to local advertisers, the stations usually get to keep a higher percentage of these revenues than of comparable spot sales. The growth of local advertising in recent years has far outpaced the growth in other areas. Although some of this apparent growth may be due to changes in reporting procedures, i.e., reclassification of what was formerly considered spot sales to local sales, a good part of it does indeed reflect growth in local sales.

(Note: For radio stations, the terminology is similar, but the breakdowns are somewhat different in that local revenues are a larger part of the mix. Because most of the broadcasting profits of the publicly held group station owners' companies derive from their television operations, we will limit our discussion here to the television end of their business.)

Dynamics of the Business

The television station business is characterized by the same kind of leverage as the network business in terms of both costs and ratings. For station owners, as for the networks, costs are largely fixed. Increased advertiser demand results in higher prices and profits, decreased demand in lower prices and profits. The major difference between the two businesses lies in the nature of their cost structures. With 60 to 70 percent of their program schedules supplied by the networks, stations that are network affiliates have average, according to FCC figures, pretax margins of over 30 percent. Remember, they *are paid* to carry programs rather than *pay for* them. "Independents," i.e., stations not affiliated with a network, which must buy all their own programming, and networks themselves average much lower pretax margins. Until recently, in fact, independents, in many cases, operated at a loss.

Ratings, too, can have a significant impact on a station's performance. As with the networks, the stations with the highest ratings in a market can command the highest prices. For network affiliates, their ratings performance is often—but not always—dependent on the performance of the network with which they are affiliated. Thus for the 20 years that CBS led its competitors in the prime-time ratings, the CBS affiliate in a given market tended to dominate its competition. In recent years, however, with ABC's rise to the top, this situation has changed in many markets.

Growth of Local Advertising

Because of the volatility of the national spot market, the group station business has largely been perceived as a cyclical business, in that historically a station's profits were largely determined by the flow of national spot business. In recent years, however, the growth of local advertising on television has triggered a significant change in the long-term earnings outlook for the station business. As a commodity business in which pricing strength or weakness is a direct function of supply and demand, prices will clearly strengthen in response to a new source of demand, i.e., retailers of all varieties. Furthermore, retail advertising, unlike national advertising, tends to be rather stable, increasing each year in direct relation to the increase in retail sales. Therefore, to the extent that an ever larger percentage of a station's revenues in the coming years will be derived from this more stable and predictable source, it would follow that the flow of earnings at many stations around the country will become less volatile and probably more predictable in the years ahead than it has been historically.

The reasons for the continuing growth of local advertising on television are several. The retailing business has become increasingly dominated by the large national chains. With many outlets in a given market, the large retailer would incur less wasted circulation in a television buy than was true previously and would tend to be putting more emphasis on image rather than item advertising to attract customers to his store. In addition newspaper advertising rates have increased sharply in the last few years, in large measure to offset spiraling newsprint costs, while newspaper circulation has overall grown minimally, if at all. The cost per thousand to the advertiser in newspapers has, therefore, risen dramatically, thereby reducing the cost differential between the two media significantly. All of these factors have tended to benefit local advertising on television, while still leaving the lion's share of this business with newspapers. In the years ahead, we foresee no significant change in these trends.

Recognizing the many inherently attractive characteristics of the station business—the high operating margins, the generous cash flows, the absence of foreign involvements—many companies having until now no interests in the broadcasting business have recently been acquiring them. These include newspaper companies like Knight-Ridder and Gannett, as well as such other diversified giants as General Electric. In each case, the acquirer paid a substantial premium to the market price. With more such combinations possible in the future, stockholders—individual, institutional, or insider—will all reap the benefits.

POTENTIAL PITFALLS

In recent years, some observers have questioned whether the networks will be able to maintain their audience dominance. Regardless of their current success, such critics cite the following as factors which might lead to a decline in the networks' power:

1. The possibility of increased government intervention with regard to program and advertising content and/or network-affiliate relations
2. The possibility of significant network audience splintering as a result of wide public acceptance of pay cable TV, video discs, or video cassettes
3. The development of direct satellite-to-home transmission which would bypass the local station system as we now know it
4. The possibility of no growth or even declines from current levels in time spent viewing television per home
5. The sharply escalating costs of programming
6. The nearly total saturation of television in United States households
7. The absence currently of any new technological developments, such as color television, to stimulate new interest in television buying and television viewing

All of these represent valid long-term concerns that should be monitored by the careful investor. Given the industry's rather rapid recovery from the 1971 congressional ban on cigarette advertising and its extremely strong profit performance in the last few years, none would appear to be an immediate threat.

QUESTIONS TO ASK YOURSELF BEFORE MAKING AN INVESTMENT IN THE BROADCASTING INDUSTRY

1. Are you aware that broadcasters are basically an advertising or consumer-spending play?
2. Are you certain that the leverage of this industry will be working for you rather than against you?
3. What is happening to network cost per thousand? Are they strengthening or weakening?
4. Are you aware that you would do best to buy broadcasting stocks in periods of economic uncertainty or recession? (They will quickly discount an improved economic outlook, and you may be buying too late if you wait until there's solid evidence of a pickup in advertising.)
5. Are you aware that you could realize substantial leverage, in terms of both company earnings gains and stock price gains, by buying the stock of the network with the lowest ratings at the time of an important management change or hint of a schedule's success?
6. Are you aware that certain kinds of government rulings, whether from the FCC, Congress, or the courts, can have, temporarily at least, a negative impact on these stocks?

CHAPTER 7

THE BUILDING AND RELATED INDUSTRIES

Ned W. Davis

KEY TO ANALYZING THE INDUSTRY

1. Being able to determine where you are in the building cycle.
2. Having a good feel for long-term demographic trends, especially the growth in new households, the mix of the population by age, and the "scrappage" of old homes.

MOST COMMON INVESTOR MISTAKE

Thinking that building-related companies move cohesively as a group. Most building-related companies depend heavily upon other industries for their profits. The average company in the building-related universe derives less than 35 percent of its earnings from sources directly dependent upon new residential construction activity.

WHEN TO BUY BUILDING STOCKS

The time to buy building-related companies is at the beginning of a recession, as credit conditions are easing. The tighter the credit has been, the earlier and faster the building market will come back when interest rates decline and the fundamentals of the housing markets turn favorable.

SOME GENERAL POINTS TO REMEMBER ABOUT THE INDUSTRY

1. While the housing industry was essentially a no-growth industry for the postwar era as a whole, certain companies, such as Masco and Owens-Corning, emerged during these stretches and became rewarding investments. The more successful building-related companies did this by maneuvering in a variety of ways, including:

   a. the diversification into attractive areas outside the residential industry: U.S. Gypsum
   b. concentration on products serving the home improvement market, which experienced a fairly rapid rate of secular growth: Masonite and Armstrong Cork
   c. development of new products or service concepts for residential construction and related industries, often with proprietary market positions: Masco and MGIC

   The key to investment success with building-related issues no doubt will continue to derive from finding companies capable of exploiting such opportunities and investing in them with a watchful eye on the likelihood and timing of cyclical change.
2. Most building-related companies heavily depend upon other industries for their profits. The average company in the building-related universe derives less than 35 percent of its earnings from sources directly dependent upon new residential construction activity; a few that are popularly categorized as building stocks actually derive none. Nevertheless, the stock market psychology for most issues in this group should continue to primarily depend on how the residential housing picture unfolds.
3. The demographic realities of the United States, if taken on their own merits, are positive for housing's future. Although the adult population growth rate will be slightly slower in the 5-year period through 1982 than it was in the previous 5 years, the change in the age mix of the population (as the babies from the post-war boom enter their late twenties and early thirties) holds

favorable implications. Persons progressing through their thirties traditionally have shown a strong propensity to upgrade
their shelter standards by purchasing single-family homes.

4. Aside from the special importance that demographic trends
have for residential construction, the housing industry is special
in many ways. Home ownership is looked upon in a very favorable light in this country, and it is not inconceivable that the
consumer might choose to dedicate a larger portion of his
income to shelter in the future than he has in the past. This
would particularly be the case if inflation continues at a high
rate over a long time period. Furthermore, the demand for and
production of shelter is closely tied to the mortgage market, a
strange animal that to a great extent functions independently of
the economy. Investors therefore should differentiate the housing sector from other consumer areas. It is unique and peculiar
in so many ways that its outlook cannot and should not be
viewed as being closely analogous to such industries as autos,
appliances, or retailing.

5. The "residual" characteristics of the housing sector, and therefore its chronic susceptibility to inflation, swings in credit conditions, and the vagaries of its position in the priorities of the
government, make forecasts of specific annual levels of activity
beyond a year or so most unreliable.

6. Although most investors focus on residential construction in
evaluating the potential for building-related companies, the role
of nonresidential activity in their fundamental outlook should
not be ignored. The nonresidential construction sector has consistently been more than two times as large as the new residential sector and has exhibited dependable long-term growth with
fairly moderate cyclicality.

7. Each of the eight major housing industry contractions since the
Second World War has been initiated by a process which begins
with a slowing of money supply growth in reaction to overheating of the economy and governmental fear of excessive inflation.
The growth of capital available for mortgage lending has proven
during the postwar period to be highly sensitive to fluctuations
in short-term interest rates, because the ability of savings intermediaries to compete on a yield basis for financial savings is
very limited. When credit conditions tighten, short-term interest

rates rise, and under such circumstances, the primary sources of mortgage capital, savings intermediaries, have tended to lose share of the net new savings generated by households.*

8. Since the mid-1960s the pattern of housing-start cyclicality has closely paralleled the pattern of seasonally adjusted savings flows into savings and loan associations. These lenders have accounted for approximately one-half of all residential lending since that time.

9. To a very great extent the mortgage market operates independently of the credit markets in general.

    a. The S&L's have little choice about where they will invest their funds, except in a very short-term sense. They are obliged by charter and regulation to keep the vast majority of their assets in mortgages.

    b. The rates they charge on mortgages are based only partly on supply/demand conditions for mortgage money. The most important determinant of the trough level that mortgage rates will reach in a period of easing credit conditions is the interest rate paid for savings and the future expectations for those rates.

10. The building material companies depend mainly on the level of commercial construction which runs in a cycle different from that of the housing industry. The housing industry tends to get going in the early parts of an economic advance, while commercial construction tends to lag the economic cycle. Thus, the combination of housing and commercial construction tends to give a stabilizing effect to the building industry. Unfortunately, many investors look at building materials companies as dependent on the housing industry, which is a wrong and misleading approach.

FACTORS INVOLVED IN ANALYZING SHELTER DEMAND

The demand for shelter is basically related to the desire and ability of the nation's population both to expand the size of its housing stock and

---

*With the first-time availability of floating-rate savings certificates (as of June 1978) this tendency may be reduced.

to improve the qualities of the units within that stock. Numerous factors influence this desire and ability over the long term. Certain of these factors take on particularly great importance in determining the dimensions and timing of cycles:

1. The availability of new capital for mortgage lending. This availability fundamentally depends upon the extent of net savings capital increases experienced by the two major classes of thrift institutions, mutual savings banks and savings and loan associations, which are the backbone of the residential construction industry.

2. Changing consumer economic expectations. Shelter demand and production are influenced by the willingness of consumers to make new major financial commitments, their ability to make job moves, and their propensity to form new households. All of these are highly sensitive to cyclical changes in consumer economic expectations and attitudes. Such expectations and attitudes can change very quickly.

3. The extent of federal assistance to the industry during both contractions and expansions. Federal assistance to the housing industry has some semipermanent aspects: Federal Housing Administration and Veterans Administration credit insurance programs, tax-deductibility of mortgage interest, accelerated depreciation on real estate investments, and the Federal Reserve Board's Regulation Q. It also takes on more transient forms, which influence residential cyclicality.

These more transient forms of federal involvement in the industry have been modified considerably from cycle to cycle. Basically, however, they all involved one of several basic approaches:

   a. Encouraging the rationing of securities market funds into mortgage investment during tight credit periods, primarily through the efforts of the federal housing agencies

   b. Stimulating shelter demand by subsidizing the monthly housing expenditures of certain home buyers and apartment renters

   c. Improving the ability of thrift institutions to compete for funds. The creation of the floating-rate savings certificate in June 1978 was a step in this direction

SOME POTENTIAL PROBLEMS AND STRATEGIES IN FORECASTING DEMAND

It is no more appropriate to make forecasts of shelter production based on a perception of needs than it is to make projections on the same basis for any other product or service where quality characteristics demonstrate great variability over time. A forecast based on needs is only appropriate for a product or service that is a pure necessity. Shelter in its simplest form is a basic necessity. But the upgrading of shelter conditions through enlargement and/or improvement of the shelter stock is primarily a function of standard-of-living change, just as is true for the saturation and quality upgrading that occurs with automobiles and most other consumer durables. Housing units do not tend to wear out if maintained, so that even the scrappage rate in housing's case is more a standard-of-living factor than a function of physical deterioration over time.

Most demographic trends, and particularly those involving net household formations, are closely related to changes in economic conditions. The same is true for vacancy rate shifts, second home demand, and most other shelter demand factors. The only primary factors in shelter demand that are independent of economic factors are accidental removal (due to catastrophe) and adult population growth, which is highly predictable over future time spans of 18 years or less, barring significant change in mortality rates or immigration.

In forecasting housing production over the long term, you should attempt to define the amount of shelter demand that can be expected to assert itself effectively in the marketplace, assuming certain economic conditions. The perceived need for shelter has no relevance unless you expect it to assert itself effectively in the marketplace. Furthermore, demographic vacancy and second-home trends of the past are greatly dependent upon past economic conditions and rising living standards. It is unreasonable to extrapolate such trends into the future unless the economic environment of the future is expected to be identical or very similar to that of the past.

The effective demand for new shelter units over time depends upon changes in the desire and the ability of the population to *enlarge* and *upgrade* its housing stock. The desire to enlarge and upgrade, at least historically, has been limited by a host of factors, the most important of which has been the finite amount of income that the population has had at its disposal to pay financial constants and occupancy costs on the housing stock.

The creation of new housing units requires both investment and consumption outlays by households. In a cyclical sense, investment considerations (and therefore, housing's status in the nation's capital-allocation process) become key. Most shelter investments are financed with fixed-interest-rate mortgages. Investment in shelter units as a cyclical determinant depends greatly upon changes in the mortgage market environment.

In a longer-term sense, the level of shelter demand is a function of the population's ability to enlarge and upgrade its shelter stock because rises in disposable income permit the assumption of greater financial constants and occupancy costs. (We include in the term "occupancy costs" all consumer expenditures that are necessary for the normal use of shelter units, including utilities, maintenance, and insurance. Obviously furnishings, appliances, and property taxes are closely related to shelter occupancy, but we believe that expenditures on these items are determined somewhat independently of the shelter stock enlargement and upgrading process.)

A long-term forecast of shelter production can best be approached by first examining the basic demographic processes and other key demand factors and then viewing the outlook for continuation of these factors in light of inflation's impact on the population's ability to afford shelter. The demand factors to be examined are: (1) household headship rates by age, sex, and marital status; (2) varying growth rates among age groups in the adult population; and (3) characteristics of the existing housing stock in terms of its propensity for scrappage.

The income- and inflation-related factors of greatest concern are: (1) the price and terms of financing which will prevail for housing both of new and transferred existing units; and (2) the probable trade-off between the growth of personal income and the growth of costs associated with the housing stock.

HOW TO ANALYZE CYCLICAL AND DEMOGRAPHIC FACTORS

The two critical factors in analyzing the building and building-related products area are the cyclical considerations and the longer-term trends. Any contemplated investment in this industry requires a close look at the position and outlook of these two areas.

Why Building Is Cyclical in Nature

1. Housing activity is highly cyclical because it represents a form of capital investment by consumers and business. A single-family home is a major family commitment; it can be postponed indefinitely, and thus there is an inherent volatility to the housing area.

2. Multifamily housing requires a long lead time in construction and is motivated in large part by the confidence builders have in the economic future. That confidence can change dramatically, thereby adding to the cyclical forces.

3. Total availability and cost of credit is also an important consideration. (And when we say cost of credit, we don't mean only the level of interest rates; the actual terms of the financing can be just as important as the level of interest rates.) Since 85 percent of all housing is financed by mortgage debt, the availability of mortgages can have a significant effect on swings in building. By the same token, the terms of mortgage lending are extremely important in evaluating whether consumers will or will not be able to purchase homes.

4. The savings flow into thrift institutions is a key variable in determining the availability of mortgage money. Most of the mortgage financing is made by thrift institutions, and a lot of the savings capital which goes into the thrifts is yield-sensitive. (That is to say, if money-market interest rates are higher than the interest rates savings and loans are allowed to pay, the new inflows of funds to S&L's may slow or stop completely.) For instance, if the interest rates on Treasury bills and other money-market instruments rise to a certain level, new savings deposits may not flow into the thrift institutions, and less money will be available for housing. Thus, the first question to ask yourself in analyzing this industry is what is the likelihood of a change in credit conditions, and how large could that change be? History shows that periods of significant change in credit conditions are relatively short-lived; most of the time there's an equilibrium (i.e., interest rates are stable).

5. The government has become increasingly involved in the housing industry in the postwar period in an attempt to smooth out the cycles in housing. When credit conditions get tight, the government attempts to make mortgage money available through

other means. However, there is only so much that the government can do.

Secular Long-Term Trends

The most important aspect of the long-term trend is the outlook for demographics, specifically, the rate of household formation. Interestingly, since 1790, when the first census was taken, the growth of households has been greater than the growth of the adult population. This is because more families now tend to live independently of each other. In former years, grandparents might have lived with their children, but rarely does this occur nowadays. What's more, young people tend to move out of their parents' houses at an earlier age. Both of these trends have come about because real incomes increased, thereby allowing more people to afford housing. But a key question for the future is whether households will continue to grow faster than adult population. If not, then secular demand for new housing could slow somewhat.

Another important demographic factor to consider is the current and future average age of the population. For example, the baby boom offspring are now approaching adulthood, which, all things being equal, should add to demand for housing. You should also look at the ratio of single to married people, the rate of population growth, the changes in lifestyle, and the affordability of shelter.

It's also critical to study the aspiration to and affordability of shelter. In the middle of 1978 there was an obsession with home ownership. This had happened for a variety of reasons, not the least of which was that the tax system promotes home ownership. What's more, consumers, aware of the destructiveness of a high rate of inflation, respond to it by purchasing houses as an inflation hedge. Thus, if inflation stays high, there will be a continued demand for new homes. As in a bull market in stocks, people are buying houses because they are afraid that the prices will run away from them.

The income of wives is now being included in analyzing the amount of monthly or annual income that's available to cover mortgage payments, which increases the affordability of new housing. Finally, the use of private mortgage insurance has helped in reducing the initial down payment on a home. Thus, even though real incomes declined in the early and middle 1970s and home prices rose dramatically, other ways were found to enable consumers to continue purchasing homes.

The next factor to analyze is the scrappage rate, which can be considerable, since housing starts and mobile home shipments exceed the rate of household formation year in and year out. In fact, there are some estimates that 31 percent of the annual demand for new housing is based on scrappage of old homes.

Scrappage basically depends on the following factors:

1. Immigration into urban centers of poor blacks, who thereby vacate their former rural housing.
2. Tearing down of inner-city houses.
3. The destruction of homes due to new highways and roads.
4. Mobile home shipments during the past 10- to 15-year period. Since mobile homes have a shorter life than houses do, mobile home scrappage has become an important factor now.
5. Economic conditions in various parts of the country. As people leave one area for another one with greater opportunity, scrappage often results.
6. Rising aspirations. A lot of scrappage occurs because people want bigger and better homes.

In the future, scrappage may be less important because the great migration from the rural areas to the cities has already occurred.

HOMEBUILDERS

These are entrepreneurial companies, and the key to a successful investment is the ability to judge management. All of the questions you will want to know about relate to the ability of management to take advantage of opportunities and to stay away from problems. What separates one company from another is management philosophy and judgment. You'll want to know what part of the country the company does most of its business in, and what the economic outlook there is.

This is a very difficult industry to evaluate, and all but the most sophisticated investors should avoid stocks of this industry. However, the industry has now grown to the point that several companies are large enough to insure some consistency of performance.

THE APPLIANCE INDUSTRY

While some of the companies in the building materials industry may not compete head-on, the appliance industry has direct competition. Therefore you must evaluate market share of each major product, analyze costs, and think of these companies as manufacturers and assembly businesses.

Also look at backward integration. For example, General Electric makes its own motors. Whirlpool sells 54 percent of its products through Sears, which gives it certain critical advantages in production. GE, on the other hand, owns its own distributors, and therefore it is critical to know what the dealer relationship is, as well as the level and quality of the dealerships.

While a building material like insulation is not really a brand product, the brand is a very important part of a washing machine. You must learn what's going on in the general area of product distribution. Is the company's product gaining or losing market share? Where is the pricing of the company in the industry? Is it better or worse than the competition? And how efficient a producer is the company? Can it manufacture products more cheaply than the competition?

Scrappage is even more important for the appliance industry than it is for the housing industry. Appliances wear out physically, and they must be repaired and/or replaced. What's more, obsolescence comes into play much sooner than with a house. An appliance built in the 1950s is probably out of date at present, while a house built then is probably very satisfactory.

In order to analyze the demand for appliances, one must study the change in the number of households, the replacement demand based on scrappage, and the saturation of demand—in other words, one must learn the percentage of households that already own appliances. (Remember that the introduction of a new product, such as a frost-free refrigerator, adds to demand, since a consumer might replace an existing unit with a frost-free refrigerator much sooner.) Of course, saturation depends largely on real-income growth and the relative cost of the product. Take as an example microwave ovens, which, when initially brought out, were extremely expensive. As the prices of the ovens fell, demand and saturation rose.

The appliance industry is not too dependent on housing activity. It depends on economic activity, the level and growth of employment, real personal incomes, and the amount of general consumer confidence. Technological innovation is also important, as we've seen above, because it can hasten replacement and increase the total market. Only about 20 percent of the industry is directly attributable to new housing.

However, a major shift in that 20 percent figure can have a huge impact on earnings. A 5 percent increase in revenues from housing, for instance, can have a 15 percent impact on the bottom line. Therefore, the association that investors make between appliance companies and the housing industry is correct, when you consider the effect that the housing industry has on profits.

HOW TO GET ADDITIONAL INFORMATION ON THE BUILDING INDUSTRY

Investors interested in following the building industry closely should read the *Housing Affairs Letter,* available for $100 by writing to Community Development Services Publishers, 399 National Press Building, Washington, DC 20045. This letter discusses all the government activity related to the housing industry as well as other key factors which might influence it. Another important publication is the *National Real Estate Investor,* published by Communications Channel Corp. If you're interested in monitoring credit conditions, the St. Louis Federal Reserve Bank sends out, free of charge, weekly publications on all aspects of the money supply, economic conditions, and interest rates. You can get on its mailing list by writing directly to it.

QUESTIONS TO ASK YOURSELF BEFORE MAKING AN INVESTMENT IN THE BUILDING MATERIALS INDUSTRY

1. What market is the company basically dependent upon? It's important to break out each aspect of the company and determine what the different degrees of cyclicality are.
2. Is the company dependent on commercial construction, consumer demand, the housing market? Many building-related companies have diversified out of the construction industry into such remote areas as minerals. It's very hard to make a generalization about this industry, as there's very little homogeneity and there's a great variation in stock and company performance during an economic cycle.
3. What is the relative profitability that each company derives from each market? While it may be relatively easy to get a sales breakdown for the company, earnings breakdowns are harder to come by. But that's no reason to give up without a fight.
4. What is the company's market share in its major products?
5. Does the company have control over the pricing of its products?

6. Is the company the low-cost producer in its area? This is a regional industry, and the cost of production varies dramatically from market to market.

7. What is the company's energy efficiency? (This is an industry which tends to be very energy-intensive.)

8. Where is the company strongest and what is happening to its markets in those areas? This is a regional business that is characterized by oversupply in one area and undersupply in another; competition might be tough in Florida and nonexistent in Colorado. Thus, for example, when you know that a company does half its business in the Southeast at a time when pricing there is poor, you'll know that the outlook for the company is not good. You should even think in terms of learning about a specific facility and knowing how efficient that facility is.

9. Where are you in the economic and housing cycle?

10. What's the outlook for interest rates, mortgage availability, and affordability of houses?

11. What is it that separates your company from others in the industry? Be sure to analyze the performance of the company during the last period of tight credit conditions. Did earnings go up more or less than the competition?

12. What is the outlook for the various segments of the building-products area? For example, insulation prices might be going up while gypsum prices are going down, which could affect different companies in different ways.

13. What are the demographic trends? Are they long-term favorable? What's the level of household formations? What's the future outlook for same? What's the demand for second homes? Is scrappage increasing because of migration?

CHAPTER 8

THE CATV INDUSTRY

Ellen Berland Sachar

BACKGROUND

To get the proper perspective on the CATV (cable television) industry, one must go back to the early 1970s, when this industry was viewed as a classic emerging-new-technology area. Investors anticipated then that within a few short years the nation would be fully "wired" for cable, that people would have available to them a wide variety of programming alternatives from cable's multichannel capacity, that they would be doing most of their shopping at home through a CATV connection, that their homes would be made safe from burglars and fire through CATV-connected security systems, and that, in fact, the cable-to-home hookup would obviate the need for the daily newspaper as we now know it. Subsequent events, especially skyrocketing interest rates in 1974, proved these expectations to be overly optimistic, but enumerating them now gives some idea of the promise this form of communication has held over the years.

Simply put, cable television is the technology of transmitting program signals by coaxial cable. With its broadband capacity, CATV makes available to subscribers a large number of channels in a variety of modes. In its early stages, CATV was used most effectively to improve signal reception. Now, with the introduction of pay cable services and, in some markets, two-way capability, CATV has made possible a variety of specialized and localized services.

To obtain cable services, subscribers must pay anywhere from $6 to $10 per month, depending on the market involved. Pay cable costs an additional $6 to $10 per month. At the present time, just under 20 percent of United States households subscribe to cable. Markets with poor signal reception and only two VHF over-the-air signals, the so-called classic systems, have penetration rates of 60 to 70 percent. Elsewhere the numbers are much lower.

Not all United States markets are wired for cable. Several big cities, like Chicago and Boston, in fact, have not yet even awarded cable franchises. Because of the expense involved in building these large systems, and because of the many entertainment alternatives available in these markets, systems in places like New York and Los Angeles have tended to be far less, if at all, profitable than the smaller classic systems.

Since 1976, the industry has basically come into its own. With the high start-up costs on "new-builds" behind them and the successful introduction of pay cable services, cable operations since then have been showing impressive earnings gains. In addition, various regulatory restrictions, in force since the late 1960s, have one by one been dropped or overturned by the FCC and the courts. The result: expansion of cable in the top 100 markets, increased distant signal importation, elimination of "leapfrogging"* restrictions, relaxed program exclusivity protection for the broadcasters, and an increased number of movies available for pay cable.

Another interesting development in the cable industry has been the consolidation of operations over the last few years. Begun originally as small, individually owned community antenna companies in the 1950s, these operations were quickly gobbled up by larger, new companies known in the trade as "MSO's" (multiple systems operations). In a later phase of consolidation, MSO's began acquiring each other, and more recently yet, the larger MSO's have been bought out by such

---

*"Leapfrogging" refers to the industry practice of bypassing the closest major market stations and selecting more remote ones.

diversified communications giants as Time Inc. and the Times Mirror Company. If present trends continue, there will be few if any small operations left in this field.

INVESTMENT CONSIDERATIONS

In evaluating an investment in the CATV industry, one must consider carefully the future prospects for the industry. On the one hand, one could argue that basic cable penetration is reaching its outer limits, that revenue and profit growth in the business is coming more from increasing the revenue yield per subscriber than from actually adding new subscribers, that a new technology, yet undetermined, will supplant cable, that the regulatory environment might change and once again put limits on cable's growth—in sum, that the industry is rapidly approaching its maturity point. On the other hand, one could look ahead to the development of new technology (e.g., fiber optics or inexpensive hardware permitting "per-program" billing) that would make building in the big cities economically viable, to the introduction of further services and additional programming alternatives that would lead to increased subscriber growth and still higher revenue yield per subscriber, and to the development of either a sizable cable "network" or a series of definable minority audiences that would enable systems to sell advertising time and hence provide them with yet another source of revenue. Either scenario is possible; more likely, there will be some combination of the two. In either case, some wholly unforeseen regulatory change, from either the FCC, the courts, or Congress, could alter the picture entirely. The question then boils down to one of investment risk. At current prices, are the stocks undervalued or overvalued? Is one willing to gamble on the future or only to invest in what is known in the present?

One cushion that investors should bear in mind: The large, publicly held companies that have been buying out the smaller, publicly held CATV companies have all paid a substantial premium to the market price in making these purchases. More of that could well occur in the future. If not on their own merits, then, these stocks could certainly be viewed as attractive buy-out candidates, for those who choose to play that game.

We would point out in this connection that in recent years the major advances in the cable business—the launching of Home Box Office, the Time Inc. subsidiary that through satellite transmission has, in effect, created a pay cable network, and the QUBE experiment of Warner Cable in Columbus, Ohio, that permits two-way transmission and per-program billing—have both required substantial capital investments that small companies on their own could not have made. The next phase of development in the cable business, whatever that may be, will also likely require substantial capital commitments. Merging with a proverbial rich uncle is an easy and logical solution to a problem of this kind.

CATV, STV, AND OVER-THE-AIR BROADCASTING

From the earliest days of cable transmission, broadcasters have viewed this new technology as a direct threat to their financial well-being. At current levels of cable penetration, however, this has hardly proved the case. In fact, since 1972, nothing—not the wage and price controls of 1971–1973, nor the recession of 1974–1975—has had a seriously adverse effect on the profitability of the television broadcasting industry (see Chapter 19). Their official stance notwithstanding, many group station owners today are among the larger cable television system owners (as are a number of newspaper groups as well). In other words, it would appear at this time at least that the two businesses, broadcast and cable, can coexist in peace and profitability.

The current "new kid on the block" is over-the-air subscription TV (STV), which is being developed by broadcasters as well as entrepreneurs. Using an over-the-air signal, usually an existing underutilized UHF station, the STV operator programs the daytime schedule as before but in the nighttime hours sends out a scrambled signal that may be decoded only by a black-box device attached to the subscriber's television set. For a set monthly fee, usually comparable to the combined monthly basic-pay cable charge, or in some cases for a per-program fee, the subscriber can see first-run entertainment or exclusive sports features uninterrupted by commercials. Currently, the kind of programming being offered on STV channels is not substantially different from what is offered by pay cable, except that the combined basic-pay cable package offers the subscriber much more than one channel of entertainment. It would appear then, at this time at least, that STV can offer a viable alternative to commercial television programming in big-city markets—or even sections of those markets—that are not wired or cannot be wired for cable.

Conclusion: At current levels of penetration, basic cable, pay cable,

STV, and over-the-air broadcasting each appear to be filling a clear market need. The regulators and the politicians notwithstanding, it remains to be seen in the years ahead whether one technology will necessarily win out, be it one of the existing ones or an as yet undeveloped one, such as videodisc or direct satellite-to-home transmission, or whether the current peaceful coexistence can continue.

QUESTIONS TO ASK YOURSELF BEFORE MAKING AN INVESTMENT IN THE CATV INDUSTRY

1. What is the capital and financial situation of the company? Can the company finance additional systems from internally generated funds, or will it have to seek external financing? How soon will those systems become profitable? Will they generate a sufficient return on investment to make the whole process worthwhile?
2. What is the level of turnover or "churn" of existing subscribers? Is the subscriber count growing, stagnating, or decreasing?
3. What additional services do the systems offer and at what additional cost to the operator? Do they require extensive "rebuild" work? If so, what will the payback period be?
4. What is the average income level of the subscribers in the areas where the CATV systems are located? Can they afford to pay for incremental services?
5. What is the population growth of the area where the cable system is located? Are a lot of people moving into that region?
6. Are there any peculiar terrain problems in the areas to be built that would sharply increase the cost of building the system?
7. Are there problems for any of the company's systems on the local political level? What has the history been on rate increases? Does the local city government, which regulates all such rate increases, approve them readily?
8. Are there any discernible trends or attitudes at the federal level, from the FCC, Congress, or the courts, that could potentially harm cable's growth?

CHAPTER 9

THE CHEMICAL INDUSTRY

Peter E. Butler

KEY TO ANALYZING THE INDUSTRY

Evaluating macroeconomic trends correctly and judging when the industry will be in a favorable variable cost/price relationship.

MOST COMMON INVESTOR MISTAKES

Buying these stocks too late, that is, when the stocks have already discounted the good news.

The chemical industry is not a homogeneous industry; on the contrary, it is characterized by three types of companies: large, multinational companies; middle-sized, mostly domestic companies; and specialty chemical companies. (The same rules that apply to the large, multinational companies also hold for the medium-sized companies, excluding, of course, the international aspect.) From time to time, each of these three types of companies will be going in a different direction and will have a different outlook.

HOW TO ANALYZE MULTINATIONAL CHEMICAL COMPANIES

1. The product mix of multinational companies is heavily dependent on the worldwide trade of commodity chemicals. The outlook for the industry, therefore, is dependent on economic production in the major markets the company serves. These
   companies derive 20 to 40 percent of sales from foreign markets,
   including local production as well as export sales. (Canada and
   Europe are characterized by local manufacturing, while the Far
   East and South America are export markets.) It's very difficult for
   the average investor to follow and analyze the economic trends
   outside the United States, because timely economic data are
   unavailable.
2. The significance of trends in production can be seen in the
   following statistic. For every 1 percent change in volume, there
   will be a 3 to 4 percent change in earnings for the major
   companies.
3. Even more important than changes in volume are changes in
   product pricing, as a 1 percent change in pricing can cause a 9
   percent change in earnings. Over a long period of time, pricing is
   dependent on the cost of manufacture (raw materials, labor, capital costs, etc.); over the short term, however, prices are a function
   of the level and direction of operating rates. When operating rates
   are high, prices usually go up faster than costs; but when operating rates are low, the reverse is true.

   An important aspect of the pricing question is the relationship
   of the dollar to foreign currencies. Most foreign sales are made in
   the local currency and then converted into dollars. So, if an
   American chemical company had significant sales in, say, Germany, and the Deutschemark increased 10 percent against the
   dollar, this, in effect, would amount to a 10 percent price increase
   for the company.
4. The relationship of the dollar to other currencies can also have a
   big effect on export pricing. Thus, when the U.S. dollar declines
   against other currencies, it tends to make our products more
   competitive in world markets.
5. On the cost side of the equation, labor is a fairly predictable item,
   representing some 20 to 25 percent of sales. Raw materials usually represent some 30 percent of sales, but this is more difficult
   to forecast. Petrochemical feedstocks and energy are two

extremely important aspects of raw materials, and both are subject to political pressures. Despite the political aspects, raw materials, wage, and capital costs are generally easier to predict than product pricing; they are a function of what is happening in a particular country and what the financial condition of that country is.

6. Because of the exposure that many of these multinational companies have to foreign markets, their earnings are sensitive to foreign currency fluctuations. Unfortunately, however, it's very difficult to evaluate the geographic asset-liability exposure of these companies, as they do not generally release such information. This foreign currency exposure question has reduced the earnings visibility of these companies and therefore the relative earnings multiple that investors will pay for the stocks. Another potential uncertainty is that union pressure on the U.S. government could result in controls on foreign investment on the grounds that such investments take away domestic jobs.

UNIQUE ASPECTS OF THE CHEMICAL INDUSTRY

1. The chemical industry is not homogeneous but comprises thousands of different products. In this sense, it is different from other basic industries, which have only a few product varieties. For this reason, it is difficult, or at times impossible, to analyze every product of a chemical company. From time to time, however, there will be key products that are important to concentrate on. Thus, an investor should focus on macroeconomics, taking a top-down approach to companies, and determine the relationship between pricing and costs. Then you can separate one company from another on the basis of which one will benefit most from macroeconomic trends and of the foreseeable price/cost relationship.

2. Another unique aspect of this industry is its high foreign sales component. In fact, it has the highest foreign sales component of all the basic manufacturing industries.

STRUCTURAL CHANGES TAKING PLACE IN THIS INDUSTRY

1. There is a long-term downward trend in the inventory-to-sales ratio for chemical companies' customers. Because the cost of carrying inventories has risen, there is pressure on managements

to run their businesses more efficiently. Thus, through the use of computer and other financial controls, inventories as a percentage of sales have been reduced on a secular basis, with the result that chemical demand growth has slowed. Formerly, chemicals typically grew at a rate 2 to 2½ times the GNP growth; however, this has been reduced significantly of late to 1 to 1½ times, and it would not be surprising if the price/earnings multiples of these stocks were reduced accordingly.

2. The U.S. government has gone from fostering investment in chemicals, as it did 20 years ago, to discouraging it now. What's more, there are price controls in several key foreign countries, which hamper profitability. Furthermore, there are strong, militant unions outside the United States which are working hand in hand with local governments to discourage American competition in foreign markets. Environmental considerations have also reduced growth. (Note that environmental problems are significant both internationally and domestically.) All these negatives have reduced the expected growth rate of the industry to 1 to 1½ times the GNP.

3. The small entrepreneur is being inundated with government red tape and restrictive regulations, which means there will be a further concentration of the industry in the hands of a few large companies.

4. Another important development is that the substitution of chemicals for labor and for other materials is slowing.

5. Many chemical markets are mature.

6. The role of foreign governments will be a key to the outlook of multinational chemical companies. The squeezing of profitability and the lower earnings visibility are factors not fully discounted in the price of the stocks. There are now only a few places where an American company can make an investment on a 100 percent ownership basis. The trend in third world investment is joint ventures, a poor way of doing business, as a company's options are reduced and its government partner is likely to have a motivation different from the company's for doing business.

WHEN TO BUY/SELL THE STOCKS

1. In 1973 and 1974, the chemical industry was in a seller's market in spite of the fact that GNP growth was declining because of the

approaching 1974–1975 recession. So, a generalization about the outlook for economic growth may not always be right as it applies to these companies.

2. It's very rare for the dividends of these companies to be cut. Very rarely will a company show earnings deficits for an extended period of time. Perhaps for a quarter or so, but generally not more than that. Thus, you can, and should, focus on dividend yields as a means of downside protection in major companies.

3. The time to buy these stocks is when the fundamental news is terrible. Usually at this point, every conceivable piece of bad news has already occurred and an even worse case is being discounted. It usually isn't long before the news improves, however. You should look for a particular stock which you estimate will have better earnings than the consensus thinks it will. You should look for a stock which will record above-average earnings gains and which has a low relative p/e ratio in relation to its past history.

4. It's important to remember that the very large commodity-oriented companies are very volatile. Over a 10-year period, there are likely to be several opportunities to buy or sell the stocks. These are not long-term investments, and it's difficult for the small investor to play this industry.

5. You should analyze the financial resources of the company, its technology, and its product position. What is the company's market share for its products, what kind of franchise does it have, and how will it translate its resources into earnings growth?

6. You should never consider these stocks as long-term investments, as many investors did in the 1974–1975 period. When cyclical stocks become viewed by analysts as noncyclical, that is usually a good signal to sell them.

7. The factors which motivate these stocks over the long term are the outlooks for earnings and dividends, or total return; over the short term, it's the outlook for earnings and positive or negative news.

CHAPTER 10

THE CONSUMER PACKAGED GOODS INDUSTRY

Edward A. Jones

EXAMPLES OF CONSUMER PACKAGED GOODS

Toiletries, cosmetics, fragrances, proprietary drugs (sold over the counter without a prescription), food, tampons, first aid products, and many others are considered consumer packaged goods.

KEY TO ANALYZING THE INDUSTRY

1. Being able to correctly evaluate management's responsiveness to change and innovation and its marketing skills. Events take place so rapidly in this industry that it's almost impossible for the average investor to keep track of what's going on (e.g., a new advertising program can be introduced in 30 to 60 days). The best way around this quandary is to develop a confidence that management can respond effectively and quickly to any changes or competitive innovations that occur.
2. Having a clear understanding of what constitutes successful marketing skills and realizing that marketing is an art. (Note that the manufacturing cost for these products is more or less the same throughout the industry.)

MOST COMMON INVESTOR MISTAKES

1. Focusing too much on individual products.
2. Not paying enough attention to what constitutes successful marketing skills.
3. Not knowing how to evaluate marketing management, marketing success, and the criteria necessary for continued success.

BACKGROUND ON THE INDUSTRY

Consumer packaged goods are basically a people business. The success of the companies in the industry depends on flair, insight, marketing strategy, and marketing research. It's also important to have a broad line of existing products with sufficient cash flow to finance new ventures and new products, which, in the final analysis, determine the outlook for the future. Another key criterion is to know how to evaluate market share for a given product: the larger the market share is, the more profits will increase as the market share grows, and the less spending will be needed on advertising for this product. For example, Noxzema and Vaseline are two products which are not advertised much but which dominate their markets and generate a large cash flow.

This is basically a $1-to-$5–item business: items that are used up, bought again, used up, and bought again. These items are highly useful to the consumer, but they are certainly not necessities.

It's important to remember that you cannot easily categorize most of the companies in this industry, because they have been diversifying into many fields, such as medical supplies and food. So you are not just looking at a cosmetic or toiletry company, as may have been the case 10 or 15 years ago.

Therefore, the first step in analyzing a consumer packaged goods company is to evaluate its existing product lines. How does the company maintain its current market share and growth rate? Does the company achieve this by spending a lot of money? If the company suddenly stopped spending money on advertising and promotion, would sales fall off dramatically?

In answering these questions, it is very important to look at what is called the multimedia spending of the entire industry. There are two types of spending: "measured media," which includes advertising in newspapers, TV, and magazines, and "unmeasured media," which includes giveaways, coupons, and displays. Typically, measured media spending goes for sustaining the market share of existing products, while unmeasured media spending is devoted to the promotion of a new product.

Such firms as Nielsen, Sami, and Point-Of-Sale evaluate measured media advertising expenditures and the results of such spending. Sami, a subsidiary of Time Inc., prepares what is called a "warehouse" audit, analyzing the turnover of a product at the warehouse level. On the other hand, Nielsen takes a "retail take-away" audit, which, in the final analysis, is the key piece of information. In advance of a large advertising campaign, a company might build up a huge warehouse of various products. Thus, a warehouse audit could be misleading in terms of how well the product is doing with the consumer.

Of course, one must not limit one's analysis to measured spending, since giveaway campaigns, in-store promotions, coupons, and point-of-purchase displays can be significant in terms of cost and effectiveness. As you can gather, then, it is hard to determine the actual level of promotion expenditures, since the information on many forms of spending is not available through conventional methods. This poses a major obstacle to the average investor, one that can be surmounted, however, through the use of imagination and effort.

The best way for you to get the advertising information you'll need to properly evaluate one of these companies is to get to know as many marketing people as you can—whether from an advertising agency, the marketing department of a corporation, or sales in general. The more marketing people you know and the better they are at what they do, the better will be your lines of communication.

It is recommended that you pay most attention to those who are very successful at what they do. The whole marketing business is a great party circuit, and a lot of information can be obtained by keeping in close contact with the people in the industry. It's easy in the advertising business to throw around a lot of buzz words and sound as if you really know what you're doing, and people who do can be quite misleading. In evaluating the information of your industry source, ask yourself how successful that individual has been in marketing and how successful his firm has been. If the answer to both these questions is favorable, then you can rely heavily on the input that you receive.

Just as determining the level of advertising is difficult, so is getting a fix on the true performance of these companies. What frequently happens is that a company will launch an assortment of new products at the same time, spend a lot of money on promotion, and thereby cut deeply into profits for several years. And just as these new products become very profitable, the company will spend money on promoting and developing other new products. This process tends to even out earnings over a considerable period so that no one year will show a huge jump in profitability due to the introduction of a new product. Procter & Gamble and Revlon, for example, follow this pattern closely. They believe in maximizing growth over the long term and try to avoid wherever possible having a few dramatically successful years that might soon be followed by down or flat years as the new product's impact wears off.

For this reason, it should come as no surprise that an important factor affecting the stocks of these companies is the introduction of a new product. New products tend to get investors excited, and this is especially so if the new product appears to offer other potential new avenues of exploitation. For example, a name that was used successfully in one area could be used in several other new product lines as well.

The second critical factor in evaluating these companies, and one that is tied closely to the first point, is the ability of management to adapt to change. Since this is a consumer business, a manager must be able to sense and anticipate the changing habits, customs, likes, desires, and dislikes of the American consumer.

There are two main categories of consumer packaged goods—cosmetics and toiletries—and there are a lot of differences between the two. Toiletries are basically utilitarian and price-sensitive. Typical examples of toiletries are shampoos, deodorants, hair conditioners, hair colors, hair spray, and toothpaste. Cosmetic sales are more sensitive to fashion and individual taste, and therefore more personal selling is required.

On the other hand, the ease of entry into the toiletries business is very high. Toiletries is a very volatile business and thus, an investment in toiletry stocks should be made only after careful scrutiny. The cosmetics business is more individualistic and therefore has more control. In other words, cosmetics won't be plagued by price wars: cosmetics are fashionable, and that is the key to their success. Toiletries, on the other hand, are extremely price-sensitive and are influenced by the business cycle. Most consumer packaged goods companies are in a wide variety of businesses, and one must discover the most important products of these companies in order to fully understand whether they're a cosmetics or a toiletries company.

Another important aspect of these companies relates to the introduction of new products, which generally go in spurts. For example, in the mid 1950s hair sprays were the very latest thing. But after the advent of the 1974–75 recession, hair sprays became a lackluster business, while shampoos and home permanents became big winners. (Inflation and recession increased the desire to save money on hairdressers.)

In summary, then, the key to success in this business is the judgment of management. Do they have the insight into the subliminal and psychological feelings of the buyer, and can they develop products that will appeal to those buyers? (Chemical companies, for instance, have a strong emphasis on quality control and employ a disciplined, scientific method in the production of their basic materials. But in consumer packaged goods, such formulas and disciplines are not possible. Being able to gauge what the consumer wants and then developing a product that satisfies those wants and selling it imaginatively are the critical factors.) Another reason management is so important to this industry is that one can be misled by merely looking at the growth potential in existing product lines; for instance, innovative, management can find new and different uses for products or increase their market shares. A classic example of this is the new market area for Pampers—adults who have bladder problems.

Therefore, in evaluating different companies in the industry, analyze the management carefully. Is the caliber of management stronger or weaker than the competition's? In order to get effective answers to that question, you have to evaluate the competition. Is it strong or weak in the product lines your company competes against? Also take into consideration the price/earnings ratio of the company. In other words, a problem that might bother you in a company selling at twenty times earnings might not bother you in a company selling at five times earnings.

Timing of new-product introduction is also very critical. (Charlie was a great success for Revlon because it came out at exactly the right time.) You also should stay with companies that are of a certain size. Big companies have the money that's needed to get a new product going, and small companies have difficulty competing against that kind of marketing muscle. What's more, the packaged goods industry is becoming more and more professional. For instance, at the purchasing end of the pipeline, and in the whole pipeline process, in fact, more and more people are getting involved. Where formerly you might have had to deal with just one person in the buying end, now you may have to deal with a whole range of people in the store. Now, you have to "sell" not just the buyer, but also all of these other people.

SOME CRITERIA FOR MARKETING SUCCESS

1. The company should have someting to clearly differentiate its product(s) from others on the market. The product doesn't necessarily have to be better, only different. This, then, will help the company to advertise and push the product successfully before the public.
2. The marketing plans should be well-thought-out and should have good follow-through. The marketplace should be well assessed and the long-term demand studied closely.
3. The company should be *structured* for success. Even if the company has an exciting new product, it may come to naught if there isn't considerable follow-through with retailers and promotion. In other words, the company should have skills all up and down the line.
4. The greater the company's market share of existing products, the better. Greater market share means more profits, which means more money for promotion of new products.
5. Ideally, a company should build a consumer franchise for its products. That way, the company can free itself from dependence on retail stores, which often involves discounts or other incentives. To develop a consumer franchise, a personality or a social status must be developed for the product.
6. Management should have a long-range focus with special emphasis on (a) building a solid consumer franchise and (b) developing and introducing new products which will contribute to profits.
7. The company should be adept at "line extension"—in other words, developing high- and low-end versions of its products. (Procter & Gamble, for instance, has twelve different detergents.) Line extension is important for several reasons:

    a. If a company doesn't do it, the competition most likely will.
    b. The larger the line extension, the greater the diversification and the greater the appeal to the whole market.

10-6

8. Research and development spending should be large and continuous.

QUESTIONS TO ASK YOURSELF BEFORE MAKING AN INVESTMENT IN A CONSUMER PACKAGED GOODS COMPANY

1. What is the capability of management?
2. What is the company's marketing strategy? How good is it?
3. What is the competitive strength of the company's major brands?
4. What is the company's new-product capability? Does it frequently introduce a lot of successful new products, or is it living off past successes?
5. What percentage of earnings or cash flow is being spent on new products?
6. What percentage of the company's earnings comes from abroad and is therefore subject to currency fluctuations?
7. What is the company's competitive position abroad? (As foreign markets offer more potential than the United States market, a strong and expanding position abroad is a major plus.)
8. What is the nature of the company's competition?
9. How easy or hard is it to introduce a new product?
10. Are there any important changes taking place which might affect the ground rules of a particular aspect of the business? For instance, if instant coffee were just being introduced for the first time, you'd want to ask yourself how dominant or how active a participant your company was in this line of business.
11. If the company has a losing or weak operation, what is management doing about it? Is it trying to get rid of it, cutting out the losing part of the operation?
12. What is the depth of managerial talent? Are the good people only at the top, or is the company developing a good marketing staff at all levels?
13. What is the quality of earnings? How large is the spending on developing and introducing new products? (In other words, a company may be generating good current earnings but at the sacrifice of new-product development, a sacrifice which could present problems over time, and which the stock market would certainly anticipate well in advance.)

14. What are the company's strengths and weaknesses? (For example, Colgate-Palmolive is highly successful internationally and knows how to minimize earnings losses due to foreign exchange fluctuations.)

15. How does the financial community feel about management?

16. How forthright is management and how well does it deal with the financial community? If a company has problems and the management is forthright about it, then the problems become less of a concern. That's even more true if management appears to be taking action to solve the problems. You would not want to learn suddenly about a negative development that took place. Nor, for that matter, should that negative development have come as a surprise to the company.

17. Can the company identify problems and start to deal with them effectively? In other words, can the company respond to change?

18. What are the overall demographics, and is your company responding to them? For instance, the average age of the population in the United States is steadily increasing, and there is a pronounced increase in the number of single households and working women. This will open up good opportunities for alert management.

19. What are the unusually optimistic areas for growth in the industry? Is your company involved in them? For instance, the medical field, especially pharmaceutical products and hospital supplies, was one of the most attractive areas for growth in 1978.

CHAPTER 11

THE CONTAINER AND PACKAGING INDUSTRY

H. Edward Schollmeyer

KEY TO ANALYZING THE INDUSTRY

Being able to anticipate what type of container bottlers and brewers think their customers want.

MOST COMMON INVESTOR MISTAKE

Taking an oversimplified view of these companies. It takes a lot more than an analysis of GNP, personal income, etc., to correctly forecast demand. Such unpredictable factors as the weather and the price of sugar can have a greater effect on this industry than, say, an economic slowdown.

SOME GENERAL POINTS TO REMEMBER ABOUT THE INDUSTRY

1. This industry is a chess game with no checkmate. Glass container companies, metal container manufacturers, and aluminum producers are constantly vying with one another for an

increased share of the container market. New products, new designs, and new market strategies are constantly being employed to that end.

2. The major food companies went into in-house manufacturing of cans but stayed away from glass, because glass container manufacturing is an art, not a science.

3. About 20 percent of the retail price of Coca-Cola or Pepsi-Cola is accounted for by the container. Thus, the soft drink companies have a big incentive to keep container prices down.

4. There are no basic yardsticks or ground rules for this industry. The critical factor to watch is what makes the bottlers and brewers decide on one form of packaging instead of another.

5. The outlook for the aluminum industry is important in evaluating the future of the container industry. The period 1983–1984 is a critically important time, since that is when the hydroelectric power contract with aluminum companies comes up for renewal. If the contract isn't renewed because the Northwest's need for energy is too large, or if its content is severely affected by new legislation enacted by that time, you could see a significant increase in energy costs for aluminum producers that would raise the price of an aluminum can and make glass or steel much more competitive. What's worse, even though some plants in the Northwest are fully depreciated, producing aluminum there is a break-even proposition, even with the current low cost of power. And it's worth noting that the price of aluminum has already gone up dramatically.

6. Container companies are viewed as defensive and yield investments.

7. It's hard to forecast demand for this industry, because weather can be a major factor. For instance, a lot of rain or cold weather could reduce the demand for soft drinks, and good crops, good weather, and a successful planting season can increase the demand for cans for vegetables and fruits. Therefore, the best approach is to analyze this industry on a company-by-company basis. Unfortunately, however, most companies don't break out profits by line of business.

8. Environmental legislation on disposable cans and glass bottles should be closely watched.

9. The key to analyzing this industry is to pick out a basic long-term trend and analyze which companies will be beneficiaries of

that trend. One of the ways to do that is to watch the introduction of new products, such as the 7-ounce beer bottle and the 64-ounce soft-drink container, and then determine what companies will benefit from the trend. If such a product catches on, the company promoting the new product could be an attractive investment.

10. Pricing and the ability to pass along increased costs is a key factor in the metal can industry, because that industry is caught between what can best be described as strong suppliers and strong customers.

11. The glass and metal container companies tend to resort to cutthroat competition during prosperous periods in an attempt to increase their market share. Thus, one should always be attuned to such a development and be cautious when times appear to be too good.

12. Historically, there has been some seasonality to the stock market action of common stocks of packaging companies, particularly glass container companies. They tend to reach a zenith late in the summer or early in the fall, and then to enter a period of consolidation until the early part of the next year.

QUESTIONS TO ASK YOURSELF BEFORE MAKING AN INVESTMENT IN THE CONTAINER AND PACKAGING INDUSTRY

1. What are the economics of steel versus aluminum for beer and soft drink cans?

2. What percentages of sales of your company come from food, beer, and soft drink markets?

3. What percent of the company's operations are in foreign markets and would be subject to foreign currency fluctuations? And to what degree are profits subject to foreign currency fluctuation?

4. Where did the company invest its funds in the last 5 years? What percent of those funds were used in cost-reduction equipment and productivity improvement?

5. What percent of the container market does the company have? What is the company's corporate strategy? What is the financial condition of the company? How has the company handled any major problems that occurred in the last 10 years? How good was the company in getting itself back into shape?

6. How competitive is the company in terms of aluminum, steel, and glass container manufacturing?
7. Will plastic continue to replace glass and metal containers?
8. What is the risk that the company's major customers might go into in-house container manufacturing?
9. What are the company's major customers, and is the company dependent on any one for a sizeable percentage of its volume? (Some 70 percent of the beer produced in this country is produced by the top five brewers. What are those companies doing in terms of containers and packaging?)
10. What is happening in the area of types and sizes of containers? And how involved is your company in each area?
11. What are the basic trends in aluminum, glass, steel, and plastic? What research and development is being done in these areas? Can steel or aluminum cans be produced that are even lighter than the ones that currently exist? Can steel or aluminum cans be produced at a lower price?
12. What is the status of environmental legislation? If you want to get up-to-date information on this you can talk to your local congressional representative or state legislator. This is a very important factor, because if certain legislation is passed, either at the state or the national level, the bottlers of beer and soft drinks will be using mainly returnable glass bottles, with the result that the demand for many types of containers will be drastically reduced.

CHAPTER 12

THE DATA PROCESSING INDUSTRY

Sanford J. Garrett

MOST COMMON INVESTOR MISTAKES

The most common investor mistake is to base buying decisions on short-term criteria rather than on longer-term considerations. Most frequently this takes two forms:

1. Buying companies, particularly "secondary" (small, growing) ones, because of rapid earnings growth, which generally is not sustainable over the long term.
2. Buying companies at the peaks of their product cycles, just prior to the advent of a new generation of equipment.

IMPORTANT POINTS TO REMEMBER ABOUT THE INDUSTRY

1. *The only constant is change.* The data processing industry is a high-growth industry with a foundation built on its participants' ability to continually improve the cost/performance of its product line through the rapid introduction of advanced technology. It is more important to

discern what is on the horizon than to analyze the current state of the market. Today's wonder device may be tomorrow's obsolete chunk of iron.

2. The market for computers is highly elastic in response to the ongoing improvement in cost/performance. This derives from the explosion in information, which needs to be compiled and processed, and inflation, which increases dramatically the need for improved productivity.

3. The advent of the microprocessor is accelerating the pace of technological change and in retrospect may eventually be viewed as being as important as the development of the transistor. New markets are continually being created, and these can be exploited for a period of time by one or more companies clever enough to recognize them.

4. Since the microprocessor is greatly facilitating the ease of market entry for small or emerging companies, the well-established industry leaders are attempting to maintain market share by reducing the value from hardware and recouping it through support areas such as maintenance and software. Hence, the price umbrella over hardware per se will be declining even more rapidly than technological advances would suggest, and the staying power of new companies will erode.

5. The advent of the microprocessor and the accelerating pace of technological advances is causing a blurring of the distinctions between what had previously been discrete industries. Mainframe and minicomputer data processing, telecommunications, electronics, office equipment, and even instrumentation are now all beginning to merge into one giant high-technology industry. This will increase competition, raise the stakes for being successful, and enlarge the market.

6. Because of expected high growth and the pervasiveness of increased computing requirements, competition is becoming more international. Japan in particular is making a significant effort to compete in the international markets for computing capability.

7. One cannot analyze a company in this industry without studying the position of the company relative to the largest factor in the business: IBM. Generally, smaller companies can be successful only if they are able to take advantage of a pricing or product development strategy of IBM, or if they become a supplier of peripheral products compatible with IBM equipment.

The larger computer manufacturers must also be responsive to the pricing strategies of IBM and to the cycle of new product introduction.

In the future, the Japanese computer industry may also call the tune in these matters. To sum up, there is room for several successful strategies in this industry because of its rapid growth, but investors must always keep a watchful eye on IBM and in the future on Japan.

FACTORS WHICH DETERMINE THE INDUSTRY'S PROFITS

1. Product Cycle

In the past, the industry experienced a 4- to 7-year product cycle characterized by the following:

1. Lower profit growth as a new product was introduced, since economies of scale had not yet been achieved, marketing costs were high, and customers were reluctant to purchase the older products at the end of their cycle and preferred to lease instead
2. High profit growth in the middle of the cycle
3. Lower growth again as the cycle neared its end and a new one began.

This is now changing, however. The product cycle is shortening to 3 to 5 years because of increasing competition and the development of the microprocessor. Profitability toward the end of the cycle is being maintained by switching from a high-lease component to predominantly outright sale (see below). This is possible because the growing importance of software has assured that new generations of computers will be entirely compatible with older ones. Hence, users are now more responsive to purchasing older product families.

2. Sales/Lease Ratio

The changing mix between outright sales and equipment leasing is a critical factor to short-term revenue and earnings growth. Since computers represent large capital outlays to the customer, such factors as pricing policies, the stage in the product cycle, the cost of capital, and corporate liquidity all have a major influence on the user's decision to buy or lease. The increasing spread between software and hardware costs and the increase in competition brought about by the advent of the microprocessor have created an environment that is now evolving more toward sale than lease. Nevertheless, short-term aberrations can occur which will result in a decline in the sales/lease ratio with a negative impact on profitability. The lease typically represents a lower profit to the manufacturer over the short term, but greater revenue and profits over the long haul.

3. Capital Spending Cycle

The ability and willingness of corporations to spend money on capital equipment influences computer shipments with an impact on profitability from two standpoints:

1. The changing sales/lease mix as discussed above.
2. Changing unit volumes which modestly impact expenses and, in turn, margins.

4. Market Share

Traditional analysis suggests that a company's market share determines its profitability because the larger the share, the greater the control the company has over its pricing. Superficially, this might appear to be the case in the data processing industry as well when one compares IBM's high margins to those of the other mainframe companies. Closer examination, however, reveals that many smaller participants in the market (such as Data General, for example) also have high profitability. This stems from the fact that the data processing market is not homogeneous in nature, but rather is broken down into a large number of specialized submarkets, each with its own pricing characteristics. The investor must constantly be aware, however, of the changing nature of these segments as evolving technology breaks down some barriers while at the same time creating new ones.

HOW TO INVEST IN THE INDUSTRY

Due to inflation on one hand and continuing cost/performance improvements for computers on the other, the data processing industry is expected to continue to gain share of worldwide GNP for the foreseeable future. As such, it represents one of the few areas where a long-term investment strategy makes the most sense. This creates two key avenues where opportunity might present itself:

1. Systematically, when the stock market sells off for comparatively short-term cyclical reasons or otherwise (e.g., concern about a

pending energy shortage) and relative price/earnings ratios compress, the data processing group as a whole begins to look highly attractive. It is unlikely that the long-term growth rate of the industry will be affected.

2. From a specific (as opposed to systematic) standpoint, the stocks of the industry have historically been characterized by a cyclicality associated with computer product cycles. On the introduction of any major new product line, cost/performance parameters improve sharply and questions always seem to arise about the industry's ability to maintain margins. The stocks sell off, and occasionally there are even short-term dislocations in earnings that seem to justify it. Inevitably, the elasticity of demand in the market exerts itself, unit placements accelerate, and profitability recovers (if it falls off in the first place). The weakness in the stocks immediately following major product introductions has typically provided outstanding buying opportunities in most of the well-established companies. It is the smaller companies that miss the change in technology that do not recover, and it is here that the investor must be cautious and reassess his appraisals.

Investing in the smaller companies in the industry which are suppliers to or competitors of the larger companies actually requires a strategy all its own. Ideally, the investor should understand very thoroughly the technological and market position of the company and feel confident that a high level of earnings growth can be sustained for at least a five-year period. If possible, an investor should be confident that sales are at least keeping pace with the growth rate of the total market for the company's products. If growth rates are slower than those of the market, it means the company is losing market share and will ultimately find itself at a major competitive disadvantage. In other words, do not be fooled by a high growth rate which is low by comparison to the rate of growth of the rest of the industry.

Once you have bought one of the smaller computer companies, be alert to any signs of a slowing in the growth rate or a loss of market share. If you see an increasing drop in sales or the introduction and rapid success of a new product by a competing company, you would do well to sell the stock at once.

The problem with investing in small companies is that regardless of how well the situation is analyzed, the resulting image is only a snapshot in time. Due to the rapidly changing advances in technology and the reasonably high probability of unforeseeable events, the risk associated with such an investment is extremely high. However, you can greatly reduce this risk without sacrificing potentially large rewards by pursuing a diversified portfolio strategy.

The best approach to participating in the extraordinary growth of the small data processing concerns is to purchase a market basket of companies in essentially noncompetitive submarkets. This reduces the specific risk of events turning any individual investment sour, but it allows the investor to partake in the systematic growth of the industry as a whole. Needless to say, the cautionary notes mentioned above in regard to investing in any small company still apply to the market-basket approach.

QUESTIONS TO ASK BEFORE MAKING AN INVESTMENT IN THE DATA PROCESSING INDUSTRY

1. Where is the industry in relation to its latest product cycle? Is it at the beginning or at the tail end of a major generation of computers? When is the next generation of equipment likely to be introduced?

2. Have the latest price cuts or cost/performance improvements in the industry radically departed from historical rates? If so, are they justified on the basis of improving technology or structural changes which recoup revenues from other sources?

3. What is the status of competition in the industry particularly as it relates to Japan or to technological innovations that may be causing structural changes?

4. How is the nature of competition changing due to the breakdown of barriers between mainframe computers, minicomputers, telecommunications, office equipment, and electronics? Does the potential reward of owning your company justify the increasing pressure and risk? What new opportunities are presenting themselves, and who is best positioned to take advantage of them? What companies are now at a disadvantage?

5. What is the future strategy of IBM in regard to pricing and product development? What effect will this strategy have on your company? What effect will alternate strategies have?

6. What is the outlook for capital spending? Combined with product cycle, what impact will this have on the sales/lease ratio?

7. What is happening to your company's market share? Is your com-

pany growing as fast as its major market (submarket)? Have any developments occurred, particularly technological in derivation, which would cause you to redefine your company's market (submarket)? If so, how does your company's performance measure up under this new definition? Is the outlook better or worse because of this change?

CHAPTER 13

THE DRUG INDUSTRY

J. Peter Gaskins

KEY TO ANALYZING THE INDUSTRY

Being able to predict the relative level of earnings. Although new-product development is critical to the industry, it is not as important as many drug stock analysts would have you believe.

MOST COMMON INVESTOR MISTAKES

1. Attempting to play the new-product game before a new product has proved itself. This is a very risky approach and is stacked 4- or 5-to-1 against success.
2. Relying on doctors' advice about new drugs. Doctors generally don't know and can't evaluate nationwide or worldwide demand for a new drug. While it may be worthwhile to check into a new drug product which a doctor recommends, you should view his recommendation skeptically.
3. Buying drug stocks just because they are cheap. The trouble with this strategy is that a drug stock can always get cheaper. The life

cycle for drug products is very long, and any structural change takes place very slowly in this industry. When things are going well they tend to stay well, and when things are going badly they tend to keep getting worse. There seems to be considerable resistance to change, and it takes 1 to 2 years to turn things around. Thus, there's no need to rush in and buy these stocks when things appear to be bad; there will be plenty of time to evaluate whether there really is a fundamental turnaround taking place.

HOW TO ANALYZE THE INDUSTRY

You can't make too many generalizations about the industry. It has historically been a very heterogeneous industry, and company performance, both in earnings and in the stock market, has varied widely from company to company over the years.

Many analysts get bogged down in details with drug companies, which is a mistake. The best way to view these companies is as a consumer product business. It's important that investors not be scared away by technical terms and expressions, and they should make every attempt to use commonsense reasoning in approaching the industry and analyzing the potential for new products.

The first step in analyzing a drug company should be to discover which markets the company serves. For example, is the company involved in antibiotics, antihypertension products, or drugs for the treatment of diabetes? After you have discovered which market the company serves, the next question to ask is, what is the growth rate of those markets, and what is the company's position in those markets? This is important, because markets may grow at different rates, in terms of both units and overall sales. A key aspect of analyzing the company's position in each market is to know what the size of that market is. The position that a company has in its market is critical. The more a company dominates its market, the more it is able to determine pricing, and the more profitable its position will be in that particular market.

Regulation: the Food and Drug Administration

Government regulation is also an extremely important aspect of analyzing the industry. For one thing, the government, through the FDA (Food and Drug Administration), controls new-product introduction and existing-product usage.

There are two stages of drug development. The first stage involves extensive clinical work and amassing of data by the drug company. When this has been completed, the results are sent to the FDA for review. The amount of time the FDA takes to analyze the material and to form a decision can dramatically affect the time it takes to bring a new product out. But contrary to popular expectations, the FDA has not increased the amount of time for new-product approval since around 1968. In fact, FDA approval time has remained constant since 1968.

A second way the FDA can affect drug companies is through its control over existing products, either by taking them off the market or by narrowing or broadening their use. Typically, after a drug has been introduced on a mass scale, there are additional side effects or benefits discovered that were not apparent in the preintroduction clinical work. (In the initial investigation and clinical studies by the company, there is generally no opportunity to observe the effectiveness of a drug and its side effects on a long-term user. Thus, when you have mass-scale usage by different types of people with different types of physiological and biological problems, certain unforeseen effects can come to the fore.) If side effects start to mount, there is a definite possibility that the FDA will begin to investigate the drug.

The FDA controls the labeling of a drug, which involves a complete description of the product, its side effects, its chemical composition, and its approved indications for use. The FDA can increase the warning about certain side effects and it can narrow the applications of the drug.

Because of the ability of the FDA to affect existing products, it is very important that investors be aware whether the FDA is currently investigating a drug that represents a large part of a drug company's sales and earnings. One of the best ways to anticipate FDA problems of this nature is to monitor the clinical data that are released concerning the side effects of drugs. For example, if many doctors around the country are writing reports about bad side effects of a certain drug, this could be an early warning that investigation by the FDA may soon be on the way.

The FDA can also permit the label for the drug to indicate broader usage. This, however, is done only in response to an active request by the maker of the drug based on additional clinical trials. Thus, expansion of approved claims for a drug can occur after introduction but will typically take much longer than a narrowing of approved claims does when the need arises.

In 1962 there was an amendment to the Food and Drug Act which required drug companies to prove efficacy of a new drug. For this reason, it took a lot longer between 1962 and 1968 than it had up to that time to get a new drug approved. Not only did it take more time for the company to do its clinical work, but it also took longer for the FDA to evaluate the material that the drug company sent in. However, this was purely a function of experience, or lack thereof, and once the FDA became more familiar with the mass of data being sent in, it was able to handle new drug applications in a more efficient fashion.

Thus, we can see that the FDA can control the future of a drug company significantly. It can remove a company's products from the market, or it can alter the therapeutic claims made for them, which in turn can change the product's usage and, hence, sales and profits.

New Products

The next-most significant area for investors to study is new-product development. To begin with, it generally is not wise for investors to speculate on new products. The best strategy is to wait until the new product has been available on a mass basis for a period of 6 to 18 months, either in the United States or in European markets. Such a time period will enable you to determine the extent of the drug's usefulness and to evaluate its side effects.

A typical pattern is that a drug company's stock will advance sharply in price prior to the introduction of a new drug, fall off sharply after the new drug has been introduced, and increase in price gradually *if* the drug turns out to be a significant therapeutic advance in a major market. On the other hand, if the drug does not turn out to be a significant improvement over existing therapy, the stock may languish for a number of years. Therefore, by taking this cautious approach, which stresses the purchase of the drug stock only after the new product has demonstrated its effectiveness, you can avoid major errors. You can bypass the loss in the drug's stock price which occurs right after the new drug is introduced, and also avoid a period of lackluster stock prospects if the product does not measure up to investor expectations.

It is easy to become excited about a new drug product, and investors should have a fail-safe mechanism to protect them from their own exuberance. Here are some questions to ask concerning the outlook for a new product: Has this new product, which is being touted to the skies, been introduced to any other markets? If so, how long ago was it introduced and how is it doing? If not, then when will it be introduced on a wide-scale basis? (If you discover that the new product may not be introduced to the United States market for some 3 years, the drug represents a zero value to you as an investor, since you are likely to have only relatively limited clinical data on the product.) What is the potential size of the new market? Also, what's wrong with current therapy? Is the new product going to do more or better for less? (There's no need for investors to be involved in the technical terms of this discussion. A commonsense evaluation of the answers to these questions permits the average investor to understand whether there is a need for such a drug product and whether it is applicable to the overall health care needs of the nation. Be sure not to let some professional overwhelm you with complicated names.)

Earnings

While new products and their introduction may affect stock prices of drug companies over the short term, the long-term fortunes of drug stocks are basically motivated by relative earnings gains. And as we discussed earlier, the key to predicting earnings is being able to distinguish what the company's markets are, its position in those markets, and the growth potential for each market. Drug stocks' relative prices typically turn up about 6 to 12 months in advance of an earnings turnaround.

Regulation in Foreign Markets

Government involvement has ramifications beyond the Food and Drug Administration. For instance, in many nations outside the United States, the government pays for, directly or indirectly, the vast majority of the drugs that are consumed. Since government is, in effect, a monopoly purchaser, it can set prices, and, as we all know, prices are an important determinant of profitability.

Therefore, in a period of rapidly accelerating inflation, governments may attempt to hold down prices and in turn affect the profitability of a company's foreign operations. For this reason, you should find out what the most important countries are with which your drug company does business, what the behavior pattern of these countries has been in the past in terms of pricing of drug products, and what the behavior pattern is at present and what the outlook is for the future.

In the United Kingdom, for instance, all drugs are paid for by the government as part of the national health program. Therefore, during the period of sharply rising inflation in the late 1960s and early 1970s, drug prices were not allowed to rise materially in Great Britain, and drug prices there became the lowest in the world. It was not until 1974 that the British government decided to let prices increase enough to offset the effects of past and present inflation.

Bear in mind that this area lends itself to some sensationalism from time to time. It is important that you not be overwhelmed by what may be described as an overly dramatic activity on the part of a foreign government. It is very rare for a foreign government to take drastic action on drug prices or products—what happens invariably is a gradual evolution, and for this reason it is important to watch the trends, because they will give you a better indication of what is happening than some sensational report stating that this government or that country plans to do this or that to the product of a given drug company.

Since about 45 percent of major drug companies' earnings comes from abroad, this matter of foreign governments is important to watch. It is also necessary to remember that we are not talking about a United States market and a foreign market, but rather a United States market and 125 foreign markets.

We can, however, divide foreign markets into the developing countries and the developed. In developing nations, the basic economic needs are three in number: education, jobs, and health. Of these three, health and education are the most important, since they are the determinants of jobs. A healthy nation is able to be more productive than a nation of sick and unhealthy citizens; its population lives longer; and, as a result, its economic growth is better. And since drugs are the most cost-effective form of health care and most undeveloped nations are short of trained medical personnel and medical facilities, there is considerable impetus for underdeveloped nations to devote a larger portion of their national health care budget to drugs.

Therefore, you can make the generalization that a good market position in a developing country is a solid plus for a drug company. But here again, as we discussed earlier, the profile of the company in the different markets is an important factor. For instance, anti-infective therapy is the most important aspect of health care for developing nations; drugs which treat hypertension may not be nearly so important to developing nations, many of which have not had the high incidence of high blood pressure that the United States has.

In summary, then, you want to know if the drug company is a General Motors, a Ford, or a Chrysler in each one of its markets. Remember that a small market share may appear to be more profitable than it really is, so long as that market is growing fast. But when a market stops growing, a small market share can turn unprofitable almost overnight.

SOME LONG-TERM STRUCTURAL CHANGES

A lot of major drug products will lose patent protection by the early 1980s. Therefore be sure to learn about the status of your company in this area. Does your company derive a lot of its earnings from several products which may lose patent protection in the next few years? If that's the case, will there be price competition in those products when the patent protection expires?

Generally speaking, if a drug is used mainly in a hospital, it tends to be more price-sensitive than if it is used by consumers. (That's because hospitals tend to buy in bulk and their purchasing departments tend to be much more price-conscious.) Also, if the particular product has won a brand recognition, it may be less affected by the loss of patent protection.

Another important structural change is the increasing intervention of states into the whole drug area. Certain states are considering legislation which would favor the substitution of equivalent generic drugs when proprietary drugs are prescribed. Depending on the particular law, this could mean that the pharmacist has to supply the cheapest generic drug to the purchaser or inform him that such a drug is available. That, in turn, might put considerable pressure on product prices where the patent has expired. The key to evaluating this area is to learn whether it is easy or hard to make the product. Clearly, the harder the production process is, the more protection the drug company has. Generally speaking, the more countries that produce a given drug product, the easier it probably is to produce, and therefore the more subject to price pressures, as discussed above.

QUESTIONS TO ASK YOURSELF BEFORE MAKING AN INVESTMENT IN THE DRUG INDUSTRY

1. Are you attempting to play the new-product game? If so, do you realize that the odds are 4 or 5 to 1 against success?
2. Are you buying a drug stock on a doctor's recommendation concerning a new product? If so, are you aware that doctors are notoriously bad at judging market potential for drug products?

3. Are you buying a drug stock simply because it's cheap? If so, are you aware that the stock could always get cheaper?

4. If you're contemplating an investment in the drug industry because you like the group, have you done your homework to determine which company (or companies) will benefit most?

5. Are you getting bogged down in details, or are you evaluating these companies as consumer products businesses?

6. Do you know what markets your company serves, what its position is in those markets, and what their growth rate is?

7. What is the FDA doing with new-product development? Is approval time increasing or decreasing?

8. Is the FDA investigating any of your company's products? If so, why? Is there the possibility the drug could be taken off the market or have its usage narrowed?

9. Has your company just introduced a new drug on a mass basis? If so, how are doctors around the country evaluating the drug's efficacy and side effects?

10. If you must play the new-product game, are you doing so in accordance with the strategy discussed earlier? If you cannot wait for more conclusive data, have you asked the following questions concerning the new drug:

    Has the new drug been introduced to any major markets?
    If so, how long ago was it introduced?
    What is the potential size of the new market?
    What is wrong with current therapy?
    Is the new product going to do more and better for less?

11. How dependent is your company on foreign earnings? What is the trend of intervention in those countries? What is the company's market position abroad and how fast are its markets growing?

12. Is your company going to lose patent protection for any major product by the early 1980s? What effect will that have on earnings?

13. What's happening to intervention on the state level? Are more and more states requiring that druggists fill a prescription with the cheapest drug available?

CHAPTER 14

THE EQUIPMENT AND MACHINERY INDUSTRY

Eli S. Lustgarten

KEY TO ANALYZING THE INDUSTRY

1. Correctly anticipating the outlook for capital spending, which is influenced by several factors, including the outlook for the Federal Reserve Board "Index of Industrial Production" and the level of capacity utilization.
2. Being right on corporate cash flow trends.
3. Knowing whether corporations will be able to finance their capital spending.

MOST COMMON INVESTOR MISTAKES

Being negative because these stocks sell at a high price/earnings multiple caused by depressed earnings, or being overly excited by a low price/earnings multiple caused by cycle-peak earnings.

SOME GENERAL POINTS TO REMEMBER ABOUT THE INDUSTRY

1. Capital spending is a lagging indicator of the economy, and equipment and machinery stocks are dependent on capital spending.

2. These are very cyclical stocks and are far from homogeneous. Each one is different and must be considered on the basis of the markets it serves.

3. If there is any question about the outlook for economic growth, these stocks will be affected. The two factors which affect these stocks most are:

    a. The Federal Reserve Board "Index of Industrial Production" and the level of capacity utilization. When production and capacity utilization reach a certain point, additional capital spending is made. (Although some analysts use the 85 percent level for capacity utilization as the turning point, you should not use this figure in a black-and-white fashion.)

    b. Corporate cash flow, money supply, and the level of interest rates. These will help you to determine if corporations can pay for or finance the equipment they want.

4. In the second year after a recession, capital goods companies generally are in a cost/price squeeze. That's because demand for their products has slowed and a profit squeeze is on. Then, as the economic cycle starts to pick up, the machine tool and construction industries generally come back first. Orders pick up and backlogs start to grow. Soon thereafter, the short-cycle capital goods, such as bearings and tools, start to pick up. After that, if capacity and economic activity continue strong and there is a reasonable level of cash flow and a moderate rate of inflation, capital spending will pick up in the longer-lead-time areas.

5. These stocks sell at high multiples on depressed earnings and low multiples on cyclical peak earnings. (At the bottom of an economic cycle, the earnings of an equipment company will be generally cut in half, and that's why the stocks will be selling at a high multiple on depressed earnings.)

6. There's a typical pattern which these stocks follow in an economic advance. The first stock move comes as backlogs and orders start to grow; then, the stocks flatten out for a while until earnings increases come through, at which time the stocks move upwards again.

7. You should be aware of the various segments of the industry that are capital goods—sensitive, and you should relate how each segment might participate if government policy changed, export demand picked up, or a new technology came on the

scene. For example, the outlook for government policy on the energy industry is a critical determinant of the performance of certain energy-related capital spending stocks.

Another example of government action which can affect the industry is in the machine tool industry, which began booming in 1976–1977 because the automobile companies were forced by the government to make more fuel-efficient cars and needed to spend billions of dollars on retooling. Thus, the external factors which influence this industry can be very significant and should always be watched carefully.

Tax policy is also a critical factor, because it either gives or takes away incentive for business to spend money. The outlook for world trade is an essential variable, too. And changing technology can have a major effect on demand; the introduction of the computer, for example, gave business an incentive to automate in order to reduce costs and improve productivity. One should also consider the effect of changing economics, such as a rise in energy prices, which makes diesel engines relatively more attractive than gasoline engines.

8. The demographics are also important. For example, several years ago engineers were in surplus, while now they're in high demand and expensive. Thus, the trade-off between capital and labor is constantly changing. If engineers, say, are in tight supply, business might have an inducement to substitute capital for labor, and when the reverse is true, labor might be substituted for capital.

9. Another aspect to look into is whether business truly needs the equipment and whether the prospective annual return promised by the equipment can justify the expense. (Part and parcel of evaluating this element, as we discussed above, is whether interest rates are high or low and whether there's money available to finance the new equipment.)

10. Watch the relationship between supply and demand for the products of this industry's major customers. When there's more demand than supply, you'll be in a seller's market, and additional capacity will be needed. On the other hand, if there's a lot of excess capacity in various basic industries, you can rest assured that very little additional capital spending will be made.

The whole basic industry thesis of the 1973–75 period is an example of what can happen when demand exceeds supply.

Because of the limited availability of basic industry capacity, these industries were able to raise prices and increase profits, and the market went from a buyer's to a seller's market.

11. It's also important to analyze government policy when you come out of a recession. For instance, capital spending as a percent of the gross national product averaged 10.4 percent between 1964 and 1974. However, between 1974 and 1976 it dropped to 9.5 percent of gross national product, and one of the subsequent aims of government policy was to get spending back to trend line.

Thus, if you see that capital spending is way below par as a percentage of the GNP, you can bet that sooner or later it may get back and exceed the norm for a few years in order to account for the previous lackluster period.

WHEN TO BUY/SELL THE STOCKS

The time to buy equipment stocks is when you perceive that the economic outlook for the group has improved and is beginning to accelerate. The time to sell is when everything looks great and you can get a premium multiple on good earnings. Remember, however, that investors will pay only a low multiple on so-called cyclical peak earnings. Also recall that when things do look good, many things could go wrong, any one of which could cause the stocks to fall.

THE FARM EQUIPMENT INDUSTRY

1. The outlook for farm equipment is dependent on three things: (a) the level of farm cash receipts (which is a function of the size of the crops); (b) the level of interest rates, i.e., the cost of financing the equipment; and (c) the change in the amount of total farm acreage. (Total acreage projections can be obtained from the Department of Agriculture.)

2. Other important factors for the farm industry are (a) farm prices, which in turn influence farm cash receipts; (b) the cost of crop production; and (c) weather. (Note that farmers have their own cycle, which is independent of economic activity.)

3. The real growth in farm equipment in the industrialized countries is about 2 percent a year. (The capital equipment industry is growing roughly at the same rate as the gross national product, or

3½ to 4 percent a year.) Thus, with this kind of low growth rate, you should concentrate on trying to anticipate bad weather and crop failures on the one hand; and on the other hand, high crop prices and higher cash receipts, and consequently more spending on farm equipment.

4. Unit demand for farm equipment in nondeveloped countries is greater than in the United States, because these nations are increasingly substituting capital for labor. Thus, when selecting a farm equipment stock, you want to evaluate its penetration in overseas markets.

5. Farm consolidation is still continuing, which means greater interest in large pieces of equipment. For example, 30 percent of the farms today produce nearly 90 percent of the output in the United States. Europe is 10 years behind us and just recently began to purchase bigger and bigger pieces of farm equipment. It is important, therefore, that companies have a strong position in higher-horsepower equipment.

QUESTIONS TO ASK YOURSELF BEFORE MAKING AN INVESTMENT IN EQUIPMENT AND MACHINERY STOCKS

1. Where does the demand for your company's products come from? What makes customers buy the equipment? What is the length of time for the cycle of the equipment and where are you now in the cycle?

2. Where are the stocks in their normal pattern of movement? Are they moving because of improving backlogs, or because of increased earnings?

3. Are you attracted to these stocks because of their low p/e on (cyclical peak) earnings or afraid of them because of their high p/e on (cyclical bottom) earnings?

4. What is the attitude of the federal government towards business? Does the government favor changes in the tax law which will stimulate business capital spending?

5. What is the outlook for inflation? Will labor cost increases be such that industry has plenty of incentive to automate? Can business generate a sufficient return on investment to justify additional capital spending? Has the outlook for inflation unsettled the horizon to such an extent that businesspeople are dominated by uncertainty?

6. What was the status of industry profit margins during the last cycle? Was the industry able to generate enough profitability in the good times to provide a good reserve for the next down cycle?
7. What is happening on the international scene in terms of industrialization, particularly in the less developed nations? Is there sufficient demand (and the means of paying for it) to generate a good export potential?
8. What is the cash flow situation of the customers of machinery equipment producers? (This is the basic factor that really determines the level of spending.)
9. What's the debt level of major industrial companies? If debt is high and there's a concern about having too much debt, then the ability to finance additional significant capital expenditures may be in question.
10. What's the level of orders in relation to shipments? Ideally, you want orders to be well above shipments so that backlogs continue to build.
11. What is the outlook for world trade? Is protectionism growing? This could be a bad sign for those machinery companies that depend heavily on export markets.
12. What is the current competitive situation in the industry? Is anyone taking any steps to gain market share using, for example, aggressive pricing? What about merger and acquisition trends within your industry?
13. What is the current level of capacity utilization in your industry? How fast is new capacity coming on stream and who is adding it? Will it change the competitive structure?
14. Are there any significant technological changes taking place in the industry? How will these changes affect the current competition structure and types of products sold?

CHAPTER 15

FINANCE COMPANIES

Harold M. Levine

KEY TO ANALYZING THE INDUSTRY

1. Being able to determine the future growth of loan volume. (Note that this figure is relatively predictable.)
2. Being able to determine the nature and magnitude of financing costs to gauge the net interest spread between the cost of funds and the effective loan rate.
3. Apart from interest costs, the major costs of finance companies are generally predictable. For instance, the loan loss reserve is fixed at a certain percentage of receivables. Thus, the loan loss provision can be calculated by estimating loan losses plus the target year-end reserve. Also, overhead costs generally keep in line with the growth in receivables; thus, this figure can be readily estimated.

MOST COMMON INVESTOR MISTAKE

Overreacting to rising (or falling) interest rates. The major finance companies don't get hurt badly when rates rise, as 70 to 80 percent of their borrowings are long-term in nature and therefore unaffected by short-term swings in interest rates.

WHO SHOULD CONSIDER FINANCE COMPANY STOCKS

These stocks are generally most suitable for income-oriented investors, as yields are generally above those of most stocks. With a reasonable growth rate, these companies can increase the dividend at quite satisfactory rates, thereby insuring a higher current return in the future.

SOME GENERAL POINTS TO REMEMBER ABOUT THE INDUSTRY

1. The key determinant of the market valuation of lending institutions is investor perception of (a) their ability to maintain profit margins during periods of volatile credit demand and interest rates, and (b) the quality of their assets.
2. Besides the above, the outlook for financial companies also depends heavily on the rate of inflation. The reason is that potential profit gains from inflation-swollen lending volume are sooner or later eroded by narrowed spreads stemming from rising interest rates.
3. Because of the greater flexibility of rates on business loans, the companies more heavily oriented toward business lending are less affected in volatile periods than those concentrating on consumer credit.
4. The business finance companies have generally been able to maintain their share of the overall credit market. The key has been the ability to find niches for specialized lending activities in which the major competitors are money-center banks. The finance companies' comparative advantage lies in their ability to blanket the country with lending offices and thus bring their expertise to regions that the large banks find difficult to reach. In addition, finance companies discover that local banks often prefer to work with them rather than with big correspondents that might ultimately capture the customer relationship between the smaller banks and local corporations. The defining characteristic of finance companies is the fact that they deal in loans that have higher servicing costs than those handled by most other financial institutions.

Consumer Finance Companies

1. The consumer finance companies (CFCs) have seen their share of the market gradually but steadily erode in recent years, first because of bank competition and more recently because of the rapid growth of credit unions. Thus, asset growth has lagged growth in nominal GNP and in total personal lending. In addition, because of ceilings on asset yields, profitability has suffered as inflation has accelerated and as money costs have risen. The industry has attempted to offset these factors by diversifying. The favored and most successful area has been insurance. Over the long term, these companies are likely to continue to lessen their dependence on consumer lending and stress other fields. Success is likely to vary from company to company.

2. It is important to note that on a cyclical basis, the CFCs have reached their low absolute and relative prices virtually simultaneously with the overall market and that in two of the three recent stock market cycles, the absolute high has correlated with overall market peaks. (The exception was in 1965–1966, when these equities peaked on an absolute basis in September 1965, five months prior to the general market top; the relative peak was in August 1965.) In 1968 the absolute and relative peaks corresponded with the market top in November. In 1972–1973, the absolute peak preceded the January 1973 overall market top by 2 months.

   In sum, the CFC stocks have historically been high-beta (highly volatile) market stocks, albeit at progressively lower levels of price/earnings values, reflecting investor hopes and fears in regard to interest rates and inflation.

3. The consumer lending industry consists of about 2500 companies throughout the nation, ranging in size from Household Finance, with $3.1 billion in receivables and 1800 offices, to companies with single offices and only $100,000 to $1 million in outstandings.

4. The market share of the CFCs of the entire household credit market has fallen in recent years. The main reason for this loss of market share has been the accelerating growth in credit unions. A slight loss of share to banks also occurred, but it was mainly in 1965–1968.

   The growth of credit unions stems from several important

factors. First, they are identified with a particular employment unit, making it convenient to deposit funds with them, often by payroll deduction. Second, they can often offer higher rates of interest on passbook deposits than can commercial banks or savings and loans. Third, their convenience also makes borrowing easy. Fourth, interest rates charged are often lower than those of CFCs because of lower operating costs due to their nonprofit orientation, partly voluntary staff, partial subsidy of office expenses by employers, and lower loss ratios than those of CFCs. The latter may result from peer group pressure from fellow employees not to default on a loan from *their* credit union. Although their share of the consumer loan market should eventually stabilize, it is very difficult to say when that might occur.

The major part of the commercial banks' gain in market share came in the mid-1960s, probably spurred by two factors. The first was that consumer lending seemed especially attractive then, given the relatively low level of interest rates; the second was the introduction of a new form of lending, overdrafts on checking accounts.

5. On a long-term basis, the key factor affecting earnings growth is volume. Nevertheless, spread is more important on a shorter-run basis and is influenced mainly by the level of short-term interest rates.

The income side of the equation is relatively stable, with income from receivables continuing to account for about 80 percent of gross. Roughly half the remainder is derived from credit life and credit accident and health insurance.

6. The largest item of operating expense is wages and salaries, accounting for nearly half of noninterest expenses. These expenses in total range between 55 and 58 percent of gross revenues. The most volatile item has been the cost of borrowed funds, ranging from 22 to 32 percent of revenues. The major yearly swings in earnings as a percentage of revenues or earnings assets have been closely related to interest rate swings. This is not to say that other factors have not been important in certain years—for example, good expense control and a reduced tax rate offset rising rates in 1970 and 1974—but their movements have been more random in nature and not as identifiable with major macroeconomic trends.

7. The consumer finance business is characterized by rapid turn-over of outstanding receivables. For example, large companies such as Household Finance have nearly 50 percent of average outstandings repaid on a cash basis each year. Including refi-nancing and additional borrowings by existing customers, even moderate annual growth requires new loan volume nearly equal to existing outstandings. One large company estimates that about 60 percent of its loans made were in the form of additional borrowings by present customers, although this accounted for only 28 percent of the dollar amount of new loans. This rapid turnover is the reason the industry funds its earning assets one-third by short-term borrowings despite inflexible asset yields: to maintain flexibility on the balance sheet in case of sudden changes in loan demand.

8. Surveys have shown that the largest single reason for borrowing from a CFC is to consolidate existing bills, accounting for 33 percent of loans made. Automobile purchase or repair, travel, home furnishings, appliances, and household repairs constitute 28 percent. All other reasons make up the balance.

9. The typical borrower from a CFC is relatively young, of moder-ate income, and in a skilled or semi-skilled occupation.

10. Despite their national scope, CFCs in a sense have fifty separate operations, as each state has its own consumer finance laws, regulations, administrative procedures, and creditor remedies. Nevertheless, certain broad trends are evident. In general, CFCs sprang up in the second and third decades of the twentieth century as the various states passed in one form or another the Uniform Small Loan Act. This law was drafted primarily under the impetus of a movement started by the Russell Sage Founda-tion to attract capital to consumer lending. Until then low state usury ceilings had left the field to the loan sharks. The act permitted substantially higher rates than before in return for loan limits, prepayment refunds, periodic examination, and the restricting of the field to those lenders whose operations contrib-uted to the "convenience and advantage of the community." This last item was and still is subject to widely varying interpre-tations. As a result, in some states, it is almost impossible to start a new company or even open a new office, while in others it is very easy.

11. The interest yield on consumer loans is much higher than that

on most other forms of lending. This is required, of course, by the greater operating costs per dollar incurred by CFCs than by other lenders. The yield varies from state to state and is generally limited by either law or regulations. In addition, rates are usually on a sliding scale so that the smallest loan in dollar size carries the highest return—as the economics of the business would dictate. A typical scale would be 3 percent per month for the first $300, 2 percent for $300 to $1000, and 1½ percent over $1000. There is sometimes a further break at, say $2500, with amounts above that returning 1 percent or ¾ percent. Thus, a $1000 loan would yield 27.60 percent per annum; a $2500 loan, 21.84 percent; and a $5000 loan (with a 1 percent rate above $2500), 16.92 percent.

12. The distribution of finance company loans by state generally follows the pattern of personal income. For example, eight of the top ten states in personal income are also in the top ten in finance company loans outstanding.

13. Since consumer loans are usually made at statutory rate ceilings, there is normally no room for imposing price increases if interest rates rise. Lenders need to maintain a certain proportion of liquidity to fund portfolio turnover each year, which requires some reliance on short-term borrowing. The result is that when interest rates rise, spreads come under pressure—but how much pressure and how bad an earnings impact depend on the rise in rates.

14. Recent industry results indicate the larger companies have reversed the market share erosion that occurred in the early 1970s. But since the industry itself is losing credit market share, a company must do better than finance companies in the aggregate to hold its own. Thus, to see how well a company is growing, it is necessary to track market share against all consumer goods lenders.

15. The industry should continue its consolidation, which puts into question the financial and economic viability of smaller, nonautomated companies, whose borrowing costs are as much as 60 percent higher than those of major companies and whose overhead expenses take a huge bite out of every dollar of receivables. This redistribution of receivables through consolidation should enable the survivors to experience faster overall growth in earning assets relative to industry trends. Eventually, the consolida-

tion may proceed until there are no more than a dozen or so larger companies remaining.

Commercial Finance Companies

INDUSTRY BACKGROUND

Commercial financing is the term applied to various types of business loans that are secured by specific assets of the customer rather than by his general credit. To dramatize the contrast, one could say that banks (in their unsecured lending) advance funds on the basis of balance sheet and income statement analysis, with little regard for the collateral value of specific assets, while commercial finance companies lend on the basis of the security of specific assets, with little regard for financial statement analysis.

The two main forms of secured lending are accounts receivable financing, and factoring. Accounts receivable financing consists basically of the advancing of funds against the assignment to the lender of specific receivables. The maximum loan is generally 70 to 85 percent of the receivables' face value and is repaid as the borrower collects from his customers. Certain types of accounts cannot be assigned, such as those delinquent or disputed. The borrower retains flexibility by borrowing only as funds are needed; there is no minimum amount and no compensating balance requirement.

Factoring is a service made up of two parts. First, the factor performs for his client the function of the client's accounts receivable department. That is, he checks and polices the credit of the client's customers, keeps the books, collects funds and overdue accounts, and bears the credit risk. For this, the factor receives a commission of ¾ to 2 percent (usually averaging 1 to 1⅜ percent) of the dollar amount (volume) of receivables handled. Second, the factor may advance funds to the client (in proportion to the receivables outstanding) before their average maturity date and charge interest at several points over the prime rate. This is called "old-line" factoring. If funds are paid to the client only on the receivables' average due date, the service is called maturity factoring. Note that in contrast to accounts receivable financing, the factor acquires the receivables and bears the credit risk that his client's customers will pay.

Another form of commercial finance is inventory lending. This is closely related to accounts receivable financing and is generally done only in conjunction with it. Inventory lending is most suitable for seasonal businesses, in which a substantial inventory must be acquired and processed before receivables can be generated. Loans as a percent of the cost of inventory are, of course, smaller than in accounts receivable financing, and only raw materials and finished goods are suitable collateral. Work-in-process requires additional investment to be salable and therefore is not acceptable collateral. As inventory is depleted, loans against it are repaid by the proceeds of accounts receivable financing or factoring before they are liquidated by the cash collection of sales made.

Other types of loans made by commercial finance companies include equipment loans and leases, first and second mortgages on industrial plants, loans for acquisitions, and occasionally construction loans for plant expansion.

Commercial finance companies in the United States number in several hundreds, but most of the business is handled by the twenty-five to thirty-five largest firms. Many of these have in the past 10 years been acquired by bank holding companies or industrial companies, leaving only a few large independent operations. The attraction of bank holding companies to commercial financing is a natural one, since commercial finance is in many ways an extension of traditional bank commercial and industrial (C&I) lending to businesses not qualifying for unsecured credit. In addition, the growth of secured lending has been quite rapid in recent years, although slightly below the growth rate of C&I lending itself.

Further bank acquisitions in this field are limited by the reduced number of acquisition candidates. Start-ups are difficult because of the significant differences of the business from ordinary bank lending. There is also an important economic function performed by the independent companies. Through their regional or nationwide operations they can bring the advantages of secured lending to the customers of banks not active in the field. Indeed, the major source of new business for the industry is the referral, by banks lacking secured lending capability, of small- and medium-sized companies in need of funds beyond what their bank can provide on an unsecured basis. Only a few score of the nation's 14,000 banks have a commercial finance department. Although they account for the bulk of C&I loans on a dollar basis, most of the commercial finance volume is generated by companies with annual sales of $500,000 to $50 million, which are less likely to be customers of the largest banks. Thus, the independent commercial finance company can enable a medium-size or small bank to compete with large banks in the major financial centers.

Commercial finance and, in particular, factoring have long been identified with the textile and garment industries. Indeed, the first factors in the United States were agents of British textile exporters who, as on-the-spot representatives, found it easier to perform the credit checking and collection functions than the distant mills. The textile and garment industries are still the largest clients of factoring companies, but good customers of commercial finance firms are also found in other industries, such as metals, building materials, food processing, electronics, sporting goods, and transportation parts and equipment.

INVESTMENT CONSIDERATIONS

1. Short-term earnings trends—those lasting several quarters to several years—are most heavily influenced by swings in short-term interest rates. Longer-run trends depend most heavily on volume. The reason is that the match between interest rate–sensitive assets and liabilities is relatively good but not perfect, and not all variable-rate assets float immediately or by the full amount of rate changes. Thus, a rapid change in rates can cause temporary openings and closings of the interest rate margin. Longer-term, once the margin has adjusted to the new rate level, volume becomes the dominant factor.

2. Historically, commercial finance equities have tracked the market, reaching absolute and relative peaks and bottoms consistent with the S&P 400. It appears these equities are beginning to trade in a pattern more consistent with that of bank stocks, which have traditionally lagged the market.

3. Commercial finance profits are, in the long run, inextricably tied to volume growth. Despite a rate structure that may appear to be noncompetitive with bank lending (secured loans on accounts receivable and inventory typically are priced at 4 to 5 percent over prime, while advances to factoring clients are priced anywhere from 2 to 3 percent over prime), the ability of commercial finance companies to provide credit for only that period of time it is actually needed, with no commitment fees or compensating balance requirements, often results in a more attractive financing arrangement for the borrower.

4. What effect, if any, is the increasing level of competition exerting on the industry and how can it be measured? Although the industry is highly competitive among the major firms, competition takes place in a positive manner. In other words, there do not seem to be instances of wholesale price cutting and lowering of credit standards and quality in order to increase business. These practices would surface in volume figures, but ultimately profits would suffer as ensuing chargeoffs would quickly negate the benefits of higher volume. Since there are relatively few companies in the industry, market share data trends, rather than the year-to-year distributions, bear closer scrutiny. For this reason market share trends of the industry in general are fairly reliable.

5. Volume alone does not translate into profit, but it is a useful tool in determining a company's position vis-à-vis its competition. A company need not increase its market share each year in order to improve its profitability. However, patterns are important. A sharp change in volume relative to the market may reflect the gain or loss of a client and foreshadow future trends. Because of a high incidence of customer loyalty in the industry, steady relative volume declines often signal a fundamental problem at a company that is likely to sustain such a trend. On the other hand, overly aggressive growth does not appear to be a sustainable trend either.

6. Unlike consumer finance companies, which are limited in increasing their loan yields, commercials can and do vary the price of their loans in accord with short term interest rates. Portfolios generally are responsive to changes in the prime rate within 3 months.

   During periods of slack loan demand, typically in the early stages of economic recovery, interest rates generally have declined from earlier inflated levels. Loan losses increase, reflecting the fallout from the contraction just past. However, lower rates mean a lower cost of funds which, because of their greater elasticity relative to loan yields, results in wider margins. During periods of expansion, especially toward a cyclical peak, rising interest rates lead to narrower spreads. But the faster pace of economic activity is accompanied by accelerated loan demand.

7. Many firms that borrow from commercial finance companies would not find great receptivity at commercial banks; size, earnings seasonality, and/or earnings potential may not meet stan-

dards considered acceptable. It is fair to say, then, that commercial finance credits are more risky than those of a commercial bank. Several points are worth noting in this regard: (a) the level of risk is clearly reflected in the rates charged these customers; (b) year-to-year swings can be less dramatic on a relative basis, since the absolute level is higher than, say, that of banks; (c) since commercial finance companies have a generally higher credit risk horizon, most loans are either secured or collateralized. These companies typically work much closer with problem loans than do banks and have vast experience in "workout" situations.

CHAPTER 16

THE INSTRUMENTATION INDUSTRY

Thomas H. Mack

SOME GENERAL POINTS TO REMEMBER ABOUT THE INDUSTRY

1. The instrumentation companies, of which there are only a handful with large stock capitalizations, are very individualistic and tend not to be homogeneous. What's more, these companies are not directly competitive; it's rare for one company to be in competition with another for more than 20 percent of its sales.
2. The industry is extremely fragmented. It designs finished products to meet specific customer needs.
3. The industry is not especially cyclical and, even in an economic downturn, does not experience much of a decline in sales. That's because its products are sold to an end user, and since the product is not usually incorporated into another product, it is not susceptible to an inventory cycle.
4. Typically the industry has annual sales growth of between 12 and 15 percent a year. That might mean 20 to 25 percent in a good year and flat revenues in a poor year.
5. The industry is somewhat tied to the capital spending market,

since corporations do spend money on instrumentation to expand capacity and to improve efficiency and productivity. It's important to look at the trend in expenditures on research and more generally the trends in capital spending.

6. One of the key areas in the future for instrumentation companies is the interweaving between instrumentation and data processing. Since computers are now "talking" to each other and to instrumentation devices, the key to the instrumentation industry over the next 5 to 10 years is to see how well each company handles the data processing side of the business.

7. Instrumentation companies are very dependent on new-product flow, and investors must keep a watchful eye to insure that new products keep coming. Equally important is an accurate perception of what the customer needs, combined with the ability to incorporate that need into a design which will satisfy the customer.

8. Instrumentation devices perform measurement, control, and automation functions in a variety of applications. For example, a waveform analyzer might be used to monitor a TV station's signal and automatically adjust the station's transmitter in order to correct any deficiencies in the signal.

There are two major categories of instruments: electronic test and measurement, and analytical instruments. Electronic test and measurement equipment is involved in such applications as electronic design, product checkout, determining the malfunction of electric equipment, and certain types of maintenance. (Note that electronic test and measurement instruments are heavily involved in the computer and communications industries.)

Analytical instruments are primarily involved with chemistry: analyzing the composition of chemicals, using a variety of techniques; breaking down chemical compounds; process control; and forensic uses (to detect chemicals in human blood, for instance). They are also used to test for certain chemicals in persons' blood in a pure question-and-answer format.

9. These stocks tend to lag the stock market and the economic cycle, and they turn in a better performance in the latter part of a bull market.

10. Unfortunately, there is no single source of data for the industry. Therefore the best way of analyzing the outlook for the industry

is to amalgamate the financial performance of the individual companies.

11. Instrumentation companies do not have much backlog, since their products are usually shipped directly from the shelf. For this reason, you shouldn't focus too much on the relationship between orders and shipments.

12. Instrumentation stocks are somewhat more volatile than the market (because they tend to sell at a premium to the market), but not nearly as much as the semiconductor industry.

13. In analyzing a company you should look for a leading market position, a strong product line, and excellent marketing. Also be sure the company has digital electronics capability, which is necessary these days.

CHAPTER 17

THE LEISURE INDUSTRY

Lee S. Isgur

KEY TO ANALYZING THE INDUSTRY

Being able to predict the public taste, and guessing how consumers will want to spend their leisure time.

MOST COMMON INVESTOR MISTAKES

1. Judging the potential for a leisure product according to your own personal, individual tastes, which may conflict with those of the vast majority of the population.
2. Buying leisure stocks when their price/earnings multiple is considerably in excess of the p/e of the S&P 400.

GENERAL POINTS TO REMEMBER ABOUT THE INDUSTRY

1. The leisure industry is composed of two main categories: durables; and services, or entertainment. In other words, the companies in the industry either produce a durable, manufactured

product, such as a bicycle, a golf club, or a camping outfit, or they are in the service side of the business, which includes the production of movies and other entertainment-related services.

2. The conglomerates involved in the business are rarely attractive investments. The best way to invest in the industry is via the "pure play": a company exclusively in a particular line of business.

3. The leisure industry can be categorized as a form of escapism. Whether you're walking down Main Street in Disney World or going to a movie on 59th Street in New York City, you are basically trying to get away from the day's worries and escape into a world of unreality. Therefore, the key aspect of this business is to be able to predict what form of escapism the public wants next. Needless to say, whether you're an investor or a company president, trying to guess what the consumer will want next can be exceedingly tricky and risky.

For instance, there may be a 2½-year lag between the time a movie script is conceived and the time a movie actually reaches the public. Therefore, a movie producer must try to anticipate what the public mood will be 2½ years in the future.

Take the success of *Star Wars* as a case in point. Up until *Star Wars*, no science fiction movie since *2001* had been successful. Therefore, on the basis of past experience, it would have been difficult to predict the spontaneous and ebullient reaction accommodated *Star Wars*.

In summary, then, it is very hard to predict in advance how successful a movie will be. It is rarely possible to know how well a movie will do until the first day's viewing, and generally it will take 2 weeks before you have a real idea how successful the film will be.

4. Leisure products are increasingly seeming like a necessity. There's no doubt that leisure products have a much higher priority for consumers today than they did 20 years ago. For example, when times get rough nowadays, the high-powered boat or the summer home is frequently the last thing to go. That's because people feel that they owe it to themselves to have a good time when times are bad. By the same token, after a difficult period, one of the first things that people buy during an economic rebound is a "leisure necessity," such as the new boat

or new golf club they wanted. People feel that, having suffered through some rough times, they owe themselves a little bit of indulgence.

5. Part and parcel of estimating the direction of public moods and taste are demographic trends and the level of consumer incomes.

6. Investors often apply their own taste in evaluating the potential for a leisure product. That is unwise: just because you like a particular product or are crazy about a particular sport does not mean that the rest of the country will feel the same way. For instance, some people prefer to own a big boat and ride in a Volkswagen, while others prefer to have a big car and forgo the boat. On the other hand, some prefer to ride public transportation and not own a car at all, in order to have a fancy summer home. Thus, you should look at this industry as if there were a given amount of purchasing power fluctuating from area to area (even between necessities and nonnecessities), given varying consumer desires and interests. Consumers will frequently cut back in one area to buy something they consider more important. As a result, there may be a lot of volatility and flexibility in leisure products.

7. In general, the leisure industry has been misunderstood. However, it is gaining a better understanding, and more investors and analysts are now following the group.

8. The durable side of the leisure industry is dependent on the overall growth of the economy and the growth in consumer incomes. If consumer incomes are growing in real terms, there will be more money available for the purchase of consumer durables.

9. In evaluating a specific company within the leisure industry, look at its share of market and its trend in market share, and pick the company which has been showing the biggest gains in this area.

10. The time to sell leisure stocks is when they are selling at a premium in terms of price/earnings ratios to the S&P 400. The greater the premium is, the more incentive you have to sell your stocks. On the other hand, there does appear to be a long-term upward bias in this industry.

11. It is also wise to buy a package of stocks to spread your risks.

HOW TO ANALYZE THE INDUSTRY

The key to a successful investment strategy in the leisure industry is to correctly anticipate public taste. Once you feel that you have noticed a developing trend, it is important to analyze the potential market for the product. (For example, the potential market for an expensive speedboat will never be very large.) Often, you will have a number of years to evaluate the trend before Wall Street catches on, and thus you'll have plenty of time to do your homework.

You can liken this industry to a gold mine: once you hit a vein you mine it for all it's worth. Likewise, if one area in the leisure industry strikes a vein, i.e., hits if off with the public, you can bet that there will be a raft of other products that attempt to duplicate the public response.

For this reason, it is important to see how many products or potential products the company has which can be employed to capitalize on an emerging or developing trend.

Once you have decided that a given part of the leisure industry or a particular product is starting to develop a trend, then you need to determine if the trend is sustainable. Ask yourself, why is this trend developing? Is it because of the business cycle, the baby boom, the concern with physical fitness, or what?

Let's analyze the bicycle industry as an example. Let's say you notice that bicycles have become increasingly socially acceptable: Add to that the increasing concern for health and physical fitness and you have the beginning of a potential trend.

The next step is to analyze how sustainable this trend is and where you are in the sales cycle. To get answers to these questions, you could go to various retail outlets and see how bikes are selling. Then, look around you and ask yourself whether this trend seems to be gathering force. Are more bike trails under construction? Are certain retail outlets offering special sales on certain types of bicycles? Do an increasing number of retail stores carry bicycles?

Next, ask yourself if competition could alter this trend. In other words, what will the popularization of mopeds do to the demand for bicycles? Remember, however, to avoid being influenced by your own preference; whether you do or do not like bicycles is not of concern here, but what counts is whether the overall trend for bicycles is up.

In analyzing a developing trend you need to assess all the statistics that are available on the product. The need to get accurate and complete industry statistics cannot be overestimated. (One of the reasons why many investors had losses in snowmobile stocks was that the industry's statistics were wrong and misleading. Had the right statistics been available, the problems that subsequently arose might never have happened.)

In gathering industry statistics, you must be very careful not to rely too heavily on estimates provided by a company's marketing staff, which invariably tend to be overly optimistic. Be sure to confirm the statistics you get with investigations of your own. For example, in the case of snowmobiles, if you went to a snowmobile shop in March or April and found out that this particular dealer usually sells 100 snowmobiles each year and he still had 15 on his floor, you might question optimistic sales assumptions.

Another way of evaluating the validity of statistics is to look for too much or too little numerical rounding. If there's too much rounding, you should be somewhat leery of the figures. By the same token, a statistic which is precise to the last unit can also be viewed suspiciously. A statistic which demonstrates a consistent growth rate year in and year out should also be viewed somewhat skeptically. In any of these cases, the company may be only manipulating figures instead of doing the needed research.

Most industries have a trade association, which should be a good source of industry information. What's more, you can get on its mailing list for free. Be sure to get as much historical data as you can.

Another way to invest in the industry is to follow an area in which you have an interest, and where you are something of an expert already. If a new product comes out, evaluate it yourself and see if you find it worth owning.

At all costs, avoid buying these stocks when they are selling at a premium to the market. Generally speaking, the stocks alternate between a 50 percent discount and the p/e multiple of the market in general. This is the range that you should keep in mind. Thus, attempt to buy the companies when they are selling at around a 50 percent discount to the market, and sell them when they are at a market multiple, that is to say, at a p/e ratio of the market as reflected by a proxy, such as the S&P 400.

INDUSTRY BACKGROUND

The Music Industry

In simple terms there are two aspects of the music industry: (1) making music oneself and (2) listening to others make music. For a long time, these two markets were nearly equal in size. But in recent years recorded music sales have begun to handily exceed music instrument sales.

A prerecorded tape or phonograph record is relatively inexpensive, while a musical instrument is not. Tighter school budgets, at least temporarily, have curtailed many school music programs, which played a large part in musical instrument sales. (However, it should be noted that today's guitars and organs now account for well over half the unit sales of musical instruments. Rarely is proficiency in these instruments taught in the formal public school music program.)

In the musical instrument area the greatest unit growth has been in electronic instruments (guitars, synthesizers, organs, etc.). While the prices of these items have risen, they have gone up less than those of most other musical instruments. Thus it could be argued that there is more strength in the musical instrument figures than the total figures indicate (because of the more rapid growth in the electronic music area, which is relatively inflation-resistant). On the other hand, the recorded music figures are stated in terms of retail list prices. Since price discounting has grown in recent years, it can be argued that the growth of recorded music is not as fast relative to musical instruments as it first appears.

Nevertheless, it can be concluded that both the recorded music sector and the musical instrument sector of the music industry have been growing fairly steadily and rapidly, with the recorded music area showing the faster growth in recent years. In the recorded music field the worldwide market was about $6 billion in 1977 in terms of retail sales of records and tapes.

Domestically, Warner Communications dominates recorded music, with over a 25 percent market share. Warner's foreign market share is probably closer to 10 percent, since Philips is the dominant company abroad. Recorded music operations account for nearly half of Warner's pretax operating earnings. CBS is the second largest company, with a market share estimated at over 20 percent. However, because of the sheer total size of CBS, its recorded music business accounts for a smaller portion of total revenues and profits (about 25 percent of revenues and under 20 percent of profits).

In the domestic musical instrument business, Norlin Corporation is the dominant factor, with about a 14 percent market share. Norlin's foreign operations have a far lower market share, probably closer to 5 or 10 percent. Yamaha Music appears to be the dominant company in the foreign market.

The Filmed Entertainment Industry

There are basically eight major companies in this industry: Columbia Pictures Corp., MCA, MGM, Paramount (a division of Gulf & Western Industries), Twentieth Century Fox, United Artists Corp. (a division of Transamerica Corp.), Walt Disney Productions, and Warner Communications. Although there are many other film companies, it is the eight companies listed above that dominate the distribution of broad-appeal films in the United States.

Within the entire leisure field, the filmed entertainment area stands out as a seller's market, where ease of entry is nearly nonexistent and the chance of demise is currently nearly nil. At the same time, this is an industry whose basic business is generating more capital than needs to be reinvested. It's also an industry that has received very favorable treatment under the federal tax laws. Although it is a cyclical business, cycles result from internal, rather than external, macroeconomic factors.

What's more, the post-1945 filmed entertainment industry is the special beneficiary of three factors: the *Paramount* case (1948), television, and inflation.

In the *Paramount* case, the film production and distribution divisions of the eight previously mentioned movie giants, together with RKO Pictures, signed a consent decree in which, among other things, they agreed that they would henceforth own no domestic movie theatres if they were to remain in the movie distributing business.

The decree was considered a landmark event, and it was generally thought that the result would be the entrance of many new companies into the filmed entertainment production and distribution business. Up until this time, most of the major film product producers and distributors were businessmen who had started their careers as operators of motion picture theater chains; they originally went into film production to assure themselves of a continuing supply of films. Following the

Paramount consent decree, many new, independent filmmakers and distributors sprang up to fill the vacuum. Nevertheless, as you will see shortly, the majority of film revenues still go to the eight aforementioned companies.

Not only do these companies dominate film distribution, but also, because of a shift in moviegoing habits, perhaps attributable largely to television, the same eight companies are probably much better off not owning theatre chains. The reason is that nowadays people see movies primarily on vacations and holidays. Thus, the box office peak extends from the Fourth of July weekend through Labor Day. The Christmas–New Year's period is next-most important, and other peak times are around Washington's Birthday, Easter, and Memorial Day.

In the nonholiday season, the 2-day, 3-night period from Friday night through Sunday night every week normally accounts for 75 percent of the whole week's box office revenues. Since in hours of potential viewing time this period accounts for less than one-third of the optimum level, this skewing effect has interesting ramifications: essentially it means theater chain operators have several short seasons during the year, followed by long periods when they approach capacity utilization of their physical facilities only during a very limited time.

Thus, as a result of the *Paramount* consent decree, the major filmed entertainment companies became unsaddled from real estate that is underutilized much of the time. Moreover, freed from this real estate monster that they otherwise would have had to feed year-round product, the major studios were able to tailor their film release patterns to get the broadest exposure during the prime film viewing time—the holiday periods.

A great deal of criticism has been leveled at the major film companies by theater owners, who claim they don't get enough product. What the theater owners really mean is that at times other than the Fourth of July and Christmas they don't have enough product. For this reason, they scramble to maximize profits during the prime periods, end up paying astronomical advance guarantees, and oftentimes incur dire economic consequences.

Television has benefited film production companies in another very material way. Quality films are one of the few consistently high–audience share products in the television market; hence network demand for first-run product during prime time is great, while films have also become a staple for non–prime-time television, both on and off network. All this has created a terrific appetite for theatrical film product in the television industry, and lease prices paid for showing films on television have risen dramatically. These increases have been most noticeable in the prices paid for product distributed by the majors.

To try to alleviate some of this price inflation, the television networks have been willing in recent years to buy the right to show a film on television sight unseen (before it has been released theatrically) and agree not to show the film until it has completed its first theatrical run. This willingness on the part of the networks to commit early has enabled a film production company, when it wishes, to finance several million dollars, or about half, of its production costs simply by selling the right to show the film once or more on television.

So television, initially the motion picture industry's major threat, has become an important customer and, in effect, its single biggest outside financier. Today one could certainly make the case that television is benefiting the filmed entertainment business more than it's hurting it.

Inflation has also worked to the industry's advantage. Like everything else, theatrical ticket prices have risen, as you can see from Table 17-1.

TABLE 17-1

Year	Average Admission Price	Paid Admissions	Admission Revenues
1967	$1.20	$927,000,000	$1,110,000,000
1971	1.65	820,000,000	1,350,000,000
1974	1.89	1,011,000,000	1,909,000,000
1975	2.05	1,033,800,000	2,115,000,000
1976	2.13	957,000,000	2,036,000,000
1977	2.23	1,063,000,000	2,372,000,000
1978 (Est.)	2.33	1,150,000,000	2,680,000,000

Of course, the cost of making movies has risen concomitantly. But the number of feature films released by the majors has declined (Table 17-2).

Although there aren't any precise figures on this trend, the releases by major companies, while declining in number, have increased in the percentage of the total box office receipts they account for. This is due

TABLE 17-2

Year	Number of Films Released
1948	248
1954	225
1958	237
1963	142
1967	157
1971	183
1976	150
1977	152

to inflation as much as to anything else. Filmmaking is more expensive now than formerly.

Because they have less access to capital, the independents have generally had to make lower-quality, commercial, general-interest films. Thus, the small amount of product being made by the majors is what is most in demand. Roughly speaking, the proportion of the box office ticket price kept by the major distributors has risen from about 35 percent in 1948 to 50 to 55 percent in 1977. In addition, since in business, time is money, the majors, as of 1978, frequently receive advances even before a film is shown, and the bulk of the rentals on the average domestic film is collected in the first 90 days after release. In 1948, advances were rare to nonexistent; it was often 6 to 12 months or more before most of a film's rental receipts came in.

Despite their spiraling costs, therefore, the major filmed entertainment companies have benefited from inflation, which has enhanced their strength relative to the independents and the theater owners.

To sum up: the filmed entertainment business today is dominated by a relatively small number of companies. If it is cyclical, its cycles are a function of the company's own actions, rather than macroeconomic factors. It is a cash-rich industry; its basic business throws off more money than it can utilize internally in any given year. Finally, it is a business that is relatively immune from concerns about such government activity as energy or taxes.

It is important to be aware of the four major mysteries of this industry: (1) unpredictability, (2) the people aspect, (3) copyright issues, and (4) technology. Normally, investors are interested in stocks whose quarter-to-quarter earnings appear relatively predictable. However, predictability in the film industry is dubious at best.

Since theatrical film releases are the basic product of the filmed entertainment industry and no one can consistently guess how a film will do, it is next to impossible to determine prior to release what a film will generate in revenues. As the major distribution companies enjoy a seller's market, they will normally suffer a small loss on a dud release, make a modest sum on an average product, and reap windfall profits on box office hits. With anything over seven to ten releases a year, it becomes hard to lose money.

Films are written, directed, and acted in by people. They are packaged by people. Until it is recorded and copyrighted, whatever a person does is proprietary to him or her. Thus, other than its library, the only real asset a studio has is its relationship with the people that create the product. Hence, if these people leave, investors become uncertain about the continuity of the company's product.

Mel Brooks has been a great money-maker for Twentieth Century Fox in recent years (*Young Frankenstein*, *Silent Movie*, and *High Anxiety*). Prior to this he did *Blazing Saddles*, another successful film, for Warner. Even if every release of his is considered money in the bank, investors in Twentieth Century Fox can count as money in the bank only Brooks's past successes. It would be imprudent to count on him to do another successful film for the company before it is completed or close to completion. Hollywood is filled with stories about projects that commenced at one studio but ended up at another.

This looks very bad for predictability. But for the most part a large number of talented people involved in making films remain for a long period of time with a single studio. At the same time, the defections usually even out. MCA's Universal Studio turned down the *Star Wars* project. But Twentieth Century Fox had earlier turned down the *Jaws* project. In both cases the person responsible for the decision is no longer an employee of the studio.

In the final analysis, however, people go to see films in order to see other people perform. It doesn't matter much to the film viewer what the brand name on the film is. At present, the name Mel Brooks will draw people to a film whether the brand name is Warner, Twentieth, or XXX.

Once the product has been made, it normally becomes the studio's property. Thus if it has continuing value, as do *Snow White*, *Young Frankenstein*, and *Gone with the Wind*, much, if not most, of this continuing value will accrue to the studio.

Film libraries are therefore becoming increasingly valuable assets for the major film companies. But we are now entering a period when there is a widespread ability to duplicate video product. In fact, we could rapidly be approaching the time when the value of these libraries peaks and begins an almost catastrophic descent. (Both the publishing and the music recording industries have successfully faced the challenge of duplication technology. However, as you play an audio recording over and over you unconsciously write off the capital cost of a prerecorded disk or tape over the multiple-play life of the item.) Film libraries today consist mostly of product whose multiple play in the home is probably very limited.

Hence, it may be, in the 1980s or later, at a time when there is wide-scale private use of video duplicating equipment, that the price of film product, in terms of first-run theatrical ticket prices and sale prices to network television, will be up. But in terms of rerelease potential and subsequent sales to television (for showings after the network premiere), prices will slide dramatically.

This by no means implies a dire future for the industry. After all, in the 1940s and much of the 1950s, film library sales contributed only a small amount to film company income statements. But this does imply that an area from which the companies are getting a healthy amount of income today may indeed not be important in the future. (One could even argue that the sale of prerecorded disks or tapes to the home market will be a much bigger market than library sales are today.) We have linked here the future value of copyrighted video product to changing technology.

While technology can be viewed as a threat to the financially healthy status quo that now exists in the industry, it also points to a potentially even more lucrative future. This, more than any other reason, is why the filmed entertainment industry could be the recipient of increasing amounts of investor attention in the future.

No matter which horse wins the race (cable, disk, tape, etc.), in the mid-1980s many of the relatively affluent of the world will for the first time be able to watch what they want, when they want, and where they want. For by that time the age of special-interest programming should have arrived. It could very well be that well-acted movies complete with special effects will account for only a small part of the total future market. In any case, whether it be Mel Brooks or Julia Child, the product will probably be there. It is up to today's filmed entertainment companies to determine what the public will want in terms of form and content. If they do this, then their virtual monopoly of the filmed entertainment market today will be preserved well into the future.

Video Technology

As you can see in Table 17-3, video tape recording (VTR) is the newest communications medium to enter the home. It took television some 12 years from the time it was introduced into the home on a mass scale to reach $1 billion in retail sales. It is estimated that VTR will have reached that mark after only 3 years. If this projection is correct, VTR will be the most rapidly accepted product in the consumer field.

TABLE 17-3

Device	Years in Home
Mail	200
Telephone	65
Radio	55
Audio Records	50
Television	30
Audio Tape Recording	15
Video Tape Recording	1
Video Disks	Yet to come

At the end of 1977, approximately fifteen brands of video tape recording devices were on the market, including units by Sony, Quasar, JVC, Sanyo, Toshiba, RCA, Sears, Magnavox, Panasonic, Akai, and Sylvania. Since the various systems utilize four different standards, buyers may find that cassettes recorded on one unit cannot be played back on another unit.

If the home video playback/record industry is to develop a real mass market, like that for the phonograph record industry, pricing will have to come down substantially from present levels (somewhere between $100 and $400 for hardware and $5 to $10 for three-quarters of an hour of software). This will happen, but probably not until at least 1980.

What exists at the moment is a number of competing, incompatible hardware systems vying for market share. The system or systems that should eventually achieve dominance will probably be those that first reach a price level allowing them to capture the mass market. In the kind of market we have today, despite all the publicity, the number of units in use will probably stay relatively small for some time. The amount of software actually consumed by these units will also be relatively small and probably, because of the high average income and education levels of current buyers, will not reflect the type of software that will be most in demand when this product finally reaches a mass market stage in the 1980s.

Pirating is a problem, one that can be controlled only by rigorous enforcement and obviated by the availability of inexpensive prerecorded software.

At present, it seems premature to try to pick what hardware form will become dominant, although it is certainly likely that home video playback systems will eventually concentrate on a single, virtually universal, compatible form of hardware. The first horse out of the gate, moreover, is not necessarily the winner. In the field of audio tape, it initially appeared that eight-track systems were achieving a dominant share; today it's clear that cassettes will eventually capture this market.

Software, although growing in importance, will probably produce no more earnings in the near term than a good theatrical film's network television sale. This can be appreciated if one realizes that there are well over 100 million audio tape and record playback systems in American homes. Yet, with all these units, even the most popular recording artist sold far too few units in 1977 to have much of an impact on near-term earnings.

So even if there are 3 million video playback systems in United States homes by 1980, one could not realistically expect blockbuster titles like *Jaws, The Sting,* or *Star Wars* to sell 300,000 albums, or an ordinary title to sell more than 10,000 to 50,000 albums. *Star Wars* has already earned over $100 million in rentals for Twentieth Century Fox; the company would have to realize an average of $333 per album to earn the same amount on the sale of 300,000 home video albums.

Since the price after distribution costs, including retail markup, will probably be substantially less than $10 per album, it is easy to see that a great many more hardware systems will have to be in homes by 1980 than will probably be there if a film, even a blockbuster, is to garner meaningful revenues. (Twenty percent of 3 million systems is 600,000. At $5 profit to the production company per unit of software, you get $3 million profit for a blockbuster. As these are admittedly optimistic assumptions, the profit for a normal film realistically will be negligible until the number of home playback systems in use becomes substantially more than 3 million units. This probably won't occur until the mid-1980s.)

Notwithstanding all the excitement, it should be some time before one can define what hardware system or systems might manage to establish a permanent foothold in the emerging home video market. That this market will consume a great deal of software seems clear. What is still unclear, though, is when this consumption will become economically significant, and what form of software will become most popular, e.g., entertainment or educational material. In any case, filmed entertainment companies active in both theatrical and television production should find in this new market a fresh outlet for selling their wares.

QUESTIONS TO ASK YOURSELF BEFORE MAKING AN INVESTMENT IN THE LEISURE INDUSTRY

1. Have you used your own experience and individual expertise to evaluate the quality of a product and the responsiveness of it to a given sociological trend?
2. Have you done your homework as to the sustainability of the trend?
3. Have you compiled all the industry data available concerning the trends of the industry?
4. Have you confirmed those statistics on your own to determine whether you're being misled by overly optimistic current-sales and future-sales estimates?
5. Are you sure that you're not being misled by your own personal tastes and biases?
6. Where are the stocks selling in relation to the S&P 400? If they're selling at a premium, is it possible that most of the improvement in industry fundamentals has already been discounted?
7. Are you evaluating this industry in terms of public taste and mood? Have you historically been successful at gauging swings in public mood and opinion? If not, do you know someone who is?
8. Are you trying to forecast the unpredictable? In other words, are you gambling that a certain movie soon to be released will be a big hit? If so, shouldn't you reconsider, as the odds will be heavily against you?

CHAPTER 18

THE MEDICAL PRODUCTS INDUSTRY

Robert G. Bruce

FACTORS WHICH AFFECT THE OUTLOOK FOR THE INDUSTRY

1. The availability of new or continuing funds is most important. If the government decides to spend money, then typically the demand for a new product or service increases dramatically. The company or companies that supply the service or produce the product will be in a favorable position.
2. The general incidence of illness in the population is also key. If there's a high incidence of flu one year relative to the year before, there will be more hospitalization, and hence more business for hospital supply companies. The composition of the population is also a consideration. The older people get, the sicker they tend to become, and the more often they need to be hospitalized. The key users of hospital services are those 40 years old and up, particularly people over the age of 65.
3. You should also consider the trend in total U.S. employment. Most health care is funded through either employers or the government, and the more people who are employed, the more people there will be who can get employer or government hospi-

tal benefits. Thus, generally speaking, if the trend in employment is up, health care coverage will increase, and thus so will access to and use of physicians and medical services.

4. Technology can add to demand, too. A new piece of medical equipment which either improves upon patient care delivery or treatment, or reduces costs, implies increased usage by health care providers. Typically, most new products these days tend to be more efficient and are improvements on existing products, rather than revolutionary new ideas.

5. Regulation and government involvement are critical factors. Regulation has created a consolidation in the industry: typically regulation hurts the small business and helps the big operator. The government is also becoming more cost-conscious, and the result will be further weeding-out of inefficient producers in this industry. Remember, too, that government regulation can have a detrimental effect on large hospital supply companies. Their products can be recalled, as was the case in the early 1970s with intravenous solutions of a number of companies.

6. Another important consideration is the amount of business that a company does overseas. Overseas markets tend to be growing faster than domestic markets, because the practice of medicine is not quite as modernized and the transition from reusable to disposable products is still not complete.

7. Another influence on demand is the number of practicing physicians. More physicians normally means more patients being seen, and more patients being seen usually means more treatment being administered. In addition, the more physicians in a locale, the higher the rates normally. The level of fees has not been a significant drawback heretofore.

TRENDS IN FORCE IN THE INDUSTRY CONTINUE FOR A LONG TIME

Once a momentum starts on a certain health care procedure, it tends to keep going for quite a while. For example, coronary bypass surgery, which is a comparatively easy procedure for a thoracic surgeon to master, has grown from none per year in the late 1960s to over 75,000 in 1977. This has happened because there was significant need for the treatment, it was an easy procedure to learn, and this expensive surgery was generally paid for by the government or by a private insurance plan which, in turn, provided physicians with meaningful financial incentive.

SOME INVESTMENT CONSIDERATIONS

1. One of the challenges in analyzing these companies is that, generally speaking, they do not supply a definitive breakdown of the percentage of their sales and earnings by markets.
2. It has been relatively easy to forecast profits and to get a good handle on general industry fundamentals—but it is relatively hard to predict what the stocks will do in reaction to these fundamentals.
3. The stock market's valuation of these companies has changed dramatically. In the early 1970s, many hospital supply companies were selling at a price/earnings ratio three or four times that of the S&P 400. In recent years, the stocks have sold anywhere from 1½ to 2 times the market.
4. These companies often are involved in high-technology or esoteric medical fields, which can frequently be hard for individual investors to identify with. There are over thirty medical disciplines, and over 1000 different products service those disciplines.
5. The medical community will rarely suddenly jump on a new product. It will study and evaluate the products over time. Thus, investors should not rush into these stocks just because of some new technology or product.
6. A key determinant in the industry is the evaluation of whether there will be funds available to medical providers for the purchase of new products or services.
7. Hospital care is already pretty well funded in the United States; government pays for basically 45 percent of it, private insurance pays for about 45 percent, and the individual pays for the rest.

QUESTIONS TO ASK YOURSELF BEFORE MAKING AN INVESTMENT IN THE MEDICAL PRODUCTS INDUSTRY

1. What is the outlook for government spending on health care, particularly individual facets or treatment modalities?

2. What is the general incidence of particular illnesses among the population?
3. What is the average age of the population and the outlook for that average? (The older the population, the more susceptible it will be to illness and hospitalization.)
4. What are the trends in total employment, and thus the trends in total health care insurance coverage?
5. Is the company you're interested in introducing new products or technology? Are they adaptations, or are they truly revolutionary in nature? What has been the reception in the medical community?
6. What is the trend toward government regulation? Is the consolidation in the industry still going strong? What effect will the government's cost-consciousness have?
7. What is the growth in practicing physicians?
8. Is your company heavily involved in markets outside the United States, where growth typically will be much stronger?
9. How exposed is your company to government regulatory action—i.e., is it producing the type of item that is closely scrutinized? Could a federal temporary restraining order or outright ban on a *single* product line at the company seriously reduce profit growth?
10. Does your company have a good record of a continuous flow of new products, which it will need to sustain its growth?
11. Have you tried to differentiate the company's product lines and markets and attempted to get a fix on the growth rates of same?

CHAPTER 19

THE NEWSPAPER INDUSTRY

Ellen Berland Sachar

From an investor's point of view, the most important fact to remember about the newspaper business is that it is a monopoly business. In over 95 percent of the newspaper markets in the United States today, either there is only one newspaper, or there are two newspapers both belonging to one company. More important from a business perspective, newspapers are an unregulated monopoly business—the only such monopoly business in the entire country, in fact. This unique situation gives a newspaper considerable control over its pricing structure. With the only game in town and a flexible inventory situation, a newspaper can pretty well charge whatever the traffic will bear. Unlike that of broadcasting, therefore, a newspaper's pricing structure is by and large not subject to the vagaries of supply and demand. The result: the ability to pass along cost increases as they occur and a media business that, barring such uncontrollable external phenomena as wage and price controls, is, in many instances, recession-resistant, in that advertising linage and circulation declines can, to a large degree, be offset by price increases.

RECENT DEVELOPMENTS

Over the last 10 years, the newspaper industry has undergone a number of changes, all of which have produced a business that is considerably more efficient and more profitable than in the past.

Automation

As recently as the 1970 census, newspapers were among the top 10 employers in the country. With the computerization of phototypesetting and the introduction of other operating efficiencies, the number of production employees at newspapers has declined significantly. As a result, the operating margins at most newspapers around the country have improved dramatically. As a by-product of this successful automation, the power of the labor unions in the newspaper industry has declined considerably. The *Washington Post*, for example, in 1975 and 1976, was able to continue publishing despite a lengthy and even violent strike by its pressroom union. Other instances abound in the industry. Consequently, in most areas, newspaper labor unions are no longer in a position to demand (or receive) inordinate wage increases or to threaten a newspaper with a total shutdown, as they could in days gone by.

Consolidation

In the early 1960s the newspaper industry consisted primarily of numerous individual, family-owned operations. Since then, more and more of these individually owned papers and even some of the smaller groups have been bought out by the large newspaper chains. Currently, newspapers accounting for over 50 percent of United States daily circulation are owned by groups. This trend toward consolidation has had two important consequences for the industry: (1) group ownership has resulted in various economies of scale in the daily operation of newspapers, thereby leading to increased profitability for all involved; and (2) continued acquisition activity by the various publicly held newspaper groups has considerably enhanced their earnings growth potential. In this respect, newspapers have an advantage over broadcasters, in that there are no government restrictions on the number of newspaper properties any one company can own. Newspaper companies have thus been able to expand in the business they know best, without running the risk that broadcasters have of entering businesses that are less attractive than their own.

Public Ownership

Since the mid 1960s, a good number of the large newspaper chains have become publicly owned companies. With shareholders to report to (and each other to impress), all of these companies have brought in professional management, applied modern management techniques to their operations, and become far more efficiently run and profitable enterprises than in the past. Investors should always remember that privately held companies are run in such a way as to minimize their tax burden, and publicly held companies, to maximize their earnings per share. Hence the move toward public ownership has led the newspaper industry to an increased awareness of profits and efficiency.

HOW TO INVEST IN THE INDUSTRY

In the early 1970s newspaper stocks were viewed basically as recession-proof advertising plays. However, since the severe recession of 1974 and 1975, when advertising linage, particularly classified advertising linage, declined and newsprint prices skyrocketed, the image of these companies in investors' eyes has changed somewhat. While the newspapers are still viewed as being more recession-resistant than other media businesses, they are also clearly seen as being more sensitive to swings in the economic cycle than was previously assumed. For this reason, it should come as no surprise that the stocks of certain of the well-run newspaper companies are selling at a fraction of their former p/e ratios.

In addition, as more and more retailers begin to use the electronic media, especially television, with greater frequency (see discussion in Chapter 6), newspapers' advertising revenue mix—now generally 55 to 65 percent retail, 20 to 30 percent classified, and 10 to 15 percent national—will swing more heavily in the direction of classified and national advertising. Since both these categories are more readily affected by economic downturns than is retail advertising, it would stand to reason that over the long term the newspaper business could come to be perceived as an even more cyclical business, if current trends continue. At the present time, however, such a judgment seems premature, since newspapers in total still are the largest single advertising medium in the United States, attracting approximately 30 percent of the total ad dollars spent in the United States, compared to television's 20 percent; and newspapers' retail advertising revenue base is still five times the size of the local television number.

As with a broadcasting stock, the best time to buy a newspaper stock is at the depth of a recession. Expectations of an economic recovery lead investors to anticipate strong increases in advertising spending and hence sharply higher earnings for all media-connected businesses. As more newspaper companies diversify into the broadcasting business and vice versa, however, investors' ability to make categorical distinctions between these two businesses will diminish significantly. Both, after all, have similar operating characteristics: generous cash flows, high operating margins compared to the rest of American industry, no foreign involvements, and no mandatory heavy reinvestment in plant and equipment; and both represent protected ways to play consumer spending or a recovery in consumer spending. In some respects, then, it might be safe to say that investment in a diversified media company, i.e., one with significant holdings in both the newspaper and broadcasting businesses, represents the best vehicle of all among the media stocks. For these companies, the shifts in retail advertising dollars out of newspapers into television will be of little consequence. Given their substantial holdings in each business, whichever way the retail pendulum swings, they will stand to benefit. Moreover, their earnings growth will likely reflect the best of both worlds: consistency and stability, regardless of swings in the economic cycle, because of their heavy exposure in the local and retail areas; and significant upside leverage in presidential-election and recovery years, from their considerable exposure in classified and national "spot."

In deciding which newspaper company's stock to invest in, you should consider the markets its newspapers serve—the growth prospects of those markets and the degree, if any, of union strength there; the degree to which their ad revenue mix is dependent on classified rather than retail advertising strength; the size contribution to profits of their broadcasting operations; and the timing of the economic cycle. In times of economic downturn, one might favor investing in a company with a heavy classified component, on the theory that an economic recovery would lead to sharp gains in this area and hence dramatic earnings increases. If one were less risk-oriented, however, one would seek out companies more clearly dependent on local advertising, since the growth in this category appears to be rather consistent, regardless of the swings in the economy overall.

POTENTIAL PROBLEMS

The careful investor in newspaper stocks should monitor the following trends:

1. Continued decline in newspaper circulation, especially among the younger demographic group, 18–35, that advertisers seek out so consistently.
2. Massive shifts of retail advertising dollars out of newspapers into television, as opposed to the current gradual changeover.
3. Consistent growth of advertising or circulation revenues through price increases alone, with no concurrent unit gains.
4. Dramatic increases in the number of print alternatives for the local advertiser—preprints, shoppers, weeklies, and direct mail offerings—which would eat into newspapers' retail revenue base.
5. A pronounced increase in distribution problems, whether on the cost side or the control side, making it more difficult and/or more expensive for the newspaper to reach the home.
6. Adoption of legislation restricting the number of newspaper properties an individual or a company can own.
7. Sudden development and acceptance of some electronic technology that would replace newspapers as we know them today.

As with the broadcasting industry, all of these concerns are long-term and present no immediate danger. In the years ahead, however, these straws in the wind could become definite hurricane warnings.

QUESTIONS TO ASK YOURSELF BEFORE MAKING AN INVESTMENT IN THE NEWSPAPER INDUSTRY

1. What is the general mix of this company's advertising revenues? What was it 5 years ago? Has retail advertising declined significantly as a percent of the total?
2. Has the company been aggressive in its pricing strategy? Has it been so aggressive that ad linage and circulation units are showing little growth?
3. Has the company demonstrated an ability to control costs? Have margins improved significantly over the last 5 years?

4. Is the population in the markets which this newspaper company serves growing faster or slower than the national average?
5. Are retail sales in the markets which this newspaper company serves growing faster or slower than the national average?
6. Are any new industries or companies locating in the markets this company serves?

CHAPTER 20

THE OIL SERVICE INDUSTRY

John B. Walker

KEY TO ANALYZING THE INDUSTRY

1. Correctly anticipating the spending patterns of the oil industry.
2. Being right on the price of oil and gas and the profitability in exploring for them.

MOST COMMON INVESTOR MISTAKE

Focusing too intently on the fundamentals and not paying enough attention to investor psychology. For instance, energy legislation, the price of energy, or political demagogy can have a major effect on the psychology of investors, without having any effect on the underlying earnings trend of the companies.

HOW TO ANALYZE THE INDUSTRY

1. The outlook for the oil service companies is dependent on the capital spending pattern of the oil industry. Unfortunately, how-

ever, there are a lot more players in this game now, and it is harder and harder to determine what actual spending patterns are. The major oil companies continue to lose market share, as national oil companies, such as the Arabian Oil Company, and independent producers continue to increase their share of overall capital spending.

In fact, to give you an indication of how small the major companies are in the total picture, you should know that the major oil companies drilled only some 16 percent of the wells in the United States in 1978.

For this reason, it is very difficult to get a consensus on what the spending will be for the industry. The independent oil companies, which account for the vast majority of spending, are a tremendous swing factor in terms of spending for oil equipment.

One other complication has entered the picture, and this is that Russia and China, among others, are increasingly using Western technology in searching for oil. This has added another uncertainty in estimating the amount of money likely to be spent on oil exploration.

2. The second major consideration which affects the oil service industry is the profitability of looking for oil and gas. If there is not adequate financial incentive to do so, then it is clear that money will not be spent looking for oil or gas. Needless to say, if the price of oil increases dramatically, as it did in 1973—in effect, a quadrupling of the price—then it is safe to say that oil companies will spend a lot of money looking for it, as their profitability will be increased accordingly.

In analyzing the profitability of looking for oil or gas, one cannot just make a generalization about it. One must look on an area-by-area basis and evaluate the profitability in each place. For example, price controls are still in effect in the United States.

3. When you consider the outlook for the oil service industry, be sure to remember that there are many different aspects of the business—and each one may be affected in a different way. For example, there are contract drillers, expendable-supply companies, oil field services, capital equipment manufacturers, and marine construction companies.

4. In order to get a handle on what the spending of the industry is, it's important to know what the major oil companies are doing,

but even more important, as we've seen above, is to find out what the independent oil companies are doing. (That's because they are such an important swing factor in terms of spending.) The Independent Petroleum Association of America in Washington, D.C., is a useful organization in this regard and can supply some indications of spending.

5. One of the key statistics for this industry is new rig additions. If you can get a handle on this, it will help significantly in coming up with a revenue forecast for the oil service industry. If you have an excess of rigs, then oil service revenues will fall off sharply and profits will get squeezed; conversely, if there's a shortage of rigs, prices will rise and rig utilization will be at a high level, as will profits.

   Note that the *Oil and Gas Journal* publishes a forecast for spending by the major and independent oil companies for the lower forty-eight states. Chase Manhattan estimates historical capital spending on a worldwide basis, although there is a time lag of 1½ years.

6. The level of seismic activity, lease acquisitions, and rank wildcat drilling are normally leading indicators of drilling intentions for 3 to 5 years. So, be sure to keep abreast of these statistics.

HOW TO ANALYZE INDIVIDUAL COMPANIES

1. A critical factor in evaluating particular companies is figuring out which ones have a proprietary product. Here's why:

   In the 1960s, the industry was dominated by a few major companies. After the North Sea discoveries, the Europeans were able to get into the contract drilling business very successfully. The Japanese are making headway in the marine construction market. But now, because the cost of failure is so much higher than in any other industry, drillers are constantly trying to reduce the cost of drilling.

   The rental of a drilling rig can represent as much as 40 percent of the cost of drilling. What's more, a lot of the drilling is currently taking place at deeper and deeper levels. For this reason, oil companies are interested only in buying premium products—in which the United States happens to be dominant. That's because they cannot afford to make a mistake using a shoddy product, since such a mistake could idle the entire drilling rig and thus raise costs dramatically. For this reason, the United States remains in a dominant position for certain proprietary products.

2. The oil service industry is in a consolidation phase: the large companies are taking over the small companies. By the early 1980s, it is likely that seven or eight major companies will dominate the industry and will be offering a package deal for a wide range of products and services. Most companies at present deal on an individual basis, providing an individual product packaged to meet a particular company's needs.

    Government's increasingly interventionist role will further the consolidation trend. Government's heavy restrictions on the pricing of oil and offshore drilling is hampering profitability and requires a large number of reports to be submitted.

3. In the marine and contract drilling side of the business, the utilization of equipment and the rates for rig rentals are the key factors affecting industry profitability. In the expendables market, the key to profitability is the type of drilling that's being done, the amount of it, its location and depth, and the type of product mix used to do the drilling (whether, for example, a premium or nonpremium drilling bit is being used).

    The service business is a very-high-margin operation because of its technology, and it is priced in relation to total oil well costs. Therefore, if the cost of drilling continues to escalate, so will the revenues for service companies. What's more, service companies are often getting additional sales by developing offshoots from one basic product or service. The outlook for capital equipment companies is dependent on the ordering of new rigs.

4. The service part of the industry is the strongest, as it is the most proprietary.

5. In getting a fix on where you are in the industry spending cycle, you should survey the output of and demand for rig builders, rig utilization statistics, and monthly drilling statistics.

6. This industry is not so much economy-related as it is dependent on profit expectations for the oil industry. Note that capital spending for the oil industry could stay high even after oil

company profits have dropped off. (It seems to take the independents a while to notice that drilling profits are in a downtrend.)

7. When you are analyzing a particular drilling company, be sure to compare its rig utilization to the overall industry utilization rate.

8. Other important industry statistics to get hold of are the level of oil field activity (which includes the amount of wildcat drilling, seismic activity, and lease rate activity), government offshore lease sales, and action on oil and gas pricing. All of these factors can have a significant effect on what is happening in the industry.

9. These stocks have a certain pattern; for example, they do poorly in the first quarter of every year, having peaked in December, and decline into an April–May trough.

10. These stocks used to be very good trading vehicles, but they won't be as volatile as they were formerly.

11. Typically, contract drillers sell at a slight discount to the market's p/e, the expendables sell at around the same multiple as the market, and the service companies sell at a premium to the market.

12. Between 1972 and 1976, this industry was practically exploding at the seams. The industry needed huge amounts of capital, and these companies had to rely largely on external financing. A company's cash flow position remains an important factor in looking at individual companies, as it will determine dividends and the amount of new stock which must be sold.

13. This industry only started to be closely watched in the early 1970s, and many investors made a lot of the classic mistakes.

QUESTIONS TO ASK YOURSELF BEFORE YOU MAKE AN INVESTMENT IN THE OIL SERVICE INDUSTRY

1. What was last year's rig activity versus what it is now, and what are the forecasts for the next two years?

2. What are the expectations in the United States and world-wide for rig activity?

3. What is the activity in the leading indicators for the industry, i.e., lease sales, seismic activity, etc.?

4. Of the rigs that are currently available, how many of them are active? (Eighty-five percent is about as high as you can go.)

5. How many rigs will be added worldwide this year? (Most rigs are built in the United States.)

6. What's the utilization of land rigs? What's the utilization of offshore rigs in the United States and outside the United States?

7. Are new-rig backlogs building? Note that one of the hardest oil field statistics to obtain is the annual rig-building capacity of United States rig manufacturers. This information is important, because most of the world's rigs are produced in the United States. One problem in measuring rig capacity is that there is no such thing as a "rig manufacturer." It takes over 100 separate vendors to supply one complete rig. For this reason, the most commonly used measure of rig capacity involves parts of a rig, i.e., the annual capacity to build drawworks, rotary tables, or derricks.

   Another problem is that the industry carefully guards information on rig parts capacity, for fear of export controls. In any case, most oil field forecasters assume that about 200 rigs per year is the rig capacity level. However, some knowledgeable sources claim that 250 to 300 rig additions per year is an achievable number.

8. Which sectors of the capital equipment and expendables markets are in a shortage or surplus condition?

9. What are the expectations for oil and gas pricing in the United States and outside the United States?

10. What are the general expectations of capital spending this year versus last year on drilling rigs by the major oil companies and by the independents on a national and international basis?

11. Are there major government activities contemplated which will affect the energy field?

12. Are the stocks likely to be impacted psychologically by any government activity?

13. What is the current profitability of looking for oil and gas?

14. What is the pricing in the oil service industry itself? In other words, what's happening to the rates on rig rentals, marine construction barges, expendables, and prices of drilling bits and services?

15. What's the trend in the cost of drilling? What's the total world cost?

16. What sectors of the industry are seeing increasing foreign competition? What's the internal competition like within the various sectors of the oil service industry?
17. What's happening to the overall market share in the industry? And in the various sectors of the industry?

CHAPTER 21

THE PAPER AND FOREST PRODUCTS INDUSTRY

Lawrence A. Ross

GENERAL BACKGROUND

There is often debate about whether paper and forest products constitute one or two industries. Our answer is "both." From a product and
market viewpoint they are two industries, serving different segments of
the economy and utilizing different types of productive facilities. But
from a raw materials viewpoint they are one industry, both dependent
on the forest and timber. Timberland ownership, to varying degrees,
characterizes both product lines. Let's begin by briefly describing each
one. The largest market for forest products, of which lumber and
plywood are the most important parts, is residential construction,
which accounts for 40 to 50 percent of usage. The largest end use for
paper products is packaging, which accounts for about 55 percent of
tonnage. Not only is residential construction the largest end use, it's
the most volatile, and this adds to its importance in the total picture.

   Forest products are durable in nature; lumber that was produced in the 1950s is still in use today. On the other hand, little of the paper which was produced in the 1950s is in use today. Forest products are durable products which service a durables demand, while paper serves primarily a nondurables demand.

As indicated above, both wood products and pulppaper are forest resource industries, but the timber economies of the United States vary widely by area. In the Pacific Northwest, timber is harvested for use in lumber and plywood production processes that give rise to wood waste in the form of chips and sawdust. These residuals are then used in paper production. In the Pacific Northwest, a tree is rarely cut down solely to be used for pulp and paper. The forest economy of the Pacific Northwest is basically an integrated system, with pulp paper and solid wood products dependent on each other. In other parts of the country, small-size timber (pulpwood) is used directly in the production of pulp and paper, and trends in lumber and plywood can be quite irrelevant.

Both types of companies have concerns regarding the availability of raw materials, and a forest products company will sometimes compete against a paper company for raw materials. However, the various markets each segment serves do not necessarily have similar market cycles.

Forest Products Companies

THE FACTORS WHICH DETERMINE THE OUTLOOK

First and foremost among factors that determine the outlook for the forest products industry is the level of housing activity. In going back in the chain of causation, the primary determinant of housing activity, in the long run, is demographics and income levels. But the year-to-year determinant of housing activity is typically the availability of credit (i.e., mortgage money). What is it, then, that determines the availability of mortgage money?

Savings and loan organizations plus mutual savings banks originate 70 to 80 percent of the mortgages. They cannot legally compete for funds when interest rates rise above certain levels. And if they lose their "raw material" (savings deposits) they are unable to make new mortgage loans. Therefore, the outlook for short-term interest rates is a critical factor affecting mortgage availability, and in turn new home construction, and thus demand for forest products. Therefore, rising interest rates are normally a threat to forest product companies and will normally have a negative effect on forest product stocks.

Of course, if such stocks are undervalued to begin with, rising interest rates may not cause them to decline, and in fact, in the spring and summer of 1978, rising interest rates were accompanied by rising forest product stock prices.

In summary, then, regardless of the outlook for future earnings, or the current earnings gains experienced by these companies, this industry will usually do badly in the stock market if interest rates are rising or are thought likely to rise. (Interest rates typically rise late in a business cycle, as the rate of inflation begins to accelerate.)

UNIQUE ASPECTS OF THE INDUSTRY

1. One unique aspect of the forest products industry is that it operates on a *renewable* and *domestically owned* natural resource base.

2. Another unique aspect is special tax treatment. To encourage the long-term (25 to 50 years or more) investments necessary in growing timber, the federal government allows capital gains treatment of that portion of income derived from timber profits, with timber profits defined as the difference between original cost and current market value for timber owned more than 6 months and used in the production process (or sold) in any given year.

3. Another unique aspect is large government ownership of the raw material. In the Pacific Northwest, for example, the government owns some 60 percent of the timber.

4. The United States is a raw materials supplier to other nations (primarily Japan). This is one of the few industries where we have a strong raw materials export position. The United States exports about 5 to 7 percent of its softwood timber harvest.

5. There is a wide range of costs between various producers in this industry. One of the reasons for this is that some companies own their own timber, while others buy at current market prices. The big timber companies generally tend to be lower-cost producers, because they have owned their timber for a long period of time and initial timber cost was low. In effect, these timber companies have had an inflation hedge which has worked.

STRUCTURAL CHANGES TAKING PLACE

Increasingly, the industry is moving to the South. Two-thirds of the plywood and three-quarters of the lumber is still produced in the West, but the environmental movement there is strong and has effectively limited the growth in government-supplied raw materials.

Timber supply varies from region to region. In the Pacific Northwest, private supplies are declining, and the government is unable (at present) to increase its supply of timber to the open market. Government supplies may or may not become more available in the future, depending on regulation and environmental concern. The argument for increasing the government harvest is that it will help inhibit inflation, but environmentalists claim that a step-up would disturb the environment and exhaust a precious natural resource. Congress and the various state legislatures have already enacted several laws favoring the environmentalists' position.

As a result of this situation, other regions are being encouraged to produce more. For example, some observers estimate that the South, which produced only 30 percent of the softwood products in the United States in 1970, will supply up to 50 percent by the end of the century. And, of course, the level of consumption should be much higher by then.

HOW TO DETERMINE WHERE YOU ARE IN THE INDUSTRY CYCLE

In trying to figure out where you are in the industry cycle, you should first track the length of previous cycles in housing and industrial production. Look at the amount of time elapsed since the uptrend or downtrend occurred, and compare that against a set of previous temperature readings.

Try to determine the probable length of an average housing cycle, and prepare, based on that, a rough estimate of where you are. However, remember that every economic expansion has a different length, and it is hard to make generalizations. Look at recent housing levels versus secular trend. For example, based on demographic trends, housing is sustainable at 1.7 to 1.8 million units per year. If the number has been below that, there is cause for optimism about the future, and vice versa.

WHEN TO BUY/SELL THE STOCKS

Traditionally, the time to buy forest products companies is when short-term interest rates have peaked and a decline in the outlook for interest rates is imminent. And conversely, the time to sell the stocks has been when the outlook for interest rates is up. From a timing point of view, it's best to buy when one thinks short-term interest rates are at their highs or close to their highs. But there is a different approach, and that is to ignore cyclical timing and concentrate on the long-term growth rates of the various companies and buy whenever shares are available at reasonable prices in relation to those growth rates. Some investors define that to be any time the price/earnings ratio, on normal current earnings, is lower than the growth rate. For example, if a forest products company can grow at 11 to 12 percent per year, a good purchase price might be anything lower than a ratio of 10.

MOST COMMON INVESTOR MISTAKES

The most common mistake investors have made in the forest products area is to buy the companies because current earnings look good. In an up cycle the earnings in this industry can be exceptional. For example, Georgia Pacific earned $203 million in its wood products division in 1976, and $358 million in 1977. But the stocks trade on the outlook for housing (against a background of valuation), not current earnings. Another frequent mistake is to buy the forest product companies simply because the price of lumber is going up. That's no true indication of the underlying health of the industry or the sustainability of demand.

HOW TO AVOID THE MAJOR INVESTOR ERRORS

One of the ways of avoiding an investment mistake in this industry is to hold off buying the stocks until the outlook for short-term interest rates is clearly positive. Another key is for the investor to have a good grasp of the earnings outlook for the industry and the companies in particular, as well as their potential earning power. Finally, investors should discipline themselves to buy the stock at a reasonable price. Investors should always have some kind of parameter of value and know when a company is reasonably or unattractively priced.

QUESTIONS TO ASK YOURSELF BEFORE MAKING AN INVESTMENT IN A FOREST PRODUCTS COMPANY

1. Is the outlook for higher or for lower short-term interest rates?
2. Is the housing industry above or below its normalized trend? (Sustainable demand is currently estimated at between 1.7 and 1.8 million housing starts, exclusive of mobile homes, annually. Therefore, one should consider buying the stocks when housing starts are and have been well below secular trend, and one should consider selling them when they are and have been well in excess of sustainable trend.)
3. What is happening to savings flows at S&L's?
4. What is the government's policy concerning its timber?
5. What is the outlook for pulp and paper? Do you have an idea of what "value" represents in this industry? Do you have a discipline which will keep you from an overvalued forest products stock?

Paper Companies

FACTORS WHICH AFFECT THE INDUSTRY'S OUTLOOK

First and foremost among factors that affect the outlook for the paper industry is the operating rate, which is a measure of the supply-demand balance. Nothing helps this industry more than a high operating rate. (Anything in excess of 94 percent of capacity is considered high.) It takes 2 to 3 years to add capacity, and so one generally knows in the near term what industry capacity will be.

In analyzing the outlook for the industry, it's important to look at both the supply and the demand side of the equation. If either changes, the operating rate can be altered. For instance, significant decreases in productive capacity due to closings related to pollution requirements came about in the paper industry in the early 1970s.

Paper mills are generally large and capital-intensive. Shutdowns are generally impractical, and because of this, paper companies are often forced to accept whatever prices they can obtain. On the other hand, wood products plants are not large and can be shut down when demand is slack. For example, Weyerhaeuser recently built a 300 million–foot (annual capacity) sawmill at a cost of $45 million. This facility should generate about $60 million in annual sales, and therefore $1.33 of sales per dollar of capital invested. On the other hand, some paperboard mills cost up to $250 million to construct and generate sales of $70 million a year, or only 28 cents of sales per dollar invested.

In summary, the paper industry is a basic manufacturing industry, the key determinant of which is general economic conditions. Remember, however, that it is hard to generalize about this, because the industry can be in an up or down cycle apart from the general economic environment. In fact, the general economy may be booming, but things may not be especially good for the paper industry. Conversely, in 1974 and 1975, when the economy had a severe recession, the paper industry was in a general up cycle and therefore fared better versus the economy than it had in many prior cycles.

UNIQUE ASPECTS OF THE INDUSTRY

Unique aspects of the paper industry include partial ownership of raw material needs (timber) plus a domestic, rather than foreign, resource base. Otherwise, it is a conventional, capital-intensive manufacturing industry. However, at present, the United States *is* the low-cost producer in the world. The reason for this is that timber costs here are lower, and our growing cycle is shorter. (It takes 80 years to grow a tree in Scandinavia, for instance, and only 25 years in the United States.) In certain product areas (e.g., market pulp) Canada may be lower-cost, but taken on a weighted-average basis, the United States is lower-cost.

Because the United States is the low-cost producer, we don't suffer from lower-priced imports. Canada supplies a good part of United States newsprint, but even that capacity is partly owned by United States companies.

It is important to watch what is happening to international currencies, where a drastic change could affect the ability of the United States to remain the low-cost producer. In this regard, Canada has lowered its timber costs considerably in recent years versus the United States by the continued depreciation of its currency against the U.S. dollar.

STRUCTURAL CHANGES TAKING PLACE

The paperboard side of the business has historically been concentrated in the South, which means these companies will tend to be the prime beneficiaries of the major geographical evolution towards increased wood products production from the South. Paper companies are starting to go increasingly into the wood products business, and somewhere down the road it will be very difficult to tell the difference between a paper and a wood products company.

Plastics and paper are in a constant fight for market share, and generally, paper products are losing more markets than they are gaining. But this has been going on for many years and is reflected in the unit growth rate.

THE FACTORS THAT INFLUENCE PROFITS

The outlook for profits in the paper industry, as in any industry, is dependent on volume, prices, and costs. Paper products are growing, on a unit basis, at about 3 to 3.25 percent per year. However, wage increases have recently been running around 10 percent a year. Thus, the unit growth rate is not adequate to maintain profitability, and therefore price is, at present, a more critical variable in the outlook for profits than it was a decade ago.

WHEN TO BUY/SELL THE STOCKS

The paper industry is normally dependent on economic activity. So, generally speaking, the time to sell the stocks is when you would sell all cyclical stocks, that is, at the top of the economic cycle, if you can determine when that is. By the same token, the time to buy the stocks is at the trough of a recession.

However, it's important to remember that the industry may be operating on a different cycle from that of the rest of the economy.

In evaluating the business cycle of the postwar period, the paper industry's profits have historically increased between 50 percent and 75 percent from trough to subsequent peak. But during the 1972–74 period, industry profits increased fivefold. The reason for this is that the paper industry was operating at the highest rates of the postwar period and sellers' markets prevailed. Such a situation is not likely to be repeated soon, even though *selected* markets can do particularly well in any given cycle. Currently, coated papers are experiencing what might be termed sellers' markets.

There are times when you may not want to buy paper stocks even at the bottom of an economic cycle. And by the same token, there will be times when you'll want to buy paper stocks even though the business cycle may be ending. Both cases depend on valuation.

It's also important to remember that an individual paper company can be attractive even though the industry isn't. That's because an individual company may be improving relative to the rest of the industry. In the early 1960s, for example, the paper companies by and large weren't attractive, but some companies were. For example, let's say one company reported earnings of $2 a share, consisting of $4 of earnings at one division and a $2 loss at another. If this company then decided to sell the losing division, reported profits would jump by 100 percent, and the company would turn out to be a good medium-term investment.

An important thing to watch is trends in vertical integration. Some companies are large buyers of raw materials, so whenever a company decides to integrate backwards, thereby keeping some of the profits currently being paid to others, the result could be an improved profit situation for that company.

The paper industry is a large ($40 billion) industry, and for that reason, it's usually easy to find attractive situations at any time. Certain segments of the industry may be operating at only 85 percent of capacity and be unattractive, while other segments may be operating at 100 percent of capacity and are therefore very attractive.

One investor strategy already alluded to is to look for internal change. This could be a financial change, an acquisition, or the disposal of a losing operation. This event may be so positive that you would want to buy the stock regardless of industry conditions and the business cycle.

Another important thing to remember is that price may make generalizations meaningless. At a certain price, a company like Georgia Pacific or Weyerhaeuser may be a buy, and conversely at a certain price these strong companies would be a sale, regardless of the outlook for earnings, dividends, and operating rates.

MOST COMMON INVESTOR MISTAKES

The major investor mistake with paper stocks is to become infatuated with good current earnings or disgruntled with bad ones. Current conditions usually have been discounted. Investors also tend to be somewhat too optimistic about the pricing flexibility of paper producers.

QUESTIONS TO ASK YOURSELF BEFORE MAKING AN INVESTMENT IN A PAPER COMPANY

1. What is the industry's operating rate?
2. What is happening to the industry's productive capacity? Is it expanding or decreasing?
3. What is the outlook for the economy?
4. Is the industry in or likely to be in a separate up or down cycle from the economy as a whole?
5. Is the United States still the lowest-cost producer? Is this likely to change in the near future?
6. What is happening to the Canadian dollar versus the U.S. dollar? Has this affected United States competitiveness vis-à-vis Canada?
7. Are plastics currently making or expected to make in the future any significant inroads into the market for paper products?
8. What is the relationship between wage increases and unit growth? If wage increases are increasing faster than unit growth, can prices be raised to offset the higher costs?
9. Are you looking for either certain segments or a particular company in the industry which might be attractive given a high operating rate, internal change, or backward integration?

CHAPTER 22

THE PETROLEUM INDUSTRY

Bruce E. Lazier

KEY TO ANALYZING THE INDUSTRY

Being able to determine the true worth of a company on the basis of the asset value of its oil reserves. The best way of doing this is to calculate the net present worth of future cash flow from existing assets. Another way is to look at the value or price the petroleum market (where billions of dollars worth of oil reserves are bought and sold each year) is putting on the company's assets. In other words, if all the company's petroleum reserves could be sold for price X, then the liquidating value of the company is price X divided by the number of shares outstanding. If that price is significantly above the price of the stock, an investment in the company should be considered.

MOST COMMON INVESTOR MISTAKES

1. Being overly concerned with typical measures of value, such as past and present p/e ratios, etc.
2. Failing to look at a company from the standpoint of what price its reserves could be sold for today.

SOME GENERAL POINTS TO REMEMBER ABOUT THE INDUSTRY

1. Investors always have an alternative to the stock market to determine the true worth of an oil company: the active petroleum marketplace, where billions of dollars of assets are sold each year.

2. Once investors get the slightest hint that an oil company is about to sell off its assets, its stock often appreciates significantly, almost overnight.

3. Investors in recent years have been skeptical about this group, because they were uncertain whether oil prices would remain high or whether governments might confiscate or nationalize the oil companies' assets.

4. The advantage of the oil industry so far in the 1970s is that petroleum reserves represent one of the closest things to liquid money. An investor can have an assurance that there is a demand for petroleum and that it can be turned into money in a relatively short period of time.

5. Both small and large domestic oil companies are operating under a price umbrella provided by the Organization of Petroleum Exporting Countries (OPEC). A dominant figure in an industry (in this case OPEC) is a bullish development for other companies in that industry, because prices are held high and stable. Price stability, which is the net result of this, is an important ingredient for a company's success. Even more important, and unusual, is the fact that OPEC, unlike dominant figures in most other industries, is willing to cut back on production to keep prices firm.

6. There is plenty of new oil available in the world; the important factor to remember, however, is that the days of cheap oil are gone. It now costs about $15 to $20 a barrel to find and produce new oil.

7. There are three basic types of oil company: the small companies, where a major oil find could increase the stock value overnight; the middle-sized companies, which are starting to pay dividends and to which a major find will still have an impact, albeit less than for a small company; and the large companies, which are mature, pay very high dividends, and are often regarded as income bonds, but can still experience a small rate of growth.

Which one of these you choose to invest in should depend upon your proclivity for risk and desire for gains.

8. Like other natural resource companies, the oils present particularly difficult problems to the analyst trying to assign relative or absolute p/e ratios to current book earnings. For example, what kind of p/e should one assign to earnings from a company formed solely to find oil on a North Sea block that hits one big field? Such a company would clearly be reporting liquidating earnings. Thus, estimating discounted cash flow to calculate a net asset value indicator is the best way of comparing the various oils with each other.

9. Generally speaking, you should look for an oil company which derives all of its earnings from "safe" areas: the United States, Canada, and Western Europe. Since all these areas import large quantities of oil from OPEC, it is OPEC imports that absorb the fluctuations in domestic petroleum demand. These companies' earnings are therefore relatively independent of general economic conditions. Also, until price ceilings on domestic oil and gas reach world oil prices, prices will rise steadily, although under mandated escalations. For some time to come, indigenous energy producers should, generally speaking, produce oil and gas at maximum technical capacity under firmly rising prices.

10. Here are some positives and negatives that currently exist for the oil industry. First the positives:

   a. Conventional oil and gas will still supply most of the energy demand of the United States and the free world, at least through the next 25 years.
   b. Including "synthetic" oil and gas (from coal, oil shale, and oil tar sands), most of the world's energy through the twenty-first century should continue to be fossil fuel.
   c. Exploration experts say that over 300 billion barrels of non-OPEC and non-Communist oil can be added, by oil exploration and enhanced recovery, in the free world's existing non-OPEC oil fields to the approximately 100 billion barrels of recoverable reserves now there.
   d. Over 1800 TCF (trillion cubic feet) of existing natural gas reserves and exploration potential remain in the non-OPEC free world.

e. Although government-owned oil companies will probably become increasingly common, the technical, managerial, and risk-taking abilities of the private oil companies make them likely partners with the former (i.e., Brazil, U.K., Norway, Chile).

f. Even in the OPEC nations, private companies should be able to profitably contribute their expertise, because advanced oil recovery techniques will become necessary as OPEC oil fields mature.

g. Huge private oil company investments in oil refining and marketing and in chemicals are likely to become more profitable (from current, very low levels) and remain necessary, as the hydrocarbon era continues into the next century. (To a refinery or a petrochemical plant, synthetic oil and gas from coal, oil shale, or tar sands are not much different as feedstock from conventional oil and gas.)

h. In the United States, Canada, Western Europe, and most other Western nations, the idea of nationalization (or worse, confiscation without compensation) seems to be past its high point in appeal for at least the next decade.

i. The extremely big discontinuous jumps in real oil prices are, one hopes, behind us; the steady 1 to 5 percent per year rise in real prices is unpleasant but less frightening than the 350 percent increase between 1973 and 1974.

These are the negatives for the petroleum industry:

a. The energy (including petroleum) industry is so essential that government regulation will increase in virtually every area and country. (This need not be irrational and can, in fact, provide some protection against a "know-nothing" reaction from some industry critics.)

b. A slower economic growth (and higher unemployment) scenario could sharpen the focus on income redistribution, rather than income creation; this could possibly lead to greater socialism, probably hurting all private capital, not just oils.

c. The stability of even the slower world economic growth scenario diminishes as certain political problems intensify, e.g., Middle East politics, world financial imbalances, and environmental concerns.

      d. Saudi Arabia's importance in financial and political affairs
will grow, with all that implies about the long-term concern for its internal political stability. If Saudi society
becomes radicalized, the country might conceivably have
an anti-American regime in place by 1990.

11. It is probable that Saudi Arabia will continue to be the swing
factor in the supply/price equation for petroleum and that, under
a wide variety of assumptions, the world is likely to require
Saudi Arabia to produce far more than its present ceiling of 8.5
million barrels per day (B/D). By 1985 the Saudis could be asked
to produce 15 million B/D, and by 1990, 20 million B/D, assuming economic growth worldwide is moderate and real oil prices
constant. A hardheaded look at the financial, economic, and
political realities facing the Saudis indicates sustained production of no more than 12 million B/D in 1985. If that is true, real
oil prices must rise, or the West's economic growth will be
extremely slow.

QUESTIONS TO ASK YOURSELF BEFORE MAKING AN INVESTMENT IN THE PETROLEUM INDUSTRY

1. Fundamental questions investors face about the petroleum industry are:

      a. How did the present situation in oil demand, supply, and
prices develop?

      b. What lies ahead for petroleum supply/demand?

      c. Which way will real and nominal prices go?

      d. What are the likely political consequences of all the above
for the United States and the oil companies?

2. Specifically regarding petroleum stocks, investors need to ask:

      a. Will high real prices of energy be either maintained or
increased?

      b. Will governments confiscate, in any further manner, the
high current present worth (cash value) of the oil
companies?

      c. Can each company keep reinvesting funds at or above its
risk-adjusted cost of capital so that its present worth will
continue to increase?

CHAPTER 23

THE PHOTOGRAPHY INDUSTRY

William A. Relyea

KEY TO ANALYZING THE INDUSTRY

Being able to correctly judge the timing and success of new-product cycles. However, increasing competition has rendered product cycles shorter and more uncertain and volatile.

MOST COMMON INVESTOR MISTAKE

Becoming infatuated with a new product and imagining that earlier, spectacular successes will be repeated.

SOME GENERAL POINTS TO REMEMBER ABOUT THE INDUSTRY

1. No two companies in the industry are alike. Eastman Kodak is the largest, with approximately 25,000 different products. Polaroid, on the other hand, is a fraction the size of Kodak and has only a few hundred products.
2. There are some major changes currently taking place in the

industry. For 13 years, Eastman Kodak's prices were very steady, but in the 1976—78 period, prices began fluctuating markedly.

3. It is very difficult to enter the film manufacturing segment of the photography industry. The manufacturing process for black-and-white—sensitized products is extremely difficult, and the manufacturing of color photographic systems is harder still. (For example, du Pont has never successfully entered the color market, although it has been an important factor in black-and-white products for a number of years.) The multiple emulsion layers of color films are coated at high speeds in the dark, and the opportunities for error are numerous. The difficulty of manufacture makes it unlikely that any new producers will enter the color film market. On the other hand, it is easier for companies to enter the camera or photo equipment manufacturing business.

4. The reputations of products, particularly film, are an important aspect of this industry. Even though Kodak films are more expensive than other films, they hold a majority of the United States market because of consumer confidence.

5. One of the most significant developments in recent years is the plethora of antitrust suits against Kodak. Under the settlement of the *Bell & Howell* suit, Kodak agreed to predisclose the details of new conventional-film cartridges to hardware manufacturers. The pattern of predisclosure begins 18 months before Kodak's introduction of the film. (In one instance, some Japanese film manufacturers benefited from this sort of predisclosure. On examining Kodak's new film cartridge, the companies discovered that their own new products were competitive and thus were able to beat Kodak to the market.) Lawsuits by Berkey and GAF accuse Kodak of attempting to monopolize certain areas of the industry. Any investment in Kodak should be made with an eye to the status of any pending suits and some confidence that the potential negative effects of the suits has been reasonably discounted in the stock price.

6. In some areas, as technology has matured, price competition has become a more important factor. In 1973, Kodak had more than 90 percent of the market of color photofinishing paper, but by holding its prices up in the face of lower-price, good-quality competitive papers, its market share by 1977 had slipped to only 50 percent. In late 1977 Kodak significantly reduced its prices, too.

7. In the past, new systems or new product introductions have typically expanded the total amateur photographic market.

8. Instant photography was a Polaroid monopoly from that company's introduction of its first system in 1947 until the entry of Kodak in 1976. As such, instant photography is an example of a field that was beautifully cultivated for the benefit of the monopolist. New product introductions through the 1950s and 1960s were carefully controlled by Polaroid to exploit as fully as possible each major system. The first cameras for both the black-and-white and Polacolor systems were sold at high prices, typically at about $175. These were followed by a lower-priced camera, about a year later, then, by still lower-priced versions, spread out over time, so that an optimum number of cameras could be sold at each price level. The more sold at high prices the better, as the higher the camera price and profit, the better the camera, and the greater the commitment of the user, which probably yields higher film usage than later, lower-priced models. For example, it took 6 years after introduction of the Colorpack system in 1963 for Polaroid to bring the camera price to below the $50 level.

The entry of Kodak in 1976 changed the nature of the instant business, as it:

a. Ended Polaroid's control over instant-product introductions
b. Destabilized the pricing of instant cameras
c. Changed the cost structure and to some degree the style of marketing
d. Very probably changed the level of profitability of instant photography.

LONG-TERM STRUCTURAL CHANGES

1. Kodak's technological lead has shrunk.
2. Price competition is increasing. In September 1977 Kodak cut prices on color paper for the first time in its history. This is the first time that Kodak had to respond to competition in the color area. (Note that the color side of the business is the most profitable and represents a huge portion of Kodak's earnings.)
3. Electronic photography is becoming more and more competitive with silver halide photography for certain uses and can be expected to take an increasing share of the photography market.

4. Another important change is the addition of competition in the instant photography area. Kodak entered this field with its own system in 1976.

5. In the 1960s, the industry took huge strides forward in terms of increasing the number of picture takers in the United States and in trading these picture takers up from black-and-white prints and color slides to color prints. To look at the 1960s as a benchmark would be misleading, as several factors were in place to allow record profitability: fast rate of film growth, price stability, and trading customers up to more expensive film types. Also, Kodak and Polaroid were not direct competitors in the 1960s as they have become in instant photography in the last couple of years.

HOW TO ANALYZE THE INDUSTRY

1. The outlook for photography is dependent on certain outside factors. First is the general economic outlook and particularly the outlook for personal discretionary income, as the amateur market represents the largest single factor in most photographic companies' earnings.

   Other longer-range factors to evaluate are demographics, including the birthrate and order of children. For example, more pictures are taken of the first child than of subsequent children. Other important factors are how much traveling the population is doing and what special opportunities there are to take pictures: e.g., such important events as the Bicentennial or the Olympics.

2. The key to analyzing the industry is to correctly analyze the product cycle. Therefore, you must study any major new product and try to determine the extent of the additional demand it will create.

3. The outlook for prices is a key factor in analyzing the industry. For many years, Kodak had very stable prices, but increased competitive pressures have forced Kodak to become more responsive with price changes.

4. Silver costs are important for the industry, as they are significant in sensitized-goods manufacturing costs; and because they are easily identifiable, they can have an effect on stock prices of photo companies.

5. One strategy for investing in the smaller companies of this indus-

try is to find a company which exercises a high degree of control over some segment of the business.

6. While much attention has been focused on the historical advantages that foreign manufacturers have had in low labor costs, particularly in Asia, much less attention has been paid to the increasingly competitive position the Japanese have developed in photographic technology. One indication of the amount of innovation being practiced by the United States photographic industry compared to that of its major competitor, the Japanese photographic industry, is the number of patents that each has been granted over time. Take the 8-year period 1967–1975 as an example. In looking at the patents granted to five major United States manufacturers principally concerned with photography, these companies received 528 in 1967. By 1971 this number had risen 71 percent, to 904. By 1975 the number of patents granted for these same companies had declined 46 percent, to 485, partly as a result of the increasing use of research disclosure as a means of protecting a company's access to a particular idea.

   The comparison becomes interesting when you compare the results at eleven major Japanese photographic manufacturing companies. In 1967 these eleven Japanese photographic companies had only forty-one patents granted in the United States. By 1971 the number granted to these companies had risen to 339, an increase of 720 percent. By 1975 the number of patents had risen further to 653, an increase of 93 percent over 1971 and 1293 percent over 1967. Thus, in 1967 the five United States companies were granted better than twelve times the number of patents than the eleven Japanese companies were granted. By 1971 the advantage had decreased to 2.7 times, and in 1975, the American companies only had 70 percent as many patents granted as the Japanese companies.

7. Vital to any long-range forecasting of Eastman Kodak's corporate progress is the outlook for its conventional amateur still-photography–related business, the largest single category of the company's worldwide business, accounting for about 30 percent of sales and, as discussed above, 50 percent of earnings. The outlook for this product sector rests largely on technological developments, in the form of new products coming as a result of Kodak's and other companies' efforts; the benefits of these new products for consumers and the effect they have on stimulating picture

taking, since this translates into sales of equipment, film, and photofinishing services; and economic developments in United States and world markets that affect consumers.

An underlying assumption in Kodak's snapshot business is that people want pictures of their families, friends, and travels. The easier a camera is to use, the better the results, the lower the price, and the more pictures more people will take. Kodak sees its job as providing the means to get these pictures with whatever technology is available at the current time. Kodak attempts to provide the simplest means possible for the amateur snapshot taker to get his or her picture. George Eastman summed up this philosophy in 1885 with his advertising slogan, "You push the button, we do the rest."

In 1963 Kodak introduced the Instamatic system, which incorporated technological advances to overcome several major barriers to picture taking that were characteristic of typical snapshot systems then in use, including the popular Brownie system. The Instamatic's most important features included: (a) cartridge loading of film, overcoming the difficulty of loading roll film; (b) color negative film, color slide film, and black-and-white film all having the same speed, so that all could be used in simple cameras with no adjustments necessary; (c) a smaller camera than its predecessor, with a small, built-in flash reflector that retracted into the camera body when not in use; and (d) a film in which each frame was exactly positioned by the camera for each shot.

The Instamatic system, assisted by advances in flash, stimulated picture taking considerably beyond previous levels. Despite this considerable success, Kodak remained convinced that major opportunity remained. The greatest barrier to snapshooting among Instamatic owners appeared to be the camera's size. Portability difficulties kept people from having the camera with them when picture-taking opportunities arose. Kodak's aim in developing the pocket Instamatic was to make the system much more portable. Diminishing overall size was part of this, but reducing the thickness to 1 inch enabled the camera to be inserted in a pocket.

The success of a new amateur photographic system, as measured by camera sales and eventual film usage, should reflect how well it overcomes the principal limitations of the major system that preceded it. Two ways to appraise a system's limitations are

(a) to look at what it does least well and how that inhibits further usage and (b) to look at what keeps the system from being used in the first place. In order to measure how well a new Kodak pocket system might succeed, an investor should attempt to define the principal problems of the current system.

On the other hand, remember that some limitations are readily perceived by consumers using the cameras and by the retailers selling to them and that others may not be, because they are too basic to be perceived or are overshadowed by another restriction that is currently more annoying.

WHEN TO BUY/SELL THE STOCKS

The time to sell these stocks is when people get overenthusiastic about a new product of the company. The time to buy the stocks is when the benefits of new products are invisible to investors.

QUESTIONS TO ASK YOURSELF BEFORE MAKING AN INVESTMENT IN THE PHOTOGRAPHY INDUSTRY

1. What is the status of new-product introduction? How much of the prospect for the new product has already been discounted by the stock? Is the new product revolutionary in scope? Or is it just evolutionary? How well does the new product overcome the limitations of the previous product? What were those limitations?
2. How enthusiastic are investors about the new product? Or conversely, are the benefits of new products totally ignored by, or invisible to, investors? (The answers to these two questions should help you judge from a psychology standpoint whether the stock is underpriced or fully priced.)
3. How long will the product cycle last?
4. How close is the competition? If a company is about to introduce a new product or system, how soon will competitors be able to follow suit? What is the state of technological competition from abroad?
5. What is happening to industry pricing? Is it stable, or is it subject to increased competition?
6. What's the outlook for the Japanese yen in relation to the U.S. dollar? As the most significant competition in conventional pho-

tographic materials (in terms of quality and price) comes from Japanese manufacturers, Fuji being clearly the prime competitor, fluctuations of the yen against the dollar affect the willingness and/or ability of these competitors to maintain significant discounts to Kodak's prices.

7. How competitive has electronic photography become?
8. What is the status of antitrust suits? Is your company liable to monopoly charges?

CHAPTER 24

THE RAILROAD INDUSTRY

John V. Pincavage

KEY TO ANALYZING THE INDUSTRY

The major determinants of rail stock prices are, in order of importance, the levels of dividends, the demand for transportation of natural resources, government policy, and wage increases.

MOST COMMON INVESTOR MISTAKES

Investors frequently pay too much for these stocks for the wrong reason and hold onto them for too long a period of time. The only reason to buy a rail stock is to look forward to selling it.

GENERAL POINTS TO REMEMBER ABOUT THE INDUSTRY

1. The railroad industry is a capital-intensive, labor-intensive business, with an operating and financial leverage greater than that of most industries.
2. The outlook for the industry is heavily dependent on the ability

to pass wage increases on to customers through higher prices. (Labor represents about 50 percent of costs.)

3. Another key consideration is the outlook for new and existing traffic sources. For instance, are coal shipments going up? What's happening to grain shipments? And what is the overall trend between railroad and trucking shipments?

4. Productivity is also a key factor. The key to the future for the railroad industry is to get better asset utilization. The average railroad car, for instance, goes only 100 miles a year. Thus, a lot of the industry's capital and assets are not being productively used. (What's more, the "100-mile rule" necessitates changing the crew or paying them overtime after 100 miles of travel.)

5. The industry is only as good as its weakest link. Even though the railroad you like is productive and efficient, if that railroad's tie-in is not efficient, then the overall efficiency of transportation on that line may not be very good.

6. The industry is highly regulated; it is also a service industry and thus is highly labor- and capital-intensive—which means that it gets hurt in a period of inflation through rising interest rates and labor costs.

7. It is the most fuel-efficient of all forms of transportation.

8. One cannot underestimate the role of government in the outlook for the industry. The regulation is so heavy and so complex that the industry is unable to do anything without the say-so of the government.

9. Trucks are basically the carriers of finished products, while the rails are carriers of raw materials. Thus, the rails go up first in a capital spending–based economic recovery, while the truckers go up first in a consumer-spending economic recovery.

10. One way of evaluating railroads is through the use of relative price/earning ratios. Typically rail stocks' p/e ratios alternate between 50 and 100 percent of the S&P 400 p/e. Thus, they should be purchased when they are selling close to 50 percent of the S&P 400 p/e and should be sold when they get close to 100 percent.

11. It is also important to learn about the potential for a strike against key customers of the industry, such as coal, steel, and other basic industries.

12. Dividends are a very important factor for the rail industry. You

buy these stocks for dividends, not for growth, as it is a very mature industry. So far, the major motivating factor for the stocks has been a change in dividend policy. (Energy costs and availability, demand for transportation of natural resources, and government policy are also important factors in influencing stock prices.)

13. For the first time in 30 years, railroads are starting to increase their market share of transportation of goods. This has mainly occurred through piggy-backing, which has enabled the railroads to get back a considerable amount of auto-hauling traffic.

14. One must also examine how much potential a railroad has in developing its nonrail assets (in many cases land, minerals, and oil), and what this contributes to present and future earnings. Union Pacific is becoming less a railroad and more a natural resources company because of its development of nonrail assets.

15. In summation, the farther you are away from a recession, the more nervous you should be about holding a rail stock.

LONG-TERM STRUCTURAL CHANGES TAKING PLACE IN THE INDUSTRY:

The railroad industry will either consolidate or become nationalized. The key to evaluating these alternatives is what happens in the Midwest, where several bankrupt railroads are in the process of being liquidated. Will these railroads follow in the steps of Conrail, or will they be spun off into the private sector? Needless to say, the nationalization of the industry would be very bad for even the most profitable carriers, as it would then be harder for the private railroads to compete in price against public rail systems. One less disastrous alternative of nationalization would take the form of nationalizing the roadbed, whereby government would maintain the roadbeds as it now maintains the highways.

THE MAIN DETERMINANTS OF INDUSTRY PROFITABILITY

1. The current and future direction of the economy.
2. Whether the railroad can get adequate rate relief to offset rising costs.
3. The long-term trend of track maintenance. A railroad is only as

good as its track—trains can go faster, have less damage, and require less maintenance overall if the tracks are well maintained. This problem tends to feed on itself, and those railroads which have not had an adequate maintenance of their system tend to find themselves in increasing difficulty as those maintenance problems magnify over the years.

One of the ways of gauging the amount of maintenance that needs to be done is to get hold of a figure called the "amount of deferred maintenance." This figure is put out once a year by the Interstate Commerce Commission (ICC) and includes such information as what percentage of railroad ties need to be replaced. It is important to remember that inflation makes these statistics understated, and thus you must make calculations for that in your analysis.

If a railroad wants to play with earnings, the best way to do it is to cut back on maintenance. The most successful railroads have been able to cut back on maintenance when traffic demand falls off. It is the unsuccessful railroads which have to keep on doing maintenance even when demand is slack and the economy is slowing.

4. The cash position of the railroad. This is basically a balance sheet industry, as opposed to the trucking industry, which is an income statement industry. The more cash a railroad has, the better.

Railroads are harder to analyze than truckers, because they are more complex and their leverage is so much greater. Earnings leverage can be two to three times more for rails than for trucks. That's because rails have so much fixed overhead costs; thus any incremental increase in demand can substantially affect the bottom line.

Just as the trucking industry has a great increase in incremental profits coming off the bottom of a recession, so do the railroads. The big improvement in earnings and margins will come in the early months of an economic recovery. And the further you get from the bottom, the less margin improvement and the less earnings improvement you will see. Thus as soon as operating margin improvements slow, you should consider selling the stock.

QUESTIONS TO ASK YOURSELF BEFORE MAKING AN INVESTMENT IN THE RAILROAD INDUSTRY

1. What is the status of labor negotiations?
2. What is the region the industry serves? For example, in Mississippi railroads will have to compete not only with trucks, but also with barges.
3. What is the status of new traffic sources?
4. What is the ability of management to control costs?
5. Does the railroad utilize its equipment well?
6. What is the cash position of the railroad?
7. Has the company been able to keep paying dividends in a down economy?
8. What is the outlook for major existing traffic sources?
9. What is the overall trend of market share between trucks and rails?
10. What is the outlook for regulation? Are price increases permitted quickly and in the size which the railroad wants and needs?
11. What's the outlook for inflation?
12. What is happening to bankrupt railroads? Is the trend toward nationalization, or toward dependence on the private sector?
13. Has the railroad been doing a good job of maintaining its track?
14. Is it able to cut down on maintenance costs in an economic downturn?
15. What is happening to capital spending?
16. What is the amount of deferred maintenance for the railroad?
17. Are you aware of the great operating leverage of the rails—on both the up and down cycles?
18. Has margin improvement slowed? If so, hadn't you better consider selling the stock?
19. What is the relative p/e for the industry in relation to the S&P 400? Is it at the high or the low end?
20. What's the potential for a strike at one of your railroad's biggest customers, e.g., coal?
21. What natural resources does the company have to develop and what will they add to future earnings?
22. Are all earnings sources of a railroad/resources company accurately valued in the price of the stock?

CHAPTER 25

RETAILING INDUSTRY

Stuart M. Robbins

KEY TO ANALYZING THE INDUSTRY

In a simplistic sense, analysis of the retail industry involves judging four general areas of activity: new store site selection, merchandising, distribution of products to stores, and financial controls.

MOST COMMON INVESTOR MISTAKES

1. Allowing personal shopping experiences to excessively influence judgments about a company.
2. Underestimating the substantial leverage that accelerating or decelerating sales gains have on both operating ratios and gross margins.
3. Placing too much emphasis on short-term (i.e., quarterly or weekly) sales/earnings results.
4. Overanalyzing the numeric (number of new stores, etc.) and ignoring overall corporate strategies.

HOW TO ANALYZE THE INDUSTRY

1. How you analyze a company depends on its size. The rules that apply to a large retailer don't necessarily apply to a small one. And drug chains, for instance, are different from supermarket chains and department stores. However, a retailer is basically a retailer, and what applies to one, in broad generalities, applies to the entire group.

2. Market share represents the end result of all retailer activities; moreover, share is directly related to profitability. Strong market positions can result from highly productive stores and from a saturation approach to expansion in individual areas. Greater penetration allows wide promotional impact, disperses distribution and advertising costs, and generally produces higher margins.

   Proper analysis of future growth potential requires careful scrutiny of corporate volume breakdowns and market shares. Investors should do two things in analyzing the retail industry:

   a. Locate accurately sales volume for the largest merchants and review carefully their share positions. This should provide useful information on market performance relative to competitors' and on area importance to the company analyzed.

   b. Get hold of projective input concerning retailing trends and their importance to various retailers. This should help in judging future volume and earnings performance by both large retailers and smaller merchants.

3. This is both an easy and a hard industry to analyze. It's easy in the sense that there are few technical terms to understand. On the other hand, it's a hard industry to analyze because of its people-sensitivity, both personnel and consumer. In retailing there are no backlogs or orders in process; on January 1 every merchant starts from scratch looking for customers.

4. Retailing is a play on the consumer; it is a people business, and the key to success in it depends on how well management can anticipate and react to consumer demands and desires.

5. Retailing is not a very profitable business.

6. Retailing is a low-growth industry. Most of it is domestically related and is therefore tied to the United States economy. It is a

mature business and can be categorized as well stored. Thus, retailing is basically a reflection of the economy. In investing in a company which is going to grow no faster than the economy, one looks for a company which is better managed than the competition. You also want to look for a company with a product that is experiencing considerable growth, such as CB radios, for example.

7. There are three basic things to understand in this industry: first is what makes each individual company tick, second is what makes the consumer tick, and third is how the stocks react to changing fundamentals.

HOW TO ANALYZE A RETAILER

There are four basic aspects of retailing which separate a successful retailer from an unsuccessful one. They are: (1) site selection, (2) merchandising, (3) distribution, and (4) financial controls. Almost all the analysis you do in retailing will relate to one or the other of these factors.

Site Selection

Site selection is the most important aspect of retailing. A company can be a wonderful merchant, but if its store is not located in a good location, there will not be enough floor traffic to generate adequate revenues and insure profitability. For example, if you were to put Bloomingdale's, which is a merchant par excellence, on a slow street corner with little traffic, the store would not be profitable. Conversely, if you were to put a W. T. Grant store at an excellent location, one where it would be conspicuous and accessible to a lot of traffic, it would be able to operate successfully.

The first step in analyzing the effectiveness of a company's site selection is to get an overview of the company's demographics. For instance, the Northeast is a highly competitive market, and a company which is doing business primarily in the Northeast may not be as attractive as a discounter in the Southwest with only a few stores and an opportunity to grow through the addition of more stores. Thus, a good company should have a large portion of sales volume coming from an area where the demographics are good—where there is large growth in consumer incomes and population and no saturation of retail stores.

It is not as hard as you might think to come to conclusions about demographics. For example, the migration from the Northeast and industrial heartland into the South, the Southwest, and the Mountain region has been fairly obvious for some time now. On the other hand, a demographic trend need not be long-term in nature for you to take advantage of it. For example, if farm income rises dramatically, you might want to consider retailing companies located in farmlands.

The next question to ask concerning site selection is whether the company has clever marketing practices. For instance, if the company is a drugstore, does it locate itself with a top-grade supermarket? Also, your company should be participating in high-traffic shopping entities (i.e., enclosed malls). Also, suburban shopping areas have been gaining over urban areas over the years—thus, you would want your company to be more involved in the suburban than the urban areas.

It's important to remember in the analysis of site selection that one store cannot stand by itself. For example, in analyzing Sears versus J. C. Penney, you would have to analyze the Sears regional mall versus the J. C. Penney regional mall. That would entail keeping track of the entire shopping complex and comparing one with the other.

The next aspect of site selection to consider is the concept of convenience. The average person in the United States drives no more than 1½ miles to the grocery store or drugstore. Thus, you want to make sure that your company has chosen sites which are convenient to the largest number of potential consumers in the areas it operates in.

In order to gauge the effectiveness of a company's site selection, an individual investor can ask several important questions:

1. How many stores has the company closed in the last 5 years? If there have been a large number of stores closed, this could be an indication that the site selection of the company was poor.
2. What portion of new stores over the next 12-month period will be placed in areas that have good markets, such as the Southwest? A company which is going to open 50 percent or more of its stores in a booming market is a company that you can be optimistic about.
3. How many stores is the company planning to open in the next year? There is a fine line between opening too many new stores and not opening enough. Ideally, you'll want to see the same number of new stores (as a percentage of total stores) opened next year as were opened in each of the last five years. You should be

nervous about a company which has wide distortions in new store openings. Such distortions often indicate something bad has happened somewhere along the line and should raise a caution flag immediately.

The best retailing companies generally open stable numbers of stores from year to year. By the same token, if a company is increasing the number of new stores by 30 percent annually, you should have a somewhat cautious attitude. That would entail a lot of start-up costs and could hurt earnings for several quarters, even years. (Generally speaking, the major retailing companies increase their selling space by about 4 or 5 percent annually.)

Merchandising

The key to looking at merchandising is to think about the retailing industry and the individual company as they think about themselves. (The best way to define merchandising is the way a retailer gets you to spend more dollars at a given store.) Merchandising is the least scientific aspect of this industry, since changes in fashion and consumer moods and sentiments must constantly be dealt with.

One of the key aspects of merchandising is that there's nothing that any retailer can do that will remain secret for long. As soon as a new merchandising concept is tried, the competition immediately knows about it. A second key to merchandising is that one retailer can always undersell another retailer, and thereby attract customers. Thus, any product or product line can be reduced in price as far as is necessary to attract attention and customers.

In understanding merchandising, the first major goal for an investor should be to learn the basic image of the company. Is it price, value, or quality? Is it a department store or discount store, fashion-related or value-oriented?

It's important that each company know what its image is, and you should have no doubt in your mind what that company's image is. For example, Bloomingdale's has an image of quality fashion and quality furniture. But W. T. Grant's image was harder to figure out. When management doesn't have a clear image of the company's direction, that spells trouble. Thus, it's very important that you evaluate the company's success in establishing an image.

Ideally, you want a company to stick with an image once it's been established. For example, if K Mart started to sell fur coats, you might be worried. If a retailing firm starts changing its product mix and plays around with its image, it's an indication that the firm doesn't know what it is and where it's going. Furthermore, it's an indication that all is not well; otherwise, why change the present strategy?

The next major aspect of merchandising is how much inventory a retailer should carry at any given time. Part and parcel of being successful here is the quality of financial controls. This can best be measured by getting hold of the figures stating the company's annual inventory turnover. This statistic should tell you whether what it bought sold well. Be sure to evaluate inventory turnover in terms of the company's historical performance and in comparison with the rest of the industry. Ideally, you like to see a stable inventory turnover with a constant, steady improvement.

The next merchandising consideration is the company's marketing or sales ability. A dirty store, a supermarket with food on the floor, or a department store with boxes lying around is not an auspicious selling environment. Oftentimes when you buy a product, it represents an extension of your personality, and you want the buying to be a pleasurable experience. Of course, a single store's bad performance could always be an aberration.

As an example of a company that sells its products well, take Federated (Bloomingdale's, Lazarus, and other department stores). Products are neatly lined up with a colorful display. Note that the best merchants in the world are supermarkets—they have the lowest gross margins, and therefore they have to be effective. One of the first things you'll notice when you enter a supermarket is the colorful fresh produce display, which is an attempt to make you feel comfortable in the environment.

If your mental image of the retailer is reaffirmed when you walk in, that's a good sign. This is important, because the high cost of labor has led retailers to hire fewer sales clerks in relation to sales volume, and now merchandise generally must sell itself. Therefore, it's very important to analyze whether the store looks and makes you feel good when you walk in.

Another criterion for measuring a retailer's merchandising ability is to find out the retailer's sales per square foot. Naturally, the higher the sales per square foot, the more productive is each individual store and, by inference, the company.

You should also study the relationships between markups and markdowns. Ideally, you like to see gross margins remain constant. If you see margins jump all over the lot, you should begin asking yourself questions. It could imply that the company was selling goods at the wrong prices, ended up with too much slow-moving inventory, and had to sell off the excess at a discount, thereby hurting gross margins. Because of the lack of ability to control operating costs, retailers' gross margins are extremely important. (Gross margins are a function not only of price, but also of product mix. For example, house brand names tend to be more profitable than other lines.)

In summary, merchandising consists of literally thousands of little clever tools that are employed to get the customer to buy more.

Distribution

Distribution is less important than site selection or merchandising, but it can be important, because if a product is out of stock, a potential sale is lost forever. For this reason, the efficiency of distribution is a critical factor. You'll want to know how distribution is done and how efficient it is. Is the warehouse in back of the store? Or are the goods shipped in from a warehouse many miles away?

Distribution is increasingly important, given the ever-rising cost of transportation. That's especially true, for example, if a company that has 100 stores in a tight, four-state area suddenly acquires a chain of stores 1000 miles away. There could well be some distribution problems in such an event.

Financial Controls

The key areas to watch are gross margins, operating ratios, and debt ratio patterns. Are these improving, or are they deteriorating; and how is the company doing in comparison with the industry? (When analyzing debt ratios, be sure to include lease obligations, which is considered an off–balance sheet item but nevertheless constitutes a fixed obligation.) Don't be overly concerned with a high debt ratio in this industry: a 40 to 50 percent debt-to-equity ratio is not excessive for retailers. Other items to analyze are the return on investment, and liquidity ratios; the trends in both; and how the company rates in comparison with the industry.

You should also ask what the problem markets are for each individual company, and what is being done to improve those markets. Try to learn why the retailer is doing significantly better or worse than the average.

ECONOMIC CONSIDERATIONS

All retailing stocks are basically affected by the economic cycle. If you are worried about the state of the economy, you may want to become involved in companies whose products are relatively inelastic in demand, such as drug or supermarket chains. You will also want a company with a strong market share, which is apt to hold its traffic longer in uncertain economic conditions. A value image may also tend to do well in slow times.

In analyzing the economy, there are several factors which you should consider:

1. Discretionary spending is very important. If the economy is strong and discretionary spending is rising, the high-quality gift store, for instance, may do better, as will consumer electronics stores; both of these may grow faster than the basic retail company. This added growth will give more leverage to the earnings of these companies.

2. Clothing demand is also a critical factor. For example, clothing sales account for two-thirds of Federated Department Stores' revenues, and an estimated $6 to $7 billion of Sears's sales. Thus, you want to ask where you are in the demand cycle for apparel. A rough rule of thumb, which does not always work, is that consumer durables lead clothing in the early stages of an economic recovery.

3. There are three basic areas of consumer sales: autos, homes, and general merchandising. Generally, it is very rare that all three will boom at the same time. Therefore, apparel and general merchandise, for example, may be emphasized at a stage in the economic recovery where homes are not.

4. The difference between discretionary and necessity spending is much more vague than it was 10 years ago. One good way to differentiate is to use your own common sense and analyze how you yourself are spending your money. In recent years, for example, leisure time and services have taken greater portions of typical family incomes.

5. In evaluating the macroeconomic picture, you must become a mini-economist. Here are some of the economic statistics which should be analyzed:

a. The savings rate is not as useful as some make it seem. Savings are basically residual in nature; i.e., they are what is left over after all spending has been done. It is the last thing that one does with one's money, and it is an indicator of what has happened, not what may happen in the future.
b. Consumer confidence can similarly be a misleading indicator, at times. It is an indication of what's happening now, but not what may happen in the future. By the same token, if consumer confidence indexes do develop a major trend, that could be meaningful.
c. Inflation is perhaps the most important indicator to watch. Consumers are affected by inflation very dramatically, not only in the psychological aspect, but also in reducing purchasing power. In analyzing inflation, keep track above all else of food prices. (The most important component of food prices is meat.) Consumers spend more time in food stores than at any other type of retail outlet, shopping daily or, at least, several times per week. Thus, projections for rising food-price inflation could mean a slowing in consumer sales.
d. Real disposable income is also a critical factor. Is it on the increase or on the decrease? Needless to say, incomes that are rapidly rising in real terms suggest a good environment for retail sales.
e. Unemployment is often misleading. It can gyrate from season to season and may be influenced by segments of the population that do not generate huge increases in retail sales. (On the other hand, if automobile layoffs were imminent, one would not want to own a company which has many retail outlets in the Detroit area.)
f. A tax cut is generally considered beneficial.
g. Higher interest rates are generally considered detrimental to retail sales, because higher interest rates will eventually slow the economic recovery, which will eventually hurt retail sales.

In analyzing these statistics, one should never hang one's hat on a single month's figures. That is especially true of the government's retail sales figures, which are often revised later and the results of which may have no effect at all on a particular company. Take note of a trend only if it continues over a period of 3 to 4 months.

h. The level of consumer debt is useful, but often misleading. The best way to evaluate consumer debt is to find out what the percentage of monthly income is that must go to debt service, and to place the current figure in a historical context.

STOCK MARKET CONSIDERATIONS

In analyzing the stocks of retailers, there are several important things to remember:

1. These companies pay relatively low dividends and are basically used as capital-appreciation plays.
2. The fastest growing retailers have low dividend payout ratios.
3. The average retailing company is growing no faster than the economy (and thus the overall stock market), and therefore an investor should be careful about purchasing a large retailing stock with a p/e higher than the stock market.
4. Dividends will likely grow faster than earnings for these companies. (The leading retailers pay out roughly 30 percent of earnings.)
5. Most retailers trade as a group.
6. Conventional wisdom says that retailing stocks lead the market in the first phase of a bull market. This does not always work; however, it was the case in the 1975–76 market expansion.
7. You should buy major retailing stocks when they sell at a discount to the market, or when the economy is moving towards its bottom.
8. There are three measures of value for a retailer: the price/earnings multiple of the stock in relation to the overall stock market, the growth rate of the company in relation to the growth rate of the economy, and the yield of the stock in relation to the yield of the market. If there is any wide discrepancy in any of these three areas, you should take the opportunity to buy (or sell) the stock.
9. Christmas season is an all-important quarter for most retailers. In fact, 55 percent of earnings are derived in the fourth quarter for the average leading mass merchant.
10. Supermarkets are generally viewed as defensive stocks.

11. Purchase programs for specialty retailers should emphasize companies that stress single or limited products and, thus, don't compete across the full product mix of large merchants.

HISTORICAL INFORMATION AND SECULAR TRENDS

1. Retailing competition continues to accelerate. For some time, general merchandise sales have become increasingly dominated by the leading national merchants, which in 1977 represented an estimated 31.8 percent of total "GAF" (general merchandise–furniture–apparel) volume. During the 5 years previous to 1977, sales for the retailing leaders grew by nearly 12 percent annually, while overall retail sales rose by less than 10 percent per year.

   All 300 of the nation's Standard Metropolitan Statistical Areas (SMSAs) are now serviced by at least one of the largest merchants, while 282 SMSAs, or 94 percent, have operations of three or more of the leaders. More than four-fifths of the United States population has access to one of the leader's units, and the vast majority of the populace can choose between outlets from two or more companies.

   Despite such penetration, the most capable specialty retailers and major regionals have recently impeded the national companies' market share advances. At the end of 1977, the eleven major national retailers (Allied Stores, Associated Dry Goods, Carter-Hawley-Hale, Dayton-Hudson, Federated Department Stores, K Mart Corporation, R. H. Macy, Marcor, May Department Stores, J. C. Penney, and Sears Roebuck) had not significantly increased market position since 1974, and eight of the eleven biggest merchants began to derive more volume from markets where they were losing share than from markets where they were gaining share.

2. A shakeout of less efficient retailers is occurring. Most sectors of retailing decline annually in unit numbers as smaller chains and independents find they lack sufficient financial and merchandising capability. The decline is most apparent among general merchandse firms. Although major regionals and leading specialties may continue to prosper, the shakeout of the less capable firms is likely to continue. The growth of specialty chains has had a definite impact on major portions of general merchan-

dise sales. W. T. Grant may not be the last substantial firm to be forced from business.

3. Following World War II, United States economic growth clearly benefited the consumer sector and, therefore, the retail industry. From 1955 to 1970, real disposable personal income grew at an average annual rate of 4.2 percent, and retailers captured a significant share of those gains.

   However, this is changing. There are only three basic ways to achieve sales growth: increase the price of merchandise sold, increase the volume of merchandise sold in existing stores, and increase the number and/or size of stores. After more than 20 years of implementing the basic growth programs, retailers now find these avenues less open. New-store opening rates are slowing, and trading down is a new trend among major retailers.

4. The largest merchants, as a group, have consistently improved their market penetration during the last 2 decades. However, this trend appears to be moderating. Since 1974, the eleven major retailing companies have not improved their combined market penetration. These companies represented an estimated 28.6 percent of "GAF" sales in both 1974 and 1976. The improving position of the leading specialties, the elimination of many less capable merchants, and the exceptional penetration already achieved by the majors are limiting current market share gains by the leading retailers. Nevertheless, their broad product mixes, advertising strength, and consumer franchises should allow them some further impact in both metropolitan and rural markets.

5. The largest merchants remain primarily metropolitan. They represent about 30 percent of total "GAF" sales in the SMSAs and derive more than 88 percent of their combined volume from these markets. Although they generate more than 21 percent of total rural "GAF" volume, only Penney, Marcor, and K Mart derive large portions of their revenues outside the metropolitan markets.

6. The Midwestern and Western states continue to experience the greatest market penetration by the major chains and department stores. The top eight companies represent more than one-third of "GAF" volume on the Pacific Coast, in the Mountain area, and throughout much of the industrial Midwest and the farm belt.

Most of the eight retailers derive significant portions of their sales from the Midwest. K Mart and Dayton-Hudson, for instance, are particularly sensitive to the industrial Midwest, while more farm-related areas are important to May and Dayton-Hudson.

7. The Northeast is most critical to Macy's, Associated, and, to a lesser extent, Federated and Allied. Department stores tend to be more important in this region.

8. Recent expansion has made the Pacific Coast and the Southeast more important. Obviously, Carter-Hawley is most sensitive to Western trends. Marcor and Allied derive the largest portion of their volumes from the South, although the other three chains and Federated also enjoy relatively strong Southern exposure.

9. The chains have limited sensitivity to individual metropolitan areas. No single city represents as much as 5 percent of total sales to Penney, Sears, Marcor, or K Mart. The top ten volume-producing locales represent less than one-fourth of each chain's sales.

10. Department stores, on the other hand, have more concentrated volumes; their top ten markets generate approximately 40 to 70 percent of each department store's totals. Macy's, Carter-Hawley, and Dayton-Hudson generate about one-fourth of sales from their most important city.

11. The demographic potential of a retailer's markets and the company's real estate strategies in relation to them significantly influence volume position and earnings growth. None of the leading companies has exceptional demographic favorability. Their combined sales show less than 20 percent of total volume derived from highly attractive areas. Macy's, May, and Associated seem to have the least propitious current locations. Most companies appear to be improving demographic positions via expansion, particularly Federated and Macy's. May is the only leading merchant with less than half of its immature volume in acceptable markets.

12. Store maturation and internal productivity improvement can strongly influence both retailer market share and profitability. Excluding K Mart, the leading merchants seem to have few maturation advantages. Associated and Dayton-Hudson are the only department stores with more than 10 percent of footage

new since 1974. Allied, May, and Penney appear to have the least maturation potential.

13. The department stores have generally improved their store productivity more than the chains. K Mart and May have exhibited the most significant improvement, while Sears and Penney appear to have achieved the lowest sales per foot growth.

HOW TO USE CORPORATE STRATEGY ANALYSIS IN LOOKING AT RETAILERS

Corporate strategy analysis is both applicable to and useful for analyzing the retail industry. In the mid-1970s, the sales and earnings of the leading retailers became extremely sensitive to fluctuations in the economy. What's more, extensive competition, maturing demographics, and limited financial structures forced retailers to reevaluate their strategic decisions. Since the retail industry is no longer in the rapid expansion phase of the 1960s, one's focus should consequently be on the competitive strategies of various companies.

Good retailers, like good manufacturers, use organized strategies to achieve leadership positions in growth markets. These companies understand their markets and their relative market positions. Most important, they maximize cash flows in mature areas and redirect them to newer markets or to dividends.

Here are some of the key factors to analyze in a corporate strategy:

1. A retailer's base assets are its locations. Most strategies relate to the placement of units and market emphasis.
2. Retail companies are identified more by broad categories of product than by individual items. Their stores carry many products and generally attempt to project overall images.
3. Consumer loyalty is founded on many nonproduct factors, such as convenience, price, service, and habit.
4. Site selection is generally considered one of the most important retailing functions, if not the key one. The most impressive merchandisers must contend with formidable problems in overcoming location difficulties.
5. There is substantial evidence that market favorability has a strong bearing on success potential. For example. rates of store failure or

decline have been significantly higher in unfavorable New England–Northeastern markets than in other areas.

Rapidly growing areas generally need to be supported by cash generated in mature markets. This implies that single-market retailers are unlikely to be as successful as multimarket merchants. It also indicates that companies with consistently weak market shares have less stability than strongly positioned retailers. Limited-market or weak–market share companies often lack debt capacity and must finance improvements through outside financing or higher margins. Maintaining high margins is extremely difficult if one is competing with dominant or leading merchants that can heavily invest in growth areas through cash flows from mature areas.

Like manufacturing businesses, the retail industry can be analyzed according to its use of certain financial, marketing, and investment strategies. For example:

1. Markets with high real-growth characteristics should be managed with the intent of optimizing market share and generating growth.
2. The highest percentage of incremental market growth must be achieved during a market's rapid-growth stage.
3. Heavy and carefully planned investment is required during a market's rapid-growth phase. It usually results in a negative cash flow during this period. If funding is insufficient to achieve strong market share, the market or business usually becomes a permanent cash drain.
4. Company investment strategy should be designed to discourage competition and prevent rivals from gaining a large market share and return on investment.
5. Pricing (or its equivalent) is critical.
6. Pricing strategy can utilize a variety of "price substitutes," such as heavy advertising, innovative product promotion, multi-store operations, and superior warranty service. Price substitutes are nonprice mechanisms that increase the cost of effective competition.
7. If an important market position cannot be obtained, divestiture is an appropriate maneuver.
8. Markets with slow real-growth characteristics should be man-

aged to maximize cash flow in order to support growth areas or to pay dividends. Since most domestic retail markets are low-growth, a retailer must manage resources to quickly and efficiently move these areas to cash-producing positions.

QUESTIONS TO ASK YOURSELF BEFORE MAKING AN INVESTMENT IN THE RETAILING INDUSTRY

1. How good is the company in the four major aspects of retailing? In other words, is its new store site selection good, how well can it merchandise its products, what's its distribution efficiency, and how good are its financial controls? How does the company compare in these areas with the competition?
2. What is happening to the company's market share, both in its strongest and weakest markets?
3. What are the major trends in retailing and what effect will these have on the company's outlook?
4. What are the demographic trends for the area where your company is located?
5. Have you determined the effectiveness of the company's site selection policy by asking the questions discussed earlier?
6. What is the company's merchandising image? Is this image clear to all concerned (the company, the consumer, and you)? Has the company done anything to alter that image? If so, why? What effect will that have on the business?
7. What is the company's annual turnover of inventory? How does this compare with historical experience and with comparable retailers?
8. Do you have the conviction that this company knows how to successfully sell its products?
9. What is the company's problem market, if any? What's being done about it?
10. What's the economic outlook, particularly concerning the rate of inflation, and most especially the outlook for food prices?
11. What's happening to the three mainstays of consumer spending, autos, homes, and general merchandising? Are you aware that it is rare for all three to boom at the same time?
12. Have you compared the p/e of your company with the stock market as a whole, the growth rate of your company with the economy in general, and the yield of your company to the

overall yield of the market? On the basis of that comparison, does your company still represent value?

13. Have you remembered the importance of the fourth quarter to earnings of retailers?
14. Does the retailer compete head-on with a major firm?
15. Is the high growth potential market for your company being managed to optimize market share and growth?
16. Is the highest percentage of incremental market growth being achieved during the market's rapid-growth stage?
17. Is company strategy designed to discourage competition and to prevent rivals from getting a foothold in the market?
18. Are markets with slow growth characteristics being used to maximize cash flow to support the growth areas?

CHAPTER 26

THE SAVINGS AND LOAN INDUSTRY

Ronald I. Mandle

KEY TO ANALYZING THE INDUSTRY

1. Correctly assessing the outlook for short-term interest rates.
2. Being able to anticipate and evaluate a change in the amount of interest S&L's can pay on savings deposits.

MOST COMMON INVESTOR MISTAKES

Buying too late and selling too late. For instance, in the rally from the 1974 bottom, if you had been 1 week late in buying the stocks, you would have missed one-third of the move. If you had been 16 weeks late, you would have missed three-quarters of the move.

HOW TO ANALYZE THE INDUSTRY

1. In evaluating a savings and loan company, cash flow is most important. The two vital aspects of cash flow are savings deposit growth and repayments of existing loans, the latter of which

account for 40 to 45 percent of total cash flow. If an S&L has more money to lend because it has had a cash inflow, it can make more loans and generate more profit.

In analyzing the outlook for deposit growth, the most important variable is the relationship between open-market interest rates and the interest rates S&L's are allowed to pay under regulation. At present, S&L interest rates on a 30-day passbook have a ceiling of 5¼ percent, and 8 percent is the ceiling for an 8-year savings certificate. (Note that only 10 percent of assets can be in the longer-term savings certificates.) There is also the new kind of account tied to the yield on 6-month Treasury bills.

2. There are certain structural changes taking place which may have some long-term favorable implications for the industry. For one thing, the industry is changing its method of borrowing. For example, there is now a mortgage-backed security, collateralized by mortgage holdings. The Federal Home Loan Bank is another source of cheap credit for savings and loans, as are Mortgage Pass-Through Securities.

3. In order to evaluate profitability, you must analyze the yield on the various mortgage loans in a savings and loan portfolio. After you've done that, you should analyze the cost of savings. (For instance, the cost of savings in California is about 7¼ percent.) Note that in the recent past, cost of savings has been growing at about 5 to 10 basis points a year, while yields on the mortgage portfolio have been increasing at around 25 basis points a year.

4. Some 8 percent of the industry's assets are invested in liquid securities, generally government securities of a short-term nature. Usually one-half are in securities maturing in 1 year, one-half maturing within 7 years. As market interest rates rise, the yields on these securities rise.

5. Rising interest rates are negative for the S&L industry; the higher interest rates get, the worse the prospect.

6. Changes in Regulation Q can have a major impact on the industry. Until 1966 there was no restriction at all on the amount of interest that savings and loans could pay. But in 1966 a limit of 4½ percent on passbooks and 5 percent on 90-day deposits was instituted. In 1970, the passbook interest rate ceiling was raised to 5 percent, and a 2-year certificate paying 6 percent was permitted. (The 6 percent certificate became so successful that

between 1970 and 1973, 2-year certificates grew to represent 45 percent of total deposits.)

Then, in 1973, the ceiling on passbook interest rates went from 5 percent to 5¼ percent, and the rate on the 2-year certificate rose to 6¾ percent; finally, a 7½ percent, 4-year certificate and a 6-year, 7¾ percent certificate were introduced. Initially, this change was costly for the industry, because its cost of funds rose dramatically. For this reason, 1974 was a down year for the industry.

Note that the new T-bill–related account was created on June 1, 1978, as an alternative to further increases in Regulation Q.

In summation, any increase in interest rates under Regulation Q will have a negative impact at first but will be positive for the industry over a longer period of time.

7. Taxation is also a critical factor for the industry. At present, the industry can deduct 40 percent of pretax earnings and put it in a bad debt reserve. As a result, the industry doesn't pay any taxes on the amount going into the bad debt reserve. It should come as no surprise, then, that the effective tax rate for savings and loans in, say, California is 37 to 38 percent.

But, by the same token, reported earnings aren't fully available for dividend payouts. In fact, on a dollar of earnings, typically only 42 cents is available for dividends. (If earnings go into the bad debt reserve, they can't be used for other purposes, such as dividends.)

There is some talk at present of reducing the amount that can be put into the bad debt reserve. One suggestion is to lower the bad debt reserve to 30 percent, and to offset that by reducing the corporate tax rate from 48 percent to 44 percent. If that were to happen, the amount of dividends that could be paid out on a dollar's worth of earnings would rise from 42 cents to 55 cents. (At present, only 17 to 20 percent of total earnings is paid out, as cash dividends were just initiated a few years ago.) Although these figures are very tentative, they can give you some idea of the impact that taxation can have on dividend policies for savings and loans.

8. Another key factor affecting the industry is the new competitive environment among all financial institutions. (Savings and loans are allowed to pay ¼ percent more for savings than com-

mercial banks.) With the introduction of NOW (Negotiable Order of Withdrawal) accounts, automatic transfer of funds from savings to checking accounts, and other, similar services, the difference between the various types of financial intermediaries is diminishing.

9. Another factor which must be watched is the increasing competition that S&L's are facing. Credit unions are the most rapidly growing type of financial institutions in the country. (Note that they have just recently gotten the right from the regulators to write checks against passbook accounts, upon which they pay 6 to 7 percent interest. That's a higher rate than either banks or S&L's can pay.) The question also remains whether savings and loans will be able to keep the ¼ percent interest rate advantage over commercial banks. If they were to lose that edge, there would be no difference between a savings account at an S&L and one at a commercial bank.

10. The optimum situation for the savings and loan industry is a period when interest rates are falling, loan demand is strong, a housing boom is under way, and all is quiet on the political front. Another favorable development occurs when interest rates on new mortgages rise above the existing portfolio rates. (This means new mortgages are being put out at increasingly higher rates.)

11. Savings and loan stocks are interest rate–sensitive. When short-term rates peak, these stocks can move very fast on the up side. (Typically, short rates peak after the beginning of a recession. For example, short-term rates peaked in January 1970, while the recession began in November 1969. Conversely, there was a mini-recession which began in the fourth quarter of 1966, and interest rates peaked very late in 1966.) On the other hand, when interest rates rise, these stocks do not immediately decline. Interest rates can rise considerably without having an effect on the stocks.

12. The recent move to start paying dividends means that these stocks won't be quite as volatile as they have been in the past. They certainly will not go down nearly as much in a period of rising interest rates as they did formerly. (For example, in 1973 and 1974 many of these stocks fell in price by as much as 85 percent.)

13. Loan loss reserves are not a major factor these days, because savings and loans don't make construction loans any more; they make only "permanent" loans. That's because the California real estate market had a real boom/bust in the mid-1960s and many of these savings and loans made loans and investments which turned out to be even worse than those made in the Real Estate Investment Trust (REIT) debacle of the mid-1970s.

14. Most of the publicly held savings and loans are in California.

15. This is a very homogeneous industry, although there are some distinguishing factors. Some S&L's are more involved in land and property development, which is a risky business, and the stock market pays less for that kind of company.

    Other factors to evaluate relate to the marketing ability of the company. A savings and loan is a retail outlet, the goal of which is to get the customer's savings deposit. Therefore, you should watch very closely the trend in market share of the company in question. If industry growth rate is, say, 10 percent (which is roughly what it has been in the past), you'll want a company which is growing above that rate. You should also look at loan production. Evaluate the amount of loans originated in one year as a percent of the loans in the S&L's portfolio. The higher the percent, the faster assets turn over. Rapid asset turnover is favorable when interest rates rise over a long period of time.

16. Variable-rate mortgages will have a major effect on the industry. (Variable-rate mortgages are based on a cost-of-funds index which is published every 6 months. The rate on a loan can't move more than 2½ percent in total, and it can only change ¼ percent every 6 months.) Some S&L's now have more than half of their portfolios in variable-rate mortgages. This factor, along with some of the other ones mentioned previously, makes the industry less interest rate—sensitive than it was previously, all of which is a long-term plus for the industry.

QUESTIONS TO ASK YOURSELF BEFORE MAKING AN INVESTMENT IN THE SAVINGS AND LOAN INDUSTRY

1. What is the outlook for short-term interest rates?
2. Is a change in Regulation Q interest rates likely in the foreseeable future?

3. What is the outlook for the size of bad debt reserve allowed S&L's?
4. What is happening to dividend payout ratios?
5. What are credit unions doing? Are they taking away market share from S&L's?
6. How has the new competitive environment for financial institutions affected S&L's?
7. Have you evaluated your particular S&L in terms of marketing ability, market share, and loan production?

CHAPTER 27

THE SEMICONDUCTOR INDUSTRY

Thomas H. Mack

KEY TO ANALYZING THE INDUSTRY

Knowing the trend-line growth rate for semiconductor shipments, and accurately determining whether shipments are above or below trend.

MOST COMMON INVESTOR MISTAKE

Holding onto the stocks too long, and as a result suffering from the stocks' enormous downside volatility.

SOME GENERAL POINTS TO REMEMBER ABOUT THE INDUSTRY

1. The growth of the semiconductor industry has come from its success at putting more and more electronic functions on a small area, or chip, as it is called. As this has occurred, the cost of producing semiconductor functions has dropped, and the demand for them has increased substantially. In fact, the average price of semiconductor functions has fallen at about 15 percent a

year, while the average use of semiconductors has increased by about 30 percent a year. This has translated into average annual revenue gains of about 15 percent.

You may reasonably ask whether the past and present rate of price reduction and increased application can continue in the future. It appears that there is considerable room left for price reduction and increased usage. However, semiconductor growth may depend more on consumer and computer usage than it has in the past.

2. The semiconductor industry is very cyclical, and it is highly dependent and highly leveraged on the economy. In fact, semiconductor companies are categorized by sharp inventory cycles, where end users hoard excessively or cut back significantly on inventories. You often get a multiplier effect, therefore, in inventory building or dishoarding. For this reason, semiconductor prices can change dramatically, depending on whether you're in a weak or a strong period of demand. During the 1974–75 inventory recession, for instance, the rate of semiconductor shipments dropped 40 percent from peak to trough, but actual semiconductor consumption during this period was flat. This illustration should give you something of an idea of the potential volatility in the industry.

3. It is important to remember that this industry is characterized by one or two high-quality companies and many small companies. Such a situation could represent some problems for investors down the road, as the small companies may sooner or later come into direct confrontation with the big companies, resulting in a shakeout. For this reason, it is advisable for most investors to stick to the high-quality companies.

HOW TO ANALYZE THE INDUSTRY

1. In order to successfully analyze this industry, you must know what the trend-line growth rate is for semiconductors, and where shipments are running currently in relation to that long-term trend line. Thus, if you see 20 to 25 percent more semiconductor shipments than you think the economy can reasonably use, you should take a very cautious stance. Conversely, if the industry is shipping considerably less than the economy can use or the trend line indicates is reasonable, you can begin to anticipate better

times ahead. The trend line of increased annual shipments appears to be on the order of 15 to 17 percent.

2. Semiconductor stocks respond to several things. First and most important is the level of orders. Other factors which influence the stocks are overall changes in earnings gains, a change in market share between companies, and the introduction of a new product.

3. The ability to produce semiconductors at the lowest cost level is also a critical factor in evaluating individual companies. Those companies which have the greatest amount of experience in semiconductor technology will generally have a lower cost basis and can generally either increase market share or be more profitable than the competition.

4. During a recession, the efficiency of semiconductor companies goes up dramatically; many inefficient workers are laid off and costs are cut back dramatically. The reverse happens, of course, during a boom, and that's why productivity tends to go down in an up cycle.

WHEN TO BUY/SELL THE STOCKS

1. The best time (and some think the only time) to buy semiconductor stocks is at the bottom of an economic cycle or at a stock market bottom. These companies tend to move off the bottom very quickly, and as you can see from Exhibit 27-1, much of the increase in stock price off the 1974 stock market bottom came within the first several months of 1975.

   On the other hand, because these stocks did so well coming off the bottom in 1974, it is not unreasonable to assume that a certain amount of that performance will be anticipated in future cycles. Therefore, these stocks could well bottom on the next go-round before the general market does.

2. Because these companies are so fast-paced and so cyclical, it is very hard for individual investors to buy and sell these stocks successfully. On the other hand, semiconductors do represent an excellent way of participating in a bull market recovery, and for the nimble-footed trader, they are perhaps one of the best ways of getting upside leverage.

3. You should consider selling these stocks quite early in an economic cycle, more specifically, when things are going well for the companies and good earnings gains are starting to come through.

EXHIBIT 27-1
Trends in Semiconductor Stock Relative Prices, an Eight-Company Weighted Average Divided by the S&P 400.

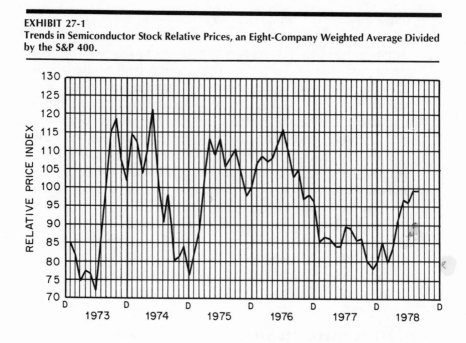

You can never predict in advance when these companies will fall off the track, and because of their volatility you don't want to be caught holding them as the fundamentals begin to deteriorate and the stocks slide.

QUESTIONS TO ASK YOURSELF BEFORE MAKING AN INVESTMENT IN THE SEMICONDUCTOR INDUSTRY

1. How long have the industry's shipments been going up? And how long have this company's shipments been increasing?
2. How recently has the economy or the inventory cycle bottomed out? The more time that has elapsed between the last bottom and the present, the more questionable any investment should be in these stocks.
3. Where are industry orders relative to shipments? If orders are more than 10 to 15 percent above shipments, this may be a bad sign. The reason for this is that you don't want a backlog that's building too quickly, since that implies a possibly excessive jump in shipments and a boom/bust down the road.
4. What's happening to the profit margins of the companies in the

industry and the particular company that you are interested in? If, for example, one company is suddenly generating 13 to 14 percent profit margins when it traditionally only makes 7 percent, the industry could well be in a seller's market, which is a time of great overexposure and a probable sell signal for the stocks.

5. What is the market share and the particular focus of the company you are interested in? Does the company have market share in favorable areas? Be sure to avoid companies that are growing rapidly and don't have a high market share. It's very possible they could run head-on against a large company somewhere down the road and suffer a real profit squeeze.

6. What is the nature of the company's products, and what is the amount of competition it has in its major product lines? You want to make sure that the company isn't doing so well that it attracts significant competition.

7. What is the overall stock market environment? In a period of declining stock prices, people will be very anxious to avoid the leverage of this group, and therefore these stocks should be avoided in any period that even faintly sniffs of a decline in stock prices.

8. What is the company's participation in consumer products? This area offers growth potential but is not very profitable.

CHAPTER 28

THE SPECIALTY RETAILERS

Margo N. Alexander

KEY TO ANALYZING THE INDUSTRY

Being able to judge whether the retailer can grow through (1) higher prices for its products, (2) expansion of new units, and (3) introduction of new products.

MOST COMMON INVESTOR MISTAKE

Paying too much for these stocks. The managements are unseasoned and untested, and thus an investor faces a large risk if something goes wrong.

SOME LONG-TERM STRUCTURAL CHANGES AFFECTING THE INDUSTRY

1. Retailers grow in three simple ways: building new stores, adding new products, and trading up. The growth opportunities from these sources are quite limited for the major retailers, largely

because they already exploited these simple strategies over the 10-year period ending 1977. In addition, the future retail environment will be more competitive, as the growth rate of consumer spending slows and the largest retailers try to maintain past growth rates by gaining share of market, competing more aggressively on price and service in existing product lines, and competing for a larger share of consumers' dollars.

While the largest merchants try to serve an ever-broader customer base (i.e., cover a broader range of merchandise or a wider spectrum of the product price point curve), small specialty retailers, concentrating on specific customers and product segments, may be able to service those customers better. Thus, they will be able to grow in the traditional—and most simple—ways.

2. Consumers respond favorably to differentiation. (By contrast, in the 1950s, consumers just wanted the lowest price.) But now, consumers frequently look for service and avoid the huge, monolithic store.

The desire for convenience is an important plus for a retailer. Take, for example, a 7-Eleven store: although you might pay more for a quart of milk at a local 7-Eleven store, you'll buy it there simply for the convenience. It's the same with the specialty retailer: when you want a certain thing and you know the specialty retailer carries it, you're more likely to buy it there and save the time required to hunt through a large store.

3. The specialty retailer will be able to use the management and financial controls already instituted by the majors, thereby improving cost controls and efficiency.

4. At present, the small specialty retailers are small enough to still have considerable opportunity in terms of unit expansion.

HOW TO ANALYZE THE INDUSTRY

1. The outlook for the macroeconomic picture is less important to specialty retailers than to the majors. These companies might have a large amount of unit expansion in hard times, and therefore sales could trend up even though economic factors are negative.

2. These companies specialize in a particular line of goods or aim themselves at a special target. Find out what that line of goods or

that target is, and evaluate the future opportunity for growth there.

3. Within 3 years of opening, a new store is generally profitable.
4. During the early development of a retail company, new stores are usually the most important source of growth; other sources become relatively more important as the rate of unit expansion slows and/or management alters its initial strategy.
5. In analyzing these companies, the key number to get your hands on is the same-store sales growth. If a company is growing only through the expansion of new stores, there could be some trouble down the road when that expansion is forced to slow for competitive reasons.
6. Always ask about the sources of growth for the company. What are they? Basically, there are three ways for a company to grow: through higher prices, new units, and new products. A company can build new stores, it can introduce higher-priced items (trading up), or it can add new products to its line. (Investors typically give less value to sales that come from new stores.) In analyzing past, present, and future growth, get answers to the following questions:

   a. Can the company keep adding new stores, given the competition and given its own internal financial situation?
   b. Where is the company in its store cycle? This is an important question, for two reasons. First, because stores typically build volume at a rapid rate in the first 3 years of operations, the high rate of new-store addition in the latter 2 years will provide built-in sales gains over the next several years as those stores proceed through their normal maturation cycle. Thus, a company's growth could be slipping, even though record revenues and profits are coming through from stores opened a couple of years ago. Second, it's important to know how much longer the company can count on unit expansion to generate growth.
   c. What is the outlook for the economy? Will it be easier or harder to sell products in the economic environment that you forsee? Will this affect the sales of the company?
   d. What is the quality of management? Since specialty retailers are small companies, it's very important to evaluate the

quality and level of management. These are basically untested management and tend to fall into the trap of expanding too quickly.

e. Is the company in the low or the high end of its new-store profitability cycle? Are new stores close to break-even yet? (It's important to remember that these companies tend to be volatile and vulnerable to problems.)

f. Is there room in the country for new stores of this kind? Is the opportunity for adding new stores wide open?

g. Is there widespread demand for the retailer's product?

h. Will there be competition in new areas where stores can and are being opened?

i. How many stores does the company have and how many more can it add?

j. Is all the growth coming from new stores? What percentage of sales growth is coming from old stores? If most of the growth is coming from new stores and old store sales are stagnant, this says something about the company, and you should be cautious.

k. Is there the potential to increase same-store sales? Can the company introduce a new product to add to existing products? For example, McDonald's is now trying to capture the breakfast market, while Tandy is introducing more sophisticated equipment into its stores.

7. An industry recommendation is not appropriate for this group; you must analyze it company by company.

8. Also, there should be a "story" that makes conceptual sense to you. Ask yourself why the company is doing well, why it has done well, and why it should continue to do well in the future. Also ask yourself, what new product could the company introduce that might boost sales? For example, Tandy is getting into the home computer market, which could be a big seller.

9. Another factor to remember is that the major retailers are increasingly aware of the strength of specialty retailers, and there may be either increased competition from the majors or acquisitions by them.

QUESTIONS TO ASK YOURSELF BEFORE MAKING AN INVESTMENT IN A SPECIALTY RETAILER

1. Does this kind of store make common sense? What are the real reasons why the store should do well? What is the potential market for its products?
2. Does the store deliver real value? Does the consumer have a real reason to stop here? How broad is the product line and how wide will its appeal be?
3. Is the company filling a gap, or are there lots of other retailers competing with it?
4. Does management have the ability to deliver? Is the store dirty? Is it frequently out of stock? If the store is not well run, even though the concept may be good, the company could have difficulties.
5. What's the level and trend of earnings? What is causing earnings and profits to go up? Is it same-store sales or is it new store expansion? What is the outlook for dividends? (At some point, growth will slow, and profits should be translated into more of a payout for shareholders.)
6. Is everyone on the bandwagon for this particular kind of specialty retailer? (If so, you should be very leery and analyze whether the prospects have been fully discounted.)
7. Does the outlook for the future of the retailer depend on something changing? Is the market mature? Identify what's going to stay the same and ask yourself, will the company have to do something new to keep its growth rates up? Is the company doing what it knows how to do well and is it likely to be able to continue that into the future? The risk comes in when companies get into new areas—either literally (new locales) or figuratively (new products)—and you do not have a certainty that they can deliver there as they have already delivered in more familiar areas. Therefore, as long as the company has a prospect of being able to do what it has done successfully in the past, you can be relatively at ease on its ability to do so into the future.
8. Are you anticipating too much? Typically, the stocks don't react until the actual proof of success is there. If the company is developing a new marketing tack, investors should generally wait until evidence is available.

9. What are the major retailers doing to combat the penetration of the specialty firms?
10. Has the management been tested in tough times?
11. Are you sure you're not paying too much for the stock, given its inherent leverage, risk, and volatility?
12. Have you asked all the questions relating to growth discussed earlier?

CHAPTER 29

THE STEEL INDUSTRY

Peter F. Marcus

KEYS TO ANALYZING THE INDUSTRY

1. Having a good feel for the ebb and flow of steel's pricing power.
2. Being able to anticipate 1 to 2 years in advance when the industry will regain pricing power (which always happens in a shortage).

MOST COMMON INVESTOR MISTAKE

Buying the stocks for yield. Like most other stocks, they should be bought to be sold.

SOME GENERAL POINTS TO REMEMBER ABOUT THE INDUSTRY

1. Many of the same factors influence all the major steel mills—especially trends in the American and the worldwide capital equipment cycles.
2. Being a derived-demand industry tied into capital spending, the steel industry is extraordinarily volatile.
3. Typically, the rate of inflation has been higher than the rate of

technological advance for the industry. This has boosted revenues (i.e., the price of steel) and added to the value of existing plants.

4. Most steel companies, sooner or later, will for a while substantially out-perform the others. In other words, the timing of each company's cycle is independent of other companies. One company will lay off people, install new equipment, benefit from a high demand for particular products, or have better or worse nonsteel earnings on a cycle not necessarily in phase with the competition. This often creates wide differences in the performance of individual steel stocks.

5. Shifts in pricing power (that is to say, the relationship of price to cost) are the key to analyzing the industry. The question to ask when pricing power appears to be coming back into the hands of the steel companies is, how long will such power last? If it lasts for a considerable period of time, the stocks can be expected to appreciate.

6. At certain times, the stocks will be either so depressed or so highly priced that they should be bought or sold irrespective of the outlook for the economy.

7. When the Western world steel industry operates at 90 percent or more of capacity, we will probably be in the "shortage" zone. This is a time when the pricing power has passed to the seller and domestic users must pay a premium to purchase foreign steel.

8. Historically, the time to buy steel stocks was at the end of a bear market, when steel operating rates were low and earnings were depressed. Then, when operating rates increased, investors would first look upon the dividends as being safer and then begin to expect dividend increases. In 1973 and 1974, however, the steels were a "buy," even though interest rates were high and still climbing and the economy entering a recession. So, past rules do not always hold.

BACKGROUND

The steel industry's profit performance has been poor since the late 1950s. In fact, despite the rise in domestic steel prices, there was no evidence of an uptrend in pretax profits per ton shipped from the late 1950s to the early 1970s. We can separate the industry's performance since World War II into three categories:

1. 1946 to 1957: good times. This was a period of high operating rates, low import penetration, and price premiums in world steel export markets. During these years, profit margins were generally quite satisfactory—returns on equity, for example, generally averaged about 12.5 percent, although interest rates were low.
2. 1958 to 1971: bad times. During this time, the operating rate exceeded 90 percent only in 1969 (when it was about 94 percent), import penetration was steadily rising (from 1.3 percent in 1958 to a peak of 21 percent in 1971), and the world export price of steel frequently dropped well below the United States price level. The industry's return on equity averaged only about 7.5 percent.
3. 1972 to 1978: volatile times. We observed huge swings in most of the variables. During this period, the United States yearly operating rate ranged from 75 percent to 101 percent; steel prices in export markets fluctuated by 350 percent; and the major mills' operating profits ranged from a quarterly peak of $1322 million in the third quarter of 1974 to a negative figure in the third quarter of 1977, if Bethlehem Steel's major write-offs are taken into account.

If one didn't know steel's financial record, one might expect a highly profitable industry, since:

1. It is extremely capital-intensive and virtually impossible to enter on an integrated basis.
2. The transport of steel is expensive relative to its selling price— producers normally possess an economic advantage within their geographic locations. It often costs about 20 percent of the selling price of steel in a home market to deliver it to a customer in a foreign market.
3. Established producers have seldom been hurt by new technological developments; they have usually been able to adapt new processes to their older plants. Thus, their assets have usually had a much greater value on a replacement-cost than on a carrying-cost basis.
4. The industry's structure is oligopolistic. Some economists would argue that the larger producers have the advantage over the smaller ones and thus should perform better over time.
5. The United States market for steel is large and diverse, granting domestic producers many economy-of-scale opportunities; and the United States is blessed with a sophisticated infrastructure,

permitting: (a) the transport of raw materials and finished steel on an efficient basis; and (b) the purchase by domestic steel producers of a myriad of key miscellaneous materials (refractories, spare parts, lubricating oils, etc.) at a favorable price.

6. Although the carbon steel business requires large numbers of skilled workers, it is not labor-intensive on a per ton basis (there are only about 8 man-hours per ton shipped). (Note: direct employment in the domestic steel industry in 1977 was about 500,000 people.)

7. The leading domestic producers have maintained strong raw materials positions over the years. The ownership of iron ore and, especially, coal properties seems vital to the interests of an integrated steel producer.

8. Production costs for steel in the United States in 1977 were among the lowest in the world.

Despite these positives, the performance of the major steel companies has been poor since the late 1950s, reflecting the following:

1. The industry has an international structure that frequently involves, directly or indirectly, governments throughout the world. This no doubt causes steel prices to remain at extremely depressed levels in export markets during periods of oversupply, since governmental aid often is not available to support resulting losses. Given the structure of the American private sector, low-priced foreign steel has been attractive to domestic steel buyers and thus has hurt many U.S. mills.

2. U.S. governmental policymakers have frequently interfered with, and influenced, decisions of steel company executives. Time and again the industry has been accused of being an engine of inflation and taking actions contrary to the interests of the general public. Being an exceptionally visible industry, steel has been a favorite target of anti–big business groups. Throughout the 1960s it was commonly held that the United States steel industry was antiquated—although its productivity levels were the best in the world at that time.

3. Steel shipments have grown at relatively slow rates, for several reasons. The United States is a mature economy; markets have been lost to other materials, and market share has been eroded by imports and nonintegrated producers. Thus, it has become harder

for producers to achieve productivity gains to offset cost increases. And, because shipments have expanded slowly, domestic steel capacity has usually been excessive, preventing "capital cycle" forces from lifting price levels.

4. The bad news about steel's slow rate of technological progress is that cost reduction efforts usually cannot offset inflationary cost increases, so that steel prices increase faster than those of many other products. The good news is that the assets have a prolonged life, which makes them increasingly valuable during periods of high inflation.

5. Steelworkers are paid one of the highest wage scales in the country. This no doubt is attributable to the efforts of their union, the United Steelworkers of America. But the government and steel company managements also played a contributory role. Wage boosts granted steelworkers in the mid-1970s seemed tied more to prevailing economic trends than to industry economics.

6. Some steel managements were slow to respond to a changing environment. Few showed timely awareness of the threats posed by the Japanese steel industry and American nonintegrated mills. Substantial cash flow was not diverted to other fields in many cases.

Three factors stand out when one contemplates the steel industry's present condition:

1. The vast disparity between the carrying value and replacement costs of steel plants.
2. The sharp cutbacks currently being made in the rate of supply additions in the Western world, indicative of the way free world steel producers tend to react to economic stimuli.
3. The industry's increasing internationalization: steel technology is for sale, and so developing nations are building steel plants.

There are myriad correlations between domestic and foreign steel activities. For example, steel export prices and prices of copper and aluminum often seem to have parallel movements. This is also true for domestic steel scrap prices versus the world steel export price. And Treasury bill rates have moved with many of these commodity prices for the 15-year period ending in 1978. Changes in export orders from Europe seem to lead movements in the world export price for steel.

HOW TO ANALYZE THE INDUSTRY

1. Most steel companies seem to operate on the basis of cash flows, not earnings. Yet the stock market judges companies in just the opposite manner.

2. There is a thin margin between successful and unsuccessful financial results. Price levels just a few percent higher or lower over time have a dramatic influence on capital spending capabilities, balance sheet ratios, etc.

3. The ultimate force determining profit levels in steel over the longer run seems to be the level of capital expenditure requirements. And these capital needs are very difficult to forecast when considering (a) the unclear impact of inflation on construction costs and (b) the enormous difference between outlays for expanding capacity and for just maintaining it.

4. Slower economic expansion leads to slower technological progress, which is, of course, the domestic steel industry's classic problem. Steel's rate of technological progress might be 1 or 2 percent per annum, versus an overall rate of technological progress in the U.S. economy of 3 or 4 percent.

5. One key relationship to monitor is the industry's capital expenditure requirements relative to the level of sales revenues. If an industry's sales/capital ratio is rising steadily, it would seem that there has been either: (a) good gains in the capital productivity rate, enabling new plant builders to expand capacity at a lower capital cost; or (b) a greater surge in unit prices than in volume. Ultimately, if demand grows and new capacity is needed, one should expect some adjustment (shortage conditions, and thus higher profits) to raise the level of capital relative to sales.

6. Inflation tends to raise the pricing power of established integrated steel producers. This applies mostly in robust economic times, for when demand is weak, steel companies are subject to significant price/cost pressures.

7. Exhibit 29-1 plots monthly data for the composite export and domestic price of steel since 1951. We have adjusted the figures so that, when the lines cross, we calculate that a domestic user must pay a 5 to 10 percent price premium to purchase foreign steel. This is our definition—and importantly, a price-related one—of what could be called a steel "shortage." The ebb-and-

EXHIBIT 29-1
PWMH Composite Export vs. Shadow Price *(Paine Webber Mitchell Hutchins Inc.)*.

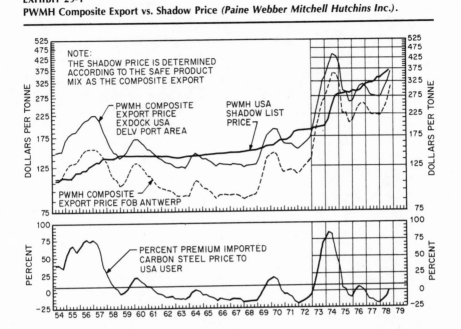

flow of the price premium for foreign steel seems to track rather well with the overall performance of the American steel industry (as well as with that of steel distributors and metal traders, who frequently seem to capitalize on periods of uncertainty and volatility).

8. Table 29-1 presents a theoretical weighing for sixteen factors that influence the relative position of the major American steel producers. You can work up the industry's position by evaluating certain items, such as stature with the government, "economic rent" in raw materials, technological advantages, the rate of growth of the free world economy, and the loss of market to other materials. Experience indicates that there is a strong correlation between these conceptual ratings and the financial performance of the major mills.

9. Exhibit 29-2 sheds some light on steel's capital intensity and rate of technological progress compared to other industries. We see that:

   a. Steel, plus a number of other mostly basic industries with poor long-term profit records, combine great capital inten-

TABLE 29-1   THEORETICAL WEIGHTING OF FACTORS INFLUENCING THE COMPETITIVE POSITION OF THE MAJOR STEEL MILLS

International Factors	WW II to Mid-1950s	Most of 1960s	1974–75	1977	Late 1978	Early to Mid-1980s	Comments on Mid-1980s
1. Relative advantage in raw materials							
a. Iron ore	+ 3	+ 1	+ 2	+ 1	0	0	International ore prices below USA
b. Metallurgical coal	+ 3	0	+ 5	+ 3	+ 2	+ 2	New sources developing abroad
c. Energy	+ 1	0	+ 2	+ 2	+ 1	0	Energy prices rising in USA
2. Labor costs:							
a. Productivity level	+ 7	+ 5	+ 3	+ 3	+ 3	+ 2	Only Japan to be much better
b. Wage cost per hour	– 7	– 7	– 6	– 5	– 3	– 2	Faster growth of wages abroad
3. Financial strength:							
a. Granted profit system standards	+ 3	+ 2	+ 2	+ 1	+ 1	+ 1	Steel industry just OK
b. Compared to producers elsewhere	+ 2	+ 2	+ 3	+ 3	+ 4	+ 3	Foreign mills still greatly over-borrowed
4. Relative operating rate	—	– 2	—	—	+ 3	—	Same operating rate as abroad
5. Economy of scale advantage	+ 5	+ 4	+ 2	+ 2	+ 2	+ 2	Still significant due to market size
6. Technological lead over foreign mills	+10	+ 5	+ 1	+ 1	+ 1	0	Technology has been for sale
7. Equipment situation:							
a. Pollution control costs	—	—	– 1	– 2	– 2	– 2	Relative cost disadvantage not to worsen
b. Ability to keep existing plants modern	+ 5	+ 5	+ 3	+ 2	+ 2	+ 1	Old plants closing
c. Ability to expand existing plants on an economic basis	+ 4	+ 2	0	0	– 1	– 3	Older plants have higher operating costs
d. Ability to build "greenfield" plants	+ 3	+ 2	– 1	– 2	– 2	– 3	Only U.S. Steel can conceive of greenfield

8. Rate of capacity expansion elsewhere:							
a. Japan	− 5	− 8	− 5	0	+ 2	+ 2	Slower expansion in Japan
b. Europe	− 4	− 6	− 4	0	+ 2	+ 1	Slower expansion in Europe
c. Developing nations	0	− 1	− 1	− 2	− 2	− 4	Fast expansion in developing nations
9. Stature with government:							
a. Government attitude towards private sector in general	+ 4	− 3	− 2	− 1	+ 1	+3	Seems to be improving
b. Government attitude towards steel	+ 2	− 7	− 5	− 3	− 1	0	Neutrality at best
10. Relative value of U.S. dollar	−10	−10	− 7	− 5	+10	+1	A major unpredictable
11. Pretax costs versus major competitors	+10	− 5	− 7	− 3	+ 6	+3	Depends very much on #10
Industrial Structure Factors							
12. Technological threats to existing processes	+ 7	+ 4	+ 4	+ 4	+ 4	+ 3	Minor threat is posed by direct reduction process
13. Rate of loss of market share to other materials	− 3	− 3	− 3	− 5	− 3	− 3	Steady losses, because steel price rise faster
14. Steel import penetration	+ 9	− 5	0	− 5	− 2	− 6	Developing nations a threat
15. Growth in size of nonintegrated producers	+ 3	+ 2	− 3	− 3	− 3	− 6	Steady entrepreneurial expansion
16. Carrying value versus replacement value of assets	+10	+ 5	+ 6	+ 7	+ 8	+15	Replacement value zooms with high inflation
TOTALS*	+62	−18	−10	− 7	+33	+10	

*Many of the items are duplicative, and the weightings subjective. The reader is encouraged to make his own judgments. Items in boxes seem least predictable.

EXHIBIT 29-2
Portrayal of Various American Industries' Capital Intensities, Rates of Technological Progress, and Unit Growth Rates. *(Paine Webber Mitchell Hutchins Inc.)* Rate of Technological Progress is advancements in the utilization of labor, materials, and capital. Capital Intensity is ratio of Sales Revenues to Total Capitalization; this may vary from ratio of Gross Plant to Capital.

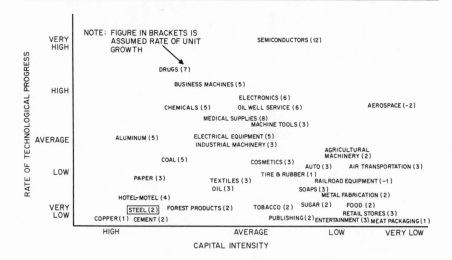

sity (the ratio of sales to capital) with a slow rate of technological progress (as measured by the relatively higher rate of price increases over the years).

b. Many of the industries in the lower left-hand portion of the exhibit (although not steel or copper) are now in a shortage situation (and/or, like coal, are quite profitable because of earlier huge price boosts). This is because inflation pushes up the cost of maintaining capacity to such an extent that capacity often cannot be sustained during extended periods of low profitability.

c. Inflation widens the disparity between the carrying value of existing assets (about $225 per tonne shipped for the American steel industry) and replacement value. This is because steel plants remain productive for many years— since new processes usually can be adapted to existing steel plants. Republic Steel Corporation, for example, has a book value of $85 per share, versus an average stock price in 1978 of $23. Yet, if we put a replacement value of $600 per tonne on Republic's shipment capability of 7.7

million metric tonnes, versus the cost to build "green-field" facilities of at least $1200 per tonne, we derive an adjusted real value for Republic of $4.6 billion. This comes to about $250 per share after subtracting the company's long-term debt.

d. Inflation boosts revenues as long as the increase in costs is greater than the potential that exists from cost reduction efforts. As a result, the sales price realization for carbon steel for the major steel mills in the United States currently averages about $450 per metric tonne versus only $280 in 1974. If steel prices go up an average of 7 percent per annum and unit growth by 2 percent per annum, in just 10 years this boosts revenues by 2.4 times (the unit price of steel in 1988 would be about $885 per metric tonne).

e. Inflation makes new entry into the industry increasingly difficult. Thus, it adds to the "economic rent" of established producers.

All in all, the industries in the lower left-hand portion of Exhibit 29-2 possess inflation-hedge characteristics because of the prolonged life of the assets—in many ways, this is the traditional concept of an inflation hedge. Of course, anything which goes up in value is an inflation hedge—thus, this also would apply to the common stocks of companies in non–capital-intensive industries, such as semiconductors, that turn in profit growth due to the maintenance of technological leads over the competition.

QUESTIONS TO ASK YOURSELF BEFORE MAKING AN INVESTMENT IN THE STEEL INDUSTRY

1. Are you aware that this is an extraordinarily volatile industry? Where are you coming in? At the very beginning of the cycle, or possibly at the tail end? You don't want to buy these stocks when the news of steel shortages has reached the headlines of major newspapers. Buy 1 or 2 years before the shortage, or not at all, if the stocks have already moved well ahead.

2. Have you done a thorough analysis of pricing power? Does the relationship between price and cost look favorable 1 to 2 years out?

3. How sustainable will be the existence of pricing power in the hands of the major steel mills? Long enough to get the stocks moving on the up side?

4. Have the stocks reached such a low valuation based on book value, historical p/e, and price that they represent good value based on price alone?

5. What is the present worldwide operating rate for steel? Once it has exceeded 80 percent, a shortage may not be far away if capacity has been overestimated.

6. What is happening to import penetration of steel into the United States?

7. What is the price of steel scrap doing?

8. What is happening to the sixteen factors listed in Table 29-1 which affect the relative position of United States steel producers?

9. What is the outlook for raw steel capacity on a worldwide basis?

10. What is the political environment for the steel industry? Is there evidence of jawboning and political interference in the pricing structure?

11. What is the status of technological progress for the industry? New inventions are bad for established producers.

12. What is happening to union wage rates?

13. How are managements of United States steel companies responding to the competitive environment?

14. What is the level of the steel industry's capital expenditure requirements? If it is huge, this can be a force that pulls up profit results.

CHAPTER 30

THE TRUCKING INDUSTRY

John V. Pincavage

KEY TO ANALYZING THE INDUSTRY

The two major determinants of profits—and thus the driving forces behind stock prices—are the level of industry tonnage (weight of goods shipped) and whether wage increases of the Teamsters' Union can be passed on to customers in the form of higher prices.

MOST COMMON INVESTOR MISTAKES

1. Holding onto these stocks too long. The only reason you should ever consider buying a trucking stock is if you have a firm intention of selling it.
2. Buying small, unknown companies with little, if any, sponsorship or following.

GENERAL POINTS TO REMEMBER ABOUT THE INDUSTRY

1. The level of tonnage is the number one factor in analyzing the industry. The trucking industry is a cyclical industry, and

demand is a function of economic activity. In order to have increased trucking activity, you must have a growing economy. There is a direct correlation between the Federal Reserve Board "Index of Industrial Production" and the "Intercity Truck Tonnage Index," which is prepared by the American Trucking Associations. If you had a graph of those two indexes, you'd see they are practically parallel.

2. The next-most vital concern is the ability to apply for and get rate increases. Sixty-five percent of trucking costs is labor related, and, therefore, when union drivers get a wage increase, that increase must be passed on in the form of higher rates to the end user.

3. The next-most important factor is the availability and price of fuel.

4. There are ten major rate bureaus around the country, and these must apply to the Interstate Commerce Commission for a rate increase. The geographical location of the bureau is not a concern, but the ability of the bureau to do a good job of preparing the argument for a rate increase is critical.

5. Demographic trends can be very important. For instance, the building of the Interstate Highway System and the move from the inner cities to the suburbs has had a tremendously beneficial effect on the trucking industry. The Interstate Highway System enabled truckers to travel much faster than they would normally be able to. Before the interstates were built, the average mileage of a trucker was some 350 miles per day. Now a trucker might be able to log as much as 500 miles a day. Thus, truckers and the trucking industry became more productive because of the Interstate Highway System.

At the same time that the trucking system was on the rise, the railroads were on the decline and the truckers were able to take a lot of business from the railroads. This happened because trucks could deliver goods faster than the railroads.

As trucks increased their length and cubic capacity, they could transport more weight and more goods at a cheaper price. Also, technological advances, such as diesel trucks with greater fuel economy, helped in achieving productivity gains. The computer, which enabled truckers to keep track of their trucks around the country, the amount of goods being delivered to certain places, and the need for transportation, also helped improve productivity.

6. The trucking industry is highly regulated, both at the state and at the national level. It is one of the few industries which has an antitrust exemption to fix rates—although this is in the process of changing.

7. The trucking industry has historically been able to earn a very high return on shareholders' equity—between 13 and 15 percent a year.

8. It is a domestic industry with very little foreign exposure.

9. The industry competes on service, not on price. Good service consists of consistently delivering goods on schedule without damage.

10. Since 1970, the ICC has been generally good to the trucking industry. In fact, during 1976 and 1977, the trucking industry had considerable economic problems, and two big carriers went out of business. However, the ICC stood behind the industry and helped ease some of the problems.

11. Typically the trucking industry has been "one big happy family"—but if one big trucker starts to confront another big one, this happy family could dissolve, and without regulation, rate wars could ensue.

12. Historical experience indicates that any acquisition which amounts to more than 20 percent of the purchasing company's revenues presents problems. The reason for this seems to be that it is just too hard for one company to absorb such a large acquisition. Therefore, if you are aware that your company is making such a large acquisition, you should consider selling the stock or at the very least be prepared for several years of unpleasant surprises in earnings.

13. Another thing to be aware of is when a trucking company reaches the level of $100 million in annual revenues. For some reason this is the cutoff between the small operator and one needing a professional manager. Professional management needs to be added at around the $100 million sales level, and typically, as that is being done, the company experiences several years of slow earnings.

LONG-TERM STRUCTURAL CHANGES TAKING PLACE IN THE INDUSTRY

1. The industry is consolidating. In 1968, there were some 21,000 independent regulated trucking companies, while in 1978 there were only 16,000. In fact, this is one of the secrets of past growth in the trucking industry—the larger companies have grown through mergers.
2. The Interstate Highway System has practically been completed, so there will be no improved productivity coming from better roads.
3. Larger equipment, such as double trailers, and piggybacking, however, may allow further productivity increases.
4. There is the potential for considerable reduction of government regulation. The implications of this for inefficient carriers cannot be underestimated. The ICC bases rates on the industry's average cost. Thus a low-cost producer can make considerable profits, because its trucking rates may be set at a much higher level than its costs. If government deregulation gains force, many small and inefficient carriers may be put out of business.
5. The trend of big truckers' acquiring small ones may be coming to an end. As a consequence, the big companies may end up competing against one another, which could cause price wars and a decline in profitability.
6. For the 30-year period through 1977, the trucking industry took business away from the railroads, a trend which appears to be coming to an end.
7. The trucking industry generally grows at the same rate as the overall economy. But now that a lot of the industry consolidation has taken place, the ability of big companies to grow faster than the industry in real terms may diminish. Formerly, a large carrier could grow at 2 to 2½ times the industry rate; this may now slow down to 1.5 to 1.8 times.
8. The good return on shareholder's equity should continue as long as pricing problems don't develop in the industry.

HOW TO PICK A TRUCKING STOCK

The best way to evaluate a trucker is to see how well it performs in an economic downturn. This is the time when the men are separated from the boys. Does a trucker know where and how to cut costs? (This will have to be done very quickly, otherwise profits will suffer.) All truckers, for example, pay over-the-road drivers only when the trucks are actually being run. Thus, if there is not the necessary tonnage to move the trucks, fixed overhead is not that large.

WHEN TO BUY/SELL THE TRUCKING STOCKS

You should buy the stocks only at a trough of a recession or at the bottom of a bear market. And remember to be very careful of relative price/earnings ratios. This is a regulated industry, and if the stocks ever sell at a large premium to the market, they should be sold. That's especially true if the industry trend towards consolidation and deregulation continues, as it will increase the industry's instability.

The rationale behind buying the stocks at the trough of a recession is that the industry will have laid off a lot of people and will be very efficient and lean. Then, when the economic recovery begins, you'll see a great boost in profit margins and earnings gains. (It's important to remember that the outlook for earnings is what motivates these stocks; there is little dividend yield.)

A frequent investor mistake is to hold these stocks too long. The only reason you want to buy a trucker stock is to sell it. What happens typically is that the stocks are halfway down to the bottom before investors realize that the economic fundamentals have changed.

BACKGROUND ON THE TRUCKING INDUSTRY

The trucking industry's earnings grew at a 9.9 percent compound annual rate from 1966 to 1976, which compares very favorably to a 6.1 percent rate for the S&P 400.

The reasons for this above-average growth rate can be traced back to the birth of the industry in 1935:

1. Tonnage growth matched or exceeded real economic growth because the regulated trucking industry consistently gained share of market of intercity revenue from the railroads.
2. Regulation protected the industry from ruinous competition by limiting new entrants and setting rates designed to insure adequate service.
3. The industry was able to offset some increased expenses with

improved productivity, mainly legislated increases in weight and length limits and construction of the Interstate Highway System by the government.

Trucks Gained at Railroads' Expense

Transportation expenditures, including passenger and freight, have consistently accounted for approximately 20 percent of the Gross National Product (GNP) of the United States. Freight outlays alone represent 9 percent of the GNP, and the cost of regulated motor carrier service 1.4 percent of the GNP. The distribution of revenue among the various regulated freight carriers has changed dramatically over the past 35 years.

The biggest change has been the increase in market share of trucks at the expense of railroads. Some of the factors responsible for this include:

1. The suburbanization of population and decentralization of industry, which created a demand for a more flexible distribution system
2. The increase in consumer demand for a wide variety of products
3. Demand for improved transportation service to allow inventory costs to be reduced
4. The construction of the Interstate Highway System at government expense

Regulation Protected the Industry

Regulation of the interstate trucking industry by the ICC is another main reason for the industry's growth record. The ICC began to regulate the trucking industry in 1935, when the Motor Carrier Act was passed. The ICC's authority extends over rates, routes, types of service, types of commodities hauled, accounting and financial procedures, mergers and acquisitions, and operating procedures.

Since the Motor Carrier Act makes the ICC responsible for the industry's financial health and adequate service to the shipping public, the ICC has granted rate increases in the past that permit many inefficient carriers to remain in business. The rates are set to allow for a 93 to 94 percent industry average operating ratio, with the result that the more efficient carriers are able to translate a greater percentage of the rate increases into profits. At the same time, the service levels must remain high to justify the higher rates, or freight will be diverted to private carriage or other less expensive modes.

The motor carrier industry enjoys antitrust immunity on rate setting via the Reed-Bullwinkle Amendment to the Motor Carrier Act. This exemption allows for collective rate making, whereby carriers arrive at uniform rates for their service on a collective basis when underlying conditions are similar. An individual carrier retains the right to act independently. These rate-making associations of carriers started as tariff-publishing bureaus, a function they still serve. However, their most important function is the proposal and filing of rates and charges with the ICC with justification of the reasonableness and compensatory nature of the rates. The ICC judges the rate requests and provides a forum for hearing protests against, and evidence for, the proposals.

The entry restrictions mean that nonregulated intercity carriers are not allowed entry into the regulated carriers' market and are restricted to hauling exempt commodities such as farm products and foods. Additionally there are legal restrictions on private carriers (company-owned) as to whom they work for and the freight they haul. Generally they are allowed to haul only for a single specific company and only products used directly in the product's manufacture (e.g., tomatoes, glass bottles, boxes, spices, and finally full catsup bottles could all be hauled for a catsup manufacturer). A conglomerate with a number of unrelated subsidiaries is prohibited from hauling for each of them with the same truck fleet.

Productivity Gains from Bigger and Faster Equipment

Productivity advances are responsible for some of the industry's record of growth. The area where the greatest productivity improvement has been accomplished is in line-haul operations, where trailer capacities (weight and length) have increased significantly and where an improved highway system has helped to speed service. Consider that in 1935 the capacity of a trailer was 10,000 pounds, while today loads of 40,000 to 60,000 pounds are easily handled, and some states allow loads of over 80,000 pounds on highways. A modern diesel tractor, as we all know, is powerful enough to pull loads at high speeds and to do so relatively efficiently while withstanding increased torques and stresses. Widespread computer applications have allowed improved analysis and scheduling of operations and more accurate cost controls.

The terminal and platform categories are the biggest cost center and are extremely labor-intensive. Productivity gains from automation have been meager, and state-of-the-art technology consists of a dragline pulling carts loaded with freight around a circle. Further automation, along the lines achieved by United Parcel Service, where conveyor belts and sorting tables are used, is difficult if not impossible, because of the wide variety of shipment sizes and weights. Possibly the biggest advance has come from the increased professionalism of managers who are increasingly skilled in worker motivation techniques.

Large Carriers Grew Even Faster

The large trucking companies, of which Roadway Express, Yellow Freight, and Consolidated Freightways are prime examples, grew substantially faster than the general freight industry in the same operating environment.

The reasons for this faster growth include the following:

1. Market share gains were accomplished by acquisition of other carriers and their operating rights and/or by more intensively developing existing franchises through terminal additions.
2. Regulation minimized competition and indirectly rewarded efficient carriers by setting rates to keep inefficient carriers in business.
3. Economies of scale were realized which allowed spreading of overhead and allowed even greater productivity gains to be realized.

Market Share Grew Rapidly

The main reason for the substantial growth rates at the larger carriers is growth of tonnage, which forms the basis for the increased share of market in revenue. Tonnage growth has historically correlated closely with real GNP and the Federal Reserve Board "Index of Industrial Production."

A close examination of this relative growth reveals that large carriers acquired other carriers to expand into new markets and that each added many new terminals. Yellow, for instance, doubled its size in 1966 with the Watson Wilson acquisition, added another one-third with Norwalk in 1969, 20 percent with Adley in 1972, and most recently, 5 to 10 percent with Braswell and Republic Freight in 1976–1977. Roadway, on the other hand, expanded from 104 terminals in 1966 to 178 in 1971 and to 328 in 1976.

Regulation Rewards Efficiency

The large carriers, notably Roadway and Yellow, have been extremely successful in segmenting the market and attracting the types of shipments they find desirable (high-yield). As a result they have been able to consistently achieve higher yields per ton (two to three times) than the industry. This in turn has helped lead to better operating margins, since more revenue is available to cover the costs of operation. How, in an industry where inherent in the right to be in business is an obligation to provide service to all shippers, can a carrier be selective in the freight it hauls? The answer is to avoid soliciting and even to discourage undesirable freight, the first by sales-force direction, and the second by giving poorer service than a carrier that is actively soliciting that freight because it fits his system.

It's possible to do this because the industry competes on a service, not price, basis and rates are fixed. Collective rate making has also had another beneficial effect for those carriers with better-than-industry operating margins. Because the ICC has the financial health of the industry as one of its responsibilities, it has seen fit to provide rate relief in amounts large enough to keep inefficient carriers in operation. This has had the effect of providing a rate umbrella for efficient carriers, thereby rewarding them for their efficiency.

Economies of Scale Help Marketing and Productivity

Economies of scale can be achieved in the trucking industry, and this impact is felt both in marketing and in the cost control and productivity aspects. In marketing, a larger carrier has more locations to serve and therefore more potential points to sell to a customer. This means he can capture a larger percentage of available freight than a more geographically limited carrier.

This same diversity (size and a large number of service points are related) creates opportunities to develop a system designed to minimize cost and maximize efficiency by allowing freight flows to be balanced. This eliminates costly empty miles and allows higher average loads.

The trucking industry has historically been labor-intensive, meaning that 60 percent of each revenue dollar has gone to labor (65 percent of operating expenses). While the industry has managed to maintain much management flexibility with regard to labor control, it has done so at a high price. Today, the teamster is one of the highest paid blue-collar workers in America. The industry has been willing to accede to union demands for higher pay and improved benefits because it has been able to pass these costs through to the shipping public with little difficulty.

Energy was not a large concern before 1974, when fuel prices tripled. In the process, fuel expenses rose to 6 to 8 percent on revenue, and a new series of rate hikes had to be asked for. Coupled with other nonlabor expenditures that rose rapidly with high inflation rates, it placed motor carrier margins under pressure, since the industry had somewhat more difficulty getting rate increases approved. Before 1973 these other costs increased little.

Summary of Success Forces

1. Regulation, which minimized competition and rewarded efficient carriers by setting rates to keep less efficient carriers in business
2. Tremendous expansion via acquisitions, addition of terminals, or both, which pushed tonnage growth up much faster than industry rates
3. The fact that competition in new areas was in many cases against smaller, more regional carriers
4. Implementation of marketing programs based on providing superior service for a selected shipper group having desirable freight over a carefully constructed route system designed to minimize costs and maximize yields
5. Productivity gains from using larger equipment over better roads and introducing computer-based cost control systems and more professional management
6. Cheap and abundant energy

It is important to remember that these trends are not at present operating in the industry's favor.

QUESTIONS TO ASK YOURSELF BEFORE MAKING AN INVESTMENT IN THE TRUCKING INDUSTRY

1. Can the company grow further through acquisition? If a trucking company already operates in the 100 largest cities, a further acquisition may not be possible or may not be very meaningful in terms of profits.

2. What is happening to intercarrier competition?

3. Where is the trucker located? Is it in a growing part of the country?

4. What is the outlook for energy prices?

5. When is the next Teamsters' Union contract due to expire?

6. Is it likely that new wage increases can be passed on in the form of higher prices?

7. Are you making the mistake of buying these stocks when economic conditions are good, instead of waiting until the trough of a recession?

8. Are you aware that these stocks are only bought to be resold?

9. Are you buying the top companies in the industry?

10. Is your company about to make a large acquisition? If so, shouldn't you consider selling the stock? (See the earlier discussion of this.)

11. Is your company approaching the $100 million annual sales level? (See previous discussion.)

12. What is happening to government regulation? If deregulation is the order of the day, are price wars likely?

13. How well did your company perform in the last economic downturn?

14. How quickly can your trucker cut costs if economic growth slows?

15. What is the trend and outlook for productivity in the industry?

16. What is the outlook for return on shareholders' equity?

17. What is happening to the respective shares of shipping that go to rails and trucks? Is the trend favoring rails or trucks?

CHAPTER 31

THE UTILITY INDUSTRY

Charles A. Benore

KEY TO ANALYZING THE INDUSTRY

1. Correctly judging the level and direction of the political and regulatory environment. The regulatory environment controls the translation of sales into earnings and dividends.
2. Being able to judge the level and direction of financial integrity.

MOST COMMON INVESTOR MISTAKE

Not paying enough attention to the financial integrity differences of various utilities.

How to Avoid the Most Common Errors

1. For electric utilities, buy only those stocks which can be defined as having financial integrity, or be sure the price of the security provides fair compensation for the lack of adequate financial integrity. In order to meet this definition, an electric utility must:

    a. generate at least 50 percent of its construction program internally

b. have a high bond rating
c. be able to sell new common stock at book value or higher
d. have sufficient financial strength and financial flexibility
e. provide investors a competitive return of good quality
f. have no higher than a satisfactory level of financial integrity
   so that rates charged are fair

The financial ratios which measure financial integrity are shown in Table 31-1 and indicate an improvement between 1974 and 1977.

TABLE 31-1   INDICATORS OF FINANCIAL INTEGRITY FOR INVESTOR-OWNED ELECTRIC POWER INDUSTRY

	Cash Flow to Construction, %	Price to Book Value*	Pretax Interest Coverages	Common Equity Ratio, %	Effective Federal Income Tax Rate, %	Return on Avg. Common Equity, %
1977	38	0.9×	2.9×	37	34	11.4
1976	41	0.8×	2.8×	36	32	11.5
1975	37	0.7×	2.7×	35	30	11.1
1974	27	0.7×	2.5×	34	25	10.6
1973	28	1.0×	2.8×	35	26	11.5
1972	27	1.1×	3.0×	35	27	11.7
1971	27	1.3×	2.9×	35	28	11.6
1970	29	1.2×	3.1×	35	31	11.8
1969	35	1.6×	3.7×	36	37	12.2
1968	39	1.7×	4.3×	36	39	12.3
1967	45	1.9×	4.7×	37	38	12.7
1966	53	2.0×	5.1×	38	39	12.7
1965	63	2.3×	5.3×	39	40	12.5

*Moody's 24 Electrics
Sources: Edison Electric Institute; Moody's

2. Be sure that you have analyzed the quality of the utility's earnings, and by inference, dividends. The best way to do this is to make sure the company follows conservative accounting policies and has a reasonable dividend payout ratio (about 75 percent for most electric companies). You should also check to see how your company compares with the industry measurements listed above.

UNIQUE ASPECTS OF THE UTILITY INDUSTRY

1. It is a monopoly business.
2. The utility industry is the most capital-intensive of all major

31-2

industries, and for this reason it makes little sense to have competition. This is the basic reasoning behind the utility monopoly.

3. Because of the essential nature of electric service and because it is a monopoly business, the industry is regulated to prevent possible abuses. The monopoly status is positive because of the absence of other electric energy suppliers, but it introduces a risk to investors that regulation will cause financial integrity to be insufficient.

4. Since the public is highly dependent on the service a utility provides (in terms of employment and living standards), the industry has public responsibilities, and often management must lean over backwards to satisfy public needs, even at the expense of the shareholders.

5. Because of the above, a utility cannot just institute a price increase; it must first apply for one to the appropriate regulatory authority.

STRUCTURAL CHANGES IN THE INDUSTRY

1. There is a continuing increase in the cost of building a new power plant. Ten years ago, it cost about $300 per kilowatt to add new capacity. Now it costs as much as $1000 per kilowatt, or over three times as much.

2. Environmental and safety obligations have caused the industry to invest a lot of money in non–income producing areas.

3. Inflation has increased from a 2 percent rate in the early 1960s to above 7 percent currently.

4. The cost of providing electric service has rapidly increased and caused the industry's need for financing and rate increases to rise sharply. Rate relief over the last decade has not been sufficient to maintain the industry's financial integrity level of the mid-1960s.

INDUSTRY REGULATION

1. More than 90 percent of the industry is regulated by state regulatory authorities. Less than 10 percent is regulated by the Federal Energy Regulatory Commission. This means that both regulation and financial integrity of electric companies vary dramatically from region to region and state to state.

2. A good regulatory environment is one where the utility is allowed a fair return of good quality *and is able to achieve the return it is allowed.*

SOME GENERAL COMMENTS ON UTILITY STOCKS

1. Utilities are viewed as defensive stocks with respect to market risk and tend to act somewhat in accord with the long-term bond rates, with which they are competitive.
2. Because of their defensive nature, utilities typically outperform industrial stocks in a bear market. From the second quarter through the eighth quarter after a stock market bottom, industrial common stocks generally outperform utilities. After the eighth quarter, industrials and utilities generally perform about equally.
3. The largest buyers of utility stocks are individuals, and they frequently do not perceive the differences in the quality of various utility issues.
4. In evaluating the financial integrity of a utility, be sure to make financial comparisons with the industry average discussed above. Where is the company in relation to the industry average? Is the quality above or below the industry average? If it's below, will it soon be corrected? Has the stock already discounted the worst?
5. The earnings and dividend growth prospects of electric utility companies are relatively modest, and the principal return to investors is income.
6. The risk in electric utility common stocks has increased from what it was a decade ago, as can be seen in the decline in the industry's indicators of financial integrity.

QUESTIONS TO ASK YOURSELF BEFORE MAKING AN INVESTMENT IN THE UTILITY INDUSTRY

1. Is the regulatory commission fair to investors? Is there a balance between consumer and investor interests?
2. Does the utility have good management?
    a. How does management plan? What strategies is it employing to achieve goals, and is it following through on them?
    b. What is management doing to reward shareholders? Is there a balance between consumer and investor interests?

3. What is the boiler fuel mix of the utility? Coal and hydro are preferable to a heavy reliance on oil.
4. Does the utility have or will it have financial integrity?
5. Is the combination of prospective dividend growth and current yield attractive relative to other investment alternatives, and is the price of the security fair for its combination of risk and reward?

PART TWO
FIXED-INCOME ANALYSIS

SOME BASIC INFORMATION ABOUT FIXED-INCOME SECURITIES

CHAPTER 32

HOW TO PREDICT THE DIRECTION OF LONG-TERM INTEREST RATES

Lawrence A. Kudlow

Robert M. Sinche

GENERAL SUMMARY

The major determinant of long-term interest rates is investors' expectations concerning the future rate of inflation. As investors conclude that inflation is likely to cause a deterioration in the real value of financial assets in the future, they will refuse to supply funds to borrowers without adequate protection against inflation. This protection is often called the "inflation premium," or the increase in the rate of interest needed to compensate the holder for his loss of purchasing power over the holding period of the security. Numerous studies indicate that long-term government bonds require a real return of about 2½ percent, and so with long-term interest rates at about 8½ to 9 percent, the implied inflation premium is about 6 to 6½ percent.

HOW TO PREDICT THE OUTLOOK FOR INFLATION

Because the long-term outlook for inflation occupies such a central role in forecasting movements in long-term interest rates, fixed-income economists spend a good deal of time analyzing prospective changes in the inflation outlook. (Remember to distinguish between a short-term inflationary outlook and a long-term one. For instance, a crop failure, with resultant temporary rises in food prices, should not be viewed as seriously as a change in the structural, built-in rate of inflation.)

Relationship between Money Supply Growth and Inflation

Monetary economists have spent much time analyzing the relationship between the growth of the money supply and the rate of change of the price level. While changes in the money supply are not all that matters, over the past 10 to 15 years it has become clear that a *sustained* increase in the general rate of price increase (inflation) cannot take place without a corresponding increase in monetary growth. For this reason monetary economists carefully monitor movements in the money supply. However, as a guide to inflation forecasting, weekly changes in the money supply have very little meaning. In fact, the rule of thumb used by many monetary economists is that inflation over the next 1 to 2 years can be approximated by the growth in the narrow money stock (M1) over the latest 2-year period. (One of the best ways to monitor the movements in the money supply is to subscribe to the St. Louis Federal Reserve Bank publication *Monetary Trends*, which can be obtained free by writing to that institution.)

Monetary Policy and Fiscal Policy

Of course, monetary policy should be viewed in conjunction with fiscal policy and against the background of general economic trends. Specifically, expansionary trends in monetary and fiscal policy can be expected to become more inflationary in later stages of the business cycle, when labor and product markets begin to tighten, than they would be in earlier stages of an economic recovery, when additional supplies of resources are more readily available. However, even during a period of excess resources in labor and output market it cannot be expected that inflation will slow sharply. First, long-term contracts, particularly in labor markets, tend to maintain inflation despite changes in underlying economic conditions. In addition, recent evidence shows that individuals and businesses now anticipate future rates of inflation and act to preserve their income and wealth against rising prices. As a result, economic participants analyze trends in monetary and fiscal policy, review those trends relative to trends desired by the appropriate authorities, and form judgments about the prospects of achieving the stated goals in the areas of employment, real economic growth, and inflation. Individuals plan various activities, including wage demands, product pricing, and purchases of goods and services, on the basis of these expectations. Financial market participants also anticipate compensation on the same basis, bringing this process of rational expectations to the marketplace for stocks and bonds. In this process, financial markets increasingly have come to discount the impact of the variations in economic activity on various assets well in advance.

REQUIREMENTS FOR A LONG-TERM BULL MARKET IN BONDS

In order that long-term rates of inflation might be reduced and a long-term bull market for bonds be launched, there must be: (1) a gradual deceleration in the rate of growth of the money supply; (2) a reduction in federal government deficits, which generally are financed through higher interest rates and/or faster money supply growth; and (3) a long-term economic plan that deals with the general rate of inflation, rather than short-term palliatives that deal only with the prices that are rising most rapidly over the near term.

CHAPTER 33

THE IMPORTANCE OF FIXED-INCOME CREDIT ANALYSIS

H. Russell Fraser

FREQUENT DOWNGRADINGS IN CREDIT RATING

The whole area of bond credit research has come into its own in the past decade. A primary reason for this is the fact that credit rating assignments have changed so rapidly between the late 1960s and the mid-1970s. For example, Detroit Edison and Boston Edison were considered AAA-rated credits in 1968. By 1978, these two credits had slipped to Baa/BBB credits and were considered overrated even at such a low rating. Thus, if an investor had bought those bonds in 1968 thinking that he or she had good quality paper, that would have proved to be a major misconception.

The yield differential between an Aaa or AAA credit and a Baa or BBB credit in mid-1978 was some 150 basis points in yield, or approximately 15 points in price for a long-term bond. Back in 1974, when the credit differences were viewed as even more important, there might have been a 30-point difference in price between those quality parameters (and even the lack of a reasonable bid in some cases). Over the course of the 1968–78 period, there were upwards of 200 rating changes a year, the majority of which represented downgradings.

In the early to middle 1960s, there was very little change in the bond market. There was considerable stability—until inflation began to accelerate in the late 1960s, with a dramatic impact on many industries that were very labor-intensive. For example, telephone, steel, tire and rubber, and textiles are all very labor-intensive and suffered tremendously from labor cost increases between the late 1960s and the mid-1970s. Also, inflation and labor cost increases raised prices of materials, production costs, and manufactured equipment. Additionally, the cost of money and bank financing increased sharply. These factors changed the level of creditworthiness of many companies and hastened the day of bond credit analysis.

In the future, the relationship between stocks and bonds will be followed much more closely than in the past. The trade-off between the two types of securities may be much more difficult, and investors should keep their eyes on the total rate of return provided by each type of security.

CHAPTER 34

CORPORATE BONDS

Corporate Bond Research Department

Of all the investment opportunities readily within the means of the average investor, few offer a greater return with more security than corporate bonds. Yet many individuals neglect them because they see them as conservative, gilt-edged securities for the institutional buyer or for the very rich. That is not the case. Today, individual investors in search of reliable fixed income own something like $60 billion worth of corporate bonds.

WHAT ARE CORPORATE BONDS?

A corporate bond is an IOU or loan agreement between a lender and a borrower, in some cases backed by specific collateral and in others by the general credit of the issuing corporation. It is literally a piece of paper, a contract that obligates the borrower to repay the lender by a specific date the full amount being loaned. The contract also states how much interest the borrower will pay the lender each year for the use of his money. Corporate bond interest payments are generally not exempt from federal, state, and municipal taxes. This sets them apart from municipal bonds, which are exempt from federal taxes and, in many cases, from state and municipal taxes as well.

WHO ISSUES CORPORATE BONDS?

Generally speaking, corporate bonds are issued by large organizations, usually corporations, to raise the money they need to buy new plant and equipment and to modernize their operations. Foreign governments or their agencies often raise money in the same market. The Kingdom of Norway, for example, issues debt obligations that are traded as corporate bonds. However, the overwhelming number of corporate bond issues being traded today come from large, publicly held companies and fall into three general classifications: utility bonds, industrial bonds, and bank and finance company bonds.

WHO BUYS CORPORATE BONDS?

Financial institutions, banks, pension funds, corporations, and professional money managers responsible for large portfolios have traditionally been the principal buyers of corporate bonds. And for good reason. Good-quality corporate bonds combine relative safety with an annual yield that is generally higher than that available elsewhere. In fact, over recent years, yields on corporate bonds have exceeded the dividend yields on most listed common stocks. This development has not escaped the notice of the sophisticated individual investor. As a result, a major change has taken place in the bond market over the past 10 or 15 years.

WHY DO PEOPLE BUY CORPORATE BONDS?

Corporate bonds should be carefully considered as an investment alternative by individuals looking for current income. While it is possible to realize long-range capital gains by buying deep-discount bonds, generally speaking, those in search of significant capital appreciation in a short period of time should prospect elsewhere. Corporate bonds are an ideal investment for those who have no immediate need for a portion of their capital but may need it a number of years down the road. Their aims are to make their money work as hard as possible for them now, and yet to be reasonably assured of protection later.

HOW SAFE ARE CORPORATE BONDS?

First of all, it's important to bear in mind that the corporate bonds a conservative investor might be interested in are generally issued by large, well-managed utility companies, industrial firms, and bank and finance companies. Historically, these have provided safety. Secondly, when a corporation issues a bond, it is acknowledging a debt, not an investment in the company. What this means is that if a company files for bankruptcy, it must, by law, pay off its debts before it meets any of its obligations to shareholders. Finally, while a company may decide to reduce or even do away with dividend payments on its common stock at its discretion, interest payments to bondholders are a contractual obligation.

WHAT BACKS UP CORPORATE BONDS?

Bondholders can anticipate receipt of a fixed amount of interest each year, usually paid semiannually. How the actual payment is made depends upon the kind of bond held. There are two types. Coupon bonds are certificates to which are attached a series of coupons. These are also called bearer bonds. When the payment date falls due, the owner simply clips off the proper coupon and presents it to the bond issuer or its agent. The other kind of bond has no coupons. This is a registered bond. The company or its agent keeps a record of the owner, making necessary changes in documentation each time the bond changes hands, and sends the owner of record automatic payments when they are due.

HOW IS THE PRINCIPAL REPAID?

A corporate bond, you'll remember, is an IOU. The company issuing the bond agrees to repay the principal in a given number of years—let's say 25—and furthermore agrees to pay the bondholder a certain fixed interest each year until the bond comes due or matures. In theory, then, repayment of principal is simple. Barring a collapse so extensive that the issuing company is unable to pay off its creditors, the principal will be returned to the lender, or bondholder, on the date of maturity. If a buyer lends a company $1000 for a period of 25 years at 8½ percent annual interest, he will receive that interest each year for 25 years and then, at the end of that time, will get the full $1000 back. That is the concept underlying all corporate bonds, and a transaction can happen exactly in that way. But in practice it seldom does. That's because corporate bonds are negotiable; they can be bought and sold before they reach their maturity date in a busy secondary trading market.

HOW IS A CORPORATE BOND EVALUATED?

With so many to choose from, how does one shop around for the most suitable and attractively priced bond? The first thing to remember is that the best bond for one person may not be the best for another. But, speaking generally, most buyers are interested in bonds that give them the largest return on their money with the greatest safety. So, two things to look for are yield and the credit rating of the company issuing the bond. Other things being equal, a bond paying 7 percent interest a year is not going to attract as many buyers as one that pays 8 percent. But all things are seldom equal.

Yield

Yield is probably the most important factor for the individual investor to take into consideration, because it represents the return he gets on the dollars he invests. On the surface, it would seem that determining the yield of a bond is a simple matter. After all, it is part of the contract obligation of the issuer and is printed directly on the bond itself. However, this would be true only if all corporate bonds were to be bought and sold at their par value price of $1000. But they are not. It's possible to buy bonds at a discount, paying $800 for a bond with a par value of $1000, and it's equally possible to pay $1080 for another bond with the same par value. As a result, there are two types of bond yield: current yield and yield to maturity (or effective yield). "Current yield" merely refers to current return on the money invested. This is determined by dividing the interest rate by the price paid for the bond.

If a bond is purchased at par for $1000, the yield is what the coupon rate says it is. For example, an 8 percent bond purchased at par has a yield of 8 percent, and the $80 each year this represents is both current yield and yield to maturity. However, if this bond were to be bought at a premium price, or at a figure higher than $1000, the yield to maturity would be less than the coupon rate. The reverse is equally true. An 8 percent bond that is purchased for $900, or at a discount, will have a yield to maturity of over 8 percent (considering the additional $100 the holder will get when the bond matures). Two examples will help illustrate how and why these changes occur.

Let's assume that you have bought a corporate bond in the primary market (a new issue never before offered to the public), that you paid $1000 for your bond, and that it gives you a yield to maturity of 7 percent. Obviously, your interest income from that bond, as long as you hold it, will be $70 a year. But let's assume that, after 3 years, with another 17 years to go before the bond matures, you decide you want to sell it. However, when you bring it to market, you discover that other companies are putting out issues at a yield to maturity of 8 percent. How do you compete? The only way possible is to somehow make your bond yield 8 percent, too.

You do this by lowering your asking price so that the $70 annual interest results in an 8 percent yield to maturity. In this case, in order to be competitive, you would be forced to sell the bond you paid $1000 for 3 years earlier at a price of approximately 90¾, or $907.50. You lose $92.50.

But it works the other way as well. Let's say you come to sell your 7 percent bond and find the market flooded with issues paying only 6½ percent. Under these circumstances, you should not sell your bond for what you originally paid. You can ask 105, or $1050, for your bond, because whoever buys it will then receive 6½ percent yield to maturity, which is the going, competitive rate at that time. When you sell, you're ahead by $50.

Yield to maturity is influenced by the coupon rate of the bond, its price, and the length of time to maturity. Perhaps the best way to explain the importance of yield to maturity is to present an extreme example.

Let's take that same $1000 bond yielding 7 percent that you sold at a discounted price of $907.50. Let's assume that it is a security you originally purchased 19 years ago, and that it is due to mature in one year. Remember that the issuing company has agreed to pay the bond-holder of record $1000 on maturity date, and that it is further obligated to pay $70 a year in interest. This means that the fortunate purchaser of your bond will receive $70 for the year he holds it, and that, in addition, he will be sent a check for $1000 by the issuing company when the bond matures, giving him a total return for the year of $162.50, or almost 18 percent.

But, of course, under those circumstances, you would never have sold him your bond for $907.50, because you would have calculated your bond's yield to maturity. Your original problem, you'll remember, was that you had to compete with bonds paying 8 percent. That's why you dropped your price to $907.50. But your bond had only one more year of life. So to make it as fully competitive as other securities paying $80 a year, all you would have had to do was drop your asking price by $10, to $990 instead of $907.50. The buyer would still get $80 that year ($70 interest from the issuing company and a profit of $10 when the bond matured). As you can see, yield to maturity plays a critical role in judging the value of a bond.

Credit Rating

Also important in evaluating a bond is an assessment of the company issuing it. The quality of corporate bonds is judged by two independent services that rate the credit of the company backing the bonds. The two services, Moody's Investors Service, Inc., and Standard & Poor's Corporation, use the following symbols for their four highest ratings:

Moody's	Aaa	Aa	A	Baa
Standard & Poor's	AAA	AA	A	BBB

There are lower ratings as well, but these top four are for what are known as investment-grade bonds. If you wish to buy bonds with a lower rating, they may not qualify as collateral for loan purposes. Also, you'll be incurring greater financial risk but, of course, always with the expectation of a greater yield than you'd normally get from investment-grade bonds. The quality rating of the bonds you buy or sell is extremely important, because it exerts a powerful influence on both price and yield. Generally speaking, the higher the rating, the lower the yield and the stronger the market.

Early Redemption

Many companies retain the option of redeeming or "calling" their bonds before they mature. This constitutes protection for them. For example, suppose a company puts out a new issue at a time when money is tight. In order to find buyers, it may be forced to offer a very attractive yield, say 9 percent. A few years later, however, the money supply loosens and there is less of a buyer's market, with new issues paying 7 percent. Under these circumstances, it would be to the company's advantage to get rid of the 9 percent debt as soon as possible and

34-6

replace the issue at the lower prevailing interest rate. The company can do this in two ways. It can redeem its bonds by *calling* them. This involves exchanging a part, or all, of an outstanding issue for cash. In return for this privilege, the issuing company must usually pay a premium, which declines over the life of the bond to 0 shortly before the bond matures.

It can also redeem its bonds by *refunding* them, or offering another issue at a lower interest rate. The proceeds of this issue are then used to redeem the earlier, more costly one. Again, the issuing company will generally pay bondholders an extra fee for calling in bonds before they mature. However, it isn't likely that a new issue of bonds will be redeemed shortly after it is offered, simply because the company wouldn't have issued the bonds in the first place unless it needed to raise the cash. There is no rule, but bondholders usually have a minimum of 5 years protection before a new issue can be refunded. This can go as high as 10 and even 15 years in some cases.

Investment Strategy for Callable Bonds   An example of a callable bond was the $100′ million issue of New Jersey Bell Telephone, due June 1, 2010, with a coupon value of 9.35 percent. This was issued in 1970, with 5 years of call protection, and those bonds were called shortly after the call protection expired. However, under the terms of this issue, New Jersey Bell was obligated to pay $1077.40 (through June 1, 1977) for each bond it redeemed. This indicates that, for maximum protection of principal, it would have been unwise for an investor to pay more than the call price of that bond, or for any bond that is currently callable.

What If Your Bond Is Called?   If your bond is called, you may want to reenter the bond market. Beyond the ways already mentioned, how can you make a wise investment decision? Clearly, one way is to select a bond whose price is likely to increase after you've bought it. Bond prices are influenced, more than anything else, by the prevailing interest rate. As interest rates fall, the price of corporate bonds rises. Conversely, bond prices decline as interest rates go up.

To find out why this is so, let's go back to that $1000 bond with a 7 percent coupon. If you had purchased it (with 17 years until maturity) at a time when the prevailing interest rate was 6 percent, the price of your bond at that time would be $1106. That's because, at that particular point in the economic cycle, about the best a lender could get for his money was 6 percent. You, however, with a return on your $1000 investment of $70, would be doing better than the average. Your bond, in other words, would represent an attractive investment, given the prevailing interest rate. As a result, the price of your bond would be above par.

On the other hand, if interest rates increase to 8 percent, your bond is no longer as attractive as it once was, and its price will slide accordingly. These fluctuations in the prevailing interest rate could influence your investment or reinvestment decision. If you believe that interest rates are headed for a decline, then you could consider the purchase of bonds with lower coupons.

Sinking Funds

A given bond issue can run up to many millions of dollars, and, of course, it's all due for repayment at the same time. To make sure the money is available for repayment, many companies create what is known as a sinking fund. The fund is used to buy back some of the issue each year, thus gradually retiring the debt over a period of time instead of in one bite. In one way, that's good for investors, because it provides insurance that their money will be returned. On the other hand, if it's your bond that is being retired by the sinking fund, you might be losing 8 percent a year at a time when the highest yielding bonds available are paying only 7 percent. Bondholders, however, have a certain amount of protection.

First of all, issuers will generally try to meet their sinking-fund requirements on the open market. They'll try, in other words, to buy from those willing to sell. This is particularly true if the bond is currently being valued below par. Second, bonds chosen to be retired by the sinking fund are selected by lottery. Third, no matter what the current value of the bond, the issuer must pay the bondholder unwilling to part with his holding at least par value and sometimes a premium as well. Finally, and most important, sinking funds don't usually start until several years after a new issue first comes out. Not all corporate bonds have provisions for sinking funds. Before buying, it's important to find out if the issue you're interested in has one, and when it begins.

A Checklist Before You Buy

Here, then, are the principal factors that you should take into consideration before buying a bond. Yield, both current yield and yield to maturity; the length of time to maturity; whether or not the bond has a sinking fund; rating; call or redemption date; call price; and finally, the direction interest rates are most likely to take in the near future.

HOW BONDS ARE TRADED

The par value, or principal value, of a corporate bond is $1000, and it's possible to buy on margin. Trades are executed within multiples of that figure, with higher commissions or fees per bond due on smaller transactions. Bonds are bought and sold on exchanges and over the counter. There is no specialist system on the New York Stock Exchange for bonds as there is for stocks. However, all orders for nine or less of a bond *listed* on NYSE must first be entered on the floor. If the order cannot be executed *within a reasonable period of time* it may be offered for trade in the OTC (over-the-counter) market.

If a bond changes hands on an exchange, the trade usually takes place in the following way: The broker representing the seller places the sell order in what is known as the cabinet. Brokers with buy orders go through the offerings currently in the cabinet to see if their customers' needs can be met by what is available. Sell orders can be placed in the cabinet with a firm price. If that price is attractive, the bonds will probably move quickly. If the price is high, they might stay in the cabinet for weeks. An alternative is for the sell order to come into the cabinet with no specific price. Then, if a buyer is interested in the bonds being offered, a trade will be consummated at the highest buyer's price.

When bonds are sold over the counter, individual dealers make the market. They buy bonds for their own account and hold them for later resale. This, of course, means a market risk for the dealer, who is paid for that risk by factoring a profit into the prices he quotes. The over-the-counter market is heavily used by large, institutional investors moving substantial blocks of securities. As a result, many institutional dealers won't even bother to make markets for anything under 100 bonds.

How Bonds Are Quoted

Corporate bonds are quoted as a percentage of par value in multiples of ⅛. For example, a bond quote of 92¼ means that the bond is selling for $922.50. This is how bond market information appears in daily newspapers, such as the *Wall Street Journal*.

For instance, the *Wall Street Journal* corporate bond table illustrated in Table 34-1 indicates that AMAX Inc. subordinated debentures that have an 8 percent coupon and mature in 1986 are currently yielding 8.4 percent. The column labeled for volume gives the number of bonds

TABLE 34-1

Bonds	Cur Yld	Vol	High	Low	Close	Net Chg
ARA 4⅝s96	cv	13	73	70½	70½	−1¼
ATO 4⅜s87	cv	12	55¼	55¼	55¼	+⅛
AddM 9⅜95	10.9	28	86⅞	85½	86¼	+⅝
AirRe 3⅞87	cv	7	104	103½	103½	+½
AlaB 5.90s99	5.9	5	100½	100½	100½	. . . . . .
AlaP 9s2000	9.3	2	96½	96½	96½	+¼
AlaP 7⅞s02	9.3	2	85⅛	84¼	84¼	−⅞
AlaP 8⅞s03	9.4	20	94½	94½	94½	+½
AlaP 9¾s04	9.6	27	101⅜	101¼	101⅜	+⅛
AlaP 10⅞05	10.1	25	107¾	107½	107¾	+¼
AlaP 10½205	10	5	105½	105½	105½	+1½
Alaska 6s96	cv	26	73¼	73	73¼	. . . . . .
Alexn 5½296	cv	18	53½	53	53	. . . . . .
AllnG 11½94	cv	25	121½	121	121	. . . . . .
AlldPd 7s84	9.2	9	76¼	76	76	. . . . . .
AldSu 5¾487	cv	18	54	53¾	54	+1
Alcoa 4¼s82	5	3	85½	85½	85½	+½
Alcoa 5¼s91	cv	25	110	109½	110	. . . . . .
AMAX 7½278	7.6	1	99	99	99	−1
AMAX 8s86	8.4	103	96½	95¼	95½	−7½
Amerce 5s92	cv	10	68½	68½	68½	. . . . . .
AFoP 4.8s87	7.1	2	67¼	67¼	67¼	. . . . . .
AForP 5s30	9.4	2	53	53	53	−1
AAirFil 6s90	cv	5	82½	82⅜	82½	. . . . . .

traded on that day; 103 AMAX 8s of '86 were traded. The next two columns report the highest and lowest prices paid for that bond on that day. In this case, the AMAX bonds sold for a high price of $965 and a low price of $952.50. As the table shows, the price for the bonds at the end of trading on that day was $955, a decline of $7.50 from the previous day's close.

A Short Directory of Bonds

While there are many different kinds of securities traded on the bond market, these are the ones the individual investor most commonly encounters:

Collateral Trust Bonds These are generally considered to be the safest and most secure bonds on the market. That is because they are backed by securities or real property that the issuing company has deposited with a third-party trustee. Railroads, for example, often issue what are called "equipment trust certificates" to raise the money they need to buy cars and locomotives (rolling stock). People who buy these certificates are theoretically buying ownership in that equipment, because the railroad turns it over to a trust, which then leases it back to the company. No matter what happens to the railroad company, the rolling stock can always be sold to meet any obligations under equipment trust certificates.

Mortgage Bonds These, too, are generally considered safe, because they are secured by a lien or mortgage on real property. The lien may be a first, second, or subsequent mortgage. First-mortgage bonds are the best secured of all mortgage bonds and have the first claim on earnings and assets of the company, ahead of other creditors and security holders.

Debentures These bonds are not backed by real property. Instead, they are issued on the general credit of the corporation. As a result, individual investors considering the purchase of debentures should examine the credit rating of the issuing company carefully before buying.

Sinking Fund Debentures These are exactly what the name declares them to be. They are debentures with a provision for a sinking fund that sets aside a certain amount of money each year to retire the obligation.

Subordinated Debentures These, too, are the same as debentures, but with one significant difference. They are junior to any outstanding debentures, which means that, in the event of default, holders of mortgage bonds and debentures and general creditors will be paid first. Buyers of these securities are usually exchanging security for a higher return on their investment.

Floating-Rate Notes Actually, several different types of bonds can also be floating-rate notes. This is a term that applies to the note's coupon rate, which changes at regular intervals as other specific interest rates change.

Price

Buying a bond purely on the basis of its price is not a good idea. There are many other variables that should be taken into consideration, not the least of which is the individual's investment objectives. It is perfectly possible to find a $1000 par value bond selling for $800 (or 80, as it is normally listed). But before snapping it up as a bargain, a buyer should realize the possible consequences of his purchase. Quality *discount bonds* generally have lower yields. If the coupon rate is high and the price is low, then the bond is probably not of investment grade. On the other hand, deep-discount bonds usually provide good call protection and offer the possibility of capital gains at maturity.

At the other end of the scale, *premium bonds* (those selling above par) provide attractive current yields, but offer less in the way of call protection. Furthermore, the buyer will have no capital gain when the bond matures, which may be exactly what he wants. Table 34-2 lists the principal features of the four broad classifications of corporate bonds.

TABLE 34-2

	Price Range	Coupon Rate	Current Income	Call Protection	Capital Gains at Maturity
Premium (or cushion)	102+	9%+	Highest	Minimal	Loss
Current	97–102	7⅞%–8⅞%	High	Medium	Minimal
Moderate Discount	80–97	5%–7¾%	Moderate	Good	Moderate
Deep Discount	80 and below	Below 5%	Low	High	Highest

CHAPTER 35

SOME QUESTIONS AND ANSWERS ABOUT CONVERTIBLE BONDS

Corporate Bond Research Department

INTRODUCTION

Convertible bonds represent one sector of the securities market that is often neglected by investors when structuring their portfolios. Many individuals tend to think of "stocks and bonds." However, convertible bonds are instruments that fall into the middle section of a company's capitalization structure. They're neither fish nor fowl. But, because of this unique in-between state, convertible bonds may be especially appropriate for certain investors.

WHAT IS A CONVERTIBLE BOND?

A convertible bond (convertible subordinated debenture) is a debt instrument of an issuing corporation. It states a par value (the bond's redemption value at maturity), a maturity date (the repayment date of the principal amount to bondholders, at par), a call price (the price to be paid to bondholders if the corporation wishes to retire the bond prior to maturity), and an interest rate. Also, a convertible bond is exchangeable, at the holder's option, into a predetermined number of the corporation's common shares (assuming it is convertible into the issuing company's common stock) during a certain period of time, generally until the maturity date of the bond.

WHAT ARE SOME OF THE DIFFERENCES BETWEEN A CONVERTIBLE BOND AND COMMON STOCK?

Convertible bonds offer some of the stability and relative safety associated with straight debt issues such as regular bonds. Although a convertible bond may not appreciate as much as stock might in a bull market, neither will it lose value as rapidly in a dwindling market. The issuing corporation's obligation to pay interest associated with debt before common stock dividends might further enhance a convertible bond's investment merit for the more conservative investor.

WHAT ARE SOME OF THE DIFFERENCES BETWEEN A CONVERTIBLE BOND AND A STRAIGHT DEBT BOND?

A convertible bond, unlike a straight debt bond, offers appreciation possibilities linked to the earnings and growth of the issuing company. Since the convertible bond is linked to the common stock of the issuing corporation in a given ratio, as the common stock rises in value to reflect a firm's growth, the price of the convertible bond increases. Conversely, as the stock declines in value, so does the convertible bond's price decline, although its price fluctuations are generally less severe than the corresponding common stock.

HOW MUCH INTEREST CAN YOU RECEIVE FROM AN INVESTMENT IN A CONVERTIBLE BOND?

Interest rates paid on convertible bonds vary from issue to issue. However, these bonds will generally yield more than the dividends on common stock of comparable quality and less than the interest on nonconvertible bonds of comparable quality and maturity. The issuing company has a commitment to pay interest on convertible bonds prior to its payment of dividends on preferred and common stock.

ARE ALL CONVERTIBLE BONDS CONVERTIBLE INTO COMMON STOCK?

No. Some may be wholly or partially convertible into preferred and/or equities. Sometimes the bond may be convertible into securities of another corporation.

MUST AN INVESTOR CONVERT HIS OR HER CONVERTIBLE BONDS INTO STOCK?

It is not necessary to convert a convertible bond in order to realize its investment merit. Convertible bonds are often sold many times before they are converted into stock. Also, some investors choose to retain ownership of the bond until its maturity date.

ARE WARRANTS, RIGHTS, AND OPTIONS THE SAME AS CONVERTIBLE BONDS?

No. Warrants, rights, and options are names for certificates or contracts which are often considered to be convertible securities but which have no real value based on ownership interest or debt. Rather, these contracts give their owners the right to buy or sell specified securities at a predetermined price called the "exercise" price.

WHERE ARE CONVERTIBLE BONDS TRADED?

Convertible bonds are traded on the New York Stock Exchange, on other exchanges, and over the counter. Currently, more than 350 issues of convertible bonds are traded on the NYSE alone.

WHAT IS THE CALLABILITY OF CONVERTIBLE BONDS?

Callability is the right of an issuing corporation to redeem its convertible bonds before maturity at a stated price slightly above par (or face value). There is usually an initial period after issuance when the bond is noncallable. When a convertible bond listed on the New York Stock Exchange is called for redemption, holders of record of registered bonds are notified directly. Notice is also given in a newspaper of general circulation to permit bondholders to convert to stock prior to the redemption date or sell the bond to someone who may convert it.

HOW ARE CONVERTIBLE BONDS USED IN HEDGING?

A sophisticated hedging technique is the buying of convertible bonds and, simultaneously, the selling short of the stock into which the bonds are convertible. If the stock goes up, there should be a profit on the bond side of the transaction but a loss on the stock shorted. If the stock goes down, the opposite relationship should be true. For successful investing, the profits obviously must exceed the losses and expenses. Like many investment techniques, hedging has potential risks as well as rewards. These potential gains and losses should be fully understood by the investor before he enters into a hedging program.

CHAPTER 36

SOME QUESTIONS AND ANSWERS ABOUT GOVERNMENT NATIONAL MORTGAGE ASSOCIATION (GNMA)

GNMA Department

WHAT IS GNMA?

The Housing and Urban Development Act of 1968 set up the Government National Mortgage Association (GNMA) to attract new funds into housing by appealing to a broader spectrum of the investment community than traditional mortgage investors alone. GNMA certificates are attractive to a wide range of individual and institutional investors, notably pension funds, credit unions, state and municipal retirement funds, commercial banks and insurance companies, real estate investment trusts, and individuals with substantial portfolios.

WHAT ARE GNMA SECURITIES?

Certain GNMA mortgage-backed securities, or pass-throughs, represent a share in a pool of Federal Housing Administration (FHA) or Veterans Administration (VA) single-family or multifamily mortgages. They are issued by an FHA-approved mortgagee and guaranteed as to payment of principal and interest by GNMA. This guarantee is backed by the full faith and credit of the United States Government, lending the highest degree of quality to this investment. As they come due, monthly payments of principal and interest are "passed through" GNMA to investors.

ARE ALL GNMA SECURITIES PASS-THROUGHS?

No. Some GNMA-type securities are mortgage-backed rather than pass-through. Mortgage-backed bonds guaranteed by GNMA have been issued by the Federal National Mortgage Association (FNMA) and also by the Federal Home Loan Mortgage Corporation (FHLMC), a subsidiary of the Federal Home Loan Bank Board. These securities are mortgage-backed rather than pass-through. Both carry a GNMA guarantee, although the pass-throughs are directly backed by an FHA or VA mortgage pool.

IS THERE ANY OTHER DIFFERENCE BETWEEN MORTGAGE-BACKED BONDS AND PASS-THROUGH SECURITIES?

Yes. Mortgage-backed bonds pay interest semiannually and have a fixed maturity date for full payment of principal. Pass-through securities pay each certificate holder monthly a pro rata share of all principal and interest payments on the pooled mortgages plus a pro rata share of all principal prepayments collected on those mortgages.

HOW GOOD IS GNMA'S GUARANTEE?

GNMA's guarantee is backed by the full faith and credit of the United States. GNMA has full authority to borrow without limitation from the U.S. Treasury to meet its obligations under the various mortgage-backed securities guarantee agreements.

DOES GNMA BUY THE MORTGAGES TO BE POOLED?

No. GNMA guarantees the pool. The mortgages to be pooled are held by a custodiam, usually the trust department of a bank.

WHAT IF ONE OF THE POOLED MORTGAGES GOES INTO DEFAULT?

The holder of a GNMA security will not be aware of the default or any ensuing foreclosure action. The issuer continues to pay the principal and interest payments due on the mortgage until it is liquidated. At that time, the pool and, in turn, each security holder is paid at par just as if the mortgage had been prepaid by the owner.

IF THERE ARE A LARGE NUMBER OF FORECLOSURES, IS THE ISSUER'S ABILITY TO CONTINUE PAYMENTS ENDANGERED?

The diversification of risk on the mortgages included in most pools makes this unlikely. However, in the event of default the issuer advances payments, which are then repaid by GNMA.

WHAT IS THE STATED MATURITY AND AVERAGE (PREPAID) LIFE OF PASS-THROUGHS?

Stated maturities on GNMA certificates depend on the mortgages that underlie them. Most residential mortgages carry a stated maturity of 30 years. Actual, or expected, maturity is often considerably less than 30 years because of prepayments and regular amortization. Although the certificates are not callable, mortgages may be prepaid at any time. Prepayments are distributed proportionately to all certificate holders in the pool. Market practice is to quote GNMA yields to a 12-year prepaid life.

WHAT INTEREST RATES ARE AVAILABLE ON GNMA SECURITIES?

Single-family mortgage pools are issued at a coupon rate ½ of a percentage point below the current FHA/VA mortgage rate. Thus, 8½ percent mortgages create 8 percent GNMA securities. The ½ percent difference provides the issuer's servicing fee and 0.06 percent represents GNMA's guarantee fee. Common rates on single family issues are 9 percent, 8½ percent, 8¼ percent, 8 percent, 7½ percent, 7 percent, and 6½ percent, with a few issues outstanding at 5½ percent and 5¼ percent.

CAN THE YIELDS QUOTED ON GNMA SECURITIES BE COMPARED WITH THOSE QUOTED FOR CORPORATE BONDS?

Not exactly. Since most bonds pay interest only semiannually and principal at maturity, the monthly payments of principal and interest on GNMA pass-through securities have a compounding effect which must be adjusted if an accurate comparison is to be made. See Table 36-1.

TABLE 36-1

If the GNMA Yield Is	Add This to Get Semiannual Payment Equivalent
6.73 to 7.07	0.10
7.40 to 7.71	0.12
8.02 to 8.30	0.14
8.59 to 8.85	0.16
9.12 to 9.37	0.18
9.63 to 9.86	0.20

WHEN ARE PAYMENTS MADE TO INVESTORS?

Monthly payments to certificate holders are made the fifteenth day of the month following the month in which collections are made by the issuer of the certificates. The certificate holder receives payment regardless of whether the issuer is paid or not. Each check carries a breakdown of principal and interest and states the balance due under the certificate and the aggregate balance of the mortgages underlying that particular issue.

WHAT IS THE MINIMUM PURCHASE?

$25,000.

WHAT HAPPENS IF I WANT TO SELL BEFORE THE SECURITY MATURES?

No problem. There is an active secondary market for GNMAs. Hundreds of millions of dollars in GNMAs are traded in the secondary market each year.

WHY INVEST IN GNMAS?

GNMA pass-throughs offer the individual investor:

1. a dependable, monthly cash flow from interest and amortization
2. a more active secondary market than is commonly encountered in most bonds
3. a guarantee backed by the full faith and credit of the U.S. Government that makes GNMA securities eligible as collateral to meet the requirements of mutual savings bank and savings and loan associations.

CHAPTER 37

PREFERRED STOCK AND THE CORPORATE INVESTOR

Preferred Stock Research Department

THE NEED FOR A DIVIDEND EXCLUSION

As an investment officer of a corporation, you are no doubt painfully aware of the need to invest for the highest possible after-tax return. With today's seemingly all-encompassing corporate tax laws, the task is not an easy one. However, the tax laws have also provided a solution: the 85 percent dividend exclusion.

THE EXCLUSION

The exclusion exempts a corporation from taxes on 85 percent of the dividend income it receives through qualified common and preferred stock investment in the securities of other corporations. This advantage is particularly rewarding for corporate investors holding "new money" preferred issues.

New money preferreds are those issued after October 1, 1942, for purposes other than refunding. ("Old money" preferreds, a portion of whose dividends are tax-deductible—although not a full 85 percent—

were issued prior to October 1, 1942, or for refunding purposes after that date.) Here's what investment in a 9 percent new money preferred can mean for your corporation's after-tax yield:

$$\frac{\text{Taxable Portion of Dividend}}{15\%} \times \frac{\text{Corp. Tax Rate}}{48\%} = \frac{\text{Portion of Dividend Taxed}}{7.20\%}$$

$$\frac{\text{Portion of Dividend Retained after Tax}}{92.80\%} \times \frac{\text{Dividend Rate (Assume 9\%)}}{9.00\%} = \frac{\text{After Tax Yield}}{8.35\%}$$

In other words, a 9 percent preferred can yield a hefty 8.35 percent after taxes.

DIVIDEND ROLLOVER

This return could be enhanced even further by a technique called a "dividend rollover." The concept is simple. A corporate account sells a preferred which has gone X-dividend. It uses the proceeds to invest in another preferred issue which is about to go X, thereby enabling the corporation to collect more than four quarterly dividends during a 12-month period. This strategy can substantially enhance after-tax return. But like any investment opportunity, it involves a certain degree of risk.

DETAILED INFORMATION ABOUT FIXED-INCOME SECURITIES

INTRODUCTION

THE KEY FACTORS WHICH AFFECT THE PRICE OF A CORPORATE BOND

B. Daniel Evans, Jr.

There are six main factors that affect the price of a bond:

1. The direction of interest rates in general
2. The relative creditworthiness of the issuer
3. The outlook for the issuer's industry, be it tire and rubber, steel, autos, electric utilities, finance companies, or anything else; how the company fits into the big picture of the industry; and how management deals with past and present problems
4. The particular indenture and technical features of an issue, e.g., issue size, call features, sinking funds, etc
5. The supply and demand for a particular issue, a particular industry group, or a particular sector, such as municipals, corporates, or governments
6. Expectations of investors and issuers

CHAPTER 38

THE ESSENCE OF FIXED-INCOME CREDIT ANALYSIS

B. Daniel Evans, Jr.

THE IMPORTANCE OF CASH FLOW AND YIELD TO MATURITY

1. The goal of most fixed-income investors is preservation of capital commensurate with a satisfactory rate of return.
2. Bondholders and bond purchasers are typically defensively oriented. For example, a bondholder is primarily concerned with buying issues which will at least maintain relative creditworthiness, especially in view of the deterioration of credits in recent years.
3. Since the time horizon for bondholders is long, the horizon for bond research analysis must also be long.
4. Bond analysts follow many more companies than do equity analysts, and they use equity research as an aid in analysis. Roughly speaking, there are 1900 companies to follow in the corporate bond sector, upwards of 75,000 different issuers of municipal bond securities, 50 international issuers, and some 50 government and federal agency securities.
5. Bond analysts can be described as professional skeptics. They

generally tend to look first for the pitfalls and then for the positives, balancing each against the other to arrive at a decision concerning the relative creditworthiness of an issuer.

6. A bond analyst would probably not recommend selling a bond just because the company will stay stagnant for 5 years. On the other hand, a stock analyst faced with such a prospect might very likely recommend a switch into a company expected to have a better growth rate. Thus, generally speaking, stability and predictability are positives to a bond analyst.

7. A bond analyst is more concerned with the overall level of earnings than with earnings per share; equity analysts, on the other hand, primarily focus their attention on earnings per share. To a bond analyst, cash flow is the most important piece of financial information, for it is cash flow that pays off debts. While an equity analyst may be mostly concerned with the growth rate of a company, a bond analyst might view too rapid growth as a threat to the company's working capital and financial position. Even though a bond analyst may agree that business is great for the company, he will want to know if there is enough working capital and cash flow to finance accounts receivable, inventories, and capital expenditures.

8. Between common stocks and bonds there are two major differences. Bonds have a fixed interest rate (coupon) and carry a promise to pay back principal upon maturity. One can compare all existing bonds by one benchmark: yield to maturity. That gives all bonds a common reference mark in terms of analysis and helps greatly in the selection and comparative process.

   This yield to maturity is based on a *contractual* obligation to pay interest and to repay principal in full at a particular point in the future. Payments of dividends, on the other hand, are subject to the discretion of the board of directors. What's more, stockholders are not promised a particular sum of money at maturity, as common stocks do not have a maturity or a sinking fund. Basically, then, the price of a bond in the marketplace is a function of the prospects of continuing to receive interest (on time) and the likelihood of receiving total payment upon maturity.

   In summary, the focus of most analysts in the stock market is on the potential for price appreciation and dividends, while a bond analyst concentrates upon yield to maturity.

SOME GENERAL GUIDELINES FOR BOND CREDIT ANALYSIS

As previously mentioned, cash flow is the be-all and end-all of the bond analyst. For this reason, much effort is spent on this area, because it is cash flow which pays off debts.

Cash Flow

In analyzing cash flow, one wants to know where the money is coming from and what would happen if certain events affected the continuity of that flow; also, one should study the amount of growth necessary to offset inflation. The first step in analyzing cash flow is to separate *gross cash flow* from *net cash flow*. Gross cash flow is a total of various items, including earnings, depreciation, deferred taxes, and the investment tax credit. (As long as a company continues to grow and has large capital expenditures, it can defer taxes, but when it stops growing and investing, those taxes become payable. Oil companies, for instance, have such a high depreciation and write-off of drilling expenditures that they pay very little tax in the United States. When an oil company stops its drilling expenditures, the effective tax rate for the company can go up sharply, affecting its cash flow and other financial ratios.)

Net cash flow is computed by subtracting dividends from gross cash flow. Once having arrived at a net cash flow figure, compare it with past, present, and future capital expenditures. The more that a company is able to finance internally, the greater protection there is for bondholders. What's more, the less a company has to finance externally, the less supply of its issue there will be in the bond market, and the more financial flexibility it will have for raising capital. Many companies' stocks are now selling below book value, which encourages them to raise money through debt financing. But a company with a large amount of debt may have no alternative to equity financing and thus may have to sell stock below book value.

It's also important to analyze cash flow from division to division and the flow of cash within a corporation. Is there one particular aspect of the company or one particular product that is generating most of the cash? If that's so, then what would happen if something went wrong with that particular aspect of the business? Example: depreciation and amortization alone should be high enough to generate sufficient cash flow should the company not earn any money in a given year.

One of the best ways of evaluating the cash flow of industrial companies is to look at the *cash flow–to–long-term debt ratio.* (Long-term debt is defined as funded or contractual debt.) If a company has a 33 percent ratio, that means it could theoretically retire all of its debt in 3 years if all of its cash flow were dedicated to retirement of debt. An Aaa/AAA-rated credit should have a 75 to 100 percent ratio—in other words, all of the funded debt could be paid off in 1 year or slightly more.

An AA/Aa credit should have at least a 50 percent ratio, i.e., the means of paying off all the debt within 2 years. An A/A credit should have a 35 to 40 percent ratio, representing the potential to pay in 3 years, and a Baa/BBB credit should have a 25 percent ratio, or a 4-year payment potential.

Probably the ratio which receives the most attention is the *fixed charge coverage ratio.* The most widely used fixed charge coverage ratio is the *pretax interest coverage ratio,* which is computed by dividing the sum of pretax net income and interest expense by interest expense. Frequently, this ratio will present an accurate picture of bondholder protection. For instance, a company could have a net income of 0 and pay no taxes *but still be able to pay 100 percent of interest expense.*

Another fixed charge coverage ratio is the after-tax fixed charge ratio, which is computed by dividing the sum of interest payments, annual obligations, and after-tax income by the sum of interest payment and rental obligations. Ideally a good Aa/AA industrial bond should have at least a 4 × after-tax coverage ratio. When this fixed charge ratio slips below 3 ×, it can indicate potential problems or a deteriorating credit. (Retail companies have high lease payments and can get away with lower ratios. Generally a 1.5-to-1 is considered acceptable for a retailer.)

The importance of leases cannot be underestimated in a true cash flow analysis, as leases are an alternative to a capital outlay. Many corporations do not realize that when they sign a lease, they are increasing the capital commitment of the company. And if a company overcommits itself to lease obligations, this can dramatically affect its overall creditworthiness. Typically, the decision for a lease is made at a low level of management. By adding lease payments into the fixed charge coverage ratio, a bondholder can assess the potential of excessive off–balance sheet financing, which could add a tremendous financial burden to a company. (Note that Financial Accounting Standards Board Statement #13—*Accounting for Leases,* instituted in 1977, now forces a company to capitalize more leases, thereby increasing long-term debt and interest charges.)

Another important ratio to look at is the *debt service ratio.* This would include rental payments, interest payments, and principal repayments. In other words, one looks at the level of cash flow and analyzes the ability of the company to service interest, principal, and lease payments. If the overall debt burden is becoming a real problem for the company, it may lose flexibility of financing alternatives. Ideally, one does not want to invest money in the bonds of a company which may be stretched unduly and has little financial flexibility.

Bank Relationships

In analyzing the credit of a corporate bond, it is important to get a handle on the credit agreement with the company's bank(s). Is the company paying a premium over the prime interest rate? Does the company have a contractual arrangement with the bank which guarantees credit availability, or does it have just a short-term line of credit, which could be canceled at any moment? The better the relationship between the company and the bank, the more flexibility the company will have in obtaining financing. (This information can usually be obtained in either the annual report or the 10-K statement.)

Bond Indenture Agreement

Next, one should study the indenture provisions of the bond. Are there any restrictions concerning the ability of the company to finance, or is there an obligation to meet certain coverage formulas? (For example, a typical indenture ratio for an industrial company is that net tangible assets must be maintained above 250 percent of long-term debt in order for the company to issue additional debt.) Is there a dividend payment test? (This usually restricts the payment of dividends according to various formulas.)

Indenture provisions are provided to keep companies out of trouble and to act as a restraint on management. (On the other hand, it is much better to have a strong financial management than all the tough indenture provisions in the world.)

Many low-grade bonds do not provide any indenture protection. If one has a choice of two bonds of an equal nature with the same yield, always pick the one which has the indenture protection.

It may be very difficult for individuals to get hold of the indenture provisions; however, an abbreviated version of the indenture is provided in the original prospectus or offering circular. Above all, an investor should be aware of the technical features (i.e., refunding, sinking fund, etc.) that apply to a particular bond. A copy of the issuing prospectus would contain what is needed; however, a prospectus is often difficult to locate if a bond has been outstanding for several years.

Note that expert help may be needed to interpret the indenture provisions. The company's 10-K, and sometimes the annual report, states in the footnotes whether debt tests (that is, protective covenants) exist and how restrictive they are.

Leverage

The next area to analyze is leverage. There are two types of leverage: operational leverage and financial leverage. The more leverage the company has, the greater the swings can be in terms of earnings.

Leverage is a two-edged sword; it can both help and hurt the company and the bondholder or stockholder. The number one reason for using leverage in recent years has been that it is a hedge against inflation, enabling the company to pay back borrowed money in cheaper dollars, which could be interpreted as a justifiable means of protecting shareholders.

If a company has both financial and operational leverage, it may have potential problems in terms of the volatility of results in down cycles. The steel, auto, and tire and rubber industries are good examples of what can happen in down years. Therefore, the degree of leverage should be studied carefully.

One of the best ways of analyzing leverage is to compute a *sales-to-employees ratio*. You take the total amount of sales and divide it by the total number of company employees. Normally, one would not want to see a company have less than $25,000 of sales per employee. Ideally, the figure should be above $50,000. If a company has a low sales-to-employees ratio and is heavily unionized, that is worse still. It means that in bad times the company would have problems in laying off employees and would have continued high labor costs. This ratio basically enables you to determine how labor-intensive and how productive a company is.

The cost of employee benefits has risen so dramatically in recent years (as has the cost of labor) that companies in the future are going to have to reduce their labor component. Companies just will not be able to afford to spend an increasing percentage of revenue on labor. Thus, companies which are increasing productivity through mechanization and automation should be in a better competitive position in the years ahead. (Western Electric, for example, reduced total employment 30 percent between 1973 and 1978.)

Another type of ratio to determine financial strength of a company is the *operating ratio*. Two examples are: cost of goods sold as a percentage of total sales, and net income as a percentage of total sales. In analyzing cost of goods sold as a percentage of total sales, the key is to compare this ratio with those of comparable companies and to look at the historical trend for the company. In the net income–to–sales ratio, also compare the trend of the company and its performance relative to others in its industry. A rule of thumb: One should be concerned if a company has an after-tax margin of only 1 to 2 percent, unless, of course, the company is a supermarket chain and thus is expected to have notoriously low margins. Generally speaking, one would like to see margins of at least 5 percent for an industrial company.

CHAPTER 39

INDUSTRIAL BONDS

B. Daniel Evans, Jr.

William F. Fannon

DEBT RATIOS

Before purchasing a long-term corporate bond, you should evaluate several financial ratios. Here are some of the more important ones:

Long-Term Debt–to–Total Capitalization Ratio

There are two important debt ratios. The first one is computed by dividing the company's long-term debt by its total capitalization. (Capitalization is defined as stockholders' equity plus long-term debt.) Typically a ratio of long-term debt to total capitalization of 33 percent is about as high as you would want to go for a good, solid company. Any ratio higher than that should serve as a warning signal to you. A company with a ratio considerably less than 33 percent, say 18 percent, may be a high caliber credit.

Total Liabilities–to–Net Worth Ratio

A second debt ratio of importance is computed by dividing total liabilities by net worth, or stockholders' equity. Ideally, a ratio of total liabilities to net worth of about 1 to 1, or 100 percent, is needed for a good, solid company. Any ratio higher than that is evidence of high financial leverage and should be viewed with caution.

Some Ratio Parameters for Various Industries

It is important to remember that these ratios can vary from industry to industry. For example, the capital-intensive industries, such as steel and autos, could have higher ratios than the ones mentioned above. Total liabilities as a percentage of net worth could be as high as 115 to 120 percent for a capital-intensive company without raising a warning flag. Likewise, the long-term debt–to–capitalization ratio could be as high as 37 percent for these companies without being cause for concern. Capital-intensive companies need more debt to survive. These companies need to spend more for producing facilities in order to be able to build different types of automobiles or to add capacity. Just doing business requires more capital, and therefore such capital-intensive companies have generally employed a high degree of leverage.

The retailing industry also has certain special quirks which should be carefully considered. Typically, many retailing stores will rent or lease their stores rather than own them. Thus, in analyzing debt ratios for retailers, one should "capitalize" the leases. (That's a way of saying "include the leases as indebtedness of the company on its balance sheet.") One way to capitalize a lease is to take the company's annual rental payments and multiply that figure by 8. The resulting number can then be added to long-term debt to provide a total debt figure for the company which can be used in debt-ratio calculations. (On the balance sheet, the number needs to be added to assets, also, to avoid undue penalty to the company.)

Remember in analyzing debt ratios: *be consistent in analyzing the trend of such ratios, and be consistent from company to company as you make comparisons.*

BALANCE SHEET MEASURES OF LIQUIDITY
Current Ratio

After calculating the debt ratios for a company, one should look closely at several balance sheet measures of liquidity. (It is important to measure the cash position of a company, because that is the final determinant of its immediate financial flexibility.) The first ratio to calculate is the ratio of current assets to current liabilities (or current ratio). In the old days, when cash management and the level of interest rates did not receive the attention they do today, a current ratio of 2 to 1, that is, twice as many current assets as current liabilities, was considered necessary for a good, solid company. But in the 1970s, when money became so costly, companies discovered they could get along with less cash, and the minimum acceptable current ratio decreased. For example, automobile companies, which are big advocates of low current ratios, get away with a 1.5 to 1.6 current ratio. For this reason, the current ratio is not as important to the analyst or investor as it used to be.

Quick Ratio

The second ratio important to measurement of working capital is the quick ratio, or acid test ratio: the cash and receivables divided by current liabilities. Ideally, this ratio should be 1 to 1 or better. Here again, though, this ratio isn't as important as it used to be, and typically the ratio may fall to 0.5 without causing concern; however, anything below that figure should raise a red flag to an investor.

INTEREST RATE COVERAGE

The next step in analysis involves looking at the income statement and calculating interest rate coverage. Interest coverage is an important figure to investors, because a bondholder's prime concern is whether he or she will continue to receive interest in the future. Therefore, it is important to analyze how much protection and security a bond has in terms of earnings and cash flow to cover the projected interest payments in the years ahead.

Pretax Interest Coverage Ratio

The first ratio to work up in this regard is the pretax coverage ratio,

$$\frac{\text{pretax income} + \text{interest}}{\text{interest}}$$

A 6 × coverage would be considered a good ratio for a typical industrial company. Anything less than that should be viewed as potentially troublesome.

After-Tax Interest Coverage Ratio

The next ratio to get is the after-tax interest coverage,

$$\frac{\text{after tax income} + \text{interest}}{\text{interest}}$$

A 4.0 × ratio is considered good here. (It is important to note that in arriving at the pretax or after-tax income figure, one should exclude extraordinary charges or losses or gains, or income from discontinued operations.) For comparisons, the pretax ratio is considered more useful, because of differing tax rates.

After-Tax Interest Coverage plus Rents

The next ratio to calculate is after-tax coverage of interest expense plus annual rentals,

$$\frac{\text{after-tax income} + \text{interest and rents}}{\text{interest and rents}}$$

This ratio is especially important for those companies which lease a lot of their property, such as retailers, and therefore have a lot of long-term lease obligations. Three-times coverage is considered good for this ratio.

PROFIT MARGINS

Also to be considered is the profit margin of the company. The best ratio to use for this analysis is after-tax income as a percent of sales. (Here again, you should exclude extraordinary items and losses or gains from discontinued operations in arriving at the after-tax income figure.)

The after-tax margins of companies will fluctuate widely from industry to industry, and therefore it is not so important what the profit margins are for the company as it is to see how that company compares with the other companies in the industry. Supermarket chains and commodity processors, for example, typically have unusually low margins, running somewhere in the area of 1 percent, which can be considered quite good for a company in those industries. In making comparisons from company to company, one should look at a 5-year period; unusual distortions can make one year's comparison misleading.

CASH FLOW RATIOS
Cash Flow as a Percent of Long-Term Debt

Cash flow ratios can never be underestimated in importance for correctly assessing the financial situation of a company. This is how investors determine whether a company will be able to pay off its debt. The first ratio of cash flow measurement to look at is cash flow as a percentage of long-term debt. (Cash flow, for our purposes, is defined as net earnings plus depreciation plus deferred taxes.) A cash flow–to–long-term debt ratio of 40 percent and above is considered a good ratio for an A/A industrial credit.

Cash Flow–to–Capital Expenditure Ratio

Next is the net cash flow–to–capital expenditure ratio (net cash flow equals funds from operations minus cash dividends). You can get the most recent year's capital expenditures from the "sources and uses of cash" statement in the company's annual report. Be sure to observe the trend of this ratio, because it can give you an indication of the company's need to finance externally, its ability to finance internally, and the outlook for its financial liquidity.

There is no rule of thumb for the net cash flow/capital expenditure ratio apart from general observations on the trend. For example, if a company has a very low cash flow–to–capital expenditure ratio and the trend continues to deteriorate, this should be a red flag to investors. This is one of the most important indicators to watch for an advance idea of when a credit rating might be changed. If you learn that a company is planning to make major capital expenditures over a number of years, and you make assumptions as to exactly how much it might spend, then you can see how much debt the company would be able to add without affecting its ratio. Upon learning that a company may have to borrow so much that its key financial ratios will be diluted, one can get an advance indication of potential deterioration of a company's credit rating.

Some Guidelines for the Key Financial Ratios

Appendix III provides the ratios previously discussed for all the major industry categories of corporate bonds. These ratios are provided to give holders an idea of the financial position of each industry group. Thus, when it comes time to evaluate the creditworthiness of a particular company, you will have meaningful frame of reference. All you need to do is compare the financial ratios of your company with others in the same industry. Be sure to remember that what is most important is the trend of the financial measurements of a company, particularly in comparison to other companies in the industry. It is critical to know before it is too late whether a company is stagnating while the rest of the industry is improving. That should raise a red flag, because when things get tough and the industry experiences a downturn, a particular company could really suffer, and its financial ratios could deterioriate markedly in a short period of time.

CHAPTER 40

ELECTRIC UTILITY BONDS

Alfred G. Mazzorana

WHY CREDIT ANALYSIS OF UTILITY BONDS IS SO IMPORTANT

In the 1960s, very little credit analysis was done on electric utilities. Investors typically didn't even ask what state the utility was located in. However, during the early 1970s, when the fundamental weaknesses of this industry began to surface and subsequently many high-quality utilities were downgraded, credit analysis of this industry became extremely important. What's more, this industry is capital-intensive, is subject to the vicissitudes of a tight capital market, is vulnerable to inflation, and will have increased construction expenditures, all of which adds to the need for careful analysis.

WHAT ARE THE KEY FACTORS TO EVALUATE IN UTILITY BOND CREDIT ANALYSIS?
State Regulation

State regulation determines whether rate increases will be allowed, and whether financial ratios will improve or deteriorate.

The Fuel Mix of a Utility

A utility's fuel mix is something which doesn't change quickly, and investors can get a good handle on it. A reliance of 80 to 90 percent on a combination of coal and nuclear energy is a good sign. On the other hand, 80 to 90 percent reliance on oil could present problems, for the obvious reasons. Be sure the utility has a fuel adjustment clause, so that it can immediately pass on higher energy costs to consumers.

Financial Ratios

You want to see pretax interest coverage of at least 2.7×. A net cash flow–to–capital expenditure ratio of 30 percent or less is considered troublesome. (You should be able to get hold of the estimated capital expenditure program for at least the next 3 years, and in many cases for as long as 5 years.) In analyzing expected capital expenditures, you should view it in relation to the level of demand. If the company is overly optimistic about demand and it plans to engage heavily in external financing to expand capacity, you should be quite leery.

The industry average of net cash flow to capital expenditures is roughly 40 to 42 percent. The twenty utility companies which fell from Aaa/AAA rating to Baa/BBB over the last 8 years all exhibited depressed levels (less than 30 percent) of cash flow as a percentage of capital expenditures. The net cash flow–to–capital expenditure ratio acts as a warning of potential credit deterioration during periods of financial and economic stress. A utility with a ratio less than 30 percent lacks financial flexibility and is more subject to financial stress as the ratio declines.

It should be noted here that a 40 percent net cash flow–to–capital expenditure ratio has a different meaning today from what it had in 1974. This is due to the impact of inflation on new plant equipment and labor. With a 40 percent ratio in 1974, one $100 million bond offering might have been sufficient; now, two offerings of debt might be necessary.

Generally speaking, pretax interest coverage should be 3.5 × for Aa/AA bonds, 2.7 × for A/A, and 2¼ × for Baa/BBB bonds.

The debt-to-equity ratio for the utility industry on average is 51 percent.

The short-term debt as a percentage of total capital is also a useful ratio. As this ratio rises above 2½ percent, you should become a little wary.

Factors to Consider in Analyzing the State Regulatory Environment

1. Take the major rate cases decided during a given test period of at least 18 months and anlyze the allowed rate or return authorized by the regulatory commission. Has it turned up, headed down, or stabilized?
2. What was allowed in the utility's rate base? Has construction work in progress been included in the rate base?
3. What test period is being used to calculate the rate of return? You don't want too much of a regulatory lag; so, the most recent available period is the most desirable.
4. Regulatory lag is the next factor to consider. The greater the difference between the test period and the date the increased revenues go into effect, the less likely the utility will be able to earn the allowed rate of return.
5. Does the regulatory commission allow interim rate increases to go into effect during the lag period? The allowance of interim rate relief has the effect of nullifying, to some extent, the negative impact of regulatory lag. However, interim rate relief is usually implemented subject to refund, and therefore an unfavorable rate decision could require a refunding.
6. What is the utility's return on equity? How does that relate to what the commission allows? (Ideally, you would want a utility to be earning what it is permitted.) If it is earning above what it is allowed, there's always a possibility that rates could be rolled back so that the return would be more in line with what the commission had authorized.

CHAPTER 41

TELEPHONE COMPANY BONDS

B. Daniel Evans, Jr.

James R. Bulfin

In analyzing telephone company bonds, there are certain things which an investor should be aware of. Here's a list:

1. The telephone industry is regulated by state commissions, and therefore fifty different regulatory bodies are involved. It's important to learn whether the regulatory environment is deteriorating or improving. Rate relief often is subject to political pressure and does not necessarily respond to economics.

2. One should investigate the growth rate of each territory where your company is involved. What is the growth dependent upon? In general, rate relief has not been satisfactory of late, and as a result, household formations and industrial growth are assuming increased importance. Note that the worst of all possible worlds is fast population growth and inadequate rate relief.

3. One of the best ways to evaluate the status of regulation is to look at the overall rate of return on capital which the telephone company is allowed. (Rate of return is defined as annual after-tax earnings taken as a percentage of stocks, bonds, and preferred

stock outstanding.) The rate of return allowed for most Bell System subsidiaries in 1977 was around 9 percent, with the independents doing better. Is your company doing better or worse than that? Another way of getting a handle on how responsive the regulatory authorities are is to learn how long it took for them to make a decision on a rate increase. A decision in less than a year is considered satisfactory.

4. The next area to analyze is the company's rate base. Needless to say, the larger the rate base, the better for the company. Therefore, if the authorities are using a very current rate base to determine the allowed rate of return, it's a sign of favorable regulatory posture.

5. In analyzing telephone growth, investigate the demographics of the state and the region in which the company is located.

6. Financial ratios for telephone companies should also be studied. The first one to look at is *fixed charge coverage*, which can be computed by taking net income before interest charges and dividing that by interest expenses. The next ratio to analyze is the *long-term debt ratio*, which can generally be higher than for industrial companies because of the more predictable and steady demand for the telephone company's services. *Net cash flow as a percentage of capital expenditures* is important to watch, because a deteriorating relationship is an indication that additional financing may soon have to be done.

It's also important to examine the refunding protections of the telephone issue you're interested in. For example, all telephone issues with a coupon of 10 percent had been called by the first quarter of 1978. You can be sure that telephone companies won't pay interest on high-coupon issues if they can replace them with a lower-coupon debt security.

CHAPTER 42

NATURAL GAS PIPELINE AND DISTRIBUTION COMPANY BONDS

Heather M. Kenny

NATURAL GAS PIPELINE COMPANIES

In analyzing the bonds of a natural gas pipeline company you should consider the following factors:

1. What is its gas supply position? What is the *ratio of total reserves to the amount of gas sold* in the most recent year? (Total reserves would include those under contract from others and owned by the company itself.) Ideally you would like to see a reserve life index ratio of at least 9 or 10 to 1.
2. Next, you want to evaluate *gas sales volume over the last 5 or 6 years.* Is it stable, declining, or increasing? (This is a way of double-checking the total reserve–to–amount sold ratio mentioned above. A declining sales volume can camouflage a deteriorating trend of reserves.)
3. Where does the company get its reserves? The more reserves a company owns or buys directly from gas producers, the better. On the other hand, if it buys from other pipelines, the outlook is less stable, because availability and price are less certain.

4. What is the pipeline's exploration subsidiary doing in the field of drilling and exploration? Is it exploring in the areas which have the most optimistic outlook for exploration?

5. What is the relationship between the company's distribution of interstate versus intrastate gas?

6. What customers does the pipeline company sell to? This is an important question, because low-priority users will be the first to be cut back in a period of shortage. Generally speaking, a residential customer is preferable to industry, because residential users are high-priority.

7. What are the financial ratios for the company? Generally, *a debt-to-capitalization ratio* for a pipeline company should be no higher than 50 percent. *Pretax interest coverage* should be at least 3.5 to 1, and annual cash flow as a percentage of long-term debt should be at least 35 percent.

8. What is the status of the depreciation allowance? Typically, you'd want to see annual depreciation charges at least 4 percent of the balance sheet's gross plant item. The pipeline companies generally have a limited economic life, and therefore depreciation should be more rapid than for other utilities.

On the other hand, *you can't rely too heavily on general financial measurements for this industry. The better companies are diversified into other industries and other forms of energy, and thus their financial ratios may be misleading.*

GAS DISTRIBUTION COMPANIES

1. Distribution companies are regulated by state utility commissions and often have difficulty in receiving an adequate rate of return, because they are close to the end user, which makes their rate levels susceptible to political pressures to hold down rate increases.

2. Generally speaking, maturity of the bonds of distribution companies is longer than for pipeline companies, and their sinking funds are less active.

3. While pipeline companies are thought to be somewhat safer investments, the rating companies generally put higher ratings on distribution companies. Those ratings may soon change, as

there are a lot of vulnerable Aa/AA distribution companies at the present time.

4. In analyzing a distribution company, you should look extremely closely at the customers it serves and the industries it is involved with. Note that pipeline companies can sell gas anywhere along their pipelines, while distribution companies are less flexible.

5. Financial ratios are much more important for distribution companies than for pipeline companies. Depreciation, for example, for distribution companies tends to be much lower than that for pipeline companies.

6. *The same ratios that apply to pipeline companies are generally applicable to distribution companies, too.*

CHAPTER 43

FINANCE COMPANY BONDS

Randy F. Schmidt

There are three main types of finance companies: consumer, commercial, and captive finance. In general, the key to analyzing finance companies (there are 54 of them) is determining the quality of management. Here are some important things to remember in looking at a finance company:

1. If management is good and there are conservative accounting practices, then, generally speaking, the finance company's portfolio will be good.
2. The three most important statistics you should be familiar with in analyzing a finance company's receivables portfolio are "delinquencies," "chargeoffs," and "recoveries." (Delinquencies are the delinquent consumer loans a finance company has, chargeoffs are delinquent loans which have been written off, and recoveries are previously charged off loans which turned out to be good.) It's important to evaluate these three in relation to what frequently are dramatically differing accounting practices among various companies. For example, one company may have a very conser-

vative chargeoff policy while another doesn't. Therefore, comparing the two companies only on the basis of the numbers could be misleading.

One of the best ways of determining the conservativeness of a company's chargeoff policy is to look at the relationship of recoveries to chargeoffs. If the recovery rate is high—in other words, upwards of 15 percent—you can bet that the company's method for accounting for chargeoffs is fairly conservative. (Some finance companies will have recovery rates almost as high as 30 percent, while others' may be less than 10 percent.) The recovery rate may be hard to obtain, as some companies don't disclose it. Also, companies don't all report the recovery rate in the same fashion. If it is available, you will be able to find it in the company's 10-K or in a prospectus, if the company has recently come to market. Also, it may be obtainable in the financial supplement to the annual report which most finance companies issue.

Be sure to analyze the figures on a trend basis, and compare them against the general figures for the industry. If the industry trend on delinquencies is down and the delinquencies of the company you're investigating are up, you should be somewhat concerned. It could indicate poor management, or it could be an indication of what will happen to the rest of the industry at some point in the future.

Note that the trend of delinquencies may be more meaningful over the short term than the amount of chargeoffs, since chargeoffs are delinquencies that, in effect, were usually at least 6 months late.

3. Rising interest rates are bad for the industry. That's because there is no ceiling on the industry's cost of funds, while there are restraints on the rate that finance companies can charge for their loans, and they usually charge the maximum allowable rate.

4. Because of the susceptibility of finance companies to changes in interest rates, you should evaluate the relationship of "liability" management to "portfolio" management. (In other words, observe the relationship between the finance company's earning assets and how they are funded.) Ideally, you want a company which attempts to match fixed–interest rate liabilities with fixed–interest rate receivables of like maturities, as well as matching rate-sensitive receivables with rate-sensitive debts of like maturities.

In the early 1970s, many finance companies got burned by rising interest rates, and as a result many companies now have better matching of debt and receivables. The industry used to finance itself with short-term borrowing from the commercial paper market, and it normally got 60 percent of its financing needs in that way; only 40 percent of funds came through long-term financing. After the commercial paper market dried up in 1970 and experienced further confidence problems in 1974, finance companies began to finance more of their requirements through long-term debt.

At the present time, the industry is getting approximately 40 percent of its total debt from short-term borrowing and 60 percent from long-term funds. Any finance company which is not in line with those ratios, i.e., has more short-term debt than long-term debt, should be analyzed carefully before an investment is made. Also, be wary of finance companies which have a longer maturity for their loans than for their borrowed money.

5. In general, the funding of loans through longer-term money has improved the overall financial situation of the industry. On the other hand, remember that finance companies generally do not have close relationships with their bankers. (That's because finance companies have typically relied on the commercial paper market, which has been and is one of the prime competitors for bank financing.) Thus, finance companies are subject to the vagaries and indifference of the commercial paper market rather than what can often be the more friendly attitude of a bank.

A key question to ask, therefore, is whether a company has 100 percent bank line coverage of its commercial paper borrowings. (Of course, some captive finance companies, such as GMAC, have only 50 percent coverage; but if a financing problem ever arose, General Motors would most likely advance the necessary money to its subsidiary, because GMAC plays an important role in marketing General Motors' products.) It is important that consumer and commercial finance companies maintain at least 100 percent bank line coverage of net short-term debt. When the commercial paper market dries up, it is generally the smaller and weaker companies which find access to the market difficult.

6. The increasing use of computers has also improved the general performance of finance companies. The computer enables finance companies to identify lending opportunities, improve their own

liquidity, and keep a better handle on delinquent loans, so that if a problem crops up, the finance company is able to take quick action and avoid a major problem.

7. Management in the finance company area is possibly more important than in any other industry. That's because the receivables in a given portfolio may turn over 100 percent within a relatively short period of time. (Thus, the portfolio will turn over frequently between the time the bonds are issued and their maturity.)

In analyzing management, you should look at the depth of management, promotions, pay scales and incentives, and management turnover, as well as management's operating philosophies. Be sure to find out how management performed and reacted in previous industry crises. Does management anticipate problems or does it merely react to them? Also, what does management do when faced with a problem? Does it take the necessary tough action to minimize long-range damage?

8. Be sure to watch credit unions, presently the fastest growing financial intermediaries and a potentially negative force for finance companies. Fortunately, to compensate for the effects of this competition, finance companies in general are becoming more diversified, which is a good sign. They are getting into leveraged leasing, are buying savings and loan companies, etc., and are, in effect, becoming financial conglomerates of a sort.

CHAPTER 44

CAPTIVE FINANCE COMPANY BONDS

Randy F. Schmidt

Captive finance companies are different from consumer finance companies in the sense that they don't have their own management team. They are owned and run by a parent company. For a captive finance company that is a subsidiary of a major company, such as General Motors or Sears Roebuck, rating agencies will generally be satisfied with fewer restrictions between the captive finance company and the parent because of the parent's abundant resources. But if you're thinking of investing in a captive finance company which has a relatively weak parent, you should look for considerable backing from the parent in the operating agreement.

Generally, high-quality captive finance companies, such as GMAC or SRAC, will yield only ⅛ percent more than high-grade industrial bonds. However, lower-quality captive finance companies may yield ¼ to ½ percent more than comparably rated industrials. One of the best opportunities for investing in finance companies is in the small and not well-known companies with good credit. Interest rates on bonds of unknown companies can often be higher than their credit would normally indicate.

HOW TO ANALYZE A CAPTIVE FINANCE COMPANY

1. The first step in analyzing a captive finance company is to look at leverage. Typically, you'll have more leverage in a commercial finance company than in a consumer finance company. (Commercial finance companies finance larger loans, and they are generally more highly leveraged.) Typically, a consumer finance company shouldn't be leveraged more than 4½ or 5½ to 1 in terms of debt-to-equity. A 7× debt-to-equity ratio is considered quite high. For a commercial finance company, a 6× to 7× debt-to-equity ratio is normal, and over 9× is considered excessively high. However, a captive finance company can get away with leverage as high as 12 to 1, depending on the quality of the parent and the amount of total debt in relation to total resources of the parent.

2. Is the finance company really important to the parent? Is this just a way to get debt off the balance sheet of the parent? Or does the credit company do so much financing for the parent that it is indispensable? If the parent company has nationwide dealerships, does the finance company do a lot of dealer financing which would be unobtainable otherwise? If this is the case, then the parent and finance company will have a close relationship, and the creditworthiness of the subsidiary will be closely tied to the creditworthiness of the parent.

3. What does the indenture say? Note that the indenture is more important for captive finance companies than for other finance companies. (See pages 38-9 and 38-10 for a discussion of indenture provisions.)

4. What is the operating agreement between the parent and the captive finance company? Ideally, you want to see that the parent will agree to maintain pretax earnings for the captive of at least 1.5 × fixed charges. (By fixed charges we mean interest expense and annual rental charges.) Next, inquire as to whether this maintenance agreement is a direct obligation of the parent. (Ideally, you would like the parent to have a direct obligation to maintain stated fixed charge coverage.) Frequently, the parent

and the captive will have an indirect agreement to maintain fixed charge coverage; but that's not as desirable as a contractual obligation.

5. Is there a "keep well" agreement? In other words, does the parent have a contractual obligation to keep the finance company healthy? Does it have an obligation to keep the equity of the captive at a certain level, and is it obligated to put in funds if the equity falls below a certain point?

6. Does the parent have an obligation to repurchase defaulted receivables from the captive? This is one of the most reliable ways for a captive finance company to avoid losses, and it is an arrangement you should look for.

7. Is there a so-called contract withholding account? (A contract withholding account is a reserve which enables the captive finance company to set aside 10 to 15 percent of the purchase price of the paper it buys in a reserve against which future losses can be written off. Such a reserve is a good arrangement for a captive finance company.)

SOME OTHER CONSIDERATIONS

1. Typically, it is very hard for an investor to get information concerning write-offs for captive finance companies. However, as long as the parent company is healthy and it repurchases defaulted accounts, the level of losses is not a significant factor.

   Generally speaking, it is easy for investors to get information about a captive finance company's operating statements, and hard to find out about the quality of the receivables from published reports.

2. The operating statement of a captive finance company is only as good as the parent's ability to live up to it. It is better to have a strong parent and a weak operating agreement than a weak parent and a strong operating agreement.

3. Captive finance companies are easier to analyze than other finance companies, but investors seem to find them to be the hardest to analyze. Most investors make up their minds about a captive finance company bond on the basis of their like or dislike of the parent company. This is not always a wise way to invest in captive finance companies.

4. The best time to buy bonds of finance companies is in an economic downturn, when investors question the industry fundamentals. At such times, the yields on these instruments can get quite high relative to the market.

5. Be sure to watch the trend of upgradings and downgradings for finance companies. Have the upgradings been too quick? If so, there could be some readjustments down the road, with a concomitant drop in price and rise in yield.

CHAPTER 45

INTERNATIONAL DOLLAR-DENOMINATED BONDS

Karen S. W. Friedman

International dollar-denominated bonds, usually called "Yankee" bonds, are generally issued by a foreign country or by a financing institution subscribed to by several countries and are denominated in U.S. dollars and thus are not subject to foreign exchange fluctuations.

If one is considering buying international dollar bonds, here are some important questions to ask about the credit of the foreign country which is issuing the bonds:

1. What is the current status of the economy of the country in question? What is its rate of inflation, unemployment, GNP per capita, personal income per capita, and debt per capita? Most important, what has been the trend of these economic measurements over the last 15 years, and what is the future outlook?
2. What is the main source of revenue for the country? How heavily taxed is the population, i.e., what is the tax burden?
3. What is the status of the political situation? How stable is the government and what kind of concern does it have for private enterprise? One of the best ways to keep track of politics in a

country is to follow the political polls and to attempt to get a feel for the sentiments and moods of the populace. Much of this can be ascertained merely through reading major U.S. publications. Certain countries thought of as healthy prior to an election may soon be in dire straits if the new administration promotes policies that interfere with economic growth. What's more, there could be nationalistic trends which would militate against repayment of foreign debt obligations.

4. What is the balance-of-payments situation, and how dependent is the country on foreign trade and the level of imports? One does not want to see a country highly dependent on a few exports. Something could adversely affect the supply or pricing of those exports, thereby causing a serious deterioration in the overall outlook for the economy.

5. Having analyzed the major export markets for the country, it is important to learn about the outlook for those markets. How long will they remain strong and receptive to the goods of the exporting country?

6. What are the international monetary reserves of the nation?

7. To what international organizations, such as the IMF (International Monetary Fund), does the country belong? This could be a major strong point, since such an organization could provide a further source of revenues for the country.

8. What is the trend of the nation's population? Is there structural unemployment?

9. What is the basis of the country's industry? Is it a primary industry, such as raw materials, metals, or mining? Or is it mainly a secondary manufacturing economy? Ideally, one does not want to see too heavy a concentration in one area or the other. One should always look for economic diversification.

10. What sectors of the economy contribute most to gross national product? Is there one dominant industry? What is the possibility that an unfavorable change will occur in the general trend or structure of the economy?

11. What are the country's capital investment plans? Do they relate to areas which contribute most to the nation's revenues? If a country plans to spend a lot of money in a new area—not a productive or a profitable way to generate revenues—will it lead to potential problems down the road?

12. What are the major issues addressed in the country's budget?

Have there been budgetary deficits, and if so, how substantial are they? Also, how are these deficits being financed? What is the government expenditure burden per capita? What is the relationship between growth in expenditures and growth in revenues?

13. Does the country have a manageable level of debt outstanding? One clearly would not want a country that is overleveraged, i.e., one that has excessively high debt burdens.

14. One way to determine value for these bonds is to evaluate them in terms of yields on domestic securities. Historically, Yankee bonds generally have provided a good premium over other domestically rated issues. Some of these bonds also offer attractive inducements for investor participation. (For example, most Canadian bonds offer a 15-year call protection, which is much greater than can be obtained on a normal corporate issue in the United States. Most corporates usually have only 5 to 10 years of refunding protection.)

CHAPTER 46

TECHNICAL FEATURES OF BOND RESEARCH

Nancy M. Drucker

One of the most troubling areas for the individual investor is the technical features contained in the bond indenture. Many bondholders have been hurt over the last several years when the high-coupon bonds they owned were called by the issuing company at a dollar price substantially below where the issue was trading in the market.

Bonds are issued with varying lengths of *call protection*: usually a utility issue cannot be refunded (refinanced) for 5 years; an industrial bond carries 10 years of refunding protection; some finance company bonds cannot be called at all for 10 years. This protection is for the benefit of the bondholder. Without it a company would be able to substitute a lower–interest rate bond for a high-coupon bond as soon as interest rates dropped.

Most long-term bonds have *sinking funds* of various types which provide for an orderly retirement of the issue over a period of years. Bonds are callable by the company to satisfy the sinking fund requirement at a price around par ($1000) called a "special redemption price." When a company refunds an issue, it must pay a substantial premium above par. This price is called the "regular redemption price." (See Table 46-1.)

TABLE 46-1   MOST TYPICAL PROVISIONS FOR LONG-TERM CORPORATE
BONDS

	Cannot Be Refunded	Call Prices Start	Sinking Fund, %	Sinking Fund Begins	Typical Long Maturity, Years
Electric Utility	5 years	Immediately	20–60	Year after offering date	25–30
Bell Telephone	5 years	5 years	None	. . . .	30–40
Natural Gas	5 years	Immediately	85–95	5 years	20–25
Finance	10 years	10 years	Seldom	Varies	25
Industrial	10 years	Immediately	90–99	10 years	25
Canadian	15 years	15 years	Invested (bonds can't be called for sinking fund)	. . . .	25

These technical features became crucial to investors in 1971, when Georgia Power called in $7.8 million of its 8⅞ percent–coupon debentures at the "special redemption price." Since this issue still had 3 years of refunding protection left to run, the company's action created a great amount of consternation in the market place, and the price of the bonds fell significantly. For the first time, investors became aware that sinking funds can operate at this special price, *which usually does not have any refunding protection.*

Georgia Power was able to call in the bonds before refunding protection expired by using what is called a "blanket" or "funnel" sinking fund, a provision written into the indenture. This particular provision allowed Georgia Power to meet all its sinking fund requirements on numerous outstanding securities by calling the securities of one particular issue, which in this case was the issue with the highest coupon. This unusual development created quite a stir in the bond market and hastened the day of the importance of analyzing technical features.

Further havoc resulted in 1977, when Florida Power and Light called in half of its highest-yielding bond issue, using another provision in the indenture called a "maintenance fund provision," written to insure that the company maintains the property and other assets securing its bond issues. Each utility is generally required to spend a certain amount of its revenues each year on maintenance. And if this maintenance figure is not met, the deficiency may be made up by calling bonds, again, at the special redemption price *without* refunding protection. When the oil embargo occurred and oil prices quadrupled, the revenues of utilities with fuel adjustment clauses skyrocketed. Thus, their maintenance fund requirements also jumped, and deficiencies were created. At this writing, four companies have called portions of their highest-yielding issues, using this provision, three of them through money raised at lower interest cost than the issues called. The investors not only lost their high-yielding investments, but also many of them lost their capital gains when the market price of these issues plummeted.

In order to be protected from such developments, investors should keep in mind the following considerations when contemplating a bond purchase:

1. What kind of call protection does the bond have? If it is noncallable for a period of time, a high-coupon investment is safe from call. If it is nonrefundable, be aware that the company will probably refinance the high-coupon bonds as soon as refunding protection expires and call them in.
2. It's important to remember that most issues of bonds can be called prior to the expiration of refunding protection if the company has excess cash in its treasury. Such a call, however, is always done at the regular redemption price (the higher one), so that the investor will at least receive a premium price if his bonds are called.
3. Consider buying discount bonds especially during periods of lackluster markets. The issuing company is unlikely to call bonds having lower coupons, and the capital gain is built in when the issue is redeemed for $1000 at maturity.

SECTION THREE

TAX-EXEMPT SECURITIES

INTRODUCTION

Tax-Exempt
Research Department

In analyzing the outlook for the credit of a tax-exempt security, one should focus most of one's attention on the past, present, and future ability of the issuer to generate cash flow. Most rating services and credit evaluation services tend to concentrate on the issuer's balance sheet, which is not the most effective method and one which should be avoided.

There are two basic types of tax-exempt securities: general obligation bonds, and revenue bonds. We will take each one and discuss it at length. The cash flow potential of revenue bonds is generally easier to analyze, because the system is relatively closed by the defined revenue stream. One can work from historical figures and/or estimate that revenues should increase at thus-and-so level, and thus one can evaluate whether that revenue flow will be sufficient to service the prical and interest payments of the bonds. Generally speaking, the more times that debt service is covered by the revenues pledged to the payment of a revenue bond, the better the bond tends to be.

On the other hand, many investors feel more secure with general obligation bonds. States, which are the major issuers of general obligation bonds, are considered to have relatively unlimited taxing authority and substantial resources. Thus, many investors used to think that these were safer investments than revenue bonds. But the debacle of New York City and the related problems which affected New York State have eroded that viewpoint. It is now a good question whether a state actually does have the ability to raise tax revenues at will, and whether it does have superior net resources at its disposal.

UNCOMMON FEATURE

Do your bonds have what is called the "invested sinking fund"? This feature, which was used until arbitrage regulations forbade further issues so secured, enables the municipality to make a balloon payment at maturity (i.e., to make most of the repayment at maturity) but to pay slightly lower interest, because the municipality must set up reserves to meet that balloon payment by investing the funds in U.S. government securities. In a sense, once the reserve reaches a certain level, these bonds represent a form of tax-exempt securities backed by the U.S. government.

CHAPTER 47

GENERAL OBLIGATION BONDS

Joan R. Perry

Karen A. Hessing

Charles E. F. Sandmel

In analyzing the credit of a general obligation bond, one should consider the following factors:

ECONOMICS

1. What is the wealth of the area? What is the gross state product? What are the significant economic trends?
2. What's the trend of personal income? This is important, because personal income is a powerful indicator of economic strength and, viewed over time, can reveal strong basic trends. Income is also a major fiscal resource of state governments and, therefore, is the standard against which debt and taxes are compared. If income is rising more rapidly than in the nation and/or region as a whole, favorable shifts in economic base composition are a strong possibility. Growth in consumption can be expected, as can growth in government revenues from sales and income taxes.

     What is the relationship between population and personal

income? Ideally these two should be increasing together at somewhat the same rate.

Per capita income below the national average can have both favorable and unfavorable aspects. On the negative side, low incomes are associated with low-quality public education and, consequently, low-skilled labor. More positively, low per capita incomes are often associated with a low level and a limited scope of government services, and a low debt burden. Usually, low-income states historically have been characterized by low wages and below-average public and private unionization, which have been attractive to specific types of firms. It is currently unclear whether and at what point low but rising incomes explain increased pressures for unionization and for better and broader public services.

(Personal income consists of the sum of private and government wages, salaries, and other payments for labor; farm and nonfarm proprietors' income; and interest, rent, royalties, dividends, and transfer payments; less personal contributions for social insurance. Per capita personal income is total personal income divided by total population. Total and per capita income are measured in current dollars, and the primary source used is the U.S. Bureau of Economic Analysis. Total personal income for the United States is the sum of state total incomes and excludes the income of District of Columbia residents and the income disbursed to government personnel stationed abroad.)

3. What's the trend of employment? Employment is a powerful analytic tool, and nonagricultural employment figures are more useful for comparison than total employment, because the agricultural job data component of total employment is often unreliable or unavailable. Relatively high growth in nonagricultural jobs is a favorable sign, and increases at rates faster than population growth may indicate positive changes in labor force participation.

(Nonagricultural employment consists of total wage and salary employment in mining, contract construction, manufacturing, transportation and public utilities, wholesale and retail trade, finance, insurance and real estate, services, and government. Government employment includes federal, state, and local employees. Employment data are available from *Employ-*

ment and Earnings, published by the U.S. Bureau of Labor Statistics.)

4. What's the trend of government employment? Government employment, a portion of nonagricultural employment, indicates the contribution of public jobs to employment. If government employment is growing faster than private sector employment, there may be a new commitment to higher public service standards, or government may be taking up the slack in a deteriorating economic base. Similarly, relatively high proportions of government jobs within nonagricultural employment may indicate a potentially harmful economic mix.

One must be sure to watch the trends in government employment versus the trend of employment in the private sector. A very large increase in government employment could present problems, as it may mean deficits and financing gimmickry later on.

Is state and local government employment growing faster than nonagricultural employment for the same area? In other words, is the area increasingly taxing the private sector to support an expanding bureaucracy?

What is the government employment burden (state, local, and federal employees as a percentage of nonagricultural employees)? Is it higher than the average for the United States? If so, that may present a problem.

In analyzing the answers you get for questions 1–4, be sure to compare the figures you get with those for other credits. If you're talking about an investment in a city, you would want to compare the city to the state, the state to the region, and the region to other regions and to the United States as a whole. The purpose of such comparisons is to judge whether the area you're interested in is doing better or worse than the trend in other credits. It is important to remember, however, that it takes an unusual city not to go in the general direction of its region and of the United States economy. Therefore, if the general economy is going up in terms of its major economic trends and your city is going down, you should have some serious questions about the viability of the city as a potential investment.

5. What are the sources of revenues and what provides the impetus to the local economy? (For example, petroleum is the backbone

of the economy in the state of Louisiana, and an understanding of the outlook for Louisiana would necessitate evaluating the future for the oil business there. Therefore, in analyzing the outlook for the locale, you want to analyze the health of the industries which are important to the economy of that area.)

6. What are the energy and water resources of the area? What is the current and future demand for energy and water versus its availability? Does it seem that there will be a shortfall of either some time in the future?

7. What is the quality of the labor force? If you have consistently high unemployment, you can probably assume that there is structural unemployment, and therefore a high quotient of low-skilled workers. Furthermore, unemployment figures may understate the problem, because many people may be too discouraged to enter the work force and others may have given up looking for jobs.

8. What are the relative growth rates of the eight major industrial categories: mining, wholesale and retail trade, finance, construction, manufacturing, transportation and utilities services, insurance and real estate, and government? You want to know the growth rates of those categories over the past 10 to 15 years in the state, the region, and the United States. Then you'll be able to compare the growth of these key sectors in the area you're analyzing with trends elsewhere.

9. What are the big-growth industries in the nation as a whole? Are any of these located in the area you're studying?

10. Where is exciting new research being done? Typically, an area which is prominent in research and development will generate jobs and employment as ideas move off the drawing board.

11. How did the area do in the last recession? How did it perform in comparison to other states?

12. What is the structure of employment? Is it diversified or concentrated? Is the area dependent on one industry? (Durable goods manufacturing concentration during a period of expansion is generally good, because it tends to generate high personal income and growth.)

POLITICS

1. What are the values of the electorate? Are they conservative or are they liberal? Do they want and support big public spenders?
2. What is the level of scandal in the area? This is something of an indication of what the electorate will tolerate, and whether there is graft, corruption, and waste in the government.
3. What is the level of conflict between persons or groups within a locale? Are the political leaders playing one group off against another and arousing tensions and hostilities?
4. What kind of emphasis does the area place on its outlook? In other words, how does it view itself and how is it trying to promote itself? Is the credit trying to promote itself for industrial development, retirement, or tourism? If so, what are the ramifications of that type of development in terms of availability of water, energy, roads, etc.? In other words, different types of growth require different resources and public services and fit in better in different areas.
5. What is the general quality of management in the public sector?
6. What is the outlook for federal aid? If debt burdens are high and public spending is high, substantial federal aid could alter the financial situation of the area significantly.

   Federal aid is an important and growing source of revenue for states and localities. Relatively high levels and growth indicate a shift of national resources into a state, and relatively low levels and growth highlight a redistribution of state resources to other jurisdictions. Historically this shift has been from the Northeast to the South, and a dampening or reversal would be particularly significant. Federal aid, although a major policy tool, is only one of several redistribution devices that are used by Congress. This set of tools includes direct federal expenditures, especially for defense, highways, and agriculture, and various loan guarantee programs that favor suburban and rural development. Federal aid itself refers to amounts received from the federal government for expenditures by state and local governments.

7. Politics is the wild card in the deck here and must always be watched carefully, for politicians may promise more than the local economy can support.

DEMOGRAPHICS

1. What are the population trends? Is the area growing through migration or internal growth, or both? Population is a fundamental indicator of economic health. Growth in population is associated with increases in retail sales and with growth in consumer-related jobs. Population increases attributable to migration are often additionally associated with construction and durables-manufacturing job expansion. Growth at faster rates than the national average indicates an increasing share of the United States market. Similarly, population growth exceeding regional rates indicates favorable economic shifts within the region.

    (Population for each state, for purposes of this discussion, is the total resident population, estimated for July 1 of every year. The basic source of data is *Current Population Reports* (Series P-25) published by the Bureau of the Census. Population for the United States is the sum of the populations of all the states and excludes residents of the District of Columbia.)

2. What are the current and likely future sociological trends? Are certain fundamental changes taking place which may affect how money is spent by local governments or how it is collected? For example, is there a general rural-to-urban shift within the state or region?

3. What's the demand for education, schools, and highways?

4. Since population is a key factor, you should be aware of birth and death rates, as well as migration from outside the state or region, changes in the rural/urban mix, and shifts in the age distribution of residents.

    Starting in 1970, all of the states in the Southeast with the exception of Louisiana began experiencing migration. If such a trend starts, it's important to consider why such migration is taking place. Is it happening because of a change in the perception of opportunities? If there really are opportunities, then the trend will continue, and the original jump in employment will soon be followed by an increase in secondary industries, such as retailing, construction, and health care.

FINANCES

1. What is going on in the area of court decisions? Sometimes a court decision can mandate major spending, which might affect the finances of the area. (For example, some recent court decisions required that money be spent on improving prison conditions in certain states.)

2. What is the quality of accounting and reporting? How good are the financial controls? Is it possible for the government to back-charge and manipulate revenues and expenditures? What is the adequacy of disclosure? Without accurate accounting and reporting, any type of financial analysis can be imprecise and misleading.

3. What is the status of the pension system? How well funded is it, and how large are the unfunded pension liabilities? What is the quality of the pension portfolio? (For instance, if a pension portfolio is invested in low-grade issues, a serious problem could emerge at some point in the future.)

4. Learn whether the locale is made up of new or old buildings. Neither one is necessarily bad or good. Old buildings require major expenditures for repairs and refurbishments, while a new area could require major expenditures in order to build the necessary infrastructure. A newly developing area could suffer from mistakes in the placement of various facilities, and sometimes poor public control over the patterns of development leads to traffic congestion and decreased amenities for living.

5. What does the locality spend its money on? Be particularly sensitive to a major change in the capital budget, especially if there is a dramatic increase in borrowing for projects.

6. What are the tax and debt burdens of the area? Is the tax burden so high that it is discouraging economic growth? The way to calculate this number is to take general revenues (excluding enterprise sales) and divide that by personal income (excluding those welfare payments which are funded from area taxes).

   Debt burden indicates the extent that prior borrowing limits future spending flexibility. Trends in debt burden can reveal an urbanizing credit, a deteriorating credit position, emerging reliance on borrowing for operations, and a credit with insufficient capital flexibility at a time when public facilities require replacement or expansion. Relatively low and stable debt patterns are generally favorable unless lack of adequate infrastructure (e.g., highways, schools, mass transit, libraries, and hospitals) is retarding economic growth. Per capita debt figures facilitate comparisons among states and within a state over time.

(Debt burden is calculated by dividing long-term debt outstanding by adjusted personal income. Adjusted personal income excludes welfare transfer payments paid from area taxes.)

7. What is the reliance on the federal government? Generally speaking, too heavy a reliance on the U.S. government represents a vulnerability. On the other hand, money from all levels of government tends to represent stability during a recession.

8. What is the trend of credit ratings, both in the particular area you're analyzing and in general obligation bonds everywhere? If there is a trend taking place there, whether it's downgrading or upgrading, is it likely to continue?

9. What are state and local direct expenditures (i.e., excluding intergovernmental transfers)? What is public expenditure per capita in the state? Is the ratio above or below the national average? Government expenditure levels are particularly revealing of the extent of government participation in the area economy. If expenditures are increasing more than revenues from own sources and federal aid, increasing reliance on debt and accounting gimmicks is a possibility. Rising per capita expenditures may indicate broader-scope and higher-quality public services, increasing welfare burdens, and/or rising public employee compensation. Below-average expenditures that show a sudden surge may indicate a shift to an urban economy characterized by high-skilled industries. Per capita figures facilitate comparisons among jurisdictions and within a state over time.

(State and local direct expenditures are payments to employees, suppliers, contractors, beneficiaries, and other final recipients of government payments, that is, all expenditures other than intergovernmental transfers. The main sources of expenditure, revenue, federal aid, and debt data are *State Government Finances* (GF3) and *Governmental Finances* (GF5) of the U.S. Bureau of the Census.)

10. What is the relationship of government debt to personal income? Is personal income increasing faster than debt, or the

reverse? Ideally, you'd like to see personal income increasing at least as fast as debt. On the other hand, if debt-supported spending is increasing much faster than personal income, there may be problems down the road.

11. How heavily is personal income taxed? How responsive to income growth are total revenues?

12. Who are the major taxpayers and employers? How healthy are the major sectors of the economy? Any company that represents more than 5 percent of assessed value of the area should be investigated to determine the potential for adverse effects on government revenues.

13. What is the rate of payout of the debt? Ideally, you'd want to see at least 25 percent of principal paid off in 5 years and 50 percent in 10 years.

14. What percentage of expenditures goes to debt services? If debt payout is slow and expenditures for debt service are high, the ability to pay for future capital and operating expenses is limited. A high proportion of spending on debt service is not necessarily bad if it takes place in a growing community which is putting in a large amount of infrastructure. In contrast, if the economy is losing population and the tax base is eroding at the same time that debt is increasing, a credit problem may be emerging.

15. What is the current real property tax collection rate? A way to get to the bottom of this is to ask how much of this year's tax levy was collected in the period when it was supposed to be collected. (Although more of the taxes may eventually be collected, it could take several years.) A 90 percent collection of levy in the current year is a reasonable expectation. Also ask what has been the collection rate over the past several years and whether there is a reserve for uncollectible amounts.

CHAPTER 48

REVENUE BONDS

Joan R. Perry

Karen A. Hessing

Charles E. F. Sandmel

SOME GENERAL POINTS TO REMEMBER ABOUT ALL REVENUE BONDS

1. Learn the exact terms of the indenture agreement. Is the pledge of revenues for gross revenues, or for net revenues? (See #2 below.) Is it a senior or a subordinate pledge of revenues? In other words, does your issue have first call on the revenues, or does some other issue, political body, operating expense, or whatever, have first call?

2. If the revenue pledge is gross revenues, is it reasonable to expect that the municipality will pay debt service before operating and maintenance expenses? In other words, will the bondholders be paid before trade bills, employee's salaries, etc.? Ideally, you want assurances that ballooning operating expenses won't divert so much revenue that your issue can't be serviced adequately, or a covenant that the issuer will maintain a fee structure sufficient to generate a minimum level of coverage by *net* revenues.

   At the very least, there should be some general specification as to what the payment order will be. A typical order is operating and maintenance expenses, then interest, then principal, then sinking fund payments, then allocation to reserves.

3. What is the level of revenue coverage of debt service? You will probably want a minimum of 110 percent coverage, which is usually considered thin, and you should even look carefully at 120 percent to 150 percent; anything above 150 percent provides a reasonable margin for the unexpected. In recent years, Moody's Investor Service has published median coverage ratios for several categories of enterprises issuing revenue bonds. These are a useful beginning guideline.

4. Is there a restraint on the issue of additional bonds if certain financial tests are not met? Such a restraint gives you some security and prevents additional issuance of debt by an enterprise which is already financially overextended. (The issuance of additional bonds could dilute the stream of revenue coverage for your issue, and thus any constraint on additional bonds is a good thing for existing bondholders.) An additional bond test requiring that last year's revenues provide a certain level of coverage of future debt is preferable to a test demanding merely projected coverage.

5. Is there a debt service reserve fund? This is money put aside by the issuer as a reserve against future debt service. There are three basic types of reserve funds, all subject to variation: a reserve fund that is equal to next year's debt service requirement (i.e., one year's security); a reserve equal to the maximum annual debt service over the life of the bond; and a reserve equal to the total outstanding principal requirement (bonds so secured are "collateralized"). Naturally, the greater the proportionate amount of the reserve fund, the greater the security for investors. For all debt service reserves, those capitalized from issuer contribution or bond proceeds are preferable to those to be funded from future revenues.

FEASIBILITY STUDIES

As investors become more cautious and demand more disclosure, the feasibility study becomes more important to revenue bond analysis. A feasibility study is an analysis of the economic factors influencing the future ability of an enterprise to generate cash flow; it includes projected balance sheets, revenue and expenditure tables, and hard projections of future cash flow and cash positions. Feasibility studies are usually prepared by CPA firms and engineering firms.

Feasibility studies vary both in their inherent quality and in the extent to which they indicate the consultants' level of confidence with the projections. Quality can be estimated from the name and reputation of the firm which prepared the study, although even "big eight" accounting firms and first-rank consulting engineers can produce unsatisfactory work. Level of assurance can be determined by scrutinizing the introductory letter. Look for an assertion that the consultant has reviewed the client's assumptions and found them reasonable. Check any items on which the consultant offers no opinion; if the consultant provides no opinion as to the feasibility of the project, or does not state that, without major qualifications, he or she believes the enterprise will be able to generate sufficient cash flow to cover debt service, caution is surely advised.

There are many different types of tax-exempt revenue bonds. A discussion of the most important ones follows.

PUBLIC POWER REVENUE BONDS

Public power revenue bonds constitute the largest dollar amount outstanding of all types of revenue bonds. They are issued by government-owned electric utility authorities, departments, and districts. In analyzing these issues one should keep in mind the following considerations:

1. Evaluate the issue as you would a normal utility bond. (See Chapter 40.) To what extent is it subject to regulation? Is it controlled by the state regulatory authorities? (In some cases it will not be.) Where does its power come from? What is the status of its fuel supply? For how long are contracts? Is there an escalator clause for fuel price increases? Where does the fuel come from? If the fuel is mainly coal, what is the sulfur content? Does the coal meet Environmental Protection Agency standards? What is the magnitude of the utility's future construction costs? What is the outlook for spending requirements for the next 5 years? What is the historical net margin for the utility? To what extent was debt service covered last year? What are the growth trends in power usage in the area? (Rapid growth necessitates heavy con-

struction. Slow, steady growth is to be preferred because it spreads out construction costs.) How good have the issuer's past growth estimates proven to be?

2. You should also rely heavily on regional analysis and the economic outlook for the region where the utility is located. (See Chapter 47.)

3. Is the utility management expecting growth in population and electricity usage that seems unreasonable to you on the basis of common sense or regional analysis? Be sure to do some sort of independent check on growth projections. (Be wary of any figures provided by a chamber of commerce; they tend to be overly optimistic.) The best figures for population growth come from the U.S. Census Department.

4. What is the economy of the service area like? What industries serve the area and what are their prospects? (For example, Youngstown, Ohio, is dominated by Youngstown Sheet and Tube Company, while Puget Sound and San Diego are dominated by the defense industry.) Ideally, you want industrial and employment diversification, which will spread risks.

5. Look closely at the utility's feasibility study and contrast its conclusion with your own study of regional and demographic trends. Some credence can be placed on the report of a reputable consultant, but an independent check will increase the confidence with which you can invest.

6. How does the utility compare with the rest of the industry? Is it outperforming or underperforming the industry? What's the trend in its net profit margins?

UNIVERSITY REVENUE BONDS

There are four types of university revenue bonds: dormitory revenue bonds, tuition revenue bonds, collateralized bonds, and tax-supported university bonds. In analyzing these types of bonds, you should ask the following questions:

1. What is pledged as security?
2. What is the demand for the university? How broad is it in terms of curriculum? A comprehensive university often is preferable to a

2-year junior college. What is the ratio of applicants to available places?

3. What is the trend of enrollments for the portion of the university by which the bonds are secured?

4. What kind of reserves for future debt service is established in the bond indenture?

5. How substantial is the university's endowment?

6. If the issuer is a state university, will the state have an obligation to support the bonds? Despite recent bad press on "moral obligation" issues, which have reserve replenishment mechanisms requiring legislative appropriations, these seem to be gaining in stature, because states realize that their good name is directly linked to an issue which they back in this manner. If there is not a moral obligation, has the legislature provided some other kind of backing for the issue?

AIRPORT REVENUE BONDS

The most important thing for one to remember about airport bonds is the quality of the lien, which is key in evaluating the quality of airports. In understanding airport credit, one should bear in mind the following considerations:

1. Do holders of other bonds have a prior lien?

2. What is the trend of the airport's market share of total airport traffic? How close are competing airports?

3. What is the economy of the area like? (For example, certain airport service areas are experiencing stronger economic trends than others.)

4. Do the leases of the airlines in the airport run as long as the bonds? (The leases could expire before the bonds are due, and they might not be renewed.)

5. What power does the airport have to raise rents? (This, too, is critical, since operating expenses for running the airport can be expected to increase.)

6. Is there any tax support available for the airport?

7. Has the airport building already been constructed, or is the current debt issue for an addition? What's the level of competition

among local airports? (For example, Newark has a fine new airport, but it is underutilized because of the dominance of JFK and LaGuardia Airports.)

8. What's the quality of access to the airports? Is there a public transportation link? What's the distance from the town to the airport? And to other airports?

HOSPITAL REVENUE BONDS

There are certain risks inherent in hospital revenue bonds which should be discussed first:

1. Certain cost-containment legislation has been proposed, and could affect the future profitability of hospitals.
2. There's no guarantee that medicare or medicaid will continue to provide 60 to 80 percent of hospital costs. On the other hand, the odds that medicare and medicaid will be cut back are very low, because the increasing percentage of voters who are over 65 makes public financing of medical care a politically sensitive issue.

Here are the questions you should ask before you make an investment in hospital revenue bonds:

THE BOND ISSUE

1. What are the terms of the indenture?
2. Is interest capitalized? (One wants it to be.)
3. What is the mortgage on? Is it on hospital equipment or is it on bricks and mortar, or both?
4. One must be sure to analyze the feasibility study. Are the projections realistic? In evaluating projected usage into the future, one should look into the following aspects: What is the competition with other hospitals? What is the market share of the hospital in that geographical location? (Generally the larger the hospital is in comparison to its neighbors, the better off the investment.) What is the affiliation of the hospital? Is it connected with a nursing school, a medical college, a clinic with geographical or contrac-

tual ties, or some other institution? It's generally wiser to buy the preeminent hospital in a given area. A monopoly is best of all.

5. What's the purpose of the bond? (Generally speaking, an expansion is better than a relocation, as there's no certainty that patients and doctors will follow the hospital to a new location.)

6. Does the hospital have certification from the local health systems agency? If it doesn't, the hospital may not be able to get Blue Cross reimbursement.

7. One should remember that hospital bonds are not as liquid as some other bonds, because there is a relatively small secondary market for them. It's often hard to get annual reports from hospitals if they have not been recently to market.

FINANCES OF THE HOSPITALS

1. Who pays patients' bills? If it's largely a self-paying hospital usage, then one may have more bad debt problems than one would if patients were mostly covered by insurance.

2. What is the debt load of the hospital? An average debt load per bed was $50,000 in 1977. More than $80,000 debt load per bed may legitimately cause concern. (On the other hand, if the hospital is connected with a teaching facility, a higher debt per bed ratio is allowable, since the cost of such a facility is usually inordinately high.)

3. What is the occupancy rate of the existing facility? For a 300-bed hospital or larger, one prefers at least a 75 percent occupancy rate. On the other hand, smaller hospitals may be organized to operate with a 55 percent to 60 percent occupancy rate.

4. What are the services provided by the hospital? Does the hospital have a local monopoly or referral on any particular service? Ideally one would like to see a good amount of specialty; a general practitioner emphasis entails greater exposure to competition.

5. How many doctors are there in relation to the number of beds? What is the turnover rate of doctors? A high turnover rate indicates something may be wrong with the management or the location. What is the average age of the doctors? (Generally speaking, the younger the doctors, up to a point, the better, because they are more likely to provide a long-term source of

admissions.) How many of the doctors are certified by the local board in their specialty?

6. What is the ratio of coverage of future debt service by historical revenues? Take the most conservative approach here, and for a large bond issue, you want a minimum of 1-to-1 coverage, and ideally 1.5 to 1.

FEASIBILITY OF THE HOSPITAL

1. Is the area already overbedded? If so, then occupancy and revenue projections will be hard to achieve.
2. One should look very closely at the financial projections and feasibility study made by a construction company. (Was the feasibility study done by a reputable firm? What is the track record of that firm? Are the criteria used in the study conservative and reasonable? Is the firm expecting a large hospital rate increase, which may not be possible or realistic?) One should look ahead for at least 5 years and analyze the debt service coverage which the firm is projecting for the new project. Ideally, in the first 2 years after the new project has been completed, one would like to see an estimate of revenues covering debt service by a ratio of at least 1.8 times.
3. One certainly doesn't want a surplus of beds upon completion, so one should ask whether any other hospitals in the area are planning new construction.
4. Are the doctors in favor of the hospital and will they send their patients there? What is the supply of doctors in the area? How much of the hospital's business is done by what percentage of the doctors? (For example, if there are fifteen doctors in a hospital and five of them are over 60 and account for 50 percent of the new patients, one should be somewhat cautious. If those doctors were to retire, the hospital could lose quite a bit of business in the future.)
5. Are the services provided by the hospital appropriate for the service area? (For example, extensive maternity services are not likely to have high utilization in a retirement community.)
6. Is the hospital associated with a nursing school? A nursing school is a plus, because the hospital benefits from a low-cost supply of nurses.
7. What are the demographics in the area? Is it growing?

8. One should avoid investing in a hospital that may be overbuilding; a Taj Mahal image, where the hospital is buying *all* the latest equipment and building many unnecessary expensive additions, is a negative for investors, because luxury facilities and supersophisticated equipment may not gain adequate usage.
9. One of the ways of getting good information on analyzing the hospital facility is to get in touch with a hospital administrator, who can help an investor analyze the viability of a new project.

TAX-EXEMPT HOUSING BONDS

State housing agencies were set up to facilitate the expansion of low- and moderate-income housing, which is achieved by issuing tax-exempt housing bonds to the general public and funneling the proceeds into the purchase of mortgages. There are two broad types of housing authority bonds: multifamily and single-family.

MULTIFAMILY

Here are some things to consider before investing in a multifamily housing bond:

1. One should look for a federal guarantee, or a guarantee by the Federal Housing Administration. Ideally, one would prefer 100 percent coverage for the entire project in the event of default.
2. One would prefer to see a project with 100 percent Section 8 assistance, as opposed to Section 236.
3. A lot of state agencies have a reserve replenishment mechanism requiring an appropriation by the state legistature ("moral obligation"). Part of the bond proceeds will be credited to a reserve account, which the state has an obligation to keep at a certain level.

   Although such moral obligation features have suffered some criticism, they offer valuable protection for investors. To date, states have acted in every instance where bond reserves have fallen low enough to trigger the replenishment mechanism. Moral obligation backing is likely to continue to be valuable, because states realize the importance of honoring commitments to bondholders to protect the states' own credit standing and access to the market place. In evaluating a state's moral obligation mechanism, one needs to know whether the resources of the state are sufficient to provide assistance to its bonding authorities.

4. In summary, then, one wants to look for as many layers of security as possible, be it a federal government guarantee or a state moral obligation.

5. Also, one should look for an authorization limit on the amount of new debt that can be raised for similar types of projects.

6. Finally, many states have set up a loan loss reserve to protect these issues in the event of default. Ideally one should buy only bonds which have such a loan loss reserve.

7. The housing agency's portfolio of multifamily developments should not be dominated by large mortgage loans to a few projects; many small loans are preferable.

SINGLE-FAMILY

Generally, the bond market perceives single-family housing bonds as a safer investment than multifamily housing bonds, because individuals who own houses are thought to be more reliable financially than persons living in a multifamily housing complex. Here again, one should look for FHA or VA insurance, or some other kind of government guarantee for the project. Another acceptable alternative is a combination of FHA, VA, and private mortgage insurance. A typical arrangement is for private mortgage insurance to cover 20 percent of the value of the mortgage. Here again, look for a state reserve replenishment mechanism and a mortgage reserve fund.

TURNPIKES AND TOLLWAYS

In order to analyze turnpike and tollway bonds, one should consider the following:

1. Debt service coverage is usually very high for turnpikes and tollways; recently, however, construction cost overruns and traffic falloffs have impaired coverage of bonds that appeared well protected only a few years ago.

2. One should learn about the trend of usage of the turnpike or tollway. Is there any existing or planned competition? Is a new

interstate highway (which has no toll) likely to be competitive with the turnpike or tollway?

3. What is the lien that bondholders have on revenues? Is it a first, a second, or a third? (Clearly, a first lien is superior.)
4. Will there be enough automobile traffic to generate revenues adequate to meet debt service? What is the outlook for gasoline prices? Are tolls at or near practical limits?
5. What is the quality of maintenance? What has been happening to maintenance unit costs in recent years? Is the roadway in good repair? Are deposits from revenues being made to maintenance and repair funds on a reasonable basis?

APPENDIX I

CHANGES IN THE AUTOMOBILE OVER THE NEXT DECADE

Ronald A. Glantz

Government safety, pollution, and mileage regulations are going to lead to huge, and perhaps revolutionary, changes in the automobile industry. There is no question that Detroit is going to meet the mandated mileage requirements. The penalties are too severe not to. For example, in 1978 the automobile companies are to be fined $5 per car for every tenth of a mile that their fleet average is below 18 mpg. The penalty could be increased to as much as $10, beginning in the 1982 model year. This may not sound like much, but if Ford's United States sales and fleet average were to be the same in 1978 as in 1977 (2.6 million cars and 16.1 mpg), then Ford would be fined $250 million. Since this fine can't be deducted from income taxes, Ford's earnings would be reduced by $2.10 a share. Similarly, in 1985 a 22 mpg average (a 37 percent improvement over Ford's current average) with a $10 fine would lead to a $1.4 billion fine. This is why Ford's capital spending jumped from $1 billion in 1976 to $2.8 billion in 1978 and is forecast at $3.5 billion in 1979. It is cheaper to meet government regulations than to pay that kind of fine.

New safety and pollution regulations will make it even harder for

Detroit to meet the mandated improvement in mileage. So it is obvious that these laws will create opportunities for new technologies, materials, and manufacturing techniques.

There are six major ways of improving mileage:

Substituting lighter materials
Miniaturizing components
Improving aerodynamics
Reducing tire friction
Reducing power
Improving engine efficiency

Let us evaluate each one.

MATERIALS

The substitution of aluminum and plastics for iron and steel is already well advanced and expected to continue.

The average 1985 car will be 8 percent aluminum, versus 3 percent in 1978. The reasons why aluminum won't make greater inroads are that it is more expensive than steel and that there are problems in processing, welding, corrosion, and surface finish.

Plastics are expected to account for 8.5 percent of a 1985 car's weight, as opposed to 5.3 percent today. Here there are problems in fastening, finishing, and production speed. (A production rate half that of steel means that twice as much plant and equipment is required.)

Other materials will also become less important. Glass will become thinner, lighter, and stronger. Tires will become lighter. Gas tanks and engines will become smaller, requiring less fluid capacity.

TYPICAL CAR

Material	Weight, lb		% Change, ±
	1978	1985	
Plastic	185	225 to 230	+22 to +24
Aluminum	108	200 to 240	+85 to +122
Steel	2,083	1,500 (1,500)	−28
Iron	573	350 (350)	−39
Other	524	380 to 425	−27 to −19
Total	3,473	2,655 to 2,745	21 to 24% less

Aluminum

Aluminum has gradually won applications in such areas as bumpers, brake drums, wheels, master cylinders, transmission covers, hoods, trunks, cylinder heads, manifolds, and air conditioning compressors. Despite the well-publicized problems of the Vega engine, Honda and Renault use aluminum engine blocks exclusively, and the $30,000 Porsche 928 has an aluminum V 8. Ford plans to die-cast aluminum V 6 engine blocks by 1982. An aluminum block would probably weigh half as much as a 400-pound iron block. Hayes-Albion predicts that aluminum casting will become a $1 billion market by the mid-1980s.

Aluminum water pumps, aluminum honeycomb door components, and aluminum radiators are also being developed.

Plastics

Plastics are ubiquitous in the interior of the American car. They are used for seats, trim, steering wheels, dashboards, and heating ducts. Plastic is also used for battery cases, oil pans, light-duty camshafts, and covers for compressors, electronic devices, gasoline tanks, and pumps.

Many front ends of cars are being made of fiberglass-reinforced plastic. Fender liners and sight shields are also being made of plastic. McCord Corporation expects urethane bumpers to be on at least 20 percent of all American cars in 1979 as opposed to 6 percent in 1977. It wouldn't be surprising if plastic bumpers existed on 80 percent of all cars by 1985. This would require the development of an inexpensive and durable chrome finish, since Detroit believes that large cars look better with brightwork. (All plastic bumpers currently in production are colored.)

Detroit has to think specifically of plastic when designing a part, rather than just interchanging it with other materials. Plastics can cost ten times as much per pound and twice as much per piece as steel or zinc. One piece of plastic, however, can replace ten or fifteen metal parts, enabling the total cost to be less, once labor is taken into consideration. For example, a plastic-metal–composite door that weighs half as much as and costs about 20 percent less than a conventional steel door has been proposed.

It takes a while to educate engineers about plastic's advantages and to convince the public that a properly designed plastic part can be just as safe as metal. Most of the near-term developments will be in areas not thought of as requiring strength. For instance:

The 1978 Corvette has an all-plastic seat, including the adjustment mechanism. Eventually all seats will have a thin layer of foam on a hard shell, reducing thickness to obtain additional room.

In 1980, high-strength plastic will be used on Ford radiator supports and Pontiac transmission supports.

Plastics are being considered for transmission valve bodies, fiberglass-reinforced wheels, bumper reinforcements, and side windows.

The next step will be to use plastics for body components, such as roofs and doors. The difficulty is less with plastic's engineering characteristics than with molding techniques affecting surface finish and production speed.

The cost of finishing to cover up "valleys" and other imperfections has prevented the use of low-cost sheet molding compounds for large body panels. GM, however, has developed a polyurethane primer which is said to eliminate or cover up surface imperfections when applied prior to assembly. This primer enables use of a one-piece front header panel made of fiberglass-reinforced polyester on GM's 1979 compact Pontiac Phoenix. The panel contains the hood extension, grille surround, and fender extension, and is said to weigh 7 to 12 pounds less than the metal assembly it replaces.

In addition to front header panels, GM is looking at roofs, station wagon tailgates, deck lids, doors, hoods, and other body panels as potential applications for in-mold–coated SMC. GM reportedly will have a glass-reinforced SMC station wagon tailgate on its 1980 model Oldsmobile 88. It will weigh 36 percent less, replace 7 steel parts, and obviously eliminate corrosion problems.

Plastics, perhaps reinforced by carbon fibers, may even be used on engines. These advanced plastic composites probably will make their debut in push rods, connecting rods, oil pans, rocker arms, water pump impellers, engine brackets, or other moving parts where high endurance limits are needed. The weight reductions gained from use of push rods, rocker arms, and connecting rods will permit similar reductions in the crankshaft counterweights, permitting smaller engines with the same power output.

Iron

It isn't always necessary to replace iron or steel with lighter materials. To give an example, Chrysler will chop 105 pounds off its venerable 225–cubic inch six-cylinder engines by 1981 by using thinner iron castings. This is possible because the engine block was built heavier than needed to reduce the chance of breaking during handling and to ensure a low rate of defective casting.

Some castings can even be made hollow.

Steel

Steel itself is also undergoing a change. It is becoming thinner, lighter, and stronger. However, thinner steel requires more antirust protection. Zinc is currently being used to protect the unpainted side of steel sheet used in areas especially susceptible to rusting. If thinner steel becomes pervasive, zinc will likely have to be applied to both sides of the sheet, even underneath paint, which itself will be thinner to reduce weight. Chemicals may be developed which protect even better than zinc.

A similar problem is also posed by aluminum, which corrodes when in contact with certain other metals.

Graphite

Some materials which are currently very expensive may also be used in cars. For example, the price of high-strength–grade carbon or graphite fibers suitable for automotive applications currently ranges from $20 to $32 a pound. Engineers are excited by the fact that advanced composites, such as carbon fiber–reinforced epoxy or polyester, have the potential of reducing automotive component weights by 70 percent or more, compared with 50 percent savings possible with current plastics, 40 to 50 percent savings with aluminum, and 10 to 30 percent savings with current high-strength steel. When the price goes below $10 a pound, graphite should take the place of steel in truck driveshaft and leaf springs. Below $5 a pound, fiber-reinforced composites could even take the place of steel or cast iron in engine push rods, wrist pins, connecting rods, bumpers, driveshaft yokes, hoods, deck lids, transmission supports, frame cross members, and door beams.

Other

Another material substitution already under development is ceramics, which can be used to replace metal in engine parts such as rocker arms, turbocharger and turbine rotors, cylinder liners, heat exchangers, and manifolds. Ceramics could reduce weight in certain applications by 50 percent, provided engineers can figure out a way to avoid its inherent brittleness.

Hydrogen or alcohol may eventually take the place of gasoline. GM prefers methanol because it is compatible with current storage and metering systems and because there are plentiful resources for current needs (methanol can be made from coal). Because methanol provides about half as much energy per gallon as gasoline, fuel tank size would have to be doubled. In addition, the fuel tank and all fuel system components would have to be made of highly corrosion-resistant materials. Ethanol is also a possibility. While expensive, it contains more energy per gallon and has less risk of poisoning than methanol.

COMPONENTS

As far as components are concerned, the major change underway is the fact that engineers are now taking size and weight into consideration. (In the past the emphasis was on ride, comfort, and cost, rather than fuel economy.)

This means that Detroit is going towards (1) more sophisticated designs, (2) components which previously weren't cost-effective, and (3) shaving weight off current parts. For example:

Even though harder to engineer, rack-and-pinion steering is replacing heavier steering systems.

Front-wheel drive is gradually taking over from conventional layouts because it eliminates the weight and space taken up by the driveshaft and rear differential.

Two-speed rear axles could be useful for light trucks. Although the axles would weigh 80 to 100 pounds more, they would improve overall mileage by 5 percent. (The economy axle speed would be used when the truck wasn't loaded.)

Forged gears are replacing cast gears to permit smaller and lighter axles.

Viscous fan drives are being installed in trucks, to obtain 4 to 8 percent fuel savings.

Chrysler offered a lock-up automatic transmission in 1978, which improved fuel economy by 3 to 5 percent.

Another 10 percent improvement in fuel economy is possible with overdrive. Ford will build a four-speed lock-up automatic with overdrive for 1980 models.

Chrysler bought rotary air conditioning compressors for its 1978 models that weighed 20 pounds less than previous compressors.

Speed control devices have jumped in popularity, because they reduce gasoline consumption.

Quartz halogen headlights draw less power, permitting lighter batteries and alternators.

AERODYNAMICS

An aerodynamically efficient car can reduce fuel consumption by at least 5 percent over current designs. It is possible that the surface finish itself can be modified to increase slip.

TIRES

Detroit has asked the tire companies to reduce the noise, weight, and rolling resistance of their tires to improve fuel economy, and to further improve tire life, reliability, and traction.

There don't seem to be any major changes about to take place in tire technology over the next few years. The molded tire would be less expensive to build and might have a lower reject rate. However, molded tires appear to have poor durability, restricting their use to low-speed, lightweight "urban" cars.

The "closed torus" tire developed by Caterpillar and licensed to General Tire may become important by the mid-1980s. A continuously wound loop of wire—similar to a "slinky" toy—is inserted into a rubber tube, which is then encased in rubber. The wound wire deflects like a spring at the point where the tire touches the pavement, distributing tension equally throughout the tire body. This is supposed to enable the tire to double the mileage attained by a steel-belted radial, provide better fuel economy though lower rolling resistance, run flat for considerable distances, and be built completely by machine, reducing the quality control problems of current tires, which are built with at least some hand labor. The problem with this tire is that the new plant it requires would cost several hundred million dollars, and the tire industry is short of capital while long on excess capacity.

Radial tires are the current state of the art. Radials reduce rolling resistance, although they weigh more than previous tires, and last longer.

But this doesn't mean the radial can't be improved. Tires can be made lighter and perhaps last longer through the use of Aramid or some other synthetic fiber instead of steel in the belt. Widespread use of front-wheel drive may lead to different specifications for tires which go on the front (which both drives the car and bears most of the weight) and those which go on the rear.

Tires can also improve handling, thus reducing weight and saving money otherwise spent on the suspension. Michelin's wide, low profile TRX and Pirelli's P6 are the leaders in radial technology. Pirelli has placed a nylon belt on top of the steel wire undertread belts. This shrinks as it warms up and tightens down onto the steel belts, keeping them precisely in place under stress and allowing them to be made of thinner wire. That means the P6 rides more softly and shock-absorbently over rough roads. Small belts in the sidewall, close to the rim, stiffen the tires, sharpening steering response and improving the car's stability under very hard cornering. Also, unlike the TRX, the P6 can be used on a standard wheel.

One industry objective is to eliminate the spare tire and jack, reducing weight and increasing useful trunk space. The definitive tire will be one which doesn't fail at all. The solution which currently appears to be most likely is the ultra-low-profile radial, which improves handling without any deterioration in ride or mileage. When punctured, the tire can still be driven on to the nearest service station.

Other solutions are possible. For example, you could use controls that constantly monitor tire pressure, thereby eliminating the need for a spare tire. GM is rumored to be doing this on its 1980 compacts. The dashboard will signal when a tire is losing air, enabling the driver to repair the tire before it goes flat.

ENGINES

The introduction of new engines will take place over many years, because cars will have to be reduced in size before they can have adequate performance with a smaller engine. There are about a dozen different engines with substantial research support. Each company might develop a different engine, depending upon tooling already in place and the cost of labor and raw materials at a given point in time. Chrysler, for example, is working on a sixth-generation turbine. There doesn't appear to be hope that this engine can be built for less than twice the cost of a conventional engine, but it is always possible that there will be a breakthrough in the seventh or eighth generation.

GM has already submitted documents to congressional committees and government agencies laying out in detail how it plans to improve mileage. By 1985, GM believes that 25 percent of all the cars it builds and perhaps 40 percent of trucks may have to be diesels (which improve mileage by 30 percent) and that most V 8 and in-line six-cylinder gasoline engines will be dropped in favor of thriftier V 6 and four-cylinder engines. (Stricter particulate and nitrogen oxide emissions standards, however, may prevent widespread diesel use.)

Buick expects to deliver 125,000 turbos in the 1979 model year ($450 extra cost option) supplied by the Garrett AIResearch Division of Signal. By mid-1979, Garrett will be able to supply 400,000 turbochargers a year. Turbocharger demand will really jump by 1981, when Ford introduces new 1.3- and 1.6-litre four-cylinder engines (1.1 million annual capacity) designed to easily accept a turbo. Finally, turbochargers will be necessary for all diesels built in 1983, when they will be needed to meet stricter particulate standards for passenger car diesels.

PROCO

Other engines, of course, are probable. After working on a stratified-charge piston engine known as PROCO (for programmed combustion) for more than a decade, Ford is planning to build 100,000 of these engines in the 1981 model year and then move to 500,000 a year by 1983. Ford believes that PROCO can boost fuel economy by 20 to 25 percent (nearly matching a diesel); what's more, it does a better job on controlling emissions and achieves those pluses without performance losses, while eliminating the diesel's noise, smoke, and odor problems. Moreover, tooling and the unit cost of production would be less expensive than for the diesel. The PROCO uses conventional manufacturing techniques, except for electronic fuel injectors not much different from injectors currently being made for diesels.

Electric

Even with the most optimistic forecasts of the ability of the internal combustion engine to improve mileage, it is nevertheless clear that alternative engines must be developed if the United States is to reduce its dependence on oil. So far no electric car has been invented which can be considered a serious competitor with the internal combustion engine, if comparisons are made with gasoline engines of similar performance characteristics, such as lawnmower engines. Nevertheless, GM has indicated that by 1985 it will build a battery-operated car for urban or commuting use, where range, acceleration, and carrying capacity aren't important. Daihatsu, a subsidiary of Toyota, is reportedly planning to manufacture a ferro-nickel battery–powered car by 1981.

The problem is the comparatively low energy density of batteries and the length of time it takes to discharge. One thousand pounds of the best lead-acid batteries contain energy equal to only 1 gallon of gasoline. Nickel cadmium cells are just too expensive. Exxon's lithium disulfide cell has an energy density two to three times present lead-acid batteries and is able to operate at ambient temperatures. However, Exxon has had problems with the battery exploding.

There are scores of batteries under development, among them nickel-zinc, zinc-nickel oxide, nickel-iron, and zinc-air. But when battery "breakthroughs" are discussed, the conversation eventually turns to some highly exotic high-temperature technology. The lithium-sulfur/lithium-metal sulfide battery is one promising example. But this cell operates in a temperature range of 570 to 930 degrees Fahrenheit. Because of the high temperatures involved, glass seals are generally required, and the containers are vulnerable to the corrosive materials inside the cells. GM has been able to operate a lithium-iron sulfide battery for 10,000 hours of continuous operation and over 700 complete discharge cycles. If 25 percent of the vehicle's weight is allocated to a lithium-iron sulfide battery, the car could have a 200-mile range and sufficient performance to obtain highway speeds.

Argonne National Laboratories hopes to begin road tests next spring on its lithium-iron battery. The 309-pound battery operates at 840°F and should double the range of the same vehicle powered by ordinary lead-acid batteries. Argonne predicts that an improved version should double that performance level again in 1983.

Ford, meanwhile, is finishing its fourteenth year of working on a sodium-sulfide battery which operates between 570 and 750°F, where both the sulfur and the sodium are molten. Ford originally predicted a prototype would be delivered in 1981, but it now puts the date at 1983.

A possible solution to the high temperature problems of such super-batteries as sodium-sulfur, iron-sulfur, lithium-metal, and lithium-sulfur is a zinc-chlorine unit under development by Energy Development Associates, a subsidiary of Gulf & Western and Occidental Petroleum. Energy Development plans next spring to show how its battery can double the range of an electric van built for conventional lead-acid power. It is expected to be able to power a car 150 miles at an average speed of 55 mph and a top speed of 75 mph.

Next spring should also see the debut of what researchers say is probably, pound for pound, the most powerful of the superbatteries. The 500-pound lithium-water battery developed by the Continental Group, Inc., would hold sufficient power for 2000 miles at cruising speed. The lithium-water battery, like its somewhat less powerful but cheaper sister, the aluminum-air battery, cannot be recharged. Instead, such batteries are renewed by replacing their electrodes, a possible recycling problem.

Other problems which must be solved include:

Reliability and noise of controls
Durability of the regenerative braking system necessary to permit adequate range
Availability of recharging stations

The ultimate solution will probably be a hybrid, with a small-displacement, two-cylinder engine (operating at constant speed to maximize efficiency) charging a battery which powers the car. Daihatsu is rumored close to placing one into production.

ELECTRONICS

Although the first automotive electronic application was in 1960, when Plymouth introduced the solid-state alternator to replace the generator, until 1975 electronics made serious inroads only in entertainment devices. This was primarily because cars operate in a more hostile environment than such applications as ballistic missiles, making the cost prohibitive for components with sufficient reliability and durability. To give an example, the useful lifespan of a microprocessor in a missile warhead can be measured in minutes, while circuitry which affects emissions has to last for 50,000 miles (1000 to 2000 hours) by federal regulation. Also, a missile's microprocessor operates in an environment between 50 and 100 degrees, while an automobile must function in the heat of the desert, in the Alaskan cold, in a summer shower, and on unpaved, dusty roads. The car engine itself can exceed a temperature of 400 degrees in normal operation, which is why most sophisticated circuitry has had to be placed inside the passenger compartment. In addition, automobile electronics require different speed and reliability parameters. All of this is why electronics companies haven't been able to sell existing technology but instead have had to design entirely new devices for Detroit.

Nevertheless, as of the 1978 model year, electronics had replaced mechanical devices in about two dozen applications, clearly pointing the way toward the day when a microprocessor would feed and control the engine. By 1982, there should be about forty automotive electronic systems in production. The average 1978 model had about $57 worth of electronic entertainment devices and $47 in other electronics, such as ignitions, voltage regulators, and speed control devices. TRW estimates that by 1987 entertainment applications will average $66 (in constant dollars) and other applications will reach a staggering $608.

The future of automobile electronics can be divided into five categories: engine control, substitution for the driver, displays, diagnosis, and interconnection systems.

Engine Control

In the early 1970s, Chrysler introduced solid-state electronic ignition, which eliminated points and condensers, thereby lengthening the time between major tune ups. By the 1981 model year, almost every car will have an electronic engine control system which will, in effect, tune the engine after every firing of the spark plugs.

Electronic engine control will permit use of the three-way catalysts necessary to meet 1981 model year emission requirements. The microprocessor which will be at the heart of the control system will cost less than $10 and will be able to execute several million operations a second. It will be programmed to control most of the engine's functions. The microprocessor will directly measure oxygen in the exhaust, engine speed, temperature, humidity, and atmospheric pressure to adjust the air/fuel mixture and spark plug timing to their optimum setting under all running conditions to avoid knocking, while maximizing both mileage and effective catalyst performance.

At the present time, electronic carburetors and electronic fuel metering are less expensive than electronic fuel injection, which is currently a $702 option on certain Cadillacs. However, single-point electronic throttle body fuel injection is expected to be on the majority of GM's 1981 models, when Bendix estimates the cost will fall to $100, below that of electronic carburetors. Fuel injection enables the engine to maximize efficiency by permitting greater control over the air/fuel ratio (the ability to run "lean"), the amount of fuel delivered to each cylinder, the option to cut off fuel during deceleration, elimination of fuel accumulation in the manifold, and better distribution to each cylinder. Fuel injection can provide up to 15 percent more power or alternatively 15 percent better economy than a conventional carburetor by eliminating the intake pressure loss of the carburetor and by providing optimum fuel/air ratios and optimum manifold design. In addition, catalyst efficiency is about 40 percent with a mechanical carburetor, but improves to around 85 percent with fuel injection, permitting reduced use of scarce platinum and rhodium.

Electronics will represent about 30 to 40 percent of the total electronic fuel injection system cost. In addition to mechanical parts, the engine control system will need sensors for measuring air temperature, coolant temperature, crankshaft position, manifold pressure, engine speed, oxygen concentration in the exhaust, air flow measurement, exhaust gas flow, and possibly the throttle position. Actuators will be necessary to translate the processor output into action to control fuel flow, spark timing, and exhaust gas recirculation.

Electronics will also make possible such developments as Eaton's valve selector, which can make an engine operate on any number of cylinders according to power demands. This will cost the consumer $100 to $150, but might improve mileage by 10 percent.

Drive Substitution

Before long, the computer will take over part of the driver's function. The first example of this will probably be the transmission. Fiat has an experimental electronically controlled automatic transmission with five forward gear ratios, expected to improve mileage by 17 percent. The driver will only be able to select neutral, reverse, and drive. After the car is put into motion, gear selection would be made automatically to achieve maximum economy and performance under the existing conditions of engine revolutions, road speed, and accelerator pedal position. The accelerator wouldn't be directly linked to the carburetor, but would signal the driver's power demands to a potentiometer. The vehicle's actual operating data, as obtained from sensors, would be compared with pre-established optimal operating data, and the appropriate throttle opening and gear ratio would then be automatically selected and actuated.

The second substitution of the computer for the driver may be in automatic anti-skid braking. Mercedes already offers such a device at about the same price as an automatic transmission. The system can reduce the stopping distance on a slippery road by as much as 25 percent, while largely eliminating the risk that the car will slide out of control during a panic stop.

Off in the future, with the development of an inexpensive memory to store radar signatures, radar brakes are also a possibility. Some feel that the "bubble memory" will be cheap enough by 1985 to 1990. The problem is that the car must be able to distinguish between the radar signatures of a falling leaf, a bicycle, and a concrete abutment. The car would begin to stop before the collision, not as the result of a collision.

Displays

Several cars offer electronic digital readout clocks and radios. GM's 1978 Cadillac Seville offered an electronic instrument panel. By 1980, this display may be less expensive than conventional instruments. It will certainly take up less space, be more reliable, and offer the potential for increased information retrieval. The initial information offered will be such items as speed, fuel level, miles traveled, transmission gear, and time.

Additional functions will be added. The 1978 Continental Mark V offered an optional computer-controlled gauge beneath the regular fuel gauge to show the number of miles a car can be driven with its current supply of fuel. The Ford device uses a large-scale integrated circuit less than a quarter of an inch square containing approximately 3600 transistors. (In comparison, electronic ignition requires only seven.) The circuit receives information from two sensors, one in the fuel tank sensing fuel level and the other linked to the transmission, sensing speed. This device also improves the accuracy of the speedometer and odometer, while eliminating a mechanical drive's noise, risk of failure, and possibility of tampering by unscrupulous sellers of used cars.

With the electronic display, within a few years the dashboard will be able to signal when it is time to tune up the car, specify which spark plug needs to be replaced, indicate when a tire is running low, monitor the condition of the radiator, and signal when a car needs oil or gasoline.

Robert Bosch has proposed a "Driver Guidance and Information System." The driver taps out his destination on a small coding device which looks like a pocket calculator. From then on, all the information needed concerning where and how to drive is flashed on a small display face the size of your hand. This display will give the driver the quickest route—you won't need a road map, or even need to know where you are. The display will flash an arrow signaling a left turn. It will also give you advance warnings of unfavorable weather and traffic conditions and propose alternate routes.

An induction loop buried in the road surface before every intersection will receive and transmit information to and from an electronic station mounted at the side of the road, which in turn will be linked to a central computer. As the vehicle passes over the induction loop, it transmits its speed, destination, and whether it is a passenger car or truck. The central computer in turn calculates the ideal speed and route for each individual vehicle.

While the cost of the car electronics would be under $150, that of installing induction loops, stations, and central computers would be in the billions of dollars.

Once a microprocessor is placed on the car, it is reasonably inexpensive to add additional functions:

One of the most obvious is a sensor to activate an air bag.

Doors can be automatically locked some period of time after the engine is turned on or off.

The suspension can be controlled to produce a better "feel." GM already offers a version of this on its 1979 E bodies.

Theft prevention can be added, through the use of codes to start the car.

Drivers can be tested for intoxication.

One idea is for the computer to give the driver a 10-second test of his reflexes, using the steering wheel to control a needle on a dashboard dial. Another is for the computer to flash a number which the driver has to remember and then punch back into a keyboard. A third is for a display to flash questions, such as "What is your social security number?" or "What is 9 plus 9?" One problem is that in order to leave your car at a parking lot, you would have to give the attendant the code to operate your car, which is less secure than giving a key. Another problem is that about 5 percent of all drivers can't remember their social security number or add 9 plus 9. Finally, drivers really don't want to add 9 plus 9 if they are stalled on a railroad track with a train bearing down on the car at 60 miles per hour.

Diagnosis

Another application of electronics just beginning to appear on cars is in diagnosis. While the Germans lead in this field, GM has offered a diagnostic plug on every new car line introduced since the 1976 model year. The mechanic is able to measure such factors as distributor dwell angles, revolutions per minute, advance angle, and charging circuits on a portable apparatus which is simply plugged into the car.

With the development of more sophisticated instrument panels, the car will increasingly diagnose itself, offering the possibility of advances in other areas.

For example, Texas Instruments is trying to persuade Detroit to use its new electronic sensing device which alerts car owners when the engine coolant turns corrosive, signaling that it is time to add or change antifreeze. The device is expected not only to prevent corrosion in the cooling system, which leads to engine overheating and cracked engine blocks, but also to eliminate a major stumbling block in the substitution of lighter and less expensive aluminum for copper in radiators: the fear of corrosion. This device will also enable the use of lighter and smaller engine blocks, since passageways for circulation of coolant can be reduced in size.

Similar devices can be expected for engine oil, which will enable use of synthetic oils which last longer and have reduced friction, extending engine life and increasing mileage. This kind of diagnosis will make possible the use of lifetime batteries (already available in the aftermarket) and lifetime platinum-tipped spark plugs (introduced on a Chrysler engine line in the 1974 model year).

Interconnection Systems

Somewhere around 2600 feet of wire is currently used to control an average car, and this figure will increase as new electronic functions are offered. Detroit would like to eliminate the clumsy wiring harness now used, which has many connections liable to assembly errors and deterioration over time and which is costly to diagnose and repair.

The most promising idea is a system of multiplexing, similar to what the telephone company uses on voice transmission. This could use either electric wire or fiber optics. Multiplexing means that many coded signals are sent along a common wire. Theoretically only two wires are necessary, although three are more likely. In addition to electronics, multiplexing would control such mundane items as the radiator fan, horn, lights, windshield wiper, power windows and locks, and rear window defogger. Each function is equipped with an electronic module to decode the signals it needs to operate. One system already available repeats individual codes for each component 1000 times a second. When the electronic module has received four consecutive similar codes (a safety precaution to prevent incorrect operation due to random voltage transients on the code wire) the accessory to which it is connected will be actuated. If for some reason the accessory fails to function, then a fail signal is sent back along the code wire to the logic box, which in turn triggers a warning indicator on the electronic dashboard. This, of course, makes it easy to add options to a car. Instead of having to run a separate wire through the car to add a light in the trunk, the assembly line worker only needs to splice into the multiplex wire already running through the trunk to activate the tail lights.

To sum up, there will be a remarkable amount of technology added to cars of the future. The car is being re-invented. There is an industry cliché that someone who went to sleep in 1910 could wake up and operate a new car without any problem. By and large, model change-overs have consisted of just "shuffling the deck" differently. In the future, however, cars will be much more complex, but also easier to drive, easier to park, safer, less harmful to health, more efficient, and probably more reliable. When it breaks down, the car will be able to limp into a service station through a fail-safe system. The dashboard will inform the driver where there is a problem. The mechanic will test the car with a $100 diagnostic device, probably made by Sun Electric, and inform the driver that, say, the number seven electronic module needs replacing. This will reduce the need for mechanics, just as the development of automatic switching reduced the need for telephone operators. And it could prove to be a boon for the do-it-yourselfer.

THE MOST FREQUENTLY ASKED QUESTIONS CONCERNING CORPORATE BONDS

What is a corporate bond?
A corporate bond is an obligation representing debt incurred by incorporated companies, including utilities, industrial companies, banks and financial institutions, and transportation and real estate companies. Most corporate bonds have a fixed coupon rate and maturity.

Why are corporate bonds issued?
Prudent financial policies require corporations to permanently finance their debt capital needs. Long-term corporate bonds assure the permanency of money needed for capital improvements.

Who buys corporate bonds?
Individuals, insurance companies, savings banks, mutual funds, investment counselors, pension and trust funds.

What is a unit of trade in corporate bonds?
The "par value," or principal value, of a corporate bond is $1000. Trades are usually in multiples thereof.

Is interest on corporate bonds subject to income taxes?
Yes. Interest on corporate bonds, unlike interest on municipal bonds, is subject to federal, state, and local income taxes.

Is a profit from a corporate bond transaction subject to capital gains tax?
Yes. And many people in high tax brackets use deep-discount bonds to take

their profits as capital gain rather than as ordinary income. The income attributable to the discount can be deferred to maturity of the bond.

With a corporate bond, is it possible to incur a loss?

If a bond is sold before maturity, a loss may be realized. This depends on the market at the time of sale. The prices of bonds vary inversely with interest rates. The loss, for tax purposes, is either long- or short-term.

What is a first mortgage bond?

A first mortgage bond is the highest claim on the property specified in the loan agreement. It is somewhat similar to the mortgage on a house or real estate.

What is a debenture?

A debenture is a bond that is junior in rank to a mortgage bond and is secured by the general credit of a corporation. Debentures can be senior or subordinated to other obligations.

What is a discount bond?

A discount bond is a security trading below its principal, or par, value: e.g., a bond trading at 85.

What is a current-coupon bond?

This is a bond whose coupon rate coincides with the then prevailing market rates and generally would be trading at or close to par.

What is a premium bond?

A premium bond is a security trading above its principal, or par, value: e.g., a bond trading at 105.

What is a cushion bond?

A cushion bond is usually a high-coupon security trading at a premium, usually above the initial call price. The call potential causes the security to trade at a lower price than otherwise would be warranted, hence the cushion, which protects the holder from some market risk.

What is "current yield"?

A relation stated as a percent of the market price of the bond, similar to stock yield. It is determined by dividing the price of the bond into the coupon rate.

What is "yield to maturity"?

The annual percentage return if a particular call feature is exercised. Yield to call would often be referred to with high-coupon or cushion bonds.

Are all corporate bonds callable?

Most corporate bonds may be redeemed before the maturity date. An exception would be most Equipment Trust Certificates. It is most important when selecting bonds to check the various methods of bond redemption.

How is interest on a corporate bond paid?

Interest on a corporate bond is paid semiannually on the bond's "interest payment dates." Some securities are traded "flat," or ex-interest; that is, the interest is paid to the bondholder of record on the interest payment date, much as the payment of a dividend on a stock. The price of the bond is reduced by the amount paid.

What is a serial bond?
A serial bond issue is composed of issue bonds with multiple annual maturities. Railroad companies frequently offer this type of security, called Equipment Trust Certificates. (Serial maturities relate to the depreciation rate of the pledged assets.)

What is a bearer (coupon) bond?
A bond with interest coupons attached. The coupons are clipped as they come due and deposited at the issuer's paying agent. In many instances, they may even be deposited at a bank for payment of interest. Bearer (coupon) bonds are highly negotiable, with ownership passing by delivery. When purchasing a coupon bond one has to be sure that all coupons are attached.

What is a registered bond?
A bond with the name of the owner specified on the books of the issuing company. Corporate bonds can be registered as to principal and interest and are thus termed "fully registered." Interest on registered bonds is paid by check directly to the holder of record.

When trading, does it matter whether the holder has coupon or registered corporate bonds?
Yes. Sometimes there are different markets for an issue: one market for registered, another for coupon. Always specify the type of bond held when selling.

What are some of the prominent investment features of a corporate bond?
1. It provides an opportunity to invest in large, quality corporations.
2. Since corporate bonds have a stated coupon rate, they provide a fixed rate of return.
3. Promise of payment of principal at maturity.
4. Discount bonds can provide capital gains.

Where are corporate bonds traded?
The two forms of trading are:
1. Agency trade. This takes place via the auction market, which puts the buyer and seller together at a mutually agreed price, less a specified commission.
2. Principal trade. If there is no auction possible, bonds are purchased for the firm's account or sold to customers from a firm's inventory at a negotiable net price. Corporate bonds are quoted and executed on a dollar price expressed as a percentage of par.

What is the NYSE nine bond rule?
There is no specialist on the NYSE for bonds as there is for stocks. However, all orders for nine bonds or less of a bond listed on the NYSE must first be entered on the floor. If the order cannot be executed within a reasonable period of time it may be offered for trade in the OTC market.

Can the market on the NYSE and OTC vary?
Yes. The NYSE market is generally limited to odd-lot executions, while the OTC market represents a round lot. This variance, at times, can be substantial. Also, the NYSE is an auction market without a specialist. Thus, at times disparities develop between what a bond is worth and where it trades.

What is considered an odd lot in corporate bonds?
Generally, a trade involving fewer than 250 bonds is considered an odd lot. Many times, however, only 100 or higher is considered a round lot (i.e., an amount large enough not to be an odd lot).

What should you know to evaluate a corporate bond?
One must have a full description, including the name of the issuer, number of bonds, type of bond, coupon rate, exact maturity, redemption features, and rating if the security is assigned one.

Who rates corporate bonds?
Moody's, Standard & Poor's, and Fitch rate corporate bonds. For individuals purchasing nonconvertible bonds, only securities which have the four highest ratings are recommended:

Moody's	S&P	Fitch
Aaa	AAA	AAA
Aa	AA	AA
A	A	A
Baa	BBB	BBB

These are known as "bank-grade," or "investment-grade," securities and therefore qualify for margin or use as collateral for loan purposes.

What is a primary market?
The first offering of newly issued bonds.

What is the secondary market?
Where bonds are traded after the initial offering.

What influences price levels of the corporate bond market?
The prevailing level of interest rates, both domestic and international, the rate of inflation, supply and demand for corporate bonds and competitive instruments, and Federal Reserve policy.

What is a convertible bond?
A convertible bond is a hybrid security that has a fixed coupon rate but also has the option of being exchanged for the common stock of the issuing company.

What is preferred stock?
Preferred stock is a class of stock which has a fixed dividend rate, usually paid quarterly. It ranks senior in classification to common stock but is junior to bonds of a company. It has tax advantages for corporate owners, as most preferred dividends are 85 percent tax exempt to corporations.

Can a corporate bond be sold prior to maturity?
There are ready markets for most corporate bonds. Marketability depends on quality, overall size of issue, amount to be sold, and general market conditions.

SOME CORPORATE BOND DEFINITIONS

evaluation	A general quide to the approximate value of a security.
quote	This reflects the bid side or offering side of the market in a security. Many factors are involved for a quote to be "workable."
bid	The price to be paid for a bond. A bid may be firm or subject.
firm	A definite commitment to bid or offer bonds at a specific price for a specified period of time.
subject	An indication that it may be possible to trade a bond at a given price.
nonredeemable	Describing a period during which a bond may not be called for any reason.
nonrefundable	Describing a period during which a bond may not be called by the issuance of a security at lower interest costs to the company.
short- and intermediate-term corpo-rate bonds	Bonds with maturities of up to 10 years.
interest coverage	The multiple by which the interest costs of a company's debt are covered.
debt-to-equity ratio	Debt expressed as a percent of stockholder's equity.
accrued interest	Interest earned on a bond since the last coupon payment. Bonds usually trade "plus accrued interest."
settlement date	The date on which payment for a bond is due.
"free crowd"	An area in the floors of the NYSE bidroom where listed convertible securities are traded. A quote—but not a market size—is available.
subordinate debenture	As the name implies, this is junior in rank to a debenture. Convertible bonds are often issued in this form.
sinking fund debenture	This is a bond which may be retired by a company through periodic purchases with monies appropriated for this purpose. The sinking fund may also be certified by bonds purchased in the open market, or by property additions, in the case of certain utility issues. There are various types of sinking funds, and terms have to be checked carefully.

APPENDIX III
RATIO TREND ANALYSIS*

INTRODUCTION

Ratio Trend Analysis is designed to assist a portfolio manager, individual investor, or analyst in reviewing the financial trends of a particular corporate credit or industry over the most recent 5 years. The most pertinent and frequently used financial ratios and performance measurements for a large number of widely owned industrial, manufacturing, and service companies in some thirty industries are arranged for easy reference. Examination of these measurements will be helpful in evaluating, for example, the progress a company is making in internal cash generation, in maintaining a structurally sound capitalization, or in improving liquidity.

Using the ratios we have compiled, a company can be readily compared (1) with other credits in the same industry group to assess how well it is performing against its competition, and (2) with management's previously stated objectives. Industry trends may also be used to evaluate whether a company is using opportunities to improve its debt

---

*This appendix contains sample data extracted from the Compustat data base.

quality position or is struggling to maintain it during both healthy and difficult economic periods.

Ratio Trend Analysis contains twelve ratios displayed for the companies within some thirty industries arranged alphabetically. Ratios for the most recent 5-year period available at date of publication are presented with comparative ranking numbers for each year. Moody's and Standard & Poor's ratings are also listed.

DATA BASE LIMITATIONS

All data are as originally reported in a company's financial statements. In order to provide information as accurately as possible, certain footnotes are included. The listing for these footnotes is found at the end of this introductory chapter.

No adjustment has been made to offset the impact of capitalized interest on net income and income taxes.

No adjustment has been made to show the impact on the balance sheets and income statements of those companies that retroactively complied with FASB statement #13 during 1977. This ruling, dealing with the capitalization of nonoperating leases, will be enforced on all companies during 1978.

All data reflect foreign currency translation with no adjustments made to distinguish between realized and unrealized gains or losses.

For the purpose of computing net tangible assets, the data item "other assets" has been treated as an intangible, even though it may include assets which are tangible.

Fixed Charge Coverage is adjusted to exclude unremitted earnings of unconsolidated subsidiaries when this amount appears on the source and use of funds statement. In cases where the portion of the unremitted earnings of unconsolidated subsidiaries is not reported on the source and use of funds statement, the total amount of earnings of unconsolidated subsidiaries has been excluded from income available for fixed charges.

In certain cases, interest expense is reported net.

Finally, if one of the key data items necessary to compute a ratio is not available, the ratio will appear as N.A. In the computation of averages, the N.A. items are not included.

HOW TO USE RATIO TREND ANALYSIS

An individual's time and analytical needs vary, but one way to use the data presented in this publication follows. Let's say one is interested in comparing one company with others in its industry.

First, turn to the Industry Comparisons to examine the trend and strength or weakness of selected ratios as well as the ranking of the company's measurements within its industry in each of the five years presented. Very often the trend may signal problems experienced by a credit, a change in business mix, or a basic change in an industry fundamental. For example, one may look for signals of increased use of leverage, narrowing product margins, increased volatility in earnings performance, or reduced liquidity.

Next, you should obtain the company's most recent financial ratios, to insure a current picture of where your company is today. Your local office of Paine, Webber, Jackson & Curtis should be able to supply you with any current financial information you may need.

RATING ORDER SUPPLEMENT

A companion product to the Ratio Trend Analysis is the Ratio Trend Analysis Rating Order Supplement, which is located in Appendix IV. This publication ranks similarly rated companies with the objective of providing an easy-to-use format for determining the relative creditworthiness of industrial companies statistically within their respective rating categories. It also provides averages and medians for each ratio within each rating category. This edition includes 291 industrial companies, and the ratios calculated are based on the latest available data as of press time. Only those companies that have senior debt rated investment-grade by either Moody's or Standard & Poor's are included in this study.

EXPLANATION OF FINANCIAL MEASUREMENTS

Fixed Charge Coverage

Fixed charge coverage (the number of times interest expense is covered by earnings) is probably the most frequently examined ratio in reviewing a corporate credit. It can serve as an indicator of both earnings performance and the use of leverage. Pretax relationships are being given increasing emphasis by analysts and the rating agencies, since they eliminate the impact of the variety of forms of prevalent tax accounting practices, which tends to invalidate after-tax coverage. After-tax coverage, however, may be a better measure of debt quality for some industries (e.g., integrated oil companies, since certain foreign taxes may be included in the cost of crude oil and pretax coverage would not accurately compare different credits). Fixed charge coverage including rents indicates the use of rentals as a substitute for ownership and also the balance sheet financing of assets. A thin coverage may signal poorer earnings protection and less financial flexibility. In the computation of this ratio, no adjustment has been made to offset the impact of capitalized interest on net income and income taxes.

Debt Measurements

These ratios indicate the mix of debt or equity financing employed to fund operations and fixed plant. A trend may be reflective of a shift of industry fundamentals, a changing corporate philosophy on the use of debt, economic conditions, and/or alterations in a company's business composition. Leverage and interest coverage together reflect the current level of financial risk as well as a company's ability to raise more debt should the need arise. The maintenance of appropriate leverage ratios is essential for a company's rating. The asset protection afforded a debt holder is shown in the net tangible assets–to–long-term debt ratio. This value may be greatly understated for natural resources companies, such as those in the oil, metals, and paper industries, which do not show the replacement or economic value of their holdings. Nevertheless it provides some indication of the value of assets protecting debt outstanding.

Cash Flow Measurements and Liquidity Measurements

For many companies cash flow and working capital ratios are good indications of (1) ability to sustain a general recession or a cyclical downturn of a particular industry and still make debt service payments; (2) potential need for additional financing; (3) adequacy of operating funds; (4) the amount of spending which is funded from internal cash generations; and (5) dependence on short-term sources of funds.

Operating Ratios

Operating income divided by net sales measures cost efficiency of a company, while net sales–to–employees and net sales–to–assets shows the efficiency of use of employees and assets.

Performance Measurements

The return on common equity reflects not only a company's earning ability but also its degree of leverage. This measurement may also indicate its ability to raise capital through equity financing. The ratio net income as a percent of sales shows the history of a company's profit margins and the influence of industry factors. For the retail industry, inventory turnover ratios are included to indicate any adverse trends such as holdings of excessive inventories which expose an enterprise to added costs (storage, insurance, taxes, etc.) as well as the risks of loss of value through obsolescence or physical deterioration. Receivables turnovers are shown to allow detection of any lengthening of time required for collections which could add to working capital requirements.

Financial Data

The basic financial data examined individually may point to corporate actions not reflected directly in the selected ratios, such as a reduction in debt or an increase in sales. The size of a company as measured by its net sales or stockholders' equity is of importance in credit rating considerations, as is its relative strength in its industry. The amount of cash flow can be compared to capital expenditures to assess a company's spending pattern in relation to its cash generation and stated borrowing philosophy. Permanent alterations in these areas may show a change in industry fundamentals or may be due to an increase in replacement costs. For many industries, especially those that are labor-intensive, the amount of unfunded prior service pension liability should be factored in the analysis of a company's leverage position.

Aerospace Industry

PRETAX COVERAGE

	RATINGS	FYR END	78		77		76		75		74	
MCDONNELL DOUGLAS CORP	Ba /BBB*	12/78	41.98 (	1)	22.25 (	1)	8.39 (	3)	4.06 (	4)	4.36 (	4)
RAYTHEON CO	A /AA	12/78	24.36 (	2)	14.93 (	3)	14.55 (	1)	11.87 (	1)	8.42 (	2)
BEECH AIRCRAFT CORP	Ba /BBB*	9/78	23.34 (	3)	15.40 (	2)	10.28 (	2)	7.10 (	2)	6.21 (	3)
UNITED TECHNOLOGIES CORP	Aa /AA	12/78	11.99 (	4)	10.24P(	4)	7.50P(	4)	6.99P(	3)	9.72 (	1)
ROCKWELL INTL CORP	A /A	9/78	8.07 (	5)	5.65 (	5)	4.61 (	5)	2.97 (	6)	3.86 (	6)
SUNDSTRAND CORP	Ba /BB-*	12/78	5.35 (	6)	4.19 (	7)	3.73 (	6)	2.46 (	7)	2.31 (	7)
LOCKHEED CORP	B /NR*	12/78	3.20 (	7)	3.21 (	8)	2.74 (	8)	2.34 (	8)	1.34 (	8)
GRUMMAN CORP	B /BB*	12/78	3.12 (	8)	5.01 (	6)	2.96 (	7)	3.13 (	5)	4.34 (	5)
AVERAGE			15.18		10.11		6.85		5.12		5.07	
MEDIAN			10.03		7.95		6.06		3.60		4.35	

AFTER TAX COVERAGE

	RATINGS	FYR END	78		77		76		75		74	
MCDONNELL DOUGLAS CORP	Ba /BBB*	12/78	24.35 (	1)	12.96 (	1)	5.43 (	3)	3.06 (	4)	2.96 (	4)
RAYTHEON CO	A /AA	12/78	14.42 (	2)	8.82 (	2)	8.59 (	1)	7.33 (	1)	5.13 (	2)
BEECH AIRCRAFT CORP	Ba /BBB*	9/78	11.88 (	3)	8.37 (	3)	5.92 (	2)	4.24 (	2)	3.93 (	3)
UNITED TECHNOLOGIES CORP	Aa /AA	12/78	6.64 (	4)	5.63P(	4)	4.27P(	4)	4.08P(	3)	5.51 (	1)
ROCKWELL INTL CORP	A /A	9/78	4.57 (	5)	3.30 (	5)	2.97 (	5)	2.10 (	6)	2.67 (	6)
SUNDSTRAND CORP	Ba /BB-*	12/78	3.86 (	6)	3.10 (	7)	2.80 (	6)	2.03 (	7)	1.87 (	7)
GRUMMAN CORP	B /BB*	12/78	2.26 (	7)	3.30 (	5)	2.18 (	7)	2.22 (	5)	2.82 (	5)
LOCKHEED CORP	B /NR*	12/78	2.25 (	8)	2.11 (	8)	1.73 (	8)	1.67 (	8)	1.23 (	8)
AVERAGE			8.78		5.95		4.24		3.34		3.26	
MEDIAN			5.60		4.46		3.62		2.64		2.89	

AFTER TAX COV (INCL RENTS)

	RATINGS	FYR END	78		77		76		75		74	
BEECH AIRCRAFT CORP	Ba /BBB*	9/78	6.78 (	1)	5.09 (	1)	4.29 (	1)	3.36 (	1)	3.10 (	1)
RAYTHEON CO	A /AA	12/78	4.21 (	2)	3.36 (	2)	3.03 (	2)	2.62 (	2)	2.39 (	3)
UNITED TECHNOLOGIES CORP	Aa /AA	12/78	3.23 (	3)	3.00P(	3)	2.57P(	3)	2.48P(	3)	2.75 (	2)
MCDONNELL DOUGLAS CORP	Ba /BBB*	12/78	2.78 (	4)	2.54 (	4)	2.35 (	4)	1.86 (	4)	1.94 (	5)
ROCKWELL INTL CORP	A /A	9/78	2.68 (	5)	2.14 (	5)	1.99 (	5)	1.67 (	5)	1.96 (	4)
LOCKHEED CORP	B /NR*	12/78	1.60 (	6)	1.64 (	7)	1.43 (	7)	1.43 (	7)	1.17 (	7)
GRUMMAN CORP	B /BB*	12/78	1.54 (	7)	1.95 (	6)	1.63 (	6)	1.63 (	6)	1.81 (	6)
SUNDSTRAND CORP	Ba /BB-*	12/78	NA (-)		NA (-)		NA (-)		NA (-)		NA (-)	
AVERAGE			3.26		2.82		2.47		2.15		2.16	
MEDIAN			2.78		2.54		2.35		1.86		1.96	

NET INCOME AS % NET SALES

	RATINGS	FYR END	78		77		76		75		74	
SUNDSTRAND CORP	Ba /BB-*	12/78	6.8 (	1)	5.4 (	2)	5.5 (	2)	4.3 (	2)	3.9 (	2)
BEECH AIRCRAFT CORP	Ba /BBB*	9/78	6.7 (	2)	6.1 (	1)	5.9 (	1)	5.8 (	1)	5.2 (	1)
RAYTHEON CO	A /AA	12/78	4.6 (	3)	4.0 (	3)	3.5 (	3)	3.2 (	3)	3.0 (	5)
MCDONNELL DOUGLAS CORP	Ba /BBB*	12/78	3.9 (	4)	3.5 (	5)	3.1 (	4)	2.6 (	5)	3.5 (	3)
UNITED TECHNOLOGIES CORP	Aa /AA	12/78	3.7 (	5)	3.5 (	4)	3.0 (	5)	3.0 (	4)	3.1 (	4)
ROCKWELL INTL CORP	A /A	9/78	3.7 (	6)	2.5 (	6)	2.3 (	6)	2.1 (	6)	3.0 (	6)
LOCKHEED CORP	B /NR*	12/78	1.6 (	7)	1.6 (	8)	1.2 (	8)	1.3 (	8)	0.7 (	8)
GRUMMAN CORP	B /BB*	12/78	1.5 (	8)	2.1 (	7)	1.6 (	7)	1.8 (	7)	1.8 (	7)
AVERAGE			4.07		3.59		3.26		3.02		3.02	
MEDIAN			3.82		3.50		3.06		2.83		3.07	

LTD/CAPITALIZATION (%)

	RATINGS	FYR END	78		77		76		75		74	
MCDONNELL DOUGLAS CORP	Ba /BBB*	12/78	5.9	(1)	7.0	(1)	12.7	(2)	22.5	(2)	11.9	(1)
RAYTHEON CO	A /AA	12/78	9.0	(2)	11.5	(2)	12.1	(1)	16.3	(1)	17.2	(2)
BEECH AIRCRAFT CORP	Ba /BBB*	9/78	14.2	(3)	23.4	(4)	25.9	(4)	29.9	(3)	33.5	(4)
ROCKWELL INTL CORP	A /A	9/78	25.5	(4)	29.4	(5)	31.6	(5)	38.7	(4)	35.4	(5)
UNITED TECHNOLOGIES CORP	Aa /AA	12/78	29.9	(5)	15.6	(3)	22.9	(3)	40.0	(5)	19.6	(3)
SUNDSTRAND CORP	Ba /BB-*	12/78	33.6	(6)	41.4	(7)	46.1	(6)	53.3	(6)	57.5	(7)
GRUMMAN CORP	B /BB*	12/78	45.9	(7)	38.6	(6)	48.4	(7)	59.0	(7)	55.3	(6)
LOCKHEED CORP	B /NR*	12/78	58.2	(8)	71.0	(8)	77.1	(8)	91.5	(8)	96.9	(8)
AVERAGE			27.77		29.74		34.62		43.90		40.90	
MEDIAN			27.70		26.43		28.79		39.31		34.43	

LTD/NET PLANT (%)

	RATINGS	FYR END	78		77		76		75		74	
MCDONNELL DOUGLAS CORP	Ba /BBB*	12/78	18.3	(1)	24.6	(1)	49.9	(2)	91.3	(3)	35.9	(1)
RAYTHEON CO	A /AA	12/78	18.5	(2)	26.3	(2)	29.0	(1)	39.4	(1)	45.0	(2)
ROCKWELL INTL CORP	A /A	9/78	50.9	(3)	61.3	(3)	67.8	(4)	84.6	(2)	74.2	(4)
SUNDSTRAND CORP	Ba /BB-*	12/78	67.1	(4)	80.2	(5)	84.8	(5)	106.9	(5)	113.3	(5)
UNITED TECHNOLOGIES CORP	Aa /AA	12/78	84.1	(5)	37.2	(3)	55.2	(3)	100.1	(4)	51.8	(3)
BEECH AIRCRAFT CORP	Ba /BBB*	9/78	128.3	(6)	192.0	(7)	230.1	(8)	246.7	(7)	271.5	(7)
GRUMMAN CORP	B /BB*	12/78	140.2	(7)	100.3	(6)	131.5	(6)	182.4	(6)	145.6	(6)
LOCKHEED CORP	B /NR*	12/78	160.9	(8)	209.3	(8)	226.9	(7)	317.6	(8)	322.5	(8)
AVERAGE			83.54		91.41		109.40		146.11		132.46	
MEDIAN			75.61		70.74		76.26		103.51		93.71	

TOT LIABILITY/TOT STK EQUITY

	RATINGS	FYR END	78		77		76		75		74	
BEECH AIRCRAFT CORP	Ba /BBB*	9/78	82.5	(1)	105.0	(2)	107.7	(1)	144.6	(2)	147.1	(3)
SUNDSTRAND CORP	Ba /BB-*	12/78	116.4	(2)	135.8	(4)	153.2	(5)	200.4	(6)	245.5	(6)
UNITED TECHNOLOGIES CORP	Aa /AA	12/78	129.8	(3)	104.5	(1)	111.0	(2)	182.1	(5)	109.6	(1)
MCDONNELL DOUGLAS CORP	Ba /BBB*	12/78	158.2	(4)	133.7	(3)	125.3	(3)	160.7	(4)	188.2	(5)
ROCKWELL INTL CORP	A /A	9/78	161.0	(5)	170.9	(5)	145.0	(4)	156.3	(3)	177.8	(4)
RAYTHEON CO	A /AA	12/78	178.9	(6)	190.8	(7)	181.9	(6)	122.0	(1)	127.6	(2)
GRUMMAN CORP	B /BB*	12/78	183.9	(7)	190.4	(6)	228.9	(7)	256.9	(7)	252.3	(7)
LOCKHEED CORP	B /NR*	12/78	503.7	(8)	617.0	(8)	851.3	(8)	1989.5	(8)	6066.4	(8)
AVERAGE			189.31		206.02		238.05		401.56		914.31	
MEDIAN			159.62		153.34		149.12		171.37		183.01	

NET TANG ASSETS/LTD (%)

	RATINGS	FYR END	78		77		76		75		74	
MCDONNELL DOUGLAS CORP	Ba /BBB*	12/78	1631.1	(1)	1409.3	(1)	773.8	(2)	440.1	(2)	827.6	(1)
RAYTHEON CO	A /AA	12/78	1043.5	(2)	810.7	(2)	798.8	(1)	590.7	(1)	560.9	(2)
BEECH AIRCRAFT CORP	Ba /BBB*	9/78	704.1	(3)	425.3	(3)	384.4	(4)	333.6	(3)	297.1	(4)
ROCKWELL INTL CORP	A /A	9/78	370.2	(4)	319.5	(5)	294.1	(5)	241.3	(5)	261.6	(5)
UNITED TECHNOLOGIES CORP	Aa /AA	12/78	319.0	(5)	634.3	(3)	432.2	(3)	247.7	(4)	502.7	(3)
SUNDSTRAND CORP	Ba /BB-*	12/78	284.7	(6)	230.1	(7)	212.9	(6)	183.9	(6)	170.7	(7)
GRUMMAN CORP	B /BB*	12/78	206.2	(7)	249.1	(6)	202.7	(7)	167.9	(7)	179.2	(6)
LOCKHEED CORP	B /NR*	12/78	67.0	(8)	58.0	(8)	40.6	(8)	41.5	(8)	91.3	(8)
AVERAGE			578.21		517.05		392.46		280.85		361.38	
MEDIAN			344.59		372.40		339.28		244.53		279.31	

CASH FLOW/LTD (%)

	RATINGS	FYR END	78		77		76		75		74	
GRUMMAN CORP	B /BB*	12/78	22.4	(1)	41.4	(2)	25.3	(2)	19.0	(2)	29.8	(3)
UNITED TECHNOLOGIES CORP	Aa /AA	12/78	49.4	(2)	116.1	(6)	83.1	(6)	36.7	(5)	85.3	(6)
LOCKHEED CORP	B /NR*	12/78	53.0	(3)	33.3	(1)	21.3	(1)	17.3	(1)	7.9	(1)
SUNDSTRAND CORP	Ba /BB-*	12/78	59.8	(4)	43.0	(3)	37.0	(3)	23.5	(3)	20.3	(2)
ROCKWELL INTL CORP	A /A	9/78	65.8	(5)	52.2	(4)	46.0	(4)	31.9	(4)	37.8	(4)
BEECH AIRCRAFT CORP	Ba /BBB*	9/78	184.0	(6)	87.8	(5)	74.7	(5)	62.1	(7)	52.7	(5)
MCDONNELL DOUGLAS CORP	Ba /BBB*	12/78	292.3	(7)	233.3	(8)	116.6	(7)	57.7	(6)	188.7	(8)
RAYTHEON CO	A /AA	12/78	320.8	(8)	224.5	(7)	191.4	(8)	131.9	(8)	112.4	(7)
AVERAGE			130.93		103.94		74.44		47.51		66.85	
MEDIAN			62.79		70.00		60.33		34.32		45.21	

NET CASH FL/CAP EXP (%)

	RATINGS	FYR END	78		77		76		75		74	
BEECH AIRCRAFT CORP	Ba /BBB*	9/78	677.2	(1)	290.3	(2)	388.4	(1)	341.4	(3)	469.7	(2)
LOCKHEED CORP	B /NR*	12/78	376.4	(2)	340.1	(1)	362.7	(2)	356.3	(2)	284.0	(3)
SUNDSTRAND CORP	Ba /BB-*	12/78	187.2 V(3)		175.5	(4)	134.4	(7)	112.3	(6)	66.4	(8)
UNITED TECHNOLOGIES CORP	Aa /AA	12/78	125.8	(4)	158.9	(5)	189.6	(4)	148.3	(4)	143.7	(5)
MCDONNELL DOUGLAS CORP	Ba /BBB*	12/78	121.1	(5)	155.7	(6)	236.5	(3)	375.2	(1)	472.3	(1)
RAYTHEON CO	A /AA	12/78	110.9	(6)	123.9	(7)	144.3	(6)	109.1	(7)	113.7	(6)
GRUMMAN CORP	B /BB*	12/78	106.1	(7)	179.9	(3)	161.7	(5)	128.7	(5)	246.1	(4)
ROCKWELL INTL CORP	A /A	9/78	102.3	(8)	99.5	(8)	124.4	(8)	91.7	(8)	73.2	(7)
AVERAGE			225.86		190.47		217.76		207.87		233.64	
MEDIAN			123.41		167.18		175.65		138.47		194.88	

AFT TAX RET ON COM EQTY (%)

	RATINGS	FYR END	78		77		76		75		74	
BEECH AIRCRAFT CORP	Ba /BBB*	9/78	24.3	(1)	23.3	(2)	22.8	(2)	21.2	(2)	19.9	(2)
LOCKHEED CORP	B /NR*	12/78	21.3	(2)	29.1	(1)	31.5	(1)	60.2	(1)	87.5	(1)
RAYTHEON CO	A /AA	12/78	20.3	(3)	18.2	(3)	15.9	(3)	15.3	(4)	14.3	(4)
SUNDSTRAND CORP	Ba /BB-*	12/78	16.4	(4)	13.7	(6)	15.0	(5)	11.1	(6)	10.6	(8)
ROCKWELL INTL CORP	A /A	9/78	15.0	(5)	11.0	(8)	9.6	(8)	8.2	(8)	11.0	(7)
UNITED TECHNOLOGIES CORP	Aa /AA	12/78	14.7	(6)	14.8	(5)	15.0	(4)	13.4	(5)	12.7	(6)
MCDONNELL DOUGLAS CORP	Ba /BBB*	12/78	13.4	(7)	11.6	(7)	11.5	(7)	10.1	(7)	13.8	(5)
GRUMMAN CORP	B /BB*	12/78	10.2	(8)	16.5	(4)	14.1	(6)	16.2	(3)	16.0	(3)
AVERAGE			16.97		17.28		16.92		19.45		23.23	
MEDIAN			15.70		15.67		14.99		14.33		14.07	

RET ON TOT ASSETS (%)

	RATINGS	FYR END	78		77		76		75		74	
BEECH AIRCRAFT CORP	Ba /BBB*	9/78	28.6	(1)	23.7	(1)	22.9	(1)	19.0	(1)	17.0	(1)
SUNDSTRAND CORP	Ba /BB-*	12/78	15.3	(2)	13.0	(3)	13.9	(3)	10.7	(4)	10.4	(5)
RAYTHEON CO	A /AA	12/78	13.2	(3)	11.9	(5)	10.8	(4)	12.9	(2)	12.8	(2)
ROCKWELL INTL CORP	A /A	9/78	13.2	(4)	10.4	(7)	9.4	(7)	9.0	(7)	9.3	(7)
UNITED TECHNOLOGIES CORP	Aa /AA	12/78	12.9	(5)	15.0	(2)	14.4	(2)	9.9	(6)	12.3	(3)
MCDONNELL DOUGLAS CORP	Ba /BBB*	12/78	9.3	(6)	9.2	(8)	9.6	(6)	7.5	(8)	10.2	(6)
GRUMMAN CORP	B /BB*	12/78	8.9	(7)	12.4	(4)	10.8	(5)	11.6	(3)	10.8	(4)
LOCKHEED CORP	B /NR*	12/78	8.9	(8)	10.9	(6)	9.3	(8)	10.0	(5)	8.4	(8)
AVERAGE			13.78		13.31		12.63		11.33		11.42	
MEDIAN			13.02		12.15		10.80		10.37		10.58	

Auto Parts Industry

PRETAX COVERAGE

	RATINGS	FYR END	78	77	76	75	74
CHAMPION SPARK PLUG	Aa /AA	12/78	19.03 (1)	27.84 (1)	32.62 (1)	31.96 (1)	39.82 (1)
FEDERAL-MOGUL CORP	A /A	12/78	14.72 (2)	10.22 (3)	7.95 (3)	2.01 (7)	3.50 (6)
DANA CORP	Aa /AA	8/78	14.30 (3)	13.16 (2)	10.73 (2)	8.01 (2)	10.54 (2)
BORG-WARNER CORP	A /AA-	12/78	8.96 (4)	7.48 (5)	6.41 (5)	2.63 (6)	2.75 (7)
TRW INC	A /A	12/78	7.69P(5)	7.40P(6)	6.71 (4)	4.72 (3)	4.77P(4)
ARVIN INDUSTRIES INC	Baa/BBB	12/78	6.14 (6)	8.28 (4)	6.37 (6)	1.69P(8)	1.49 (8)
BENDIX CORP	A /A	9/78	5.54 (7)	5.89 (7)	5.86 (7)	4.07 (4)	4.20 (5)
EATON CORP	A /A	12/78	4.79 (8)	5.37 (8)	5.64 (8)	3.61 (5)	6.01 (3)
AVERAGE			10.15	10.70	10.29	7.34	9.14
MEDIAN			8.33	7.88	6.56	3.84	4.49

AFTER TAX COVERAGE

	RATINGS	FYR END	78	77	76	75	74
CHAMPION SPARK PLUG	Aa /AA	12/78	9.79 (1)	14.40 (1)	16.14 (1)	16.21 (1)	20.59 (1)
FEDERAL-MOGUL CORP	A /A	12/78	8.41 (2)	5.86 (3)	4.74 (3)	1.60 (7)	2.49 (6)
DANA CORP	Aa /AA	8/78	7.79 (3)	7.22 (2)	6.25 (2)	4.75 (2)	6.05 (2)
BORG-WARNER CORP	A /AA-	12/78	5.67 (4)	4.71 (5)	3.84 (5)	2.06 (6)	2.18 (7)
TRW INC	A /A	12/78	4.49P(5)	4.28P(6)	4.07 (4)	3.05 (3)	3.04P(4)
ARVIN INDUSTRIES INC	Baa/BBB	12/78	3.71 (6)	4.78 (4)	3.64 (7)	1.34P(8)	1.42 (8)
BENDIX CORP	A /A	9/78	3.52 (7)	3.72 (7)	3.77 (6)	2.94 (4)	2.75 (5)
EATON CORP	A /A	12/78	2.69 (8)	3.07 (8)	3.27 (8)	2.23 (5)	3.56 (3)
AVERAGE			5.76	6.00	5.71	4.27	5.26
MEDIAN			5.08	4.74	3.95	2.59	2.89

AFTER TAX COV (INCL RENTS)

	RATINGS	FYR END	78	77	76	75	74
CHAMPION SPARK PLUG	Aa /AA	12/78	5.73 (1)	6.57 (1)	7.29 (1)	7.79 (1)	10.11 (1)
FEDERAL-MOGUL CORP	A /A	12/78	4.25 (2)	3.58 (3)	3.11 (2)	1.40 (6)	2.00 (5)
BORG-WARNER CORP	A /AA-	12/78	4.05 (3)	3.43 (4)	2.53 (5)	1.67 (5)	1.81 (6)
ARVIN INDUSTRIES INC	Baa/BBB	12/78	3.21 (4)	3.87 (2)	3.06 (3)	1.28P(7)	1.33 (7)
TRW INC	A /A	12/78	2.60P(5)	2.58P(6)	2.37 (7)	2.05 (3)	2.09P(4)
BENDIX CORP	A /A	9/78	2.60 (6)	2.66 (5)	2.67 (4)	2.23 (2)	2.15 (3)
EATON CORP	A /A	12/78	2.21 (7)	2.48 (7)	2.53 (6)	1.83 (4)	2.78 (2)
DANA CORP	Aa /AA	8/78	NA (-)	NA (-)	NA (-)	NA (-)	NA (-)
AVERAGE			3.52	3.60	3.37	2.61	3.18
MEDIAN			3.21	3.43	2.67	1.83	2.09

NET INCOME AS % NET SALES

	RATINGS	FYR END	78	77	76	75	74
CHAMPION SPARK PLUG	Aa /AA	12/78	8.0 (1)	8.7 (1)	8.8 (1)	10.2 (1)	10.9 (1)
FEDERAL-MOGUL CORP	A /A	12/78	6.2 (2)	5.7 (4)	5.4 (4)	1.1 (8)	2.9 (6)
DANA CORP	Aa /AA	8/78	6.0 (3)	6.0 (3)	6.2 (2)	5.5 (2)	5.7 (2)
BORG-WARNER CORP	A /AA-	12/78	5.8 (4)	5.1 (5)	4.4 (7)	2.7 (6)	2.9 (7)
ARVIN INDUSTRIES INC	Baa/BBB	12/78	4.7 (5)	6.3 (2)	5.8 (3)	1.4 (7)	4.1 (4)
TRW INC	A /A	12/78	4.6 (6)	4.7 (7)	4.5 (6)	4.0 (3)	4.1 (4)
EATON CORP	A /A	12/78	4.3 (7)	5.0 (6)	5.0 (5)	3.0 (5)	5.1 (3)
BENDIX CORP	A /A	9/78	3.6 (8)	3.6 (8)	3.6 (8)	3.1 (4)	3.1 (5)
AVERAGE			5.39	5.65	5.47	3.88	4.51
MEDIAN			5.23	5.40	5.21	3.05	3.57

LTD/CAPITALIZATION (%)

	RATINGS	FYR END	78		77		76		75		74	
CHAMPION SPARK PLUG	Aa /AA	12/78	11.8	(1)	5.6	(1)	6.3	(1)	8.3	(1)	9.2	(1)
BORG-WARNER CORP	A /AA-	12/78	14.5	(2)	14.5	(2)	14.7	(2)	19.2	(2)	26.9	(4)
FEDERAL-MOGUL CORP	A /A	12/78	18.4	(3)	19.7	(3)	26.1	(3)	35.9	(7)	36.7	(6)
DANA CORP	Aa /AA	8/78	20.8	(4)	25.1	(5)	28.5	(5)	31.5	(4)	24.9	(2)
BENDIX CORP	A /A	9/78	26.9	(5)	23.0	(4)	26.4	(4)	28.1	(3)	25.6	(3)
TRW INC	A /A	12/78	29.5	(6)	30.2	(6)	30.9	(6)	35.7	(6)	38.5	(7)
ARVIN INDUSTRIES INC	Baa/BBB	12/78	37.9	(7)	39.1	(8)	44.0	(8)	42.2	(8)	44.8	(8)
EATON CORP	A /A	12/78	44.3	(8)	32.4	(7)	36.6	(7)	35.5	(5)	32.0	(5)
AVERAGE			25.52		23.70		26.70		29.55		29.84	
MEDIAN			23.86		24.01		27.44		33.48		29.48	

LTD/NET PLANT (%)

	RATINGS	FYR END	78		77		76		75		74	
CHAMPION SPARK PLUG	Aa /AA	12/78	31.0	(1)	16.0	(1)	17.9	(1)	22.5	(1)	25.4	(1)
BORG-WARNER CORP	A /AA-	12/78	33.3	(2)	33.3	(2)	33.8	(2)	41.1	(2)	59.8	(4)
FEDERAL-MOGUL CORP	A /A	12/78	37.9	(3)	40.7	(3)	53.9	(3)	69.4	(5)	67.5	(7)
DANA CORP	Aa /AA	8/78	48.7	(4)	62.5	(5)	67.7	(5)	70.1	(6)	46.8	(2)
BENDIX CORP	A /A	9/78	60.7	(5)	47.1	(4)	59.3	(4)	67.6	(4)	52.7	(3)
TRW INC	A /A	12/78	68.1	(6)	66.3	(6)	68.9	(6)	79.2	(8)	89.3	(8)
ARVIN INDUSTRIES INC	Baa/BBB	12/78	88.3	(7)	102.4	(8)	115.3	(8)	61.4	(3)	63.1	(5)
EATON CORP	A /A	12/78	88.8	(8)	71.5	(7)	82.4	(7)	73.9	(7)	66.7	(6)
AVERAGE			57.11		54.96		62.38		60.65		58.93	
MEDIAN			54.72		54.77		63.46		68.50		61.45	

TOT LIABILITY/TOT STK EQUITY

	RATINGS	FYR END	78		77		76		75		74	
CHAMPION SPARK PLUG	Aa /AA	12/78	56.4	(1)	39.3	(1)	36.5	(1)	37.2	(1)	42.0	(1)
BORG-WARNER CORP	A /AA-	12/78	71.0	(2)	66.4	(2)	74.1	(2)	73.1	(2)	91.7	(2)
FEDERAL-MOGUL CORP	A /A	12/78	75.1	(3)	74.8	(3)	94.2	(4)	108.5	(5)	120.1	(4)
DANA CORP	Aa /AA	8/78	91.2	(4)	82.7	(4)	91.7	(3)	90.6	(3)	93.4	(3)
ARVIN INDUSTRIES INC	Baa/BBB	12/78	92.3	(5)	90.3	(5)	125.2	(8)	205.0	(8)	273.4	(8)
BENDIX CORP	A /A	9/78	118.7	(6)	115.9	(7)	117.6	(5)	114.3	(6)	131.7	(6)
TRW INC	A /A	12/78	125.3	(7)	122.4	(8)	122.7	(7)	121.4	(7)	138.2	(7)
EATON CORP	A /A	12/78	184.6	(8)	108.6	(6)	118.9	(6)	105.9	(4)	121.6	(5)
AVERAGE			101.84		87.54		97.62		106.99		126.51	
MEDIAN			91.76		86.47		105.87		107.24		120.83	

NET TANG ASSETS/LTD (%)

	RATINGS	FYR END	78		77		76		75		74	
CHAMPION SPARK PLUG	Aa /AA	12/78	791.1	(1)	1698.3	(1)	1519.3	(1)	1155.0	(1)	1043.1	(1)
BORG-WARNER CORP	A /AA-	12/78	677.6	(2)	681.2	(2)	667.3	(2)	511.4	(2)	364.2	(3)
FEDERAL-MOGUL CORP	A /A	12/78	527.0	(3)	494.5	(3)	374.2	(3)	272.9	(5)	267.2	(6)
DANA CORP	Aa /AA	8/78	464.2	(4)	386.5	(5)	339.4	(5)	307.7	(4)	391.8	(2)
BENDIX CORP	A /A	9/78	342.9	(5)	397.6	(4)	344.6	(4)	322.3	(3)	345.6	(4)
TRW INC	A /A	12/78	277.5	(6)	274.3	(7)	265.8	(6)	228.3	(7)	212.7	(7)
ARVIN INDUSTRIES INC	Baa/BBB	12/78	254.5	(7)	247.8	(8)	217.1	(8)	224.6	(8)	208.2	(8)
EATON CORP	A /A	12/78	207.4	(8)	299.0	(6)	264.7	(7)	270.0	(6)	297.5	(5)
AVERAGE			442.78		559.90		499.05		411.51		391.29	
MEDIAN			403.55		392.03		341.99		290.29		321.57	

Auto Parts Industry

CASH FLOW/LTD (%)

	RATINGS	FYR END	78		77		76		75		74	
CHAMPION SPARK PLUG	Aa /AA	12/78	150.7	(1)	317.2	(1)	254.8	(1)	214.1	(1)	231.1	(1)
FEDERAL-MOGUL CORP	A /A	12/78	119.6	(2)	106.2	(3)	71.9	(3)	28.7	(8)	36.3	(7)
BORG-WARNER CORP	A /AA-	12/78	115.8	(3)	109.8	(2)	91.6	(2)	50.6	(4)	40.2	(5)
DANA CORP	Aa /AA	8/78	99.7	(4)	75.3	(4)	65.3	(4)	50.6	(3)	72.8	(2)
TRW INC	A /A	12/78	65.1	(5)	63.1	(6)	58.1	(6)	41.0	(5)	39.7	(6)
BENDIX CORP	A /A	9/78	55.9	(6)	73.7	(5)	64.3	(5)	50.7	(2)	56.5	(3)
ARVIN INDUSTRIES INC	Baa/BBB	12/78	36.8	(7)	46.9	(8)	38.6	(8)	31.4	(6)	25.6	(8)
EATON CORP	A /A	12/78	35.8	(8)	51.5	(7)	38.8	(7)	30.4	(7)	52.9	(4)
AVERAGE			84.91		105.45		85.42		62.20		69.39	
MEDIAN			82.37		74.48		64.76		45.82		46.55	

NET CASH FL/CAP EXP (%)

	RATINGS	FYR END	78		77		76		75		74	
EATON CORP	A /A	12/78	196.8	(1)	181.4	(4)	157.9	(7)	79.4	(8)	117.4	(3)
DANA CORP	Aa /AA	8/78	168.7	(2)	192.7	(3)	224.2	(5)	164.2	(4)	106.1	(4)
TRW INC	A /A	12/78	156.6	(3)	161.7	(6)	176.9	(6)	111.0	(6)	101.1	(5)
CHAMPION SPARK PLUG	Aa /AA	12/78	146.6 V(4)		199.2 V(2)		236.7 V(4)		166.8 V(3)		251.4 V(1)	
FEDERAL-MOGUL CORP	A /A	12/78	136.0	(5)	152.8	(7)	367.4	(2)	145.3	(5)	75.8	(7)
BORG-WARNER CORP	A /AA-	12/78	130.8	(6)	165.5	(5)	249.7	(3)	100.7	(7)	88.2	(6)
ARVIN INDUSTRIES INC	Baa/BBB	12/78	128.1	(7)	222.3	(1)	427.9	(1)	345.6 V(1)		29.4 V(8)	
BENDIX CORP	A /A	9/78	104.2	(8)	106.5	(8)	157.3	(8)	176.6	(2)	142.1	(2)
AVERAGE			145.98		172.75		249.75		161.20		113.94	
MEDIAN			141.33		173.44		230.42		154.73		103.58	

AFT TAX RET ON COM EQTY (%)

	RATINGS	FYR END	78		77		76		75		74	
DANA CORP	Aa /AA	8/78	18.3	(1)	17.9	(2)	17.7	(2)	14.4	(2)	15.7	(2)
FEDERAL-MOGUL CORP	A /A	12/78	17.6	(2)	15.8	(3)	14.9	(3)	2.2	(8)	7.5	(6)
TRW INC	A /A	12/78	15.4	(3)	15.0	(4)	14.1	(5)	11.7	(3)	12.1	(4)
ARVIN INDUSTRIES INC	Baa/BBB	12/78	15.3	(4)	22.7	(1)	22.8	(1)	6.4	(6)	5.9	(8)
CHAMPION SPARK PLUG	Aa /AA	12/78	14.9	(5)	14.5	(5)	14.3	(4)	15.9	(1)	17.6	(1)
EATON CORP	A /A	12/78	14.3	(6)	14.2	(6)	13.4	(7)	7.5	(5)	14.9	(3)
BENDIX CORP	A /A	9/78	13.8	(7)	14.0	(7)	13.4	(6)	10.1	(4)	10.2	(5)
BORG-WARNER CORP	A /AA-	12/78	13.7	(8)	11.8	(8)	10.8	(8)	6.3	(7)	7.4	(7)
AVERAGE			15.43		15.73		15.16		9.31		11.41	
MEDIAN			15.09		14.76		14.20		8.75		11.18	

RET ON TOT ASSETS (%)

	RATINGS	FYR END	78		77		76		75		74	
FEDERAL-MOGUL CORP	A /A	12/78	20.7	(1)	19.9	(4)	17.2	(4)	5.9	(8)	9.0	(6)
CHAMPION SPARK PLUG	Aa /AA	12/78	20.6	(2)	21.6	(2)	22.5	(1)	24.4	(1)	25.2	(1)
DANA CORP	Aa /AA	8/78	20.2	(3)	20.7	(3)	18.8	(3)	16.1	(2)	16.9	(2)
ARVIN INDUSTRIES INC	Baa/BBB	12/78	17.6	(4)	24.7	(1)	22.1	(2)	10.2	(6)	6.9	(8)
TRW INC	A /A	12/78	16.1	(5)	16.4	(6)	15.2	(6)	13.8	(3)	13.7	(4)
BORG-WARNER CORP	A /AA-	12/78	15.0	(6)	13.9	(8)	13.5	(8)	8.5	(7)	8.6	(7)
BENDIX CORP	A /A	9/78	14.1	(7)	14.2	(7)	13.7	(7)	10.9	(4)	11.8	(5)
EATON CORP	A /A	12/78	13.9	(8)	17.8	(5)	15.2	(5)	10.7	(5)	15.7	(3)
AVERAGE			17.27		18.64		17.27		12.57		13.49	
MEDIAN			16.83		18.81		16.22		10.79		12.76	

Beverage Industry

PRETAX COVERAGE

	RATINGS	FYR END	78	77	76	75	74
PEPSICO INC	Aa /AA	12/78	8.70 (1)	9.01 (1)	10.16 (1)	6.30P(3)	4.55P(4)
ANHEUSER-BUSCH INC	Aa /AA	12/78	8.12 (2)	7.36 (2)	4.84 (4)	8.31 (1)	11.26 (3)
HEUBLEIN INC	A /A	6/78	5.80 (3)	4.20 (3)	8.56 (2)	8.24 (2)	12.64 (2)
SEAGRAM CO LTD	A /A	7/78	3.67 (4)	3.29 (4)	2.88 (5)	2.64 (5)	3.58 (5)
SCHLITZ (JOSEPH) BREWING	Baa/BBB	12/78	2.35 (5)	3.09 (5)	6.62 (3)	5.19 (4)	12.94 (1)
AVERAGE			5.73	5.39	6.61	6.14	8.99
MEDIAN			5.80	4.20	6.62	6.30	11.26

AFTER TAX COVERAGE

	RATINGS	FYR END	78	77	76	75	74
PEPSICO INC	Aa /AA	12/78	5.34 (1)	5.45 (1)	6.00 (1)	3.95P(3)	3.05P(4)
ANHEUSER-BUSCH INC	Aa /AA	12/78	4.84 (2)	4.44 (2)	3.06 (4)	4.75 (1)	6.40 (3)
HEUBLEIN INC	A /A	6/78	3.42 (3)	2.59 (3)	4.76 (2)	4.60 (2)	6.53 (2)
SEAGRAM CO LTD	A /A	7/78	2.45 (4)	2.32 (4)	2.23 (5)	2.07 (5)	2.69 (5)
SCHLITZ (JOSEPH) BREWING	Baa/BBB	12/78	1.78 (5)	2.18 (5)	3.90 (3)	3.13 (4)	7.23 (1)
AVERAGE			3.57	3.40	3.99	3.70	5.18
MEDIAN			3.42	2.59	3.90	3.95	6.40

AFTER TAX COV (INCL RENTS)

	RATINGS	FYR END	78	77	76	75	74
PEPSICO INC	Aa /AA	12/78	3.78 (1)	3.93 (1)	3.47 (1)	2.81P(2)	2.41P(3)
HEUBLEIN INC	A /A	6/78	2.24 (2)	1.91 (2)	2.75 (2)	2.55 (3)	2.65 (2)
ANHEUSER-BUSCH INC	Aa /AA	12/78	NA (-)	NA (-)	NA (-)	3.58 (1)	4.01 (1)
SCHLITZ (JOSEPH) BREWING	Baa/BBB	12/78	NA (-)	NA (-)	NA (-)	NA (-)	NA (-)
SEAGRAM CO LTD	A /A	7/78	NA (-)	NA (-)	NA (-)	NA (-)	NA (-)
AVERAGE			3.01	2.92	3.11	2.98	3.02
MEDIAN			3.01	2.92	3.11	2.81	2.65

NET INCOME AS % NET SALES

	RATINGS	FYR END	78	77	76	75	74
SEAGRAM CO LTD	A /A	7/78	6.7 (1)	7.0 (1)	7.4 (1)	7.6 (1)	9.2 (1)
PEPSICO INC	Aa /AA	12/78	5.3 (2)	5.3 (2)	5.0 (4)	4.5 (4)	4.2 (5)
ANHEUSER-BUSCH INC	Aa /AA	12/78	4.9 (3)	5.0 (3)	3.8 (5)	5.2 (3)	4.5 (4)
HEUBLEIN INC	A /A	6/78	4.7 (4)	4.2 (4)	5.7 (2)	5.5 (2)	5.6 (3)
SCHLITZ (JOSEPH) BREWING	Baa/BBB	12/78	1.3 (5)	2.1 (5)	5.0 (3)	3.3 (5)	6.0 (2)
AVERAGE			4.59	4.73	5.38	5.21	5.91
MEDIAN			4.91	5.00	4.99	5.15	5.59

Beverage Industry

LTD/CAPITALIZATION (%)

	RATINGS	FYR END	78		77		76		75		74	
SCHLITZ (JOSEPH) BREWING	Baa/BBB	12/78	28.3	(1)	35.5	(5)	38.5	(5)	39.4	(5)	31.3	(3)
PEPSICO INC	Aa /AA	12/78	29.1	(2)	30.6	(1)	27.0	(1)	31.0	(1)	38.5	(4)
SEAGRAM CO LTD	A /A	7/78	32.1	(3)	33.5	(3)	38.2	(4)	34.1	(2)	25.2	(1)
HEUBLEIN INC	A /A	6/78	32.3	(4)	33.8	(4)	35.1	(2)	38.6	(4)	40.4	(5)
ANHEUSER-BUSCH INC	Aa /AA	12/78	36.2	(5)	33.2	(2)	35.5	(3)	36.6	(3)	26.4	(2)
AVERAGE			31.59		33.31		34.85		35.95		32.38	
MEDIAN			32.05		33.51		35.52		36.56		31.33	

LTD/NET PLANT (%)

	RATINGS	FYR END	78		77		76		75		74	
SCHLITZ (JOSEPH) BREWING	Baa/BBB	12/78	26.7	(1)	34.8	(1)	38.1	(1)	40.7	(1)	35.9	(2)
ANHEUSER-BUSCH INC	Aa /AA	12/78	38.5	(2)	39.8	(2)	39.8	(2)	47.2	(2)	31.0	(1)
PEPSICO INC	Aa /AA	12/78	42.1	(3)	50.9	(3)	55.8	(3)	65.2	(3)	81.0	(4)
SEAGRAM CO LTD	A /A	7/78	66.8	(4)	76.5	(5)	90.2	(5)	77.4	(4)	53.7	(3)
HEUBLEIN INC	A /A	6/78	67.6	(5)	74.8	(4)	79.1	(4)	90.3	(5)	103.7	(5)
AVERAGE			48.33		54.51		60.59		64.16		61.08	
MEDIAN			42.11		50.93		55.75		65.16		53.74	

TOT LIABILITY/TOT STK EQUITY

	RATINGS	FYR END	78		77		76		75		74	
SCHLITZ (JOSEPH) BREWING	Baa/BBB	12/78	94.9	(1)	103.7	(2)	106.9	(3)	105.3	(2)	79.4	(2)
HEUBLEIN INC	A /A	6/78	107.0	(2)	110.8	(5)	121.0	(4)	128.9	(5)	134.5	(4)
PEPSICO INC	Aa /AA	12/78	107.2	(3)	110.7	(4)	104.7	(1)	117.5	(3)	147.8	(5)
SEAGRAM CO LTD	A /A	7/78	111.7	(4)	100.2	(1)	123.9	(5)	118.1	(4)	103.8	(3)
ANHEUSER-BUSCH INC	Aa /AA	12/78	118.4	(5)	106.3	(3)	105.0	(2)	102.5	(1)	73.2	(1)
AVERAGE			107.85		106.34		112.30		114.45		107.73	
MEDIAN			107.20		106.32		106.85		117.47		103.77	

NET TANG ASSETS/LTD (%)

	RATINGS	FYR END	78		77		76		75		74	
SCHLITZ (JOSEPH) BREWING	Baa/BBB	12/78	331.9	(1)	267.4	(4)	249.1	(4)	239.5	(4)	293.1	(3)
PEPSICO INC	Aa /AA	12/78	301.4	(2)	286.1	(3)	314.2	(1)	265.3	(3)	212.5	(4)
SEAGRAM CO LTD	A /A	7/78	294.5	(3)	290.6	(2)	256.4	(3)	286.2	(1)	388.4	(1)
ANHEUSER-BUSCH INC	Aa /AA	12/78	274.0	(4)	299.1	(1)	274.5	(2)	268.7	(2)	371.5	(2)
HEUBLEIN INC	A /A	6/78	266.4	(5)	252.1	(5)	239.4	(5)	211.8	(5)	196.4	(5)
AVERAGE			293.66		279.07		266.71		254.30		292.38	
MEDIAN			294.53		286.11		256.37		265.28		293.08	

CASH FLOW/LTD (%)

	RATINGS	FYR END	78		77		76		75		74	
PEPSICO INC	Aa /AA	12/78	79.0	(1)	68.7	(1)	75.2	(1)	63.0	(1)	42.4	(5)
ANHEUSER-BUSCH INC	Aa /AA	12/78	51.8	(2)	56.0	(2)	45.6	(3)	45.4	(2)	64.8	(1)
SCHLITZ (JOSEPH) BREWING	Baa/BBB	12/78	48.6	(3)	43.5	(3)	45.2	(4)	31.5	(5)	53.4	(2)
SEAGRAM CO LTD	A /A	7/78	41.8	(4)	39.4	(4)	30.7	(5)	32.9	(4)	47.5	(3)
HEUBLEIN INC	A /A	6/78	41.6	(5)	36.3	(5)	48.3	(2)	40.6	(3)	43.6	(4)
AVERAGE			52.55		48.78		49.01		42.67		50.33	
MEDIAN			48.57		43.47		45.61		40.61		47.52	

NET CASH FL/CAP EXP (%)

	RATINGS	FYR END	78		77		76		75		74	
SCHLITZ (JOSEPH) BREWING	Baa/BBB	12/78	377.0	(1)	184.1	(1)	73.0	(4)	28.5	(5)	38.1	(5)
SEAGRAM CO LTD	A /A	7/78	119.4	(2)	163.6	(2)	108.3	(3)	96.7	(3)	106.0	(2)
ANHEUSER-BUSCH INC	Aa /AA	12/78	80.5	(3)	100.1	(3)	62.8	(5)	81.3	(4)	77.6	(4)
HEUBLEIN INC	A /A	6/78	77.4	(4)	80.0	(5)	138.8	(1)	108.1	(2)	109.8	(1)
PEPSICO INC	Aa /AA	12/78	75.6	(5)	86.6	(4)	134.1	(2)	193.3 V(1)		105.5 V(3)	
AVERAGE			145.98		122.88		103.39		101.60		87.41	
MEDIAN			80.50		100.14		108.31		96.67		105.54	

AFT TAX RET ON COM EQTY (%)

	RATINGS	FYR END	78		77		76		75		74	
PEPSICO INC	Aa /AA	12/78	19.3	(1)	19.3	(1)	18.1	(2)	16.7	(2)	15.7	(2)
ANHEUSER-BUSCH INC	Aa /AA	12/78	14.7	(2)	13.5	(2)	9.0	(4)	14.3	(3)	11.9	(4)
HEUBLEIN INC	A /A	6/78	13.6	(3)	12.6	(3)	19.7	(1)	19.1	(1)	19.2	(1)
SEAGRAM CO LTD	A /A	7/78	8.3	(4)	8.5	(4)	8.3	(5)	8.1	(5)	9.4	(5)
SCHLITZ (JOSEPH) BREWING	Baa/BBB	12/78	3.4	(5)	5.5	(5)	14.0	(3)	9.5	(4)	15.5	(3)
AVERAGE			11.88		11.89		13.82		13.53		14.36	
MEDIAN			13.63		12.60		14.00		14.27		15.54	

RET ON TOT ASSETS (%)

	RATINGS	FYR END	78		77		76		75		74	
PEPSICO INC	Aa /AA	12/78	18.7	(1)	18.5	(1)	17.9	(2)	16.2	(2)	13.8	(4)
HEUBLEIN INC	A /A	6/78	15.3	(2)	15.4	(2)	19.7	(1)	18.9	(1)	18.3	(1)
ANHEUSER-BUSCH INC	Aa /AA	12/78	14.2	(3)	14.0	(3)	10.3	(4)	15.6	(3)	14.3	(3)
SEAGRAM CO LTD	A /A	7/78	10.0	(4)	10.6	(4)	8.8ˑ	(5)	9.2	(5)	9.8	(5)
SCHLITZ (JOSEPH) BREWING	Baa/BBB	12/78	5.2	(5)	7.1	(5)	15.4	(3)	11.3	(4)	18.0	(2)
AVERAGE			12.70		13.12		14.43		14.25		14.84	
MEDIAN			14.24		14.01		15.44		15.63		14.32	

PRETAX COVERAGE

	RATINGS	FYR END	78	77	76	75	74
TIMES MIRROR CO	Aa /AA	12/78	89.87 (1)	75.08 (1)	56.85 (1)	37.83 (1)	43.90 (1)
CBS INC	Aa /AA	12/78	38.15 (2)	43.15 (2)	33.62 (2)	31.51 (2)	25.54 (2)
STORER BROADCASTING CO	Ba /B*	12/78	18.49 (3)	19.61 (4)	15.07 (4)	7.08P(5)	4.61P(5)
TIME INC	Aa /AA	12/78	17.53 (4)	16.22 (5)	10.88 (5)	8.20 (3)	9.43 (4)
AMERICAN BROADCASTING	A /A	12/78	17.09 (5)	15.43 (6)	10.45 (6)	3.94 (7)	15.04 (3)
METROMEDIA INC	Baa/BB+*	12/78	8.22 (6)	28.52 (3)	25.91 (3)	7.80 (4)	3.00 (8)
MACMILLAN INC	Baa/A-	12/78	5.59 (7)	5.28 (7)	5.85 (7)	4.01 (6)	4.32 (6)
WARNER COMMUNICATIONS INC	A /A	12/78	4.49P(8)	4.36P(8)	4.64 (8)	3.74 (8)	3.26 (7)
AVERAGE			24.93	25.96	20.41	13.02	13.64
MEDIAN			17.31	17.92	12.97	7.44	7.02

AFTER TAX COVERAGE

	RATINGS	FYR END	78	77	76	75	74
TIMES MIRROR CO	Aa /AA	12/78	48.53 (1)	40.77 (1)	31.14 (1)	20.69 (1)	25.19 (1)
CBS INC	Aa /AA	12/78	19.53 (2)	21.77 (2)	16.96 (2)	15.78 (2)	12.85 (2)
STORER BROADCASTING CO	Ba /B*	12/78	9.96 (3)	10.44 (4)	8.11 (4)	2.75P(6)	1.57P(8)
TIME INC	Aa /AA	12/78	9.92 (4)	9.37 (5)	6.97 (5)	5.20 (3)	5.77 (4)
AMERICAN BROADCASTING	A /A	12/78	8.56 (5)	7.84 (6)	5.55 (6)	2.41 (8)	7.82 (3)
METROMEDIA INC	Baa/BB+*	12/78	4.55 (6)	14.71 (3)	13.33 (3)	4.38 (4)	2.03 (7)
MACMILLAN INC	Baa/A-	12/78	3.29 (7)	3.19 (7)	3.51 (7)	2.52 (7)	2.77 (5)
WARNER COMMUNICATIONS INC	A /A	12/78	3.19P(8)	3.12P(8)	3.35 (8)	2.98 (5)	2.51 (6)
AVERAGE			13.44	13.90	11.12	7.09	7.56
MEDIAN			9.24	9.91	7.54	3.68	4.27

AFTER TAX COV (INCL RENTS)

	RATINGS	FYR END	78	77	76	75	74
TIMES MIRROR CO	Aa /AA	12/78	9.33 (1)	8.37 (1)	7.56 (1)	5.69 (1)	7.13 (1)
CBS INC	Aa /AA	12/78	4.71 (2)	5.19 (2)	5.15 (2)	4.64 (2)	4.32 (2)
TIME INC	Aa /AA	12/78	4.05 (3)	4.15 (3)	3.37 (3)	2.61 (3)	2.98 (4)
STORER BROADCASTING CO	Ba /B*	12/78	3.65 (4)	3.33 (5)	3.32 (4)	1.36P(8)	1.18P(8)
AMERICAN BROADCASTING	A /A	12/78	3.49 (5)	3.36 (4)	2.80 (6)	1.54 (7)	3.05 (3)
WARNER COMMUNICATIONS INC	A /A	12/78	2.39P(6)	2.53P(7)	2.79 (7)	2.48 (4)	2.16 (5)
METROMEDIA INC	Baa/BB+*	12/78	2.29 (7)	2.85 (6)	2.91 (5)	1.77 (5)	1.35 (7)
MACMILLAN INC	Baa/A-	12/78	1.80 (8)	1.77 (8)	1.81 (8)	1.57 (6)	1.73 (6)
AVERAGE			3.96	3.94	3.71	2.71	2.99
MEDIAN			3.57	3.34	3.12	2.12	2.57

NET INCOME AS % NET SALES

	RATINGS	FYR END	78	77	76	75	74
STORER BROADCASTING CO	Ba /B*	12/78	12.8 (1)	11.7 (1)	11.6 (1)	10.7 (1)	9.1 (1)
TIMES MIRROR CO	Aa /AA	12/78	10.1 (2)	8.5 (3)	7.2 (5)	5.9 (5)	8.0 (2)
METROMEDIA INC	Baa/BB+*	12/78	9.5 (3)	10.7 (2)	11.4 (2)	6.6 (3)	3.3 (8)
AMERICAN BROADCASTING	A /A	12/78	7.2 (4)	6.8 (5)	5.4 (7)	1.6 (8)	5.1 (6)
TIME INC	Aa /AA	12/78	7.0 (5)	7.2 (4)	6.5 (6)	4.9 (6)	6.1 (5)
WARNER COMMUNICATIONS INC	A /A	12/78	6.3 (6)	5.8 (7)	7.4 (3)	7.5 (2)	6.7 (3)
CBS INC	Aa /AA	12/78	6.1 (7)	6.6 (6)	7.4 (4)	6.3 (4)	6.2 (4)
MACMILLAN INC	Baa/A-	12/78	4.0 (8)	3.8 (8)	3.5 (8)	2.7 (7)	3.4 (7)
AVERAGE			7.87	7.65	7.54	5.79	5.97
MEDIAN			7.11	7.04	7.28	6.12	6.14

TOT LIABILITY/TOT STK EQUITY

	RATINGS	FYR END	78		77		76		75		74	
TIMES MIRROR CO	Aa /AA	12/78	60.2	(1)	54.0	(2)	54.0	(1)	51.7	(1)	47.6	(1)
STORER BROADCASTING CO	Ba /B*	12/78	61.3	(2)	53.6	(1)	65.0	(2)	60.4	(2)	97.7	(5)
AMERICAN BROADCASTING	A /A	12/78	75.2	(3)	91.1	(5)	109.6	(6)	105.9	(6)	86.5	(2)
CBS INC	Aa /AA	12/78	88.4	(4)	87.6	(3)	81.2	(3)	85.1	(3)	89.0	(3)
TIME INC	Aa /AA	12/78	94.7	(5)	91.0	(4)	92.2	(4)	91.1	(5)	100.9	(6)
MACMILLAN INC	Baa/A-	12/78	100.0	(6)	96.3	(6)	95.4	(5)	86.4	(4)	93.3	(4)
WARNER COMMUNICATIONS INC	A /A	12/78	239.6	(7)	214.1	(8)	216.0	(8)	193.1	(8)	163.3	(8)
METROMEDIA INC	Baa/BB+*	12/78	341.0	(8)	121.7	(7)	110.6	(7)	116.0	(7)	132.2	(7)
AVERAGE			132.57		101.18		103.00		98.73		101.31	
MEDIAN			91.57		91.06		93.81		88.78		95.49	

LTD/CAPITALIZATION (%)

	RATINGS	FYR END	78		77		76		75		74	
TIMES MIRROR CO	Aa /AA	12/78	6.1	(1)	6.2	(1)	7.4	(1)	8.4	(1)	10.1	(1)
CBS INC	Aa /AA	12/78	10.0	(2)	10.7	(2)	11.5	(2)	13.3	(2)	15.4	(2)
TIME INC	Aa /AA	12/78	22.7	(3)	18.8	(3)	23.5	(3)	22.9	(3)	25.2	(4)
AMERICAN BROADCASTING	A /A	12/78	23.4	(4)	28.3	(6)	31.9	(6)	36.5	(7)	24.1	(3)
MACMILLAN INC	Baa/A-	12/78	27.1	(5)	28.2	(5)	29.1	(5)	23.9	(4)	26.5	(5)
STORER BROADCASTING CO	Ba /B*	12/78	27.2	(6)	23.8	(4)	27.0	(4)	28.6	(5)	39.2	(6)
WARNER COMMUNICATIONS INC	A /A	12/78	39.9	(7)	44.7	(8)	47.7	(8)	47.7	(8)	42.4	(7)
METROMEDIA INC	Baa/BB+*	12/78	69.5	(8)	38.9	(7)	33.1	(7)	36.4	(6)	43.9	(8)
AVERAGE			28.23		24.96		26.39		27.20		28.36	
MEDIAN			25.28		26.00		28.05		26.25		25.87	

LTD/NET PLANT (%)

	RATINGS	FYR END	78		77		76		75		74	
TIMES MIRROR CO	Aa /AA	12/78	10.3	(1)	10.6	(1)	12.2	(1)	13.4	(1)	15.6	(1)
TIME INC	Aa /AA	12/78	32.3	(2)	38.0	(3)	43.2	(3)	38.5	(2)	45.2	(2)
CBS INC	Aa /AA	12/78	32.8	(3)	37.3	(2)	42.4	(2)	47.1	(3)	51.0	(3)
STORER BROADCASTING CO	Ba /B*	12/78	57.3	(4)	49.7	(4)	62.1	(5)	49.5	(4)	63.6	(5)
AMERICAN BROADCASTING	A /A	12/78	88.2	(5)	98.2	(6)	106.5	(6)	116.7	(6)	62.7	(4)
WARNER COMMUNICATIONS INC	A /A	12/78	103.8	(6)	132.3	(7)	155.5	(7)	166.6	(8)	176.4	(8)
METROMEDIA INC	Baa/BB+*	12/78	145.3	(7)	72.8	(5)	55.9	(4)	65.8	(5)	84.8	(6)
MACMILLAN INC	Baa/A-	12/78	165.4	(8)	170.4	(8)	173.1	(8)	124.5	(7)	148.0	(7)
AVERAGE			79.42		76.18		81.35		77.77		80.91	
MEDIAN			72.77		61.28		58.99		57.62		63.15	

NET TANG ASSETS/LTD (%)

	RATINGS	FYR END	78		77		76		75		74	
TIMES MIRROR CO	Aa /AA	12/78	1341.6	(1)	1399.5	(1)	1192.0	(1)	1032.3	(1)	837.3	(1)
CBS INC	Aa /AA	12/78	851.7	(2)	787.3	(2)	767.3	(2)	645.0	(2)	546.9	(2)
AMERICAN BROADCASTING	A /A	12/78	363.3	(3)	297.7	(4)	285.5	(4)	244.4	(6)	369.2	(3)
TIME INC	Aa /AA	12/78	349.8	(4)	463.9	(3)	388.7	(3)	393.2	(3)	351.6	(4)
MACMILLAN INC	Baa/A-	12/78	257.9	(5)	246.6	(6)	232.6	(5)	262.8	(4)	242.8	(5)
STORER BROADCASTING CO	Ba /B*	12/78	213.4	(6)	266.6	(2)	222.9	(6)	244.6	(5)	186.8	(6)
WARNER COMMUNICATIONS INC	A /A	12/78	172.2	(7)	169.4	(7)	166.6	(8)	161.8	(7)	181.4	(7)
METROMEDIA INC	Baa/BB+*	12/78	71.1	(8)	143.1	(8)	167.9	(7)	155.4	(8)	132.9	(8)
AVERAGE			452.64		471.76		427.93		392.42		356.11	
MEDIAN			303.87		282.15		259.04		253.65	e	297.19	

Broadcasting/Publishing Industry

CASH FLOW/LTD (%)

	RATINGS	FYR END	78		77		76		75		74	
TIMES MIRROR CO	Aa /AA	12/78	409.6	(1)	381.7	(1)	289.1	(1)	211.4	(1)	203.0	(1)
CBS INC	Aa /AA	12/78	240.0	(2)	213.9	(2)	207.7	(2)	147.0	(2)	134.2	(2)
AMERICAN BROADCASTING	A /A	12/78	82.4	(3)	63.6	(5)	52.9	(6)	21.5	(8)	61.3	(4)
STORER BROADCASTING CO	Ba /B*	12/78	62.7	(4)	67.2	(4)	54.3	(5)	49.6	(4)	39.4	(5)
TIME INC	Aa /AA	12/78	62.3	(5)	101.4	(3)	77.2	(3)	62.8	(3)	62.5	(3)
WARNER COMMUNICATIONS INC	A /A	12/78	47.2	(6)	33.6	(8)	33.2	(8)	27.5	(7)	26.1	(7)
MACMILLAN INC	Baa/A-	12/78	37.6	(7)	35.3	(7)	34.0	(7)	46.1	(5)	34.2	(6)
METROMEDIA INC	Baa/BB+*	12/78	24.7	(8)	53.7	(6)	62.0	(4)	41.6	(6)	22.1	(8)
AVERAGE			120.82		118.82		101.31e		75.94		72.85	
MEDIAN			62.53		65.44		58.14		47.85		50.35	

NET CASH FL/CAP EXP (%)

	RATINGS	FYR END	78		77		76		75		74	
MACMILLAN INC	Baa/A-	12/78	373.3	(1)	409.2	(1)	546.8	(1)	407.3	(1)	401.6	(1)
AMERICAN BROADCASTING	A /A	12/78	192.5	(2)	177.0	(5)	296.9	(3)	89.5	(7)	98.8	(8)
METROMEDIA INC	Baa/BB+*	12/78	189.1 V(3)		227.4 V(3)		215.3 V(5)		174.0 V(4)		148.2 V(4)	
CBS INC	Aa /AA	12/78	185.7	(4)	232.2	(2)	326.9	(2)	315.1	(2)	335.6	(2)
WARNER COMMUNICATIONS INC	A /A	12/78	150.9	(5)	158.6	(6)	270.4	(4)	278.7	(3)	167.1	(3)
TIMES MIRROR CO	Aa /AA	12/78	142.8	(6)	150.2	(7)	146.4	(7)	167.2	(5)	107.0	(7)
TIME INC	Aa /AA	12/78	121.6	(7)	209.5	(4)	182.9	(6)	89.3	(8)	112.4	(6)
STORER BROADCASTING CO	Ba /B*	12/78	115.2	(8)	101.7	(8)	107.4	(8)	125.2	(6)	140.7	(5)
AVERAGE			183.89		208.21		261.62		205.79		188.92	
MEDIAN			168.31		193.23		242.86		170.61		144.48	

AFT TAX RET ON COM EQTY (%)

	RATINGS	FYR END	78		77		76		75		74	
METROMEDIA INC	Baa/BB+*	12/78	34.1	(1)	21.1	(3)	21.1	(3)	11.7	(3)	6.1	(8)
TIMES MIRROR CO	Aa /AA	12/78	22.8	(2)	17.6	(5)	14.7	(6)	11.1	(5)	14.7	(3)
WARNER COMMUNICATIONS INC	A /A	12/78	21.1	(3)	20.3	(4)	22.1	(1)	17.6	(2)	13.3	(5)
CBS INC	Aa /AA	12/78	20.9	(4)	22.5	(1)	21.9	(2)	18.9	(1)	18.9	(1)
AMERICAN BROADCASTING	A /A	12/78	20.3	(5)	21.8	(2)	17.8	(4)	5.0	(8)	15.0	(2)
STORER BROADCASTING CO	Ba /B*	12/78	14.5	(6)	12.3	(7)	13.8	(7)	10.5	(6)	9.8	(6)
TIME INC	Aa /AA	12/78	12.7	(7)	16.5	(6)	14.9	(5)	11.3	(4)	13.5	(4)
MACMILLAN INC	Baa/A-	12/78	8.0	(8)	7.4	(8)	7.0	(8)	5.5	(7)	6.6	(7)
AVERAGE			19.29		17.42		16.67		11.47		12.24	
MEDIAN			20.62		18.93		16.36		11.24		13.40	

RET ON TOT ASSETS (%)

	RATINGS	FYR END	78		77		76		75		74	
TIMES MIRROR CO	Aa /AA	12/78	26.9	(1)	21.5	(3)	18.0	(4)	14.1	(3)	18.2	(2)
AMERICAN BROADCASTING	A /A	12/78	26.2	(2)	25.7	(1)	19.5	(3)	6.9	(8)	17.7	(3)
CBS INC	Aa /AA	12/78	22.2	(3)	24.4	(2)	25.2	(1)	21.6	(1)	21.3	(1)
STORER BROADCASTING CO	Ba /B*	12/78	18.5	(4)	16.6	(5)	17.7	(5)	14.7	(2)	12.6	(5)
METROMEDIA INC	Baa/BB+*	12/78	17.9	(5)	19.8	(4)	21.1	(2)	12.5	(4)	7.6	(8)
TIME INC	Aa /AA	12/78	12.6	(6)	16.4	(6)	13.9	(7)	11.4	(6)	13.5	(4)
WARNER COMMUNICATIONS INC	A /A	12/78	12.4	(7)	13.1	(7)	14.0	(6)	11.5	(5)	11.0	(6)
MACMILLAN INC	Baa/A-	12/78	9.6	(8)	9.0	(8)	8.3	(8)	7.8	(7)	8.3	(7)
AVERAGE			18.29		18.32		17.21		12.55		13.78	
MEDIAN			18.21		18.22		17.86		12.00		13.04	

Building Industry

PRETAX COVERAGE

	RATINGS	FYR END	79	78	77	76	75
OWENS-CORNING FIBERGLAS CORP	A /A+	12/78	18.91 (1)	16.71 (1)	10.44 (2)	6.53 (4)	5.31 (9)
U S GYPSUM CO	Aa /AA	12/78	18.56 (2)	11.31 (2)	7.58 (6)	5.96 (5)	5.68 (8)
IDEAL BASIC INDUSTRIES INC	A /A	12/78	14.65 (3)	10.83 (3)	9.38 (3)	12.05 (2)	27.66 (1)
JOHNS-MANVILLE CORP	A /AA	12/78	11.49 (4)	10.39P(4)	7.57P(7)	4.60 (9)	6.33 (7)
BLACK & DECKER MFG CO	A /AA	9/78	9.81 (5)	7.95 (9)	5.97 (11)	4.24 (11)	7.62 (5)
ARMSTRONG CORK CO	Aa /AA	12/78	9.81 (6)	7.39 (11)	8.89 (4)	4.67 (8)	6.42 (6)
VULCAN MATERIALS CO	A /A	12/78	9.76 (7)	7.86 (10)	6.72P(10)	7.57P(3)	11.47P(3)
STANLEY WORKS	A /A+	12/78	9.35 (8)	8.73 (6)	8.04 (5)	4.46 (10)	3.81 (11)
GENERAL PORTLAND INC	Baa/BBB	12/78	8.99 (9)	4.72 (12)	0.85 (17)	0.82 (17)	3.06 (16)
CORNING GLASS WORKS	Aa /AA	12/78	8.97 (10)	8.12 (8)	6.91 (9)	1.95 (15)	3.50 (12)
MASCO CORP	A /A	12/78	8.63 (11)	10.28 (5)	12.75 (1)	12.12 (1)	13.71 (2)
FISCHBACH & MOORE INC	Ba /BB*	9/78	7.36 (12)	8.69 (7)	6.93 (8)	4.92 (7)	4.93 (10)
FLINTKOTE CO	Baa/BBB+	12/78	5.95P(13)	4.38P(13)	2.41 (16)	2.89 (13)	3.14 (14)
LONE STAR INDUSTRIES	Baa/A	12/78	4.27 (14)	3.17P(16)	3.43 (14)	2.42 (14)	3.16 (13)
WALTER (JIM) CORP	Baa/BBB	8/78	3.39 (15)	3.64 (15)	3.57 (13)	3.13 (12)	3.07 (15)
WICKES CORP	Baa/BBB	1/79	2.85 (16)	3.89 (14)	2.57 (15)	1.39 (16)	3.02 (17)
SHERWIN-WILLIAMS CO	Baa/BB	12/78	1.52 (17)	0.40 (17)	3.85 (12)	5.28 (6)	8.01 (4)
AVERAGE			9.07	7.56	6.35	5.00	7.05
MEDIAN			8.99	7.95	6.91	4.60	5.31

AFTER TAX COVERAGE

	RATINGS	FYR END	79	78	77	76	75
OWENS-CORNING FIBERGLAS CORP	A /A+	12/78	10.93 (1)	9.51 (1)	6.18 (3)	4.08 (5)	3.39 (9)
U S GYPSUM CO	Aa /AA	12/78	10.34 (2)	6.51 (3)	4.80 (6)	4.25 (4)	3.94 (8)
IDEAL BASIC INDUSTRIES INC	A /A	12/78	9.82 (3)	7.37 (2)	6.67 (2)	7.94 (1)	19.18 (1)
VULCAN MATERIALS CO	A /A	12/78	6.34 (4)	5.18 (7)	4.93P(5)	4.99P(2)	7.04P(2)
JOHNS-MANVILLE CORP	A /AA	12/78	6.26 (5)	5.97P(5)	4.42P(7)	2.95 (9)	4.02 (7)
GENERAL PORTLAND INC	Baa/BBB	12/78	5.75 (6)	3.33 (12)	1.31 (17)	1.10 (17)	2.43 (14)
CORNING GLASS WORKS	Aa /AA	12/78	5.66 (7)	5.24 (6)	4.28 (9)	1.60 (15)	2.52 (12)
BLACK & DECKER MFG CO	A /AA	9/78	5.51 (8)	4.45 (10)	3.49 (11)	2.67 (11)	4.28 (5)
STANLEY WORKS	A /A+	12/78	5.31 (9)	4.80 (9)	4.32 (8)	2.80 (10)	2.51 (13)
ARMSTRONG CORK CO	Aa /AA	12/78	5.21 (10)	3.72 (11)	5.04 (4)	3.13 (7)	4.10 (6)
MASCO CORP	A /A	12/78	4.92 (11)	6.04 (4)	7.19 (1)	6.72 (2)	7.19 (2)
FISCHBACH & MOORE INC	Ba /BB*	9/78	4.20 (12)	4.85 (8)	3.97 (10)	3.00 (8)	2.96 (10)
FLINTKOTE CO	Baa/BBB+	12/78	3.84P(13)	2.99P(13)	2.14 (15)	2.55 (12)	2.78 (11)
LONE STAR INDUSTRIES	Baa/A	12/78	3.19 (14)	2.56P(14)	2.91 (12)	1.91 (14)	2.32 (16)
WALTER (JIM) CORP	Baa/BBB	8/78	2.32 (15)	2.47 (16)	2.46 (14)	2.22 (13)	2.16 (16)
WICKES CORP	Baa/BBB	1/79	1.97 (16)	2.51 (15)	1.84 (16)	1.28 (16)	2.08 (17)
SHERWIN-WILLIAMS CO	Baa/BB	12/78	1.29 (17)	0.60 (17)	2.60 (13)	3.48 (6)	4.76 (4)
AVERAGE			5.46	4.60	4.03	3.33	4.57
MEDIAN			5.31	4.80	4.28	2.95	3.39

Building Industry

AFTER TAX COV (INCL RENTS)

	RATINGS	FYR END	79		78		77		76		75	
OWENS-CORNING FIBERGLAS CORP	A /A+	12/78	4.64	(1)	4.66	(1)	3.48	(3)	2.55	(2)	2.08	(5)
VULCAN MATERIALS CO	A /A	12/78	4.43	(2)	3.52	(3)	3.56P	(2)	3.45P	(1)	4.50P	(1)
JOHNS-MANVILLE CORP	A /AA	12/78	3.85	(3)	3.60P	(2)	2.63P	(7)	2.07	(7)	2.74	(4)
GENERAL PORTLAND INC	Baa/BBB	12/78	3.75	(4)	2.20	(9)	1.14	(13)	1.05	(13)	1.61	(11)
ARMSTRONG CORK CO	Aa /AA	12/78	3.66	(5)	2.72	(7)	3.60	(1)	2.49	(3)	3.00	(3)
BLACK & DECKER MFG CO	A /AA	9/78	3.51	(6)	3.07	(5)	2.65	(6)	2.19	(4)	3.14	(2)
CORNING GLASS WORKS	Aa /AA	12/78	3.40	(7)	3.40	(4)	2.82	(5)	1.34	(11)	1.81	(10)
STANLEY WORKS	A /A+	12/78	3.11	(8)	2.90	(6)	2.84	(4)	2.09	(5)	NA	(-)
FLINTKOTE CO	Baa/BBB+	12/78	2.61P	(9)	1.84P	(11)	1.55	(10)	1.73	(9)	1.85	(9)
LONE STAR INDUSTRIES	Baa/A	12/78	2.42	(10)	2.04P	(10)	2.15	(9)	1.56	(10)	1.86	(8)
WALTER (JIM) CORP	Baa/BBB	8/78	2.10	(11)	2.28	(8)	2.27	(8)	2.08	(6)	2.03	(6)
WICKES CORP	Baa/BBB	1/79	1.68	(12)	1.70	(12)	1.40	(12)	1.13	(12)	1.52	(12)
SHERWIN-WILLIAMS CO	Baa/BB	12/78	1.12	(13)	0.86	(13)	1.47	(11)	1.75	(8)	1.87	(7)
FISCHBACH & MOORE INC	Ba /BB*	9/78	NA	(-)	NA	(-)	NA	(-)	NA	(-)	NA	(-)
IDEAL BASIC INDUSTRIES INC	A /A	12/78	NA	(-)	NA	(-)	NA	(-)	NA	(-)	NA	(-)
MASCO CORP	A /A	12/78	NA	(-)	NA	(-)	NA	(-)	NA	(-)	NA	(-)
U S GYPSUM CO	Aa /AA	12/78	NA	(-)	NA	(-)	NA	(-)	NA	(-)	NA	(-)
AVERAGE			3.10		2.67		2.43		1.96		2.33	
MEDIAN			3.40		2.72		2.63		2.07		1.95	

NET INCOME AS % NET SALES

	RATINGS	FYR END	79		78		77		76		75	
IDEAL BASIC INDUSTRIES INC	A /A	12/78	13.3	(1)	10.0	(2)	10.5	(2)	10.6	(2)	11.9	(1)
MASCO CORP	A /A	12/78	10.3	(2)	11.0	(1)	11.1	(1)	10.8	(1)	10.5	(2)
CORNING GLASS WORKS	Aa /AA	12/78	8.3	(3)	8.2	(3)	8.2	(4)	3.3	(11)	4.6	(6)
VULCAN MATERIALS CO	A /A	12/78	7.9	(4)	7.8	(4)	9.1	(3)	7.7	(3)	7.0	(3)
U S GYPSUM CO	Aa /AA	12/78	7.8	(5)	5.1	(10)	3.8	(11)	3.7	(9)	3.6	(12)
JOHNS-MANVILLE CORP	A /AA	12/78	7.4	(6)	7.0	(6)	4.1	(10)	3.5	(10)	4.6	(7)
GENERAL PORTLAND INC	Baa/BBB	12/78	7.3	(7)	4.0	(11)	0.7	(17)	0.3	(17)	2.7	(15)
OWENS-CORNING FIBERGLAS CORP	A /A+	12/78	7.0	(8)	7.6	(5)	6.7	(5)	4.7	(6)	4.2	(9)
BLACK & DECKER MFG CO	A /AA	9/78	6.9	(9)	6.4	(7)	5.7	(6)	5.4	(5)	6.9	(4)
STANLEY WORKS	A /A+	12/78	5.5	(10)	5.1	(9)	4.9	(9)	3.7	(8)	3.6	(13)
FLINTKOTE CO	Baa/BBB+	12/78	5.2	(11)	3.5	(13)	2.0	(13)	2.9	(14)	3.1	(14)
WALTER (JIM) CORP	Baa/BBB	8/78	5.1	(12)	5.6	(8)	5.6	(7)	5.7	(4)	4.9	(5)
ARMSTRONG CORK CO	Aa /AA	12/78	4.9	(13)	3.7	(12)	5.3	(8)	4.1	(7)	4.2	(8)
LONE STAR INDUSTRIES	Baa/A	12/78	4.2	(14)	3.4	(14)	3.8	(12)	3.2	(13)	3.8	(10)
FISCHBACH & MOORE INC	Ba /BB*	9/78	1.8	(15)	1.8	(16)	1.7	(15)	1.7	(15)	1.9	(16)
WICKES CORP	Baa/BBB	1/79	1.8	(16)	1.8	(15)	1.3	(16)	0.5	(16)	1.3	(17)
SHERWIN-WILLIAMS CO	Baa/BB	12/78	0.5	(17)	-0.8	(17)	1.9	(14)	3.3	(12)	3.6	(11)
AVERAGE			6.18		5.38		5.08		4.42		4.85	
MEDIAN			6.90		5.14		4.88		3.71		4.18	

III-19

LTD/CAPITALIZATION (%)

	RATINGS	FYR END	79		78		77		76		75	
BLACK & DECKER MFG CO	A /AA	9/78	16.9	(1)	18.2	(1)	22.6	(4)	22.6	(3)	14.7	(2)
CORNING GLASS WORKS	Aa /AA	12/78	18.1	(2)	19.2	(2)	21.8	(3)	24.2	(5)	25.5	(9)
OWENS-CORNING FIBERGLAS CORP	A /A+	12/78	18.1	(3)	21.2	(4)	25.3	(8)	30.0	(9)	27.5	(11)
U S GYPSUM CO	Aa /AA	12/78	18.1	(4)	22.3	(6)	18.5	(1)	19.0	(1)	17.7	(3)
ARMSTRONG CORK CO	Aa /AA	12/78	19.2	(5)	23.3	(7)	23.0	(5)	23.2	(4)	23.9	(7)
STANLEY WORKS	A /A+	12/78	23.4	(6)	23.9	(8)	24.2	(7)	28.6	(8)	25.2	(8)
FISCHBACH & MOORE INC	Ba /BB*	9/78	23.5	(7)	24.9	(10)	32.5	(13)	34.8	(14)	36.9	(16)
IDEAL BASIC INDUSTRIES INC	A /A	12/78	23.6	(8)	19.6	(3)	20.7	(2)	22.4	(2)	8.8	(1)
VULCAN MATERIALS CO	A /A	12/78	28.2	(9)	28.9	(11)	31.5	(12)	32.1	(12)	22.5	(6)
FLINTKOTE CO	Baa/BBB+	12/78	31.8	(10)	31.0	(12)	33.4	(14)	34.5	(13)	33.5	(14)
JOHNS-MANVILLE CORP	A /AA	12/78	32.4	(11)	21.5	(5)	23.6	(6)	24.3	(6)	20.2	(4)
GENERAL PORTLAND INC	Baa/BBB	12/78	32.6	(12)	24.2	(9)	26.7	(9)	30.1	(10)	29.0	(12)
LONE STAR INDUSTRIES	Baa/A	12/78	35.1	(13)	37.1	(14)	31.0	(11)	38.1	(16)	32.9	(13)
MASCO CORP	A /A	12/78	43.2	(14)	32.3	(13)	36.1	(15)	28.5	(7)	34.0	(15)
WALTER (JIM) CORP	Baa/BBB	8/78	46.3	(15)	49.2	(17)	44.0	(16)	36.0	(15)	27.2	(10)
SHERWIN-WILLIAMS CO	Baa/BB	12/78	46.9	(16)	42.1	(15)	30.5	(10)	30.9	(11)	22.1	(5)
WICKES CORP	Baa/BBB	1/79	51.6	(17)	43.4	(16)	45.8	(17)	45.6	(17)	42.6	(17)
AVERAGE			29.92		28.37		28.89		29.70		26.13	
MEDIAN			28.24		24.16		26.74		30.00		25.46	

TOT LIABILITY/TOT STK EQUITY

	RATINGS	FYR END	79		78		77		76		75	
ARMSTRONG CORK CO	Aa /AA	12/78	55.3	(1)	60.7	(3)	58.3	(2)	62.2	(3)	60.3	(3)
IDEAL BASIC INDUSTRIES INC	A /A	12/78	62.1	(2)	54.8	(1)	51.5	(1)	52.8	(1)	34.3	(1)
CORNING GLASS WORKS	Aa /AA	12/78	65.1	(3)	62.2	(4)	71.1	(5)	69.9	(5)	84.2	(11)
U S GYPSUM CO	Aa /AA	12/78	72.5	(4)	76.5	(8)	63.4	(4)	62.1	(2)	59.2	(2)
BLACK & DECKER MFG CO	A /AA	9/78	78.7	(5)	74.5	(6)	76.9	(7)	87.8	(11)	83.9	(10)
STANLEY WORKS	A /A+	12/78	79.7	(6)	75.4	(7)	79.5	(8)	84.2	(7)	94.6	(13)
GENERAL PORTLAND INC	Baa/BBB	12/78	80.4	(7)	57.3	(2)	62.0	(3)	74.5	(6)	82.5	(8)
OWENS-CORNING FIBERGLAS CORP	A /A+	12/78	82.1	(8)	81.8	(10)	83.7	(9)	89.2	(12)	77.1	(6)
VULCAN MATERIALS CO	A /A	12/78	87.3	(9)	88.2	(11)	87.1	(10)	87.6	(10)	76.4	(5)
JOHNS-MANVILLE CORP	A /AA	12/78	95.6	(10)	79.7	(9)	76.8	(6)	85.6	(8)	75.8	(4)
FLINTKOTE CO	Baa/BBB+	12/78	105.5	(11)	94.6	(12)	92.7	(12)	90.8	(13)	87.0	(12)
MASCO CORP	A /A	12/78	113.9	(12)	72.9	(5)	89.4	(11)	67.3	(4)	81.7	(7)
LONE STAR INDUSTRIES	Baa/A	12/78	123.6	(13)	124.6	(13)	114.5	(14)	107.7	(14)	108.8	(14)
SHERWIN-WILLIAMS CO	Baa/BB	12/78	136.1	(14)	126.7	(14)	94.4	(13)	86.6	(9)	83.8	(9)
WICKES CORP	Baa/BBB	1/79	201.2	(15)	179.8	(15)	176.3	(15)	191.3	(15)	148.2	(15)
WALTER (JIM) CORP	Baa/BBB	8/78	202.5	(16)	196.6	(17)	190.4	(16)	200.8	(16)	219.6	(16)
FISCHBACH & MOORE INC	Ba /BB*	9/78	212.5	(17)	194.9	(16)	213.0	(17)	215.1	(17)	236.4	(17)
AVERAGE			109.06		100.07		98.89		100.89		99.63	
MEDIAN			87.32		79.66		83.70		86.60		83.77	

Building Industry

NET TANG ASSETS/LTD (%)

	RATINGS	FYR END	79		78		77		76		75	
BLACK & DECKER MFG CO	A /AA	9/78	550.6	(1)	511.9	(1)	416.4	(5)	412.9	(4)	645.1	(2)
CORNING GLASS WORKS	Aa /AA	12/78	542.6	(2)	509.1	(2)	447.3	(3)	400.3	(5)	373.4	(8)
U S GYPSUM CO	Aa /AA	12/78	533.0	(3)	433.4	(6)	522.8	(1)	506.4	(1)	544.5	(3)
OWENS-CORNING FIBERGLAS CORP	A /A+	12/78	531.5	(4)	453.7	(4)	380.5	(8)	325.4	(8)	349.6	(10)
ARMSTRONG CORK CO	Aa /AA	12/78	514.5	(5)	419.9	(7)	423.9	(4)	418.2	(3)	408.2	(7)
IDEAL BASIC INDUSTRIES INC	A /A	12/78	417.7	(6)	506.0	(3)	479.1	(2)	444.6	(2)	1129.9	(1)
STANLEY WORKS	A /A+	12/78	416.0	(7)	405.6	(8)	397.9	(7)	334.2	(7)	346.7	(11)
FISCHBACH & MOORE INC	Ba /BB*	9/78	372.7	(8)	355.9	(9)	278.0	(14)	259.1	(15)	252.5	(16)
VULCAN MATERIALS CO	A /A	12/78	348.4	(9)	339.2	(11)	311.6	(10)	304.7	(11)	437.8	(6)
JOHNS-MANVILLE CORP	A /AA	12/78	300.8	(10)	445.9	(5)	408.3	(6)	389.3	(6)	468.4	(4)
FLINTKOTE CO	Baa/BBB+	12/78	297.4	(11)	305.6	(12)	288.7	(13)	279.3	(12)	288.0	(13)
LONE STAR INDUSTRIES	Baa/A	12/78	273.0	(12)	255.1	(14)	300.3	(12)	247.0	(16)	291.3	(12)
GENERAL PORTLAND INC	Baa/BBB	12/78	270.0	(13)	339.6	(10)	306.9	(11)	269.8	(14)	273.0	(14)
WALTER (JIM) CORP	Baa/BBB	8/78	215.2	(14)	202.2	(17)	226.0	(16)	275.9	(13)	364.6	(9)
SHERWIN-WILLIAMS CO	Baa/BB	12/78	207.5	(15)	230.6	(15)	326.4	(9)	321.7	(10)	448.6	(5)
MASCO CORP	A /A	12/78	196.3	(16)	285.0	(13)	254.5	(15)	322.3	(9)	265.6	(15)
WICKES CORP	Baa/BBB	1/79	188.7	(17)	224.1	(16)	211.9	(17)	200.1	(17)	229.5	(17)
AVERAGE			363.29		366.04		351.78		335.95		418.63	
MEDIAN			348.37		355.89		326.36		322.29		364.58	

CASH FLOW/LTD (%)

	RATINGS	FYR END	79		78		77		76		75	
U S GYPSUM CO	Aa /AA	12/78	121.7	(1)	70.1	(7)	64.6	(6)	58.6	(6)	78.0	(4)
OWENS-CORNING FIBERGLAS CORP	A /A+	12/78	113.9	(2)	119.7	(1)	87.9	(1)	75.0	(1)	56.2	(8)
BLACK & DECKER MFG CO	A /AA	9/78	107.6	(3)	93.6	(3)	68.7	(5)	62.8	(4)	117.4	(3)
CORNING GLASS WORKS	Aa /AA	12/78	105.2	(4)	97.4	(2)	78.8	(3)	42.4	(11)	51.2	(11)
VULCAN MATERIALS CO	A /A	12/78	92.4	(5)	81.9	(6)	77.3	(4)	70.4	(2)	121.0	(2)
ARMSTRONG CORK CO	Aa /AA	12/78	88.0	(6)	59.1	(9)	58.4	(9)	48.1	(8)	53.0	(9)
IDEAL BASIC INDUSTRIES INC	A /A	12/78	86.4	(7)	86.9	(4)	81.5	(2)	69.1	(3)	229.3	(1)
STANLEY WORKS	A /A+	12/78	73.3	(8)	66.7	(8)	61.9	(7)	42.7	(10)	52.2	(10)
FISCHBACH & MOORE INC	Ba /BB*	9/78	61.3	(9)	58.9	(10)	42.0	(12)	39.6	(12)	41.8	(13)
FLINTKOTE CO	Baa/BBB+	12/78	56.4	(10)	38.0	(13)	29.5	(14)	29.3	(14)	33.2	(15)
GENERAL PORTLAND INC	Baa/BBB	12/78	45.3	(11)	50.1	(12)	32.2	(13)	25.7	(16)	33.2	(16)
LONE STAR INDUSTRIES	Baa/A	12/78	34.6	(12)	34.6	(14)	43.2	(11)	23.4	(17)	35.7	(14)
JOHNS-MANVILLE CORP	A /AA	12/78	33.5	(13)	84.6	(5)	61.3	(8)	43.8	(9)	61.9	(6)
MASCO CORP	A /A	12/78	32.2	(14)	55.6	(11)	44.8	(10)	58.8	(5)	43.5	(12)
WICKES CORP	Baa/BBB	1/79	24.4	(15)	29.2	(15)	20.6	(17)	29.2	(15)	21.2	(17)
WALTER (JIM) CORP	Baa/BBB	8/78	16.9	(16)	15.8	(16)	23.1	(16)	50.8	(7)	73.3	(5)
SHERWIN-WILLIAMS CO	Baa/BB	12/78	10.2	(17)	5.7	(17)	24.9	(15)	31.6	(13)	57.1	(7)
AVERAGE			65.47		61.64		52.98		47.13		68.19	
MEDIAN			61.35		59.08		58.36		43.80		53.02	

NET CASH FL/CAP EXP (%)

	RATINGS	FYR END	79		78		77		76		75	
MASCO CORP	A /A	12/78	273.7	(1)	219.6	(2)	341.4	(1)	365.6	(1)	207.5	(1)
BLACK & DECKER MFG CO	A /AA	9/78	215.5	(2)	224.0	(1)	204.2	(5)	78.0	(14)	96.1	(7)
ARMSTRONG CORK CO	Aa /AA	12/78	201.0	(3)	129.9	(10)	100.6	(13)	116.2	(7)	76.3	(10)
U S GYPSUM CO	Aa /AA	12/78	148.8	(4)	95.7	(14)	94.0	(14)	67.5	(16)	85.1	(9)
CORNING GLASS WORKS	Aa /AA	12/78	136.8	(5)	182.5	(4)	215.8	(4)	78.0	(15)	50.5	(17)
STANLEY WORKS	A /A+	12/78	131.9	(6)	176.9	(6)	231.4	(3)	198.9	(4)	94.0	(8)
VULCAN MATERIALS CO	A /A	12/78	130.5	(7)	128.0	(11)	81.8	(15)	87.3	(11)	99.0	(6)
FLINTKOTE CO	Baa/BBB+	12/78	120.9	(8)	104.5	(13)	125.3	(10)	96.4	(10)	69.5	(14)
LONE STAR INDUSTRIES	Baa/A	12/78	104.8	(9)	46.1	(16)	107.2	(12)	82.3	(13)	72.0	(12)
SHERWIN-WILLIAMS CO	Baa/BB	12/78	96.1 V(10)		2.7 V(17)		48.9 V(17)		105.0 V(8)		175.2 V(2)	
IDEAL BASIC INDUSTRIES INC	A /A	12/78	92.3	(11)	107.2	(12)	135.5	(9)	83.2	(12)	116.6	(5)
FISCHBACH & MOORE INC	Ba /BB*	9/78	84.8	(12)	179.7	(5)	121.8	(11)	200.7	(3)	148.6	(3)
JOHNS-MANVILLE CORP	A /AA	12/78	82.0	(13)	138.5	(9)	137.3	(8)	53.7	(17)	60.0	(16)
WICKES CORP	Baa/BBB	1/79	69.2	(14)	142.7	(8)	167.1	(7)	104.7	(9)	75.3	(11)
WALTER (JIM) CORP	Baa/BBB	8/78	62.1 V(15)		61.2 V(15)		79.5 V(16)		155.6 V(6)		127.9 V(4)	
OWENS-CORNING FIBERGLAS CORP	A /A+	12/78	55.4	(16)	162.8	(7)	278.5	(2)	258.5	(2)	71.2	(13)
GENERAL PORTLAND INC	Baa/BBB	12/78	36.9	(17)	192.0	(3)	188.2	(6)	169.6	(5)	60.9	(15)
AVERAGE			120.15		134.95		156.38		135.36		99.16	
MEDIAN			104.78		138.48		135.47		104.73		85.09	

Building Industry

AFT TAX RET ON COM EQTY (%)

	RATINGS	FYR END	79		78		77		76		75	
VULCAN MATERIALS CO	A /A	12/78	19.8	(1)	17.8	(3)	18.5	(2)	16.1	(2)	19.4	(1)
OWENS-CORNING FIBERGLAS CORP	A /A+	12/78	19.6	(2)	20.3	(1)	15.8	(3)	10.6	(6)	9.4	(9)
MASCO CORP	A /A	12/78	19.5	(3)	19.1	(2)	21.5	(1)	19.2	(1)	18.6	(2)
IDEAL BASIC INDUSTRIES INC	A /A	12/78	18.4	(4)	13.1	(9)	13.2	(6)	13.1	(5)	15.2	(4)
U S GYPSUM CO	Aa /AA	12/78	18.3	(5)	11.2	(12)	7.1	(14)	5.9	(13)	6.1	(16)
STANLEY WORKS	A /A+	12/78	15.1	(6)	13.5	(7)	12.2	(8)	8.6	(9)	9.2	(10)
BLACK & DECKER MFG CO	A /AA	9/78	14.8	(7)	12.8*	(11)	11.5	(9)	10.3	(7)	13.9	(6)
JOHNS-MANVILLE CORP	A /AA	12/78	14.6	(8)	13.8	(5)	7.9	(13)	6.6	(12)	9.0	(11)
WALTER (JIM) CORP	Baa/BBB	8/78	14.1	(9)	14.1	(4)	14.0	(4)	15.0	(3)	15.0	(5)
CORNING GLASS WORKS	Aa /AA	12/78	14.1	(10)	13.8	(6)	13.9	(5)	5.7	(14)	9.0	(12)
FLINTKOTE CO	Baa/BBB+	12/78	14.1	(11)	8.5	(14)			5.1	(15)	6.3	(15)
LONE STAR INDUSTRIES	Baa/A	12/78	13.7	(12)	10.0	(13)	9.7	(11)	7.2	(11)	9.4	(8)
WICKES CORP	Baa/BBB	1/79	13.5	(13)	13.2	(8)	8.3	(12)	3.2	(16)	7.6	(14)
GENERAL PORTLAND INC	Baa/BBB	12/78	12.8	(14)	6.4	(16)	1.0	(17)	0.4	(17)	4.0	(17)
FISCHBACH & MOORE INC	Ba /BB*	9/78	12.4	(15)	13.0	(10)	13.0	(7)	14.0	(4)	16.0	(3)
ARMSTRONG CORK CO	Aa /AA	12/78	11.4	(16)	8.0	(15)	10.7	(10)	7.8	(10)	8.4	(13)
SHERWIN-WILLIAMS CO	Baa/BB	12/78	1.6	(17)	-3.5	(17)	5.9	(15)	9.6	(8)	10.4	(7)
AVERAGE			14.57		12.06		11.07		9.32		10.99	
MEDIAN			14.09		13.14		11.49		8.55		9.39	

RET ON TOT ASSETS (%)

	RATINGS	FYR END	79		78		77		76		75	
U S GYPSUM CO	Aa /AA	12/78	21.9	(1)	14.0	(9)	9.8	(10)	7.7	(12)	8.5	(15)
OWENS-CORNING FIBERGLAS CORP	A /A+	12/78	20.5	(2)	21.4	(2)	17.0	(2)	12.3	(6)	10.4	(11)
MASCO CORP	A /A	12/78	19.5	(3)	23.0	(1)	23.1	(1)	23.3	(1)	21.2	(1)
VULCAN MATERIALS CO	A /A	12/78	19.3	(4)	17.5	(4)	16.8	(3)	14.1	(3)	20.6	(2)
IDEAL BASIC INDUSTRIES INC	A /A	12/78	18.5	(5)	14.4	(8)	13.9	(8)	14.1	(3)	16.0	(4)
STANLEY WORKS	A /A+	12/78	18.2	(6)	17.6	(3)	16.5	(4)	11.5	(7)	17.6	(3)
BLACK & DECKER MFG CO	Aa /AA	9/78	18.1	(7)	16.9	(5)	15.6	(5)	14.0	(4)	10.7	(9)
ARMSTRONG CORK CO	Aa /AA	12/78	16.8	(8)	13.4	(10)	14.7	(7)	10.4	(10)	8.8	(14)
CORNING GLASS WORKS	Aa /AA	12/78	15.0	(9)	15.1	(7)	15.1	(6)	6.6	(14)	6.4	(16)
FLINTKOTE CO	Baa/BBB+	12/78	14.2	(10)	9.5	(14)	5.2	(16)	5.6	(15)	4.7	(17)
GENERAL PORTLAND INC	Baa/BBB	12/78	13.5	(11)	8.2	(16)	1.6	(17)	1.9	(17)	9.6	(13)
WICKES CORP	Baa/BBB	1/79	12.7	(12)	11.7	(12)	8.6	(13)	4.5	(16)	13.1	(5)
WALTER (JIM) CORP	Baa/BBB	8/78	12.1	(13)	12.1	(11)	12.1	(9)	13.5	(5)	13.1	(5)
JOHNS-MANVILLE CORP	A /AA	12/78	11.7	(14)	15.9	(6)	9.8	(11)	8.2	(11)	10.4	(10)
LONE STAR INDUSTRIES	Baa/A	12/78	11.7	(15)	9.1	(15)	8.1	(14)	7.6	(13)	9.7	(12)
FISCHBACH & MOORE INC	Ba /BB*	9/78	9.1	(16)	10.0	(13)	9.7	(12)	10.9	(9)	12.0	(7)
SHERWIN-WILLIAMS CO	Baa/BB	12/78	4.8	(17)	1.0	(17)	7.8	(15)	11.2	(8)	12.3	(6)
AVERAGE			15.15		13.57		12.08		10.56		11.98	
MEDIAN			14.96		14.04		12.15		10.93		10.72	

PRETAX COVERAGE

	RATINGS	FYR END	78	77	76	75	74
DU PONT (E.I.) DE NEMOURS	Aaa/AAA	12/78	10.74P(1)	6.91P(6)	6.78P(14)	4.62P(18)	11.96P(6)
WITCO CHEMICAL CORP	A /A	12/78	10.57 (2)	9.11 (3)	8.86 (4)	5.97P(13)	7.63P(13)
FERRO CORP	BAA/A	12/78	9.56 (3)	9.20 (2)	9.89 (2)	6.94 (11)	12.65 (5)
BIG THREE INDUSTRIES	A /A	12/78	9.03 (4)	8.64 (4)	8.66 (5)	9.84 (6)	10.57 (9)
AIR PRODUCTS & CHEMICALS INC	NR /NR	9/78	7.91P(5)	6.56P(9)	7.21P(9)	6.53P(12)	6.04 (17)
PPG INDUSTRIES INC	Aa /A	12/78	6.74 (6)	5.64 (13)	7.65 (8)	4.54 (19)	5.75 (18)
MONSANTO CO	Aa /AA-	12/78	6.70P(7)	7.23P(5)	8.66P(6)	10.55P(5)	14.06P(3)
NATIONAL DISTILLERS &CHEMICL	A /A	12/78	6.44 (8)	9.29 (1)	13.43 (1)	12.45 (2)	14.01 (4)
INTL MINERALS & CHEMICAL	A /A	6/78	6.37 (9)	5.72 (11)	9.04 (3)	13.30 (1)	7.28 (15)
HERCULES INC	A /A	12/78	6.30 (10)	4.02 (21)	7.19 (10)	2.12 (23)	5.73 (19)
STAUFFER CHEMICAL CO	A /A	12/78	6.27P(11)	6.58P(8)	7.16P(11)	10.67P(4)	11.53P(7)
PENNWALT CORP	A /A	12/78	5.65 (12)	5.80 (10)	6.10 (17)	4.80 (17)	4.32 (24)
AMERICAN CYANAMID CO	Aa /AA	12/78	5.44 (13)	5.71 (12)	6.99 (13)	12.11 (3)	14.65 (1)
NL INDUSTRIES	A /A	12/78	5.32 (14)	4.79 (17)	4.25 (21)	2.66 (22)	5.72 (20)
GRACE (W.R.) & CO	Baa/BB*	12/78	5.12 (15)	4.55 (19)	5.33 (19)	5.53 (15)	4.80 (23)
UNION CARBIDE CORP	Aa /AA-	12/78	4.94P(16)	4.99P(16)	7.04P(12)	8.49 (7)	14.06 (2)
ALLIED CHEMICAL CORP	A /A	12/78	4.88 (17)	5.49 (14)	5.35 (18)	5.70 (14)	9.22 (11)
CELANESE CORP	Ba /BB*	12/78	4.69P(18)	4.05P(20)	4.60P(20)	3.13P(21)	7.09 (16)
IMPERIAL CHEM INDS LTD-ADR	NR /NR	12/78	4.44P(19)	5.22P(15)	6.48P(15)	5.21P(16)	7.42P(14)
ROHM & HAAS CO	A /A	12/78	4.42 (20)	3.04 (23)	2.95 (23)	1.56 (24)	5.06 (22)
DIAMOND SHAMROCK CORP	A /A	12/78	4.24 (21)	6.64 (7)	8.47 (7)	8.29 (8)	8.18P(12)
DOW CHEMICAL	Aa /A+	12/78	4.06 (22)	4.59 (18)	6.29 (16)	7.90 (9)	10.05 (10)
REICHHOLD CHEMICALS INC	Baa/BBB+	12/78	3.39P(23)	3.56P(22)	4.22P(22)	7.82 (10)	11.00P(8)
WILLIAMS COS	Baa/BBB-	12/78	2.01 (24)	2.67P(24)	2.41P(24)	4.40P(20)	5.39P(21)
AVERAGE			6.05	5.83	6.88	6.88	8.92
MEDIAN			5.54	5.67	7.02	6.25	7.90

AFTER TAX COVERAGE

	RATINGS	FYR END	78	77	76	75	74
DU PONT (E.I.) DE NEMOURS	Aaa/AAA	12/78	6.79P(1)	4.39P(6)	4.30P(12)	3.22P(18)	7.65P(5)
WITCO CHEMICAL CORP	A /A	12/78	6.33 (2)	5.61 (2)	5.35 (7)	3.41P(16)	4.50P(16)
BIG THREE INDUSTRIES	A /A	12/78	6.08 (3)	6.48 (1)	5.83 (3)	6.53 (5)	6.91 (8)
FERRO CORP	BAA/A	12/78	5.91 (4)	5.45 (4)	5.76 (4)	4.49 (11)	7.60 (6)
AIR PRODUCTS & CHEMICALS INC	NR /NR	9/78	4.39P(5)	4.00P(10)	4.27P(13)	3.95P(12)	3.73 (20)
STAUFFER CHEMICAL CO	A /A	12/78	4.35P(6)	4.36P(7)	4.72P(10)	6.83P(4)	6.94P(7)
PPG INDUSTRIES INC	Aa /A	12/78	4.31 (7)	3.36 (15)	4.80 (9)	3.23 (17)	4.22 (17)
INTL MINERALS & CHEMICAL	A /A	6/78	4.25 (8)	4.12 (9)	5.84 (2)	8.28 (1)	4.81 (13)
MONSANTO CO	Aa /AA-	12/78	4.04P(9)	4.35P(8)	5.51P(5)	6.47P(6)	8.22P(3)
NATIONAL DISTILLERS &CHEMICL	A /A	12/78	4.03 (10)	5.55 (3)	7.45 (1)	7.23 (3)	7.88 (4)
HERCULES INC	A /A	12/78	3.92 (11)	2.53 (22)	4.20 (14)	1.90 (23)	3.96 (18)
AMERICAN CYANAMID CO	Aa /AA	12/78	3.80 (12)	3.93 (11)	4.70 (11)	7.62 (2)	8.82 (1)
UNION CARBIDE CORP	Aa /AA-	12/78	3.65P(13)	3.79P(12)	4.83P(8)	5.06 (8)	8.69 (2)
IMPERIAL CHEM INDS LTD-ADR	NR /NR	12/78	3.56P(14)	3.34P(16)	4.18P(15)	3.43P(15)	4.51P(15)
CELANESE CORP	Ba /BB*	12/78	3.42P(15)	2.73P(20)	3.03P(20)	2.39P(21)	4.59 (14)
PENNWALT CORP	A /A	12/78	3.40 (16)	3.40 (14)	3.50 (18)	3.07 (20)	2.90 (24)
NL INDUSTRIES	A /A	12/78	3.34 (17)	3.17 (17)	2.91 (21)	2.11 (22)	3.75 (19)
DIAMOND SHAMROCK CORP	A /A	12/78	3.25 (18)	4.57 (5)	5.38 (6)	5.35 (7)	5.31P(12)
GRACE (W.R.) & CO	Baa/BB*	12/78	3.15 (19)	2.94 (19)	3.29 (19)	3.50 (14)	2.95 (23)
ROHM & HAAS CO	A /A	12/78	2.93 (20)	2.32 (23)	2.29 (23)	1.58 (24)	3.51 (21)
ALLIED CHEMICAL CORP	A /A	12/78	2.73 (21)	3.61 (13)	3.94 (17)	3.88 (13)	6.32 (9)
DOW CHEMICAL	Aa /A+	12/78	2.72 (22)	3.04 (18)	4.06 (16)	4.79 (9)	5.53 (11)
REICHHOLD CHEMICALS INC	Baa/BBB+	12/78	2.38P(23)	2.56P(21)	2.87P(22)	4.68 (10)	5.92P(10)
WILLIAMS COS	Baa/BBB-	12/78	1.55 (24)	2.11P(24)	2.01P(24)	3.21P(19)	3.32P(22)
AVERAGE			3.93	3.82	4.38	4.43	5.52
MEDIAN			3.72	3.70	4.29	3.91	5.06

Chemical Industry

AFTER TAX COV (INCL RENTS)

	RATINGS	FYR END	78	77	76	75	74
DU PONT (E.I.) DE NEMOURS	Aaa/AAA	12/78	4.37P(1)	3.24P(5)	3.00P(10)	2.31P(14)	3.84P(5)
WITCO CHEMICAL CORP	A /A	12/78	3.54 (2)	3.32 (3)	3.18 (6)	2.36P(13)	3.19P(11)
STAUFFER CHEMICAL CO	A /A	12/78	3.17P(3)	3.16P(6)	3.36P(3)	3.98P(3)	3.68P(7)
AIR PRODUCTS & CHEMICALS INC	NR /NR	9/78	3.13P(4)	2.97P(7)	2.62P(12)	2.46P(10)	2.26 (18)
PPG INDUSTRIES INC	Aa /A	12/78	3.06 (5)	2.56 (11)	3.20 (5)	2.27 (15)	2.65 (16)
NATIONAL DISTILLERS &CHEMICL	A /AA	12/78	2.98 (6)	3.57 (1)	NA (-)	NA (-)	NA (-)
MONSANTO CO	Aa /AA-	12/78	2.98P(7)	3.24P(4)	3.86P(1)	4.05P(2)	4.72P(2)
AMERICAN CYANAMID CO	Aa /AA	12/78	2.71 (8)	2.80 (8)	3.08 (7)	4.10 (1)	4.44 (3)
UNION CARBIDE CORP	Aa /AA-	12/78	2.68P(9)	2.78P(9)	3.32P(4)	3.51 (4)	5.30 (1)
CELANESE CORP	Ba /BB*	12/78	2.61P(10)	2.07P(17)	2.15P(17)	1.82P(17)	3.09 (12)
HERCULES INC	A /A	12/78	2.61 (11)	1.94 (19)	2.95 (11)	1.62 (19)	3.00 (13)
DIAMOND SHAMROCK CORP	A /A	12/78	2.47 (12)	3.33 (2)	3.58 (2)	3.39 (5)	3.29P(9)
PENNWALT CORP	A /A	12/78	2.42 (13)	2.44 (13)	2.19 (15)	2.04 (16)	2.00 (20)
NL INDUSTRIES	A /A	12/78	2.33 (14)	2.26 (15)	2.21 (14)	1.75 (18)	2.89 (14)
DOW CHEMICAL	Aa /A+	12/78	2.31 (15)	2.43 (14)	3.00 (9)	3.36 (6)	3.71 (6)
ROHM & HAAS CO	A /A	12/78	2.30 (16)	1.95 (18)	1.93 (19)	1.43 (20)	2.84 (15)
GRACE (W.R.) & CO	Baa/BB*	12/78	2.29 (17)	2.22 (16)	2.14 (18)	2.37 (12)	2.09 (19)
ALLIED CHEMICAL CORP	A /A	12/78	2.09 (18)	2.69 (10)	2.45 (13)	2.39 (11)	3.21 (10)
REICHHOLD CHEMICALS INC	Baa/BBB+	12/78	1.79P(19)	1.93P(20)	2.15P(16)	2.88 (7)	4.14P(4)
WILLIAMS COS	Baa/BBB-	12/78	1.44 (20)	1.77P(21)	1.71P(20)	2.55P(9)	2.53P(17)
BIG THREE INDUSTRIES	A /A	12/78	NA (-)	NA (-)	NA (-)	NA (-)	NA (-)
FERRO CORP	BAA/A	12/78	NA (-)	NA (-)	NA (-)	NA (-)	NA (-)
IMPERIAL CHEM INDS LTD-ADR	NR /NR	12/78	NA (-)	2.46P(12)	3.06P(8)	2.55P(8)	3.47P(8)
INTL MINERALS & CHEMICAL	A /A	6/78	NA (-)	NA (-)	NA (-)	NA (-)	NA (-)
AVERAGE			2.66	2.62	2.76	2.66	3.32
MEDIAN			2.61	2.56	2.97	2.42	3.20

NET INCOME AS % NET SALES

	RATINGS	FYR END	78	77	76	75	74
BIG THREE INDUSTRIES	A /A	12/78	13.2 (1)	14.4 (1)	13.3 (1)	13.2 (2)	11.8 (2)
STAUFFER CHEMICAL CO	A /A	12/78	9.5 (2)	9.4 (3)	10.3 (5)	10.4 (5)	9.1 (7)
INTL MINERALS & CHEMICAL	A /A	6/78	8.8 (3)	8.5 (5)	10.7 (3)	12.4 (4)	6.7 (14)
DOW CHEMICAL	Aa /A+	12/78	8.4 (4)	8.9 (4)	10.8 (2)	12.6 (3)	11.9 (1)
DIAMOND SHAMROCK CORP	A /A	12/78	7.8 (5)	10.6 (2)	10.3 (4)	10.1 (6)	9.8 (5)
DU PONT (E.I.) DE NEMOURS	Aaa/AAA	12/78	7.4 (6)	5.8 (10)	5.5 (15)	3.8 (19)	5.8 (17)
AIR PRODUCTS & CHEMICALS INC	NR /NR	9/78	7.3 (7)	7.1 (6)	7.8 (8)	7.8 (9)	7.1 (12)
IMPERIAL CHEM INDS LTD-ADR	NR /NR	12/78	6.7 (8)	5.5 (12)	7.1 (7)	5.6 (12)	8.4 (8)
NATIONAL DISTILLERS &CHEMICL	A /AA	12/78	6.2 (9)	6.8 (7)	7.8 (7)	7.9 (8)	8.2 (9)
MONSANTO CO	Aa /AA-	12/78	6.0 (10)	6.0 (8)	8.6 (6)	8.5 (7)	9.2 (6)
AMERICAN CYANAMID CO	Aa /AA	12/78	5.7 (11)	5.8 (9)	6.5 (13)	7.7 (10)	8.2 (10)
FERRO CORP	BAA/A	12/78	5.6 (12)	5.0 (15)	5.3 (16)	4.7 (16)	6.1 (16)
HERCULES INC	A /A	12/78	5.3 (13)	3.4 (22)	6.7 (12)	2.3 (23)	6.1 (15)
UNION CARBIDE CORP	Aa /AA-	12/78	5.0 (14)	5.5 (11)	7.0 (10)	6.7 (11)	10.0 (4)
PENNWALT CORP	A /A	12/78	4.9 (15)	5.0 (14)	4.5 (19)	4.4 (17)	5.4 (18)
PPG INDUSTRIES INC	Aa /A	12/78	4.7 (16)	3.7 (20)	6.7 (11)	2.2 (24)	7.3 (11)
ROHM & HAAS CO	A /A	12/78	4.6 (17)	4.1 (18)	4.5 (20)	3.5 (20)	4.9 (21)
NL INDUSTRIES	A /A	12/78	4.6 (18)	4.2 (17)	4.6 (18)	2.6 (22)	4.3 (22)
WITCO CHEMICAL CORP	A /A	12/78	4.5 (19)	3.9 (19)	4.1 (21)	2.6 (21)	5.1 (20)
CELANESE CORP	Ba /BB*	12/78	4.3 (20)	3.0 (23)	3.3 (23)	4.7 (14)	3.8 (24)
GRACE (W.R.) & CO	Baa/BB*	12/78	4.0 (21)	3.5 (21)	3.6 (22)	4.7 (14)	3.8 (24)
ALLIED CHEMICAL CORP	A /A	12/78	3.7 (22)	4.7 (16)	4.8 (17)	5.0 (13)	6.8 (13)
WILLIAMS COS	Baa/BBB-	12/78	2.0 (23)	5.3 (13)	6.1 (14)	13.3 (1)	10.1 (3)
REICHHOLD CHEMICALS INC	Baa/BBB+	12/78	1.6 (24)	2.0 (24)	2.7 (24)	3.9 (18)	5.1 (19)
AVERAGE			5.90	5.92	6.77	6.69	7.30
MEDIAN			5.45	5.37	6.59	5.31	6.93

LTD/CAPITALIZATION (%)

	RATINGS	FYR END	78		77		76		75		74	
FERRO CORP	BAA/A	12/78	10.5	(1)	11.0	(1)	12.6	(1)	16.1	(1)	17.0	(1)
DU PONT (E.I.) DE NEMOURS	Aaa/AAA	12/78	18.8	(2)	23.0	(2)	24.1	(3)	18.8	(2)	17.5	(2)
BIG THREE INDUSTRIES	A /A	12/78	25.1	(3)	25.3	(4)	25.1	(4)	20.1	(3)	29.9	(10)
WITCO CHEMICAL CORP	A /A	12/78	25.9	(4)	27.8	(7)	30.7	(8)	33.5	(10)	34.9	(17)
HERCULES INC	A /A	12/78	26.6	(5)	30.3	(10)	30.5	(7)	33.5	(9)	34.1	(15)
REICHHOLD CHEMICALS INC	Baa/BBB+	12/78	28.3	(6)	29.1	(8)	35.4	(14)	25.8	(6)	29.6	(8)
UNION CARBIDE CORP	Aa /AA-	12/78	28.9	(7)	32.0	(11)	34.0	(11)	31.7	(8)	26.3	(6)
NATIONAL DISTILLERS &CHEMICL	A /A	12/78	29.1	(8)	24.7	(3)	23.7	(2)	23.7	(5)	25.9	(5)
AMERICAN CYANAMID CO	Aa /AA	12/78	29.3	(9)	27.5	(6)	27.4	(5)	21.3	(4)	19.9	(3)
IMPERIAL CHEM INDS LTD-ADR	NR /NR	12/78	30.0	(10)	34.3	(13)	34.6	(12)	34.8	(14)	33.2	(14)
PPG INDUSTRIES INC	Aa /A	12/78	30.3	(11)	32.2	(12)	31.5	(9)	34.7	(12)	29.9	(9)
ROHM & HAAS CO	A /A	12/78	30.4	(12)	34.4	(14)	40.3	(22)	38.6	(20)	30.9	(13)
MONSANTO CO	Aa /AA-	12/78	32.2	(13)	30.0	(9)	28.9	(6)	30.0	(7)	25.1	(4)
PENNWALT CORP	A /A	12/78	32.4	(14)	35.4	(15)	34.9	(13)	36.1	(15)	29.9	(11)
AIR PRODUCTS & CHEMICALS INC	NR /NR	9/78	32.8	(15)	37.2	(16)	37.6	(18)	37.9	(18)	39.6	(20)
GRACE (W.R.) & CO	Baa/BB*	12/78	34.2	(16)	38.1	(19)	37.6	(17)	34.8	(13)	42.8	(22)
INTL MINERALS & CHEMICAL	A /A	6/78	34.2	(17)	37.3	(17)	38.9	(19)	39.2	(22)	44.1	(23)
STAUFFER CHEMICAL CO	A /A	12/78	35.3	(18)	38.1	(18)	40.5	(23)	33.8	(11)	29.4	(7)
NL INDUSTRIES	A /A	12/78	36.8	(19)	26.4	(5)	33.2	(10)	37.6	(17)	35.4	(18)
CELANESE CORP	Ba /BB*	12/78	36.8	(20)	39.3	(20)	37.5	(16)	38.0	(19)	38.2	(19)
ALLIED CHEMICAL CORP	A /A	12/78	42.7	(21)	40.9	(21)	36.4	(15)	37.1	(16)	30.2	(12)
DIAMOND SHAMROCK CORP	A /A	12/78	43.2	(22)	42.3	(22)	39.8	(21)	39.8	(23)	34.7	(16)
DOW CHEMICAL	Aa /A+	12/78	46.4	(23)	43.2	(23)	39.6	(20)	38.9	(21)	39.8	(21)
WILLIAMS COS	Baa/BBB-	12/78	52.6	(24)	50.2	(24)	50.0	(24)	49.5	(24)	51.5	(24)
AVERAGE			32.20		32.92		33.53		32.72		32.07	
MEDIAN			31.28		33.24		34.76		34.73		30.57	

LTD/NET PLANT (%)

	RATINGS	FYR END	78		77		76		75		74	
FERRO CORP	BAA/A	12/78	24.2	(1)	27.3	(2)	30.5	(1)	38.0	(5)	39.4	(6)
BIG THREE INDUSTRIES	A /A	12/78	26.7	(2)	27.1	(1)	31.6	(2)	24.4	(1)	34.5	(2)
DU PONT (E.I.) DE NEMOURS	Aaa/AAA	12/78	28.6	(3)	33.2	(3)	33.3	(3)	24.7	(2)	25.4	(1)
AIR PRODUCTS & CHEMICALS INC	NR /NR	9/78	29.5	(4)	36.4	(4)	36.0	(4)	36.4	(4)	39.1	(4)
UNION CARBIDE CORP	Aa /AA-	12/78	36.0	(5)	41.7	(6)	46.6	(10)	45.9	(8)	40.0	(7)
PPG INDUSTRIES INC	Aa /A	12/78	41.1	(6)	45.7	(10)	46.5	(9)	52.0	(14)	43.1	(9)
HERCULES INC	A /A	12/78	41.4	(7)	45.7	(9)	46.7	(11)	46.9	(9)	53.2	(15)
INTL MINERALS & CHEMICAL	A /A	6/78	42.6	(8)	49.7	(14)	55.6	(16)	57.2	(17)	82.0	(24)
WITCO CHEMICAL CORP	A /A	12/78	42.7	(9)	51.3	(16)	52.7	(15)	57.5	(19)	62.6	(20)
AMERICAN CYANAMID CO	Aa /AA	12/78	42.9	(10)	40.9	(5)	45.6	(8)	35.9	(3)	37.0	(3)
REICHHOLD CHEMICALS INC	Baa/BBB+	12/78	44.1	(11)	45.3	(8)	51.7	(13)	40.2	(6)	48.2	(14)
IMPERIAL CHEM INDS LTD-ADR	NR /NR	12/78	45.7	(12)	54.4	(18)	55.9	(17)	55.9	(16)	54.1	(16)
STAUFFER CHEMICAL CO	A /A	12/78	46.0	(13)	53.2	(17)	61.3	(18)	51.1	(13)	48.1	(13)
ALLIED CHEMICAL CORP	A /A	12/78	46.4	(14)	45.8	(11)	43.9	(6)	48.4	(10)	39.2	(5)
MONSANTO CO	Aa /AA-	12/78	47.0	(15)	42.8	(7)	43.8	(5)	50.9	(12)	44.8	(10)
CELANESE CORP	Ba /BB*	12/78	48.1	(16)	48.0	(12)	44.6	(7)	44.3	(7)	45.6	(11)
DIAMOND SHAMROCK CORP	A /A	12/78	51.5	(17)	51.0	(15)	48.6	(12)	49.6	(11)	41.9	(8)
ROHM & HAAS CO	A /A	12/78	52.4	(18)	57.2	(20)	68.5	(23)	58.9	(20)	48.0	(12)
GRACE (W.R.) & CO	Baa/BB*	12/78	55.2	(19)	62.0	(22)	66.1	(22)	59.5	(21)	73.9	(23)
PENNWALT CORP	A /A	12/78	59.5	(20)	70.0	(24)	76.6	(24)	79.0	(23)	57.5	(17)
NL INDUSTRIES	A /A	12/78	60.7	(21)	48.6	(13)	65.2	(21)	79.9	(24)	73.3	(22)
DOW CHEMICAL	Aa /A+	12/78	61.7	(22)	55.8	(19)	51.9	(14)	54.2	(15)	58.4	(18)
WILLIAMS COS	Baa/BBB-	12/78	64.5	(23)	62.7	(23)	64.0	(19)	67.0	(22)	72.7	(21)
NATIONAL DISTILLERS &CHEMICL	A /A	12/78	65.3	(24)	60.9	(21)	64.9	(20)	57.5	(18)	62.3	(19)
AVERAGE			46.00		48.19		51.34		50.64		51.01	
MEDIAN			45.88		48.31		50.16		51.03		48.07	

Chemical Industry

TOT LIABILITY/TOT STK EQUITY

	RATINGS	FYR END	78		77		76		75		74	
BIG THREE INDUSTRIES	A /A	12/78	69.1	(1)	64.4	(2)	62.9	(1)	56.3	(1)	81.2	(5)
DU PONT (E.I.) DE NEMOURS	Aaa/AAA	12/78	69.5	(2)	72.1	(3)	74.0	(3)	67.5	(3)	59.4	(1)
FERRO CORP	BAA/A	12/78	75.5	(3)	60.8	(1)	71.1	(2)	68.1	(4)	87.5	(7)
NATIONAL DISTILLERS &CHEMICL	A /A	12/78	84.6	(4)	78.7	(4)	78.5	(5)	72.0	(5)	80.3	(4)
ROHM & HAAS CO	A /A	12/78	92.8	(5)	93.4	(8)	116.5	(14)	107.2	(14)	94.2	(8)
HERCULES INC	A /A	12/78	95.1	(6)	95.0	(9)	92.8	(7)	98.0	(9)	98.8	(13)
MONSANTO CO	Aa /AA-	12/78	95.2	(7)	81.2	(5)	75.8	(4)	74.6	(6)	67.4	(3)
AMERICAN CYANAMID CO	Aa /AA	12/78	101.4	(8)	90.1	(7)	80.5	(6)	64.9	(2)	63.4	(2)
PPG INDUSTRIES INC	Aa /AA	12/78	101.7	(9)	99.0	(11)	99.0	(9)	105.2	(13)	95.8	(12)
INTL MINERALS & CHEMICAL	A /A	6/78	102.8	(10)	110.8	(14)	115.1	(13)	137.5	(20)	140.8	(19)
REICHHOLD CHEMICALS INC	Baa/BBB+	12/78	104.2	(11)	102.9	(12)	120.4	(17)	82.9	(7)	94.5	(9)
WITCO CHEMICAL CORP	A /A	12/78	105.8	(12)	96.3	(10)	102.1	(11)	104.0	(12)	122.7	(17)
PENNWALT CORP	A /A	12/78	105.9	(13)	103.8	(13)	101.1	(10)	103.5	(10)	111.2	(16)
IMPERIAL CHEM INDS LTD-ADR	NR /NR	12/78	110.5	(14)	141.8	(20)	149.5	(23)	136.8	(19)	136.2	(18)
UNION CARBIDE CORP	Aa /AA-	12/78	116.2	(15)	117.9	(16)	116.7	(15)	108.9	(15)	94.9	(11)
STAUFFER CHEMICAL CO	A /A	12/78	119.0	(16)	111.3	(11)	112.5	(12)	89.1	(8)	87.4	(6)
CELANESE CORP	Ba /BB*	12/78	128.1	(17)	142.8	(22)	139.9	(21)	148.4	(23)	146.1	(20)
NL INDUSTRIES	A /A	12/78	129.4	(18)	88.3	(6)	95.1	(8)	103.7	(11)	107.3	(14)
GRACE (W.R.) & CO	Baa/BB*	12/78	133.3	(19)	139.7	(18)	138.5	(19)	134.8	(18)	187.7	(24)
DIAMOND SHAMROCK CORP	A /A	12/78	134.3	(20)	128.3	(17)	120.5	(18)	120.8	(17)	108.1	(15)
AIR PRODUCTS & CHEMICALS INC	NR /NR	9/78	144.9	(21)	142.5	(21)	148.4	(22)	157.7	(24)	165.3	(23)
ALLIED CHEMICAL CORP	A /A	12/78	153.7	(22)	139.9	(19)	118.9	(16)	114.0	(16)	94.7	(10)
DOW CHEMICAL	Aa /A+	12/78	158.9	(23)	146.2	(23)	139.0	(20)	138.6	(21)	159.2	(21)
WILLIAMS COS	Baa/BBB-	12/78	192.5	(24)	162.7	(24)	152.5	(24)	141.4	(22)	160.2	(22)
AVERAGE			113.51		108.74		109.22		105.67		110.17	
MEDIAN			105.85		103.33		113.77		104.60		97.30	

NET TANG ASSETS/LTD (%)

	RATINGS	FYR END	78		77		76		75		74	
FERRO CORP	BAA/A	12/78	916.6	(1)	885.5	(1)	775.8	(1)	605.8	(1)	564.1	(1)
DU PONT (E.I.) DE NEMOURS	Aaa/AAA	12/78	519.9	(2)	417.0	(2)	401.0	(3)	514.0	(2)	556.3	(2)
BIG THREE INDUSTRIES	A /A	12/78	394.5	(3)	391.8	(4)	392.5	(4)	488.8	(3)	328.1	(7)
WITCO CHEMICAL CORP	A /A	12/78	360.1	(4)	333.5	(8)	296.1	(9)	268.0	(13)	254.8	(19)
HERCULES INC	A /A	12/78	357.8	(5)	312.2	(10)	308.5	(8)	288.3	(9)	281.7	(15)
REICHHOLD CHEMICALS INC	Baa/BBB+	12/78	346.6	(6)	334.8	(7)	274.6	(13)	368.4	(6)	325.1	(8)
UNION CARBIDE CORP	Aa /AA-	12/78	334.6	(7)	301.5	(12)	289.3	(10)	311.8	(8)	376.3	(6)
IMPERIAL CHEM INDS LTD-ADR	NR /NR	12/78	333.4	(8)	290.1	(13)	287.5	(11)	285.8	(10)	298.7	(14)
AMERICAN CYANAMID CO	Aa /AA	12/78	331.5	(9)	352.7	(6)	354.7	(5)	454.4	(4)	484.3	(3)
NATIONAL DISTILLERS &CHEMICL	A /A	12/78	323.0	(10)	395.2	(3)	413.0	(2)	410.1	(5)	377.0	(5)
PPG INDUSTRIES INC	Aa /A	12/78	323.0	(11)	304.1	(11)	309.4	(7)	279.1	(12)	321.6	(9)
ROHM & HAAS CO	A /A	12/78	321.7	(12)	274.7	(14)	211.3	(23)	246.3	(20)	305.5	(13)
MONSANTO CO	Aa /AA-	12/78	304.0	(13)	327.2	(9)	341.1	(6)	328.9	(7)	391.9	(4)
PENNWALT CORP	A /A	12/78	295.4	(14)	269.5	(15)	272.0	(14)	262.1	(15)	312.3	(11)
AIR PRODUCTS & CHEMICALS INC	NR /NR	9/78	292.9	(15)	264.2	(16)	260.5	(15)	257.1	(16)	245.4	(20)
INTL MINERALS & CHEMICAL	A /A	6/78	286.6	(16)	260.0	(17)	249.1	(18)	238.8	(22)	218.6	(23)
CELANESE CORP	Ba /BB*	12/78	266.7	(17)	249.0	(18)	260.3	(16)	256.8	(17)	255.8	(18)
STAUFFER CHEMICAL CO	A /A	12/78	263.5	(18)	248.8	(19)	235.6	(21)	279.5	(11)	318.9	(10)
NL INDUSTRIES	A /A	12/78	258.6	(19)	363.2	(5)	287.5	(12)	254.4	(18)	268.9	(17)
GRACE (W.R.) & CO	Baa/BB*	12/78	255.9	(20)	244.9	(20)	248.8	(19)	263.6	(14)	223.5	(22)
ALLIED CHEMICAL CORP	A /A	12/78	224.7	(21)	231.5	(21)	257.5	(17)	249.5	(19)	309.8	(12)
DIAMOND SHAMROCK CORP	A /A	12/78	216.1	(22)	218.4	(23)	228.9	(22)	236.8	(23)	272.4	(16)
DOW CHEMICAL	Aa /A+	12/78	209.2	(23)	224.6	(22)	243.7	(20)	246.0	(21)	238.0	(21)
WILLIAMS COS	Baa/BBB-	12/78	178.9	(24)	189.8	(24)	190.1	(24)	191.5	(24)	183.0	(24)
AVERAGE			329.80		320.18		307.86		316.07		321.34	
MEDIAN			312.89		295.80		281.05		273.56		307.66	

CASH FLOW/LTD (%)

	RATINGS	FYR END	78		77		76		75		74	
FERRO CORP	BAA/A	12/78	189.6	(1)	153.7	(1)	130.8	(1)	94.3	(3)	119.8	(1)
DU PONT (E.I.) DE NEMOURS	Aaa/AAA	12/78	151.0	(2)	106.5	(2)	93.9	(2)	98.2	(1)	119.6	(2)
BIG THREE INDUSTRIES	A /A	12/78	87.1	(3)	76.8	(3)	67.6	(6)	96.7	(2)	67.1	(10)
AIR PRODUCTS & CHEMICALS INC	NR /NR	9/78	80.4	(4)	72.1	(4)	68.3	(5)	66.1	(7)	59.5	(13)
WITCO CHEMICAL CORP	A /A	12/78	77.9	(5)	64.1	(5)	56.5	(10)	51.3	(16)	51.9	(15)
HERCULES INC	A /A	12/78	74.0	(6)	51.1	(11)	49.3	(16)	41.1	(20)	51.1	(18)
UNION CARBIDE CORP	Aa /AA-	12/78	62.3	(7)	54.8	(10)	57.5	(9)	60.9	(10)	93.6	(3)
CELANESE CORP	Ba /BB*	12/78	59.4	(8)	48.8	(15)	55.6	(13)	47.7	(17)	51.8	(16)
IMPERIAL CHEM INDS LTD-ADR	NR /NR	12/78	57.3	(9)	58.7	(9)	74.5	(3)	51.3	(15)	71.3	(8)
PPG INDUSTRIES INC	Aa /A	12/78	57.2	(10)	60.3	(8)	55.7	(11)	41.3	(19)	50.5	(19)
MONSANTO CO	Aa /AA-	12/78	56.6	(11)	63.5	(6)	73.0	(4)	65.3	(8)	85.9	(5)
ROHM & HAAS CO	A /A	12/78	56.1	(12)	42.3	(20)	32.1	(23)	28.0	(23)	58.5	(14)
INTL MINERALS & CHEMICAL	A /A	6/78	56.0	(13)	48.9	(14)	58.1	(8)	66.2	(6)	37.8	(21)
STAUFFER CHEMICAL CO	A /A	12/78	55.9	(14)	50.5	(12)	44.9	(18)	57.0	(11)	69.2	(9)
AMERICAN CYANAMID CO	Aa /AA	12/78	54.7	(15)	60.8	(7)	53.9	(15)	80.2	(4)	88.6	(4)
REICHHOLD CHEMICALS INC	Baa/BBB+	12/78	47.0	(16)	43.1	(18)	41.4	(20)	67.8	(5)	81.4	(6)
GRACE (W.R.) & CO	Baa/BB*	12/78	46.6	(17)	42.3	(21)	38.5	(21)	53.6	(13)	36.1	(22)
PENNWALT CORP	A /A	12/78	46.1	(18)	40.0	(22)	43.0	(19)	37.5	(21)	43.5	(20)
DIAMOND SHAMROCK CORP	A /A	12/78	38.1	(19)	45.4	(17)	54.1	(14)	53.5	(14)	51.3	(17)
DOW CHEMICAL	Aa /A+	12/78	38.0	(20)	42.5	(19)	55.7	(12)	64.5	(9)	77.5	(7)
NATIONAL DISTILLERS &CHEMICL	A /A	12/78	37.9	(21)	48.5	(16)	58.6	(7)	53.7	(12)	63.0	(12)
NL INDUSTRIES	A /A	12/78	34.7	(22)	49.0	(13)	35.6	(22)	22.8	(24)	34.5	(23)
ALLIED CHEMICAL CORP	A /A	12/78	32.7	(23)	38.7	(23)	47.8	(17)	47.4	(18)	65.0	(11)
WILLIAMS COS	Baa/BBB-	12/78	20.9	(24)	23.3	(24)	21.6	(24)	31.5	(22)	28.7	(24)
AVERAGE			63.23		57.74		57.00		57.41		64.89	
MEDIAN			56.04		49.76		55.68		53.64		61.24	

NET CASH FL/CAP EXP (%)

	RATINGS	FYR END	78		77		76		75		74	
DU PONT (E.I.) DE NEMOURS	Aaa/AAA	12/78	182.2	(1)	143.5	(1)	107.3	(9)	63.5	(22)	66.9	(21)
ROHM & HAAS CO	A /A	12/78	178.4	(2)	129.6	(2)	82.9	(16)	53.3	(24)	85.7	(14)
FERRO CORP	BAA/A	12/78	164.9	(3)	119.1	(6)	208.0	(1)	138.0	(3)	203.5	(4)
HERCULES INC	A /A	12/78	152.4	(4)	98.8	(9)	83.1	(15)	68.5	(18)	66.7	(22)
WITCO CHEMICAL CORP	A /A	12/78	141.3	(5)	121.3	(5)	120.1	(7)	119.6	(4)	92.1	(12)
MONSANTO CO	Aa /AA-	12/78	120.2	(6)	89.5	(12)	87.7	(14)	86.9	(12)	134.1	(6)
REICHHOLD CHEMICALS INC	Baa/BBB+	12/78	115.4	(7)	80.3	(19)	133.6	(4)	113.9	(5)	253.4	(2)
CELANESE CORP	Ba /BB*	12/78	114.1	(8)	89.7	(11)	100.0	(10)	87.0	(11)	94.1	(11)
WILLIAMS COS	Baa/BBB-	12/78	105.5	(9)	87.6	(14)	61.0	(23)	67.5	(19)	52.1	(24)
BIG THREE INDUSTRIES	A /A	12/78	97.4	(10)	59.0 V	(23)	50.9 V	(24)	67.5 V	(20)	75.3 V	(13)
STAUFFER CHEMICAL CO	A /A	12/78	94.4	(11)	89.3	(13)	76.9	(18)	62.8	(23)	113.2	(8)
GRACE (W.R.) & CO	Baa/BB*	12/78	88.8	(12)	95.7	(10)	96.9	(11)	90.5	(10)	67.3	(20)
AIR PRODUCTS & CHEMICALS INC	NR /NR	9/78	88.0	(13)	122.2	(4)	91.0	(13)	79.7	(13)	85.7	(13)
PENNWALT CORP	A /A	12/78	86.4	(14)	107.1	(7)	126.7	(6)	138.3	(2)	75.5	(17)
AMERICAN CYANAMID CO	Aa /AA	12/78	84.8	(15)	86.1 V	(16)	69.7 V	(22)	76.0 V	(15)	106.3	(9)
INTL MINERALS & CHEMICAL	A /A	6/78	83.8	(16)	83.1	(18)	114.8	(8)	66.6	(21)	83.2	(15)
NATIONAL DISTILLERS &CHEMICL	A /A	12/78	82.3	(17)	83.7	(17)	201.6	(2)	152.3	(1)	299.9	(1)
DOW CHEMICAL	Aa /A+	12/78	81.7	(18)	68.4	(21)	73.4	(19)	94.3	(8)	103.5	(10)
UNION CARBIDE CORP	Aa /AA-	12/78	75.5	(19)	86.7	(15)	77.9	(17)	73.1	(16)	136.3	(5)
NL INDUSTRIES	A /A	12/78	71.4	(20)	78.0	(20)	92.8	(12)	71.2	(17)	128.1	(7)
IMPERIAL CHEM INDS LTD-ADR	NR /NR	12/78	70.9	(21)	103.1	(8)	145.9	(3)	105.4	(6)	211.6	(3)
DIAMOND SHAMROCK CORP	A /A	12/78	68.6	(22)	59.0	(22)	70.5	(21)	92.5	(9)	52.4	(23)
ALLIED CHEMICAL CORP	A /A	12/78	50.5	(23)	57.9	(24)	73.3	(20)·	79.6	(14)	79.3	(16)
PPG INDUSTRIES INC	Aa /A	12/78	NA	(-)	125.9	(3)	131.5	(5)	102.9	(7)	75.5	(18)
AVERAGE			104.30		94.35		103.22		89.63		114.23	
MEDIAN			88.84		89.40		91.93		83.33		88.88	

Chemical Industry

AFT TAX RET ON COM EQTY (%)

	RATINGS	FYR END	78	77	76	75	74
DU PONT (E.I.) DE NEMOURS	Aaa/AAA	12/78	17.2 (1)	13.1 (9)	11.8 (16)	7.3 (21)	11.2 (22)
DOW CHEMICAL	Aa /A+	12/78	16.9 (2)	17.8 (2)	21.4 (2)	25.1 (2)	29.8 (1)
INTL MINERALS & CHEMICAL	A /A	6/78	16.8 (3)	16.8 (4)	24.0 (1)	37.3 (1)	21.5 (2)
STAUFFER CHEMICAL CO	A /A	12/78	16.6 (4)	17.1 (3)	18.9 (4)	19.2 (4)	20.1 (6)
WITCO CHEMICAL CORP	A /A	12/78	16.3 (5)	13.5 (7)	13.9 (12)	9.0 (19)	16.6 (11)
BIG THREE INDUSTRIES	A /A	12/78	15.9 (6)	15.7 (6)	13.5 (14)	14.9 (9)	16.3 (12)
AIR PRODUCTS & CHEMICALS INC	NR /NR	9/78	15.7 (7)	15.9 (5)	17.5 (5)	18.0 (6)	16.0 (14)
FERRO CORP	BAA/A	12/78	15.5 (8)	13.2 (8)	13.9 (11)	12.0 (14)	17.6 (10)
DIAMOND SHAMROCK CORP	A /A	12/78	14.9 (9)	20.0 (1)	20.3 (3)	20.7 (3)	19.2 (7)
HERCULES INC	A /A	12/78	12.6 (10)	7.6 (23)	14.4 (10)	4.9 (23)	13.9 (21)
CELANESE CORP	Ba /BB*	12/78	12.6 (11)	8.9 (20)	9.2 (23)	6.8 (22)	14.0 (20)
AMERICAN CYANAMID CO	Aa /AA	12/78	12.4 (12)	11.9 (12)	12.2 (15)	14.1 (10)	14.9 (17)
IMPERIAL CHEM INDS LTD-ADR	NR /NR	12/78	12.4 (13)	13.1 (10)	16.0 (7)	11.7 (15)	18.7 (8)
PENNWALT CORP	A /A	12/78	12.3 (14)	12.3 (11)	10.8 (19)	10.4 (17)	9.3 (24)
GRACE (W.R.) & CO	Baa/BB*	12/78	12.2 (15)	11.5 (15)	11.4 (17)	15.6 (7)	15.3 (16)
NL INDUSTRIES	A /A	12/78	11.7 (16)	10.0 (18)	10.6 (21)	8.5 (20)	15.6 (15)
MONSANTO CO	Aa /AA-	12/78	11.7 (17)	11.4 (16)	16.2 (6)	15.3 (8)	18.1 (9)
NATIONAL DISTILLERS &CHEMICL	A /A	12/78	11.4 (18)	11.9 (13)	13.6 (13)	12.5 (12)	16.3 (13)
PPG INDUSTRIES INC	A /A	12/78	11.4 (19)	8.6 (22)	14.8 (8)	9.8 (18)	10.9 (23)
UNION CARBIDE CORP	Aa /AA-	12/78	10.8 (20)	11.3 (17)	14.4 (9)	13.9 (11)	21.2 (3)
ROHM & HAAS CO	A /A	12/78	10.4 (21)	8.6 (21)	9.4 (22)	4.4 (24)	14.4 (19)
ALLIED CHEMICAL CORP	A /A	12/78	9.5 (22)	11.6 (14)	11.3 (18)	11.1 (16)	14.9 (18)
REICHHOLD CHEMICALS INC	Baa/BBB+	12/78	5.7 (23)	7.5 (24)	10.8 (20)	12.3 (13)	20.9 (4)
WILLIAMS COS	Baa/BBB-	12/78	4.1 (24)	9.1 (19)	9.0 (24)	18.6 (5)	20.1 (5)
AVERAGE			12.80	12.45	14.15	13.90	16.95
MEDIAN			12.43	11.91	13.78	12.39	16.30

RET ON TOT ASSETS (%)

	RATINGS	FYR END	78	77	76	75	74
DU PONT (E.I.) DE NEMOURS	Aaa/AAA	12/78	18.3 (1)	15.4 (4)	13.7 (14)	8.9 (20)	12.2 (21)
FERRO CORP	BAA/A	12/78	17.1 (2)	16.6 (6)	14.3 (12)		18.1 (6)
BIG THREE INDUSTRIES	A /A	12/78	16.7 (3)	15.1 (7)	15.2 (10)	17.1 (6)	16.3 (11)
INTL MINERALS & CHEMICAL	A /A	6/78	16.1 (4)	14.5 (8)	20.3 (1)	27.3 (1)	15.1 (14)
WITCO CHEMICAL CORP	A /A	12/78	15.9 (5)	13.9 (11)	14.4 (12)	11.9 (16)	16.0 (12)
AIR PRODUCTS & CHEMICALS INC	NR /NR	9/78	14.6 (6)	14.2 (9)	15.5 (8)	15.4 (8)	13.3 (17)
STAUFFER CHEMICAL CO	A /A	12/78	14.2 (7)	16.0 (3)	17.3 (5)	18.6 (3)	19.4 (5)
DOW CHEMICAL	Aa /A+	12/78	14.2 (8)	15.2 (5)	17.9 (3)	21.3 (2)	24.1 (1)
PENNWALT CORP	A /A	12/78	14.0 (9)	15.1 (6)	14.4 (13)	12.9 (15)	11.1 (23)
MONSANTO CO	Aa /AA-	12/78	13.5 (10)	14.0 (10)	17.6 (4)	17.2 (5)	21.0 (3)
HERCULES INC	A /A	12/78	13.1 (11)	9.4 (21)	16.3 (7)	6.0 (23)	13.2 (19)
ROHM & HAAS CO	A /A	12/78	12.9 (12)	10.6 (18)	10.3 (21)	5.5 (24)	14.8 (15)
GRACE (W.R.) & CO	Baa/BB*	12/78	12.2 (13)	11.5 (15)	11.3 (18)	14.7 (10)	13.0 (20)
PPG INDUSTRIES INC	Aa /A	12/78	12.0 (14)	11.4 (16)	15.4 (9)	10.1 (19)	10.3 (24)
AMERICAN CYANAMID CO	Aa /AA	12/78	11.9 (15)	12.2 (13)	12.6 (16)	15.7 (7)	16.8 (9)
DIAMOND SHAMROCK CORP	A /A	12/78	11.7 (16)	16.4 (2)	18.1 (2)	18.1 (4)	16.8 (10)
NATIONAL DISTILLERS &CHEMICL	A /A	12/78	11.4 (17)	13.0 (12)	15.0 (11)	14.1 (13)	18.0 (7)
NL INDUSTRIES	A /A	12/78	11.0 (18)	10.6 (17)	11.1 (19)	8.3 (21)	14.5 (16)
ALLIED CHEMICAL CORP	A /A	12/78	10.4 (19)	10.4 (19)	9.6 (22)	10.3 (18)	13.3 (18)
CELANESE CORP	Ba /BB*	12/78	10.2 (20)	8.6 (22)	8.3 (23)	6.1 (22)	11.2 (22)
IMPERIAL CHEM INDS LTD-ADR	NR /NR	12/78	10.0 (21)	11.9 (14)	13.1 (15)	10.6 (17)	15.8 (13)
UNION CARBIDE CORP	Aa /AA-	12/78	9.7 (22)	9.6 (20)	12.5 (17)	14.4 (11)	20.0 (4)
REICHHOLD CHEMICALS INC	Baa/BBB+	12/78	7.2 (23)	7.8 (24)	10.7 (20)	14.0 (14)	23.4 (2)
WILLIAMS COS	Baa/BBB-	12/78	7.1 (24)	8.5 (23)	8.2 (24)	15.1 (9)	17.8 (8)
AVERAGE			12.73	12.59	13.97	13.66	16.06
MEDIAN			12.52	12.58	14.38	14.21	15.92

Conglomerates

PRETAX COVERAGE

	RATINGS	FYR END	78	77	76	75	74
TELEDYNE INC	Baa/BBB	12/78	23.24 (1)	19.96 (1)	14.35 (1)	9.09 (3)	13.45 (3)
MINNESOTA MINING & MFG CO	Aaa/AAA	12/78	21.37 (2)	14.99 (2)	12.45 (4)	7.64 (6)	15.64 (2)
MARTIN MARIETTA CORP	A /A	12/78	18.06 (3)	11.68 (4)	8.32 (7)	5.59 (9)	7.27 (7)
DART INDUSTRIES	A /A ₀	12/78	12.33 (4)	11.07 (6)	12.72 (3)	12.21 (2)	11.47 (4)
TEXTRON INC	A /AA-	12/78	11.14 (5)	11.09 (5)	8.63 (5)	6.06 (8)	10.63 (5)
MOBIL CORP	Aa /AA	12/78	10.40 (6)	12.72 (3)	13.70 (2)	13.66 (1)	27.09 (1)
COLT INDUSTRIES INC	A /A	12/78	6.57 (7)	6.27 (8)	6.26 (9)	6.31 (7)	8.27 (6)
U S INDUSTRIES	Baa/BBB	12/78	6.26P(8)	6.02P(9)	3.30P(20)	1.66 (27)	1.71 (27)
NORTHWEST INDUSTRIES	Baa/BBB*	12/78	5.80 (9)	7.37 (7)	8.41 (6)	8.80 (4)	7.11H(8)
UV INDUSTRIES INC	Baa/BBB	12/78	5.47 (10)	5.93 (11)	7.07 (8)	4.72 (11)	5.34 (11)
KIDDE (WALTER) & CO	Baa/BBB	12/78	5.42 (11)	5.95 (10)	5.85 (10)	4.53 (13)	4.15 (17)
LOEWS CORP	NR /BBB	12/78	5.29H(12)	3.76H(17)	2.82H(25)	2.31H(24)	1.86P(26)
SIGNAL COS	Baa/BBB	12/78	4.76 (13)	4.02 (16)	3.20 (22)	2.47 (22)	4.31 (16)
PULLMAN INC	Baa/BBB	12/78	4.22 (14)	3.58 (20)	5.19 (11)	3.86 (15)	4.53 (14)
GAF CORP	Baa/BBB	12/78	4.18 (15)	3.59 (19)	2.88P(24)	4.03 (14)	4.56 (13)
MISSOURI PACIFIC CORP	Baa/NR	12/78	3.83 (16)	3.71 (18)	3.03 (23)	2.39 (23)	2.46 (24)
OGDEN CORP	Ba /BB*	12/78	3.74P(17)	3.34P(22)	3.49P(18)	3.45 (18)	3.96 (18)
SCM CORP	Baa/BBB	6/78	3.28 (18)	4.26 (14)	3.88 (15)	3.14 (19)	4.59 (12)
TENNECO INC	A /A	12/78	3.21 (19)	4.02 (15)	3.83 (17)	3.46 (17)	3.64 (19)
INTL TELEPHONE & TELEGRAPH	A /A	12/78	3.08H(20)	3.21 (24)	3.24 (21)	3.01 (20)	3.09 (21)
AMFAC INC	Ba /BB*	12/78	3.06 (21)	3.47 (21)	2.37 (28)	5.26 (10)	6.00 (10)
SINGER CO	Baa/BB	12/78	2.79 (22)	3.25 (23)	2.77 (27)	0.24 (30)	1.32 (29)
CITY INVESTING CO	NR /BB	12/78	2.78 (23)	2.69 (27)	2.06 (29)	1.60 (28)	1.63 (28)
A-T-O INC	Baa/BB	12/78	2.73 (24)	2.89 (26)	3.88 (16)	3.56 (16)	2.79 (23)
IC INDUSTRIES INC	NR /NR	12/78	2.72P(25)	3.12P(25)	2.82P(26)	1.97P(25)	3.05P(22)
CRANE CO	Baa/BBB	12/78	2.70 (26)	4.35 (13)	4.39 (12)	8.19 (5)	6.15 (9)
GULF & WESTERN INDS INC	Baa/BBB	7/78	2.43 (27)	2.47 (28)	3.32 (19)	2.69 (21)	2.30 (25)
GREYHOUND CORP	A /A	12/78	2.17 (28)	4.55 (12)	3.99 (14)	4.64 (12)	4.40 (15)
AVCO CORP	Ba /B*	11/78	1.99 (29)	1.98 (29)	4.15 (13)	1.86 (26)	0.97 (30)
LTV CORP	B /NR	12/78	1.26 (30)	0.59 (30)	1.26 (30)	0.93 (29)	3.35 (20)
AVERAGE			6.21	5.86	5.45	4.65	5.90
MEDIAN			4.00	4.02	3.88	3.71	4.36

AFTER TAX COVERAGE

	RATINGS	FYR END	78	77	76	75	74
MINNESOTA MINING & MFG CO	Aaa/AAA	12/78	11.99 (1)	8.52 (2)	7.27 (3)	4.81 (5)	8.92 (3)
TELEDYNE INC	Baa/BBB	12/78	11.78 (2)	10.56 (1)	7.79 (1)	5.26 (3)	9.37 (1)
MARTIN MARIETTA CORP	A /A	12/78	10.42 (3)	6.69 (3)	5.28 (5)	4.35 (6)	4.53 (8)
DART INDUSTRIES	A /A	12/78	6.72 (4)	6.61 (4)	7.41 (2)	6.86 (1)	6.31 (5)
TEXTRON INC	A /AA-	12/78	6.59 (5)	6.13 (5)	5.01 (6)	3.89 (8)	6.31 (4)
COLT INDUSTRIES INC	A /A	12/78	4.03 (6)	3.91 (7)	4.11 (8)	4.24 (7)	5.21 (6)
NORTHWEST INDUSTRIES	Baa/BBB*	12/78	3.72 (7)	4.52 (6)	5.38 (4)	5.72 (2)	4.69H(7)
UV INDUSTRIES INC	Baa/BBB	12/78	3.51 (8)	3.59 (10)	4.43 (7)	3.09 (11)	3.40 (11)
U S INDUSTRIES	Baa/BBB	12/78	3.49P(9)	3.22P(12)	2.05P(26)	1.38 (28)	1.51 (27)
LOEWS CORP	NR /BBB	12/78	3.45H(10)	2.71H(17)	2.25H(22)	1.87H(22)	1.61P(26)
KIDDE (WALTER) & CO	Baa/BBB	12/78	3.43 (11)	3.67 (9)	3.60 (10)	2.90 (13)	2.67 (18)
MOBIL CORP	Aa /AA	12/78	3.31 (12)	3.35 (11)	3.97 (9)	2.73 (15)	8.93 (2)
SIGNAL COS	Baa/BBB	12/78	2.96 (13)	2.59 (18)	2.17 (24)	1.79 (25)	2.79 (16)
PULLMAN INC	Baa/BBB	12/78	2.85 (14)	2.58 (19)	3.11 (12)	2.90 (14)	3.00 (14)
GAF CORP	Baa/BBB	12/78	2.82 (15)	2.49 (21)	2.23P(23)	3.09 (12)	3.16 (12)
MISSOURI PACIFIC CORP	Baa/NR	12/78	2.80 (16)	2.78 (14)	2.28 (20)	1.82 (23)	1.84 (25)
SCM CORP	Baa/BBB	6/78	2.66 (17)	2.76 (15)	2.63 (16)	2.42 (17)	3.08 (13)
OGDEN CORP	Ba /BB*	12/78	2.51P(18)	2.42P(22)	2.52P(19)	2.69 (16)	2.70 (17)
INTL TELEPHONE & TELEGRAPH	A /A	12/78	2.32H(19)	2.31 (24)	2.27 (21)	2.09 (21)	2.13 (22)
TENNECO INC	A /A	12/78	2.23 (20)	2.56 (20)	2.60 (17)	2.38 (19)	2.45 (19)
AMFAC INC	Ba /BB*	12/78	2.20 (21)	2.72 (16)	1.96 (27)	3.23 (10)	3.44 (10)
CRANE CO	Baa/BBB	12/78	2.19 (22)	3.81 (8)	3.12 (11)	5.01 (4)	3.97 (9)
CITY INVESTING CO	NR /BB	12/78	2.07 (23)	2.04 (27)	1.75 (29)	1.53 (26)	1.51 (28)
IC INDUSTRIES INC	NR /NR	12/78	2.03P(24)	2.39P(23)	2.11P(25)	1.79P(24)	2.30P(20)
SINGER CO	Baa/BB	12/78	1.95 (25)	2.22 (25)	1.79 (28)	0.04 (30)	1.31 (29)
GULF & WESTERN INDS INC	Baa/BBB	7/78	1.94 (26)	2.04 (28)	2.67 (15)	2.29 (20)	2.02 (23)
GREYHOUND CORP	A /A	12/78	1.92 (27)	3.21 (13)	2.93 (13)	3.25 (9)	2.92 (15)
A-T-O INC	Baa/BB	12/78	1.84 (28)	2.06 (26)	2.56 (18)	2.41 (18)	1.96 (24)
AVCO CORP	Ba /B*	11/78	1.58 (29)	1.58 (29)	2.85 (14)	1.50 (27)	0.80 (30)
LTV CORP	B /NR	12/78	1.22 (30)	0.78 (30)	1.36 (30)	1.15 (29)	2.25 (21)
AVERAGE			3.75	3.56	3.38	2.95	3.57
MEDIAN			2.81	2.74	2.65	2.71	2.85

Conglomerates

AFTER TAX COV (INCL RENTS)

	RATINGS	FYR END	78	77	76	75	74
MARTIN MARIETTA CORP	A /A	12/78	4.66 (1)	3.82 (1)	3.15 (6)	2.64 (7)	2.81 (6)
TEXTRON INC	A /AA-	12/78	3.72 (2)	3.53 (2)	3.21 (5)	2.67 (6)	3.45 (4)
DART INDUSTRIES	A /A	12/78	3.19 (3)	3.08 (4)	3.04 (7)	2.81 (5)	2.68 (8)
NORTHWEST INDUSTRIES	Baa/BBB*	12/78	2.91 (4)	3.38 (3)	3.77 (3)	NA (-)	NA (-)
COLT INDUSTRIES INC	A /A	12/78	2.89 (5)	2.73 (6)	2.85 (8)	2.89 (4)	3.60 (3)
LOEWS CORP	NR /BBB	12/78	2.82H(6)	2.25H(9)	1.94H(15)	1.65H(18)	1.51P(24)
UV INDUSTRIES INC	Baa/BBB	12/78	2.80 (7)	2.87 (5)	3.31 (4)	2.48 (8)	2.81 (7)
SIGNAL COS	Baa/BBB	12/78	2.50 (8)	2.19 (11)	1.82 (17)	1.54 (22)	2.27 (10)
KIDDE (WALTER) & CO	Baa/BBB	12/78	2.40 (9)	2.41 (8)	2.33 (10)	2.11 (11)	2.05 (14)
U S INDUSTRIES	Baa/BBB	12/78	2.18P(10)	1.91P(15)	1.47P(27)	1.19 (27)	1.29 (27)
MOBIL CORP	Aa /AA	12/78	2.16 (11)	2.04 (12)	2.27 (12)	1.60 (21)	3.23 (5)
PULLMAN INC	Baa/BBB	12/78	2.01 (12)	1.53 (26)	1.54 (25)	1.80 (15)	2.09 (13)
TENNECO INC	A /A	12/78	1.99 (13)	2.23 (10)	2.28 (11)	2.17 (9)	2.23 (11)
GAF CORP	Baa/BBB	12/78	1.99 (14)	1.87 (17)	1.60P(24)	2.11 (10)	2.16 (12)
CITY INVESTING CO	NR /BB	12/78	1.94 (15)	1.92 (13)	1.64 (22)	1.44 (24)	1.44 (25)
MISSOURI PACIFIC CORP	Baa/NR	12/78	1.90 (16)	1.86 (18)	1.63 (23)	1.42 (26)	1.42 (26)
INTL TELEPHONE & TELEGRAPH	A /A	12/78	1.85H(17)	1.89 (16)	1.81 (18)	1.69 (17)	1.68 (22)
OGDEN CORP	Ba /BB*	12/78	1.83P(18)	1.80P(19)	1.79P(19)	1.86 (14)	1.93 (15)
CRANE CO	Baa/BBB	12/78	1.82 (19)	2.58 (7)	2.22 (13)	2.98 (3)	2.63 (9)
SCM CORP	Baa/BBB	6/78	1.78 (20)	1.76 (21)	1.66 (21)	1.61 (20)	1.79 (19)
IC INDUSTRIES INC	NR /NR	12/78	1.69P(21)	1.73P(22)	1.49P(26)	1.47P(23)	1.73P(21)
A-T-O INC	Baa/BB	12/78	1.67 (22)	1.77 (20)	1.85 (16)	1.78 (16)	1.60 (23)
GULF & WESTERN INDS INC	Baa/BBB	7/78	1.64 (23)	1.69 (23)	2.13 (14)	1.99 (12)	1.79 (20)
AMFAC INC	Ba /BB*	12/78	1.62 (24)	1.53 (25)	1.27 (29)	1.62 (19)	1.89 (17)
AVCO CORP	Ba /B*	11/78	1.51 (25)	1.51 (27)	2.41 (9)	1.42 (25)	0.83 (29)
SINGER CO	Baa/BB	12/78	1.49 (26)	1.63 (24)	1.40 (28)	0.57 (29)	1.16 (28)
GREYHOUND CORP	A /A	12/78	1.43 (27)	1.91 (14)	1.77 (20)	1.92 (13)	1.88 (18)
LTV CORP	B /NR	12/78	1.18 (28)	0.85 (28)	1.25 (30)	1.11 (28)	1.90 (16)
MINNESOTA MINING & MFG CO	Aaa/AAA	12/78	NA (-)	NA (-)	4.80 (1)	3.55 (1)	5.48 (1)
TELEDYNE INC	Baa/BBB	12/78	NA (-)	NA (-)	4.52 (2)	3.38 (2)	5.03 (2)
AVERAGE			2.20	2.15	2.27	1.98	2.29
MEDIAN			1.96	1.91	1.89	1.80	1.93

NET INCOME AS % NET SALES

	RATINGS	FYR END	78	77	76	75	74
MINNESOTA MINING & MFG CO	Aaa/AAA	12/78	12.1 (1)	10.4 (1)	9.6 (1)	8.4 (2)	10.3 (1)
TELEDYNE INC	Baa/BBB	12/78	10.2 (2)	8.8 (2)	7.0 (4)	5.9 (5)	1.8 (26)
MARTIN MARIETTA CORP	A /A	12/78	7.7 (3)	7.1 (4)	6.5 (7)	5.3 (10)	6.6 (5)
MISSOURI PACIFIC CORP	Baa/NR	12/78	7.7 (4)	7.6 (3)	6.2 (8)	4.4 (12)	4.4 (14)
UV INDUSTRIES INC	Baa/BBB	12/78	7.1 (5)	6.5 (7)	6.7 (6)	5.7 (6)	6.2 (7)
DART INDUSTRIES	A /A	12/78	7.0 (6)	6.8 (6)	6.9 (5)	6.2 (3)	5.5 (8)
AVCO CORP	Ba /B*	11/78	6.8 (7)	6.5 (8)	7.9 (2)	5.3 (9)	-1.8 (30)
NORTHWEST INDUSTRIES	Baa/BBB*	12/78	6.4 (8)	6.9 (5)	7.5 (3)	8.5 (1)	7.4 (3)
TENNECO INC	A /A	12/78	5.3 (9)	5.7 (10)	6.0 (9)	6.1 (4)	6.4 (6)
TEXTRON INC	A /AA-	12/78	5.2 (10)	4.9 (11)	4.6 (12)	3.9 (14)	5.0 (11)
LOEWS CORP	NR /BBB	12/78	5.2 (11)	4.3 (13)	3.2 (18)	2.6 (21)	7.6 (2)
COLT INDUSTRIES INC	A /A	12/78	4.8 (12)	4.6 (12)	4.9 (11)	5.1 (11)	6.8 (4)
SIGNAL COS	Baa/BBB	12/78	4.5 (13)	3.4 (18)	2.6 (21)	1.9 (26)	3.9 (17)
INTL TELEPHONE & TELEGRAPH	A /A	12/78	4.3 (14)	4.3 (14)	4.2 (14)	3.5 (16)	4.0 (16)
GULF & WESTERN INDS INC	Baa/BBB	7/78	4.2 (15)	4.1 (16)	5.9 (10)	5.4 (8)	4.4 (13)
KIDDE (WALTER) & CO	Baa/BBB	12/78	3.7 (16)	3.8 (17)	3.9 (15)	3.7 (15)	3.6 (18)
U S INDUSTRIES	Baa/BBB	12/78	3.7 (17)	3.2 (20)	2.1 (25)	0.8 (28)	1.2 (28)
IC INDUSTRIES INC	NR /NR	12/78	3.4 (18)	4.2 (15)	3.6 (17)	3.2 (18)	4.3 (15)
MOBIL CORP	Aa /AA	12/78	3.2 (19)	3.1 (22)	3.6 (16)	3.9 (13)	5.5 (9)
CITY INVESTING CO	NR /BB	12/78	3.0 (20)	2.7 (25)	2.3 (23)	1.9 (27)	1.8 (25)
OGDEN CORP	Ba /BB*	12/78	3.0 (21)	3.1 (21)	3.1 (19)	3.2 (20)	2.5 (21)
CRANE CO	Baa/BBB	12/78	2.9 (22)	5.8 (9)	4.4 (13)	5.7 (7)	4.9 (12)
GAF CORP	Baa/BBB	12/78	2.9 (23)	2.8 (23)	1.9 (27)	3.2 (19)	3.4 (19)
AMFAC INC	Ba /BB*	12/78	2.8 C(24)	2.5 C(26)	1.5 C(28)	3.4 C(17)	5.5 C(10)
SCM CORP	Baa/BBB	6/78	2.5 (25)	2.7 (24)	2.3 (24)	2.2 (24)	2.3 (23)
PULLMAN INC	Baa/BBB	12/78	2.5 (26)	1.6 (29)	1.5 (29)	2.0 (25)	2.9 (20)
A-T-O INC	Baa/BB	12/78	2.5 (27)	2.0 (28)	2.5 (22)	2.5 (22)	2.4 (22)
SINGER CO	Baa/BB	12/78	2.4 (28)	3.3 (19)	2.8 (20)	-2.0 (30)	1.1 (29)
GREYHOUND CORP	A /A	12/78	1.3 (29)	2.1 (27)	2.1 (26)	2.2 (23)	2.0 (24)
LTV CORP	B /NR	12/78	0.4 (30)	-0.5 (30)	0.7 (30)	0.3 (29)	1.8 (27)
AVERAGE			4.61	4.49	4.26	3.81	4.13
MEDIAN			3.92	4.16	3.77	3.62	4.16

LTD/CAPITALIZATION (%)

	RATINGS	FYR END	78		77		76		75		74	
MINNESOTA MINING & MFG CO	Aaa/AAA	12/78	12.3	(1)	14.3	(1)	16.8	(1)	18.9	(2)	6.0	(1)
MARTIN MARIETTA CORP	A /A	12/78	14.8	(2)	23.2	(5)	27.8	(7)	30.9	(8)	32.7	(9)
U S INDUSTRIES	Baa/BBB	12/78	19.1	(3)	17.1	(2)	19.0	(2)	15.6	(1)	24.7	(4)
TEXTRON INC	A /AA-	12/78	22.2	(4)	24.5	(6)	21.3	(4)	25.1	(5)	26.8	(6)
PULLMAN INC	Baa/BBB	12/78	22.4	(5)	22.4	(3)	20.2	(3)	21.2	(4)	30.2	(7)
TELEDYNE INC	Baa/BBB	12/78	23.2	(6)	31.4	(9)	39.0	(17)	42.5	(17)	42.3	(19)
DART INDUSTRIES	A /A	12/78	24.3	(7)	22.9	(4)	25.0	(5)	25.2	(6)	25.3	(5)
MOBIL CORP	Aa /AA	12/78	27.7	(8)	27.2	(7)	27.4	(6)	21.1	(3)	21.2	(2)
SIGNAL COS	Baa/BBB	12/78	32.8	(9)	33.1	(10)	31.6	(8)	33.5	(9)	24.4	(3)
SCM CORP	Baa/BBB	6/78	33.8	(10)	36.9	(13)	40.1	(18)	42.6	(18)	36.5	(12)
INTL TELEPHONE & TELEGRAPH	A /A	12/78	34.3	(11)	31.4	(8)	33.4	(11)	33.8	(10)	32.6	(8)
COLT INDUSTRIES INC	A /A	12/78	34.3	(12)	37.4	(14)	38.6	(16)	40.1	(16)	40.2	(18)
GAF CORP	Baa/BBB	12/78	34.9	(13)	36.8	(12)	32.3	(9)	26.9	(7)	33.6	(10)
KIDDE (WALTER) & CO	Baa/BBB	12/78	39.4	(14)	38.2	(16)	32.7	(10)	36.8	(12)	37.6	(14)
SINGER CO	Baa/BB	12/78	39.4	(15)	43.3	(18)	54.3	(25)	59.5	(26)	34.5	(11)
NORTHWEST INDUSTRIES	Baa/BBB*	12/78	41.7	(16)	43.6	(19)	36.9	(14)	34.0	(11)	39.8	(17)
GREYHOUND CORP	A /A	12/78	41.9	(17)	34.7	(11)	35.7	(12)	37.8	(14)	38.4	(15)
UV INDUSTRIES INC	Baa/BBB	12/78	42.0	(18)	47.4	(22)	35.8	(13)	44.4	(19)	48.4	(21)
TENNECO INC	A /A	12/78	46.5	(19)	43.7	(20)	46.6	(21)	48.7	(22)	49.2	(22)
AMFAC INC	Ba /BB*	12/78	49.0	(20)	41.3	(17)	42.5	(19)	37.7	(13)	39.8	(16)
CRANE CO	Baa/BBB	12/78	49.1	(21)	45.6	(21)	47.8	(23)	47.4	(21)	44.1	(20)
IC INDUSTRIES INC	NR /NR	12/78	49.2	(22)	37.9	(15)	37.7	(15)	38.6	(15)	37.6	(13)
OGDEN CORP	Ba /BB*	12/78	50.9	(23)	52.9	(24)	54.8	(26)	55.7	(25)	51.6	(23)
LOEWS CORP	NR /BBB	12/78	52.0	(24)	56.4	(26)	59.2	(28)	62.6	(28)	60.3	(27)
A-T-O INC	Baa/BB	12/78	53.4	(25)	48.0	(23)	46.9	(22)	49.2	(23)	51.9	(24)
GULF & WESTERN INDS INC	Baa/BBB	7/78	55.4	(26)	57.3	(27)	55.6	(27)	61.8	(27)	62.5	(28)
MISSOURI PACIFIC CORP	Baa/NR	12/78	57.1	(27)	62.1	(28)	66.6	(29)	80.5	(30)	82.8	(30)
CITY INVESTING CO	NR /BB	12/78	60.3	(28)	54.8	(25)	49.3	(24)	53.1	(24)	54.4	(25)
AVCO CORP	Ba /B*	11/78	73.6	(29)	74.1	(30)	43.7	(20)	46.9	(20)	55.5	(26)
LTV CORP	B /NR	12/78	74.3	(30)	73.0	(29)	73.8	(30)	72.4	(29)	73.3	(29)
AVERAGE			40.38		40.43		39.75		41.48		41.27	
MEDIAN			40.57		38.06		38.14		39.34		39.06	

LTD/NET PLANT (%)

	RATINGS	FYR END	78		77		76		75		74	
MARTIN MARIETTA CORP	A /A	12/78	21.5	(1)	35.4	(3)	42.1	(3)	45.6	(4)	49.8	(4)
MINNESOTA MINING & MFG CO	Aaa/AAA	12/78	24.8	(2)	27.2	(1)	30.3	(1)	31.7	(2)	9.2	(1)
MOBIL CORP	Aa /AA	12/78	33.6	(3)	34.0	(2)	33.5	(2)	27.8	(1)	27.4	(2)
DART INDUSTRIES	A /A	12/78	48.7	(4)	49.9	(5)	53.5	(5)	55.5	(6)	56.7	(6)
TENNECO INC	A /A	12/78	53.6	(5)	50.0	(6)	55.0	(6)	57.6	(8)	53.4	(5)
MISSOURI PACIFIC CORP	Baa/NR	12/78	57.6	(6)	60.3	(11)	63.5	(10)	66.4	(10)	67.6	(8)
INTL TELEPHONE & TELEGRAPH	A /A	12/78	59.0	(7)	53.8	(7)	61.8	(7)	62.2	(9)	58.3	(7)
PULLMAN INC	Baa/BBB	12/78	60.7	(8)	59.5	(9)	61.8	(8)	66.7	(11)	112.3	(21)
SCM CORP	Baa/BBB	6/78	62.3	(9)	71.5	(12)	81.2	(18)	78.9	(16)	73.3	(11)
IC INDUSTRIES INC	NR /NR	12/78	63.4	(10)	44.2	(4)	44.4	(4)	45.7	(5)	43.1	(3)
U S INDUSTRIES	Baa/BBB	12/78	65.9	(11)	60.0	(10)	64.8	(11)	45.5	(3)	74.1	(12)
GAF CORP	Baa/BBB	12/78	67.3	(12)	73.0	(13)	70.2	(12)	57.1	(7)	78.2	(13)
OGDEN CORP	Ba /BB*	12/78	70.2	(13)	73.4	(14)	75.6	(14)	71.8	(12)	69.8	(9)
COLT INDUSTRIES INC	A /A	12/78	79.0	(14)	85.6	(16)	79.8	(16)	77.7	(15)	91.0	(16)
TEXTRON INC	A /AA-	12/78	79.2	(15)	96.2	(19)	76.3	(15)	84.2	(17)	95.0	(17)
GREYHOUND CORP	A /A	12/78	81.8	(16)	54.0	(8)	61.9	(9)	75.5	(13)	78.3	(14)
NORTHWEST INDUSTRIES	Baa/BBB*	12/78	85.0	(17)	95.1	(18)	81.2	(17)	84.7	(18)	122.9	(23)
CRANE CO	Baa/BBB	12/78	85.1	(18)	81.6	(15)	88.9	(19)	93.5	(20)	71.7	(10)
AMFAC INC	Ba /BB*	12/78	87.8	(19)	85.6	(17)	89.5	(20)	76.8	(14)	84.0	(15)
TELEDYNE INC	Baa/BBB	12/78	92.0	(20)	128.6	(25)	134.7	(23)	143.3	(23)	136.1	(24)
LTV CORP	B /NR	12/78	98.3	(21)	99.9	(20)	106.8	(22)	96.1	(21)	116.7	(22)
SIGNAL COS	Baa/BBB	12/78	105.8	(22)	100.9	(21)	94.3	(21)	101.3	(22)	106.6	(20)
UV INDUSTRIES INC	Baa/BBB	12/78	113.9	(23)	123.7	(23)	72.6	(13)	92.0	(19)	106.1	(19)
SINGER CO	Baa/BB	12/78	116.5	(24)	125.6	(24)	157.0	(26)	145.3	(25)	99.0	(18)
GULF & WESTERN INDS INC	Baa/BBB	7/78	118.5	(25)	122.8	(22)	150.2	(25)	170.3	(26)	174.0	(26)
A-T-O INC	Baa/BB	12/78	147.1	(26)	129.5	(26)	161.1	(27)	173.8	(27)	192.3	(28)
CITY INVESTING CO	NR /BB	12/78	148.0	(27)	165.8	(27)	170.6	(28)	189.3	(28)	184.2	(27)
KIDDE (WALTER) & CO	Baa/BBB	12/78	178.6	(28)	172.2	(28)	139.6	(24)	144.3	(24)	139.3	(25)
LOEWS CORP	NR /BBB	12/78	266.8	(29)	410.2	(29)	379.9	(29)	379.4	(29)	332.3	(29)
AVCO CORP	Ba /B*	11/78	1372.0	(30)	1370.0	(30)	581.2	(30)	613.2	(30)	636.9	(30)
AVERAGE			131.47		137.98		112.11		115.10		118.00	
MEDIAN			80.54		83.57		78.04		78.28		87.46	

Conglomerates

TOT LIABILITY/TOT STK EQUITY

	RATINGS	FYR END	78		77		76		75		74	
MINNESOTA MINING & MFG CO	Aaa/AAA	12/78	57.8	(1)	55.9	(1)	62.5	(1)	65.5	(1)	67.6	(1)
U S INDUSTRIES	Baa/BBB	12/78	64.9	(2)	64.4	(2)	71.2	(2)	88.9	(5)	101.2	(6)
TELEDYNE INC	Baa/BBB	12/78	79.9	(3)	107.9	(6)	144.1	(17)	132.4	(14)	126.8	(10)
MARTIN MARIETTA CORP	A /A	12/78	81.2	(4)	89.7	(5)	89.0	(5)	87.0	(4)	92.1	(3)
DART INDUSTRIES	A /A	12/78	92.4	(5)	70.2	(3)	73.4	(3)	74.1	(2)	80.2	(2)
TEXTRON INC	A /AA-	12/78	95.7	(6)	88.6	(4)	81.5	(4)	90.0	(6)	103.2	(7)
UV INDUSTRIES INC	Baa/BBB	12/78	117.0	(7)	141.9	(14)	126.5	(11)	141.8	(15)	166.1	(19)
GAF CORP	Baa/BBB	12/78	123.3	(8)	131.3	(11)	97.3	(6)	86.1	(3)	98.1	(5)
COLT INDUSTRIES INC	A /A	12/78	124.3	(9)	120.9	(8)	124.3	(9)	131.0	(10)	128.9	(11)
SCM CORP	Baa/BBB	6/78	127.0	(10)	123.5	(9)	136.0	(14)	143.3	(18)	143.1	(14)
KIDDE (WALTER) & CO	Baa/BBB	12/78	128.9	(11)	114.9	(7)	97.7	(7)	131.3	(12)	154.0	(16)
NORTHWEST INDUSTRIES	Baa/BBB*	12/78	138.4	(12)	148.3	(16)	121.8	(8)	103.2	(7)	116.1	(8)
SIGNAL COS	Baa/BBB	12/78	142.2	(13)	146.3	(15)	129.6	(13)	131.0	(11)	95.0	(4)
GREYHOUND CORP	A /A	12/78	148.8	(14)	130.6	(10)	125.7	(10)	132.2	(13)	137.4	(12)
MOBIL CORP	Aa /AA	12/78	153.8	(15)	149.4	(17)	145.3	(18)	120.0	(8)	118.7	(9)
INTL TELEPHONE & TELEGRAPH	A /A	12/78	154.9	(16)	139.0	(13)	142.0	(15)	144.8	(19)	158.7	(17)
CRANE CO	Baa/BBB	12/78	160.8	(17)	154.7	(19)	167.0	(21)	172.2	(21)	173.7	(21)
AMFAC INC	Ba /BB*	12/78	167.9	(18)	136.5	(12)	142.1	(16)	129.5	(9)	144.4	(15)
IC INDUSTRIES INC	NR /NR	12/78	172.5	(19)	154.6	(18)	146.2	(19)	142.2	(16)	140.9	(13)
SINGER CO	Baa/BB	12/78	185.8	(20)	219.6	(24)	325.7	(27)	486.9	(28)	162.2	(18)
TENNECO INC	A /A	12/78	186.7	(21)	168.8	(20)	170.7	(22)	174.3	(23)	198.8	(24)
PULLMAN INC	Baa/BBB	12/78	207.4	(22)	173.9	(21)	179.1	(23)	174.2	(22)	172.0	(20)
MISSOURI PACIFIC CORP	Baa/NR	12/78	221.1	(23)	275.5	(26)	321.3	(26)	707.7	(29)	826.4	(30)
A-T-O INC	Baa/BB	12/78	225.5	(24)	197.6	(22)	151.1	(20)	159.5	(20)	194.7	(22)
GULF & WESTERN INDS INC	Baa/BBB	7/78	228.0	(25)	237.6	(25)	217.5	(24)	289.3	(25)	279.9	(27)
OGDEN CORP	Ba /BB*	12/78	231.9	(26)	213.9	(23)	219.8	(25)	229.1	(24)	253.7	(26)
AVCO CORP	Ba /B*	11/78	519.4	(27)	550.8	(29)	128.7	(12)	143.1	(17)	197.0	(23)
LTV CORP	B /NR	12/78	572.6	(28)	438.4	(27)	416.6	(28)	444.5	(26)	489.7	(28)
CITY INVESTING CO	NR /BB	12/78	628.8	(29)	524.5	(28)	457.8	(29)	481.3	(27)	519.3	(29)
LOEWS CORP	NR /BBB	12/78	804.8	(30)	848.2	(30)	965.8	(30)	1076.3	(30)	200.7	(25)
AVERAGE			211.44		203.91		192.58		220.43		194.68	
MEDIAN			154.32		147.30		142.07		142.03		149.20	

NET TANG ASSETS/LTD (%)

	RATINGS	FYR END	78		77		76		75		74	
MINNESOTA MINING & MFG CO	Aaa/AAA	12/78	807.4	(1)	690.0	(1)	586.5	(1)	522.1	(1)	1624.7	(1)
MARTIN MARIETTA CORP	A /A	12/78	621.1	(2)	394.7	(4)	327.7	(7)	293.0	(8)	275.6	(8)
U S INDUSTRIES	Baa/BBB	12/78	431.9	(3)	471.7	(2)	418.2	(4)	485.5	(2)	318.6	(6)
TEXTRON INC	A /AA-	12/78	426.9	(4)	387.9	(5)	440.5	(3)	371.5	(5)	347.4	(4)
PULLMAN INC	Baa/BBB	12/78	420.1	(5)	441.6	(3)	490.1	(2)	468.6	(3)	326.4	(5)
TELEDYNE INC	Baa/BBB	12/78	417.3	(6)	306.0	(8)	242.4	(13)	223.1	(17)	223.7	(18)
MOBIL CORP	Aa /AA	12/78	349.0	(7)	355.8	(7)	355.2	(5)	461.3	(4)	456.9	(2)
DART INDUSTRIES	A /A	12/78	323.9	(8)	380.4	(6)	344.9	(6)	326.4	(7)	306.7	(7)
SIGNAL COS	Baa/BBB	12/78	298.0	(9)	293.4	(10)	304.4	(8)	284.6	(9)	397.1	(3)
SCM CORP	Baa/BBB	6/78	288.9	(10)	268.3	(11)	245.7	(12)	229.2	(15)	266.0	(12)
INTL TELEPHONE & TELEGRAPH	A /A	12/78	275.9	(11)	297.1	(9)	270.1	(10)	267.3	(10)	274.3	(10)
COLT INDUSTRIES INC	A /A	12/78	272.7	(12)	250.1	(13)	241.4	(15)	231.0	(14)	235.8	(15)
GAF CORP	Baa/BBB	12/78	269.2	(13)	253.4	(12)	286.8	(9)	336.1	(6)	274.4	(9)
SINGER CO	Baa/BB	12/78	238.2	(14)	210.1	(20)	159.8	(26)	136.3	(26)	266.6	(11)
KIDDE (WALTER) & CO	Baa/BBB	12/78	227.4	(15)	235.0	(16)	269.6	(11)	231.5	(13)	226.3	(16)
UV INDUSTRIES INC	Baa/BBB	12/78	214.4	(16)	187.6	(22)	240.8	(16)	194.2	(21)	176.4	(24)
TENNECO INC	A /A	12/78	210.2	(17)	223.2	(17)	209.1	(20)	200.3	(19)	194.5	(20)
AMFAC INC	Ba /BB*	12/78	202.4	(18)	240.5	(15)	222.4	(17)	250.2	(11)	237.6	(14)
CRANE CO	Baa/BBB	12/78	201.4	(19)	215.5	(19)	204.0	(22)	205.2	(18)	225.5	(17)
GREYHOUND CORP	A /A	12/78	190.2	(20)	217.2	(18)	208.8	(21)	192.1	(22)	201.0	(19)
IC INDUSTRIES INC	NR /NR	12/78	180.4	(21)	242.5	(14)	242.2	(14)	236.3	(12)	243.5	(13)
NORTHWEST INDUSTRIES	Baa/BBB*	12/78	172.2	(22)	158.1	(25)	209.4	(19)	228.1	(16)	190.9	(21)
GULF & WESTERN INDS INC	Baa/BBB	7/78	171.1	(23)	165.3	(24)	170.5	(24)	153.0	(25)	151.4	(26)
MISSOURI PACIFIC CORP	Baa/NR	12/78	169.9	(24)	155.7	(26)	146.3	(27)	120.2	(28)	117.5	(29)
A-T-O INC	Baa/BB	12/78	166.0	(25)	192.0	(21)	197.5	(23)	190.5	(23)	178.9	(23)
OGDEN CORP	Ba /BB*	12/78	162.9	(26)	166.1	(23)	164.6	(25)	166.5	(24)	180.1	(22)
LTV CORP	B /NR	12/78	117.1	(27)	121.2	(27)	123.7	(28)	126.0	(27)	124.6	(28)
LOEWS CORP	NR /BBB	12/78	99.4	(28)	94.9	(28)	76.0	(30)	74.7	(30)	137.1	(27)
CITY INVESTING CO	NR /BB	12/78	93.2	(29)	68.9	(29)	77.3	(29)	77.3	(29)	67.6	(30)
AVCO CORP	Ba /B*	11/78	63.3	(30)	59.8	(30)	211.3	(18)	195.5	(20)	164.0	(25)
AVERAGE			269.40		258.13		256.24		249.25		280.38	
MEDIAN			220.90		237.74		241.10		228.68		231.09	

CASH FLOW/LTD (%)

	RATINGS	FYR END	78		77		76		75		74	
MINNESOTA MINING & MFG CO	Aaa/AAA	12/78	225.4	(1)	174.2	(1)	132.6	(1)	103.8	(1)	407.5	(1)
MARTIN MARIETTA CORP	A /A	12/78	143.2	(2)	78.4	(2)	60.8	(4)	52.2	(6)	54.6	(5)
TELEDYNE INC	Baa/BBB	12/78	89.7	(3)	65.5	(4)	60.3	(5)	49.1	(7)	52.1	(8)
TEXTRON INC	A /AA-	12/78	75.8	(4)	62.5	(5)	74.2	(2)	55.6	(3)	58.3	(4)
LOEWS CORP	NR /BBB	12/78	67.6	(5)	51.7	(8)	48.3	(8)	34.3	(12)	7.5	(29)
DART INDUSTRIES	A /A	12/78	67.4	(6)	68.7	(3)	62.5	(3)	53.3	(5)	69.8	(3)
U S INDUSTRIES	Baa/BBB	12/78	64.1	(7)	61.3	(6)	45.8	(9)	44.5	(10)	25.0	(23)
MOBIL CORP	Aa /AA	12/78	61.5	(8)	60.3	(7)	54.9	(6)	62.0	(2)	111.8	(2)
PULLMAN INC	Baa/BBB	12/78	60.8	(9)	41.7	(10)	40.4	(11)	48.6	(8)	32.8	(15)
COLT INDUSTRIES INC	A /A	12/78	43.2	(10)	38.0	(14)	37.4	(15)	32.8	(15)	45.0	(9)
SIGNAL COS	Baa/BBB	12/78	42.0	(11)	33.8	(19)	29.7	(19)	20.0	(22)	38.7	(13)
SCM CORP	Baa/BBB	6/78	41.3	(12)	36.3	(17)	37.0	(16)	29.4	(19)	38.7	(12)
NORTHWEST INDUSTRIES	Baa/BBB*	12/78	40.3	(13)	36.6	(16)	51.9	(7)	55.1	(4)	54.0	(7)
INTL TELEPHONE & TELEGRAPH	A /A	12/78	40.1	(14)	40.2	(12)	38.9	(13)	33.6	(13)	44.8	(10)
CITY INVESTING CO	NR /BB	12/78	38.8	(15)	49.9	(9)	39.7	(12)	15.1	(27)	19.4	(25)
GAF CORP	Baa/BBB	12/78	37.3	(16)	32.8	(20)	29.1	(20)	43.7	(11)	30.1	(18)
SINGER CO	Baa/BB	12/78	33.3	(17)	36.0	(18)	25.2	(24)	10.4	(28)	28.5	(21)
TENNECO INC	A /A	12/78	32.9	(18)	37.2	(15)	33.6	(18)	32.3	(16)	34.5	(14)
UV INDUSTRIES INC	Baa/BBB	12/78	28.5	(19)	27.0	(24)	45.5	(10)	31.1	(17)	29.3	(20)
CRANE CO	Baa/BBB	12/78	27.9	(20)	39.0	(13)	36.0	(17)	46.5	(9)	54.3	(6)
OGDEN CORP	Ba /BB*	12/78	27.7	(21)	27.3	(23)	27.0	(22)	25.7	(21)	32.6	(16)
GREYHOUND CORP	A /A	12/78	27.5	(22)	41.5	(11)	37.5	(14)	33.0	(14)	29.4	(19)
KIDDE (WALTER) & CO	Baa/BBB	12/78	26.8	(23)	26.1	(25)	29.0	(21)	27.1	(20)	28.0	(22)
MISSOURI PACIFIC CORP	Baa/NR	12/78	24.8	(24)	25.6	(26)	20.8	(26)	16.0	(26)	16.1	(27)
AMFAC INC	Ba /BB*	12/78	22.9	(25)	27.6	(22)	18.6	(28)	29.9	(18)	40.9	(11)
A-T-O INC	Baa/BB	12/78	22.7	(26)	21.2	(27)	22.5	(25)	19.4	(23)	18.3	(26)
IC INDUSTRIES INC	NR /NR	12/78	19.9	(27)	30.5	(21)	26.3	(23)	16.6	(25)	21.7	(24)
GULF & WESTERN INDS INC	Baa/BBB	7/78	17.6	(28)	13.5	(29)	20.8	(27)	17.0	(24)	16.0	(28)
AVCO CORP	Ba /B*	11/78	17.6	(29)	16.9	(28)	12.7	(29)	6.1	(29)	2.8	(30)
LTV CORP	B /NR	12/78	6.9	(30)	2.7	(30)	7.9	(30)	5.9	(30)	30.2	(17)
AVERAGE			49.18		43.47		40.23		34.99		49.08	
MEDIAN			38.07		36.90		37.23		32.54		32.70	

CONGLOMERATES — NET CASH FL/CAP EXP (%)

	RATINGS	FYR END	78		77		76		75		74	
LOEWS CORP	NR /BBB	12/78	1088.3	(1)	2865.9	(1)	1500.2	(1)	1650.7	(1)	252.1	(2)
AVCO CORP	Ba /B*	11/78	686.4	(2)	1054.8	(2)	347.6	(4)	239.1	(3)	26.5	(30)
UV INDUSTRIES INC	Baa/BBB	12/78	236.1	(3)	249.5	(6)	285.6	(5)	191.6	(6)	203.9	(5)
TELEDYNE INC	Baa/BBB	12/78	229.7	(4)	337.1	(4)	504.0	(2)	450.7	(2)	412.5	(1)
CITY INVESTING CO	NR /BB	12/78	216.3	(5)	404.8	(3)	457.1	(3)	144.8	(10)	115.0	(15)
KIDDE (WALTER) & CO	Baa/BBB	12/78	206.4	(6)	220.7	(8)	231.8	(6)	224.7	(4)	102.1	(19)
MINNESOTA MINING & MFG CO	Aaa/AAA	12/78	189.3	(7)	185.3	(12)	172.4	(13)	84.0	(23)	72.2	(25)
SIGNAL COS	Baa/BBB	12/78	182.1	(8)	273.3	(5)	170.9	(15)	82.5	(24)	143.4	(12)
A-T-O INC	Baa/BB	12/78	182.1 V(9)		73.6 V(28)		196.2 V(14)		150.4 V(9)		166.9 V(8)	
COLT INDUSTRIES INC	A /A	12/78	175.6	(10)	195.6	(10)	183.1	(11)	180.9	(7)	154.8	(10)
DART INDUSTRIES	A /A	12/78	160.7	(11)	152.5	(13)	113.3	(19)	110.9	(17)	175.9	(7)
TEXTRON INC	A /AA-	12/78	160.4	(12)	190.4	(11)	208.2	(8)	121.1	(13)	159.0	(9)
U S INDUSTRIES	Baa/BBB	12/78	148.3	(13)	142.2	(16)	158.1	(17)	156.8	(8)	58.9	(28)
SINGER CO	Baa/BB	12/78	141.7	(14)	210.1	(9)	223.6	(7)	85.0	(22)	71.7	(26)
PULLMAN INC	Baa/BBB	12/78	125.8	(15)	77.2	(26)	81.1	(28)	93.0	(20)	105.7	(18)
OGDEN CORP	Ba /BB*	12/78	124.4	(16)	220.9	(7)	178.8	(12)	49.1	(29)	75.9	(24)
CRANE CO	Baa/BBB	12/78	120.6	(17)	96.1	(23)	99.0	(22)	192.4	(5)	191.6	(6)
GAF CORP	Baa/BBB	12/78	114.0	(18)	98.5	(20)	91.6	(27)	132.3	(11)	113.4	(16)
SCM CORP	Baa/BBB	6/78	110.1	(19)	98.5	(19)	185.2	(10)	67.1	(26)	93.5	(20)
MARTIN MARIETTA CORP	A /A	12/78	106.9	(20)	150.7	(14)	167.3	(16)	124.0	(12)	145.5	(11)
AMFAC INC	Ba /BB*	12/78	101.1	(21)	99.7	(18)	81.0	(29)	112.5	(16)	131.0	(13)
NORTHWEST INDUSTRIES	Baa/BBB*	12/78	98.2	(22)	148.0	(15)	171.9	(14)	119.0	(14)	227.4	(3)
IC INDUSTRIES INC	NR /NR	12/78	95.3	(23)	81.0	(25)	110.7	(20)	66.7	(27)	52.5	(29)
MOBIL CORP	Aa /AA	12/78	93.3	(24)	112.3	(17)	94.8	(25)	65.6	(28)	110.8	(17)
INTL TELEPHONE & TELEGRAPH	A /A	12/78	92.7	(25)	84.9	(24)	107.1	(21)	99.5	(19)	85.0	(22)
GREYHOUND CORP	A /A	12/78	89.3	(26)	58.7	(29)	91.7	(26)	81.5	(25)	70.3	(27)
MISSOURI PACIFIC CORP	Baa/NR	12/78	83.9	(27)	96.5	(22)	95.7	(24)	88.8	(21)	84.4	(23)
GULF & WESTERN INDS INC	Baa/BBB	7/78	83.7	(28)	75.5	(27)	132.3	(18)	118.5	(15)	123.4	(14)
LTV CORP	B /NR	12/78	79.0	(29)	28.8	(30)	60.5	(30)	20.2	(30)	222.9	(4)
TENNECO INC	A /A	12/78	77.6	(30)	97.1	(21)	98.3	(23)	106.4	(18)	89.0	(21)
AVERAGE			186.64		272.68		219.96		180.33		134.58	
MEDIAN			125.12		145.14		169.06		115.51		114.20	

Conglomerates

AFT TAX RET ON COM EQTY (%)

	RATINGS	FYR END	78		77		76		75		74	
TELEDYNE INC	Baa/BBB	12/78	28.7	(1)	28.2	(1)	26.9	(1)	20.0	(3)	5.5	(26)
MINNESOTA MINING & MFG CO	Aaa/AAA	12/78	21.7	(2)	18.2	(5)	16.5	(6)	14.4	(8)	17.8	(8)
MISSOURI PACIFIC CORP	Baa/NR	12/78	19.9	(3)	23.4	(2)	20.2	(2)	24.4	(1)	27.2	(1)
LOEWS CORP	NR /BBB	12/78	19.6	(4)	17.9	(6)	14.9	(11)	13.5	(9)	10.7	(19)
NORTHWEST INDUSTRIES	Baa/BBB*	12/78	19.3	(5)	19.4	(4)	18.2	(3)	18.4	(4)	18.4	(6)
TEXTRON INC	A /AA-	12/78	17.0	(6)	15.6	(9)	15.2	(9)	13.2	(10)	15.7	(12)
SIGNAL COS	Baa/BBB	12/78	16.1	(7)	11.6	(19)	8.1	(23)	5.2	(24)	8.5	(23)
MARTIN MARIETTA CORP	A /A	12/78	15.7	(8)	14.1	(13)	11.9	(16)	9.1	(21)	13.8	(15)
PULLMAN INC	Baa/BBB	12/78	15.7	(9)	9.2	(24)	8.9	(22)	12.2	(15)	13.9	(14)
OGDEN CORP	Ba /BB*	12/78	14.9	(10)	14.7	(10)	14.7	(12)	16.0	(6)	18.0	(7)
COLT INDUSTRIES INC	A /A	12/78	14.9	(11)	13.0	(14)	13.7	(13)	12.8	(12)	21.5	(4)
UV INDUSTRIES INC	Baa/BBB	12/78	14.8	(12)	15.9	(8)	15.8	(7)	12.7	(13)	17.4	(9)
AVCO CORP	Ba /B*	11/78	14.4	(13)	14.4	(11)	6.7	(25)	3.3	(27)	-6.6	(30)
TENNECO INC	A /A	12/78	13.8	(14)	14.3	(12)	15.0	(10)	14.9	(7)	15.8	(11)
DART INDUSTRIES	A /A	12/78	13.2	(15)	12.4	(15)	12.8	(14)	10.9	(18)	10.2	(22)
GULF & WESTERN INDS INC	Baa/BBB	7/78	12.8	(16)	11.7	(18)	18.2	(4)	16.7	(5)	14.1	(13)
MOBIL CORP	Aa /AA	12/78	12.6	(17)	12.2	(16)	12.3	(15)	11.8	(16)	16.3	(10)
INTL TELEPHONE & TELEGRAPH	A /A	12/78	12.5	(18)	11.0	(20)	15.6	(8)	9.0	(22)	10.8	(18)
CITY INVESTING CO	NR /BB	12/78	12.3	(19)	8.9	(25)	5.7	(27)	3.7	(26)	3.9	(27)
AMFAC INC	Ba /BB*	12/78	12.1	(20)	10.1	(23)	5.7	(26)	12.2	(14)	21.3	(5)
KIDDE (WALTER) & CO	Baa/BBB	12/78	11.8	(21)	10.9	(22)	10.4	(19)	11.3	(17)	11.5	(17)
A-T-O INC	Baa/BB	12/78	11.5	(22)	8.8	(26)	10.4	(20)	10.4	(19)	10.3	(21)
SINGER CO	Baa/BB	12/78	11.5	(23)	16.0	(7)	15.5	(8)	-16.8	(30)	3.1	(28)
CRANE CO	Baa/BBB	12/78	10.5	(24)	20.3	(3)	16.9	(5)	24.2	(2)	25.5	(2)
SCM CORP	Baa/BBB	6/78	10.1	(25)	10.9	(21)	9.7	(21)	9.6	(20)	10.4	(20)
U S INDUSTRIES	Baa/BBB	12/78	8.9	(26)	7.7	(27)	4.8	(29)	1.3	(29)	2.7	(29)
GREYHOUND CORP	A /A	12/78	8.4	(27)	12.0	(17)	11.8	(17)	13.2	(11)	11.9	(16)
GAF CORP	Baa/BBB	12/78	7.7	(28)	7.1	(28)	4.2	(30)	7.3	(23)	8.1	(24)
IC INDUSTRIES INC	NR /NR	12/78	7.6	(29)	6.8	(29)	5.5	(28)	4.2	(25)	5.7	(25)
LTV CORP	B /NR	12/78	3.1	(30)	-6.7	(30)	6.9	(24)	3.0	(28)	24.3	(3)
AVERAGE			13.77		12.99		12.27		10.73		12.93	
MEDIAN			12.96		12.30		12.12		12.01		12.89	

RET ON TOT ASSETS (%)

	RATINGS	FYR END	78		77		76		75		74	
TELEDYNE INC	Baa/BBB	12/78	28.6	(1)	26.1	(1)	23.0	(1)	18.3	(2)	10.1	(21)
MINNESOTA MINING & MFG CO	Aaa/AAA	12/78	26.8	(2)	23.3	(2)	20.2	(3)	17.4	(4)	21.0	(2)
MOBIL CORP	Aa /AA	12/78	20.0	(3)	23.2	(3)	21.9	(2)	22.5	(1)	27.9	(1)
NORTHWEST INDUSTRIES	Baa/BBB*	12/78	16.8	(4)	15.4	(5)	16.5	(5)	17.1	(5)	16.1	(6)
TEXTRON INC	A /AA-	12/78	16.6	(5)	16.5	(4)	16.7	(4)	14.1	(7)	14.2	(9)
MARTIN MARIETTA CORP	A /A	12/78	16.3	(6)	15.1	(8)	12.2	(12)	8.7	(21)	15.0	(8)
DART INDUSTRIES	A /A	12/78	15.6	(7)	15.4	(6)	15.6	(6)	14.4	(6)	13.7	(10)
COLT INDUSTRIES INC	A /A	12/78	15.2	(8)	13.9	(9)	13.6	(8)	12.2	(11)	20.1	(4)
UV INDUSTRIES INC	Baa/BBB	12/78	15.0	(9)	15.3	(7)	15.0	(7)	12.7	(9)	15.3	(7)
SIGNAL COS	Baa/BBB	12/78	14.6	(10)	11.1	(17)	8.9	(22)	6.5	(23)	10.1	(20)
U S INDUSTRIES	Baa/BBB	12/78	13.4	(11)	12.8	(13)	9.1	(21)	5.1	(25)	6.2	(26)
MISSOURI PACIFIC CORP	Baa/NR	12/78	13.2	(12)	13.0	(11)	11.4	(13)	8.8	(19)	8.6	(24)
KIDDE (WALTER) & CO	Baa/BBB	12/78	12.3	(13)	11.9	(15)	12.9	(10)	12.3	(10)	11.8	(14)
SINGER CO	Baa/BB	12/78	11.8	(14)	13.2	(10)	11.3	(14)	1.1	(30)	5.7	(28)
TENNECO INC	A /A	12/78	11.3	(15)	12.8	(12)	12.6	(11)	12.7	(8)	12.5	(13)
OGDEN CORP	Ba /BB*	12/78	11.2	(16)	10.9	(18)	10.8	(17)	10.2	(16)	12.6	(12)
A-T-O INC	Baa/BB	12/78	10.8	(17)	9.1	(22)	11.3	(15)	11.2	(13)	11.5	(15)
AMFAC INC	Ba /BB*	12/78	10.4	(18)	9.1	(23)	5.6	(27)	11.9	(12)	20.3	(3)
INTL TELEPHONE & TELEGRAPH	A /A	12/78	9.9	(19)	10.4	(19)	10.2	(19)	10.5	(15)	10.9	(16)
PULLMAN INC	Baa/BBB	12/78	9.7	(20)	6.0	(27)	6.2	(25)	7.8	(22)	10.3	(18)
GAF CORP	Baa/BBB	12/78	9.5	(21)	9.1	(21)	6.0	(26)	8.9	(18)	10.2	(19)
AVCO CORP	Ba /B*	11/78	9.4	(22)	8.9	(24)	7.8	(23)	6.4	(24)	2.2	(30)
GULF & WESTERN INDS INC	Baa/BBB	7/78	9.3	(23)	8.1	(25)	11.2	(16)	9.1	(17)	8.5	(25)
CRANE CO	Baa/BBB	12/78	9.1	(24)	12.2	(14)	13.1	(9)	18.0	(3)	19.1	(5)
SCM CORP	Baa/BBB	6/78	8.8	(25)	11.8	(16)	9.8	(20)	8.8	(20)	9.5	(22)
IC INDUSTRIES INC	NR /NR	12/78	7.4	(26)	6.7	(26)	6.2	(24)	5.0	(26)	6.1	(27)
GREYHOUND CORP	A /A	12/78	6.7	(27)	10.3	(20)	10.3	(18)	11.1	(14)	10.9	(17)
CITY INVESTING CO	NR /BB	12/78	5.5	(28)	5.0	(28)	4.5	(29)	3.8	(28)	4.3	(29)
LOEWS CORP	NR /BBB	12/78	5.3	(29)	4.1	(29)	3.4	(30)	3.4	(29)	9.3	(23)
LTV CORP	B /NR	12/78	3.5	(30)	2.5	(30)	5.4	(28)	4.2	(27)	13.4	(11)
AVERAGE			12.47		12.12		11.42		10.48		12.25	
MEDIAN			11.28		11.85		11.22		10.38		11.23	

PRETAX COVERAGE

	RATINGS	FYR END	78	77	76	75	74
STERLING DRUG INC	Aa /AAA	12/78	20.15 (1)	16.53 (2)	18.51 (1)	18.59 (1)	26.19 (2)
PROCTER & GAMBLE CO	Aaa/AAA	6/78	18.53 (2)	17.35 (1)	14.89 (3)	17.03 (2)	27.80 (1)
ECONOMICS LABORATORY INC	Baa/BBB*	6/78	14.79 (3)	15.58 (3)	14.45 (4)	7.10 (5)	11.84 (4)
REVLON INC	Aa /AA	12/78	12.20 (4)	9.74 (5)	8.62 (5)	7.59 (4)	7.59 (5)
PUREX INDUSTRIES INC	Baa/BBB*	6/78	10.57 (5)	15.56 (4)	14.96 (2)	8.84 (3)	8.44 (4)
FOREMOST-MCKESSON INC	Ba /BB*	3/78	5.77 (6)	4.26 (6)	4.44 (6)	3.69 (6)	5.74 (6)
AVERAGE			13.67	13.17	12.64	10.47	14.60
MEDIAN			13.49	15.57	14.67	8.21	10.14

AFTER TAX COVERAGE

	RATINGS	FYR END	78	77	76	75	74
STERLING DRUG INC	Aa /AAA	12/78	10.86 (1)	9.15 (2)	10.44 (1)	10.73 (1)	14.46 (2)
PROCTER & GAMBLE CO	Aaa/AAA	6/78	10.37 (2)	9.70 (1)	8.55 (2)	9.61 (2)	15.36 (1)
ECONOMICS LABORATORY INC	Baa/BBB*	6/78	8.22 (3)	8.73 (3)	7.87 (4)	4.21 (5)	6.77 (3)
REVLON INC	Aa /AA	12/78	6.91 (4)	5.63 (5)	5.05 (5)	4.49 (4)	4.62 (5)
PUREX INDUSTRIES INC	Baa/BBB*	6/78	5.88 (5)	8.43 (4)	8.03 (3)	4.98 (3)	4.81 (4)
FOREMOST-MCKESSON INC	Ba /BB*	3/78	3.32 (6)	2.74 (6)	2.81 (6)	2.37 (6)	3.33 (6)
AVERAGE			7.59	7.40	7.13	6.07	8.22
MEDIAN			7.57	8.58	7.95	4.74	5.79

AFTER TAX COV (INCL RENTS)

	RATINGS	FYR END	78	77	76	75	74
STERLING DRUG INC	Aa /AAA	12/78	4.66 (1)	4.36 (1)	4.49 (1)	4.97 (1)	5.85 (1)
PUREX INDUSTRIES INC	Baa/BBB*	6/78	3.78 (2)	3.51 (3)	3.45 (2)	2.79 (3)	2.63 (4)
REVLON INC	Aa /AA	12/78	3.78 (3)	3.39 (,4)	3.24 (3)	2.92 (2)	2.94 (2)
ECONOMICS LABORATORY INC	Baa/BBB*	6/78	3.57 (4)	3.52 (2)	3.20 (4)	2.46 (4)	2.72 (3)
FOREMOST-MCKESSON INC	Ba /BB*	3/78	1.77 (5)	1.61 (5)	1.64 (5)	1.59 (5)	1.77 (5)
PROCTER & GAMBLE CO	Aaa/AAA	6/78	NA (-)	NA (-)	NA (-)	NA (-)	NA (-)
AVERAGE			3.51	3.28	3.20	2.95	3.18
MEDIAN			3.78	3.51	3.24	2.79	2.72

NET INCOME AS % NET SALES

	RATINGS	FYR END	78	77	76	75	74
REVLON INC	Aa /AA	12/78	8.9 (1)	8.6 (1)	8.5 (1)	8.3 (2)	8.2 (2)
STERLING DRUG INC	Aa /AAA	12/78	7.2 (2)	7.3 (2)	7.6 (2)	8.6 (1)	8.9 (1)
ECONOMICS LABORATORY INC	Baa/BBB*	6/78	6.5 (3)	6.5 (3)	5.9 (4)	5.3 (4)	6.0 (4)
PROCTER & GAMBLE CO	Aaa/AAA	6/78	6.3 (4)	6.3 (4)	6.2 (3)	5.5 (3)	6.4 (3)
PUREX INDUSTRIES INC	Baa/BBB*	6/78	4.2 (5)	4.5 (5)	4.6 (5)	4.2 (5)	4.0 (5)
FOREMOST-MCKESSON INC	Ba /BB*	3/78	1.5 (6)	1.3 (6)	1.3 (6)	1.5 (6)	1.5 (6)
AVERAGE			5.75	5.74	5.68	5.56	5.83
MEDIAN			6.39	6.43	6.03	5.38	6.20

Consumer Products Industry

LTD/CAPITALIZATION (%)

	RATINGS	FYR END	78		77		76		75		74	
STERLING DRUG INC	Aa /AAA	12/78	7.2	(1)	7.7	(1)	6.6	(1)	4.8	(1)	6.7	(1)
PROCTER & GAMBLE CO	Aaa/AAA	6/78	16.4	(2)	16.9	(2)	19.4	(2)	20.8	(2)	11.3	(2)
ECONOMICS LABORATORY INC	Baa/BBB*	6/78	19.4	(3)	20.7	(4)	22.7	(4)	25.3	(4)	32.7	(5)
REVLON INC	Aa /AA	12/78	21.0	(4)	25.4	(5)	28.6	(5)	33.8	(5)	23.7	(3)
PUREX INDUSTRIES INC	Baa/BBB*	6/78	23.0	(5)	20.2	(3)	21.5	(3)	23.7	(3)	25.9	(4)
FOREMOST-MCKESSON INC	Ba /BB*	3/78	42.0	(6)	47.7	(6)	45.9	(6)	50.3	(6)	49.3	(6)
AVERAGE			21.51		23.10		24.10		26.45		24.92	
MEDIAN			20.23		20.43		22.10		24.52		24.77	

TOT LIABILITY/TOT STK EQUITY

	RATINGS	FYR END	78		77		76		75		74	
STERLING DRUG INC	Aa /AAA	12/78	51.5	(1)	49.7	(1)	48.8	(1)	45.5	(1)	45.4	(1)
ECONOMICS LABORATORY INC	Baa/BBB*	6/78	66.6	(2)	64.9	(2)	68.5	(2)	74.2	(3)	110.0	(5)
PROCTER & GAMBLE CO	Aaa/AAA	6/78	71.0	(3)	71.0	(3)	74.0	(4)	72.4	(2)	58.2	(2)
REVLON INC	Aa /AA	12/78	84.3	(4)	94.2	(5)	91.5	(5)	98.1	(5)	90.4	(3)
PUREX INDUSTRIES INC	Baa/BBB*	6/78	85.4	(5)	72.4	(4)	71.5	(3)	78.7	(4)	95.5	(4)
FOREMOST-MCKESSON INC	Ba /BB*	3/78	202.9	(6)	207.2	(6)	207.2	(6)	220.0	(6)	235.9	(6)
AVERAGE			93.60		93.21		93.58		98.16		105.91	
MEDIAN			77.65		71.68		72.76		76.44		92.96	

LTD/NET PLANT (%)

	RATINGS	FYR END	78		77		76		75		74	
STERLING DRUG INC	Aa /AAA	12/78	20.1	(1)	20.8	(1)	18.5	(1)	13.9	(1)	21.1	(2)
PROCTER & GAMBLE CO	Aaa/AAA	6/78	24.0	(2)	25.9	(2)	29.8	(2)	31.9	(2)	16.1	(1)
ECONOMICS LABORATORY INC	Baa/BBB*	6/78	56.1	(3)	56.9	(3)	57.1	(3)	62.9	(3)	64.0	(3)
PUREX INDUSTRIES INC	Baa/BBB*	6/78	64.8	(4)	62.5	(4)	67.1	(4)	66.4	(4)	65.2	(4)
REVLON INC	Aa /AA	12/78	73.0	(5)	93.5	(5)	131.6	(5)	199.5	(6)	110.9	(5)
FOREMOST-MCKESSON INC	Ba /BB*	3/78	107.0	(6)	141.3	(6)	133.0	(6)	140.6	(5)	133.6	(6)
AVERAGE			57.51		66.82		72.84		85.87		68.47	
MEDIAN			60.46		59.67		62.09		64.66		64.58	

NET TANG ASSETS/LTD (%)

	RATINGS	FYR END	78		77		76		75		74	
STERLING DRUG INC	Aa /AAA	12/78	1283.6	(1)	1190.8	(1)	1364.8	(1)	1896.4	(1)	1347.0	(1)
PROCTER & GAMBLE CO	Aaa/AAA	6/78	587.2	(2)	575.6	(2)	503.5	(2)	466.1	(2)	859.8	(2)
ECONOMICS LABORATORY INC	Baa/BBB*	6/78	497.6	(3)	466.7	(3)	424.0	(3)	377.9	(3)	291.3	(5)
REVLON INC	Aa /AA	12/78	412.7	(4)	331.5	(5)	298.1	(5)	256.9	(5)	355.3	(3)
PUREX INDUSTRIES INC	Baa/BBB*	6/78	392.4	(5)	440.9	(4)	412.2	(4)	370.1	(4)	336.4	(4)
FOREMOST-MCKESSON INC	Ba /BB*	3/78	191.8	(6)	171.3	(6)	205.0	(6)	188.0	(6)	189.2	(6)
AVERAGE			560.87		529.48		534.61		592.59		563.17	
MEDIAN			455.11		453.81		418.14		374.02		345.88	

CASH FLOW/LTD (%)

	RATINGS	FYR END	78			77			76			75			74		
STERLING DRUG INC	Aa /AAA	12/78	237.9	(	1)	236.4	(	1)	263.6	(	1)	394.0	(	1)	279.6	(	1)
PROCTER & GAMBLE CO	Aaa/AAA	6/78	120.7	(	2)	116.4	(	2)	95.7	(	2)	85.3	(	2)	174.1	(	2)
ECONOMICS LABORATORY INC	Baa/BBB*	6/78	96.3	(	3)	89.9	(	3)	73.3	(	3)	57.8	(	4)	51.3	(	5)
REVLON INC	Aa /AA	12/78	89.1	(	4)	63.7	(	5)	52.9	(	5)	38.2	(	5)	62.4	(	3)
PUREX INDUSTRIES INC	Baa/BBB*	6/78	62.5	(	5)	69.8	(	4)	68.8	(	4)	65.1	(	3)	52.5	(	4)
FOREMOST-MCKESSON INC	Ba /BB*	3/78	26.2	(	6)	18.3	(	6)	20.1	(	6)	17.3	(	6)	19.5	(	6)
AVERAGE			105.46			99.09			95.73			109.63			106.58		
MEDIAN			92.72			79.84			71.02			61.47			57.47		

NET CASH FL/CAP EXP (%)

	RATINGS	FYR END	78			77			76			75			74		
STERLING DRUG INC	Aa /AAA	12/78	207.8	(	1)	191.9	(	3)	186.2	(	4)	145.7	(	4)	167.3	(	2)
ECONOMICS LABORATORY INC	Baa/BBB*	6/78	205.1	(	2)	275.4	(	1)	148.1	(	5)	164.0	(	3)	62.1	(	6)
REVLON INC	Aa /AA	12/78	166.9 V(		3)	262.2	(	2)	210.3	(	2)	345.7	(	2)	298.5	(	1)
PUREX INDUSTRIES INC	Baa/BBB*	6/78	106.8	(	4)	141.0	(	5)	217.9	(	1)	367.8	(	1)	126.6	(	3)
PROCTER & GAMBLE CO	Aaa/AAA	6/78	98.6	(	5)	143.4	(	4)	135.6	(	6)	102.7	(	6)	114.3	(	4)
FOREMOST-MCKESSON INC	Ba /BB*	3/78	87.9	(	6)	87.8	(	6)	192.2	(	3)	121.0	(	5)	109.4	(	5)
AVERAGE			145.51			183.63			181.70			207.83			146.37		
MEDIAN			136.86			167.68			189.17			154.85			120.47		

AFT TAX RET ON COM EQTY (%)

	RATINGS	FYR END	78			77			76			75			74		
REVLON INC	Aa /AA	12/78	19.2	(	1)	18.3	(	1)	17.9	(	1)	16.5	(	2)	16.1	(	5)
PROCTER & GAMBLE CO	Aaa/AAA	6/78	17.6	(	2)	17.6	(	2)	17.0	(	2)	15.8	(	4)	16.3	(	4)
ECONOMICS LABORATORY INC	Baa/BBB*	6/78	15.8	(	3)	15.9	(	3)	15.0	(	3)	13.3	(	5)	17.0	(	2)
FOREMOST-MCKESSON INC	Ba /BB*	3/78	15.5	(	4)	13.5	(	5)	14.6	(	5)	16.7	(	1)	17.0	(	3)
STERLING DRUG INC	Aa /AAA	12/78	14.3	(	5)	14.0	(	4)	14.7	(	4)	16.2	(	3)	17.2	(	1)
PUREX INDUSTRIES INC	Baa/BBB*	6/78	12.8	(	6)	13.1	(	6)	13.4	(	6)	12.7	(	6)	11.7	(	6)
AVERAGE			15.86			15.39			15.42			15.21			15.89		
MEDIAN			15.66			14.94			14.84			15.99			16.66		

RET ON TOT ASSETS (%)

	RATINGS	FYR END	78			77			76			75			74		
REVLON INC	Aa /AA	12/78	21.5	(	1)	19.9	(	2)	19.9	(	1)	18.1	(	2)	17.7	(	3)
PROCTER & GAMBLE CO	Aaa/AAA	6/78	20.3	(	2)	20.5	(	1)	19.3	(	3)	18.1	(	3)	20.0	(	2)
ECONOMICS LABORATORY INC	Baa/BBB*	6/78	19.5	(	3)	19.4	(	3)	18.7	(	4)	16.9	(	4)	16.6	(	4)
STERLING DRUG INC	Aa /AAA	12/78	19.3	(	4)	19.0	(	4)	19.3	(	2)	21.3	(	1)	22.9	(	1)
PUREX INDUSTRIES INC	Baa/BBB*	6/78	15.1	(	5)	16.1	(	5)	16.9	(	5)	16.0	(	5)	13.6	(	5)
FOREMOST-MCKESSON INC	Ba /BB*	3/78	10.5	(	6)	9.1	(	6)	9.8	(	6)	11.0	(	6)	9.4	(	6)
AVERAGE			17.69			17.32			17.31			16.89			16.70		
MEDIAN			19.38			19.19			19.02			17.50			17.17		

Containers/Packaging Industry

PRETAX COVERAGE

	RATINGS	FYR END	78	77	76	75	74
DIAMOND INTERNATIONAL CORP	Aa /AA	12/78	17.34 (1)	16.00 (2)	20.90 (2)	24.13 (1)	18.73 (1)
CROWN CORK & SEAL CO INC	A /AA	12/78	11.95P(2)	19.32P(1)	23.86P(1)	11.48P(3)	11.76P(3)
ANCHOR HOCKING CORP	A /AA	12/78	9.50 (3)	7.99 (4)	10.35 (3)	17.43 (2)	16.42 (2)
BROCKWAY GLASS CO	A /A	12/78	8.20 (4)	6.04 (6)	9.54 (4)	10.21 (4)	7.32 (6)
AMERICAN CAN CO	A /A	12/78	7.48 (5)	8.05 (3)	7.73 (5)	5.14 (8)	8.62P(5)
MARYLAND CUP CORP	A /A	9/78	6.58 (6)	6.45 (5)	6.38 (7)	5.25 (7)	5.30 (8)
BEMIS CO	Baa/BBB	12/78	4.92 (7)	5.29 (8)	4.29 (11)	3.23 (11)	4.58 (10)
FEDERAL PAPER BOARD CO	Baa/BBB	12/78	4.40 (8)	3.63 (11)	5.68 (8)	5.83 (6)	8.77 (4)
OWENS-ILLINOIS INC	A /A	12/78	4.01P(9)	3.83P(10)	4.76P(10)	4.03P(10)	4.51P(11)
NATIONAL CAN CORP	Baa/A-	12/78	3.40 (10)	4.91P(9)	4.85P(9)	4.37P(9)	4.62P(9)
CONTINENTAL GROUP	A /AA	12/78	3.16 (11)	5.47 (7)	7.03 (6)	5.92 (5)	6.54 (7)
AVERAGE			7.36	7.91	9.58	8.82	8.83
MEDIAN			6.58	6.04	7.03	5.83	7.32

AFTER TAX COVERAGE

	RATINGS	FYR END	78	77	76	75	74
DIAMOND INTERNATIONAL CORP	Aa /AA	12/78	10.61 (1)	9.77 (2)	12.78 (1)	13.70 (1)	11.62 (1)
CROWN CORK & SEAL CO INC	A /AA	12/78	7.07P(2)	10.55P(1)	12.67P(2)	6.74P(3)	6.98P(3)
ANCHOR HOCKING CORP	A /AA	12/78	5.78 (3)	5.14 (3)	6.11 (4)	10.20 (2)	9.38 (2)
BROCKWAY GLASS CO	A /A	12/78	4.89 (4)	3.87 (6)	6.22 (3)	5.84 (4)	4.32 (6)
AMERICAN CAN CO	A /A	12/78	4.52 (5)	4.74 (4)	4.69 (5)	3.31 (7)	5.11P(5)
MARYLAND CUP CORP	A /A	9/78	3.98 (6)	3.96 (5)	3.90 (7)	3.29 (8)	3.32 (8)
BEMIS CO	Baa/BBB	12/78	3.38 (7)	3.59 (8)	3.49 (9)	2.03 (11)	2.76 (11)
FEDERAL PAPER BOARD CO	Baa/BBB	12/78	3.20 (8)	2.73 (11)	3.89 (8)	3.88 (6)	5.24 (4)
OWENS-ILLINOIS INC	A /A	12/78	2.97P(9)	2.87P(10)	3.28P(10)	2.86P(9)	2.97P(9)
CONTINENTAL GROUP	A /AA	12/78	2.52 (10)	3.77 (7)	4.43 (6)	4.03 (5)	4.05 (7)
NATIONAL CAN CORP	Baa/A-	12/78	2.34 (11)	3.08P(9)	2.99P(11)	2.78P(10)	2.86P(10)
AVERAGE			4.66	4.92	5.86	5.33	5.33
MEDIAN			3.98	3.87	4.43	3.88	4.32

AFTER TAX COV (INCL RENTS)

	RATINGS	FYR END	78	77	76	75	74
ANCHOR HOCKING CORP	A /AA	12/78	3.78 (1)	3.26 (1)	3.41 (1)	4.09 (1)	3.79 (1)
BEMIS CO	Baa/BBB	12/78	2.70 (2)	2.80 (2)	2.53 (4)	1.65 (7)	2.28 (6)
FEDERAL PAPER BOARD CO	Baa/BBB	12/78	2.49 (3)	1.97 (7)	2.57 (3)	2.44 (2)	3.32 (3)
AMERICAN CAN CO	A /A	12/78	2.48 (4)	2.63 (3)	2.76 (2)	2.23 (4)	3.33P(2)
OWENS-ILLINOIS INC	A /A	12/78	2.22P(5)	2.09P(5)	2.28P(6)	2.11P(5)	2.14P(7)
CONTINENTAL GROUP	A /AA	12/78	1.85 (6)	2.23 (4)	2.44 (5)	2.33 (3)	2.47 (5)
NATIONAL CAN CORP	Baa/A-	12/78	1.72 (7)	2.07P(6)	1.86P(7)	1.90P(6)	1.98P(8)
BROCKWAY GLASS CO	A /A	12/78	NA (-)	NA (-)	NA (-)	NA (-)	NA (-)
CROWN CORK & SEAL CO INC	A /AA	12/78	NA (-)	NA (-)	NA (-)	NA (-)	NA (-)
DIAMOND INTERNATIONAL CORP	Aa /AA	12/78	NA (-)	NA (-)	NA (-)	NA (-)	NA (-)
MARYLAND CUP CORP	A /A	9/78	NA (-)	NA (-)	NA (-)	NA (-)	2.60 (4)
AVERAGE			2.46	2.44	2.55	2.39	2.74
MEDIAN			2.48	2.23	2.53	2.23	2.54

NET INCOME AS % NET SALES

	RATINGS	FYR END	78		77		76		75		74	
FEDERAL PAPER BOARD CO	Baa/BBB	12/78	5.9	(1)	3.5	(7)	5.7	(1)	5.0	(4)	6.1	(2)
CROWN CORK & SEAL CO INC	A /AA	12/78	5.1	(2)	5.1	(1)	5.1	(4)	5.0	(2)	5.2	(3)
ANCHOR HOCKING CORP	A /AA	12/78	5.0	(3)	4.7	(3)	4.4	(6)	4.4	(5)	4.0	(6)
BROCKWAY GLASS CO	A /A	12/78	4.9	(4)	4.0	(5)	5.7	(2)	5.0	(3)	4.1	(5)
DIAMOND INTERNATIONAL CORP	Aa /AA	12/78	4.9	(5)	4.8	(2)	5.6	(3)	6.3	(1)	6.6	(1)
MARYLAND CUP CORP	A /A	9/78	4.5	(6)	4.7	(4)	4.7	(5)	4.0	(6)	4.1	(4)
OWENS-ILLINOIS INC	A /A	12/78	3.5	(7)	3.3	(8)	4.1	(7)	3.8	(7)	3.9	(7)
CONTINENTAL GROUP	A /AA	12/78	3.2	(8)	3.9	(6)	3.4	(8)	3.5	(8)	3.9	(8)
AMERICAN CAN CO	A /A	12/78	3.0	(9)	3.2	(9)	3.2	(9)	2.7	(9)	3.8	(9)
BEMIS CO	Baa/BBB	12/78	2.8	(10)	2.6	(10)	2.6	(10)	1.6	(11)	3.2	(10)
NATIONAL CAN CORP	Baa/A-	12/78	2.1	(11)	2.6	(11)	2.3	(11)	2.3	(10)	2.9	(11)
AVERAGE			4.08		3.85		4.26		3.97		4.33	
MEDIAN			4.53		3.93		4.35		3.95		3.97	

LTD/CAPITALIZATION (%)

	RATINGS	FYR END	78		77		76		75		74	
CROWN CORK & SEAL CO INC	A /AA	12/78	3.2	(1)	3.4	(1)	7.6	(1)	9.2	(1)	11.6	(2)
DIAMOND INTERNATIONAL CORP	Aa /AA	12/78	15.0	(2)	11.9	(2)	13.3	(2)	11.4	(2)	14.1	(3)
ANCHOR HOCKING CORP	A /AA	12/78	24.4	(3)	27.4	(3)	27.3	(4)	15.3	(3)	8.9	(1)
BROCKWAY GLASS CO	A /A	12/78	28.6	(4)	29.7	(7)	26.8	(3)	22.2	(4)	19.2	(4)
CONTINENTAL GROUP	A /AA	12/78	31.5	(5)	28.6	(6)	30.9	(7)	31.2	(6)	31.8	(6)
MARYLAND CUP CORP	A /A	9/78	31.9	(6)	34.2	(8)	35.9	(9)	37.7	(10)	29.4	(5)
AMERICAN CAN CO	A /A	12/78	32.5	(7)	27.8	(5)	29.5	(6)	31.2	(7)	32.3	(7)
BEMIS CO	Baa/BBB	12/78	33.4	(8)	27.7	(4)	27.9	(5)	30.8	(5)	33.5	(9)
OWENS-ILLINOIS INC	A /A	12/78	37.8	(9)	34.9	(9)	35.4	(8)	40.3	(11)	41.2	(11)
NATIONAL CAN CORP	Baa/A-	12/78	39.0	(10)	37.7	(11)	39.2	(11)	33.0	(8)	36.5	(10)
FEDERAL PAPER BOARD CO	Baa/BBB	12/78	44.5	(11)	37.3	(10)	36.9	(10)	36.2	(9)	33.4	(8)
AVERAGE			29.26		27.33		28.23		27.13		26.53	
MEDIAN			31.93		28.63		29.51		31.16		31.85	

TOT LIABILITY/TOT STK EQUITY

	RATINGS	FYR END	78		77		76		75		74	
DIAMOND INTERNATIONAL CORP	Aa /AA	12/78	57.2	(1)	51.0	(1)	49.8	(1)	43.6	(1)	46.4	(1)
CROWN CORK & SEAL CO INC	A /AA	12/78	77.1	(2)	74.4	(2)	72.9	(2)	84.1	(4)	106.7	(7)
ANCHOR HOCKING CORP	A /AA	12/78	83.8	(3)	82.2	(4)	84.7	(5)	68.1	(3)	51.2	(2)
BROCKWAY GLASS CO	A /A	12/78	91.4	(4)	78.1	(3)	74.2	(3)	65.5	(2)	55.5	(3)
MARYLAND CUP CORP	A /A	9/78	94.4	(5)	87.7	(5)	94.2	(7)	89.8	(5)	86.0	(5)
BEMIS CO	Baa/BBB	12/78	105.8	(6)	92.7	(6)	84.4	(4)	90.9	(7)	104.6	(6)
CONTINENTAL GROUP	A /AA	12/78	127.4	(7)	112.7	(8)	134.5	(10)	126.3	(8)	144.4	(10)
FEDERAL PAPER BOARD CO	Baa/BBB	12/78	128.3	(8)	93.7	(7)	91.4	(6)	90.2	(6)	78.8	(4)
OWENS-ILLINOIS INC	A /A	12/78	132.5	(9)	116.0	(9)	117.9	(8)	129.7	(9)	133.6	(8)
NATIONAL CAN CORP	Baa/A-	12/78	137.5	(10)	146.2	(11)	134.7	(11)	143.3	(11)	166.3	(11)
AMERICAN CAN CO	A /A	12/78	150.9	(11)	132.5	(10)	124.8	(9)	134.8	(10)	136.9	(9)
AVERAGE			107.85		97.02		96.67		96.94		100.94	
MEDIAN			105.76		92.67		91.43		90.18		104.56	

Containers/Packaging Industry

LTD/NET PLANT (%)

	RATINGS	FYR END	78	77	76	75	74
CROWN CORK & SEAL CO INC	A /AA	12/78	4.2 (1)	4.7 (1)	10.4 (1)	11.5 (1)	14.3 (2)
DIAMOND INTERNATIONAL CORP	Aa /AA	12/78	24.0 (2)	17.6 (2)	19.7 (2)	17.5 (2)	21.9 (3)
BROCKWAY GLASS CO	A /A	12/78	36.3 (3)	38.2 (3)	32.5 (3)	29.4 (4)	26.0 (4)
ANCHOR HOCKING CORP	A /AA	12/78	38.4 (4)	43.7 (5)	46.2 (6)	22.9 (3)	13.7 (1)
CONTINENTAL GROUP	A /AA	12/78	45.5 (5)	44.7 (7)	40.3 (4)	38.4 (5)	39.1 (5)
MARYLAND CUP CORP	A /A	9/78	48.7 (6)	53.1 (10)	53.4 (10)	58.5 (10)	39.8 (6)
OWENS-ILLINOIS INC	A /A	12/78	50.4 (7)	45.5 (8)	48.2 (8)	53.8 (8)	57.7 (9)
AMERICAN CAN CO	A /A	12/78	51.9 (8)	42.6 (4)	42.8 (5)	42.1 (6)	45.3 (8)
FEDERAL PAPER BOARD CO	Baa/BBB	12/78	52.5 (9)	46.4 (9)	46.3 (7)	43.8 (7)	42.6 (7)
BEMIS CO	Baa/BBB	12/78	54.6 (10)	43.9 (6)	52.1 (9)	59.6 (11)	67.9 (11)
NATIONAL CAN CORP	Baa/A-	12/78	79.7 (11)	71.2 (11)	77.2 (1*)	54.8 (9)	58.8 (10)
AVERAGE			44.19	41.05	42.65	39.30	38.82
MEDIAN			48.68	43.90	46.23	42.12	39.83

NET TANG ASSETS/LTD (%)

	RATINGS	FYR END	78	77	76	75	74
CROWN CORK & SEAL CO INC	A /AA	12/78	3013.2 (1)	2835.1 (1)	1272.5 (1)	1041.4 (1)	823.9 (2)
DIAMOND INTERNATIONAL CORP	Aa /AA	12/78	626.7 (2)	819.5 (2)	731.2 (2)	849.6 (2)	692.0 (3)
ANCHOR HOCKING CORP	A /AA	12/78	402.1 (3)	354.9 (3)	354.1 (4)	639.5 (3)	1089.0 (1)
BROCKWAY GLASS CO	A /A	12/78	347.2 (4)	334.9 (5)	370.3 (3)	441.3 (4)	511.5 (4)
CONTINENTAL GROUP	A /AA	12/78	300.2 (5)	327.6 (7)	296.7 (7)	290.3 (7)	280.6 (8)
MARYLAND CUP CORP	A /A	9/78	299.5 (6)	290.5 (8)	271.9 (8)	261.3 (10)	335.6 (5)
BEMIS CO	Baa/BBB	12/78	280.6 (7)	336.3 (4)	329.3 (5)	299.5 (6)	274.6 (9)
AMERICAN CAN CO	A /A	12/78	277.7 (8)	332.0 (6)	316.6 (6)	300.7 (5)	294.0 (7)
NATIONAL CAN CORP	Baa/A-	12/78	248.0 (9)	257.2 (11)	241.1 (11)	284.0 (8)	255.7 (10)
OWENS-ILLINOIS INC	A /A	12/78	241.4 (10)	262.8 (10)	258.2 (10)	224.2 (11)	219.3 (11)
FEDERAL PAPER BOARD CO	Baa/BBB	12/78	224.5 (11)	266.9 (9)	270.3 (9)	275.1 (9)	296.8 (6)
AVERAGE			569.18	583.43	428.39	446.09	461.18
MEDIAN			299.50	332.05	316.61	299.47	296.84

CASH FLOW/LTD (%)

	RATINGS	FYR END	78	77	76	75	74
CROWN CORK & SEAL CO INC	A /AA	12/78	736.5 (1)	713.0 (1)	297.5 (1)	247.4 (1)	199.8 (1)
DIAMOND INTERNATIONAL CORP	Aa /AA	12/78	113.6 (2)	148.3 (2)	138.1 (2)	166.1 (2)	132.3 (3)
ANCHOR HOCKING CORP	A /AA	12/78	70.2 (3)	58.2 (3)	60.4 (5)	104.0 (3)	169.7 (2)
BROCKWAY GLASS CO	A /A	12/78	63.2 (4)	57.4 (4)	67.9 (4)	82.5 (4)	74.0 (4)
MARYLAND CUP CORP	A /A	9/78	53.9 (5)	48.2 (8)	43.7 (8)	36.0 (9)	49.8 (7)
BEMIS CO	Baa/BBB	12/78	52.8 (6)	53.0 (7)	57.5 (6)	32.5 (11)	42.7 (9)
AMERICAN CAN CO	A /A	12/78	50.9 (7)	56.2 (6)	56.7 (7)	48.9 (6)	52.3 (6)
CONTINENTAL GROUP	A /AA	12/78	50.8 (8)	56.7 (5)	68.8 (3)	62.4 (5)	69.9 (5)
OWENS-ILLINOIS INC	A /A	12/78	38.0 (9)	39.6 (9)	42.6 (10)	36.0 (10)	33.4 (11)
NATIONAL CAN CORP	Baa/A-	12/78	32.0 (10)	35.2 (10)	32.6 (11)	46.4 (7)	40.0 (10)
FEDERAL PAPER BOARD CO	Baa/BBB	12/78	31.4 (11)	32.8 (11)	43.1 (9)	38.0 (8)	47.9 (8)
AVERAGE			117.58	118.07	82.63	81.85	82.88
MEDIAN			52.83	56.24	57.47	48.90	52.32

NET CASH FL/CAP EXP (%)

	RATINGS	FYR END	78	77	76	75	74
NATIONAL CAN CORP	Baa/A-	12/78	154.8 (1)	116.4 (4)	137.2 (4)	221.3 (1)	197.8 (1)
DIAMOND INTERNATIONAL CORP	Aa /AA	12/78	120.2 (2)	109.7 (6)	89.5 (10)	126.4 (3)	107.2 (9)
MARYLAND CUP CORP	A /A	9/78	118.7 (3)	111.5 (5)	118.1 (6)	110.5 (6)	130.5 (4)
BEMIS CO	Baa/BBB	12/78	114.8 (4)	62.4 (11)	122.6 (5)	99.2 (8)	173.3 (2)
ANCHOR HOCKING CORP	A /AA	12/78	112.6 (5)	74.9 (10)	96.5 (9)	122.1 (4)	114.1 (8)
AMERICAN CAN CO	A /A	12/78	110.3 (6)	130.4 (2)	142.4 (3)	107.5 (7)	124.5 (6)
BROCKWAY GLASS CO	A /A	12/78	104.0 (7)	125.3 (3)	58.5 (11)	87.3 (10)	120.2 (7)
CROWN CORK & SEAL CO INC	A /AA	12/78	100.3 (8)	154.9 (1)	357.1 (1)	156.1 (2)	130.9 (3)
OWENS-ILLINOIS INC	A /A	12/78	100.0 (9)	87.2 (8)	115.8 (8)	90.1 (9)	96.1 (11)
CONTINENTAL GROUP	A /AA	12/78	87.2 (10)	87.3 (7)	149.7 (2)	112.7 (5)	126.8 (5)
FEDERAL PAPER BOARD CO	Baa/BBB	12/78	63.2 (11)	76.1 (9)	117.0 (7)	72.0 (11)	99.0 (10)
AVERAGE			107.83	103.29	136.75	118.64	129.12
MEDIAN			110.30	109.73	118.12	110.46	124.47

AFT TAX RET ON COM EQTY (%)

	RATINGS	FYR END	78		77		76		75		74	
CROWN CORK & SEAL CO INC	A /AA	12/78	15.3	(1)	14.9	(1)	14.6	(2)	14.2	(1)	15.1	(1)
ANCHOR HOCKING CORP	A /AA	12/78	14.0	(2)	13.0	(3)	13.0	(3)	11.2	(5)	9.0	(10)
BROCKWAY GLASS CO	A /A	12/78	13.7	(3)	11.0	(8)	14.7	(1)	12.1	(4)	8.9	(11)
MARYLAND CUP CORP	A /A	9/78	12.8	(4)	13.1	(2)	12.3	(7)	9.7	(9)	9.4	(9)
AMERICAN CAN CO	A /A	12/78	12.3	(5)	11.8	(6)	11.8	(8)	13.6	(4)	13.6	(4)
FEDERAL PAPER BOARD CO	Baa/BBB	12/78	12.3	(6)	6.9	(11)	12.4	(6)	9.7	(10)	13.0	(7)
DIAMOND INTERNATIONAL CORP	Aa /AA	12/78	11.3	(7)	11.1	(7)	12.6	(5)	13.3	(2)	14.9	(2)
BEMIS CO	Baa/BBB	12/78	10.4	(8)	9.7	(9)	9.6	(11)	5.1	(11)	13.3	(5)
CONTINENTAL GROUP	A /AA	12/78	9.8	(9)	12.4	(4)	12.7	(4)	12.4	(3)	14.7	(3)
OWENS-ILLINOIS INC	A /A	12/78	9.7	(10)	8.4	(10)	10.5	(9)	10.2	(7)	10.5	(8)
NATIONAL CAN CORP	Baa/A-	12/78	9.0	(11)	12.2	(5)	10.0	(10)	10.9	(6)	13.1	(6)
AVERAGE			11.87		11.32		12.20		10.81		12.32	
MEDIAN			12.33		11.82		12.42		10.94		13.07	

RET ON TOT ASSETS (%)

	RATINGS	FYR END	78		77		76		75		74	
CROWN CORK & SEAL CO INC	A /AA	12/78	17.0	(1)	17.1	(1)	17.1	(1)	15.6	(2)	14.7	(3)
ANCHOR HOCKING CORP	A /AA	12/78	15.1	(2)	13.7	(3)	14.2	(5)	12.7	(4)	11.7	(9)
BROCKWAY GLASS CO	A /A	12/78	15.1	(3)	13.0	(5)	15.5	(2)	15.3	(3)	12.6	(6)
MARYLAND CUP CORP	A /A	9/78	14.5	(4)	15.2	(2)	13.9	(6)	11.9	(6)	11.2	(10)
DIAMOND INTERNATIONAL CORP	Aa /AA	12/78	13.0	(5)	13.5	(4)	14.9	(3)	17.6	(1)	18.0	(1)
FEDERAL PAPER BOARD CO	Baa/BBB	12/78	12.0	(6)	9.1	(10)	14.5	(4)	12.4	(5)	17.2	(2)
BEMIS CO	Baa/BBB	12/78	10.6	(7)	10.1	(8)	8.6	(11)	8.4	(11)	14.7	(4)
AMERICAN CAN CO	A /A	12/78	10.4	(8)	10.9	(7)	11.0	(8)	9.4	(9)	11.7	(8)
NATIONAL CAN CORP	Baa/A-	12/78	8.4	(9)	11.3	(6)	10.2	(9)	11.6	(7)	12.1	(7)
OWENS-ILLINOIS INC	A /A	12/78	8.1	(10)	7.5	(11)	9.7	(10)	9.3	(10)	9.8	(11)
CONTINENTAL GROUP	A /AA	12/78	7.3	(11)	9.4	(9)	11.2	(7)	10.7	(8)	12.9	(5)
AVERAGE			11.94		11.89		12.79		12.27		13.32	
MEDIAN			11.98		11.34		13.95		11.91		12.57	

Drug Industry

PRETAX COVERAGE

	RATINGS	FYR END	78	77	76	75	74
BRISTOL-MYERS CO	Aaa/AAA	12/78	21.23 (1)	16.12 (2)	17.78 (1)	17.39 (2)	15.60 (4)
MERCK & CO	Aaa/AAA	12/78	20.65 (2)	18.52 (1)	16.41 (2)	18.66 (1)	40.21 (1)
SMITHKLINE CORP	Aa /AA	12/78	15.70 (3)	8.07 (7)	7.58 (7)	7.62 (7)	7.90 (8)
BECTON, DICKINSON & CO	Baa/BBB*	9/78	13.01 (4)	11.73 (4)	11.63 (5)	8.74 (5)	10.16 (7)
UPJOHN CO	Aa /AA	12/78	10.03 (5)	7.08 (8)	6.63 (9)	7.50 (8)	14.46 (5)
RICHARDSON-MERRELL INC	Aa /AA	6/78	9.56 (6)	10.37 (6)	8.46 (6)	7.79 (6)	17.58 (3)
WARNER-LAMBERT CO	Aaa/AAA	12/78	9.39 (7)	12.23 (3)	13.19 (4)	12.92 (4)	18.17 (2)
ABBOTT LABORATORIES	Aa /AA	12/78	8.37P(8)	6.78P(10)	5.90 (11)	4.43 (13)	4.20 (13)
AMERICAN HOSPITAL SUPPLY	Aa /AA	12/78	8.37 (9)	11.08 (5)	13.58 (3)	13.12 (3)	10.87 (6)
MORTON-NORWICH PRODUCTS	A /A	6/78	5.96P(10)	5.61P(12)	1.78P(14)	3.69P(14)	5.87P(12)
BAXTER TRAVENOL LABORATORIES	Baa/BBB*	12/78	5.68P(11)	6.81P(9)	6.06P(10)	4.77P(11)	3.15 (14)
PFIZER INC	Aa /AA	12/78	5.35 (12)	4.71 (13)	4.85 (12)	5.32 (10)	7.53 (9)
SQUIBB CORP	Aa /AA	12/78	5.33P(13)	6.39P(11)	6.70P(8)	6.35P(9)	6.13P(10)
SEARLE (G.D.) & CO	Aa /A+	12/78	4.44 (14)	3.52 (14)	3.60 (13)	4.57 (12)	5.98P(11)
AVERAGE			10.22	9.22	8.87	8.78	11.99
MEDIAN			8.88	7.58	7.14	7.56	9.03

AFTER TAX COVERAGE

	RATINGS	FYR END	78	77	76	75	74
MERCK & CO	Aaa/AAA	12/78	12.95 (1)	11.78 (1)	10.50 (1)	11.74 (1)	23.94 (1)
BRISTOL-MYERS CO	Aaa/AAA	12/78	12.00 (2)	9.23 (2)	10.37 (2)	10.22 (2)	9.26 (4)
SMITHKLINE CORP	Aa /AA	12/78	10.23 (3)	5.70 (7)	5.43 (6)	5.47 (5)	5.68 (8)
BECTON, DICKINSON & CO	Baa/BBB*	9/78	7.86 (4)	7.06 (4)	6.92 (5)	5.36 (6)	6.01 (7)
UPJOHN CO	Aa /AA	12/78	6.96 (5)	4.86 (9)	4.47 (10)	4.70 (8)	8.36 (5)
WARNER-LAMBERT CO	Aaa/AAA	12/78	5.82 (6)	7.17 (3)	7.59 (4)	7.75 (4)	10.85 (2)
RICHARDSON-MERRELL INC	Aa /AA	6/78	5.82 (7)	5.91 (6)	4.86 (8)	4.64 (9)	9.54 (3)
ABBOTT LABORATORIES	Aa /AA	12/78	5.64P(8)	4.70P(10)	4.29 (11)	3.37 (13)	3.21 (13)
AMERICAN HOSPITAL SUPPLY	Aa /AA	12/78	5.61 (9)	6.85 (5)	8.12 (3)	8.07 (3)	6.49 (6)
BAXTER TRAVENOL LABORATORIES	Baa/BBB*	12/78	4.59P(10)	5.03P(8)	4.61P(9)	4.02P(11)	2.72 (14)
SQUIBB CORP	Aa /AA	12/78	4.08P(11)	4.68P(11)	4.94P(7)	4.71P(7)	4.52P(11)
PFIZER INC	Aa /AA	12/78	3.90 (12)	3.56 (13)	3.64 (12)	3.98 (12)	5.24 (9)
MORTON-NORWICH PRODUCTS	A /A	6/78	3.90P(13)	3.67P(12)	1.83P(14)	2.42P(14)	3.64P(12)
SEARLE (G.D.) & CO	Aa /A+	12/78	3.33 (14)	2.10 (14)	3.06 (13)	4.08 (10)	5.02P(10)
AVERAGE			6.62	5.88	5.76	5.75	7.46
MEDIAN			5.73	5.37	4.90	4.70	5.85

AFTER TAX COV (INCL RENTS)

	RATINGS	FYR END	78	77	76	75	74
SMITHKLINE CORP	Aa /AA	12/78	6.18 (1)	3.94 (3)	3.68 (4)	3.76 (3)	3.93 (5)
BRISTOL-MYERS CO	Aaa/AAA	12/78	5.43 (2)	4.78 (1)	4.45 (1)	4.32 (1)	4.01 (4)
ABBOTT LABORATORIES	Aa /AA	12/78	4.32P(3)	3.70P(5)	NA (-)	NA (-)	NA (-)
BECTON, DICKINSON & CO	Baa/BBB*	9/78	4.30 (4)	4.06 (2)	3.93 (2)	3.35 (5)	3.69 (6)
UPJOHN CO	Aa /AA	12/78	4.18 (5)	3.28 (8)	3.02 (7)	3.06 (7)	4.24 (3)
WARNER-LAMBERT CO	Aaa/AAA	12/78	3.63 (6)	3.90 (4)	3.73 (3)	3.97 (2)	4.71 (1)
RICHARDSON-MERRELL INC	Aa /AA	6/78	3.61 (7)	3.65 (6)	3.16 (6)	2.99 (9)	4.28 (2)
AMERICAN HOSPITAL SUPPLY	Aa /AA	12/78	3.12 (8)	3.38 (7)	3.53 (5)	3.46 (4)	3.30 (9)
BAXTER TRAVENOL LABORATORIES	Baa/BBB*	12/78	3.11P(9)	3.22P(9)	2.87P(9)	2.92P(10)	2.31 (12)
PFIZER INC	Aa /AA	12/78	3.06 (10)	2.86 (10)	2.91 (8)	3.05 (8)	3.58 (8)
MORTON-NORWICH PRODUCTS	A /A	6/78	2.71P(11)	2.65P(12)	1.52P(12)	1.92P(12)	2.66P(11)
SEARLE (G.D.) & CO	Aa /A+	12/78	2.58 (12)	1.76 (13)	2.40 (11)	3.08 (6)	3.61P(7)
SQUIBB CORP	Aa /AA	12/78	2.54P(13)	2.75P(11)	2.84P(10)	2.72P(11)	2.70P(10)
MERCK & CO	Aaa/AAA	12/78	NA (-)	NA (-)	NA (-)	NA (-)	NA (-)
AVERAGE			3.75	3.38	3.17	3.22	3.58
MEDIAN			3.61	3.38	3.09	3.07	3.65

NET INCOME AS % NET SALES

	RATINGS	FYR END	78		77		76		75		74	
MERCK & CO	Aaa/AAA	12/78	15.5	(1)	16.1	(1)	15.4	(1)	15.4	(1)	15.8	(1)
SMITHKLINE CORP	Aa /AA	12/78	14.8	(2)	11.4	(2)	10.7	(2)	10.8	(3)	11.2	(3)
ABBOTT LABORATORIES	Aa /AA	12/78	10.3	(3)	9.5	(3)	8.5	(5)	7.5	(9)	7.2	(11)
UPJOHN CO	Aa /AA	12/78	9.7	(4)	8.1	(7)	7.6	(10)	7.5	(10)	8.7	(6)
BAXTER TRAVENOL LABORATORIES	Baa/BBB*	12/78	9.1	(5)	8.9	(4)	8.9	(4)	7.9	(6)	7.8	(9)
PFIZER INC	Aa /AA	12/78	8.7	(6)	8.6	(5)	8.5	(6)	8.9	(4)	8.8	(5)
SEARLE (G.D.) & CO	Aa /A+	12/78	8.5	(7)	4.7	(14)	8.1	(7)	11.3	(2)	11.7	(2)
BRISTOL-MYERS CO	Aaa/AAA	12/78	8.3	(8)	8.0	(8)	7.9	(9)	7.8	(7)	7.6	(10)
SQUIBB CORP	Aa /AA	12/78	7.7	(9)	8.4	(6)	8.9	(3)	8.8	(5)	8.9	(4)
BECTON, DICKINSON & CO	Baa/BBB*	9/78	7.7	(10)	7.8	(9)	8.0	(8)	7.4	(11)	7.0	(12)
WARNER-LAMBERT CO	Aa /AA	12/78	7.2	(11)	7.4	(10)	6.8	(11)	7.5	(8)	8.1	(7)
RICHARDSON-MERRELL INC	Aa /AA	6/78	7.0	(12)	6.8	(11)	6.5	(12)	6.8	(12)	8.0	(8)
MORTON-NORWICH PRODUCTS	A /A	6/78	5.6	(13)	5.2	(13)	1.4	(14)	3.3	(14)	5.1	(13)
AMERICAN HOSPITAL SUPPLY	Aa /AA	12/78	5.3	(14)	5.2	(12)	4.9	(13)	4.8	(13)	4.7	(14)
AVERAGE			8.97		8.29		8.00		8.26		8.61	
MEDIAN			8.40		8.01		8.03		7.65		8.09	

LTD/CAPITALIZATION (%)

	RATINGS	FYR END	78		77		76		75		74	
BRISTOL-MYERS CO	Aaa/AAA	12/78	7.8	(1)	9.3	(1)	10.1	(1)	11.9	(1)	13.8	(5)
MERCK & CO	Aaa/AAA	12/78	12.7	(2)	14.3	(2)	16.5	(3)	18.8	(3)	2.0	(1)
RICHARDSON-MERRELL INC	Aa /AA	6/78	13.9	(3)	15.9	(3)	17.8	(5)	23.5	(6)	7.5	(2)
BECTON, DICKINSON & CO	Baa/BBB*	9/78	14.8	(4)	17.2	(4)	20.2	(6)	22.6	(5)	27.0	(10)
SMITHKLINE CORP	Aa /AA	12/78	17.0	(5)	20.0	(6)	22.5	(7)	24.2	(7)	26.6	(9)
ABBOTT LABORATORIES	Aa /AA	12/78	19.4	(6)	21.7	(7)	25.6	(8)	34.2	(12)	35.7	(12)
WARNER-LAMBERT CO	Aaa/AAA	12/78	23.8	(7)	17.6	(5)	17.6	(4)	19.2	(4)	10.2	(3)
UPJOHN CO	Aa /AA	12/78	25.1	(8)	29.2	(12)	31.4	(11)	29.0	(9)	12.5	(4)
BAXTER TRAVENOL LABORATORIES	Baa/BBB*	12/78	25.7	(9)	29.0	(10)	32.3	(12)	28.2	(8)	43.0	(14)
AMERICAN HOSPITAL SUPPLY	Aa /AA	12/78	25.9	(10)	27.6	(8)	15.2	(2)	16.8	(2)	18.5	(6)
MORTON-NORWICH PRODUCTS	A /A	6/78	28.3	(11)	33.5	(13)	35.8	(13)	34.4	(13)	26.4	(8)
SQUIBB CORP	Aa /AA	12/78	28.4	(12)	29.0	(9)	27.6	(9)	30.0	(10)	28.2	(11)
PFIZER INC	Aa /AA	12/78	30.0	(13)	29.2	(11)	31.4	(10)	33.6	(11)	22.9	(7)
SEARLE (G.D.) & CO	Aa /A+	12/78	44.5	(14)	47.4	(14)	44.1	(14)	46.5	(14)	37.7	(13)
AVERAGE			22.67		24.35		24.87		26.65		22.29	
MEDIAN			24.45		24.61		24.06		26.21		24.67	

LTD/NET PLANT (%)

	RATINGS	FYR END	78		77		76		75		74	
MERCK & CO	Aaa/AAA	12/78	22.9	(1)	25.3	(1)	29.1	(1)	33.6	(1)	3.7	(1)
BRISTOL-MYERS CO	Aaa/AAA	12/78	25.2	(2)	29.7	(2)	34.1	(2)	38.7	(3)	42.4	(5)
BECTON, DICKINSON & CO	Baa/BBB*	9/78	38.5	(3)	46.5	(5)	54.6	(7)	58.3	(7)	61.6	(9)
RICHARDSON-MERRELL INC	Aa /AA	6/78	39.0	(4)	45.7	(4)	50.7	(5)	64.8	(9)	20.3	(3)
ABBOTT LABORATORIES	Aa /AA	12/78	46.1	(5)	50.2	(6)	60.9	(8)	70.5	(10)	73.1	(11)
BAXTER TRAVENOL LABORATORIES	Baa/BBB*	12/78	47.7	(6)	55.3	(8)	62.2	(9)	50.6	(5)	81.1	(12)
UPJOHN CO	Aa /AA	12/78	49.1	(7)	52.7	(7)	53.5	(6)	45.5	(4)	18.8	(2)
SMITHKLINE CORP	Aa /AA	12/78	49.8	(8)	59.5	(9)	69.6	(12)	77.4	(13)	85.3	(13)
MORTON-NORWICH PRODUCTS	A /A	6/78	58.4	(9)	64.5	(10)	68.5	(11)	63.9	(8)	43.7	(6)
WARNER-LAMBERT CO	Aaa/AAA	12/78	59.8	(10)	45.6	(3)	49.6	(4)	54.6	(6)	25.8	(4)
SQUIBB CORP	Aa /AA	12/78	60.0	(11)	64.9	(11)	66.0	(10)	72.2	(11)	65.7	(10)
AMERICAN HOSPITAL SUPPLY	Aa /AA	12/78	62.9	(12)	70.1	(13)	35.3	(3)	38.6	(2)	46.1	(7)
PFIZER INC	Aa /AA	12/78	75.4	(13)	67.8	(12)	70.6	(13)	72.8	(12)	48.0	(8)
SEARLE (G.D.) & CO	Aa /A+	12/78	190.6	(14)	205.3	(14)	201.1	(14)	187.6	(14)	136.5	(14)
AVERAGE			58.95		63.08		64.71		66.37		53.72	
MEDIAN			49.44		53.99		57.77		61.13		47.08	

Drug Industry

TOT LIABILITY/TOT STK EQUITY

	RATINGS	FYR END	78		77		76		75		74	
BECTON, DICKINSON & CO	Baa/BBB*	9/78	48.6	(1)	51.0	(1)	52.0	(1)	56.6	(1)	73.2	(6)
MERCK & CO	Aaa/AAA	12/78	54.7	(2)	56.0	(2)	62.6	(2)	65.7	(4)	51.1	(2)
BRISTOL-MYERS CO	Aaa/AAA	12/78	60.2	(3)	64.0	(4)	65.2	(5)	69.5	(5)	70.7	(5)
RICHARDSON-MERRELL INC	Aa /AA	6/78	64.5	(4)	59.8	(3)	62.6	(3)	78.3	(6)	47.2	(1)
SMITHKLINE CORP	Aa /AA	12/78	71.2	(5)	77.2	(6)	84.6	(8)	83.8	(8)	81.6	(8)
MORTON-NORWICH PRODUCTS	A /A	6/78	80.4	(6)	94.9	(12)	96.7	(12)	93.7	(10)	90.2	(10)
AMERICAN HOSPITAL SUPPLY	Aa /AA	12/78	84.2	(7)	80.5	(7)	65.5	(6)	59.2	(2)	55.0	(3)
BAXTER TRAVENOL LABORATORIES	Baa/BBB*	12/78	84.5	(8)	85.8	(8)	90.1	(10)	83.3	(7)	122.4	(13)
ABBOTT LABORATORIES	Aa /AA	12/78	87.9	(9)	87.4	(10)	87.2	(9)	124.1	(13)	125.4	(14)
SQUIBB CORP	Aa /AA	12/78	88.5	(10)	86.7	(9)	77.9	(7)	83.9	(9)	87.2	(9)
UPJOHN CO	Aa /AA	12/78	88.8	(11)	90.9	(11)	95.6	(11)	97.6	(11)	77.4	(7)
WARNER-LAMBERT CO	Aaa/AAA	12/78	94.0	(12)	67.4	(5)	62.9	(4)	64.6	(3)	61.7	(4)
PFIZER INC	Aa /AA	12/78	119.6	(13)	118.2	(13)	112.5	(13)	117.0	(12)	97.8	(11)
SEARLE (G.D.) & CO	Aa /A+	12/78	128.8	(14)	151.7	(14)	132.3	(14)	125.3	(14)	115.4	(12)
AVERAGE			82.56		83.67		81.98		85.89		82.67	
MEDIAN			84.36		83.16		81.26		83.52		79.52	

NET TANG ASSETS/LTD (%)

	RATINGS	FYR END	78		77		76		75		74	
BRISTOL-MYERS CO	Aaa/AAA	12/78	1151.1	(1)	968.3	(1)	888.2	(1)	749.7	(1)	642.1	(5)
MERCK & CO	Aaa/AAA	12/78	755.6	(2)	652.6	(2)	572.0	(3)	504.3	(3)	4577.8	(1)
BECTON, DICKINSON & CO	Baa/BBB*	9/78	644.9	(3)	559.9	(3)	476.5	(5)	426.2	(5)	354.5	(8)
RICHARDSON-MERRELL INC	Aa /AA	6/78	531.6	(4)	485.5	(5)	423.1	(6)	314.2	(9)	957.8	(2)
SMITHKLINE CORP	Aa /AA	12/78	530.8	(5)	440.4	(7)	385.9	(7)	352.0	(6)	330.5	(9)
ABBOTT LABORATORIES	Aa /AA	12/78	499.8	(6)	446.3	(6)	380.1	(8)	282.5	(11)	270.8	(12)
UPJOHN CO	Aa /AA	12/78	389.1	(7)	335.0	(10)	312.2	(10)	338.0	(8)	777.0	(4)
BAXTER TRAVENOL LABORATORIES	Baa/BBB*	12/78	377.1	(8)	338.2	(9)	304.5	(11)	347.0	(7)	225.7	(14)
AMERICAN HOSPITAL SUPPLY	Aa /AA	12/78	374.9	(9)	351.1	(8)	651.8	(2)	593.2	(2)	533.6	(6)
SQUIBB CORP	Aa /AA	12/78	335.1	(10)	326.8	(11)	340.0	(9)	310.9	(10)	327.8	(10)
MORTON-NORWICH PRODUCTS	A /A	6/78	333.8	(11)	279.7	(13)	255.8	(13)	253.1	(13)	319.8	(11)
WARNER-LAMBERT CO	Aaa/AAA	12/78	331.3	(12)	502.9	(4)	493.3	(4)	491.6	(4)	922.6	(3)
PFIZER INC	Aa /AA	12/78	303.1	(13)	311.8	(12)	289.8	(12)	271.2	(12)	394.8	(7)
SEARLE (G.D.) & CO	Aa /A+	12/78	215.6	(14)	198.2	(14)	218.8	(14)	202.6	(14)	248.9	(13)
AVERAGE			483.84		442.61		428.00		388.32		777.41	
MEDIAN			383.09		395.76		383.02		342.51		374.68	

CASH FLOW/LTD (%)

	RATINGS	FYR END	78		77		76		75		74	
BRISTOL-MYERS CO	Aaa/AAA	12/78	271.1	(1)	225.6	(1)	197.1	(1)	177.9	(1)	146.7	(5)
MERCK & CO	Aaa/AAA	12/78	191.7	(2)	173.7	(2)	149.5	(2)	131.0	(2)	1560.8	(1)
SMITHKLINE CORP	Aa /AA	12/78	168.7	(3)	97.7	(3)	81.2	(5)	76.6	(5)	71.1	(8)
RICHARDSON-MERRELL INC	Aa /AA	6/78	118.3	(4)	95.2	(4)	78.4	(6)	54.8	(7)	205.9	(2)
BECTON, DICKINSON & CO	Baa/BBB*	9/78	109.8	(5)	90.7	(5)	71.7	(7)	55.0	(6)	55.0	(9)
ABBOTT LABORATORIES	Aa /AA	12/78	104.0	(6)	80.9	(7)	62.7	(8)	44.9	(10)	38.0	(13)
UPJOHN CO	Aa /AA	12/78	82.9	(7)	59.1	(9)	50.0	(9)	53.7	(8)	164.0	(4)
AMERICAN HOSPITAL SUPPLY	Aa /AA	12/78	70.4	(8)	65.7	(8)	137.9	(3)	97.8	(3)	85.7	(6)
WARNER-LAMBERT CO	Aaa/AAA	12/78	63.8	(9)	90.0	(6)	83.1	(4)	80.2	(4)	174.1	(3)
BAXTER TRAVENOL LABORATORIES	Baa/BBB*	12/78	61.1	(10)	47.1	(11)	43.4	(13)	42.7	(12)	27.6	(14)
MORTON-NORWICH PRODUCTS	A /A	6/78	57.2	(11)	40.8	(14)	44.5	(12)	31.1	(13)	54.5	(10)
PFIZER INC	Aa /AA	12/78	52.2	(12)	54.7	(10)	48.3	(11)	44.5	(11)	74.1	(7)
SQUIBB CORP	Aa /AA	12/78	46.4	(13)	45.7	(12)	49.7	(10)	46.2	(9)	51.1	(11)
SEARLE (G.D.) & CO	Aa /A+	12/78	40.1	(14)	41.5	(13)	23.0	(14)	26.6	(14)	45.2	(12)
AVERAGE			102.69		86.32		80.03		68.95		196.69	
MEDIAN			76.70		73.31		67.21		54.29		72.57	

NET CASH FL/CAP EXP (%)

	RATINGS	FYR END	78		77		76		75		74	
UPJOHN CO	Aa /AA	12/78	308.0	(1)	239.1	(2)	152.9	(11)	61.3	(14)	75.0	(14)
SEARLE (G.D.) & CO	Aa /A+	12/78	271.9	(2)	263.4	(1)	157.6 V(	9)	134.1 V(	7)	164.8	(3)
RICHARDSON-MERRELL INC	Aa /AA	6/78	228.6	(3)	214.7	(3)	241.6	(3)	107.2	(10)	111.2	(9)
BRISTOL-MYERS CO	Aaa/AAA	12/78	201.3	(4)	200.8	(5)	264.4	(2)	285.1	(1)	303.1	(1)
SMITHKLINE CORP	Aa /AA	12/78	190.3	(5)	156.3	(9)	184.2	(6)	194.9	(2)	172.4	(2)
AMERICAN HOSPITAL SUPPLY	Aa /AA	12/78	182.7 V(	6)	165.6 V(	8)	270.7 V(	1)	155.7 V(	4)	119.3	(8)
PFIZER INC	Aa /AA	12/78	178.9	(7)	201.3	(4)	201.8	(5)	86.3	(12)	96.6	(12)
MERCK & CO	Aaa/AAA	12/78	175.1	(8)	143.5	(11)	141.4	(12)	72.9	(13)	99.8	(10)
ABBOTT LABORATORIES	Aa /AA	12/78	174.3	(9)	178.7	(7)	183.9	(7)	144.2	(5)	121.2	(7)
BECTON, DICKINSON & CO	Baa/BBB*	9/78	149.8	(10)	181.7	(6)	222.5	(4)	118.2	(8)	98.4	(11)
WARNER-LAMBERT CO	Aaa/AAA	12/78	134.4	(11)	151.5	(10)	161.7	(8)	157.2	(3)	161.1	(4)
BAXTER TRAVENOL LABORATORIES	Baa/BBB*	12/78	128.9	(12)	108.0	(13)	117.5	(13)	92.8	(11)	77.8	(13)
SQUIBB CORP	Aa /AA	12/78	101.3	(13)	92.4	(14)	156.5	(10)	141.7	(6)	135.2	(5)
MORTON-NORWICH PRODUCTS	A /A	6/78	95.1	(14)	128.3	(12)	93.1	(14)	113.9	(9)	128.8	(6)
AVERAGE			180.04		173.24		182.12		133.23		133.20	
MEDIAN			176.98		172.16		172.78		126.15		120.26	

AFT TAX RET ON COM EQTY (%)

	RATINGS	FYR END	78		77		76		75		74	
SMITHKLINE CORP	Aa /AA	12/78	29.9	(1)	21.1	(2)	19.9	(2)	20.1	(3)	20.6	(3)
MERCK & CO	Aaa/AAA	12/78	21.2	(2)	21.8	(1)	23.2	(1)	24.1	(1)	29.7	(1)
UPJOHN CO	Aa /AA	12/78	20.2	(3)	16.7	(5)	15.8	(5)	15.1	(8)	17.1	(5)
ABBOTT LABORATORIES	Aa /AA	12/78	19.2	(4)	17.7	(4)	16.0	(4)	17.1	(5)	15.1	(9)
BRISTOL-MYERS CO	Aaa/AAA	12/78	19.0	(5)	18.9	(3)	19.2	(3)	20.0	(4)	19.4	(4)
SEARLE (G.D.) & CO	Aa /A+	12/78	16.9	(6)	9.3	(14)	14.1	(8)	20.2	(2)	21.3	(2)
PFIZER INC	Aa /AA	12/78	16.5	(7)	15.6	(6)	15.6	(6)	15.9	(6)	15.9	(6)
WARNER-LAMBERT CO	Aaa/AAA	12/78	15.1	(8)	14.9	(7)	13.5	(10)	14.9	(9)	15.5	(7)
BAXTER TRAVENOL LABORATORIES	Baa/BBB*	12/78	15.0	(9)	14.5	(9)	13.7	(9)	11.9	(12)	13.5	(12)
RICHARDSON-MERRELL INC	Aa /AA	6/78	14.3	(10)	13.7	(10)	12.8	(11)	12.8	(10)	13.9	(10)
AMERICAN HOSPITAL SUPPLY	Aa /AA	12/78	14.3	(11)	13.5	(11)	12.8	(12)	12.1	(11)	11.3	(13)
SQUIBB CORP	Aa /AA	12/78	13.9	(12)	14.5	(8)	15.3	(7)	15.4	(7)	15.5	(8)
BECTON, DICKINSON & CO	Baa/BBB*	9/78	13.2	(13)	12.9	(13)	12.7	(13)	11.7	(13)	13.7	(11)
MORTON-NORWICH PRODUCTS	A /A	6/78	12.8	(14)	13.2	(12)	3.7	(14)	7.4	(14)	10.7	(14)
AVERAGE			17.24		15.59		14.89		15.63		16.37	
MEDIAN			15.82		14.71		14.71		15.27		15.50	

RET ON TOT ASSETS (%)

	RATINGS	FYR END	78		77		76		75		74	
SMITHKLINE CORP	Aa /AA	12/78	29.7	(1)	20.5	(3)	18.5	(3)	18.7	(3)	19.2	(4)
MERCK & CO	Aaa/AAA	12/78	23.6	(2)	23.9	(1)	24.6	(1)	25.3	(1)	29.7	(1)
BRISTOL-MYERS CO	Aaa/AAA	12/78	23.2	(3)	23.0	(2)	22.6	(2)	22.8	(2)	22.1	(2)
ABBOTT LABORATORIES	Aa /AA	12/78	18.2	(4)	17.3	(6)	15.4	(7)	14.3	(9)	12.8	(12)
UPJOHN CO	Aa /AA	12/78	18.0	(5)	16.0	(8)	15.4	(8)	15.5	(5)	18.9	(5)
RICHARDSON-MERRELL INC	Aa /AA	6/78	17.2	(6)	18.1	(4)	17.3	(4)	15.4	(6)	19.7	(3)
BECTON, DICKINSON & CO	Baa/BBB*	9/78	16.9	(7)	16.6	(7)	16.4	(6)	15.0	(7)	16.0	(7)
WARNER-LAMBERT CO	Aaa/AAA	12/78	15.2	(8)	17.6	(5)	16.6	(5)	17.4	(4)	17.7	(6)
MORTON-NORWICH PRODUCTS	A /A	6/78	14.3	(9)	14.2	(9)	4.3	(14)	9.8	(14)	12.6	(13)
AMERICAN HOSPITAL SUPPLY	Aa /AA	12/78	14.1	(10)	14.1	(10)	14.7	(9)	14.1	(10)	14.3	(10)
SEARLE (G.D.) & CO	Aa /A+	12/78	14.1	(11)	11.8	(14)	10.6	(13)	13.3	(11)	15.0	(8)
PFIZER INC	Aa /AA	12/78	13.8	(12)	13.2	(12)	13.5	(11)	13.1	(12)	14.3	(11)
BAXTER TRAVENOL LABORATORIES	Baa/BBB*	12/78	12.8	(13)	13.1	(13)	12.1	(12)	10.3	(13)	11.2	(14)
SQUIBB CORP	Aa /AA	12/78	12.7	(14)	13.4	(11)	14.6	(10)	14.4	(8)	14.4	(9)
AVERAGE			17.41		16.64		15.47		15.66		16.99	
MEDIAN			16.03		16.29		15.44		14.70		15.51	

Electrical/Electronic Industry

PRETAX COVERAGE

	RATINGS	FYR END	78	77	76	75	74
TEXAS INSTRUMENTS INC	Aa /AA	12/78	31.75 (1)	23.98 (2)	22.43 (1)	11.71 (2)	16.16 (2)
MCGRAW-EDISON CO	Aa /AA	12/78	25.48 (2)	20.94 (3)	21.36 (2)	8.98 (5)	2.84 (19)
TEKTRONIX INC	A /A	5/78	22.61 (3)	18.92 (4)	12.41 (8)	10.61 (4)	31.64 (1)
WHIRLPOOL CORP	A /A	12/78	20.57 (4)	24.95 (1)	17.85 (3)	11.23 (3)	3.80 (14)
AMP INC	Aa /AA	12/78	20.48 (5)	17.87 (6)	13.65 (6)	6.54 (10)	8.55 (6)
RELIANCE ELECTRIC CO	A /A	10/78	15.40 (6)	14.23 (9)	10.77 (9)	8.77 (6)	8.72 (5)
GENERAL SIGNAL CORP	Aa /AA	12/78	14.13P(7)	14.94P(8)	14.54 (5)	8.45 (7)	7.24 (7)
SCOTT & FETZER CO	A /A	11/78	12.34 (8)	15.17 (7)	15.42 (4)	12.52 (1)	11.00 (3)
WESTINGHOUSE ELECTRIC CORP	A /AA-	12/78	11.25 (9)	9.52 (11)	7.50 (14)	4.66 (12)	3.14 (18)
ELTRA CORP	Aa /AA	9/78	11.02 (10)	9.31 (12)	9.79 (12)	7.85 (8)	9.38 (4)
GENERAL ELECTRIC CO	Aaa/AAA	12/78	10.52 (11)	10.39 (10)	10.25 (11)	6.56 (9)	6.51 (9)
MOTOROLA INC	Aa /AA	12/78	9.00H(12)	9.28R(13)	10.74H(10)	4.85H(11)	5.91H(10)
GENERAL INSTRUMENT CORP	Ba /BB*	2/78	8.81 (13)	4.30 (19)	2.33 (19)	2.50 (18)	3.37 (16)
TICOR	Aaa/AAA	12/78	7.39 (14)	18.45 (5)	12.49 (7)	1.60 (19)	6.93 (8)
NORTH AMERICAN PHILIPS CORP	A /A	12/78	6.58P(15)	8.20P(14)	8.70P(13)	3.85P(14)	4.84P(12)
GOULD INC	A /A	12/78	5.93 (16)	6.82 (15)	4.93 (15)	4.11 (13)	4.68 (13)
RCA CORP	A /A	12/78	5.59 (17)	5.93 (17)	4.72 (18)	2.99 (17)	3.16 (17)
SUNBEAM CORP	A /A	3/78	5.23 (18)	6.07 (16)	4.80 (17)	3.15 (16)	5.75 (11)
WHITE CONSOLIDATED INDS INC	Ba /BB*	12/78	4.52 (19)	5.19 (18)	4.89 (16)	3.71 (15)	3.57 (15)
AVERAGE			13.08	12.87	11.03	6.56	7.75
MEDIAN			11.02	10.39	10.74	6.54	5.91

AFTER TAX COVERAGE

	RATINGS	FYR END	78	77	76	75	74
TEXAS INSTRUMENTS INC	Aa /AA	12/78	17.76 (1)	13.71 (1)	12.72 (1)	6.74 (2)	9.34 (2)
MCGRAW-EDISON CO	Aa /AA	12/78	13.81 (2)	11.26 (3)	11.25 (2)	5.20 (6)	2.04 (19)
TEKTRONIX INC	A /A	5/78	13.40 (3)	11.23 (4)	7.12 (8)	6.31 (3)	17.61 (1)
AMP INC	Aa /AA	12/78	11.57 (4)	10.06 (6)	7.75 (7)	3.91 (10)	4.85 (7)
WHIRLPOOL CORP	A /A	12/78	10.74 (5)	12.99 (2)	9.58 (3)	6.04 (4)	2.46 (16)
RELIANCE ELECTRIC CO	A /A	10/78	8.66 (6)	7.82 (8)	6.25 (11)	5.40 (5)	5.43 (5)
WESTINGHOUSE ELECTRIC CORP	A /AA-	12/78	7.52 (7)	6.25 (11)	5.00 (14)	3.43 (11)	2.57 (14)
GENERAL SIGNAL CORP	Aa /AA	12/78	7.48P(8)	7.82P(7)	7.99 (5)	4.89 (7)	4.29 (9)
SCOTT & FETZER CO	A /A	11/78	6.59 (9)	7.77 (9)	8.19 (4)	6.99 (1)	6.28 (3)
GENERAL ELECTRIC CO	Aaa/AAA	12/78	6.54 (10)	6.52 (10)	6.43 (9)	4.44 (9)	4.38 (8)
ELTRA CORP	Aa /AA	9/78	6.21 (11)	5.61 (12)	5.76 (12)	4.84 (8).	5.66 (4)
MOTOROLA INC	Aa /AA	12/78	5.55H(12)	5.60R(13)	6.36H(10)	3.02H(12)	3.68H(10)
TICOR	Aaa/AAA	12/78	4.99 (13)	10.83 (5)	7.86 (6)	2.09 (17)	4.96 (6)
GENERAL INSTRUMENT CORP	Ba /BB*	2/78	4.87 (14)	2.71 (19)	1.70 (19)	1.89 (19)	2.42 (17)
NORTH AMERICAN PHILIPS CORP	A /A	12/78	4.06P(15)	4.83P(14)	5.07P(13)	2.69P(14)	2.99P(13)
GOULD INC	A /A	12/78	3.74 (16)	4.40 (15)	3.45 (15)	3.00 (13)	3.03 (12)
RCA CORP	A /A	12/78	3.50 (17)	3.62 (16)	2.95 (17)	2.18 (16)	2.24 (18)
SUNBEAM CORP	A /A	3/78	3.13 (18)	3.31 (18)	2.92 (18)	2.03 (18)	3.41 (11)
WHITE CONSOLIDATED INDS INC	Ba /BB*	12/78	2.97 (19)	3.35 (17)	3.08 (16)	2.52 (15)	2.47 (15)
AVERAGE			7.53	7.35	6.39	4.08	4.74
MEDIAN			6.54	6.52	6.36	3.91	3.68

III-47

AFTER TAX COV (INCL RENTS)

	RATINGS	FYR END	78	77	76	75	74
TEKTRONIX INC	A /A	5/78	6.30 (1)	5.38 (2)	3.99 (5)	3.68 (1)	6.15 (1)
AMP INC	Aa /AA	12/78	5.76 (2)	5.47 (1)	4.41 (2)	2.65 (8)	3.50 (3)
SCOTT & FETZER CO	A /A	11/78	4.42 (3)	4.80 (3)	4.25 (3)	3.60 (2)	3.25 (4)
GENERAL ELECTRIC CO	Aaa/AAA	12/78	3.94 (4)	4.10 (4)	4.06 (4)	3.03 (7)	3.17 (5)
GENERAL SIGNAL CORP	Aa /AA	12/78	3.92P(5)	NA (-)	NA (-)	3.03 (6)	2.87 (8)
ELTRA CORP	Aa /AA	9/78	3.59 (6)	3.46 (5)	3.56 (6)	3.23 (4)	3.72 (2)
WESTINGHOUSE ELECTRIC CORP	A /AA-	12/78	3.56 (7)	3.16 (9)	2.64 (10)	2.30 (10)	2.02 (12)
TEXAS INSTRUMENTS INC	Aa /AA	12/78	3.55 (8)	3.44 (6)	3.47 (7)	2.52 (9)	3.01 (7)
RELIANCE ELECTRIC CO	A /A	10/78	3.51 (9)	3.37 (7)	3.14 (9)	3.05 (5)	3.09 (6)
MOTOROLA INC	Aa /AA	12/78	3.35H(10)	3.31R(8)	3.35H(8)	2.01H(12)	2.62H(9)
GENERAL INSTRUMENT CORP	Ba /BB*	2/78	2.91 (11)	2.07 (15)	1.45 (16)	1.67 (15)	2.00 (13)
GOULD INC	A /A	12/78	2.58 (12)	2.65 (11)	2.30 (13)	2.24 (11)	2.19 (11)
SUNBEAM CORP	A /A	3/78	2.51 (13)	2.40 (14)	2.30 (14)	1.79 (13)	2.61 (10)
RCA CORP	A /A	12/78	2.48 (14)	2.44 (13)	2.05 (15)	1.64 (16)	1.69 (17)
TICOR	Aaa/AAA	12/78	2.42 (15)	2.90 (10)	2.60 (12)	1.30 (17)	1.98 (14)
NORTH AMERICAN PHILIPS CORP	A /A	12/78	2.37P(16)	2.60P(12)	2.61P(11)	1.73P(14)	1.97P(15)
MCGRAW-EDISON CO	Aa /AA	12/78	NA (-)	NA (-)	NA (-)	NA (-)	NA (-)
WHIRLPOOL CORP	A /A	12/78	NA (-)	NA (-)	4.89 (1)	3.33 (3)	1.75 (16)
WHITE CONSOLIDATED INDS INC	Ba /BB*	12/78	NA (-)	NA (-)	NA (-)	NA (-)	NA (-)
AVERAGE			3.57	3.44	3.19	2.52	2.80
MEDIAN			3.53	3.31	3.25	2.52	2.62

NET INCOME AS % NET SALES

	RATINGS	FYR END	78	77	76	75	74
AMP INC	Aa /AA	12/78	12.2 (1)	12.0 (1)	10.0 (1)	6.8 (2)	9.6 (1)
TEKTRONIX INC	A /A	5/78	9.5 (2)	9.7 (2)	8.2 (2)	7.8 (1)	7.9 (2)
RELIANCE ELECTRIC CO	A /A	10/78	6.7 (3)	6.5 (5)	6.4 (5)	5.4 (4)	5.0 (6)
SCOTT & FETZER CO	A /A	11/78	6.3 (4)	7.6 (4)	6.7 (4)	6.0 (3)	4.7 (7)
TICOR	Aaa/AAA	12/78	6.3 (5)	7.8 (3)	8.1 (3)	2.5 (17)	5.3 (5)
GENERAL ELECTRIC CO	Aaa/AAA	12/78	6.3 (6)	6.2 (6)	5.9 (6)	4.3 (9)	4.5 (9)
GENERAL SIGNAL CORP	Aa /AA	12/78	5.9 (7)	5.5 (12)	5.1 (12)	4.5 (8)	4.4 (10)
MCGRAW-EDISON CO	Aa /AA	12/78	5.8 (8)	5.5 (11)	5.6 (9)	4.3 (10)	1.9 (18)
MOTOROLA INC	Aa /AA	12/78	5.6 (9)	5.8 (8)	5.8 (8)	3.1 (13)	5.3 (4)
TEXAS INSTRUMENTS INC	Aa /AA	12/78	5.5 (10)	5.7 (9)	5.9 (7)	4.5 (7)	5.7 (3)
GOULD INC	A /A	12/78	5.4 (11)	5.8 (7)	5.4 (10)	4.8 (5)	4.1 (12)
GENERAL INSTRUMENT CORP	Ba /BB*	2/78	4.8 (12)	3.5 (17)	1.9 (19)	2.8 (15)	3.3 (14)
WHIRLPOOL CORP	A /A	12/78	4.8 (13)	5.7 (10)	5.4 (11)	4.0 (11)	1.5 (19)
ELTRA CORP	Aa /AA	9/78	4.7 (14)	4.6 (13)	5.0 (13)	4.8 (6)	4.6 (8)
WESTINGHOUSE ELECTRIC CORP	A /AA-	12/78	4.7 (15)	4.4 (14)	3.6 (15)	3.0 (14)	2.4 (17)
RCA CORP	A /A	12/78	4.2 (16)	4.2 (15)	3.3 (18)	2.3 (18)	2.5 (16)
SUNBEAM CORP	A /A	3/78	3.8 (17)	3.3 (18)	3.5 (16)	2.7 (16)	4.2 (11)
WHITE CONSOLIDATED INDS INC	Ba /BB*	12/78	3.3 (18)	3.8 (16)	4.1 (14)	3.8 (12)	3.8 (13)
NORTH AMERICAN PHILIPS CORP	A /A	12/78	3.1 (19)	3.2 (19)	3.3 (17)	2.2 (19)	2.9 (15)
AVERAGE			5.73	5.82	5.44	4.20	4.40
MEDIAN			5.50	5.67	5.43	4.31	4.39

Electrical/Electronic Industry

LTD/CAPITALIZATION (%)

	RATINGS	FYR END	78		77		76		75		74	
TEXAS INSTRUMENTS INC	Aa /AA	12/78	2.2	(1)	3.8	(1)	5.5	(1)	7.5	(1)	11.8	(4)
MCGRAW-EDISON CO	Aa /AA	12/78	10.0	(2)	12.1	(3)	12.9	(4)	14.4	(3)	15.3	(5)
TEKTRONIX INC	A /A	5/78	10.2	(3)	12.7	(5)	14.3	(5)	12.9	(2)	0.4	(1)
AMP INC	Aa /AA	12/78	10.2	(4)	12.3	(4)	12.3	(3)	14.5	(4)	6.6	(3)
WHIRLPOOL CORP	A /A	12/78	11.3	(5)	13.5	(6)	15.6	(8)	22.5	(10)	17.2	(6)
GENERAL ELECTRIC CO	Aaa/AAA	12/78	13.1	(6)	17.8	(8)	20.1	(10)	20.3	(9)	24.4	(13)
WESTINGHOUSE ELECTRIC CORP	A /AA-	12/78	13.2	(7)	15.1	(7)	19.0	(9)	23.4	(11)	30.5	(14)
GENERAL SIGNAL CORP	Aa /AA	12/78	13.8	(8)	10.8	(2)	15.1	(7)	19.7	(8)	23.4	(11)
MOTOROLA INC	Aa /AA	12/78	18.3	(9)	20.3	(10)	12.1	(2)	16.3	(6)	20.2	(9)
ELTRA CORP	Aa /AA	9/78	19.2	(10)	20.6	(11)	21.3	(11)	15.5	(5)	18.2	(7)
SCOTT & FETZER CO	A /A	11/78	23.1	(11)	23.9	(12)	21.7	(12)	24.1	(12)	21.5	(10)
RELIANCE ELECTRIC CO	A /A	10/78	23.5	(12)	25.2	(14)	29.4	(15)	32.4	(15)	24.0	(12)
NORTH AMERICAN PHILIPS CORP	A /A	12/78	24.7	(13)	25.1	(13)	26.5	(13)	29.6	(13)	33.4	(16)
GENERAL INSTRUMENT CORP	Ba /BB*	2/78	26.3	(14)	38.3	(17)	47.1	(19)	47.9	(19)	48.9	(18)
TICOR	Aaa/AAA	12/78	27.9	(15)	18.2	(9)	14.3	(6)	16.6	(7)	2.8	(2)
SUNBEAM CORP	A /A	3/78	28.7	(16)	26.9	(16)	28.5	(14)	30.0	(14)	20.1	(8)
GOULD INC	A /A	12/78	30.5	(17)	26.8	(15)	31.2	(16)	34.9	(16)	33.2	(15)
RCA CORP	A /A	12/78	41.1	(18)	42.9	(18)	42.5	(18)	44.8	(17)	47.8	(17)
WHITE CONSOLIDATED INDS INC	Ba /BB*	12/78	44.1	(19)	46.0	(19)	37.2	(17)	46.2	(18)	49.7	(19)
AVERAGE			20.60		21.70		22.45		24.92		23.64	
MEDIAN			19.16		20.25		20.11		22.49		21.50	

LTD/NET PLANT (%)

	RATINGS	FYR END	78		77		76		75		74	
TEXAS INSTRUMENTS INC	Aa /AA	12/78	3.3	(1)	7.5	(1)	12.6	(1)	18.7	(1)	25.9	(4)
AMP INC	Aa /AA	12/78	23.3	(2)	28.1	(2)	26.8	(3)	26.9	(2)	10.4	(3)
GENERAL ELECTRIC CO	Aaa/AAA	12/78	24.7	(3)	35.8	(5)	39.4	(6)	40.5	(5)	45.7	(7)
WESTINGHOUSE ELECTRIC CORP	A /AA-	12/78	27.9	(4)	30.2	(3)	36.4	(4)	44.2	(6)	64.9	(12)
TEKTRONIX INC	A /A	5/78	31.0	(5)	41.7	(7)	43.6	(9)	36.1	(4)	1.0	(1)
WHIRLPOOL CORP	A /A	12/78	33.8	(6)	38.3	(6)	41.7	(8)	58.2	(11)	38.5	(5)
MCGRAW-EDISON CO	Aa /AA	12/78	38.9	(7)	54.4	(10)	56.3	(10)	57.0	(10)	57.1	(9)
MOTOROLA INC	Aa /AA	12/78	39.3	(8)	45.6	(8)	25.2	(2)	35.0	(3)	45.5	(6)
GENERAL SIGNAL CORP	Aa /AA	12/78	41.6	(9)	32.2	(4)	41.5	(7)	53.4	(9)	67.6	(14)
RCA CORP	A /A	12/78	59.2	(10)	61.4	(11)	58.5	(11)	63.1	(12)	66.8	(13)
RELIANCE ELECTRIC CO	A /A	10/78	61.2	(11)	66.0	(13)	77.0	(15)	85.7	(15)	56.6	(8)
NORTH AMERICAN PHILIPS CORP	A /A	12/78	65.5	(12)	67.0	(14)	74.5	(13)	79.8	(14)	85.4	(17)
ELTRA CORP	Aa /AA	9/78	65.6	(13)	67.9	(15)	72.3	(12)	49.8	(7)	62.4	(10)
GOULD INC	A /A	12/78	65.9	(14)	65.7	(12)	76.0	(14)	89.7	(16)	81.1	(16)
GENERAL INSTRUMENT CORP	Ba /BB*	2/78	68.2	(15)	99.2	(17)	132.7	(19)	137.7	(19)	138.9	(19)
SCOTT & FETZER CO	A /A	11/78	74.0	(16)	83.4	(16)	79.4	(17)	78.8	(13)	63.7	(11)
TICOR	Aaa/AAA	12/78	87.9	(17)	50.1	(9)	37.2	(5)	50.4	(8)	7.6	(2)
WHITE CONSOLIDATED INDS INC	Ba /BB*	12/78	99.9	(18)	101.0	(18)	77.5	(16)	107.5	(17)	131.8	(18)
SUNBEAM CORP	A /A	3/78	100.3	(19)	105.8	(19)	117.6	(18)	122.2	(18)	77.7	(15)
AVERAGE			53.24		56.90		59.28		64.99		59.41	
MEDIAN			59.23		54.40		56.32		57.04		62.39	

TOT LIABILITY/TOT STK EQUITY

	RATINGS	FYR END	78		77		76		75		74	
MCGRAW-EDISON CO	Aa /AA	12/78	41.1	(1)	41.3	(1)	53.7	(2)	51.7	(2)	80.0	(5)
TEKTRONIX INC	A /A	5/78	50.3	(2)	51.5	(2)	48.6	(1)	51.5	(1)	43.1	(1)
WHIRLPOOL CORP	A /A	12/78	52.9	(3)	65.2	(3)	65.5	(4)	77.0	(8)	85.7	(8)
AMP INC	Aa /AA	12/78	67.8	(4)	67.3	(4)	67.1	(5)	65.5	(6)	80.3	(6)
GENERAL SIGNAL CORP	Aa /AA	12/78	72.1	(5)	72.4	(7)	76.4	(9)	77.3	(9)	91.0	(10)
TEXAS INSTRUMENTS INC	Aa /AA	12/78	79.6	(6)	68.5	(5)	70.8	(8)	60.9	(4)	78.3	(4)
GENERAL INSTRUMENT CORP	Ba /BB*	2/78	85.0	(7)	111.8	(14)	136.9	(16)	140.6	(15)	145.0	(15)
MOTOROLA INC	Aa /AA	12/78	87.1	(8)	80.1	(8)	68.7	(7)	63.9	(5)	83.2	(7)
ELTRA CORP	Aa /AA	9/78	88.1	(9)	86.1	(9)	86.6	(10)	79.5	(10)	88.4	(9)
RELIANCE ELECTRIC CO	A /A	10/78	89.2	(10)	92.5	(11)	104.7	(12)	112.7	(11)	123.4	(13)
GOULD INC	A /A	12/78	107.3	(11)	91.1	(10)	100.0	(11)	114.5	(12)	114.9	(12)
SUNBEAM CORP	A /A	3/78	119.5	(12)	108.0	(13)	106.2	(13)	127.5	(13)	106.6	(11)
SCOTT & FETZER CO	A /A	11/78	120.9	(13)	69.0	(6)	67.4	(6)	68.2	(7)	62.5	(3)
TICOR	Aaa/AAA	12/78	125.8	(14)	100.2	(12)	60.9	(3)	56.9	(3)	43.8	(2)
GENERAL ELECTRIC CO	Aaa/AAA	12/78	128.3	(15)	130.5	(16)	129.4	(14)	139.9	(14)	152.9	(16)
NORTH AMERICAN PHILIPS CORP	A /A	12/78	132.0	(16)	130.1	(15)	141.2	(17)	150.3	(17)	177.4	(17)
WESTINGHOUSE ELECTRIC CORP	A /AA-	12/78	159.0	(17)	141.0	(17)	148.7	(18)	143.1	(16)	123.6	(14)
WHITE CONSOLIDATED INDS INC	Ba /BB*	12/78	162.0	(18)	169.2	(18)	136.3	(15)	171.3	(18)	179.3	(18)
RCA CORP	A /A	12/78	204.7	(19)	204.3	(19)	200.4	(19)	216.0	(19)	217.0	(19)
AVERAGE			103.82		98.95		98.39		103.61		109.28	
MEDIAN			89.24		91.06		86.60		79.54		90.99	

NET TANG ASSETS/LTD (%)

	RATINGS	FYR END	78		77		76		75		74	
TEXAS INSTRUMENTS INC	Aa /AA	12/78	4375.7	(1)	2454.4	(1)	1720.7	(1)	1278.4	(1)	804.4	(4)
TEKTRONIX INC	A /A	5/78	979.1	(2)	787.1	(5)	698.7	(5)	774.8	(2)	27384.6	(1)
AMP INC	Aa /AA	12/78	975.2	(3)	811.8	(3)	804.0	(3)	679.3	(4)	1508.9	(3)
MCGRAW-EDISON CO	Aa /AA	12/78	972.2	(4)	805.3	(4)	765.8	(4)	684.8	(3)	648.0	(5)
WHIRLPOOL CORP	A /A	12/78	873.3	(5)	723.5	(6)	621.6	(7)	427.5	(10)	557.8	(6)
GENERAL ELECTRIC CO	Aaa/AAA	12/78	716.5	(6)	531.5	(8)	473.8	(10)	466.1	(9)	387.3	(13)
WESTINGHOUSE ELECTRIC CORP	A /AA-	12/78	688.6	(7)	614.2	(7)	485.2	(9)	388.0	(12)	286.9	(15)
GENERAL SIGNAL CORP	Aa /AA	12/78	618.2	(8)	878.4	(2)	639.3	(6)	501.3	(8)	424.0	(11)
MOTOROLA INC	Aa /AA	12/78	538.1	(9)	480.7	(10)	805.1	(2)	597.9	(6)	482.2	(8)
ELTRA CORP	Aa /AA	9/78	521.9	(10)	486.2	(9)	469.0	(11)	645.2	(5)	550.0	(7)
SCOTT & FETZER CO	A /A	11/78	403.3	(11)	409.8	(12)	451.3	(12)	405.8	(11)	455.3	(9)
RELIANCE ELECTRIC CO	A /A	10/78	403.1	(12)	372.3	(14)	317.3	(14)	296.0	(14)	396.9	(12)
NORTH AMERICAN PHILIPS CORP	A /A	12/78	397.9	(13)	389.7	(13)	368.5	(13)	328.3	(13)	291.5	(14)
GENERAL INSTRUMENT CORP	Ba /BB*	2/78	353.8	(14)	244.5	(17)	199.4	(19)	195.8	(19)	191.2	(19)
SUNBEAM CORP	A /A	3/78	317.5	(15)	333.1	(15)	310.5	(15)	291.9	(15)	426.2	(10)
TICOR	Aaa/AA\	12/78	305.7	(16)	462.1	(11)	611.4	(8)	541.1	(7)	3298.0	(2)
GOULD INC	A /A	12/78	282.7	(17)	320.8	(16)	275.2	(16)	226.4	(16)	247.8	(16)
RCA CORP	A /A	12/78	228.6	(18)	223.2	(18)	227.9	(18)	219.2	(17)	205.8	(17)
WHITE CONSOLIDATED INDS INC	Ba /BB*	12/78	218.2	(19)	209.3	(19)	258.1	(17)	208.4	(18)	194.7	(18)
AVERAGE			745.77		607.26		552.79		481.90		2039.04	
MEDIAN			521.87		480.66		473.77		427.47		426.16	

III-50

Electrical/Electronic Industry

CASH FLOW/LTD (%)

	RATINGS	FYR END	78		77		76		75		74	
TEXAS INSTRUMENTS INC	Aa /AA	12/78	1422.6	(1)	757.3	(1)	483.9	(1)	324.9	(1)	243.1	(4)
AMP INC	Aa /AA	12/78	303.6	(2)	236.1	(2)	202.3	(2)	122.4	(3)	420.8	(2)
TEKTRONIX INC	A /A	5/78	190.9	(3)	146.6	(5)	114.5	(6)	132.1	(2)	4944.6	(1)
GENERAL ELECTRIC CO	Aaa/AAA	12/78	186.3	(4)	120.7	(7)	106.8	(7)	94.4	(5)	83.8	(6)
WHIRLPOOL CORP	A /A	12/78	174.8	(5)	169.2	(3)	135.2	(4)	77.3	(7)	76.9	(8)
MCGRAW-EDISON CO	Aa /AA	12/78	160.6	(6)	124.4	(6)	122.5	(5)	88.5	(6)	52.9	(12)
MOTOROLA INC	Aa /AA	12/78	105.4	(7)	89.9	(9)	151.8	(3)	77.2	(8)	79.0	(7)
WESTINGHOUSE ELECTRIC CORP	A /AA-	12/78	102.7	(8)	95.2	(8)	71.7	(11)	54.8	(11)	37.9	(16)
RELIANCE ELECTRIC CO	A /A	10/78	98.7	(9)	77.6	(12)	63.4	(13)	52.6	(12)	74.5	(9)
GENERAL SIGNAL CORP	Aa /AA	12/78	98.3	(10)	148.1	(4)	105.7	(8)	67.3	(9)	51.9	(13)
ELTRA CORP	Aa /AA	9/78	84.9	(11)	72.1	(13)	71.0	(12)	104.2	(4)	90.4	(5)
SCOTT & FETZER CO	A /A	11/78	80.9	(12)	80.4	(11)	84.0	(10)	66.0	(10)	69.5	(11)
TICOR	Aaa/AAA	12/78	79.7	(13)	88.3	(10)	94.2	(9)	37.8	(15)	294.4	(3)
GENERAL INSTRUMENT CORP	Ba /BB*	2/78	69.3	(14)	32.2	(18)	15.3	(19)	19.8	(19)	20.8	(19)
NORTH AMERICAN PHILIPS CORP	A /A	12/78	66.1	(15)	67.6	(14)	61.7	(14)	42.4	(13)	26.3	(17)
RCA CORP	A /A	12/78	65.4	(16)	58.9	(16)	55.5	(15)	38.5	(14)	38.5	(15)
SUNBEAM CORP	A /A	3/78	50.9	(17)	50.0	(17)	44.4	(16)	34.1	(17)	70.6	(10)
GOULD INC	A /A	12/78	48.1	(18)	59.3	(15)	44.3	(17)	34.5	(16)	39.2	(14)
WHITE CONSOLIDATED INDS INC	Ba /BB*	12/78	27.4	(19)	26.5	(19)	35.7	(18)	24.7	(18)	21.8	(18)
AVERAGE			179.82		131.60		108.63		78.61		354.57	
MEDIAN			98.31		88.29		83.97		66.02		70.63	

NET CASH FL/CAP EXP (%)

	RATINGS	FYR END	78		77		76		75		74	
TICOR	Aaa/AAA	12/78	426.0	(1)	254.7	(2)	107.3	(17)	108.2	(16)	104.4	(10)
RELIANCE ELECTRIC CO	A /A	10/78	226.2	(2)	166.3	(8)	181.1	(9)	154.6	(6)	116.2	(7)
ELTRA CORP	Aa /AA	9/78	208.4	(3)	155.8	(10)	199.7	(7)	160.4	(5)	147.8	(2)
SCOTT & FETZER CO	A /A	11/78	203.8	(4)	273.6	(1)	431.0	(1)	251.5	(1)	92.2	(15)
AMP INC	Aa /AA	12/78	194.7	(5)	208.0	(5)	325.3	(2)	165.7	(4)	96.8	(13)
GENERAL SIGNAL CORP	Aa /AA	12/78	191.3	(6)	222.9	(4)	208.3	(5)	128.3	(13)	134.9	(5)
WHIRLPOOL CORP	A /A	12/78	185.1	(7)	197.8	(6)	168.8	(10)	151.8	(8)	58.0	(17)
GENERAL INSTRUMENT CORP	Ba /BB*	2/78	172.3	(8)	135.0	(12)	98.7	(18)	124.9	(14)	146.4 V	(3)
WHITE CONSOLIDATED INDS INC	Ba /BB*	12/78	171.6	(9)	133.0	(14)	147.4	(13)	144.5	(9)	93.5	(14)
TEKTRONIX INC	A /A	5/78	144.1	(10)	245.2	(3)	223.8	(4)	118.8	(15)	126.3	(6)
NORTH AMERICAN PHILIPS CORP	A /A	12/78	139.2	(11)	147.8	(11)	189.4	(8)	143.1	(10)	98.4	(12)
WESTINGHOUSE ELECTRIC CORP	A /AA-	12/78	126.3	(12)	132.4	(15)	167.8	(11)	132.9	(11)	109.1	(8)
MCGRAW-EDISON CO	Aa /AA	12/78	126.2	(13)	161.4	(9)	318.4	(3)	205.1	(2)	29.4	(19)
SUNBEAM CORP	A /A	3/78	124.2	(14)	134.6	(13)	203.1	(6)	101.1	(18)	160.0	(1)
GENERAL ELECTRIC CO	Aaa/AAA	12/78	121.4	(15)	130.4	(16)	141.9	(14)	153.3	(7)	105.7	(9)
MOTOROLA INC	Aa /AA	12/78	112.6	(16)	113.4	(17)	123.9	(15)	101.3	(17)	74.0	(16)
GOULD INC	A /A	12/78	100.7 V	(17)	171.5 V	(7)	159.2 V	(12)	131.6 V	(12)	137.1 V	(4)
RCA CORP	A /A	12/78	89.2	(18)	100.1	(18)	57.9	(19)	43.2	(19)	43.5	(18)
TEXAS INSTRUMENTS INC	Aa /AA	12/78	74.7 V	(19)	96.6 V	(19)	117.2 V	(16)	200.6 V	(3)	104.2 V	(11)
AVERAGE			165.17		167.38		187.92		143.20		104.11	
MEDIAN			144.11		155.78		168.83		143.11		104.45	

AFT TAX RET ON COM EQTY (%)

	RATINGS	FYR END	78		77		76		75		74	
AMP INC	Aa /AA	12/78	24.8	(1)	22.7	(1)	18.3	(2)	11.1	(10)	19.6	(1)
RELIANCE ELECTRIC CO	A /A	10/78	19.7	(2)	18.6	(4)	18.0	(3)	17.1	(2)	15.9	(5)
SCOTT & FETZER CO	A /A	11/78	19.7	(3)	20.1	(2)	18.5	(1)	15.6	(3)	13.7	(6)
GENERAL ELECTRIC CO	Aaa/AAA	12/78	18.7	(4)	18.3	(5)	17.7	(5)	14.3	(4)	16.4	(4)
TEKTRONIX INC	A /A	5/78	17.4	(5)	16.0	(8)	13.0	(12)	13.0	(6)	12.2	(10)
RCA CORP	A /A	12/78	17.2	(6)	17.0	(7)	13.6	(10)	9.0	(13)	9.5	(13)
TEXAS INSTRUMENTS INC	Aa /AA	12/78	16.6	(7)	15.7	(9)	14.8	(7)	10.6	(11)	16.6	(3)
WHIRLPOOL CORP	A /A	12/78	16.3	(8)	19.9	(3)	18.0	(4)	13.6	(5)	6.2	(17)
WHITE CONSOLIDATED INDS INC	Ba /BB*	12/78	16.0	(9)	17.9	(6)	17.3	(6)	18.1	(1)	17.6	(2)
GOULD INC	A /A	12/78	14.5	(10)	15.2	(10)	12.1	(15)	11.1	(9)	12.1	(11)
MOTOROLA INC	Aa /AA	12/78	14.1	(11)	13.5	(12)	12.8	(13)	12.4	(8)	12.4	(8)
MCGRAW-EDISON CO	Aa /AA	12/78	13.9	(12)	13.1	(14)	14.0	(8)	10.2	(12)	4.9	(18)
NORTH AMERICAN PHILIPS CORP	A /A	12/78	13.3	(13)	13.3	(13)	13.9	(9)	8.7	(15)	9.5	(14)
SUNBEAM CORP	A /A	3/78	13.1	(14)	10.9	(18)	11.6	(16)	8.6	(16)	12.3	(9)
WESTINGHOUSE ELECTRIC CORP	A /AA-	12/78	12.8	(15)	11.9	(16)	10.5	(17)	9.0	(14)	7.3	(16)
GENERAL INSTRUMENT CORP	Ba /BB*	2/78	12.3	(16)	9.1	(19)	3.9	(19)	6.9	(17)	9.1	(15)
ELTRA CORP	Aa /AA	9/78	12.2	(17)	11.9	(15)	12.5	(14)	12.3	(7)	13.0	(7)
GENERAL SIGNAL CORP	Aa /AA	12/78	12.2	(18)	13.8	(11)	13.4	(11)	11.8	(8)	11.2	(12)
TICOR	Aaa/AAA	12/78	11.7	(19)	11.6	(17)	10.2	(18)	2.5	(19)	4.7	(19)
AVERAGE			15.62		15.29		13.89		11.06		11.79	
MEDIAN			14.45		15.17		13.59		11.08		12.17	

RET ON TOT ASSETS (%)

	RATINGS	FYR END	78		77		76		75		74	
AMP INC	Aa /AA	12/78	28.6	(1)	26.7	(1)	22.2	(2)	15.0	(5)	24.2	(1)
RELIANCE ELECTRIC CO	A /A	10/78	21.4	(2)	21.0	(4)	19.8	(4)	18.1	(2)	16.3	(4)
WHIRLPOOL CORP	A /A	12/78	21.2	(3)	24.1	(3)	21.7	(3)	16.1	(4)	7.7	(16)
TEKTRONIX INC	A /A	5/78	20.4	(4)	19.2	(5)	17.4	(6)	16.8	(3)	15.8	(5)
MCGRAW-EDISON CO	Aa /AA	12/78	19.6	(5)	19.0	(6)	19.0	(5)	14.4	(6)	7.3	(17)
SCOTT & FETZER CO	A /A	11/78	19.6	(6)	26.6	(2)	23.7	(1)	19.3	(1)	17.5	(3)
TEXAS INSTRUMENTS INC	Aa /AA	12/78	17.5	(7)	17.5	(7)	16.5	(7)	13.5	(9)	18.0	(2)
GENERAL ELECTRIC CO	Aaa/AAA	12/78	15.6	(8)	15.0	(11)	14.7	(11)	11.3	(13)	12.5	(12)
GENERAL SIGNAL CORP	Aa /AA	12/78	15.2	(9)	17.2	(8)	15.8	(8)	14.3	(7)	12.7	(10)
MOTOROLA INC	Aa /AA	12/78	15.0	(10)	15.1	(10)	15.2	(9)	9.9	(14)	15.0	(6)
GENERAL INSTRUMENT CORP	Ba /BB*	2/78	14.8	(11)	10.8	(18)	6.0	(19)	9.3	(15)	9.7	(13)
GOULD INC	A /A	12/78	14.7	(12)	15.7	(9)	12.2	(15)	12.6	(11)	13.5	(9)
SUNBEAM CORP	A /A	3/78	14.6	(13)	13.8	(12)	14.1	(12)	11.6	(12)	14.2	(7)
ELTRA CORP	Aa /AA	9/78	13.8	(14)	12.7	(16)	13.4	(13)	13.6	(8)	13.7	(8)
WHITE CONSOLIDATED INDS INC	Ba /BB*	12/78	13.2	(15)	13.4	(13)	14.8	(10)	13.4	(10)	12.7	(11)
RCA CORP	A /A	12/78	12.9	(16)	13.0	(15)	11.4	(16)	7.7	(16)	8.2	(14)
NORTH AMERICAN PHILIPS CORP	A /A	12/78	12.7	(17)	13.2	(14)	13.2	(14)	7.6	(17)	8.0	(15)
TICOR	Aaa/AAA	12/78	9.6	(18)	10.9	(17)	11.1	(17)	2.1	(19)	5.8	(19)
WESTINGHOUSE ELECTRIC CORP	A /AA-	12/78	8.0	(19)	8.5	(19)	7.6	(18)	7.2	(18)	7.3	(18)
AVERAGE			16.23		16.50		15.25		12.31		12.64	
MEDIAN			14.97		15.06		14.82		13.45		12.74	

PRETAX COVERAGE

	RATINGS	FYR END	78	77	76	75	74
DATA GENERAL CORP	Baa/BBB	9/78	15.55 (1)	240.65 (1)	118.95 (1)	107.58 (1)	120.78 (1)
BURROUGHS CORP	Aa /AA	12/78	13.80 (2)	9.97 (5)	7.26 (5)	7.89 (3)	8.57 (3)
HARRIS CORP	A /A	6/78	12.74 (3)	13.13 (3)	11.41 (3)	5.47 (6)	4.84 (7)
DIGITAL EQUIPMENT	Aa /A	6/78	11.16 (4)	16.06 (2)	13.08 (2)	16.45 (2)	33.04 (2)
PITNEY-BOWES INC	A /A	12/78	9.70 (5)	8.55 (6)	8.26 (4)	7.07 (4)	6.48 (5)
XEROX CORP	Aa /AA	12/78	9.59P(6)	10.32P(4)	7.26P(6)	6.27 (5)	8.41P(4)
NCR CORP	A /A	12/78	8.39 (7)	5.47 (7)	3.84 (9)	2.88 (8)	4.03 (8)
HONEYWELL INC	A /A	12/78	6.41 (8)	5.22 (8)	4.17 (8)	2.36P(9)	2.09P(9)
SPERRY RAND CORP	A /A	3/78	5.29 (9)	4.68 (9)	4.48 (7)	3.57 (7)	4.93 (6)
AM INTERNATIONAL INC	Baa/BB	7/78	4.36P(10)	0.06P(11)	2.69P(10)	1.71P(11)	1.18 (10)
CONTROL DATA CORP	Baa/BB	12/78	3.32 (11)	2.34 (10)	1.45 (11)	1.72 (10)	0.29 (11)
AVERAGE			9.12	28.77	16.62	14.81	17.69
MEDIAN			9.59	8.55	7.26	5.47	4.93

AFTER TAX COVERAGE

	RATINGS	FYR END	78	77	76	75	74
DATA GENERAL CORP	Baa/BBB	9/78	8.56 (1)	125.80 (1)	62.32 (1)	56.39 (1)	63.23 (1)
BURROUGHS CORP	Aa /AA	12/78	7.82 (2)	5.90 (4)	4.69 (5)	4.88 (3)	5.28 (3)
HARRIS CORP	A /A	6/78	7.76 (3)	7.61 (3)	6.90 (3)	3.94 (5)	3.32 (6)
DIGITAL EQUIPMENT	Aa /A	6/78	7.35 (4)	10.26 (2)	8.43 (2)	10.65 (2)	22.49 (2)
PITNEY-BOWES INC	A /A	12/78	5.56 (5)	4.90 (6)	5.03 (4)	4.35 (4)	3.90 (5)
XEROX CORP	Aa /AA	12/78	5.40P(6)	5.82P(5)	4.30P(6)	3.86 (6)	4.91P(4)
NCR CORP	A /A	12/78	5.06 (7)	3.46 (7)	2.52 (9)	2.04 (8)	2.58 (8)
HONEYWELL INC	A /A	12/78	3.78 (8)	3.30 (8)	2.81 (7)	1.84P(9)	1.66P(9)
SPERRY RAND CORP	A /A	3/78	3.11 (9)	2.81 (9)	2.72 (8)	2.31 (7)	2.90 (7)
AM INTERNATIONAL INC	Baa/BB	7/78	2.91P(10)	-0.25P(11)	1.64P(10)	1.31P(11)	1.02 (10)
CONTROL DATA CORP	Baa/BB	12/78	2.21 (11)	1.78 (10)	1.20 (11)	1.45 (10)	0.70 (11)
AVERAGE			5.41	15.58	9.32	8.46	10.18
MEDIAN			5.40	4.90	4.30	3.86	3.32

AFTER TAX COV (INCL RENTS)

	RATINGS	FYR END	78	77	76	75	74
DATA GENERAL CORP	Baa/BBB	9/78	4.89 (1)	9.14 (1)	8.90 (1)	8.66 (1)	11.65 (1)
BURROUGHS CORP	Aa /AA	12/78	4.54 (2)	3.77 (3)	3.25 (3)	3.44 (3)	3.63 (3)
DIGITAL EQUIPMENT	Aa /A	6/78	4.13 (3)	4.27 (2)	4.05 (2)	4.61 (2)	6.11 (2)
HARRIS CORP	A /A	6/78	3.37 (4)	3.48 (4)	3.23 (4)	2.40 (5)	2.29 (5)
NCR CORP	A /A	12/78	3.32 (5)	2.50 (7)	1.88 (9)	1.63 (8)	1.99 (8)
XEROX CORP	Aa /AA	12/78	3.05P(6)	2.98P(5)	2.63P(5)	2.57 (4)	2.98P(4)
PITNEY-BOWES INC	A /A	12/78	2.92 (7)	2.61 (6)	2.40 (6)	2.27 (6)	2.24 (6)
HONEYWELL INC	A /A	12/78	2.43 (8)	2.26 (8)	2.00 (8)	1.54P(9)	1.45P(9)
SPERRY RAND CORP	A /A	3/78	2.27 (9)	2.14 (9)	2.06 (7)	1.87 (7)	2.09 (7)
AM INTERNATIONAL INC	Baa/BB	7/78	1.64P(10)	0.45P(11)	1.21P(10)	1.13P(11)	1.01 (10)
CONTROL DATA CORP	Baa/BB	12/78	1.53 (11)	1.38 (10)	1.10 (11)	1.26 (10)	0.83 (11)
AVERAGE			3.10	3.18	2.97	2.85	3.30
MEDIAN			3.05	2.61	2.40	2.27	2.24

NET INCOME AS % NET SALES

	RATINGS	FYR END	78		77		76		75		74	
DATA GENERAL CORP	Baa/BBB	9/78	10.6	(1)	11.2	(1)	11.8	(1)	11.9	(1)	11.9	(1)
BURROUGHS CORP	Aa /AA	12/78	10.5	(2)	10.3	(2)	9.9	(3)	9.8	(2)	9.5	(3)
DIGITAL EQUIPMENT	Aa /A	6/78	9.9	(3)	10.2	(3)	10.0	(2)	8.6	(3)	10.5	(2)
XEROX CORP	Aa /AA	12/78	7.9	(4)	8.0	(4)	8.1	(4)	8.4	(4)	9.3	(4)
NCR CORP	A /A	12/78	7.4	(5)	5.7	(7)	3.9	(9)	3.0	(9)	4.4	(6)
PITNEY-BOWES INC	A /A	12/78	6.4	(6)	6.0	(6)	5.7	(5)	5.6	(5)	5.6	(5)
HARRIS CORP	A /A	6/78	6.0	(7)	6.2	(5)	5.2	(6)	4.1	(7)	3.6	(8)
HONEYWELL INC	A /A	12/78	5.1	(8)	4.6	(9)	4.2	(8)	2.8	(10)	2.7	(9)
SPERRY RAND CORP	A /A	3/78	4.8	(9)	4.8	(8)	4.5	(7)	4.3	(6)	4.3	(7)
CONTROL DATA CORP	Baa/BB	12/78	4.6	(10)	4.2	(10)	3.6	(10)	3.3	(8)	0.3	(10)
AM INTERNATIONAL INC	Baa/BB	7/78	3.2	(11)	-2.3	(11)	1.1	(11)	0.8	(11)	0.1	(11)
AVERAGE			6.94		6.27		6.19		5.70		5.65	
MEDIAN			6.38		6.03		5.22		4.32		4.40	

LTD/CAPITALIZATION (%)

	RATINGS	FYR END	78		77		76		75		74	
BURROUGHS CORP	Aa /AA	12/78	9.2	(1)	9.4	(1)	12.7	(2)	13.1	(2)	11.7	(3)
HONEYWELL INC	A /A	12/78	18.6	(2)	17.5	(3)	18.8	(4)	33.1	(8)	31.7	(6)
NCR CORP	A /A	12/78	21.1	(3)	33.4	(10)	41.3	(11)	45.4	(11)	42.5	(11)
CONTROL DATA CORP	Baa/BB	12/78	24.2	(4)	23.9	(4)	28.1	(7)	31.7	(7)	36.2	(8)
XEROX CORP	Aa /AA	12/78	24.6	(5)	26.4	(5)	31.5	(9)	37.2	(10)	37.0	(9)
DATA GENERAL CORP	Baa/BBB	9/78	24.6	(6)	29.0	(6)	0.0	(1)	4.9	(1)	0.0	(1)
AM INTERNATIONAL INC	Baa/BB	7/78	25.0	(7)	31.1	(9)	26.2	(6)	27.3	(5)	30.0	(5)
HARRIS CORP	A /A	6/78	25.7	(8)	30.3	(8)	22.6	(5)	24.6	(4)	33.1	(7)
SPERRY RAND CORP	A /A	3/78	26.8	(9)	29.4	(7)	30.6	(8)	30.1	(6)	24.8	(4)
DIGITAL EQUIPMENT	Aa /A	6/78	27.4	(10)	11.0	(2)	13.1	(3)	17.8	(3)	3.0	(2)
PITNEY-BOWES INC	A /A	12/78	32.5	(11)	34.6	(11)	33.4	(10)	35.6	(9)	39.0	(10)
AVERAGE			23.61		25.09		23.48		27.33		26.28	
MEDIAN			24.61		28.96		26.16		30.07		31.72	

TOT LIABILITY/TOT STK EQUITY

	RATINGS	FYR END	78		77		76		75		74	
BURROUGHS CORP	Aa /AA	12/78	53.9	(1)	57.3	(2)	69.2	(3)	86.1	(3)	80.5	(3)
DIGITAL EQUIPMENT	Aa /A	6/78	64.9	(2)	45.5	(1)	41.2	(1)	43.3	(2)	29.6	(1)
DATA GENERAL CORP	Baa/BBB	9/78	82.2	(3)	87.1	(3)	42.1	(2)	30.0	(1)	52.2	(2)
CONTROL DATA CORP	Baa/BB	12/78	85.2	(4)	90.2	(4)	101.7	(6)	119.3	(6)	114.0	(4)
NCR CORP	A /A	12/78	99.8	(5)	128.8	(8)	160.1	(11)	174.9	(11)	188.1	(11)
XEROX CORP	Aa /AA	12/78	100.2	(6)	98.4	(5)	111.7	(7)	133.7	(7)	133.2	(8)
HONEYWELL INC	A /A	12/78	103.8	(7)	101.0	(6)	95.4	(4)	160.0	(10)	185.6	(10)
AM INTERNATIONAL INC	Baa/BB	7/78	119.4	(8)	137.1	(9)	96.5	(5)	110.8	(5)	126.2	(7)
SPERRY RAND CORP	A /A	3/78	129.2	(9)	119.2	(7)	120.8	(9)	139.2	(8)	120.1	(5)
PITNEY-BOWES INC	A /A	12/78	156.7	(10)	151.9	(11)	144.2	(10)	141.1	(9)	155.6	(9)
HARRIS CORP	A /A	6/78	158.4	(11)	151.6	(10)	120.4	(8)	101.8	(4)	120.9	(6)
AVERAGE			104.87		106.19		100.29		112.75		118.72	
MEDIAN			100.25		100.98		101.73		119.34		120.91	

EDP/Office Equipment Industry

LTD/NET PLANT (%)

	RATINGS	FYR END	78		77		76		75		74	
BURROUGHS CORP	Aa /AA	12/78	18.0	(1)	18.4	(1)	23.0	(2)	22.0	(1)	18.7	(3)
HONEYWELL INC	A /A	12/78	35.7	(2)	31.3	(2)	33.0	(3)	45.5	(3)	39.3	(4)
XEROX CORP	Aa /AA	12/78	36.3	(3)	38.7	(4)	43.8	(4)	47.8	(4)	45.3	(5)
PITNEY-BOWES INC	A /A	12/78	51.8	(4)	53.6	(5)	53.9	(5)	61.2	(5)	76.5	(7)
NCR CORP	A /A	12/78	55.7	(5)	78.3	(6)	87.1	(9)	91.1	(9)	84.0	(9)
HARRIS CORP	A /A	6/78	57.0	(6)	94.3	(9)	75.6	(8)	83.0	(8)	122.8	(10)
AM INTERNATIONAL INC	Baa/BB	7/78	71.0	(7)	79.4	(7)	73.6	(7)	71.0	(7)	79.8	(8)
CONTROL DATA CORP	Baa/BB	12/78	84.1	(8)	88.8	(8)	96.7	(10)	99.4	(11)	126.6	(11)
DIGITAL EQUIPMENT	Aa /A	6/78	90.9	(9)	34.1	(3)	59.2	(6)	68.6	(6)	10.8	(2)
DATA GENERAL CORP	Baa/BBB	9/78	104.4	(10)	161.2	(11)	0.0	(1)	24.0	(2)	0.0	(1)
SPERRY RAND CORP	A /A	3/78	107.4	(11)	114.8	(10)	108.9	(11)	94.4	(10)	71.4	(6)
AVERAGE			64.75		72.08		59.52		64.36		61.38	
MEDIAN			57.00		78.28		59.24		68.57		71.39	

NET TANG ASSETS/LTD (%)

	RATINGS	FYR END	78		77		76		75		74	
BURROUGHS CORP	Aa /AA	12/78	1057.5	(1)	1035.0	(1)	769.3	(1)	738.9	(2)	836.8	(2)
HONEYWELL INC	A /A	12/78	502.9	(2)	549.5	(3)	505.1	(3)	287.3	(8)	298.6	(5)
NCR CORP	A /A	12/78	418.7	(3)	275.6	(11)	223.9	(10)	203.9	(11)	215.3	(10)
DATA GENERAL CORP	Baa/BBB	9/78	406.4	(4)	345.3	(6)	NA	(-)	2047.3	(1)	NA	(-)
CONTROL DATA CORP	Baa/BB	12/78	400.7	(5)	404.3	(4)	340.0	(6)	299.0	(7)	257.4	(8)
XEROX CORP	Aa /AA	12/78	392.2	(6)	358.6	(5)	297.0	(8)	238.9	(10)	257.9	(7)
AM INTERNATIONAL INC	Baa/BB	7/78	389.5	(7)	304.8	(9)	366.2	(5)	352.3	(5)	315.6	(4)
HARRIS CORP	A /A	6/78	374.5	(8)	318.1	(8)	424.8	(4)	389.3	(4)	288.7	(6)
SPERRY RAND CORP	A /A	3/78	370.5	(9)	333.3	(7)	319.4	(7)	319.5	(6)	387.3	(3)
DIGITAL EQUIPMENT	Aa /A	6/78	364.8	(10)	912.2	(2)	763.4	(2)	562.8	(3)	3311.8	(1)
PITNEY-BOWES INC	A /A	12/78	305.3	(11)	286.8	(10)	296.8	(9)	277.9	(9)	252.6	(9)
AVERAGE			453.01		465.77		430.57		519.74		642.19	
MEDIAN			392.21		345.30		353.08		319.48		293.64	

CASH FLOW/LTD (%)

	RATINGS	FYR END	78		77		76		75		74	
BURROUGHS CORP	A AA	12/78	254.5	(1)	250.1	(1)	182.4	(1)	151.4	(2)	197.3	(2)
XEROX CORP	Aa /AA	12/78	152.1	(2)	124.4	(4)	109.4	(4)	83.8	(3)	93.1	(3)
HONEYWELL INC	A /A	12/78	133.1	(3)	147.3	(3)	127.2	(2)	74.8	(5)	79.3	(5)
PITNEY-BOWES INC	A /A	12/78	93.2	(4)	67.3	(6)	67.8	(6)	57.1	(8)	51.0	(6)
HARRIS CORP	A /A	6/78	83.1	(5)	59.9	(7)	73.1	(5)	60.9	(7)	36.5	(8)
NCR CORP	A /A	12/78	81.1	(6)	79.7	(5)	44.9	(8)	33.5	(10)	48.1	(7)
DATA GENERAL CORP	Baa/BBB	9/78	78.7	(7)	57.4	(9)	NA	(-)	363.4	(1)	NA	(-)
AM INTERNATIONAL INC	Baa/BB	7/78	72.9	(8)	13.4	(11)	29.4	(10)	30.2	(11)	18.7	(9)
SPERRY RAND CORP	A /A	3/78	66.1	(9)	59.7	(8)	59.0	(7)	61.6	(6)	85.6	(4)
DIGITAL EQUIPMENT	Aa /A	6/78	60.9	(10)	164.4	(2)	113.8	(3)	82.6	(4)	600.0	(1)
CONTROL DATA CORP	Baa/BB	12/78	60.1	(11)	52.8	(10)	39.3	(9)	39.3	(9)	18.5	(10)
AVERAGE			103.26		97.85		84.63		94.45		122.81	
MEDIAN			81.09		67.32		70.42		61.61		65.12	

NET CASH FL/CAP EXP (%)

	RATINGS	FYR END	78		77		76		75		74	
NCR CORP	A /A	12/78	182.0	(1)	198.4	(2)	119.9	(8)	75.5	(11)	101.1	(6)
AM INTERNATIONAL INC	Baa/BB	7/78	167.1	(2)	36.5	(11)	108.5	(10)	87.6	(10)	36.5	(11)
PITNEY-BOWES INC	A /A	12/78	161.9	V(3)	113.2	V(8)	118.4	V(9)	88.3	V(9)	146.3	(2)
DATA GENERAL CORP	Baa/BBB	9/78	156.8	(4)	223.8	(1)	155.6	(4)	179.9	(1)	198.2	(1)
XEROX CORP	Aa /AA	12/78	137.7	(5)	137.0	(5)	168.8	(3)	109.8	(5)	78.9	(9)
SPERRY RAND CORP	A /A	3/78	135.4	(6)	144.7	(4)	133.7	(7)	107.0	(7)	142.0	(4)
DIGITAL EQUIPMENT	Aa /A	6/78	124.5	(7)	104.0	(9)	190.7	(1)	153.4	(2)	126.7	(5)
BURROUGHS CORP	Aa /AA	12/78	111.5	(8)	151.7	(3)	138.5	(5)	109.7	(6)	94.8	(7)
HONEYWELL INC	A /A	12/78	94.8	(9)	94.0	(10)	135.5	(6)	131.3	(3)	92.9	(8)
CONTROL DATA CORP	Baa/BB	12/78	92.1	J(10)	123.4	V(6)	86.3	V(11)	102.6	V(8)	72.8	V(10)
HARRIS CORP	A /A	6/78	75.9	V(11)	115.9	V(7)	184.6	V(2)	124.6	J(4)	143.6	V(3)
AVERAGE			130.87		131.15		140.05		115.44		112.18	
MEDIAN			135.37		123.41		135.54		109.75		101.13	

AFT TAX RET ON COM EQTY (%)

	RATINGS	FYR END	78		77		76		75		74	
DATA GENERAL CORP	Baa/BBB	9/78	21.0	(1)	19.6	(1)	17.1	(2)	14.3	(3)	21.1	(1)
PITNEY-BOWES INC	A /A	12/78	19.4	(2)	18.4	(2)	17.9	(1)	16.3	(2)	18.0	(3)
HARRIS CORP	A /A	6/78	18.8	(3)	17.4	(3)	13.4	(4)	10.6	(7)	9.5	(8)
XEROX CORP	Aa /AA	12/78	16.7	(4)	16.4	(4)	16.5	(3)	17.9	(1)	18.9	(2)
DIGITAL EQUIPMENT	Aa /A	6/78	15.7	(5)	14.8	(5)	12.1	(7)	11.7	(6)	13.1	(4)
NCR CORP	A /A	12/78	14.9	(6)	14.0	(6)	10.1	(8)	8.2	(8)	12.6	(5)
BURROUGHS CORP	Aa /AA	12/78	13.3	(7)	12.7	(7)	12.4	(6)	12.6	(4)	12.6	(5)
HONEYWELL INC	A /A	12/78	13.1	(8)	11.1	(9)	9.3	(9)	7.7	(9)	7.7	(9)
SPERRY RAND CORP	A /A	3/78	12.3	(9)	12.1	(8)	12.4	(5)	12.4	(5)	11.5	(7)
AM INTERNATIONAL INC	Baa/BB	7/78	9.7	(10)	-7.1	(11)	3.0	(11)	2.3	(11)	0.2	(11)
CONTROL DATA CORP	Baa/BB	12/78	8.1	(11)	6.5	(10)	5.3	(10)	4.9	(10)	0.2	(10)
AVERAGE			14.83		12.36		11.77		10.82		11.33	
MEDIAN			14.90		14.02		12.39		11.66		11.87	

RET ON TOT ASSETS (%)

	RATINGS	FYR END	78		77		76		75		74	
DATA GENERAL CORP	Baa/BBB	9/78	23.7	(1)	20.2	(1)	23.4	(1)	21.4	(1)	27.0	(1)
XEROX CORP	Aa /AA	12/78	19.8	(2)	19.3	(2)	18.7	(2)	18.5	(2)	19.2	(2)
BURROUGHS CORP	Aa /AA	12/78	17.5	(3)	16.4	(4)	14.4	(4)	13.7	(4)	14.0	(5)
DIGITAL EQUIPMENT	Aa /A	6/78	16.8	(4)	17.6	(3)	15.1	(3)	13.9	(3)	15.5	(3)
PITNEY-BOWES INC	A /A	12/78	16.2	(5)	15.6	(5)	14.4	(5)	13.7	(5)	14.9	(4)
NCR CORP	A /A	12/78	15.4	(6)	13.7	(7)	9.9	(9)	8.4	(8)	10.6	(7)
HARRIS CORP	A /A	6/78	13.7	(7)	13.7	(6)	11.8	(7)	9.8	(7)	8.9	(8)
HONEYWELL INC	A /A	12/78	13.3	(8)	11.9	(9)	10.3	(8)	8.0	(9)	7.8	(9)
SPERRY RAND CORP	A /A	3/78	12.8	(9)	13.3	(8)	13.6	(6)	13.1	(6)	12.1	(6)
AM INTERNATIONAL INC	Baa/BB	7/78	9.9	(10)	0.2	(11)	6.2	(11)	6.0	(11)	3.7	(10)
CONTROL DATA CORP	Baa/BB	12/78	9.2	(11)	7.3	(10)	6.6	(10)	7.0	(10)	2.2	(11)
AVERAGE			15.30		13.57		13.12		12.13		12.36	
MEDIAN			15.43		13.74		13.64		13.10		12.11	

Food Products Industry

PRETAX COVERAGE

	RATINGS	FYR END	78	77	76	75	74
HERSHEY FOODS CORP	A /A+	12/78	32.26 (1)	30.47 (1)	40.71 (1)	27.10 (2)	15.26 (2)
KELLOGG CO	Aaa/AAA	12/78	29.15 (2)	29.55 (2)	28.89 (2)	38.16 (1)	33.71 (1)
GENERAL FOODS CORP	Aa /AAA	3/79	15.54 (3)	9.77 (11)	14.86 (6)	14.24 (5)	6.47 (12)
MAYER (OSCAR) & CO	A /AA	10/78	14.06 (4)	18.16 (3)	15.46 (5)	12.83 (6)	14.75 (3)
CARNATION CO	Aaa/AAA	12/78	12.02P(5)	12.21P(6)	14.53 (7)	10.99 (7)	13.23 (5)
CONSOLIDATED FOODS CORP	Aa /AA	6/78	11.83P(6)	12.17P(7)	11.11P(9)	5.73 (16)	6.91 (11)
IOWA BEEF PROCESSORS	Baa/BBB	10/78	11.37 (7)	13.28 (5)	17.08 (4)	10.28 (8)	7.58 (8)
HORMEL (GEO.A.) & CO	A /A	10/78	11.36 (8)	16.41 (4)	7.26 (18)	8.78 (10)	7.71 (7)
KRAFT INC	Aaa/AAA	12/78	10.79 (9)	10.01 (10)	11.86 (8)	9.37 (9)	5.50 (17)
HEINZ (H.J.) CO	Aa /A	4/78	10.11 (10)	10.68 (8)	6.62 (20)	4.76 (21)	5.38 (18)
NABISCO INC	Aa /AA	12/78	9.62 (11)	9.66 (12)	8.27 (12)	5.72 (17)	4.00 (24)
GENERAL MILLS INC	A /A+	5/78	9.37 (12)	9.55P(13)	7.81P(14)	5.02P(19)	6.26P(13)
RALSTON PURINA CO	Aa /AA	9/78	8.60 (13)	8.21 (16)	8.53 (11)	6.10 (14)	6.09 (14)
QUAKER OATS CO	A /A+	6/78	7.93 (14)	8.64 (14)	7.72 (16)	3.43 (24)	4.33 (23)
CPC INTERNATIONAL INC	Aa /AA	12/78	6.94 (15)	7.09 (18)	6.94 (19)	5.80 (15)	5.93 (16)
BORDEN INC	Aa /A+	12/78	5.64 (16)	7.55 (17)	7.78P(15)	7.31P(12)	7.28P(9)
PILLSBURY CO	A /A	5/78	5.53 (17)	5.45 (21)	6.30 (22)	3.52 (23)	3.47 (25)
STANDARD BRANDS INC	A /A	12/78	5.33 (18)	5.79 (20)	6.42P(21)	5.67P(18)	4.94P(21)
INTL MULTIFOODS CORP	Baa/BBB+	2/79	5.28P(19)	6.01P(19)	5.46P(23)	4.44P(22)	3.28P(26)
NORTON SIMON INC	A /A	6/78	5.08 (20)	8.41 (15)	8.04 (13)	8.20 (11)	9.88 (6)
CENTRAL SOYA CO	A /A	8/78	4.52 (21)	2.38 (25)	7.61 (17)	2.94 (26)	5.12 (19)
AMSTAR CORP	Baa/BB*	6/78	4.40 (22)	10.28 (9)	25.03 (3)	20.82 (4)	14.19 (4)
STOKELY-VAN CAMP INC	A /BBB	5/78	3.73 (23)	2.98 (24)	3.10 (26)	3.40 (25)	4.90 (22)
ESMARK INC	A /A	10/78	3.38P(24)	3.14P(23)	3.53P(25)	6.38P(13)	7.17P(10)
CASTLE & COOKE INC	Baa/BBB	12/78	3.27 (25)	4.07 (22)	4.82 (24)	4.78 (20)	5.00 (20)
STALEY (A.E.) MFG CO	A /A	9/78	2.37 (26)	2.36 (26)	10.55 (10)	21.52 (3)	6.03 (15)
AVERAGE			9.60	10.16	11.40	9.90	8.25
MEDIAN			8.26	9.10	7.92	6.24	6.17

AFTER TAX COVERAGE

	RATINGS	FYR END	78	77	76	75	74
HERSHEY FOODS CORP	A /A+	12/78	16.82 (1)	15.88 (2)	20.42 (1)	13.70 (2)	7.92 (4)
KELLOGG CO	Aaa/AAA	12/78	15.97 (2)	16.03 (1)	15.42 (2)	19.87 (1)	17.94 (1)
GENERAL FOODS CORP	Aa /AAA	3/79	8.35 (3)	5.50 (12)	7.68 (7)	7.25 (6)	3.74 (12)
MAYER (OSCAR) & CO	A /AA	10/78	7.15 (4)	10.73 (3)	9.24 (4)	7.29 (5)	8.39 (2)
HORMEL (GEO.A.) & CO	A /A	10/78	6.88 (5)	8.99 (4)	4.53 (14)	5.35 (10)	4.51 (7)
IOWA BEEF PROCESSORS	Baa/BBB	10/78	6.72 (6)	7.71 (5)	8.85 (5)	6.01 (8)	4.49 (8)
CARNATION CO	Aaa/AAA	12/78	6.64P(7)	6.60P(6)	7.74 (6)	6.04 (7)	7.08 (5)
HEINZ (H.J.) CO	Aa /A	4/78	6.43 (8)	6.33 (10)	4.27 (19)	3.15 (19)	3.64 (14)
KRAFT INC	Aaa/AAA	12/78	6.13 (9)	5.59 (11)	6.30 (9)	5.36 (9)	3.41 (19)
CONSOLIDATED FOODS CORP	Aa /AA	6/78	5.91P(10)	6.58P(7)	6.02P(10)	3.48 (16)	4.37 (9)
GENERAL MILLS INC	A /A+	5/78	5.40 (11)	5.36P(14)	4.41P(16)	3.07P(20)	3.60P(15)
NABISCO INC	Aa /AA	12/78	5.18 (12)	6.41 (9)	4.34 (18)	3.07 (21)	2.47 (24)
RALSTON PURINA CO	Aa /AA	9/78	5.09 (13)	4.82 (16)	4.89 (12)	3.71 (14)	3.68 (13)
QUAKER OATS CO	A /A+	6/78	4.84 (14)	4.96 (15)	4.37 (17)	2.14 (25)	2.74 (23)
CPC INTERNATIONAL INC	Aa /AA	12/78	4.36 (15)	4.36 (18)	4.21 (20)	3.48 (17)	3.54 (16)
BORDEN INC	Aa /A+	12/78	3.86 (16)	4.78 (17)	4.73P(13)	4.37P(12)	4.35P(10)
STANDARD BRANDS INC	A /A	12/78	3.52 (17)	3.71 (20)	3.93P(21)	3.52P(15)	3.10P(21)
INTL MULTIFOODS CORP	Baa/BBB+	2/79	3.39P(18)	3.85P(19)	3.46P(23)	2.99P(22)	2.18P(26)
NORTON SIMON INC	A /A	6/78	3.37 (19)	5.48 (13)	5.10 (11)	5.11 (11)	6.09 (6)
PILLSBURY CO	A /A	5/78	3.27 (20)	3.23 (21)	3.62 (22)	2.28 (24)	2.25 (25)
AMSTAR CORP	Baa/BB*	6/78	3.17 (21)	6.48 (8)	13.34 (3)	12.04 (3)	8.35 (3)
CENTRAL SOYA CO	A /A	8/78	2.89 (22)	1.79 (26)	4.50 (15)	2.05 (26)	3.03 (22)
ESMARK INC	A /A	10/78	2.56P(23)	2.40P(24)	2.70P(25)	3.86P(13)	4.27P(11)
STOKELY-VAN CAMP INC	A /BBB	5/78	2.55 (24)	2.16 (25)	2.20 (26)	2.33 (23)	3.16 (20)
CASTLE & COOKE INC	Baa/BBB	12/78	2.45 (25)	2.92 (22)	3.34 (24)	3.15 (18)	3.45 (18)
STALEY (A.E.) MFG CO	A /A	9/78	1.94 (26)	2.64 (23)	6.56 (8)	11.27 (4)	3.46 (17)
AVERAGE			5.57	5.97	6.39	5.61	4.82
MEDIAN			4.97	5.42	4.63	3.78	3.66

AFTER TAX COV (INCL RENTS)

	RATINGS	FYR END	78	77	76	75	74
KELLOGG CO	Aaa/AAA	12/78	8.33 (1)	NA (-)	NA (-)	NA (-)	NA (-)
CARNATION CO	Aaa/AAA	12/78	5.44P(2)	5.24P(1)	5.15 (1)	4.50 (2)	NA (-)
GENERAL FOODS CORP	Aa /AAA	3/79	4.68 (3)	3.55 (3)	4.21 (3)	3.97 (3)	2.72 (5)
NABISCO INC	Aa /AA	12/78	3.92 (4)	3.78 (2)	2.82 (9)	2.33 (12)	2.00 (14)
HEINZ (H.J.) CO	Aa /A	4/78	3.65 (5)	3.50 (4)	2.83 (8)	2.49 (8)	2.65 (7)
RALSTON PURINA CO	Aa /AA	9/78	3.37 (6)	3.48 (5)	3.27 (4)	2.71 (6)	2.78 (4)
GENERAL MILLS INC	A /A+	5/78	3.21 (7)	3.39P(6)	3.07P(6)	2.42P(10)	NA (-)
QUAKER OATS CO	A /A+	6/78	2.98 (8)	3.07 (8)	2.79 (11)	1.76 (16)	2.11 (12)
CPC INTERNATIONAL INC	Aa /AA	12/78	2.93 (9)	3.01 (9)	2.85 (7)	2.48 (9)	2.45 (8)
CONSOLIDATED FOODS CORP	Aa /AA	6/78	2.65P(10)	2.46P(12)	2.33P(13)	1.89 (13)	2.21 (11)
STANDARD BRANDS INC	A /A	12/78	2.63 (11)	2.69 (11)	2.79P(10)	2.69P(7)	2.41P(10)
PILLSBURY CO	A /A	5/78	2.30 (12)	2.27 (13)	2.13 (15)	1.77 (15)	1.76 (15)
CENTRAL SOYA CO	A /A	8/78	2.08 (13)	1.46 (18)	NA (-)	NA (-)	NA (-)
INTL MULTIFOODS CORP	Baa/BBB+	2/79	2.06P(14)	2.03P(15)	2.00P(16)	1.86P(14)	1.65P(16)
ESMARK INC	A /A	10/78	2.04P(15)	1.95P(16)	2.17P(14)	2.76P(5)	2.90P(3)
AMSTAR CORP	Baa/BB*	6/78	1.89 (16)	NA (-)	NA (-)	NA (-)	NA (-)
NORTON SIMON INC	A /A	6/78	1.71 (17)	3.28 (7)	NA (-)	NA (-)	NA (-)
STALEY (A.E.) MFG CO	A /A	9/78	1.68 (18)	2.24 (14)	4.29 (2)	6.33 (1)	2.67 (6)
CASTLE & COOKE INC	Baa/BBB	12/78	1.50 (19)	1.82 (17)	1.74 (17)	1.72 (17)	2.04 (13)
BORDEN INC	Aa /A+	12/78	NA (-)	2.79 (10)	2.58P(12)	2.39P(11)	2.43P(9)
HERSHEY FOODS CORP	A /A+	12/78	NA (-)	NA (-)	NA (-)	NA (-)	NA (-)
HORMEL (GEO.A.) & CO	A /A	10/78	NA (-)	NA (-)	NA (-)	NA (-)	NA (-)
IOWA BEEF PROCESSORS	Baa/BBB	10/78	NA (-)	NA (-)	NA (-)	NA (-)	3.53 (1)
KRAFT INC	Aaa/AAA	12/78	NA (-)	NA (-)	NA (-)	NA (-)	NA (-)
MAYER (OSCAR) & CO	A /AA	10/78	NA (-)	NA (-)	NA (-)	NA (-)	NA (-)
STOKELY-VAN CAMP INC	A /BBB	5/78	NA (-)	NA (-)	NA (-)	NA (-)	NA (-)
AVERAGE			3.11	2.89	2.96	2.78	2.47
MEDIAN			2.65	2.90	2.82	2.48	2.44

NET INCOME AS % NET SALES

	RATINGS	FYR END	78	77	76	75	74
KELLOGG CO	Aaa/AAA	12/78	8.6 (1)	9.0 (1)	9.4 (1)	8.5 (1)	7.1 (1)
HERSHEY FOODS CORP	A /A+	12/78	5.4 (2)	5.4 (3)	7.4 (2)	7.1 (2)	4.3 (4)
CARNATION CO	Aaa/AAA	12/78	4.8 (3)	4.7 (5)	4.8 (4)	4.3 (6)	4.2 (5)
NORTON SIMON INC	A /A	6/78	4.8 (4)	5.6 (2)	5.3 (3)	4.7 (4)	4.4 (3)
NABISCO INC	Aa /AA	12/78	4.6 (5)	5.0 (4)	3.8 (11)	3.0 (13)	2.5 (17)
HEINZ (H.J.) CO	Aa /A	4/78	4.6 (6)	4.5 (8)	3.9 (8)	4.0 (7)	3.9 (6)
CPC INTERNATIONAL INC	Aa /AA	12/78	4.6 (7)	4.6 (6)	4.5 (7)	4.0 (8)	3.5 (8)
QUAKER OATS CO	A /A+	6/78	4.4 (8)	4.4 (9)	3.6 (15)	2.2 (20)	3.2 (11)
GENERAL FOODS CORP	Aa /AAA	3/79	4.2 (9)	3.2 (15)	3.6 (14)	3.8 (9)	3.3 (10)
PILLSBURY CO	A /A	5/78	4.2 (10)	4.0 (11)	3.5 (16)	2.6 (16)	2.5 (18)
GENERAL MILLS INC	A /A+	5/78	4.0 (11)	4.0 (10)	3.8 (10)	3.3 (11)	3.8 (7)
RALSTON PURINA CO	Aa /AA	9/78	3.8 (12)	3.8 (12)	3.7 (13)	3.2 (12)	3.0 (15)
CASTLE & COOKE INC	Baa/BBB	12/78	3.6 (13)	4.5 (7)	4.8 (5)	4.5 (5)	5.7 (2)
BORDEN INC	Aa /A+	12/78	3.6 (14)	3.6 (13)	3.3 (17)	2.8 (15)	2.6 (16)
KRAFT INC	Aaa/AAA	12/78	3.2 (15)	2.9 (19)	2.7 (20)	2.9 (14)	2.1 (21)
STANDARD BRANDS INC	A /A	12/78	3.2 (16)	3.2 (14)	3.7 (12)	3.4 (10)	3.4 (9)
CONSOLIDATED FOODS CORP	Aa /AA	6/78	2.8 (17)	3.0 (16)	2.8 (19)	2.1 (21)	3.0 (13)
INTL MULTIFOODS CORP	Baa/BBB+	2/79	2.6 (18)	2.7 (20)	2.4 (21)	2.0 (22)	1.7 (24)
STOKELY-VAN CAMP INC	A /BBB	5/78	2.1 (19)	1.6 (23)	1.9 (23)	2.2 (19)	2.4 (19)
MAYER (OSCAR) & CO	A /AA	10/78	1.9 (20)	2.9 (18)	2.9 (18)	2.6 (17)	3.1 (12)
HORMEL (GEO.A.) & CO	A /A	10/78	1.6 (21)	2.0 (22)	1.3 (26)	1.3 (24)	1.8 (22)
AMSTAR CORP	Baa/BB*	6/78	1.5 (22)	3.0 (17)	3.9 (9)	2.3 (18)	3.0 (14)
ESMARK INC	A /A	10/78	1.4 (23)	1.3 (25)	1.6 (24)	1.7 (23)	1.5 (25)
CENTRAL SOYA CO	A /A	8/78	1.4 (24)	0.6 (26)	2.1 (22)	1.0 (26)	1.8 (23)
STALEY (A.E.) MFG CO	A /A	9/78	1.3 (25)	2.2 (21)	4.6 (6)	6.5 (3)	2.4 (20)
IOWA BEEF PROCESSORS	Baa/BBB	10/78	1.1 (26)	1.5 (24)	1.4 (25)	1.3 (25)	1.1 (26)
AVERAGE			3.43	3.58	3.72	3.35	3.12
MEDIAN			3.57	3.44	3.66	2.93	3.00

LTD/CAPITALIZATION (%)

	RATINGS	FYR END	78		77		76		75		74	
HERSHEY FOODS CORP	A /A+	12/78	11.1	(1)	10.2	(1)	11.5	(1)	13.2	(1)	15.5	(3)
MAYER (OSCAR) & CO	A /AA	10/78	11.4	(2)	12.2	(2)	14.6	(2)	17.6	(5)	19.9	(4)
KELLOGG CO	Aaa/AAA	12/78	12.3	(3)	12.9	(3)	14.9	(3)	17.1	(4)	2.8	(1)
HORMEL (GEO.A.) & CO	A /A	10/78	14.8	(4)	15.5	(4)	16.8	(4)	17.0	(3)	6.4	(2)
GENERAL FOODS CORP	Aa /AAA	3/79	16.0	(5)	18.1	(8)	18.9	(6)	19.3	(7)	22.3	(8)
AMSTAR CORP	Baa/BB*	6/78	16.2	(6)	17.1	(5)	19.0	(7)	21.8	(9)	25.0	(13)
CPC INTERNATIONAL INC	Aa /AA	12/78	16.3	(7)	17.6	(7)	19.6	(10)	20.8	(8)	21.7	(5)
HEINZ (H.J.) CO	Aa /A	4/78	16.9	(8)	17.6	(6)	19.4	(9)	23.1	(11)	22.6	(9)
CARNATION CO	Aaa/AAA	12/78	18.9	(9)	20.8	(10)	19.3	(8)	22.0	(10)	24.5	(12)
KRAFT INC	Aaa/AAA	12/78	20.1	(10)	23.7	(11)	17.9	(5)	18.7	(6)	21.8	(6)
GENERAL MILLS INC	A /A+	5/78	24.2	(11)	27.6	(16)	30.6	(18)	35.2	(20)	38.1	(23)
QUAKER OATS CO	A /A+	6/78	24.3	(12)	24.4	(12)	25.6	(13)	28.3	(14)	33.6	(20)
CONSOLIDATED FOODS CORP	Aa /AA	6/78	26.5	(13)	19.8	(9)	21.8	(11)	24.2	(12)	23.9	(10)
IOWA BEEF PROCESSORS	Baa/BBB	10/78	27.0	(14)	26.7	(15)	29.3	(17)	36.3	(24)	45.6	(25)
BORDEN INC	Aa /A+	12/78	29.1	(15)	25.6	(14)	27.1	(15)	28.0	(13)	29.6	(17)
RALSTON PURINA CO	Aa /AA	9/78	29.6	(16)	32.1	(20)	33.0	(21)	36.8	(25)	33.7	(21)
INTL MULTIFOODS CORP	Baa/BBB+	2/79	30.2	(17)	29.2	(17)	32.0	(19)	35.5	(22)	32.6	(18)
CENTRAL SOYA CO	A /A	8/78	30.5	(18)	31.6	(19)	24.1	(12)	28.3	(15)	28.2	(16)
STANDARD BRANDS INC	A /A	12/78	31.9	(19)	32.4	(21)	27.1	(16)	33.5	(18)	38.5	(24)
STOKELY-VAN CAMP INC	A /BBB	5/78	32.0	(20)	32.6	(22)	33.1	(22)	33.9	(19)	22.1	(7)
NABISCO INC	Aa /AA	12/78	33.1	(21)	30.2	(18)	32.8	(20)	35.6	(23)	37.0	(22)
STALEY (A.E.) MFG CO	A /A	9/78	33.4	(22)	36.9	(23)	37.4	(26)	15.6	(2)	27.2	(14)
NORTON SIMON INC	A /A	6/78	33.8	(23)	25.4	(13)	26.9	(14)	29.2	(16)	24.4	(11)
ESMARK INC	A /A	10/78	38.8	(24)	37.4	(24)	36.1	(25)	32.5	(17)	27.9	(15)
PILLSBURY CO	A /A	5/78	39.5	(25)	40.0	(26)	34.8	(23)	45.4	(26)	46.7	(26)
CASTLE & COOKE INC	Baa/BBB	12/78	42.7	(26)	39.1	(25)	35.2	(24)	35.5	(21)	33.3	(19)
AVERAGE			25.40		25.25		25.34		27.09		27.12	
MEDIAN			26.76		25.51		26.25		28.14		26.11	

LTD/NET PLANT (%)

	RATINGS	FYR END	78		77		76		75		74	
MAYER (OSCAR) & CO	A /AA	10/78	14.7	(1)	15.8	(1)	18.7	(1)	24.4	(2)	30.0	(4)
KELLOGG CO	Aaa/AAA	12/78	17.7	(2)	19.0	(2)	22.8	(2)	28.4	(4)	4.2	(1)
AMSTAR CORP	Baa/BB*	6/78	20.4	(3)	21.8	(4)	24.9	(4)	31.2	(7)	34.0	(6)
HERSHEY FOODS CORP	A /A+	12/78	20.8	(4)	20.6	(3)	23.3	(3)	25.6	(3)	25.4	(3)
CPC INTERNATIONAL INC	Aa /AA	12/78	22.0	(5)	24.5	(5)	27.8	(5)	30.1	(5)	31.6	(5)
HORMEL (GEO.A.) & CO	A /A	10/78	27.9	(6)	28.2	(6)	28.4	(6)	30.4	(6)	10.8	(2)
GENERAL FOODS CORP	Aa /AAA	3/79	32.4	(7)	34.1	(7)	35.2	(7)	33.9	(8)	38.7	(8)
HEINZ (H.J.) CO	Aa /A	4/78	34.7	(8)	39.3	(10)	42.9	(10)	49.7	(12)	47.2	(11)
QUAKER OATS CO	A /A+	6/78	34.8	(9)	37.3	(9)	39.8	(9)	44.2	(10)	53.7	(13)
STALEY (A.E.) MFG CO	A /A	9/78	34.9	(10)	36.5	(8)	44.2	(11)	20.0	(1)	35.2	(7)
RALSTON PURINA CO	Aa /AA	9/78	41.2	(11)	47.6	(11)	53.0	(17)	59.9	(16)	52.1	(12)
GENERAL MILLS INC	A /A+	5/78	44.3	(12)	51.1	(16)	59.8	(21)	69.1	(21)	78.6	(23)
KRAFT INC	Aaa/AAA	12/78	47.6	(13)	56.1	(18)	36.5	(8)	36.9	(9)	45.3	(10)
BORDEN INC	Aa /A+	12/78	49.8	(14)	48.1	(13)	54.0	(18)	57.5	(15)	60.1	(17)
IOWA BEEF PROCESSORS	Baa/BBB	10/78	53.0	(15)	47.8	(12)	51.7	(14)	64.9	(17)	84.8	(25)
NABISCO INC	Aa /AA	12/78	54.9	(16)	50.6	(15)	51.3	(13)	54.5	(13)	57.8	(15)
CONSOLIDATED FOODS CORP	Aa /AA	6/78	56.1	(17)	48.7	(14)	52.2	(15)	56.7	(14)	57.7	(14)
STANDARD BRANDS INC	A /A	12/78	56.3	(18)	55.7	(17)	47.5	(12)	67.4	(20)	82.8	(24)
PILLSBURY CO	A /A	5/78	61.3	(19)	62.3	(20)	52.9	(16)	66.3	(18)	69.6	(19)
CARNATION CO	Aaa/AAA	12/78	61.9	(20)	65.6	(21)	62.3	(22)	66.8	(19)	71.9	(20)
ESMARK INC	A /A	10/78	66.2	(21)	58.4	(19)	54.5	(19)	49.3	(11)	41.5	(9)
INTL MULTIFOODS CORP	Baa/BBB+	2/79	67.9	(22)	77.7	(23)	95.1	(24)	111.5	(26)	93.7	(26)
CENTRAL SOYA CO	A /A	8/78	68.6	(23)	75.2	(22)	59.5	(20)	69.2	(22)	72.7	(21)
CASTLE & COOKE INC	Baa/BBB	12/78	81.2	(24)	80.0	(24)	70.6	(23)	75.6	(23)	69.0	(18)
STOKELY-VAN CAMP INC	A /BBB	5/78	98.2	(25)	103.4	(26)	104.9	(26)	107.6	(25)	59.3	(16)
NORTON SIMON INC	A /A	6/78	112.0	(26)	91.9	(25)	101.7	(25)	106.6	(24)	78.2	(22)
AVERAGE			49.27		49.91		50.59		55.30		53.30	
MEDIAN			48.73		48.40		51.53		55.63		55.68	

TOT LIABILITY/TOT STK EQUITY

	RATINGS	FYR END	78		77		76		75		74	
HERSHEY FOODS CORP	A /A+	12/78	48.4	(1)	52.6	(1)	42.6	(1)	52.4	(1)	62.4	(2)
KELLOGG CO	Aaa/AAA	12/78	57.7	(2)	54.1	(2)	56.4	(2)	68.7	(3)	44.3	(1)
MAYER (OSCAR) & CO	A /AA	10/78	57.8	(3)	56.3	(3)	61.7	(3)	61.3	(2)	73.8	(4)
HORMEL (GEO.A.) & CO	A /A	10/78	65.1	(4)	68.4	(4)	67.1	(4)	76.9	(4)	64.2	(3)
CARNATION CO	Aaa/AAA	12/78	71.5	(5)	70.8	(6)	68.2	(5)	77.1	(5)	92.5	(8)
AMSTAR CORP	Baa/BB*	6/78	80.8	(6)	81.0	(9)	84.6	(10)	91.6	(10)	135.2	(20)
IOWA BEEF PROCESSORS	Baa/BBB	10/78	80.9	(7)	70.6	(5)	88.7	(12)	113.5	(17)	143.8	(23)
STOKELY-VAN CAMP INC	A /BBB	5/78	85.5	(8)	85.1	(10)	85.9	(11)	93.4	(12)	74.2	(5)
KRAFT INC	Aaa/AAA	12/78	88.9	(9)	88.5	(12)	79.3	(6)	78.1	(6)	101.2	(9)
HEINZ (H.J.) CO	Aa /A	4/78	89.8	(10)	94.5	(13)	95.1	(14)	127.6	(23)	120.7	(12)
GENERAL FOODS CORP	Aa /AAA	3/79	94.2	(11)	107.3	(20)	116.1	(21)	104.7	(15)	110.1	(11)
RALSTON PURINA CO	Aa /AA	9/78	95.3	(12)	103.4	(19)	103.3	(17)	104.3	(14)	124.0	(13)
GENERAL MILLS INC	A /A+	5/78	97.9	(13)	99.7	(18)	107.5	(18)	115.1	(19)	131.0	(18)
CENTRAL SOYA CO	A /A	8/78	101.6	(14)	97.2	(15)	83.0	(8)	98.1	(13)	125.0	(14)
BORDEN INC	Aa /A+	12/78	102.0	(15)	85.5	(11)	92.8	(13)	91.8	(11)	104.7	(10)
QUAKER OATS CO	A /A+	6/78	103.1	(16)	96.1	(14)	98.0	(15)	90.9	(9)	129.4	(16)
CPC INTERNATIONAL INC	Aa /AA	12/78	111.2	(17)	99.4	(17)	102.0	(16)	114.2	(18)	126.9	(15)
INTL MULTIFOODS CORP	Baa/BBB+	2/79	111.5	(18)	97.8	(16)	109.9	(19)	123.5	(22)	141.5	(22)
NORTON SIMON INC	A /A	6/78	127.7	(19)	80.8	(8)	80.8	(7)	86.9	(8)	80.9	(6)
CONSOLIDATED FOODS CORP	Aa /AA	6/78	128.7	(20)	78.1	(7)	83.8	(9)	79.4	(7)	92.2	(7)
NABISCO INC	Aa /AAA	12/78	132.5	(21)	118.5	(21)	136.9	(24)	149.2	(25)	172.0	(25)
STALEY (A.E.) MFG CO	A /A	9/78	132.9	(22)	148.1	(25)	132.1	(23)	108.2	(16)	134.3	(19)
STANDARD BRANDS INC	A /A	12/78	134.1	(23)	129.3	(22)	113.4	(20)	121.3	(21)	144.3	(24)
CASTLE & COOKE INC	Baa/BBB	12/78	143.6	(24)	129.7	(23)	120.3	(22)	117.8	(20)	130.1	(17)
ESMARK INC	A /A	10/78	160.0	(25)	141.8	(24)	147.3	(25)	137.0	(24)	135.8	(21)
PILLSBURY CO	A /A	5/78	180.5	(26)	185.0	(26)	156.7	(26)	201.7	(26)	222.5	(26)
AVERAGE			103.20		96.91		96.68		103.26		116.04	
MEDIAN			99.71		95.29		93.95		101.18		124.50	

CASH FLOW/LTD (%)

	RATINGS	FYR END	78		77		76		75		74	
KELLOGG CO	Aaa/AAA	12/78	233.2	(1)	224.4	(1)	187.8	(1)	151.8	(3)	903.1	(1)
MAYER (OSCAR) & CO	A /AA	10/78	164.7	(2)	172.0	(2)	140.7	(3)	102.6	(5)	99.2	(4)
HERSHEY FOODS CORP	A /A+	12/78	152.1	(3)	165.9	(3)	176.2	(2)	162.9	(2)	104.0	(3)
CPC INTERNATIONAL INC	Aa /AA	12/78	149.9	(4)	125.8	(4)	101.0	(5)	103.9	(4)	85.3	(5)
GENERAL FOODS CORP	Aa /AAA	3/79	123.0	(5)	88.5	(7)	104.9	(4)	100.4	(6)	73.3	(6)
HORMEL (GEO.A.) & CO	A /A	10/78	113.2	(6)	120.3	(5)	91.7	(9)	86.8	(9)	310.6	(2)
HEINZ (H.J.) CO	Aa /A	4/78	98.1	(7)	92.8	(6)	86.1	(10)	78.3	(10)	66.2	(8)
CARNATION CO	Aaa/AAA	12/78	88.4	(8)	78.8	(10)	91.9	(8)	76.4	(11)	66.0	(9)
KRAFT INC	Aaa/AAA	12/78	86.1	(9)	66.2	(14)	93.3	(7)	91.7	(7)	63.4	(10)
QUAKER OATS CO	A /A+	6/78	77.4	(10)	75.4	(11)	57.6	(17)	45.9	(17)	42.5	(20)
GENERAL MILLS INC	A /A+	5/78	74.9	(11)	63.1	(15)	54.4	(17)	40.7	(20)	39.0	(21)
AMSTAR CORP	Baa/BB*	6/78	65.4	(12)	83.6	(9)	98.5	(6)	87.8	(8)	63.0	(11)
IOWA BEEF PROCESSORS	Baa/BBB	10/78	62.6	(13)	71.1	(13)	70.4	(12)	51.0	(13)	34.9	(25)
CONSOLIDATED FOODS CORP	Aa /AA	6/78	61.2	(14)	85.4	(8)	75.7	(11)	56.8	(12)	60.5	(12)
RALSTON PURINA CO	Aa /AA	9/78	58.6	(15)	52.5	(17)	50.3	(21)	39.3	(23)	44.9	(18)
NABISCO INC	Aa /AA	12/78	56.5	(16)	75.0	(12)	55.9	(16)	46.3	(16)	37.8	(22)
BORDEN INC	Aa /A+	12/78	56.5	(17)	58.1	(16)	52.4	(18)	45.9	(18)	44.0	(19)
STANDARD BRANDS INC	A /A	12/78	50.8	(18)	42.4	(21)	58.9	(15)	47.5	(15)	36.4	(23)
INTL MULTIFOODS CORP	Baa/BBB+	2/79	46.8	(19)	47.5	(19)	38.7	(24)	33.3	(25)	35.5	(24)
CENTRAL SOYA CO	A /A	8/78	43.9	(20)	25.1	(25)	69.3	(13)	42.2	(19)	58.0	(13)
PILLSBURY CO	A /A	5/78	43.1	(21)	40.7	(22)	50.4	(20)	38.4	(24)	33.8	(26)
STALEY (A.E.) MFG CO	A /A	9/78	42.2	(22)	46.8	(20)	51.6	(19)	210.8	(1)	69.5	(7)
ESMARK INC	A /A	10/78	36.3	(23)	40.7	(23)	43.3	(23)	49.7	(14)	56.1	(14)
NORTON SIMON INC	A /A	6/78	32.7	(24)	50.5	(18)	50.3	(22)	39.8	(22)	52.4	(16)
STOKELY-VAN CAMP INC	A /BBB	5/78	28.6	(25)	23.8	(26)	27.8	(26)	28.2	(26)	50.5	(17)
CASTLE & COOKE INC	Baa/BBB	12/78	25.8	(26)	33.2	(24)	35.6	(25)	40.4	(21)	54.2	(15)
AVERAGE			79.69		78.83		77.73		73.03		99.39	
MEDIAN			61.92		68.65		68.36		50.33		57.04	

Food Products Industry

NET CASH FL/CAP EXP (%)

	RATINGS	FYR END	78		77		76		75		74	
CARNATION CO	Aaa/AAA	12/78	205.8	(1)	247.1	(1)	254.5	(3)	211.4	(3)	144.2	(9)
GENERAL FOODS CORP	Aa /AAA	3/79	184.8	(2)	117.9	(18)	168.4	(8)	172.0	(7)	115.4	(14)
KRAFT INC	Aaa/AAA	12/78	184.0	(3)	211.7	(3)	170.5	(7)	123.0	(12)	104.6	(16)
HORMEL (GEO.A.) & CO	A /A	10/78	166.3	(4)	205.8	(4)	90.3	(23)	87.7	(24)	142.1	(10)
IOWA BEEF PROCESSORS	Baa/BBB	10/78	161.3	(5)	203.0	(5)	469.6	(1)	128.2	(10)	91.7	(20)
NABISCO INC	Aa /AAA	12/78	159.6	(6)	212.9	(2)	154.8	(10)	121.0	(13)	72.3	(25)
STANDARD BRANDS INC	A /A	12/78	155.7	(7)	131.2	(11)	76.0	(25)	89.9	(21)	97.3	(19)
CONSOLIDATED FOODS CORP	Aa /AA	6/78	139.7	(8)	156.9	(8)	154.8	(9)	119.6	(14)	128.4	(12)
CPC INTERNATIONAL INC	Aa /AAA	12/78	129.8	(9)	123.8	(14)	107.7	(17)	102.5	(17)	102.8	(17)
MAYER (OSCAR) & CO	A /AA	10/78	128.9	(10)	142.7	(9)	96.7	(20)	88.8	(23)	160.4	(6)
ESMARK INC	A /A	10/78	127.9	(11)	122.6	(15)	86.9	(24)	84.5	(25)	90.7	(21)
INTL MULTIFOODS CORP	Baa/BBB+	2/79	125.6	(12)	135.1	(10)	127.6	(13)	146.6	(8)	150.4	(8)
AMSTAR CORP	Baa/BB*	6/78	123.7	(13)	103.0	(20)	118.6	(16)	227.1	(2)	179.9	(3)
STOKELY-VAN CAMP INC	A /BBB	5/78	123.4	(14)	118.3	(17)	133.8	(11)	141.9	(9)	129.0	(11)
KELLOGG CO	Aaa/AAA	12/78	120.1 V(15)		124.2 V(13)		95.5 V(21)		106.6 V(16)		84.9	(22)
BORDEN INC	Aa /A	12/78	117.4	(16)	101.3	(21)	104.9	(19)	109.6	(15)	111.4	(15)
CENTRAL SOYA CO	A /A	8/78	114.3	(17)	58.1	(25)	177.3	(6)	93.9	(19)	197.0	(2)
NORTON SIMON INC	A /A	6/78	112.3	(18)	157.8	(7)	201.6	(5)	176.0	(5)	162.6	(5)
HEINZ (H.J.) CO	Aa /A	4/78	110.0	(19)	191.0	(6)	298.8	(2)	175.9	(6)	158.6	(7)
QUAKER OATS CO	A /A+	6/78	108.5	(20)	125.1	(12)	123.8	(15)	76.5	(26)	83.2	(23)
GENERAL MILLS INC	A /A+	5/78	104.2	(21)	115.4	(19)	127.9	(12)	96.5	(18)	99.5	(18)
HERSHEY FOODS CORP	A /A+	12/78	99.5	(22)	122.0	(16)	209.3	(4)	375.7	(1)	214.0	(1)
STALEY (A.E.) MFG CO	A /A	9/78	93.2	(23)	46.7	(26)	39.6	(26)	125.3	(11)	121.6	(13)
PILLSBURY CO	A /A	5/78	79.7	(24)	77.2	(24)	105.9	(18)	89.7	(22)	59.1	(26)
RALSTON PURINA CO	Aa /AA	9/78	79.6	(25)	94.0	(22)	126.8	(14)	91.5	(20)	73.2	(24)
CASTLE & COOKE INC	Baa/BBB	12/78	52.8	(26)	93.4	(23)	90.8	(22)	208.1	(4)	172.9	(4)
AVERAGE			127.24		136.09		150.48		137.29		124.88	
MEDIAN			123.57		124.01		127.18		120.30		118.48	

NET TANG ASSETS/LTD (%)

	RATINGS	FYR END	78		77		76		75		74	
MAYER (OSCAR) & CO	A /AA	10/78	872.1	(1)	813.5	(2)	679.7	(2)	561.1	(4)	496.2	(4)
HERSHEY FOODS CORP	A /A+	12/78	831.9	(2)	901.6	(1)	770.9	(1)	662.0	(1)	553.9	(3)
KELLOGG CO	Aaa/AAA	12/78	767.1	(3)	734.7	(3)	642.1	(3)	559.2	(5)	3337.8	(1)
HORMEL (GEO.A.) & CO	A /A	10/78	661.2	(4)	632.3	(4)	582.7	(4)	577.7	(3)	1563.2	(2)
AMSTAR CORP	Baa/BB*	6/78	608.7	(5)	575.4	(5)	519.6	(6)	451.6	(8)	393.1	(11)
GENERAL FOODS CORP	Aa /AAA	3/79	604.4	(6)	531.4	(8)	506.1	(7)	489.3	(7)	418.8	(9)
CPC INTERNATIONAL INC	Aa /AAA	12/78	586.1	(7)	535.1	(7)	480.3	(10)	448.1	(9)	423.0	(8)
HEINZ (H.J.) CO	Aa /A	4/78	573.8	(8)	551.0	(6)	497.8	(8)	417.1	(11)	428.9	(7)
CARNATION CO	Aaa/AAA	12/78	504.7	(9)	457.4	(9)	487.1	(9)	426.2	(10)	380.1	(12)
KRAFT INC	Aaa/AAA	12/78	475.3	(10)	404.7	(11)	538.0	(5)	514.3	(6)	437.8	(5)
QUAKER OATS CO	A /A+	6/78	385.1	(11)	381.5	(13)	361.6	(14)	325.5	(15)	271.3	(21)
IOWA BEEF PROCESSORS	Baa/BBB	10/78	363.7	(12)	366.7	(14)	335.7	(15)	271.5	(19)	215.1	(25)
GENERAL MILLS INC	A /A+	5/78	327.2	(13)	296.3	(19)	266.0	(22)	235.9	(24)	216.8	(24)
CONSOLIDATED FOODS CORP	Aa /AA	6/78	321.3	(14)	439.7	(10)	394.9	(12)	351.2	(12)	348.8	(14)
CENTRAL SOYA CO	A /A	8/78	313.0	(15)	301.3	(17)	409.3	(11)	345.5	(13)	346.3	(15)
RALSTON PURINA CO	Aa /AA	9/78	311.7	(16)	295.0	(20)	288.1	(19)	258.4	(22)	277.3	(18)
BORDEN INC	Aa /A+	12/78	305.1	(17)	344.7	(15)	323.3	(17)	310.2	(16)	288.1	(17)
STOKELY-VAN CAMP INC	A /BBB	5/78	303.0	(18)	297.0	(18)	292.1	(18)	285.0	(18)	434.2	(6)
INTL MULTIFOODS CORP	Baa/BBB+	2/79	298.6	(19)	309.5	(16)	281.3	(20)	254.2	(23)	273.0	(20)
STALEY (A.E.) MFG CO	A /A	9/78	295.3	(20)	267.4	(23)	262.2	(23)	629.8	(2)	357.7	(13)
STANDARD BRANDS INC	A /A	12/78	280.1	(21)	271.9	(22)	330.7	(16)	268.5	(20)	224.0	(22)
NORTON SIMON INC	A /A	6/78	269.2	(22)	382.9	(12)	364.8	(13)	335.8	(14)	402.0	(10)
NABISCO INC	Aa /AA	12/78	263.7	(23)	289.4	(21)	255.2	(25)	230.2	(25)	219.9	(23)
PILLSBURY CO	A /A	5/78	233.2	(24)	235.1	(26)	268.1	(21)	201.9	(26)	198.4	(26)
ESMARK INC	A /A	10/78	223.9	(25)	243.8	(24)	253.7	(26)	294.5	(17)	340.1	(16)
CASTLE & COOKE INC	Baa/BBB	12/78	223.0	(26)	240.6	(25)	257.7	(24)	262.9	(21)	276.4	(19)
AVERAGE			430.86		426.92		409.57		383.37		504.70	
MEDIAN			324.23		374.10		363.17		340.67		353.24	

RET ON TOT ASSETS (%)

	RATINGS	FYR END	78	77	76	75	74
KELLOGG CO	Aaa/AAA	12/78	30.0 (1)	32.4 (1)	34.1 (1)	30.6 (1)	28.1 (1)
HERSHEY FOODS CORP	A /A+	12/78	20.0 (2)	18.6 (4)	28.2 (2)	28.2 (3)	17.4 (7)
CARNATION CO	Aaa/AAA	12/78	19.5 (3)	19.4 (3)	20.8 (4)	19.2 (5)	17.9 (6)
IOWA BEEF PROCESSORS	Baa/BBB	10/78	18.8 (4)	21.4 (2)	24.7 (3)	20.7 (4)	19.0 (4)
GENERAL FOODS CORP	Aa /AAA	3/79	18.8 (5)	15.1 (14)	16.8 (12)	17.0 (10)	15.0 (11)
NABISCO INC	Aa /AA	12/78	18.4 (6)	17.4 (9)	18.0 (8)	16.1 (12)	11.8 (22)
RALSTON PURINA CO	Aa /AA	9/78	17.1 (7)	17.4 (10)	17.8 (10)	16.2 (11)	15.2 (10)
GENERAL MILLS INC	A /A+	5/78	17.0 (8)	17.7 (5)	17.3 (11)	15.2 (14)	16.1 (8)
KRAFT INC	Aaa/AAA	12/78	16.8 (9)	16.1 (13)	16.7 (13)	18.0 (7)	12.6 (19)
CPC INTERNATIONAL INC	Aa /AA	12/78	16.3 (10)	17.6 (6)	18.1 (7)	18.2 (6)	15.5 (9)
QUAKER OATS CO	A /A+	6/78	15.6 (11)	16.6 (11)	15.0 (15)	12.5 (18)	12.8 (18)
CONSOLIDATED FOODS CORP	Aa /AA	6/78	15.0 (12)	16.1 (12)	14.8 (16)	12.0 (24)	13.2 (15)
HORMEL (GEO.A.) & CO	A /A	10/78	14.1 (13)	17.4 (8)	13.3 (20)	12.0 (22)	19.7 (2)
HEINZ (H.J.) CO	Aa /A	4/78	14.1 (14)	13.4 (16)	12.9 (23)	12.9 (15)	11.5 (23)
CENTRAL SOYA CO	A /A	8/78	13.8 (15)	8.0 (25)	19.0 (5)	12.5 (19)	18.3 (5)
INTL MULTIFOODS CORP	Baa/BBB+	2/79	13.5 (16)	14.0 (15)	14.1 (18)	11.9 (25)	13.1 (16)
PILLSBURY CO	A /A	5/78	13.5 (17)	12.7 (20)	13.5 (19)	12.6 (17)	10.6 (26)
MAYER (OSCAR) & CO	A /AA	10/78	13.5 (18)	17.5 (7)	17.9 (9)	17.8 (8)	19.6 (3)
STANDARD BRANDS INC	A /A	12/78	12.7 (19)	12.8 (19)	14.7 (17)	15.5 (13)	13.4 (13)
BORDEN INC	Aa /A+	12/78	12.4 (20)	13.3 (17)	12.9 (22)	11.9 (26)	11.1 (25)
NORTON SIMON INC	A /A	6/78	12.2 (21)	13.2 (18)	13.2 (21)	12.1 (21)	12.2 (20)
STOKELY-VAN CAMP INC	A /BBB	5/78	10.5 (22)	8.1 (24)	10.3 (25)	12.2 (20)	11.1 (24)
CASTLE & COOKE INC	Baa/BBB	12/78	9.8 (23)	11.9 (21)	11.5 (24)	12.8 (16)	13.8 (12)
ESMARK INC	A /A	10/78	8.1 (24)	8.3 (23)	9.5 (26)	12.0 (23)	11.9 (21)
STALEY (A.E.) MFG CO	A /A	9/78	7.0 (25)	6.6 (26)	15.8 (14)	30.3 (2)	13.0 (17)
AMSTAR CORP	Baa/BB*	6/78	6.0 (26)	10.7 (22)	18.6 (6)	17.1 (9)	13.2 (14)
AVERAGE			14.79	15.15	16.90	16.44	14.89
MEDIAN			14.06	15.63	16.25	15.32	13.30

AFT TAX RET ON COM EQTY (%)

	RATINGS	FYR END	78	77	76	75	74
KELLOGG CO	Aaa/AAA	12/78	24.3 (1)	25.5 (1)	26.7 (1)	25.7 (2)	20.5 (2)
NABISCO INC	Aa /AA	12/78	18.7 (2)	21.3 (2)	17.2 (6)	14.5 (12)	11.8 (21)
GENERAL FOODS CORP	Aa /AAA	3/79	17.6 (3)	14.4 (11)	16.3 (9)	15.3 (9)	13.4 (13)
IOWA BEEF PROCESSORS	Baa/BBB	10/78	17.1 (4)	18.4 (3)	21.4 (2)	21.6 (3)	21.3 (1)
CPC INTERNATIONAL INC	Aa /AA	12/78	16.7 (5)	16.7 (4)	16.9 (7)	16.6 (6)	15.1 (9)
RALSTON PURINA CO	Aa /AA	9/78	15.9 (6)	16.4 (5)	16.4 (8)	14.8 (11)	15.1 (10)
GENERAL MILLS INC	A /A+	5/78	15.8 (7)	16.1 (6)	15.7 (12)	13.6 (15)	15.5 (8)
CARNATION CO	Aaa/AAA	12/78	15.7 (8)	15.3 (7)	16.3 (10)	15.6 (8)	15.8 (6)
PILLSBURY CO	A /A	5/78	15.6 (9)	14.9 (8)	14.4 (15)	13.9 (14)	12.5 (16)
QUAKER OATS CO	A /A+	6/78	15.4 (10)	14.8 (9)	12.8 (18)	8.7 (25)	11.9 (20)
KRAFT INC	Aaa/AAA	12/78	15.1 (11)	13.9 (14)	13.4 (17)	14.9 (10)	11.1 (22)
HERSHEY FOODS CORP	A /A+	12/78	14.6 (12)	13.9 (15)	19.1 (4)	19.9 (4)	12.7 (15)
STANDARD BRANDS INC	A /A	12/78	14.3 (13)	14.0 (13)	14.8 (14)	16.0 (7)	14.7 (11)
HEINZ (H.J.) CO	Aa /A	4/78	14.1 (14)	12.7 (18)	12.6 (19)	13.3 (16)	12.5 (17)
INTL MULTIFOODS CORP	Baa/BBB+	2/79	13.7 (15)	13.7 (16)	13.6 (16)	12.6 (18)	11.9 (19)
CONSOLIDATED FOODS CORP	Aa /AA	6/78	13.2 (16)	12.5 (19)	11.6 (23)	7.9 (26)	11.0 (23)
NORTON SIMON INC	A /A	6/78	12.8 (17)	11.9 (21)	11.3 (24)	10.4 (22)	10.3 (24)
BORDEN INC	Aa /A+	12/78	12.7 (18)	12.4 (20)	12.0 (21)	10.7 (20)	10.3 (25)
HORMEL (GEO.A.) & CO	A /A	10/78	12.0 (19)	14.3 (12)	10.8 (25)	10.5 (21)	14.7 (12)
CENTRAL SOYA CO	A /A	8/78	11.6 (20)	5.2 (26)	16.0 (11)	8.8 (24)	16.3 (5)
CASTLE & COOKE INC	Baa/BBB	12/78	11.6 (21)	13.0 (17)	12.3 (20)	12.6 (19)	15.7 (7)
MAYER (OSCAR) & CO	A /AA	10/78	10.2 (22)	14.5 (10)	15.4 (13)	14.0 (13)	17.2 (3)
ESMARK INC	A /A	10/78	9.8 (23)	9.0 (24)	11.7 (22)	12.6 (17)	13.3 (14)
STOKELY-VAN CAMP INC	A /BBB	5/78	8.1 (24)	5.5 (25)	7.3 (26)	9.3 (23)	8.7 (26)
STALEY (A.E.) MFG CO	A /A	9/78	6.5 (25)	11.4 (22)	19.4 (3)	30.2 (1)	12.4 (18)
AMSTAR CORP	Baa/BB*	6/78	5.1 (26)	10.5 (23)	17.4 (5)	18.1 (5)	16.7 (4)
AVERAGE			13.77	13.94	15.12	1".70	13.94
MEDIAN			14.18	13.97	15.13	13.96	13.32

Food Servicing Industry

PRETAX COVERAGE

	RATINGS	FYR END	78		77		76		75		74	
LUCKY STORES INC	A /A	1/79	7.47 (	1)	12.29 (	1)	11.18 (	2)	12.65 (	2)	9.94 (	1)
KROGER CO	A /A	12/78	6.11 (	2)	6.06 (	4)	6.18 (	5)	4.76 (	5)	6.78 (	5)
AMERICAN STORES CO	A /BBB+	3/78	5.46 (	3)	6.15 (	3)	10.49 (	3)	6.91 (	4)	7.07 (	4)
SAFEWAY STORES INC	A /A	12/78	4.73 (	4)	3.63 (	5)	18.19 (	1)	18.69P(	1)	8.82P(	2)
SOUTHLAND CORP	A /A	12/78	4.21 (	5)	7.36P(	2)	10.12P(	4)	10.65P(	3)	8.41P(	3)
FISHER FOODS INC	Ba /BB*	12/78	2.28 (	6)	1.37 (	6)	3.77 (	6)	3.47 (	6)	4.75 (	6)
AVERAGE			5.05		6.14		9.99		9.52		7.63	
MEDIAN			5.10		6.10		10.31		8.78		7.74	

AFTER TAX COVERAGE

	RATINGS	FYR END	78		77		76		75		74	
LUCKY STORES INC	A /A	1/79	4.34 (	1)	6.85 (	1)	6.30 (	2)	7.03 (	2)	5.56 (	1)
KROGER CO	A /A	12/78	3.82 (	2)	3.83 (	3)	3.81 (	5)	3.17 (	5)	4.10 (	5)
AMERICAN STORES CO	A /BBB+	3/78	3.49 (	3)	3.72 (	4)	5.91 (	3)	4.13 (	4)	4.17 (	4)
SAFEWAY STORES INC	A /A	12/78	2.97 (	4)	2.46 (	5)	10.49 (	1)	10.55P(	1)	5.41P(	2)
SOUTHLAND CORP	A /A	12/78	2.63 (	5)	4.17P(	2)	5.51P(	4)	5.77P(	3)	4.73P(	3)
FISHER FOODS INC	Ba /BB*	12/78	1.79 (	6)	1.34 (	6)	2.57 (	6)	2.43 (	6)	3.06 (	6)
AVERAGE			3.17		3.73		5.77		5.52		4.50	
MEDIAN			3.23		3.77		5.71		4.95		4.45	

AFTER TAX COV (INCL RENTS)

	RATINGS	FYR END	78		77		76		75		74	
LUCKY STORES INC	A /A	1/79	2.00 (	1)	1.88 (	1)	1.76 (	1)	1.88 (	2)	1.83 (	1)
SAFEWAY STORES INC	A /A	12/78	1.87 (	2)	1.65 (	2)	1.60 (	3)	1.96P(	1)	1.56P(	3)
SOUTHLAND CORP	A /A	12/78	1.74 (	3)	1.65P(	3)	1.57P(	4)	1.52P(	3)	1.45P(	6)
KROGER CO	A /A	12/78	1.65 (	4)	1.48 (	5)	1.43 (	6)	1.34 (	6)	1.49 (	4)
FISHER FOODS INC	Ba /BB*	12/78	1.51 (	5)	1.21 (	6)	1.51 (	5)	1.48 (	4)	1.61 (	2)
AMERICAN STORES CO	A /BBB+	3/78	1.49 (	6)	1.49 (	4)	1.69 (	2)	1.46 (	5)	1.48 (	5)
AVERAGE			1.71		1.56		1.59		1.61		1.57	
MEDIAN			1.69		1.57		1.59		1.50		1.52	

NET INCOME AS % NET SALES

	RATINGS	FYR END	78		77		76		75		74	
SOUTHLAND CORP	A /A	12/78	1.9 (	1)	1.9 (	1)	1.9 (	1)	1.9 (	1)	1.8 (	1)
LUCKY STORES INC	A /A	1/79	1.7 (	2)	1.6 (	2)	1.3 (	2)	1.5 (	2)	1.5 (	2)
SAFEWAY STORES INC	A /A	12/78	1.2 (	3)	0.9 (	3)	1.0 (	3)	1.5 (	3)	1.0 (	4)
KROGER CO	A /A	12/78	1.1 (	4)	0.9 (	4)	0.8 (	6)	0.6 (	6)	0.9 (	5)
AMERICAN STORES CO	A /BBB+	3/78	0.7 (	5)	0.7 (	5)	1.0 (	4)	0.7 (	5)	0.8 (	6)
FISHER FOODS INC	Ba /BB*	12/78	0.7 (	6)	0.3 (	6)	0.9 (	5)	0.9 (	4)	1.1 (	3)
AVERAGE			1.20		1.05		1.15		1.21		1.20	
MEDIAN			1.12		0.90		1.00		1.22		1.04	

LTD/CAPITALIZATION (%)

	RATINGS	FYR END	78		77		76		75		74	
AMERICAN STORES CO	A /BBB+	3/78	27.2 (	1)	29.1 (	1)	20.4 (	2)	21.5 (	2)	21.2 (	2)
KROGER CO	A /A	12/78	37.2 (	2)	30.7 (	2)	32.8 (	3)	28.7 (	3)	22.6 (	3)
LUCKY STORES INC	A /A	1/79	47.5 (	3)	32.5 (	3)	35.3 (	5)	35.6 (	5)	29.1 (	4)
SAFEWAY STORES INC	A /A	12/78	48.5 (	4)	49.6 (	5)	10.8 (	1)	11.8 (	1)	13.1 (	1)
SOUTHLAND CORP	A /A	12/78	55.8 (	5)	39.9 (	4)	33.5 (	4)	30.6 (	4)	30.3 (	5)
FISHER FOODS INC	Ba /BB*	12/78	57.9 (	6)	62.2 (	6)	50.8 (	6)	56.6 (	6)	55.7 (	6)
AVERAGE			45.70		40.67		30.59		30.81		28.67	
MEDIAN			48.01		36.19		33.11		29.67		25.85	

LTD/NET PLANT (%)

	RATINGS	FYR END	78		77		76		75		74	
AMERICAN STORES CO	A /BBB+	3/78	46.1	(1)	51.3	(2)	30.7	(2)	31.0	(2)	33.4	(3)
KROGER CO	A /A	12/78	52.9	(2)	48.3	(1)	53.7	(4)	41.8	(4)	31.1	(2)
SAFEWAY STORES INC	A /A	12/78	54.2	(3)	55.7	(5)	14.0	(1)	15.7	(1)	16.0	(1)
LUCKY STORES INC	A /A	1/79	69.5	(4)	54.2	(4)	59.9	(5)	61.5	(5)	43.3	(5)
SOUTHLAND CORP	A /A	12/78	69.8	(5)	54.1	(3)	45.1	(3)	41.3	(3)	41.6	(4)
FISHER FOODS INC	Ba /BB*	12/78	73.9	(6)	76.2	(6)	66.3	(6)	78.1	(6)	71.8	(6)
AVERAGE			61.09		56.63		44.96		44.90		39.53	
MEDIAN			61.86		54.16		49.41		41.53		37.49	

TOT LIABILITY/TOT STK EQUITY

	RATINGS	FYR END	78		77		76		75		74	
AMERICAN STORES CO	A /BBB+	3/78	139.2	(1)	131.9	(2)	115.5	(3)	117.7	(3)	121.1	(3)
KROGER CO	A /A	12/78	198.1	(2)	186.7	(4)	169.5	(4)	154.7	(4)	144.8	(4)
SAFEWAY STORES INC	A /A	12/78	202.8	(3)	201.9	(5)	101.3	(1)	98.2	(2)	115.0	(2)
SOUTHLAND CORP	A /A	12/78	203.0	(4)	129.7	(1)	105.8	(2)	97.5	(1)	99.8	(1)
LUCKY STORES INC	A /A	1/79	211.9	(5)	164.5	(3)	170.0	(5)	159.8	(5)	153.1	(5)
FISHER FOODS INC	Ba /BB*	12/78	272.7	(6)	311.1	(6)	243.8	(6)	264.8	(6)	297.2	(6)
AVERAGE			204.63		187.63		150.98		148.78		155.18	
MEDIAN			202.90		175.62		142.52		136.21		132.96	

NET TANG ASSETS/LTD (%)

	RATINGS	FYR END	78		77		76		75		74	
AMERICAN STORES CO	A /BBB+	3/78	366.0	(1)	342.2	(1)	488.3	(2)	463.9	(2)	470.4	(2)
KROGER CO	A /A	12/78	263.2	(2)	316.4	(2)	296.5	(3)	336.9	(3)	429.3	(3)
SAFEWAY STORES INC	A /A	12/78	203.0	(3)	197.6	(5)	923.3	(1)	844.9	(1)	757.6	(1)
LUCKY STORES INC	A /A	1/79	201.6	(4)	290.0	(3)	265.1	(5)	261.2	(5)	316.6	(5)
SOUTHLAND CORP	A /A	12/78	174.1	(5)	248.2	(4)	295.8	(4)	323.2	(4)	327.3	(4)
FISHER FOODS INC	Ba /BB*	12/78	170.3	(6)	157.3	(6)	191.8	(6)	170.5	(6)	174.1	(6)
AVERAGE			229.70		258.64		410.13		400.12		412.56	
MEDIAN			202.35		269.10		296.18		330.08		378.29	

CASH FLOW/LTD (%)

	RATINGS	FYR END	78		77		76		75		74	
AMERICAN STORES CO	A /BBB+	3/78	61.7	(1)	58.8	(2)	102.7	(2)	78.5	(2)	75.3	(3)
KROGER CO	A /A	12/78	48.7	(2)	57.5	(3)	47.9	(5)	51.8	(5)	75.1	(4)
LUCKY STORES INC	A /A	1/79	42.5	(3)	69.6	(1)	57.4	(3)	60.2	(3)	79.1	(2)
SAFEWAY STORES INC	A /A	12/78	37.9	(4)	30.5	(5)	206.8	(1)	226.1	(1)	157.3	(1)
SOUTHLAND CORP	A /A	12/78	27.8	(5)	41.6	(4)	53.4	(4)	57.7	(4)	54.1	(5)
FISHER FOODS INC	Ba /BB*	12/78	25.1	(6)	18.5	(6)	33.1	(6)	28.4	(6)	30.7	(6)
AVERAGE			40.61		46.10		83.55		83.78		78.60	
MEDIAN			40.23		49.55		55.36		58.93		75.24	

NET CASH FL/CAP EXP (%)

	RATINGS	FYR END	78		77		76		75		74	
KROGER CO	A /A	12/78	107.6	(1)	109.3	(3)	109.3	(3)	101.4	(2)	64.5	(4)
AMERICAN STORES CO	A /BBB+	3/78	97.7	(2)	136.4	(1)	133.9	(1)	67.1	(6)	112.1	(2)
SAFEWAY STORES INC	A /A	12/78	95.4 V(3)		63.0 V(5)		71.3	(6)	97.3 V(3)		47.0 V(6)	
FISHER FOODS INC	Ba /BB*	12/78	82.9	(4)	75.3	(4)	114.3	(2)	82.5	(5)	48.1	(5)
LUCKY STORES INC	A /A	1/79	81.7	(5)	113.1	(2)	101.5	(4)	133.3	(1)	134.2	(1)
SOUTHLAND CORP	A /A	12/78	64.1	(6)	59.1	(6)	74.0	(5)	86.4	(4)	79.4	(3)
AVERAGE			88.24		92.70		100.72		94.66		80.87	
MEDIAN			89.18		92.33		105.41		91.86		71.91	

Food Servicing Industry

AFT TAX RET ON COM EQTY (%)

	RATINGS	FYR END	78		77		76		75		74	
LUCKY STORES INC	A /A	1/79	24.2	(1)	21.8	(1)	18.9	(1)	21.5	(1)	20.9	(1)
SAFEWAY STORES INC	A /A	12/78	15.6	(2)	12.1	(4)	12.4	(5)	18.7	(2)	11.4	(4)
KROGER CO	A /A	12/78	15.3	(3)	12.3	(3)	10.6	(6)	8.1	(6)	10.8	(5)
SOUTHLAND CORP	A /A	12/78	15.2	(4)	13.7	(2)	13.2	(4)	12.6	(4)	12.2	(3)
FISHER FOODS INC	Ba /BB*	12/78	11.1	(5)	5.2	(6)	15.1	(2)	16.7	(3)	19.5	(2)
AMERICAN STORES CO	A /BBB+	3/78	9.8	(6)	10.1	(5)	13.4	(3)	9.0	(5)	9.0	(6)
AVERAGE			15.21		12.54		13.94		14.43		13.96	
MEDIAN			15.25		12.18		13.32		14.66		11.83	

RET ON TOT ASSETS (%)

	RATINGS	FYR END	78		77		76		75		74	
LUCKY STORES INC	A /A	1/79	17.3	(1)	17.1	(1)	14.5	(1)	17.1	(2)	17.7	(1)
SOUTHLAND CORP	A /A	12/78	13.0	(2)	13.8	(2)	14.3	(2)	14.1	(3)	13.6	(2)
SAFEWAY STORES INC	A /A	12/78	12.4	(3)	9.9	(3)	11.8	(4)	18.5	(1)	10.6	(4)
KROGER CO	A /A	12/78	11.1	(4)	9.1	(5)	8.4	(6)	·6.9	(6)	9.3	(5)
AMERICAN STORES CO	A /BBB+	3/78	9.0	(5)	9.9	(4)	13.3	(3)	9.1	(5)	9.0	(6)
FISHER FOODS INC	Ba /BB*	12/78	8.5	(6)	5.2	(6)	10.4	(5)	10.9	(4)	11.0	(3)
AVERAGE			11.88		10.84		12.14		12.77		11.90	
MEDIAN			11.73		9.92		12.56		12.51		10.85	

PRETAX COVERAGE

	RATINGS	FYR END	78	77	76	75	74
ARA SERVICES	Ba /BBB*	9/78	7.97 (1)	9.09P(1)	10.71P(1)	8.19P(2)	8.38P(2)
HILTON HOTELS CORP	NR /BB*	12/78	7.69 (2)	7.07 (2)	6.31 (3)	7.60 (3)	3.07 (6)
HOST INTERNATIONAL INC	B /BB*	12/78	7.18 (3)	5.60 (4)	5.24 (6)	0.23 (9)	6.22 (3)
HARRAH'S	NR /A	6/78	5.77 (4)	5.85 (3)	8.57 (2)	8.53 (1)	8.55 (1)
METRO-GOLDWYN-MAYER INC	Baa/BBB	8/78	5.63 (5)	5.06 (6)	5.77 (5)	6.26 (4)	5.28 (5)
MCDONALD'S CORP	A /A	12/78	5.54 (6)	5.49 (5)	6.13 (4)	5.52 (5)	6.16 (4)
HOLIDAY INNS INC	NR /BBB	12/78	4.74 (7)	4.39 (7)	3.60 (7)	3.52 (6)	2.91 (7)
MARRIOTT CORP	NR /NR	12/78	4.35 (8)	3.19 (8)	2.61 (8)	2.30 (7)	2.84 (8)
RAMADA INNS	NR /B*	12/78	1.57 (9)	1.50 (9)	1.25 (9)	0.90 (8)	1.50 (9)
AVERAGE			5.60	5.25	5.58	4.78	4.99
MEDIAN			5.63	5.49	5.77	5.52	5.28

AFTER TAX COVERAGE

	RATINGS	FYR END	78	77	76	75	74
ARA SERVICES	Ba /BBB*	9/78	5.15 (1)	5.58P(1)	6.49P(1)	4.95P(2)	5.21P(2)
HILTON HOTELS CORP	NR /BB*	12/78	5.08 (2)	4.71 (2)	3.80 (4)	4.89 (3)	2.09 (6)
HOST INTERNATIONAL INC	B /BB*	12/78	4.15 (3)	3.24 (6)	3.22 (6)	0.83 (9)	3.98 (3)
METRO-GOLDWYN-MAYER INC	Baa/BBB	8/78	3.87 (4)	3.68 (3)	4.37 (3)	4.28 (4)	3.45 (5)
HARRAH'S	NR /A	6/78	3.58 (5)	3.62 (4)	4.92 (2)	5.09 (1)	5.21 (1)
MCDONALD'S CORP	A /A	12/78	3.36 (6)	3.30 (5)	3.60 (5)	3.29 (5)	3.57 (4)
HOLIDAY INNS INC	NR /BBB	12/78	3.12 (7)	2.96 (7)	2.59 (7)	2.53 (6)	2.09 (7)
MARRIOTT CORP	NR /NR	12/78	2.91 (8)	2.29 (8)	1.96 (8)	1.74 (7)	2.08 (8)
RAMADA INNS	NR /B*	12/78	1.37 (9)	1.36 (9)	1.19 (9)	1.04 (8)	1.40 (9)
AVERAGE			3.62	3.42	3.57	3.18	3.23
MEDIAN			3.58	3.30	3.60	3.29	3.45

AFTER TAX COV (INCL RENTS)

	RATINGS	FYR END	78	77	76	75	74
HILTON HOTELS CORP	NR /BB*	12/78	4.15 (1)	3.52 (1)	2.77 (3)	3.33 (2)	NA (-)
METRO-GOLDWYN-MAYER INC	Baa/BBB	8/78	3.55 (2)	3.36 (2)	3.84 (1)	3.69 (1)	2.99 (2)
HARRAH'S	NR /A	6/78	2.95 (3)	2.96 (3)	3.37 (2)	3.11 (3)	3.44 (1)
MCDONALD'S CORP	A /A	12/78	2.44 (4)	2.41 (4)	2.26 (5)	2.11 (5)	2.10 (4)
ARA SERVICES	Ba /BBB*	9/78	2.13 (5)	2.12P(5)	2.30P(4)	2.23P(4)	2.57P(3)
MARRIOTT CORP	NR /NR	12/78	1.95 (6)	1.55 (7)	1.47 (7)	1.33 (7)	1.45 (6)
HOLIDAY INNS INC	NR /BBB	12/78	1.83 (7)	1.81 (6)	1.58 (6)	1.62 (6)	1.47 (5)
HOST INTERNATIONAL INC	B /BB*	12/78	1.39 (8)	1.38 (8)	1.34 (8)	0.98 (9)	1.38 (7)
RAMADA INNS	NR /B*	12/78	1.32 (9)	1.28 (9)	1.15 (9)	1.03 (8)	1.33 (8)
AVERAGE			2.41	2.27	2.23	2.16	2.09
MEDIAN			2.13	2.12	2.26	2.11	1.79

NET INCOME AS % NET SALES

	RATINGS	FYR END	78	77	76	75	74
HILTON HOTELS CORP	NR /BB*	12/78	15.2 (1)	10.8 (2)	9.0 (3)	12.1 (2)	4.6 (5)
METRO-GOLDWYN-MAYER INC	Baa/BBB	8/78	12.3 (2)	11.5 (1)	12.0 (1)	12.5 (1)	9.5 (1)
MCDONALD'S CORP	A /A	12/78	9.9 (3)	9.9 (3)	9.5 (2)	9.4 (3)	9.4 (2)
HARRAH'S	NR /A	6/78	9.1 (4)	9.1 (4)	8.3 (4)	8.3 (4)	8.2 (3)
HOLIDAY INNS INC	NR /BBB	12/78	5.3 (5)	5.1 (5)	4.1 (5)	4.5 (5)	3.3 (8)
HOST INTERNATIONAL INC	B /BB*	12/78	4.4 (6)	4.0 (6)	3.7 (6)	-0.2 (9)	4.0 (6)
MARRIOTT CORP	NR /NR	12/78	4.3 (7)	3.5 (7)	3.5 (7)	3.0 (6)	3.9 (7)
RAMADA INNS	NR /B*	12/78	3.3 (8)	3.2 (8)	2.0 (9)	0.5 (8)	4.8 (4)
ARA SERVICES	Ba /BBB*	9/78	2.7 (9)	2.5 (9)	2.9 (8)	2.5 (7)	3.0 (9)
AVERAGE			7.40	6.62	6.11	5.83	5.64
MEDIAN			5.29	5.12	4.13	4.54	4.55

Hotel Industry

LTD/CAPITALIZATION (%)

	RATINGS	FYR END	78		77		76		75		74	
ARA SERVICES	Ba /BBB*	9/78	27.6	(1)	26.2	(1)	22.5	(1)	24.9	(1)	30.9	(2)
HOLIDAY INNS INC	NR /BBB	12/78	36.8	(2)	38.1	(2)	36.0	(4)	40.0	(4)	44.2	(3)
HILTON HOTELS CORP	NR /BB*	12/78	37.3	(3)	48.1	(5)	30.8	(2)	36.0	(3)	46.8	(5)
HARRAH'S	NR /A	6/78	38.1	(4)	43.6	(3)	35.8	(3)	26.1	(2)	27.9	(1)
HOST INTERNATIONAL INC	B /BB*	12/78	40.5	(5)	45.3	(4)	45.7	(5)	46.6	(6)	46.1	(4)
MARRIOTT CORP	NR /NR	12/78	44.7	(6)	49.1	(6)	54.8	(8)	58.7	(8)	55.7	(8)
METRO-GOLDWYN-MAYER INC	Baa/BBB	8/78	47.1	(7)	49.9	(7)	52.2	(7)	40.3	(5)	48.1	(6)
MCDONALD'S CORP	A /A	12/78	49.6	(8)	51.7	(8)	48.6	(6)	51.7	(7)	51.7	(7)
RAMADA INNS	NR /B*	12/78	69.7	(9)	65.9	(9)	69.7	(9)	72.4	(9)	67.6	(9)
AVERAGE			43.49		46.43		44.00		44.10		46.55	
MEDIAN			40.47		48.09		45.70		40.35		46.83	

TOT LIABILITY/TOT STK EQUITY

	RATINGS	FYR END	78		77		76		75		74	
HARRAH'S	NR /A	6/78	79.1	(1)	96.8	(2)	78.8	(2)	57.5	(1)	54.9	(1)
ARA SERVICES	Ba /BBB*	9/78	100.5	(2)	88.8	(1)	80.7	(3)	89.6	(2)	100.9	(2)
HILTON HOTELS CORP	NR /BB*	12/78	101.6	(3)	133.7	(4)	77.0	(1)	95.9	(3)	128.0	(4)
HOLIDAY INNS INC	NR /BBB	12/78	116.5	(4)	105.9	(3)	98.4	(4)	109.4	(4)	126.1	(3)
HOST INTERNATIONAL INC	B /BB*	12/78	124.4	(5)	142.9	(5)	145.2	(6)	137.3	(5)	132.4	(5)
MARRIOTT CORP	NR /NR	12/78	138.9	(6)	145.9	(6)	167.7	(7)	189.8	(8)	177.3	(7)
MCDONALD'S CORP	A /A	12/78	145.3	(7)	155.8	(7)	144.4	(5)	158.1	(7)	158.2	(6)
METRO-GOLDWYN-MAYER INC	Baa/BBB	8/78	163.3	(8)	170.3	(8)	171.3	(8)	153.3	(6)	203.0	(8)
RAMADA INNS	NR /B*	12/78	299.9	(9)	257.2	(9)	302.1	(9)	336.6	(9)	260.3	(9)
AVERAGE			141.07		144.15		140.62		147.51		149.02	
MEDIAN			124.40		142.90		144.42		137.28		132.44	

LTD/NET PLANT (%)

	RATINGS	FYR END	78		77		76		75		74	
HOLIDAY INNS INC	NR /BBB	12/78	41.8	(1)	42.4	(1)	38.9	(2)	44.4	(3)	47.7	(2)
ARA SERVICES	Ba /BBB*	9/78	44.6	(2)	43.9	(2)	36.8	(1)	44.3	(2)	57.5	(5)
MARRIOTT CORP	NR /NR	12/78	45.4	(3)	49.8	(3)	56.1	(6)	61.8	(7)	59.2	(6)
MCDONALD'S CORP	A /A	12/78	49.0	(4)	51.6	(4)	48.9	(5)	52.9	(4)	53.6	(3)
HARRAH'S	NR /A	6/78	49.7	(5)	58.0	(6)	42.1	(3)	26.5	(1)	29.0	(1)
HOST INTERNATIONAL INC	B /BB*	12/78	51.6	(6)	55.7	(5)	60.6	(7)	58.7	(6)	62.5	(7)
HILTON HOTELS CORP	NR /BB*	12/78	55.5	(7)	72.1	(7)	47.3	(4)	54.4	(5)	56.2	(4)
METRO-GOLDWYN-MAYER INC	Baa/BBB	8/78	66.5	(8)	73.9	(9)	78.2	(9)	75.0	(8)	90.3	(9)
RAMADA INNS	NR /B*	12/78	86.8	(9)	73.4	(8)	77.3	(8)	79.3	(9)	81.6	(8)
AVERAGE			54.54		57.86		54.00		55.25		59.74	
MEDIAN			49.66		55.71		48.89		54.38		57.50	

NET TANG ASSETS/LTD (%)

	RATINGS	FYR END	78		77		76		75		74	
ARA SERVICES	Ba /BBB*	9/78	314.9	(1)	332.9	(1)	384.6	(1)	342.6	(2)	277.7	(2)
HOLIDAY INNS INC	NR /BBB	12/78	264.6	(2)	255.9	(2)	269.5	(3)	234.9	(4)	213.8	(3)
HILTON HOTELS CORP	NR /BB*	12/78	264.1	(3)	205.4	(4)	320.3	(2)	272.8	(3)	211.3	(5)
HOST INTERNATIONAL INC	B /BB*	12/78	226.8	(4)	212.7	(3)	213.9	(5)	208.7	(5)	211.9	(4)
HARRAH'S	NR /A	6/78	224.7	(5)	189.6	(6)	247.5	(4)	381.5	(1)	356.6	(1)
MARRIOTT CORP	NR /NR	12/78	214.6	(6)	193.3	(5)	172.5	(7)	159.4	(8)	166.8	(7)
MCDONALD'S CORP	A /A	12/78	192.9	(7)	184.4	(7)	195.4	(6)	183.5	(6)	181.4	(6)
METRO-GOLDWYN-MAYER INC	Baa/BBB	8/78	161.8	(8)	159.0	(8)	150.3	(8)	173.2	(7)	148.4	(8)
RAMADA INNS	NR /B*	12/78	121.2	(9)	145.9	(9)	138.8	(9)	132.5	(9)	144.3	(9)
AVERAGE			220.63		208.80		232.52		232.12		212.47	
MEDIAN			224.71		193.33		213.85		208.71		211.26	

CASH FLOW/LTD (%)

	RATINGS	FYR END	78		77		76		75		74	
ARA SERVICES	Ba /BBB*	9/78	61.8	(1)	64.6	(1)	81.6	(1)	67.9	(1)	55.9	(3)
HOST INTERNATIONAL INC	B /BB*	12/78	54.3	(2)	41.1	(3)	39.3	(4)	60.3	(4)	33.7	(4)
METRO-GOLDWYN-MAYER INC	Baa/BBB	8/78	51.5	(3)	44.9	(2)	33.5	(7)	66.4	(2)	72.5	(1)
HILTON HOTELS CORP	NR /BB*	12/78	50.5	(4)	27.8	(7)	41.6	(2)	28.9	(7)	22.0	(8)
HOLIDAY INNS INC	NR /BBB	12/78	38.5	(5)	40.2	(4)	40.3	(3)	33.5	(5)	30.4	(5)
HARRAH'S	NR /A	6/78	37.1	(6)	30.9	(5)	38.9	(5)	63.3	(3)	56.1	(2)
MARRIOTT CORP	NR /NR	12/78	36.0	(7)	27.7	(8)	22.9	(8)	19.4	(8)	22.2	(7)
MCDONALD'S CORP	A /A	12/78	32.7	(8)	30.8	(6)	34.0	(6)	30.9	(6)	29.7	(6)
RAMADA INNS	NR /B*	12/78	10.2	(9)	11.4	(9)	7.6	(9)	6.8	(9)	9.3	(9)
AVERAGE			41.40		35.48		37.74		41.95		36.88	
MEDIAN			38.53		30.91		38.92		33.51		30.40	

NET CASH FL/CAP EXP (%)

	RATINGS	FYR END	78		77		76		75		74	
HOST INTERNATIONAL INC	B /BB*	12/78	123.2	(1)	84.6	(5)	113.6	(4)	227.8	(2)	55.8	(7)
HILTON HOTELS CORP	NR /BB*	12/78	120.3	(2)	52.8	(9)	126.1	(3)	174.9	(3)	79.0	(4)
HARRAH'S	NR /A	6/78	104.9	(3)	79.5	(6)	82.5	(7)	86.1	(6)	74.6	(5)
METRO-GOLDWYN-MAYER INC	Baa/BBB	8/78	93.5	(4)	76.1	(7)	318.1	(1)	615.0	(1)	175.1	(1)
MARRIOTT CORP	NR /NR	12/78	86.7	(5)	129.4	(2)	58.9	(9)	44.2	(8)	56.0	(6)
ARA SERVICES	Ba /BBB*	9/78	83.9	(6)	91.9	(4)	99.7	(5)	134.9	(5)	119.6	(2)
MCDONALD'S CORP	A /A	12/78	68.6	(7)	68.3	(8)	71.7	(8)	61.4	(7)	NA	(-)
HOLIDAY INNS INC	NR /BBB	12/78	62.9	(8)	97.9	(3)	133.1	(2)	153.7	(4)	100.5	(3)
RAMADA INNS	NR /B*	12/78	61.5	(9)	154.6	(1)	87.8	(6)	35.1	(9)	31.2	(8)
AVERAGE			89.50		92.78		121.26		170.33		86.49	
MEDIAN			86.69		84.56		99.67		134.86		76.83	

AFT TAX RET ON COM EQTY (%)

	RATINGS	FYR END	78		77		76		75		74	
METRO-GOLDWYN-MAYER INC	Baa/BBB	8/78	26.2	(1)	21.0	(2)	22.1	(1)	25.8	(1)	20.4	(1)
HILTON HOTELS CORP	NR /BB*	12/78	23.1	(2)	18.3	(3)	13.6	(5)	20.2	(3)	8.6	(7)
MCDONALD'S CORP	A /A	12/78	20.4	(3)	21.3	(1)	20.9	(2)	21.0	(2)	20.4	(2)
HOST INTERNATIONAL INC	B /BB*	12/78	19.3	(4)	17.4	(4)	16.1	(3)	-1.1	(9)	15.8	(3)
HARRAH'S	NR /A	6/78	15.2	(5)	15.6	(5)	14.3	(4)	14.6	(4)	14.3	(4)
MARRIOTT CORP	NR /NR	12/78	13.0	(6)	10.2	(8)	9.8	(7)	8.6	(7)	10.9	(6)
ARA SERVICES	Ba /BBB*	9/78	12.3	(7)	11.1	(6)	12.1	(6)	10.9	(5)	13.3	(5)
HOLIDAY INNS INC	NR /BBB	12/78	11.4	(8)	10.4	(7)	8.4	(8)	9.3	(6)	7.6	(8)
RAMADA INNS	NR /B*	12/78	6.9	(9)	6.3	(9)	3.9	(9)	0.9	(8)	6.5	(9)
AVERAGE			16.41		14.61		13.47		12.25		13.10	
MEDIAN			15.15		15.56		13.56		10.88		13.28	

RET ON TOT ASSETS (%)

	RATINGS	FYR END	78		77		76		75		74	
HILTON HOTELS CORP	NR /BB*	12/78	21.2	(1)	14.4	(5)	14.8	(4)	18.8	(4)	9.7	(7)
HOST INTERNATIONAL INC	B /BB*	12/78	19.6	(2)	17.9	(2)	15.5	(3)	0.6	(9)	14.2	(4)
MCDONALD'S CORP	A /A	12/78	19.5	(3)	19.8	(1)	20.2	(1)	19.6	(1)	18.9	(1)
METRO-GOLDWYN-MAYER INC	Baa/BBB	8/78	19.5	(4)	14.7	(4)	13.9	(5)	19.5	(2)	14.5	(3)
HARRAH'S	NR /A	6/78	18.9	(5)	17.7	(3)	17.5	(2)	19.4	(3)	18.7	(2)
MARRIOTT CORP	NR /NR	12/78	12.4	(6)	10.2	(8)	9.9	(7)	9.2	(7)	10.3	(6)
HOLIDAY INNS INC	NR /BBB	12/78	11.8	(7)	11.3	(7)	9.6	(8)	10.2	(6)	9.1	(8)
ARA SERVICES	Ba /BBB*	9/78	11.3	(8)	11.5	(6)	12.9	(6)	11.7	(5)	13.0	(5)
RAMADA INNS	NR /B*	12/78	7.3	(9)	7.4	(9)	6.2	(9)	4.7	(8)	6.7	(9)
AVERAGE			15.72		13.87		13.41		12.64		12.81	
MEDIAN			18.91		14.37		13.93		11.69		13.02	

PRETAX COVERAGE

	RATINGS	FYR END	78	77	76	75	74
BALLY MFG CORP	BA /BB*	12/78	15.14 (1)	12.44 (1)	7.38 (1)	5.29 (2)	5.56 (2)
TWENTIETH CENTURY-FOX FILM	Ba /BB*	12/78	8.53 (2)	11.79 (2)	3.86 (5)	8.59 (1)	7.32 (1)
BRUNSWICK CORP	Ba /BB*	12/78	4.92 (3)	4.84 (5)	5.60P(3)	2.60 (5)	4.18 (4)
AMF INC	Baa/BBB	12/78	4.66 (4)	4.87 (4)	4.72 (4)	3.60 (4)	2.57 (5)
OUTBOARD MARINE CORP	A /BBB	9/78	4.52 (5)	6.46 (3)	6.35 (2)	4.52 (3)	5.06 (3)
AVERAGE			7.55	8.08	5.58	4.92	4.94
MEDIAN			4.92	6.46	5.60	4.52	5.06

AFTER TAX COVERAGE

	RATINGS	FYR END	78	77	76	75	74
BALLY MFG CORP	BA /BB*	12/78	8.52 (1)	6.77 (2)	4.29 (1)	2.93 (3)	3.22 (3)
TWENTIETH CENTURY-FOX FILM	Ba /BB*	12/78	5.55 (2)	8.12 (1)	2.63 (5)	5.10 (1)	4.42 (1)
BRUNSWICK CORP	Ba /BB*	12/78	3.20 (3)	3.10 (4)	3.33P(3)	1.91 (5)	2.70 (4)
AMF INC	Baa/BBB	12/78	3.06 (4)	3.05 (5)	2.99 (4)	2.35 (4)	1.80 (5)
OUTBOARD MARINE CORP	A /BBB	9/78	2.90 (5)	4.03 (3)	3.95 (2)	3.06 (2)	3.33 (2)
AVERAGE			4.65	5.01	3.44	3.07	3.09
MEDIAN			3.20	4.03	3.33	2.93	3.22

AFTER TAX COV (INCL RENTS)

	RATINGS	FYR END	78	77	76	75	74
BALLY MFG CORP	BA /BB*	12/78	4.11 (1)	3.25 (2)	2.50 (2)	2.06 (3)	2.43 (1)
OUTBOARD MARINE CORP	A /BBB	9/78	2.13 (2)	2.70 (3)	2.81 (1)	2.33 (2)	2.34 (3)
BRUNSWICK CORP	Ba /BB*	12/78	2.13 (3)	2.01 (5)	2.12P(3)	1.49 (5)	1.95 (4)
AMF INC	Baa/BBB	12/78	2.11 (4)	2.06 (4)	2.05 (4)	1.82 (4)	1.53 (5)
TWENTIETH CENTURY-FOX FILM	Ba /BB*	12/78	NA (-)	4.97 (1)	1.77 (5)	2.70 (1)	2.36 (2)
AVERAGE			2.62	3.00	2.25	2.08	2.12
MEDIAN			2.13	2.70	2.12	2.06	2.34

NET INCOME AS % NET SALES

	RATINGS	FYR END	78	77	76	75	74
BALLY MFG CORP	BA /BB*	12/78	10.4 (1)	8.1 (2)	5.8 (1)	4.5 (3)	6.9 (1)
TWENTIETH CENTURY-FOX FILM	Ba /BB*	12/78	9.6 (2)	10.1 (1)	3.0 (5)	5.1 (1)	4.5 (3)
BRUNSWICK CORP	Ba /BB*	12/78	4.2 (3)	3.7 (4)	4.6 (3)	2.2 (5)	4.7 (2)
OUTBOARD MARINE CORP	A /BBB	9/78	3.6 (4)	4.7 (3)	4.7 (2)	4.7 (2)	3.5 (4)
AMF INC	Baa/BBB	12/78	3.4 (5)	3.5 (5)	3.4 (4)	3.2 (4)	2.2 (5)
AVERAGE			6.22	6.02	4.31	3.94	4.34
MEDIAN			4.16	4.73	4.56	4.51	4.47

LTD/CAPITALIZATION (%)

	RATINGS	FYR END	78	77	76	75	74
OUTBOARD MARINE CORP	A /BBB	9/78	31.4 (1)	25.2 (1)	26.8 (1)	25.6 (1)	24.4 (1)
BALLY MFG CORP	BA /BB*	12/78	32.0 (2)	27.2 (2)	27.7 (2)	30.1 (2)	34.0 (2)
AMF INC	Baa/BBB	12/78	32.7 (3)	36.8 (5)	40.2 (4)	42.3 (5)	37.0 (3)
BRUNSWICK CORP	Ba /BB*	12/78	34.7 (4)	31.6 (3)	32.8 (3)	37.2 (3)	48.3 (5)
TWENTIETH CENTURY-FOX FILM	Ba /BB*	12/78	36.8 (5)	36.5 (4)	43.5 (5)	41.6 (4)	39.9 (4)
AVERAGE			33.54	31.47	34.20	35.36	36.73
MEDIAN			32.73	31.59	32.80	37.22	37.03

TOT LIABILITY/TOT STK EQUITY

	RATINGS	FYR END	78		77		76		75		74	
OUTBOARD MARINE CORP	A /BBB	9/78	92.1	(1)	78.7	(1)	77.7	(1)	74.4	(1)	77.8	(1)
BALLY MFG CORP	BA /BB*	12/78	92.9	(2)	91.3	(2)	98.1	(2)	113.6	(3)	136.3	(2)
BRUNSWICK CORP	Ba /BB*	12/78	101.8	(3)	91.5	(3)	91.5	(3)	111.3	(2)	142.6	(3)
AMF INC	Baa/BBB	12/78	137.2	(4)	142.3	(4)	161.2	(4)	161.8	(4)	180.9	(5)
TWENTIETH CENTURY-FOX FILM	Ba /BB*	12/78	137.7	(5)	153.7	(5)	179.5	(5)	178.5	(5)	174.9	(4)
AVERAGE			112.35		111.50		123.39		127.94		142.49	
MEDIAN			101.81		91.51		100.44		113.61		142.55	

LTD/NET PLANT (%)

	RATINGS	FYR END	78		77		76		75		74	
OUTBOARD MARINE CORP	A /BBB	9/78	68.2	(1)	49.2	(1)	56.2	(1)	53.2	(1)	52.8	(1)
AMF INC	Baa/BBB	12/78	70.1	(2)	80.3	(3)	86.8	(3)	90.3	(3)	80.5	(2)
BRUNSWICK CORP	Ba /BB*	12/78	84.0	(3)	74.5	(2)	81.3	(2)	84.1	(2)	137.5	(5)
TWENTIETH CENTURY-FOX FILM	Ba /BB*	12/78	104.7	(4)	95.8	(4)	110.4	(4)	108.0	(4)	108.7	(3)
BALLY MFG CORP	BA /BB*	12/78	121.3	(5)	115.5	(5)	122.2	(5)	127.5	(5)	135.4	(4)
AVERAGE			89.65		83.05		91.38		92.62		102.98	
MEDIAN			83.98		80.26		86.83		90.35		108.68	

NET TANG ASSETS/LTD (%)

	RATINGS	FYR END	78		77		76		75		74	
OUTBOARD MARINE CORP	A /BBB	9/78	312.0	(1)	384.9	(1)	366.8	(1)	384.4	(1)	402.8	(1)
AMF INC	Baa/BBB	12/78	284.8	(2)	250.7	(4)	229.7	(4)	218.4	(4)	246.4	(2)
BALLY MFG CORP	BA /BB*	12/78	269.8	(3)	311.0	(2)	284.2	(3)	240.7	(3)	223.1	(3)
BRUNSWICK CORP	Ba /BB*	12/78	254.3	(4)	309.3	(3)	293.2	(2)	264.5	(2)	205.0	(4)
TWENTIETH CENTURY-FOX FILM	Ba /BB*	12/78	195.0	(5)	203.4	(5)	145.2	(5)	150.2	(5)	147.5	(5)
AVERAGE			263.17		291.85		263.82		251.63		244.96	
MEDIAN			269.76		309.34		284.21		240.68		223.12	

CASH FLOW/LTD (%)

	RATINGS	FYR END	78		77		76		75		74	
BALLY MFG CORP	BA /BB*	12/78	72.7	(1)	79.2	(1)	82.0	(1)	57.3	(2)	61.4	(1)
TWENTIETH CENTURY-FOX FILM	Ba /BB*	12/78	56.1	(2)	68.0	(2)	17.7	(5)	27.2	(4)	25.0	(4)
AMF INC	Baa/BBB	12/78	49.4	(3)	44.0	(4)	36.5	(4)	33.0	(3)	33.1	(3)
OUTBOARD MARINE CORP	A /BBB	9/78	46.5	(4)	67.4	(3)	60.8	(2)	59.7	(1)	58.9	(2)
BRUNSWICK CORP	Ba /BB*	12/78	35.6	(5)	41.4	(5)	47.1	(3)	26.3	(5)	21.8	(5)
AVERAGE			52.05		60.00		48.83		40.70		40.03	
MEDIAN			49.40		67.43		47.14		33.01		33.08	

NET CASH FL/CAP EXP (%)

	RATINGS	FYR END	78		77		76		75		74	
TWENTIETH CENTURY-FOX FILM	Ba /BB*	12/78	461.7	(1)	925.2	(1)	85.9	(5)	138.0	(1)	150.0	(2)
BALLY MFG CORP	BA /BB*	12/78	147.0	(2)	169.6	(2)	212.8	(2)	137.5	(2)	151.1	(1)
BRUNSWICK CORP	Ba /BB*	12/78	137.5	(3)	121.1	(4)	225.4	(1)	81.9 V(5)		92.2 V(3)	
OUTBOARD MARINE CORP	A /BBB	9/78	114.6	(4)	97.6	(5)	117.4	(3)	104.9	(3)	67.8	(4)
AMF INC	Baa/BBB	12/78	101.9	(5)	126.5	(3)	88.8	(4)	84.4	(4)	61.8	(5)
AVERAGE			192.53		287.98		146.07		109.34		104.58	
MEDIAN			137.47		126.48		117.35		104.91		92.17	

Leisure Time Industry

AFT TAX RET ON COM EQTY (%)

	RATINGS	FYR END	78		77		76		75		74	
TWENTIETH CENTURY-FOX FILM	Ba /BB*	12/78	27.1	(1)	29.7	(1)	8.7	(5)	15.0	(1)	12.9	(2)
BALLY MFG CORP	BA /BB*	12/78	23.0	(2)	19.2	(2)	14.8	(1)	11.1	(2)	18.5	(1)
AMF INC	Baa/BBB	12/78	11.8	(3)	12.6	(3)	12.2	(2)	10.8	(3)	7.7	(5)
BRUNSWICK CORP	Ba /BB*	12/78	11.1	(4)	9.7	(5)	11.7	(3)	5.9	(5)	12.4	(3)
OUTBOARD MARINE CORP	A /BBB	9/78	9.3	(5)	11.6	(4)	11.2	(4)	10.2	(4)	7.7	(4)
AVERAGE			16.46		16.55		11.72		10.61		11.84	
MEDIAN			11.77		12.55		11.68		10.83		12.41	

RET ON TOT ASSETS (%)

	RATINGS	FYR END	78		77		76		75		74	
BALLY MFG CORP	BA /BB*	12/78	24.0	(1)	21.6	(1)	16.8	(1)	14.3	(1)	19.6	(1)
TWENTIETH CENTURY-FOX FILM	Ba /BB*	12/78	19.3	(2)	19.4	(2)	7.4	(5)	11.3	(3)	10.0	(3)
OUTBOARD MARINE CORP	A /BBB	9/78	11.5	(3)	13.8	(3)	13.6	(3)	12.9	(2)	9.4	(4)
BRUNSWICK CORP	Ba /BB*	12/78	11.3	(4)	12.0	(5)	14.0	(2)	8.3	(5)	12.6	(2)
AMF INC	Baa/BBB	12/78	11.2	(5)	12.3	(4)	11.0	(4)	11.0	(4)	8.9	(5)
AVERAGE			15.46		15.84		12.54		11.56		12.10	
MEDIAN			11.52		13.83		13.58		11.28		10.03	

PRETAX COVERAGE

	RATINGS	FYR END	78	77	76	75	74
BUCYRUS-ERIE CO	A /A	12/78	12.08 (1)	11.11 (3)	9.15 (5)	7.94 (4)	8.87 (1)
PARKER-HANNIFIN CORP	Baa/BBB*	6/78	10.46 (2)	10.61 (5)	7.23 (9)	5.39 (6)	5.84 (7)
STUDEBAKER-WORTHINGTON INC	A /A	12/78	10.37 (3)	10.80 (4)	8.14 (6)	2.88 (11)	1.79 (13)
REXNORD INC	A /A	10/78	10.20P(4)	9.50P(7)	10.58P(3)	6.53P(5)	4.34P(8)
CATERPILLAR TRACTOR CO	Aa /AA	12/78	10.17 (5)	9.19 (8)	9.69 (4)	8.65 (3)	6.77 (5)
JOY MFG CO	A /A+	9/78	9.85 (6)	13.51 (1)	13.59 (1)	8.79 (2)	6.91 (4)
COMBUSTION ENGINEERING INC	A /A	12/78	9.59 (7)	12.39 (2)	13.49 (2)	10.84 (1)	8.03 (3)
ALLIS-CHALMERS CORP	A /A-	12/78	7.10 (8)	9.91 (6)	7.95 (7)	3.02 (10)	2.32 (12)
CLARK EQUIPMENT CO	A /A	12/78	7.02 (9)	4.94 (12)	3.59 (12)	2.34 (12)	2.70 (10)
DEERE & CO	Aa /AA-	10/78	5.77 (10)	7.43 (9)	7.72 (8)	4.84 (9)	8.48 (2)
INGERSOLL-RAND CO	A /AA	12/78	5.26P(11)	5.09P(11)	4.53P(11)	5.29P(7)	6.03P(6)
FMC CORP	A /A	12/78	4.98 (12)	5.70 (10)	5.99 (10)	4.88 (8)	3.55 (9)
INTL HARVESTER CO	A /BBB	10/78	3.10 (13)	3.65 (13)	3.22 (13)	2.22 (13)	2.61 (11)
AVERAGE			8.15	8.76	8.07	5.66	5.25
MEDIAN			9.59	9.50	7.95	5.29	5.84

AFTER TAX COVERAGE

	RATINGS	FYR END	78	77	76	75	74
BUCYRUS-ERIE CO	A /A	12/78	6.82 (1)	6.69 (3)	5.79 (5)	5.02 (4)	5.22 (2)
CATERPILLAR TRACTOR CO	Aa /AA	12/78	6.42 (2)	5.69 (7)	6.18 (3)	5.68 (2)	4.63 (4)
PARKER-HANNIFIN CORP	Baa/BBB*	6/78	5.99 (3)	5.73 (6)	3.99 (10)	3.15 (9)	3.47 (7)
REXNORD INC	A /A	10/78	5.85P(4)	5.48P(8)	5.95P(4)	3.87P(5)	2.72P(9)
STUDEBAKER-WORTHINGTON INC	A /A	12/78	5.75 (5)	5.99 (4)	4.58 (7)	1.99 (10)	1.48 (13)
JOY MFG CO	A /A+	9/78	5.49 (6)	7.48 (1)	7.46 (2)	5.18 (3)	4.04 (5)
COMBUSTION ENGINEERING INC	A /A	12/78	5.31 (7)	6.70 (2)	7.60 (1)	6.39 (1)	4.80 (3)
ALLIS-CHALMERS CORP	A /A-	12/78	4.25 (8)	5.87 (5)	4.50 (8)	1.98 (11)	1.73 (12)
CLARK EQUIPMENT CO	A /A	12/78	4.06 (9)	2.91 (12)	3.04 (11)	1.72 (12)	1.95 (10)
FMC CORP	A /A	12/78	3.64 (10)	3.89 (10)	4.12 (9)	3.74 (6)	2.98 (8)
DEERE & CO	Aa /AA-	12/78	3.64 (11)	4.56 (9)	4.81 (6)	3.30 (8)	5.26 (1)
INGERSOLL-RAND CO	A /AA	12/78	3.34P(12)	3.16P(11)	3.03P(12)	3.53P(7)	3.83P(6)
INTL HARVESTER CO	A /BBB	10/78	1.88 (13)	2.12 (13)	2.05 (13)	1.52 (13)	1.80 (11)
AVERAGE			4.80	5.10	4.85	3.62	3.38
MEDIAN			5.31	5.69	4.58	3.53	3.47

AFTER TAX COV (INCL RENTS)

	RATINGS	FYR END	78	77	76	75	74
STUDEBAKER-WORTHINGTON INC	A /A	12/78	3.16 (1)	3.30 (3)	2.93 (3)	1.70 (6)	1.37 (6)
JOY MFG CO	A /A+	9/78	3.16 (2)	3.97 (1)	4.15 (1)	3.32 (1)	2.52 (2)
CLARK EQUIPMENT CO	A /A	12/78	3.11 (3)	2.38 (7)	2.55 (5)	1.58 (7)	1.75 (5)
DEERE & CO	Aa /AA-	10/78	2.92 (4)	3.39 (2)	3.39 (2)	2.63 (4)	NA (-)
FMC CORP	A /A	12/78	2.74 (5)	2.84 (4)	2.93 (4)	2.82 (3)	2.39 (3)
COMBUSTION ENGINEERING INC	A /A	12/78	2.42 (6)	2.60 (5)	2.39 (7)	2.17 (5)	2.07 (4)
INTL HARVESTER CO	A /BBB	10/78	1.63 (7)	NA (-)	NA (-)	NA (-)	NA (-)
ALLIS-CHALMERS CORP	A /A-	12/78	NA (-)	NA (-)	NA (-)	NA (-)	NA (-)
BUCYRUS-ERIE CO	A /A	12/78	NA (-)	NA (-)	NA (-)	NA (-)	NA (-)
CATERPILLAR TRACTOR CO	Aa /AA	12/78	NA (-)	NA (-)	NA (-)	NA (-)	NA (-)
INGERSOLL-RAND CO	A /AA	12/78	NA (-)	2.59P(6)	2.49P(6)	2.86P(2)	3.03P(1)
PARKER-HANNIFIN CORP	Baa/BBB*	6/78	NA (-)	NA (-)	NA (-)	NA (-)	NA (-)
REXNORD INC	A /A	10/78	NA (-)	NA (-)	NA (-)	NA (-)	NA (-)
AVERAGE			2.73	3.01	2.98	2.44	2.19
MEDIAN			2.92	2.84	2.93	2.63	2.23

Machinery Industry

NET INCOME AS % NET SALES

	RATINGS	FYR END	78		77		76		75		74	
BUCYRUS-ERIE CO	A /A	12/78	10.4	(1)	9.6	(1)	8.5	(1)	8.5	(1)	7.9	(1)
CATERPILLAR TRACTOR CO	Aa /AA	12/78	7.8	(2)	7.6	(2)	7.6	(3)	8.0	(2)	5.6	(4)
DEERE & CO	Aa /AA-	10/78	6.4	(3)	7.1	(4)	7.7	(2)	6.1	(5)	6.6	(3)
REXNORD INC	A /A	10/78	6.0	(4)	5.9	(5)	5.7	(5)	4.5	(8)	3.6	(9)
INGERSOLL-RAND CO	A /AA	12/78	5.7	(5)	5.6	(7)	5.6	(6)	7.0	(3)	7.1	(2)
PARKER-HANNIFIN CORP	Baa/BBB*	6/78	5.7	(6)	5.6	(6)	4.9	(9)	4.7	(7)	4.6	(5)
CLARK EQUIPMENT CO	A /A	12/78	5.5	(7)	4.6	(10)	5.4	(7)	3.3	(9)	3.7	(8)
JOY MFG CO	A /A+	9/78	5.5	(8)	7.1	(3)	7.5	(4)	6.9	(4)	4.6	(6)
STUDEBAKER-WORTHINGTON INC	A /A	12/78	5.3	(9)	5.4	(9)	5.4	(7)	2.5	(11)	0.9	(13)
FMC CORP	A /A	12/78	4.8	(10)	5.5	(8)	5.3	(8)	4.7	(6)	3.9	(7)
ALLIS-CHALMERS CORP	A /A-	12/78	4.3	(11)	4.4	(11)	3.9	(11)	2.0	(13)	1.8	(12)
COMBUSTION ENGINEERING INC	A /A	12/78	3.4	(12)	3.3	(13)	3.0	(13)	2.6	(10)	2.8	(10)
INTL HARVESTER CO	A /BBB	10/78	2.8	(13)	3.4	(12)	3.2	(12)	2.2	(12)	2.4	(11)
AVERAGE			5.67		5.78		5.57		4.85		4.27	
MEDIAN			5.54		5.57		5.40		4.70		3.90	

LTD/CAPITALIZATION (%)

	RATINGS	FYR END	78		77		76		75		74	
JOY MFG CO	A /A+	9/78	15.7	(1)	14.6	(1)	16.6	(1)	17.7	(1)	25.2	(4)
REXNORD INC	A /A	10/78	21.6	(2)	22.5	(4)	21.9	(4)	26.0	(3)	27.5	(5)
COMBUSTION ENGINEERING INC	A /A	12/78	22.0	(3)	25.0	(7)	21.4	(3)	21.2	(2)	23.1	(2)
CLARK EQUIPMENT CO	A /A	12/78	22.1	(4)	26.0	(8)	27.8	(8)	32.1	(8)	41.6	(12)
BUCYRUS-ERIE CO	A /A	12/78	23.8	(5)	26.1	(9)	29.0	(10)	29.6	(7)	30.0	(7)
STUDEBAKER-WORTHINGTON INC	A /A	12/78	24.4	(6)	15.0	(2)	16.7	(2)	35.5	(10)	49.3	(13)
PARKER-HANNIFIN CORP	Baa/BBB*	6/78	24.5	(7)	28.0	(10)	28.3	(9)	36.1	(12)	39.2	(11)
CATERPILLAR TRACTOR CO	Aa /AA	12/78	27.0	(8)	30.1	(11)	33.8	(11)	32.6	(9)	30.9	(8)
DEERE & CO	Aa /AA-	10/78	27.4	(9)	24.4	(6)	26.4	(7)	26.2	(4)	16.9	(1)
INGERSOLL-RAND CO	A /AA	12/78	27.6	(10)	23.4	(5)	26.2	(6)	28.5	(6)	25.1	(3)
ALLIS-CHALMERS CORP	A /A-	12/78	28.3	(11)	21.3	(3)	23.2	(5)	28.5	(5)	29.8	(6)
FMC CORP	A /A	12/78	29.9	(12)	32.9	(12)	34.4	(12)	35.7	(11)	31.1	(9)
INTL HARVESTER CO	A /BBB	10/78	33.2	(13)	34.8	(13)	36.9	(13)	39.4	(13)	31.4	(10)
AVERAGE			25.19		24.94		26.35		29.93		30.85	
MEDIAN			24.47		25.01		26.38		29.55		30.02	

TOT LIABILITY/TOT STK EQUITY

	RATINGS	FYR END	78		77		76		75		74	
JOY MFG CO	A /A+	9/78	65.5	(1)	59.2	(1)	67.2	(1)	67.3	(1)	96.5	(3)
REXNORD INC	A /A	10/78	73.3	(2)	78.2	(2)	74.4	(2)	100.8	(3)	106.3	(5)
CLARK EQUIPMENT CO	A /A	12/78	77.6	(3)	87.3	(5)	97.3	(5)	124.4	(10)	162.4	(11)
PARKER-HANNIFIN CORP	Baa/BBB*	6/78	79.7	(4)	86.4	(4)	87.0	(3)	116.8	(7)	134.8	(9)
CATERPILLAR TRACTOR CO	Aa /AA	12/78	82.8	(5)	85.5	(3)	92.1	(4)	92.3	(2)	100.5	(4)
INGERSOLL-RAND CO	A /AA	12/78	99.3	(6)	92.8	(6)	101.0	(6)	109.2	(5)	110.7	(6)
BUCYRUS-ERIE CO	A /A	12/78	105.1	(7)	119.2	(10)	129.9	(12)	111.7	(6)	90.7	(2)
FMC CORP	A /A	12/78	114.3	(8)	125.0	(12)	121.1	(9)	123.9	(9)	123.2	(7)
STUDEBAKER-WORTHINGTON INC	A /A	12/78	119.7	(9)	104.4	(7)	119.8	(8)	165.1	(12)	250.4	(13)
DEERE & CO	Aa /AA-	10/78	121.4	(10)	114.3	(8)	108.8	(7)	105.2	(4)	90.4	(1)
INTL HARVESTER CO	A /BBB	10/78	130.1	(11)	118.5	(9)	126.1	(11)	143.1	(11)	143.9	(10)
ALLIS-CHALMERS CORP	A /A-	12/78	143.9	(12)	120.1	(11)	123.2	(10)	121.1	(8)	134.3	(8)
COMBUSTION ENGINEERING INC	A /A	12/78	271.9	(13)	274.6	(13)	219.9	(13)	189.0	(13)	188.4	(12)
AVERAGE			114.20		112.73		112.99		120.77		133.24	
MEDIAN			105.14		104.40		109.82		116.77		123.20	

LTD/NET PLANT (%)

	RATINGS	FYR END	78		77		76		75		74	
COMBUSTION ENGINEERING INC	A /A	12/78	31.0	(1)	33.7	(1)	31.7	(1)	32.7	(1)	36.5	(1)
JOY MFG CO	A /A+	9/78	43.9	(2)	44.7	(3)	48.5	(3)	60.7	(2)	83.0	(8)
CATERPILLAR TRACTOR CO	Aa /AA	12/78	44.6	(3)	50.6	(6)	60.9	(5)	61.2	(3)	59.1	(3)
REXNORD INC	A /A	10/78	47.4	(4)	46.6	(4)	56.7	(4)	65.4	(5)	69.6	(5)
FMC CORP	A /A	12/78	48.7	(5)	56.4	(8)	66.2	(9)	61.5	(4)	52.8	(2)
CLARK EQUIPMENT CO	A /A	12/78	51.6	(6)	56.3	(7)	65.7	(8)	65.4	(6)	105.3	(13)
ALLIS-CHALMERS CORP	A /A-	12/78	58.9	(7)	48.4	(5)	64.1	(7)	89.2	(11)	91.8	(10)
PARKER-HANNIFIN CORP	Baa/BBB*	6/78	61.3	(8)	65.6	(10)	61.9	(6)	76.1	(7)	86.7	(9)
STUDEBAKER-WORTHINGTON INC	A /A	12/78	65.8	(9)	34.8	(2)	36.6	(2)	94.5	(12)	82.0	(7)
BUCYRUS-ERIE CO	A /A	12/78	65.8	(10)	66.8	(11)	72.0	(11)	87.7	(10)	99.5	(12)
DEERE & CO	Aa /AA-	10/78	78.9	(11)	70.8	(12)	86.5	(12)	80.8	(9)	59.8	(4)
INGERSOLL-RAND CO	A /AA	12/78	82.1	(12)	62.6	(9)	66.4	(10)	79.7	(8)	70.8	(6)
INTL HARVESTER CO	A /BBB	10/78	104.8	(13)	120.1	(13)	129.6	(13)	142.7	(13)	95.5	(11)
AVERAGE			60.37		58.27		65.15		76.74		76.34	
MEDIAN			58.89		56.30		64.07		76.13		82.04	

NET TANG ASSETS/LTD (%)

	RATINGS	FYR END	78		77		76		75		74	
JOY MFG CO	A /A+	9/78	620.9	(1)	672.5	(1)	591.1	(1)	544.8	(1)	385.4	(4)
CLARK EQUIPMENT CO	A /A	12/78	453.1	(2)	384.1	(7)	359.4	(8)	311.4	(8)	240.5	(12)
REXNORD INC	A /A	10/78	450.7	(3)	429.8	(4)	439.3	(3)	375.8	(3)	357.0	(5)
BUCYRUS-ERIE CO	A /A	12/78	419.6	(4)	382.1	(8)	343.1	(10)	337.2	(7)	331.3	(6)
PARKER-HANNIFIN CORP	Baa/BBB*	6/78	401.8	(5)	352.8	(9)	348.6	(9)	271.8	(10)	250.7	(11)
COMBUSTION ENGINEERING INC	A /A	12/78	395.2	(6)	332.2	(10)	435.0	(4)	458.2	(2)	419.1	(2)
STUDEBAKER-WORTHINGTON INC	A /A	12/78	380.5	(7)	595.8	(2)	558.8	(2)	268.2	(12)	191.6	(13)
CATERPILLAR TRACTOR CO	Aa /AA	12/78	364.2	(8)	329.6	(11)	294.1	(11)	302.9	(9)	318.7	(8)
INGERSOLL-RAND CO	A /AA	12/78	359.8	(9)	424.0	(5)	378.0	(6)	346.6	(5)	391.0	(3)
DEERE & CO	Aa /AA-	10/78	354.9	(10)	399.0	(6)	369.3	(7)	374.3	(4)	578.1	(1)
ALLIS-CHALMERS CORP	A /A-	12/78	320.9	(11)	456.8	(3)	421.3	(5)	341.5	(6)	322.4	(7)
FMC CORP	A /A	12/78	320.8	(12)	291.1	(12)	279.2	(12)	269.3	(11)	306.1	(10)
INTL HARVESTER CO	A /BBB	10/78	298.8	(13)	284.4	(13)	256.0	(13)	241.8	(13)	308.9	(9)
AVERAGE			395.47		410.32		390.25		341.83		338.52	
MEDIAN			380.46		384.12		369.28		337.16		322.39	

CASH FLOW/LTD (%)

	RATINGS	FYR END	78		77		76		75		74	
COMBUSTION ENGINEERING INC	A /A	12/78	144.2	(1)	76.9	(4)	89.0	(3)	81.5	(2)	69.4	(2)
JOY MFG CO	A /A+	9/78	83.6	(2)	107.4	(2)	107.3	(2)	94.6	(1)	45.8	(6)
CLARK EQUIPMENT CO	A /A	12/78	81.2	(3)	49.2	(11)	54.4	(10)	29.4	(11)	22.6	(12)
CATERPILLAR TRACTOR CO	Aa /AA	12/78	80.4	(4)	67.5	(6)	57.3	(7)	64.1	(3)	53.2	(4)
REXNORD INC	A /A	10/78	78.0	(5)	77.0	(3)	78.7	(4)	59.7	(4)	46.1	(5)
PARKER-HANNIFIN CORP	Baa/BBB*	6/78	69.4	(6)	60.6	(10)	55.9	(9)	45.6	(7)	40.5	(8)
BUCYRUS-ERIE CO	A /A	12/78	65.8	(7)	64.0	(8)	52.9	(11)	40.0	(8)	34.8	(9)
STUDEBAKER-WORTHINGTON INC	A /A	12/78	65.7	(8)	129.3	(1)	118.2	(1)	28.8	(12)	19.7	(13)
FMC CORP	A /A	12/78	55.0	(9)	46.1	(12)	41.5	(12)	39.5	(9)	41.6	(7)
INGERSOLL-RAND CO	A /AA	12/78	52.9	(10)	65.8	(7)	56.9	(8)	54.1	(5)	64.6	(3)
DEERE & CO	Aa /AA-	10/78	51.3	(11)	62.4	(9)	58.5	(6)	50.9	(6)	90.0	(1)
ALLIS-CHALMERS CORP	A /A-	12/78	41.4	(12)	68.3	(5)	61.1	(5)	31.1	(10)	24.5	(11)
INTL HARVESTER CO	A /BBB	10/78	22.8	(13)	25.2	(13)	26.4	(13)	20.7	(13)	26.9	(10)
AVERAGE			68.59		69.21		66.01		49.23		44.60	
MEDIAN			65.82		65.78		57.32		45.56		41.56	

III-74

Machinery Industry

NET CASH FL/CAP EXP (%)

	RATINGS	FYR END	78	77	76	75	74
BUCYRUS-ERIE CO	A /A	12/78	290.4 (1)	213.8 (3)	90.6 (13)	60.4 (12)	37.3 (13)
CLARK EQUIPMENT CO	A /A	12/78	234.1 (2)	92.7 (13)	169.5 (4)	56.1 (13)	55.2 (11)
COMBUSTION ENGINEERING INC	A /A	12/78	229.9 (3)	165.2 (5)	143.9 (6)	118.3 (5)	87.7 (6)
INGERSOLL-RAND CO	A /AA	12/78	217.6 (4)	248.9 (1)	111.1 (11)	96.8 (8)	1'3.1 (5)
REXNORD INC	A /A	10/78	176.6 (5)	179.2 (4)	207.2 (2)	233.1 (1)	118.6 (3)
STUDEBAKER-WORTHINGTON INC	A /A	12/78	174.4 (6)	231.5 (2)	213.3 (1)	183.2 (2)	67.4 (10)
PARKER-HANNIFIN CORP	Baa/BBB*	6/78	135.5 (7)	153.5 (6)	155.1 (5)	117.0 (6)	125.6 (1)
CATERPILLAR TRACTOR CO	Aa /AA	12/78	120.8 (8)	105.9 (11)	94.4 (12)	98.7 (7)	72.8 (7)
DEERE & CO	Aa /AA-	10/78	113.9 V(9)	106.4 V(10)	200.4 V(3)	74.9 V(11)	117.9 V(4)
ALLIS-CHALMERS CORP	A /A	12/78	107.6 (10)	115.3 (8)	131.8 (7)	124.8 (4)	69.3 (8)
FMC CORP	A /A	12/78	105.4 (11)	102.8 (12)	130.8 (8)	80.1 (10)	52.9 (12)
JOY MFG CO	A /A+	9/78	87.5 (12)	127.0 (7)	112.8 (10)	143.4 (3)	122.9 (2)
INTL HARVESTER CO	A /BBB	10/78	69.3 (13)	106.8 (9)	113.4 (9)	83.4 (9)	68.7 (9)
AVERAGE			158.69	149.92	144.18	113.10	85.33
MEDIAN			135.51	126.99	131.76	98.65	72.81

AFT TAX RET ON COM EQTY (%)

	RATINGS	FYR END	78	77	76	75	74
CATERPILLAR TRACTOR CO	Aa /AA	12/78	20.6 (1)	19.0 (1)	18.9 (1)	22.6 (1)	15.7 (2)
BUCYRUS-ERIE CO	A /A	12/78	16.9 (2)	18.5 (2)	13.1 (9)	13.9 (7)	13.6 (5)
COMBUSTION ENGINEERING INC	A /A	12/78	16.2 (3)	15.1 (7)	13.5 (8)	12.1 (9)	11.6 (7)
PARKER-HANNIFIN CORP	Baa/BBB*	6/78	16.0 (4)	16.0 (5)	16.8 (3)	15.6 (2)	16.6 (1)
REXNORD INC	A /A	10/78	15.7 (5)	15.6 (6)	14.7 (6)	14.3 (5)	11.0 (8)
STUDEBAKER-WORTHINGTON INC	A /A	12/78	15.3 (6)	16.1 (4)	14.3 (7)	8.7 (11)	3.3 (13)
CLARK EQUIPMENT CO	A /A	12/78	15.2 (7)	12.2 (11)	14.9 (5)	11.4 (10)	13.1 (6)
DEERE & CO	Aa /AA-	12/78	15.1 (8)	16.3 (3)	17.5 (2)	15.1 (4)	15.5 (3)
FMC CORP	A /A	12/78	13.2 (9)	13.1 (9)	12.9 (10)	12.8 (8)	10.4 (10)
ALLIS-CHALMERS CORP	A /A-	12/78	13.0 (10)	12.8 (10)	12.5 (11)	6.9 (13)	5.4 (12)
INGERSOLL-RAND CO	A /AA	12/78	12.7 (11)	11.9 (12)	11.6 (12)	14.1 (6)	14.5 (4)
JOY MFG CO	A /A+	9/78	10.7 (12)	13.9 (8)	16.4 (4)	15.2 (3)	10.6 (9)
INTL HARVESTER CO	A /BBB	10/78	9.9 (13)	11.7 (13)	11.0 (13)	8.1 (12)	8.6 (11)
AVERAGE			14.64	14.77	14.47	13.14	11.53
MEDIAN			15.18	15.12	14.27	13.92	11.61

RET ON TOT ASSETS (%)

	RATINGS	FYR END	78	77	76	75	74
CATERPILLAR TRACTOR CO	Aa /AA	12/78	21.2 (1)	20.1 (1)	18.4 (2)	21.6 (1)	14.5 (4)
REXNORD INC	A /A	10/78	18.9 (2)	18.9 (3)	18.3 (3)	16.3 (4)	13.7 (6)
PARKER-HANNIFIN CORP	Baa/BBB*	6/78	18.6 (3)	19.3 (2)	16.9 (4)	18.1 (3)	16.7 (1)
CLARK EQUIPMENT CO	A /A	12/78	17.9 (4)	15.5 (7)	13.4 (9)	13.6 (7)	11.9 (8)
BUCYRUS-ERIE CO	A /A	12/78	16.4 (5)	15.9 (6)	14.2 (7)	14.2 (6)	14.2 (5)
STUDEBAKER-WORTHINGTON INC	A /A	12/78	15.4 (6)	16.9 (5)	15.4 (6)	9.5 (11)	6.6 (12)
INGERSOLL-RAND CO	A /AA	12/78	14.8 (7)	15.2 (8)	13.5 (8)	14.8 (5)	15.5 (2)
JOY MFG CO	A /A+	9/78	14.2 (8)	18.2 (4)	20.6 (1)	19.0 (2)	12.2 (7)
DEERE & CO	Aa /AA-	10/78	13.8 (9)	14.9 (9)	16.0 (5)	14.3 (6)	15.4 (3)
FMC CORP	A /A	12/78	11.6 (10)	11.5 (11)	11.6 (11)	10.3 (10)	8.1 (11)
INTL HARVESTER CO	A /BBB	10/78	10.8 (11)	13.0 (10)	12.2 (10)	10.5 (9)	10.0 (9)
ALLIS-CHALMERS CORP	A /A-	12/78	10.1 (12)	11.5 (12)	11.0 (12)	6.9 (13)	5.9 (13)
COMBUSTION ENGINEERING INC	A /A	12/78	9.7 (13)	8.7 (13)	8.9 (13)	8.7 (12)	8.6 (10)
AVERAGE			14.88	15.35	14.65	13.58	11.79
MEDIAN			14.82	15.49	14.15	13.62	12.22

Metals and Mining Industry

PRETAX COVERAGE

	RATINGS	FYR END	78	77	76	75	74
HANNA MINING CO	A /A	12/78	9.33 (1)	19.78 (1)	25.88 (2)	15.62 (2)	13.09 (6)
ALUMINUM CO OF AMERICA	A /A	12/78	6.34 (2)	4.17 (4)	3.37 (6)	1.80 (10)	6.15 (10)
REYNOLDS METALS CO	Ba /B*	12/78	4.35P(3)	3.00 (6)	2.35 (8)	2.04 (9)	3.23 (12)
CYPRUS MINES CORP	Baa/BBB	12/78	3.74 (4)	0.89 (11)	1.66 (11)	5.92 (6)	36.21 (1)
PITTSTON CO	A /A*	12/78	3.46 (5)	18.56P(2)	44.90 (1)	49.36 (1)	23.18 (2)
HUDSON BAY MINING & SMELTING	A /A	12/78	3.32 (6)	5.20 (3)	4.95 (4)	8.51 (4)	17.94 (4)
REVERE COPPER & BRASS INC	Ba /BB*	12/78	3.29 (7)	2.08 (8)	1.16 (12)	-1.91 (13)	2.91 (13)
TEXASGULF INC	A /A+	12/78	3.19 (8)	3.25 (5)	4.46 (5)	12.88 (3)	19.42 (3)
AMAX INC	A /A+	12/78	2.75 (9)	1.51 (10)	2.97 (7)	3.77 (7)	5.82 (11)
INCO LTD	A /A	12/78	2.32I(10)	2.62I(7)	5.09I(3)	6.47I(5)	13.31I(5)
ASARCO INC	A /A-	12/78	1.68 (11)	-0.17 (13)	1.99 (10)	1.42 (11)	9.52 (8)
PHELPS DODGE CORP	A /BBB+	12/78	1.55 (12)	1.60 (9)	2.01 (9)	2.19 (8)	6.64 (9)
KENNECOTT COPPER CORP	A /BBB	12/78	1.40 (13)	0.74 (12)	0.59 (13)	-0.17 (12)	11.58 (7)
AVERAGE			3.59	4.86	7.80	8.30	13.00
MEDIAN			3.29	2.62	2.97	3.77	11.58

AFTER TAX COVERAGE

	RATINGS	FYR END	78	77	76	75	74
HANNA MINING CO	A /A	12/78	7.82 (1)	14.65 (1)	18.14 (2)	10.59 (2)	9.17 (5)
ALUMINUM CO OF AMERICA	A /A	12/78	4.19 (2)	3.09 (3)	2.54 (6)	1.87 (9)	4.05 (11)
PITTSTON CO	A /A*	12/78	4.14 (3)	13.92P(2)	29.88 (1)	30.05 (1)	14.04 (2)
CYPRUS MINES CORP	Baa/BBB	12/78	3.27 (4)	1.04 (11)	1.70 (9)	4.76 (4)	23.28 (1)
TEXASGULF INC	A /A+	12/78	2.69 (5)	2.58 (5)	3.20 (4)	8.00 (3)	10.97 (4)
REYNOLDS METALS CO	Ba /B*	12/78	2.68P(6)	2.34 (6)	2.00 (7)	1.76 (11)	2.21 (12)
HUDSON BAY MINING & SMELTING	A /A	12/78	2.43 (7)	2.98 (4)	1.51 (11)	4.50 (5)	11.66 (3)
AMAX INC	A /A+	12/78	2.35 (8)	1.48 (9)	2.88 (5)	3.30 (7)	4.42 (10)
REVERE COPPER & BRASS INC	Ba /BB*	12/78	2.26 (9)	1.65 (8)	1.11 (12)	-0.92 (13)	2.01 (13)
INCO LTD	A /A	12/78	1.61 (10)	1.92 (7)	3.28 (3)	4.17 (6)	7.80 (7)
PHELPS DODGE CORP	A /BBB+	12/78	1.46 (11)	1.47 (10)	1.90 (8)	2.54 (8)	5.13 (9)
ASARCO INC	A /A-	12/78	1.10 (12)	-0.32 (13)	1.64 (10)	1.86 (10)	6.66 (8)
KENNECOTT COPPER CORP	A /BBB	12/78	1.08 (13)	1.01 (12)	1.03 (13)	0.98 (12)	8.55 (6)
AVERAGE			2.85	3.68	5.45	5.65	8.46
MEDIAN			2.43	1.92	2.00	3.30	7.80

AFTER TAX COV (INCL RENTS)

	RATINGS	FYR END	78	77	76	75	74
ALUMINUM CO OF AMERICA	A /A	12/78	3.47 (1)	2.65 (1)	2.23 (4)	1.61 (6)	2.94 (6)
TEXASGULF INC	A /A+	12/78	2.39 (2)	2.13 (3)	2.58 (2)	5.14 (1)	7.14 (1)
AMAX INC	A /A+	12/78	2.13 (3)	1.36 (7)	2.48 (3)	2.94 (4)	3.86 (5)
REYNOLDS METALS CO	Ba /B*	12/78	2.13P(4)	1.88 (4)	1.63 (6)	1.49 (7)	1.80 (7)
HUDSON BAY MINING & SMELTING	A /A	12/78	2.02 (5)	2.45 (2)	1.39 (7)	3.62 (2)	7.12 (2)
INCO LTD	A /A	12/78	1.49 (6)	1.70 (5)	2.64 (1)	3.20 (3)	NA (-)
PHELPS DODGE CORP	A /BBB+	12/78	1.39 (7)	1.41 (6)	1.78 (5)	2.33 (5)	4.51 (4)
KENNECOTT COPPER CCRP	A /BBB	12/78	1.06 (8)	1.01 (8)	1.02 (8)	0.98 (8)	6.37 (3)
ASARCO INC	A /A-	12/78	NA (-)	NA (-)	NA (-)	NA (-)	NA (-)
CYPRUS MINES CORP	Baa/BBB	12/78	NA (-)	NA (-)	NA (-)	NA (-)	NA (-)
HANNA MINING CO	A /A	12/78	NA (-)	NA (-)	NA (-)	NA (-)	NA (-)
PITTSTON CO	A /A*	12/78	NA (-)	NA (-)	NA (-)	NA (-)	NA (-)
REVERE COPPER & BRASS INC	Ba /BB*	12/78	NA (-)	NA (-)	NA (-)	NA (-)	NA (-)
AVERAGE			2.01	1.82	1.97	2.66	4.82
MEDIAN			2.07	1.79	2.01	2.63	4.51

Metals and Mining Industry

NET INCOME AS % NET SALES

	RATINGS	FYR END	78		77		76		75		74	
CYPRUS MINES CORP	Baa/BBB	12/78	25.2	(1)	1.5	(10)	1.8	(10)	8.2	(6)	12.7	(5)
AMAX INC	A /A+	12/78	9.1	(2)	5.2	(5)	12.8	(3)	14.0	(3)	12.8	(4)
TEXASGULF INC	A /A+	12/78	8.3	(3)	9.6	(2)	13.1	(2)	23.2	(1)	25.9	(1)
HANNA MINING CO	A /A	12/78	7.8	(4)	13.7	(1)	14.8	(1)	14.3	(2)	7.5	(10)
ALUMINUM CO OF AMERICA	A /A	12/78	7.7	(5)	5.7	(4)	4.9	(6)	2.8	(11)	6.3	(11)
ASARCO INC	A /A-	12/78	4.2	(6)	-2.8	(13)	3.8	(8)	2.5	(12)	9.4	(9)
REYNOLDS METALS CO	Ba /B*	12/78	4.2	(7)	3.7	(7)	3.6	(9)	3.6	(9)	5.6	(12)
INCO LTD	A /A	12/78	3.7	(8)	5.1	(6)	9.6	(5)	11.0	(5)	18.2	(2)
REVERE COPPER & BRASS INC	Ba /BB*	12/78	3.1	(9)	1.7	(8)	0.3	(13)	-8.2	(13)	3.3	(13)
PHELPS DODGE CORP	A /BBB+	12/78	3.0	(10)	1.7	(9)	4.5	(7)	5.9	(7)	11.0	(6)
PITTSTON CO	A /A*	12/78	1.9	(11)	5.9	(3)	10.3	(4)	13.3	(4)	9.9	(8)
HUDSON BAY MINING & SMELTING	A /A	12/78	1.1	(12)	1.3	(11)	0.8	(12)	5.7	(8)	17.8	(3)
KENNECOTT COPPER CORP	A /BBB	12/78	0.3	(13)	0.0	(12)	0.9	(11)	2.8	(10)	10.1	(7)
AVERAGE			6.12		4.02		6.26		7.63		11.58	
MEDIAN			4.16		3.67		4.52		5.94		10.13	

LTD/CAPITALIZATION (%)

	RATINGS	FYR END	78		77		76		75		74	
PITTSTON CO	A /A*	12/78	12.6	(1)	12.6	(2)	11.2	(2)	15.9	(2)	24.5	(7)
HANNA MINING CO	A /A	12/78	12.7	(2)	9.6	(1)	7.2	(1)	9.0	(1)	14.6	(5)
ASARCO INC	A /A-	12/78	26.5	(3)	32.7	(6)	31.8	(7)	28.4	(6)	11.9	(3)
AMAX INC	A /A+	12/78	29.6	(4)	29.3	(4)	28.9	(5)	28.8	(8)	30.3	(10)
KENNECOTT COPPER CORP	A /BBB	12/78	30.7	(5)	27.0	(3)	27.9	(4)	22.4	(3)	13.6	(4)
TEXASGULF INC	A /A+	12/78	32.0	(6)	33.1	(7)	25.1	(3)	26.6	(5)	19.2	(6)
HUDSON BAY MINING & SMELTING	A /A	12/78	32.5	(7)	30.3	(5)	31.4	(6)	28.5	(7)	11.6	(2)
ALUMINUM CO OF AMERICA	A /A	12/78	34.8	(8)	38.6	(10)	40.7	(11)	44.3	(11)	37.6	(11)
INCO LTD	A /A	12/78	39.0	(9)	34.7	(8)	35.2	(8)	29.2	(9)	26.8	(8)
CYPRUS MINES CORP	Baa/BBB	12/78	40.0	(10)	43.3	(11)	40.3	(10)	26.3	(4)	3.2	(1)
PHELPS DODGE CORP	A /BBB+	12/78	40.8	(11)	36.7	(9)	38.6	(9)	36.9	(10)	26.8	(9)
REYNOLDS METALS CO	Ba /B*	12/78	45.2	(12)	46.3	(12)	50.0	(12)	51.1	(12)	54.6	(12)
REVERE COPPER & BRASS INC	Ba /BB*	12/78	62.8	(13)	54.9	(13)	63.2	(13)	61.1	(13)	55.5	(13)
AVERAGE			33.79		33.02		33.18		31.42		25.40	
MEDIAN			32.45		33.13		31.84		28.45		24.49	

LTD/NET PLANT (%)

	RATINGS	FYR END	78		77		76		75		74	
PITTSTON CO	A /A*	12/78	16.9	(1)	19.0	(1)	20.4	(1)	30.8	(3)	39.3	(9)
AMAX INC	A /A+	12/78	33.0	(2)	35.3	(2)	35.3	(3)	37.6	(5)	38.4	(8)
TEXASGULF INC	A /A+	12/78	35.0	(3)	37.3	(3)	28.1	(2)	28.3	(1)	22.9	(4)
HUDSON BAY MINING & SMELTING	A /A	12/78	40.4	(4)	42.9	(7)	37.8	(4)	29.5	(2)	11.8	(2)
KENNECOTT COPPER CORP	A /BBB	12/78	43.9	(5)	39.1	(4)	65.6	(11)	54.8	(9)	16.1	(3)
INCO LTD	A /A	12/78	48.2	(6)	41.8	(5)	40.1	(5)	34.2	(4)	33.5	(7)
CYPRUS MINES CORP	Baa/BBB	12/78	48.6	(7)	47.9	(8)	53.7	(7)	39.2	(6)	4.5	(1)
ASARCO INC	A /A-	12/78	48.9	(8)	56.6	(9)	56.0	(8)	54.6	(8)	23.2	(5)
PHELPS DODGE CORP	A /BBB+	12/78	50.1	(9)	42.5	(6)	44.4	(6)	44.2	(7)	32.3	(6)
ALUMINUM CO OF AMERICA	A /A	12/78	52.3	(10)	57.5	(10)	59.4	(10)	65.2	(10)	54.3	(10)
REYNOLDS METALS CO	Ba /B*	12/78	82.3	(11)	85.0	(12)	88.8	(12)	88.2	(12)	90.4	(12)
HANNA MINING CO	A /A	12/78	116.3	(12)	78.0	(11)	56.5	(9)	68.8	(11)	90.8	(13)
REVERE COPPER & BRASS INC	Ba /BB*	12/78	132.7	(13)	111.5	(13)	139.6	(13)	122.1	(13)	75.3	(11)
AVERAGE			57.57		53.41		55.82		53.65		40.99	
MEDIAN			48.57		42.86		53.65		44.19		33.54	

TOT LIABILITY/TOT STK EQUITY

	RATINGS	FYR END	78		77		76		75		74	
HANNA MINING CO	A /A	12/78	38.2	(1)	34.5	(1)	29.6	(1)	31.5	(1)	40.1	(1)
ASARCO INC	A /A-	12/78	73.7	(2)	89.1	(4)	80.1	(6)	74.4	(3)	54.1	(3)
PITTSTON CO	A /A*	12/78	77.5	(3)	62.0	(2)	57.8	(2)	79.5	(4)	113.0	(11)
AMAX INC	A /A+	12/78	83.9	(4)	74.8	(3)	78.7	(5)	81.8	(5)	87.6	(8)
KENNECOTT COPPER CORP	A /BBB	12/78	90.7	(5)	91.7	(5)	65.0	(3)	57.7	(2)	53.2	(2)
ALUMINUM CO OF AMERICA	A /A	12/78	97.2	(6)	105.2	(8)	111.3	(8)	117.1	(10)	106.7	(10)
TEXASGULF INC	A /A+	12/78	97.5	(7)	96.5	(7)	72.6	(4)	84.0	(6)	74.4	(6)
PHELPS DODGE CORP	A /BBB+	12/78	98.9	(8)	95.8	(6)	98.4	(7)	85.0	(7)	67.3	(5)
INCO LTD	A /A	12/78	116.1	(9)	112.9	(9)	132.2	(10)	103.8	(9)	95.4	(9)
CYPRUS MINES CORP	Baa/BBB	12/78	122.3	(10)	139.0	(10)	125.9	(9)	87.2	(8)	59.5	(4)
REYNOLDS METALS CO	Ba /B*	12/78	151.2	(11)	147.6	(12)	165.4	(12)	165.4	(12)	191.0	(12)
HUDSON BAY MINING & SMELTING	A /A	12/78	157.8	(12)	142.9	(11)	132.5	(11)	138.3	(11)	85.9	(7)
REVERE COPPER & BRASS INC	Ba /BB*	12/78	252.0	(13)	217.2	(13)	242.3	(13)	234.4	(13)	194.2	(13)
AVERAGE			112.08		108.39		107.05		103.07		94.03	
MEDIAN			97.52		96.49		98.40		84.96		85.91	

NET TANG ASSETS/LTD (%) .

	RATINGS	FYR END	78		77		76		75		74	
HANNA MINING CO	A /A	12/78	743.9	(1)	1016.0	(1)	1365.2	(1)	1091.8	(1)	639.7	(5)
PITTSTON CO	A /A*	12/78	694.8	(2)	713.0	(2)	792.7	(2)	569.7	(2)	389.0	(7)
ASARCO INC	A /A-	12/78	369.6	(3)	300.1	(6)	307.6	(6)	343.9	(7)	823.9	(2)
AMAX INC	A /A+	12/78	331.0	(4)	337.9	(4)	343.0	(5)	347.4	(6)	329.6	(10)
KENNECOTT COPPER CORP	A /BBB	12/78	306.7	(5)	350.6	(3)	353.8	(4)	438.5	(3)	700.4	(4)
TEXASGULF INC	A /A+	12/78	292.8	(6)	284.6	(7)	377.4	(3)	362.2	(5)	500.3	(6)
HUDSON BAY MINING & SMELTING	A /A	12/78	292.4	(7)	312.2	(5)	297.7	(7)	326.1	(9)	794.4	(3)
ALUMINUM CO OF AMERICA	A /A	12/78	277.8	(8)	251.9	(10)	239.8	(11)	220.0	(11)	257.7	(11)
INCO LTD	A /A	12/78	253.0	(9)	283.1	(8)	278.4	(8)	334.9	(8)	363.6	(9)
PHELPS DODGE CORP	A /BBB+	12/78	243.8	(10)	271.5	(9)	258.2	(9)	269.7	(10)	370.5	(8)
CYPRUS MINES CORP	Baa/BBB	12/78	240.5	(11)	224.2	(11)	241.9	(10)	370.1	(4)	3009.7	(1)
REYNOLDS METALS CO	Ba /B*	12/78	206.8	(12)	201.2	(12)	187.9	(12)	184.2	(12)	171.9	(13)
REVERE COPPER & BRASS INC	Ba /BB*	12/78	152.7	(13)	180.6	(13)	157.0	(13)	162.5	(13)	178.5	(12)
AVERAGE			338.90		363.59		400.04		386.22		656.10	
MEDIAN			292.38		284.62		297.71		343.90		389.02	

CASH FLOW/LTD (%)

	RATINGS	FYR END	78		77		76		75		74	
PITTSTON CO	A /A*	12/78	124.7	(1)	163.9	(1)	280.2	(1)	263.6	(1)	147.7	(4)
HANNA MINING CO	A /A	12/78	76.5	(2)	111.1	(2)	202.1	(2)	158.2	(2)	90.2	(7)
HUDSON BAY MINING & SMELTING	A /A	12/78	50.7	(3)	59.5	(3)	60.6	(3)	72.3	(5)	197.9	(2)
ALUMINUM CO OF AMERICA	A /A	12/78	48.8	(4)	33.5	(4)	29.4	(6)	17.1	(10)	39.6	(11)
CYPRUS MINES CORP	Baa/BBB	12/78	39.6	(5)	23.8	(7)	25.3	(8)	73.0	(4)	1108.0	(1)
AMAX INC	A /A+	12/78	34.4	(6)	32.8	(5)	28.2	(7)	30.4	(7)	51.4	(9)
TEXASGULF INC	A /A+	12/78	29.7	(7)	23.8	(6)	43.5	(4)	76.5	(3)	162.5	(3)
REYNOLDS METALS CO	Ba /B*	12/78	24.9	(8)	21.2	(9)	16.0	(11)	14.3	(12)	20.0	(13)
ASARCO INC	A /A-	12/78	21.2	(9)	11.2	(12)	18.4	(10)	21.6	(8)	116.2	(6)
REVERE COPPER & BRASS INC	Ba /BB*	12/78	21.0	(10)	12.9	(11)	6.3	(12)	0.3	(13)	23.1	(12)
KENNECOTT COPPER CORP	A /BBB	12/78	18.8	(11)	5.8	(13)	1.9	(13)	17.0	(11)	132.0	(5)
INCO LTD	A /A	12/78	17.1	(12)	22.9	(8)	38.9	(5)	53.4	(6)	85.9	(8)
PHELPS DODGE CORP	A /BBB+	12/78	13.2	(13)	16.5	(10)	19.0	(9)	18.8	(9)	43.8	(10)
AVERAGE			40.04		41.46		59.22		62.80		170.64	
MEDIAN			29.70		23.78		28.24		30.37		90.17	

Metals and Mining Industry

NET CASH FL/CAP EXP (%)

	RATINGS	FYR END	78		77		76		75		74	
HANNA MINING CO	A /A	12/78	393.4	(1)	229.9	(2)	331.7	(1)	414.2	(1)	341.5	(2)
REVERE COPPER & BRASS INC	Ba /BB*	12/78	272.9	J(2)	239.3	J(1)	158.2	(2)	-15.6	(13)	510.2	V(1)
CYPRUS MINES CORP	Baa/BBB	12/78	166.7	(3)	29.5	(10)	26.3	(11)	72.5	(5)	151.1	(7)
ALUMINUM CO OF AMERICA	A /A	12/78	137.9	(4)	121.5	(4)	119.4	(6)	43.7	(8)	90.6	(10)
REYNOLDS METALS CO	Ba /B*	12/78	116.5	(5)	166.5	(3)	144.5	(4)	91.0	(4)	175.8	(6)
HUDSON BAY MINING & SMELTING	A /A	12/78	76.0	(6)	92.5	(5)	141.4	(5)	130.9	(3)	107.3	(9)
ASARCO INC	A /A-	12/78	75.1	(7)	26.6	(12)	72.2	(7)	27.2	(9)	70.6	(11)
PHELPS DODGE CORP	A /BBB+	12/78	72.1	(8)	46.2	(8)	45.6	(9)	23.9	(10)	33.8	(13)
TEXASGULF INC	A /A+	12/78	67.8	(9)	29.4	(11)	42.2	(10)	53.2	(7)	181.0	(5)
INCO LTD	A /A	12/78	62.1	(10)	30.6	(9)	46.0	(8)	62.2	(6)	221.5	(4)
PITTSTON CO	A /A*	12/78	61.1	(11)	75.6	(6)	157.1	(3)	287.2	(2)	267.2	(3)
KENNECOTT COPPER CORP	A /BBB	12/78	58.2	(12)	7.1	(13)	-6.9	(13)	10.7	(12)	142.8	(8)
AMAX INC	A /A+	12/78	47.9	(13)	46.5	(7)	23.9	(12)	23.5	(11)	45.7	(12)
AVERAGE			123.68		87.78		100.12		94.18		179.93	
MEDIAN			75.10		46.53		72.18		53.19		151.11	

AFT TAX RET ON COM EQTY (%)

	RATINGS	FYR END	78		77		76		75		74	
REVERE COPPER & BRASS INC	Ba /BB*	12/78	15.8	(1)	6.6	(5)	1.1	(12)	-23.2	(13)	10.2	(12)
ALUMINUM CO OF AMERICA	A /A	12/78	15.2	(2)	10.8	(3)	8.7	(7)	4.1	(10)	11.5	(11)
CYPRUS MINES CORP	Baa/BBB	12/78	14.4	(3)	1.3	(11)	1.4	(11)	9.2	(6)	17.2	(5)
REYNOLDS METALS CO	Ba /B*	12/78	11.3	(4)	9.0	(4)	8.8	(5)	7.5	(7)	14.9	(6)
AMAX INC	A /A+	12/78	8.2	(5)	3.4	(8)	8.8	(6)	9.2	(5)	14.8	(7)
HANNA MINING CO	A /A	12/78	7.1	(6)	12.8	(1)	15.8	(2)	16.2	(3)	7.2	(13)
TEXASGULF INC	A /A+	12/78	6.6	(7)	6.2	(6)	9.7	(4)	16.4	(2)	26.3	(2)
ASARCO INC	A /A-	12/78	5.3	(8)	-3.6	(13)	4.9	(8)	3.0	(11)	14.6	(8)
PITTSTON CO	A /A*	12/78	4.1	(9)	12.7	(2)	24.3	(1)	40.4	(1)	35.2	(1)
INCO LTD	A /A	12/78	3.7	(10)	5.9	(7)	12.6	(3)	12.6	(4)	21.4	(3)
PHELPS DODGE CORP	A /BBB+	12/78	2.5	(11)	1.4	(10)	4.8	(9)	5.2	(9)	12.6	(9)
HUDSON BAY MINING & SMELTING	A /A	12/78	2.0	(12)	1.7	(9)	1.4	(10)	6.8	(8)	17.8	(4)
KENNECOTT COPPER CORP	A /BBB	12/78	0.4	(13)	0.0	(12)	0.6	(13)	1.5	(12)	11.7	(10)
AVERAGE			7.43		5.23		7.92		8.38		16.56	
MEDIAN			6.64		5.91		8.71		7.47		14.80	

RET ON TOT ASSETS (%)

	RATINGS	FYR END	78		77		76		75		74	
ALUMINUM CO OF AMERICA	A /A	12/78	14.1	(1)	10.1	(3)	8.7	(6)	4.2	(10)	11.0	(11)
REVERE COPPER & BRASS INC	Ba /BB*	12/78	11.6	(2)	6.7	(7)	3.9	(11)	-6.8	(13)	9.9	(13)
REYNOLDS METALS CO	Ba /B*	12/78	11.1	(3)	7.8	(4)	6.7	(8)	6.3	(8)	11.5	(10)
CYPRUS MINES CORP	Baa/BBB	12/78	10.9	(4)	3.3	(11)	3.0	(12)	8.8	(6)	20.4	(4)
AMAX INC	A /A+	12/78	9.0	(5)	5.5	(9)	8.1	(7)	8.6	(7)	13.7	(6)
HANNA MINING CO	A /A	12/78	7.2	(6)	12.3	(1)	17.0	(2)	18.3	(2)	10.3	(12)
INCO LTD	A /A	12/78	6.9	I(7)	6.9	I(6)	11.9	I(3)	12.6	I(4)	21.4	I(3)
ASARCO INC	A /A-	12/78	6.8	(8)	0.8	(13)	5.7	(9)	2.5	(11)	12.9	(7)
TEXASGULF INC	A /A+	12/78	6.8	(9)	6.2	(8)	9.0	(5)	16.0	(3)	29.0	(2)
HUDSON BAY MINING & SMELTING	A /A	12/78	5.0	(10)	7.0	(5)	10.5	(4)	9.4	(5)	15.2	(5)
PHELPS DODGE CORP	A /BBB+	12/78	4.6	(11)	3.8	(10)	5.2	(10)	4.3	(9)	11.6	(9)
KENNECOTT COPPER CORP	A /BBB	12/78	3.4	(12)	1.3	(12)	1.5	(13)	0.7	(12)	11.7	(8)
PITTSTON CO	A /A*	12/78	2.5	(13)	11.2	(2)	23.9	(1)	38.2	(1)	29.4	(1)
AVERAGE			7.69		6.37		8.86		9.47		16.01	
MEDIAN			6.92		6.67		8.10		8.58		12.87	

Non-Rail Transportation Industry

PRETAX COVERAGE

	RATINGS	FYR END	78	77	76	75	74
CONSOLIDATED FREIGHTWAYS INC	A /A+	12/78	21.94 (1)	24.50 (1)	20.04P(1)	7.09 (1)	10.43 (1)
NORTHWEST AIRLINES INC	NR /NR	12/78	14.54 (2)	18.25 (2)	7.61 (2)	3.65 (2)	5.48 (3)
DELTA AIR LINES INC	Baa/A#	6/78	11.17 (3)	6.97 (3)	4.16 (4)	3.00 (3)	6.71 (2)
NATIONAL AIRLINES INC	Baa/BB#	6/78	4.64 (4)	1.25 (12)	1.21 (12)	1.79 (5)	3.91 (6)
UAL INC	Ba /BB*	12/78	4.58 (5)	2.62 (8)	1.43 (11)	0.93 (8)	4.67 (4)
WESTERN AIR LINES INC	Ba /B*	12/78	3.07 (6)	3.44 (5)	3.48 (5)	1.48 (6)	4.64 (5)
CONTINENTAL AIR LINES INC	Ba /B*	12/78	3.01 (7)	2.04 (9)	1.45 (10)	0.53 (9)	1.27 (10)
BRANIFF INTERNATIONAL CORP	Baa/BBB-	12/78	2.62 (8)	3.18 (6)	2.84 (6)	2.40 (4)	2.64 (7)
AMERICAN AIRLINES INC	Baa/BBB	12/78	2.43 (9)	4.39 (4)	4.61 (3)	-0.11 (11)	1.94 (8)
TRANS WORLD CORP	Ba /BB	12/78	2.33 (10)	2.86 (7)	1.99 (8)	-0.58P(12)	0.62P(12)
EASTERN AIR LINES	B /B*	12/78	1.94 (11)	1.84 (10)	2.02 (7)	0.46 (10)	1.26 (11)
TIGER INTERNATIONAL	Baa/NR#	12/78	1.85 (12)	1.67 (11)	1.55 (9)	1.48P(7)	1.42 (9)
AVERAGE			6.17	6.08	4.37	1.84	3.75
MEDIAN			3.04	3.02	2.43	1.48	3.28

AFTER TAX COVERAGE

	RATINGS	FYR END	78	77	76	75	74
CONSOLIDATED FREIGHTWAYS INC	A /A+	12/78	12.41 (1)	13.54 (1)	10.97P(1)	4.28 (1)	6.13 (1)
NORTHWEST AIRLINES INC	NR /NR	12/78	8.68 (2)	11.44 (2)	4.48 (2)	3.44 (2)	3.95 (3)
DELTA AIR LINES INC	Baa/A#	6/78	6.93 (3)	4.56 (3)	3.03 (4)	2.32 (3)	4.21 (2)
UAL INC	Ba /BB*	12/78	4.20 (4)	2.52 (7)	1.30 (12)	0.92 (8)	2.67 (5)
NATIONAL AIRLINES INC	Baa/BB#	6/78	3.19 (5)	1.38 (12)	1.39 (9)	1.69 (5)	2.67 (6)
CONTINENTAL AIR LINES INC	Ba /B*	12/78	2.94 (6)	2.00 (9)	1.31 (11)	0.73 (9)	1.20 (11)
WESTERN AIR LINES INC	Ba /B*	12/78	2.77 (7)	2.55 (6)	2.55 (5)	1.58 (6)	3.10 (4)
AMERICAN AIRLINES INC	Baa/BBB	12/78	2.51 (8)	4.39 (4)	3.79 (3)	0.13 (11)	1.70 (8)
BRANIFF INTERNATIONAL CORP	Baa/BBB-	12/78	2.32 (9)	2.62 (5)	2.37 (6)	2.06 (4)	2.13 (7)
TRANS WORLD CORP	Ba /BB	12/78	2.25 (10)	2.49 (8)	1.60 (8)	-0.32P(12)	0.61P(12)
EASTERN AIR LINES	B /B*	12/78	1.94 (11)	1.84 (10)	1.78 (7)	0.46 (10)	1.22 (10)
TIGER INTERNATIONAL	Baa/NR#	12/78	1.55 (12)	1.43 (11)	1.35 (10)	1.31P(7)	1.27 (9)
AVERAGE			4.31	4.23	2.99	1.55	2.57
MEDIAN			2.86	2.53	2.07	1.44	2.40

AFTER TAX COV (INCL RENTS)

	RATINGS	FYR END	78	77	76	75	74
CONSOLIDATED FREIGHTWAYS INC	A /A+	12/78	5.08 (1)	5.42 (1)	4.84P(1)	2.73 (1)	3.78 (1)
DELTA AIR LINES INC	Baa/A#	6/78	3.15 (2)	2.49 (3)	1.96 (2)	1.41 (3)	1.86 (4)
UAL INC	Ba /BB*	12/78	2.88 (3)	1.45 (6)	1.09 (12)	0.98 (8)	1.55 (6)
NORTHWEST AIRLINES INC	NR /NR	12/78	2.29 (4)	2.54 (2)	1.79 (3)	1.75 (2)	2.08 (2)
CONTINENTAL AIR LINES INC	Ba /B*	12/78	2.02 (5)	1.53 (4)	1.18 (9)	0.83 (11)	1.14 (9)
WESTERN AIR LINES INC	Ba /B*	12/78	1.81 (6)	1.38 (8)	1.31 (5)	1.13 (7)	1.65 (5)
AMERICAN AIRLINES INC	Baa/BBB	12/78	1.61 (7)	1.42 (7)	1.30 (6)	0.89 (9)	1.11 (10)
BRANIFF INTERNATIONAL CORP	Baa/BBB-	12/78	1.55 (8)	1.46 (5)	1.36 (4)	1.28 (5)	1.36 (7)
NATIONAL AIRLINES INC	Baa/BB#	6/78	1.53 (9)	1.11 (12)	1.16 (11)	1.33 (4)	1.89 (3)
TIGER INTERNATIONAL	Baa/NR#	12/78	1.48 (10)	1.28 (10)	1.22 (7)	1.21P(6)	1.19 (8)
TRANS WORLD CORP	Ba /BB	12/78	1.43 (11)	1.32 (9)	1.17 (10)	0.62P(12)	0.88P(12)
EASTERN AIR LINES	B /B*	12/78	1.41 (12)	1.17 (11)	1.19 (8)	0.84 (10)	1.07 (11)
AVERAGE			2.19	1.88	1.63	1.25	1.63
MEDIAN			1.71	1.44	1.26	1.17	1.45

Non-Rail Transportation Industry

LTD/CAPITALIZATION (%)

	RATINGS	FYR END	78		77		76		75		74	
NORTHWEST AIRLINES INC	NR /NR	12/78	11.2	(1)	11.8	(1)	15.5	(1)	28.3	(2)	26.6	(1)
CONSOLIDATED FREIGHTWAYS INC	A /A+	12/78	12.3	(2)	16.0	(2)	19.3	(2)	24.6	(1)	32.2	(2)
NATIONAL AIRLINES INC	Baa/BB#	6/78	16.5	(3)	33.8	(4)	42.0	(5)	46.7	(6)	46.4	(6)
DELTA AIR LINES INC	Baa/A#	6/78	18.5	(4)	27.7	(3)	39.3	(3)	45.1	(4)	43.7	(3)
CONTINENTAL AIR LINES INC	Ba /B*	12/78	46.7	(5)	60.0	(11)	67.7	(10)	72.8	(10)	69.1	(10)
UAL INC	Ba /BB*	12/78	49.3	(6)	47.2	(7)	53.8	(7)	55.7	(7)	54.1	(7)
AMERICAN AIRLINES INC	Baa/BBB	12/78	54.4	(7)	37.4	(5)	40.6	(4)	45.5	(5)	45.8	(4)
WESTERN AIR LINES INC	Ba /B*	12/78	57.2	(8)	39.5	(6)	48.5	(6)	43.8	(3)	46.4	(5)
BRANIFF INTERNATIONAL CORP	Baa/BBB-	12/78	61.4	(9)	55.3	(10)	56.1	(8)	58.4	(8)	59.5	(8)
TRANS WORLD CORP	Ba /BB	12/78	67.6	(10)	54.5	(9)	70.6	(11)	74.4	(11)	69.5	(11)
EASTERN AIR LINES	B /B*	12/78	68.1	(11)	53.7	(8)	62.6	(9)	68.2	(9)	67.1	(9)
TIGER INTERNATIONAL	Baa/NR#	12/78	74.4	(12)	74.5	(12)	74.5	(12)	75.6	(12)	76.6	(12)
AVERAGE			44.80		42.62		49.21		53.26		53.09	
MEDIAN			51.85		43.38		51.18		51.19		50.24	

TOT LIABILITY/TOT STK EQUITY

	RATINGS	FYR END	78		77		76		75		74	
NORTHWEST AIRLINES INC	NR /NR	12/78	75.5	(1)	73.8	(1)	73.0	(1)	94.8	(1)	90.0	(1)
CONSOLIDATED FREIGHTWAYS INC	A /A+	12/78	112.6	(2)	113.6	(2)	118.8	(2)	115.2	(2)	135.3	(2)
NATIONAL AIRLINES INC	Baa/BB#	6/78	122.0	(3)	139.2	(3)	162.4	(3)	181.6	(4)	188.8	(4)
DELTA AIR LINES INC	Baa/A#	6/78	123.5	(4)	140.4	(4)	170.7	(4)	181.3	(3)	169.3	(3)
CONTINENTAL AIR LINES INC	Ba /B*	12/78	196.3	(5)	275.1	(11)	333.2	(10)	394.4	(10)	352.7	(10)
UAL INC	Ba /BB*	12/78	212.6	(6)	225.3	(9)	258.4	(7)	245.5	(8)	229.5	(8)
AMERICAN AIRLINES INC	Baa/BBB	12/78	234.3	(7)	158.0	(5)	181.2	(5)	196.2	(5)	191.8	(5)
BRANIFF INTERNATIONAL CORP	Baa/BBB-	12/78	241.9	(8)	197.6	(6)	202.4	(6)	219.3	(7)	221.0	(7)
WESTERN AIR LINES INC	Ba /B*	12/78	254.6	(9)	200.2	(7)	268.2	(8)	204.6	(6)	199.0	(6)
EASTERN AIR LINES	B /B*	12/78	333.2	(10)	224.2	(8)	284.1	(9)	344.3	(9)	310.8	(9)
TRANS WORLD CORP	Ba /BB	12/78	342.5	(11)	244.8	(10)	402.4	(12)	475.6	(12)	377.9	(11)
TIGER INTERNATIONAL	Baa/NR#	12/78	402.0	(12)	412.9	(12)	393.5	(11)	411.1	(11)	432.8	(12)
AVERAGE			220.92		200.42		237.35		255.33		241.58	
MEDIAN			223.47		198.89		230.41		211.94		210.00	

LTD/NET PLANT (%)

	RATINGS	FYR END	78		77		76		75		74	
NORTHWEST AIRLINES INC	NR /NR	12/78	9.4	(1)	9.7	(1)	12.1	(1)	23.7	(1)	21.9	(1)
NATIONAL AIRLINES INC	Baa/BB#	6/78	11.4	(2)	27.0	(4)	36.7	(5)	38.7	(5)	38.7	(5)
DELTA AIR LINES INC	Baa/A#	6/78	12.7	(3)	18.9	(2)	28.5	(3)	33.7	(3)	33.1	(2)
CONSOLIDATED FREIGHTWAYS INC	A /A+	12/78	14.3	(4)	19.9	(3)	23.8	(2)	27.5	(2)	37.3	(3)
CONTINENTAL AIR LINES INC	Ba /B*	12/78	38.1	(5)	50.5	(8)	59.0	(9)	66.6	(9)	58.9	(8)
UAL INC	Ba /BB*	12/78	49.2	(6)	50.3	(7)	57.1	(8)	57.4	(7)	56.1	(7)
WESTERN AIR LINES INC	Ba /B*	12/78	51.1	(7)	30.6	(5)	35.8	(4)	34.8	(4)	37.4	(4)
BRANIFF INTERNATIONAL CORP	Baa/BBB-	12/78	58.6	(8)	55.2	(10)	56.9	(7)	61.2	(8)	63.5	(9)
AMERICAN AIRLINES INC	Baa/BBB	12/78	62.2	(9)	45.7	(6)	47.5	(6)	49.5	(6)	46.0	(6)
EASTERN AIR LINES	B /B*	12/78	63.1	(10)	52.0	(9)	63.7	(10)	68.0	(10)	71.9	(11)
TRANS WORLD CORP	Ba /BB	12/78	72.4	(11)	59.0	(11)	80.1	(11)	81.4	(11)	71.4	(10)
TIGER INTERNATIONAL	Baa/NR#	12/78	81.6	(12)	85.9	(12)	92.5	(12)	91.4	(12)	92.8	(12)
AVERAGE			43.69		42.07		49.49		52.83		52.41	
MEDIAN			50.14		48.00		52.23		53.45		51.05	

NET INCOME AS % NET SALES

	RATINGS	FYR END	78		77		76		75		74	
NORTHWEST AIRLINES INC	NR /NR	12/78	7.8	(1)	8.9	(1)	5.4	(1)	5.4	(1)	8.5	(1)
UAL INC	Ba /BB*	12/78	7.8	(2)	2.8	(8)	0.6	(12)	-0.2	(8)	4.3	(7)
TIGER INTERNATIONAL	Baa/NR#	12/78	7.1	(3)	5.7	(2)	5.0	(2)	5.1	(2)	4.7	(6)
DELTA AIR LINES INC	Baa/A#	6/78	6.4	(4)	5.4	(3)	4.6	(3)	3.6	(3)	7.4	(2)
CONTINENTAL AIR LINES INC	Ba /B*	12/78	6.3	(5)	3.9	(6)	1.7	(9)	-1.9	(10)	1.8	(9)
AMERICAN AIRLINES INC	Baa/BBB	12/78	4.9	(6)	3.6	(7)	2.8	(6)	-1.2	(9)	1.2	(10)
BRANIFF INTERNATIONAL CORP	Baa/BBB-	12/78	4.7	(7)	4.6	(5)	3.9	(5)	3.4	(4)	4.7	(5)
WESTERN AIR LINES INC	Ba /B*	12/78	4.6	(8)	2.1	(9)	2.5	(7)	1.0	(7)	4.9	(4)
CONSOLIDATED FREIGHTWAYS INC	A /A+	12/78	4.5	(9)	4.8	(4)	4.4	(4)	2.9	(6)	3.4	(8)
EASTERN AIR LINES	B /B*	12/78	2.8	(10)	1.7	(11)	1.9	(8)	-3.1	(11)	0.5	(11)
NATIONAL AIRLINES INC	Baa/BB#	6/78	2.4	(11)	0.6	(12)	1.5	(10)	3.3	(5)	6.7	(3)
TRANS WORLD CORP	Ba /BB	12/78	2.3	(12)	1.9	(10)	1.2	(11)	-3.3	(12)	-0.9	(12)
AVERAGE			5.15		3.83		2.96		1.25		3.93	
MEDIAN			4.78		3.75		2.64		1.93		4.47	

NET TANG ASSETS/LTD (%)

	RATINGS	FYR END	78		77		76		75		74	
NORTHWEST AIRLINES INC	NR /NR	12/78	874.1	(1)	831.6	(1)	632.5	(1)	346.6	(2)	367.9	(1)
CONSOLIDATED FREIGHTWAYS INC	A /A+	12/78	717.5	(2)	559.1	(2)	481.2	(2)	373.7	(1)	287.5	(2)
NATIONAL AIRLINES INC	Baa/BB#	6/78	563.2	(3)	279.2	(4)	227.9	(5)	204.9	(6)	205.5	(5)
DELTA AIR LINES INC	Baa/A#	6/78	534.9	(4)	354.6	(3)	252.6	(3)	219.2	(4)	228.3	(3)
CONTINENTAL AIR LINES INC	Ba /B*	12/78	207.9	(5)	162.1	(11)	144.6	(10)	137.3	(10)	144.1	(9)
UAL INC	Ba /BB*	12/78	199.3	(6)	205.8	(7)	180.4	(7)	173.3	(7)	182.2	(7)
AMERICAN AIRLINES INC	Baa/BBB	12/78	178.6	(7)	256.2	(5)	233.8	(4)	208.3	(5)	194.1	(6)
WESTERN AIR LINES INC	Ba /B*	12/78	172.9	(8)	245.9	(6)	200.3	(6)	225.8	(3)	211.2	(4)
BRANIFF INTERNATIONAL CORP	Baa/BBB-	12/78	154.8	(9)	172.9	(9)	169.7	(8)	162.3	(8)	158.7	(8)
EASTERN AIR LINES	B /B*	12/78	144.9	(10)	181.2	(8)	155.4	(9)	141.6	(9)	144.0	(10)
TRANS WORLD CORP	Ba /BB	12/78	135.1	(11)	162.5	(10)	127.8	(11)	121.3	(12)	129.8	(11)
TIGER INTERNATIONAL	Baa/NR#	12/78	128.1	(12)	127.7	(12)	121.0	(12)	126.7	(11)	127.0	(12)
AVERAGE			334.28		294.89		243.93		203.40		198.36	
MEDIAN			188.93		225.85		190.35		189.08		188.17	

CASH FLOW/LTD (%)

	RATINGS	FYR END	78		77		76		75		74	
CONSOLIDATED FREIGHTWAYS INC	A /A+	12/78	251.1	(1)	179.1	(2)	145.5	(2)	90.0	(1)	76.1	(2)
DELTA AIR LINES INC	Baa/A#	6/78	196.5	(2)	130.8	(3)	68.5	(3)	54.5	(3)	69.0	(3)
NORTHWEST AIRLINES INC	NR /NR	12/78	196.1	(3)	255.4	(1)	156.3	(1)	60.4	(2)	87.7	(1)
NATIONAL AIRLINES INC	Baa/BB#	6/78	146.3	(4)	35.9	(6)	25.2	(8)	34.1	(5)	55.1	(5)
UAL INC	Ba /BB*	12/78	50.4	(5)	35.7	(7)	23.9	(9)	20.8	(7)	42.6	(6)
CONTINENTAL AIR LINES INC	Ba /B*	12/78	39.4	(6)	27.0	(11)	18.8	(11)	12.8	(9)	17.1	(9)
WESTERN AIR LINES INC	Ba /B*	12/78	30.6	(7)	49.2	(4)	49.6	(4)	42.2	(4)	58.2	(4)
BRANIFF INTERNATIONAL CORP	Baa/BBB-	12/78	29.7	(8)	35.4	(8)	31.6	(6)	27.5	(6)	31.1	(8)
AMERICAN AIRLINES INC	Baa/BBB	12/78	27.8	(9)	42.2	(5)	45.2	(5)	17.5	(8)	31.1	(7)
TRANS WORLD CORP	Ba /BB	12/78	25.3	(10)	34.7	(9)	19.8	(10)	3.2	(12)	10.7	(11)
EASTERN AIR LINES	B /B*	12/78	25.3	(11)	31.2	(10)	27.2	(7)	10.6	(11)	16.8	(10)
TIGER INTERNATIONAL	Baa/NR#	12/78	17.3	(12)	14.2	(12)	11.9	(12)	10.7	(10)	9.6	(12)
AVERAGE			86.32		72.57		51.96		32.03		42.10	
MEDIAN			34.97		35.81		29.43		24.17		36.89	

Non-Rail Transportation Industry

NET CASH FL/CAP EXP (%)

	RATINGS	FYR END	78		77		76		75		74	
NATIONAL AIRLINES INC	Baa/BB#	6/78	261.4	(1)	264.5	(1)	261.3	(2)	73.9	(7)	318.9	(1)
TRANS WORLD CORP	Ba /BB	12/78	143.8	(2)	220.8	(3)	183.0	(5)	20.1	(12)	46.4	(11)
DELTA AIR LINES INC	Baa/A#	6/78	135.5	(3)	119.1	(7)	107.4	(10)	67.8	(9)	51.5	(9)
CONTINENTAL AIR LINES INC	Ba /B*	12/78	128.6	(4)	240.9	(2)	313.1	(1)	47.4	(11)	48.4	(10)
NORTHWEST AIRLINES INC	NR /NR	12/78	119.6	(5)	185.9	(4)	221.8	(3)	84.1	(4)	124.3	(5)
UAL INC	Ba /BB*	12/78	103.4	(6)	124.0	(6)	220.1	(4)	79.6	(5)	151.5	(3)
CONSOLIDATED FREIGHTWAYS INC	A /A+	12/78	89.0	(7)	106.1	(8)	163.5	(7)	135.5	(1)	79.2	(7)
AMERICAN AIRLINES INC	Baa/BBB	12/78	81.5	(8)	65.7	(10)	120.9	(8)	109.1	(2)	143.7	(4)
TIGER INTERNATIONAL	Baa/NR#	12/78	70.5	(9)	49.3	(12)	95.7	(11)	52.3	(10)	20.4	(12)
EASTERN AIR LINES	B /B*	12/78	56.9	(10)	131.8	(5)	170.4	(6)	77.1	(6)	183.7	(2)
WESTERN AIR LINES INC	Ba /B*	12/78	48.9	(11)	59.2	(11)	116.8	(9)	91.2	(3)	65.9	(8)
BRANIFF INTERNATIONAL CORP	Baa/BBB-	12/78	45.3	(12)	66.4	(9)	63.4	(12)	72.1	(8)	97.7	(6)
AVERAGE			107.04		136.14		169.78		75.85		110.95	
MEDIAN			96.20		121.57		166.92		75.50		88.43	

AFT TAX RET ON COM EQTY (%)

	RATINGS	FYR END	78		77		76		75		74	
UAL INC	Ba /BB*	12/78	25.7	(1)	10.1	(10)	2.3	(12)	-0.8	(8)	12.7	(6)
CONTINENTAL AIR LINES INC	Ba /B*	12/78	21.5	(2)	14.3	(4)	5.9	(10)	-6.6	(10)	5.2	(9)
WESTERN AIR LINES INC	Ba /B*	12/78	21.4	(3)	11.1	(7)	12.8	(4)	3.7	(7)	18.2	(3)
CONSOLIDATED FREIGHTWAYS INC	A /A+	12/78	21.1	(4)	22.1	(1)	19.8	(1)	11.5	(2)	18.3	(2)
BRANIFF INTERNATIONAL CORP	Baa/BBB-	12/78	18.1	(5)	16.5	(2)	13.9	(2)	12.2	(1)	16.9	(4)
DELTA AIR LINES INC	Baa/A#	6/78	17.8	(6)	14.9	(3)	13.0	(3)	10.2	(3)	20.4	(1)
AMERICAN AIRLINES INC	Baa/BBB	12/78	17.0	(7)	10.4	(9)	9.2	(7)	-3.8	(9)	3.6	(10)
TRANS WORLD CORP	Ba /BB	12/78	16.3	(8)	12.9	(5)	9.3	(6)	-26.6	(12)	-6.1	(12)
TIGER INTERNATIONAL	Baa/NR#	12/78	15.4	(9)	11.0	(8)	8.5	(8)	8.4	(4)	7.2	(8)
EASTERN AIR LINES	B /B*	12/78	14.1	(10)	9.0	(11)	10.2	(5)	-18.8	(11)	2.2	(11)
NORTHWEST AIRLINES INC	NR /NR	12/78	7.8	(11)	12.4	(6)	7.8	(9)	7.0	(5)	11.0	(7)
NATIONAL AIRLINES INC	Baa/BB#	6/78	7.1	(12)	1.6	(12)	2.6	(11)	5.8	(6)	16.3	(5)
AVERAGE			16.94		12.20		9.60		0.19		10.48	
MEDIAN			17.38		11.76		9.25		4.79		11.83	

RET ON TOT ASSETS (%)

	RATINGS	FYR END	78		77		76		75		74	
CONSOLIDATED FREIGHTWAYS INC	A /A+	12/78	19.0	(1)	20.1	(1)	18.1	(1)	11.5	(1)	15.8	(2)
DELTA AIR LINES INC	Baa/A#	6/78	15.0	(2)	12.1	(3)	9.8	(2)	8.3	(3)	15.9	(1)
UAL INC	Ba /BB*	12/78	11.7	(3)	5.3	(10)	3.3	(11)	2.1	(9)	10.9	(6)
CONTINENTAL AIR LINES INC	Ba /B*	12/78	11.3	(4)	7.8	(6)	6.4	(9)	2.6	(8)	7.4	(8)
BRANIFF INTERNATIONAL CORP	Baa/BBB-	12/78	10.5	(5)	10.9	(4)	9.6	(4)	8.7	(2)	12.3	(5)
TIGER INTERNATIONAL	Baa/NR#	12/78	10.2	(6)	8.4	(5)	7.7	(6)	7.9	(4)	7.1	(9)
WESTERN AIR LINES INC	Ba /B*	12/78	9.7	(7)	7.1	(8)	7.8	(5)	3.2	(7)	13.4	(3)
NORTHWEST AIRLINES INC	NR /NR	12/78	8.4	(8)	12.5	(2)	9.8	(3)	5.3	(6)	10.7	(7)
EASTERN AIR LINES	B /B*	12/78	7.6	(9)	6.2	(9)	7.1	(7)	0.3	(10)	5.6	(10)
AMERICAN AIRLINES INC	Baa/BBB	12/78	7.2	(10)	5.1	(11)	5.6	(10)	-0.2	(11)	3.4	(11)
TRANS WORLD CORP	Ba /BB	12/78	7.2	(11)	7.2	(7)	6.7	(8)	-1.9	(12)	2.0	(12)
NATIONAL AIRLINES INC	Baa/BB#	6/78	6.7	(12)	2.1	(12)	3.1	(12)	5.4	(5)	13.3	(4)
AVERAGE			10.37		8.74		7.91		4.44		9.82	
MEDIAN			9.98		7.48		7.38		4.25		10.79	

Oils Industry (Domestic)

PRETAX COVERAGE

	RATINGS	FYR END	78	77	76	75	74
PHILLIPS PETROLEUM CO	Aaa/AA	12/78	22.23P(1)	14.99P(2)	15.46P(3)	15.53P(5)	14.74P(5)
STANDARD OIL CO (INDIANA)	Aaa/AAA	12/78	12.63P(2)	13.85P(3)	15.99P(2)	15.88P(4)	16.06P(4)
SHELL OIL CO	Aaa/AAA	12/78	12.51P(3)	13.31P(4)	16.96 (1)	13.60 (6)	16.15 (3)
CONTINENTAL OIL CO	Aa /AA	12/78	10.52P(4)	12.15P(5)	14.27P(5)	11.50P(8)	12.46P(8)
SUN CO	Aa /AA	12/78	9.83P(5)	12.02P(6)	13.03P(7)	11.60P(7)	14.11P(6)
MARATHON OIL CO	A /A+	12/78	8.76 (6)	9.69 (8)	14.31 (4)	23.22 (1)	25.54 (1)
UNION OIL CO OF CALIFORNIA	Aa /AA	12/78	8.36 (7)	8.45P(10)	8.85P(11)	8.84P(10)	12.17P(9)
ASHLAND OIL INC	A /A	9/78	8.14 (8)	7.23 (13)	8.11 (12)	7.85 (12)	7.06 (14)
AMERADA HESS CORP	Baa/BBB*	12/78	7.81 (9)	10.85 (7)	9.13 (10)	7.35 (14)	9.10 (11)
OCCIDENTAL PETROLEUM CORP	A /BBB	12/78	7.66I(10)	8.55I(9)	7.75I(13)	7.68 (13)	8.96 (12)
KERR-MCGEE CORP	Aa /AA	12/78	6.31 (11)	8.25 (11)	10.51 (8)	16.77 (2)	19.24 (2)
QUAKER STATE OIL REFINING	A /A	12/78	6.06 (12)	7.78 (12)	9.56 (9)	16.12 (3)	13.84 (7)
SUPERIOR OIL CO	A /AA	12/78	4.83 (13)	23.28 (1)	13.37 (6)	11.22 (9)	8.40 (13)
ATLANTIC RICHFIELD CO	Aa /AA	12/78	4.64P(14)	4.19P(15)	6.18P(15)	8.05P(11)	11.54P(10)
PENNZOIL CO	Baa/BBB	12/78	3.51H(15)	3.74H(16)	4.00H(16)	4.09H(16)	4.17H(16)
CITIES SERVICE CO	A /A	12/78	3.50P(16)	6.08P(14)	6.32P(14)	4.92P(15)	5.96P(15)
STANDARD OIL CO (OHIO)	A /AA-	12/78	2.38 (17)	1.55P(17)	1.71P(17)	2.49P(17)	4.01 (17)
AVERAGE			8.22	9.76	10.32	10.98	11.97
MEDIAN			7.81	8.55	9.56	11.22	12.17

AFTER TAX COVERAGE

	RATINGS	FYR END	78	77	76	75	74
PHILLIPS PETROLEUM CO	Aaa/AA	12/78	9.50P(1)	6.82P(3)	6.38P(6)	7.31P(4)	8.00P(6)
SHELL OIL CO	Aaa/AAA	12/78	8.03P(2)	8.18P(2)	9.96 (1)	8.26 (3)	11.21 (2)
STANDARD OIL CO (INDIANA)	Aaa/AAA	12/78	5.67P(3)	6.05P(5)	7.01P(4)	6.88P(6)	9.40P(4)
SUN CO	Aa /AA	12/78	5.11P(4)	6.25P(4)	7.05P(3)	4.82P(8)	7.56P(7)
ASHLAND OIL INC	A /A	9/78	4.87 (5)	4.35 (10)	4.38 (11)	4.19 (11)	5.10 (12)
UNION OIL CO OF CALIFORNIA	Aa /AA	12/78	4.75 (6)	4.97P(7)	4.77P(10)	4.80P(9)	7.50P(8)
CONTINENTAL OIL CO	Aa /AA	12/78	4.09P(7)	4.32P(11)	5.77P(7)	4.49P(10)	5.19P(11)
KERR-MCGEE CORP	Aa /AA	12/78	3.98 (8)	5.16 (6)	6.91 (5)	10.28 (1)	11.84 (1)
QUAKER STATE OIL REFINING	A /A	12/78	3.63 (9)	4.52 (9)	5.56 (8)	8.72 (2)	8.66 (5)
AMERADA HESS CORP	Baa/BBB*	12/78	3.19 (10)	4.70 (8)	4.19 (12)	3.77 (12)	5.05 (13)
ATLANTIC RICHFIELD CO	Aa /AA	12/78	3.06P(11)	3.29P(13)	3.66P(14)	3.59P(13)	5.93P(10)
MARATHON OIL CO	A /A+	12/78	3.03 (12)	3.25 (14)	5.39 (9)	7.10 (5)	9.69 (3)
SUPERIOR OIL CO	A /AA	12/78	2.88 (13)	13.54 (1)	7.44 (2)	6.49 (7)	6.08 (9)
PENNZOIL CO	Baa/BBB	12/78	2.69H(14)	2.83H(16)	3.12H(15)	3.08H(15)	3.39H(16)
CITIES SERVICE CO	A /A	12/78	2.33P(15)	3.71P(12)	3.89P(13)	3.23P(14)	4.39P(14)
STANDARD OIL CO (OHIO)	A /AA-	12/78	1.93 (16)	1.40P(17)	1.50P(17)	1.99P(17)	3.04 (17)
OCCIDENTAL PETROLEUM CORP	A /BBB	12/78	1.11P(17)	2.86P(15)	2.70 (16)	2.90 (16)	4.19 (15)
AVERAGE			4.11	5.07	5.28	5.41	6.84
MEDIAN			3.63	4.52	5.39	4.80	6.08

Oils Industry (Domestic)

AFTER TAX COV (INCL RENTS)

	RATINGS	FYR END	78	77	76	75	74
PHILLIPS PETROLEUM CO	Aaa/AA	12/78	6.49P(1)	4.80P(2)	3.23P(8)	3.09P(5)	3.53P(7)
SHELL OIL CO	Aaa/AAA	12/78	3.97P(2)	3.76P(5)	4.62 (3)	3.82 (3)	4.65 (3)
STANDARD OIL CO (INDIANA)	Aaa/AAA	12/78	3.77P(3)	3.85P(4)	3.40P(6)	3.25P(4)	4.06P(4)
KERR-MCGEE CORP	Aa /AA	12/78	3.42 (4)	4.20 (3)	5.44 (1)	7.33 (1)	7.53 (1)
SUN CO	Aa /AA	12/78	3.15P(5)	3.44P(6)	3.69P(5)	2.78P(6)	4.05P(5)
CONTINENTAL OIL CO	Aa /AA	12/78	3.10P(6)	3.13P(7)	3.36P(7)	2.66P(7)	2.90P(11)
ATLANTIC RICHFIELD CO	Aa /AA	12/78	2.56P(7)	2.50P(10)	2.54P(10)	2.20P(11)	2.98P(9)
ASHLAND OIL INC	A /A	9/78	2.44 (8)	2.04 (14)	1.92 (14)	1.79 (13)	2.11 (13)
PENNZOIL CO	Baa/BBB	12/78	2.33H(9)	2.42H(11)	2.63H(9)	2.61H(8)	2.92H(10)
AMERADA HESS CORP	Baa/BBB*	12/78	1.74 (10)	1.89 (15)	1.89 (15)	1.70 (14)	2.09 (15)
CITIES SERVICE CO	A /A	12/78	1.73P(11)	2.25P(12)	2.27P(12)	1.94P(12)	2.71P(12)
STANDARD OIL CO (OHIO)	A /AA-	12/78	1.57 (12)	1.31P(16)	1.38P(16)	1.64P(15)	2.11 (14)
OCCIDENTAL PETROLEUM CORP	A /BBB	12/78	1.07P(13)	2.17P(13)	2.15 (13)	2.35 (10)	3.61 (6)
MARATHON OIL CO	A /A+	12/78	NA (-)	2.89 (8)	4.14 (4)	4.40 (2)	5.92 (2)
QUAKER STATE OIL REFINING	A /A	12/78	NA (-)	NA (-)	NA (-)	NA (-)	NA (-)
SUPERIOR OIL CO	A /AAA	12/78	NA (-)	7.34 (1)	5.15 (2)	NA (-)	NA (-)
UNION OIL CO OF CALIFORNIA	Aa /AA	12/78	NA (-)	2.60P(9)	2.41P(11)	2.40P(9)	3.05P(8)
AVERAGE			2.87	3.16	3.14	2.93	3.62
MEDIAN			2.56	2.74	2.93	2.61	3.05

NET INCOME AS % NET SALES

	RATINGS	FYR END	78	77	76	75	74
PHILLIPS PETROLEUM CO	Aaa/AA	12/78	10.2 (1)	8.2 (3)	7.2 (5)	6.7 (6)	8.6 (6)
STANDARD OIL CO (OHIO)	A /AA-	12/78	8.7 (2)	5.2 (11)	4.7 (14)	5.1 (8)	5.8 (14)
PENNZOIL CO	Baa/BBB	12/78	8.3 (3)	9.3 (2)	14.5 (1)	9.9 (2)	12.9 (2)
SHELL OIL CO	Aaa/AAA	12/78	7.4 (4)	7.3 (5)	7.6 (4)	6.3 (7)	8.1 (7)
STANDARD OIL CO (INDIANA)	Aaa/AAA	12/78	7.2 (5)	7.8 (4)	7.7 (3)	7.9 (4)	10.7 (3)
ATLANTIC RICHFIELD CO	Aa /AA	12/78	6.5 (6)	6.4 (6)	6.8 (7)	4.8 (10)	7.0 (10)
UNION OIL CO OF CALIFORNIA	Aa /AA	12/78	6.4 (7)	5.9 (8)	5.0 (13)	4.6 (11)	6.5 (11)
KERR-MCGEE CORP	Aa /AA	12/78	5.7 (8)	5.5 (10)	6.9 (6)	7.3 (5)	7.5 (8)
QUAKER STATE OIL REFINING	A /A	12/78	4.9 (9)	6.0 (7)	5.9 (9)	7.9 (3)	9.0 (5)
SUN CO	Aa /AA	12/78	4.9 B(10)	5.6 B(9)	6.6 B(8)	5.0 B(9)	9.9 B(4)
CONTINENTAL OIL CO	Aa /AA	12/78	4.8 (11)	4.4 (14)	5.8 (10)	4.6 (12)	4.7 (16)
ASHLAND OIL INC	A /A	9/78	4.7 (12)	3.4 (17)	3.3 (17)	3.3 (16)	3.5 (17)
MARATHON OIL CO	A /A+	12/78	4.4 (13)	4.6 (13)	5.6 (11)	4.5 (13)	5.9 (12)
SUPERIOR OIL CO	A /AA	12/78	4.2 (14)	11.5 (1)	11.4 (2)	13.6 (1)	18.3 (1)
AMERADA HESS CORP	Baa/BBB*	12/78	3.0 (15)	3.9 (15)	3.9 (15)	4.0 (15)	5.4 (15)
CITIES SERVICE CO	A /A	12/78	2.5 (16)	4.8 (12)	5.5 (12)	4.3 (14)	7.3 (9)
OCCIDENTAL PETROLEUM CORP	A /BBB	12/78	0.1 (17)	3.6 (16)	3.3 (16)	3.3 (17)	5.8 (13)
AVERAGE			5.52	6.08	6.58	6.06	8.06
MEDIAN			4.94	5.64	5.95	5.01	7.26

LTD/CAPITALIZATION (%)

	RATINGS	FYR END	78	77	76	75	74
PHILLIPS PETROLEUM CO	Aaa/AA	12/78	18.0 (1)	23.0 (5)	23.6 (5)	26.9 (8)	22.5 (6)
KERR-MCGEE CORP	Aa /AA	12/78	19.0 (2)	23.0 (4)	26.0 (6)	21.1 (3)	19.5 (2)
SHELL OIL CO	Aaa/AAA	12/78	20.5 (3)	22.2 (3)	20.4 (2)	23.5 (7)	21.5 (4)
SUN CO	Aa /AA	12/78	21.3 (4)	21.1 (2)	22.3 (4)	21.6 (5)	23.2 (8)
STANDARD OIL CO (INDIANA)	Aaa/AAA	12/78	26.2 (5)	27.0 (6)	22.2 (3)	23.4 (6)	21.8 (5)
QUAKER STATE OIL REFINING	A /A	12/78	31.5 (6)	31.7 (9)	32.0 (10)	21.5 (4)	22.5 (7)
UNION OIL CO OF CALIFORNIA	Aa /AA	12/78	32.0 (7)	29.6 (7)	30.6 (8)	27.6 (9)	25.2 (9)
CONTINENTAL OIL CO	Aa /AA	12/78	32.1 (8)	32.1 (10)	28.3 (7)	29.8 (10)	30.3 (12)
ASHLAND OIL INC	A /A	9/78	33.4 (9)	41.6 (14)	38.3 (13)	41.4 (14)	41.1 (15)
CITIES SERVICE CO	A /A	12/78	34.9 (10)	32.6 (11)	30.6 (9)	32.0 (12)	25.4 (10)
AMERADA HESS CORP	Baa/BBB*	12/78	36.0 (11)	36.7 (13)	37.0 (12)	38.0 (13)	40.4 (14)
SUPERIOR OIL CO	A /AA	12/78	36.0 (12)	11.7 (1)	11.6 (1)	15.2 (1)	20.9 (3)
ATLANTIC RICHFIELD CO	Aa /AA	12/78	37.5 (13)	36.2 (12)	34.6 (11)	30.4 (11)	26.1 (11)
MARATHON OIL CO	A /A+	12/78	42.1 (14)	43.9 (15)	47.3 (15)	19.8 (2)	17.3 (1)
OCCIDENTAL PETROLEUM CORP	A /BBB	12/78	45.6 (15)	31.3 (8)	41.5 (14)	41.5 (15)	48.7 (16)
PENNZOIL CO	Baa/BBB	12/78	54.0 (16)	51.9 (16)	50.9 (16)	58.7 (17)	60.8 (17)
STANDARD OIL CO (OHIO)	A /AA-	12/78	68.3 (17)	73.6 (17)	70.1 (17)	57.2 (16)	39.3 (13)
AVERAGE			34.61	33.49	33.36	31.15	29.79
MEDIAN			33.42	31.70	30.57	27.62	25.21

TOT LIABILITY/TOT STK EQUITY

	RATINGS	FYR END	78		77		76		75		74	
SHELL OIL CO	Aaa/AAA	12/78	71.2	(1)	68.6	(1)	70.7	(2)	79.2	(5)	72.2	(3)
KERR-MCGEE CORP	Aa /AA	12/78	85.7	(2)	82.8	(3)	78.0	(3)	71.8	(3)	77.9	(7)
SUN CO	Aa /AA	12/78	86.4	(3)	87.7	(4)	89.3	(6)	83.3	(6)	80.8	(11)
PHILLIPS PETROLEUM CO	Aaa/AA	12/78	90.7	(4)	89.1	(5)	86.3	(5)	87.5	(7)	77.2	(6)
STANDARD OIL CO (INDIANA)	Aaa/AAA	12/78	97.4	(5)	91.0	(6)	82.4	(4)	76.4	(4)	74.0	(5)
CITIES SERVICE CO	A /A	12/78	103.2	(6)	93.0	(7)	101.0	(9)	98.2	(9)	73.1	(4)
QUAKER STATE OIL REFINING	A /A	12/78	107.8	(7)	94.0	(9)	91.4	(7)	71.3	(2)	61.6	(1)
UNION OIL CO OF CALIFORNIA	Aa /AA	12/78	108.1	(8)	93.8	(8)	100.9	(8)	96.7	(8)	79.9	(9)
SUPERIOR OIL CO	A /AA	12/78	113.9	(9)	72.2	(2)	60.3	(1)	63.7	(1)	66.4	(2)
ATLANTIC RICHFIELD CO	Aa /AA	12/78	119.0	(10)	124.5	(10)	116.4	(10)	101.0	(11)	78.1	(8)
CONTINENTAL OIL CO	Aa /AA	12/78	136.5	(11)	132.5	(12)	129.2	(11)	142.9	(13)	127.5	(13)
AMERADA HESS CORP	Baa/BBB*	12/78	146.7	(12)	130.7	(11)	139.0	(12)	128.7	(12)	138.6	(14)
ASHLAND OIL INC	A /A	9/78	151.0	(13)	171.1	(16)	160.2	(14)	171.9	(14)	159.2	(15)
MARATHON OIL CO	A /A+	12/78	159.6	(14)	167.8	(14)	164.5	(15)	98.2	(10)	80.6	(10)
PENNZOIL CO	Baa/BBB	12/78	213.7	(15)	169.5	(15)	158.3	(13)	253.4	(17)	249.1	(17)
OCCIDENTAL PETROLEUM CORP	A /BBB	12/78	263.8	(16)	150.9	(13)	199.2	(16)	191.8	(16)	203.9	(16)
STANDARD OIL CO (OHIO)	A /AA-	12/78	308.0	(17)	363.1	(17)	304.1	(17)	188.8	(15)	110.8	(12)
AVERAGE			138.99		128.38		125.37		117.93		106.52	
MEDIAN			113.90		94.04		101.03		98.16		79.89	

LTD/NET PLANT (%)

	RATINGS	FYR END	78		77		76		75		74	
KERR-MCGEE CORP	Aa /AA	12/78	18.7	(1)	24.8	(4)	30.6	(5)	26.9	(5)	24.4	(2)
PHILLIPS PETROLEUM CO	Aaa/AA	12/78	19.7	(2)	25.9	(5)	31.4	(6)	36.6	(11)	30.6	(8)
SHELL OIL CO	Aaa/AAA	12/78	20.9	(3)	24.4	(2)	23.1	(2)	27.4	(6)	25.0	(3)
SUN CO	Aa /AA	12/78	25.0	(4)	24.6	(3)	24.7	(3)	23.9	(3)	26.4	(5)
STANDARD OIL CO (INDIANA)	Aaa/AAA	12/78	28.6	(5)	31.1	(7)	25.1	(4)	26.6	(4)	25.6	(4)
CONTINENTAL OIL CO	Aa /AA	12/78	34.4	(6)	36.0	(9)	33.9	(7)	32.3	(9)	36.6	(12)
QUAKER STATE OIL REFINING	A /A	12/78	35.8	(7)	36.9	(10)	40.6	(12)	28.6	(7)	31.3	(10)
UNION OIL CO OF CALIFORNIA	Aa /AA	12/78	36.0	(8)	34.5	(8)	35.5	(9)	31.4	(8)	31.1	(9)
CITIES SERVICE CO	A /A	12/78	38.0	(9)	37.0	(11)	34.4	(8)	36.8	(12)	29.5	(7)
ATLANTIC RICHFIELD CO	Aa /AA	12/78	38.4	(10)	38.1	(12)	36.8	(10)	32.5	(10)	32.4	(11)
SUPERIOR OIL CO	A /AA	12/78	38.5	(11)	12.4	(1)	14.6	(1)	19.5	(1)	27.7	(6)
OCCIDENTAL PETROLEUM CORP	A /BBB	12/78	38.9	(12)	27.4	(6)	39.7	(11)	44.3	(13)	63.4	(17)
MARATHON OIL CO	A /A+	12/78	39.9	(13)	42.3	(13)	49.0	(14)	20.6	(2)	19.2	(1)
ASHLAND OIL INC	A /A	9/78	43.9	(14)	49.9	(15)	47.3	(13)	53.7	(15)	58.4	(15)
AMERADA HESS CORP	Baa/BBB*	12/78	45.5	(15)	48.7	(14)	50.0	(15)	50.8	(14)	56.9	(14)
PENNZOIL CO	Baa/BBB	12/78	52.9	(16)	56.4	(16)	63.1	(16)	54.8	(16)	60.1	(16)
STANDARD OIL CO (OHIO)	A /AA-	12/78	72.1	(17)	81.4	(17)	74.5	(17)	59.4	(17)	45.9	(13)
AVERAGE			36.90		37.17		38.49		35.66		36.73	
MEDIAN			38.02		35.96		35.51		32.27		31.06	

NET TANG ASSETS/LTD (%)

	RATINGS	FYR END	78		77		76		75		74	
PHILLIPS PETROLEUM CO	Aaa/AA	12/78	535.5	(1)	417.2	(4)	412.0	(5)	362.6	(8)	438.2	(7)
KERR-MCGEE CORP	Aa /AA	12/78	488.0	(2)	414.2	(5)	375.1	(6)	464.9	(3)	510.6	(2)
SHELL OIL CO	Aaa/AAA	12/78	474.0	(3)	448.2	(2)	486.8	(2)	421.8	(6)	460.9	(4)
SUN CO	Aa /AA	12/78	439.5	(4)	442.2	(3)	426.1	(4)	439.2	(5)	405.7	(8)
STANDARD OIL CO (INDIANA)	Aaa/AAA	12/78	374.5	(5)	363.4	(6)	438.2	(3)	419.0	(7)	452.5	(5)
UNION OIL CO OF CALIFORNIA	Aa /AA	12/78	309.0	(6)	334.4	(7)	323.1	(9)	357.5	(9)	391.8	(9)
QUAKER STATE OIL REFINING	A /A	12/78	303.3	(7)	301.5	(10)	296.7	(10)	460.2	(4)	441.0	(6)
CONTINENTAL OIL CO	Aa /AA	12/78	299.1	(8)	300.8	(11)	340.0	(7)	322.7	(11)	314.0	(12)
ASHLAND OIL INC	A /A	9/78	289.4	(9)	233.0	(14)	255.3	(13)	237.0	(14)	240.2	(15)
CITIES SERVICE CO	A /A	12/78	284.2	(10)	304.4	(9)	323.4	(8)	324.3	(8)	314.0	(12)
AMERADA HESS CORP	Baa/BBB*	12/78	275.7	(11)	269.5	(13)	267.7	(12)	262.1	(13)	245.9	(13)
SUPERIOR OIL CO	A /AA	12/78	275.0	(12)	843.3	(1)	848.9	(1)	648.7	(1)	469.0	(3)
ATLANTIC RICHFIELD CO	Aa /AA	12/78	263.1	(13)	269.9	(12)	285.3	(11)	326.1	(10)	381.1	(11)
MARATHON OIL CO	A /A+	12/78	233.4	(14)	224.3	(15)	205.8	(15)	490.3	(2)	560.4	(1)
OCCIDENTAL PETROLEUM CORP	A /BEB	12/78	205.6	(15)	306.6	(8)	233.6	(14)	231.4	(15)	190.9	(16)
PENNZOIL CO	Baa/BBB	12/78	179.7	(16)	184.2	(16)	189.5	(16)	161.9	(17)	154.3	(17)
STANDARD OIL CO (OHIO)	A /AA-	12/78	140.3	(17)	129.3	(17)	130.4	(17)	166.8	(16)	243.6	(14)
AVERAGE			315.84		340.37		343.46		357.79		369.96	
MEDIAN			289.45		304.36		323.13		357.48		391.80	

Oils Industry (Domestic)

CASH FLOW/LTD (%)

	RATINGS	FYR END	78		77		76		75		74	
PHILLIPS PETROLEUM CO	Aaa/AA	12/78	140.7	(1)	106.3	(2)	97.1	(3)	81.1	(9)	115.2	(4)
KERR-MCGEE CORP	Aa /AA	12/78	109.5	(2)	86.4	(6)	73.7	(8)	99.3	(4)	121.4	(2)
SHELL OIL CO	Aaa/AAA	12/78	104.4	(3)	104.8	(3)	118.7	(2)	96.4	(5)	116.7	(3)
SUN CO	Aa /AA	12/78	88.8	(4)	93.5	(4)	92.9	(5)	90.3	(6)	89.8	(8)
STANDARD OIL CO (INDIANA)	Aaa/AAA	12/78	87.6	(5)	79.0	(8)	96.3	(4)	86.7	(8)	109.2	(7)
ASHLAND OIL INC	A /A	9/78	74.8	(6)	48.3	(14)	55.4	(12)	46.9	(14)	45.5	(15)
UNION OIL CO OF CALIFORNIA	Aa /AA	12/78	74.4	(7)	86.9	(5)	81.7	(7)	89.6	(7)	111.7	(5)
CONTINENTAL OIL CO	Aa /AA	12/78	68.1	(8)	66.0	(10)	81.7	(6)	80.2	(10)	71.4	(12)
QUAKER STATE OIL REFINING	A /A	12/78	62.4	(9)	67.0	(9)	61.3	(10)	119.4	(1)	110.7	(6)
ATLANTIC RICHFIELD CO	Aa /AA	12/78	58.5	(10)	50.7	(13)	55.7	(11)	57.7	(11)	78.2	(10)
CITIES SERVICE CO	A /A	12/78	58.3	(11)	55.6	(11)	66.9	(9)	53.0	(12)	77.8	(11)
AMERADA HESS CORP	Baa/BBB*	12/78	49.4	(12)	53.4	(12)	48.5	(13)	45.2	(15)	55.8	(13)
MARATHON OIL CO	A /A+	12/78	44.9	(13)	45.4	(15)	34.3	(15)	107.7	(2)	143.5	(1)
PENNZOIL CO	Baa/BBB	12/78	42.8	(14)	25.6	(16)	27.4	(16)	30.6	(16)	30.1	(16)
OCCIDENTAL PETROLEUM CORP	A /BBB	12/78	41.5	(15)	81.3	(7)	39.6	(14)	49.4	(13)	47.2	(14)
SUPERIOR OIL CO	A /AA	12/78	36.3	(16)	158.8	(1)	151.8	(1)	101.3	(3)	87.4	(9)
STANDARD OIL CO (OHIO)	A /AA-	12/78	23.7	(17)	8.7	(17)	7.4	(17)	12.5	(17)	25.9	(17)
AVERAGE			68.59		71.62		70.02		73.37		84.57	
MEDIAN			62.42		66.96		66.86		81.10		87.45	

NET CASH FL/CAP EXP (%)

	RATINGS	FYR END	78		77		76		75		74	
STANDARD OIL CO (OHIO)	A /AA-	12/78	124.6	(1)	32.6	(17)	12.7	(17)	11.7	(17)	24.4	(17)
ATLANTIC RICHFIELD CO	Aa /AA	12/78	121.0	(2)	71.4	(15)	56.3	(15)	43.9	(16)	69.6	(16)
ASHLAND OIL INC	A /A	9/78	114.7	(3)	53.7	(16)	90.0	(8)	70.1	(14)	92.4	(9)
UNION OIL CO OF CALIFORNIA	Aa /AA	12/78	113.0	(4)	97.6	(3)	82.5	(12)	83.8	(8)	93.5	(8)
STANDARD OIL CO (INDIANA)	Aaa/AAA	12/78	103.6	(5)	109.3	(2)	99.6	(5)	77.9	(13)	87.7	(10)
QUAKER STATE OIL REFINING	A /A	12/78	102.3	(6)	76.6	(11)	74.1	(14)	127.6	(1)	119.3	(2)
PHILLIPS PETROLEUM CO	Aaa/AA	12/78	97.9	(7)	76.2	(12)	93.6	(7)	86.8	(7)	104.9	(4)
SUN CO	Aa /AA	12/78	97.5	(8)	125.4	(1)	110.8	(2)	96.0	(3)	73.4	(14)
AMERADA HESS CORP	Baa/BBB*	12/78	96.3	(9)	85.6	(6)	102.3	(4)	91.1	(5)	78.5	(13)
KERR-MCGEE CORP	Aa /AA	12/78	91.5	(10)	84.1	(7)	78.9	(13)	80.7	(9)	104.5	(6)
CITIES SERVICE CO	A /A	12/78	83.3	(11)	87.7	(5)	87.5	(10)	78.6	(11)	85.4	(11)
MARATHON OIL CO	A /A+	12/78	80.9	(12)	81.3	(9)	85.5	(11)	93.1	(4)	97.9	(7)
PENNZOIL CO	Baa/BBB	12/78	79.5 V(13)		72.3 V(14)		103.9 J(3)		80.3 V(10)		70.2	(15)
CONTINENTAL OIL CO	Aa /AA	12/78	77.7	(14)	89.0	(4)	94.2	(6)	78.2	(12)	81.7	(12)
SHELL OIL CO	Aaa/AAA	12/78	77.4	(15)	73.9	(13)	89.9	(9)	87.3	(6)	129.7	(1)
SUPERIOR OIL CO	A /AA	12/78	57.4	(16)	83.4	(8)	129.4	(1)	113.9	(2)	104.9	(5)
OCCIDENTAL PETROLEUM CORP	A /BBB	12/78	42.0	(17)	80.9	(10)	51.4	(16)	69.0	(15)	108.1	(3)
AVERAGE			91.78		81.22		84.86		80.59		89.78	
MEDIAN			96.25		81.27		89.89		80.72		92.43	

AFT TAX RET ON COM EQTY (%)

	RATINGS	FYR END	78		77		76		75		74	
ASHLAND OIL INC	A /A	9/78	24.4	(1)	17.6	(1)	16.7	(4)	16.7	(3)	17.8	(8)
STANDARD OIL CO (OHIO)	A /AA-	12/78	22.1	(2)	10.8	(16)	8.9	(16)	8.7	(14)	10.2	(17)
PHILLIPS PETROLEUM CO	Aaa/AA	12/78	19.5	(3)	16.7	(2)	15.1	(6)	14.1	(6)	19.6	(6)
PENNZOIL CO	Baa/BBB	12/78	18.5	(4)	14.4	(5)	20.2	(1)	17.6	(2)	22.2	(2)
STANDARD OIL CO (INDIANA)	Aaa/AAA	12/78	15.1	(5)	15.0	(4)	14.5	(8)	14.1	(7)	18.9	(5)
UNION OIL CO OF CALIFORNIA	Aa /AA	12/78	14.4	(6)	13.6	(8)	12.5	(12)	11.7	(11)	14.6	(13)
CONTINENTAL OIL CO	Aa /AA	12/78	14.3	(7)	13.3	(10)	17.4	(2)	15.5	(5)	15.9	(11)
ATLANTIC RICHFIELD CO	Aa /AA	12/78	14.2	(8)	13.5	(9)	13.3	(10)	8.6	(15)	13.8	(14)
MARATHON OIL CO	A /A+	12/78	13.6	(9)	15.3	(3)	17.0	(3)	12.7	(9)	17.1	(10)
SHELL OIL CO	Aaa/AAA	12/78	13.3	(10)	14.0	(6)	15.4	(5)	13.2	(8)	17.4	(9)
QUAKER STATE OIL REFINING	A /A	12/78	12.5	(11)	13.7	(7)	13.9	(9)	18.5	(1)	20.1	(3)
SUN CO	Aa /AA	12/78	12.0	(12)	12.2	(11)	12.6	(11)	7.7	(17)	15.3	(12)
KERR-MCGEE CORP	Aa /AA	12/78	10.9	(13)	11.9	(13)	14.7	(7)	16.2	(4)	17.8	(7)
AMERADA HESS CORP	Baa/BBB*	12/78	8.9	(14)	12.0	(12)	11.2	(15)	10.1	(12)	19.0	(4)
CITIES SERVICE CO	A /A	12/78	6.0	(15)	10.8	(15)	12.1	(14)	8.4	(16)	12.2	(16)
SUPERIOR OIL CO	A /AA	12/78	4.6	(16)	9.7	(17)	8.6	(17)	9.6	(13)	12.3	(15)
OCCIDENTAL PETROLEUM CORP	A /BBB	12/78	-3.6	(17)	11.6	(14)	12.2	(13)	12.6	(10)	27.8	(1)
AVERAGE			12.98		13.32		13.91		12.70		17.08	
MEDIAN			13.61		13.54		13.94		12.66		17.43	

	RATINGS	FYR END	78		77		76		75		74	
PHILLIPS PETROLEUM CO	Aaa/AA	12/78	25.8	(1)	21.7	(3)	21.7	(2)	17.6	(6)	20.8	(6)
MARATHON OIL CO	A /A+	12/78	22.6	(2)	24.6	(1)	21.0	(4)	24.3	(1)	27.8	(2)
OCCIDENTAL PETROLEUM CORP	A /BBB	12/78	21.0 I(3)		24.5 I(2)		21.7 I(3)		20.2	(5)	28.3	(1)
CONTINENTAL OIL CO	Aa /AA	12/78	20.7	(4)	21.5	(4)	22.9	(1)	20.9	(4)	21.2	(5)
STANDARD OIL CO (INDIANA)	Aaa/AAA	12/78	20.4	(5)	21.2	(5)	20.8	(5)	21.3	(3)	20.5	(7)
ASHLAND OIL INC	A /A	9/78	17.5	(6)	13.4	(11)	14.9	(10)	14.1	(10)	11.7	(16)
AMERADA HESS CORP	Baa/BBB*	12/78	16.2	(7)	19.0	(6)	17.3	(6)	15.9	(8)	21.4	(4)
UNION OIL CO OF CALIFORNIA	Aa /AA	12/78	15.4	(8)	14.5	(10)	14.4	(14)	14.0	(11)	15.4	(12)
SUN CO	Aa /AA	12/78	15.2	(9)	15.6	(7)	15.7	(8)	15.1	(9)	19.9	(8)
ATLANTIC RICHFIELD CO	Aa /AA	12/78	14.7	(10)	11.4	(16)	14.4	(13)	13.8	(12)	17.3	(10)
STANDARD OIL CO (OHIO)	A /AA-	12/78	13.9	(11)	8.8	(17)	7.2	(17)	7.3	(17)	9.5	(17)
QUAKER STATE OIL REFINING	A /A	12/78	13.8	(12)	15.6	(8)	15.3	(9)	22.5	(2)	22.4	(3)
SHELL OIL CO	Aaa/AAA	12/78	13.6	(13)	15.1	(9)	17.1	(7)	13.8	(13)	16.0	(11)
PENNZOIL CO	Baa/BBB	12/78	13.0	(14)	11.8	(15)	14.5	(12)	10.7	(15)	12.0	(15)
KERR-MCGEE CORP	Aa /AA	12/78	12.4	(15)	12.9	(13)	14.7	(11)	17.1	(7)	17.7	(9)
SUPERIOR OIL CO	A /AA	12/78	8.0	(16)	12.9	(12)	12.8	(15)	13.3	(14)	13.2	(13)
CITIES SERVICE CO	A /A	12/78	7.0	(17)	12.1	(14)	12.6	(16)	9.1	(16)	12.1	(14)
AVERAGE			15.97		16.26		16.41		15.96		18.08	
MEDIAN			15.19		15.06		15.27		15.14		17.74	

Oils Industry (International)

PRETAX COVERAGE

	RATINGS	FYR END	78	77	76	75	74
HUDSON'S BAY OIL & GAS CO	A /A	12/78	70.60 (1)	62.47 (1)	44.95 (1)	39.01 (1)	29.01 (4)
EXXON CORP	Aaa/AAA	12/78	21.34 (2)	18.81 (5)	17.11 (3)	21.53 (3)	29.63 (2)
IMPERIAL OIL LTD-CL A	NR /AAA	12/78	21.25 (3)	19.30 (3)	16.29 (4)	14.23 (5)	26.98 (5)
BELCO PETROLEUM CORP	Ba /BB*	12/78	17.24H(4)	11.78 (8)	9.05 (8)	5.02 (10)	6.13 (10)
GULF OIL CORP	Aaa/AAA	12/78	16.38P(5)	21.17 (2)	21.53 (2)	25.75 (2)	34.45 (1)
STANDARD OIL CO (CALIF)	Aaa/AAA	12/78	12.50 (6)	13.17P(6)	9.70P(7)	11.29P(6)	17.22P(9)
ROYAL DUTCH PETROLEUM CO	NR /NR	12/78	10.14 (7)	13.09 (7)	15.99 (5)	17.54 (4)	25.37 (7)
NATOMAS CO	Baa/BBB	12/78	6.22 (8)	18.85 (4)	14.01 (6)	10.72 (8)	25.59 (6)
TEXACO INC	Aaa/AA+	12/78	5.94 (9)	9.79 (9)	8.30 (10)	6.95 (9)	23.57 (8)
BRITISH PETROLEUM CO LTD	Aa /AA	12/78	5.36 (10)	9.57P(10)	8.63 (9)	11.17 (7)	29.39 (3)
AVERAGE			18.70	19.80	16.56	16.32	24.74
MEDIAN			14.44	15.99	15.00	12.76	26.29

AFTER TAX COVERAGE

	RATINGS	FYR END	78	77	76	75	74
HUDSON'S BAY OIL & GAS CO	A /A	12/78	37.59 (1)	31.87 (1)	23.78 (1)	20.87 (1)	16.93 (1)
IMPERIAL OIL LTD-CL A	NR /AAA	12/78	11.92 (2)	10.44 (2)	9.44 (2)	7.96 (3)	15.77 (2)
EXXON CORP	Aaa/AAA	12/78	7.84 (3)	6.37 (7)	6.51 (5)	5.35 (5)	9.21 (6)
BELCO PETROLEUM CORP	Ba /BB*	12/78	7.64H(4)	6.48 (6)	4.73 (8)	3.54 (7)	4.80 (10)
STANDARD OIL CO (CALIF)	Aaa/AAA	12/78	7.50 (5)	6.67P(4)	5.32P(7)	3.43P(8)	5.07P(9)
GULF OIL CORP	Aaa/AAA	12/78	7.44P(6)	8.13 (3)	8.76 (3)	8.10 (2)	11.72 (5)
ROYAL DUTCH PETROLEUM CO	NR /NR	12/78	4.82 (7)	5.82 (8)	7.43 (4)	6.43 (4)	9.03 (7)
NATOMAS CO	Baa/BBB	12/78	3.77 (8)	6.64 (5)	5.90 (6)	5.17 (6)	13.07 (4)
TEXACO INC	Aaa/AA+	12/78	3.25 (9)	4.90 (9)	4.18 (9)	1.63 (10)	14.27 (3)
BRITISH PETROLEUM CO LTD	Aa /AA	12/78	1.93 (10)	2.15P(10)	1.78 (10)	1.97 (9)	7.02 (8)
AVERAGE			9.37	8.95	7.78	6.45	10.69
MEDIAN			7.47	6.56	6.20	5.26	10.46

AFTER TAX COV (INCL RENTS)

	RATINGS	FYR END	78	77	76	75	74
STANDARD OIL CO (CALIF)	Aaa/AAA	12/78	4.26 (1)	2.89P(5)	2.40P(7)	1.54P(7)	1.76P(8)
EXXON CORP	Aaa/AAA	12/78	3.39 (2)	3.09 (4)	3.60 (4)	2.84 (5)	4.12 (4)
NATOMAS CO	Baa/BBB	12/78	3.15 (3)	4.86 (2)	4.52 (3)	3.82 (3)	8.76 (2)
GULF OIL CORP	Aaa/AAA	12/78	3.00P(4)	3.38 (3)	3.49 (5)	3.12 (4)	4.05 (5)
ROYAL DUTCH PETROLEUM CO	NR /NR	12/78	2.53 (5)	2.59 (6)	3.19 (6)	2.71 (6)	3.31 (7)
TEXACO INC	Aaa/AA+	12/78	2.08 (6)	2.15 (7)	1.87 (8)	1.14 (8)	3.49 (6)
BELCO PETROLEUM CORP	Ba /BB*	12/78	NA (-)	NA (-)	NA (-)	NA (-)	NA (-)
BRITISH PETROLEUM CO LTD	Aa /AA	12/78	NA (-)	1.55P(8)	1.37 (9)	NA (-)	NA (-)
HUDSON'S BAY OIL & GAS CO	A /A	12/78	NA (-)	9.79 (1)	10.11 (1)	11.29 (1)	9.23 (1)
IMPERIAL OIL LTD-CL A	NR /AAA	12/78	NA (-)	NA (-)	5.44 (2)	4.88 (2)	7.58 (3)
AVERAGE			3.07	3.79	4.00	3.92	5.29
MEDIAN			3.07	2.99	3.49	2.98	4.09

NET INCOME AS % NET SALES

	RATINGS	FYR END	78		77		76		75		74	
HUDSON'S BAY OIL & GAS CO	A /A	12/78	27.8	(1)	27.4	(1)	28.3	(1)	30.5	(1)	31.9	(1)
NATOMAS CO	Baa/BBB	12/78	17.2	(2)	12.8	(2)	14.5	(2)	19.2	(2)	26.2	(2)
BELCO PETROLEUM CORP	Ba /BB*	12/78	12.7	(3)	10.9	(3)	8.8	(3)	6.9	(3)	14.1	(3)
IMPERIAL OIL LTD-CL A	NR /AAA	12/78	5.7	(4)	6.0	(4)	6.4	(5)	6.3	(5)	8.0	(5)
STANDARD OIL CO (CALIF)	Aaa/AAA	12/78	4.8	(5)	4.9	(6)	4.5	(8)	4.6	(8)	5.6	(10)
ROYAL DUTCH PETROLEUM CO	NR /NR	12/78	4.7	(6)	5.9	(5)	6.5	(4)	6.6	(4)	8.2	(4)
EXXON CORP	Aaa/AAA	12/78	4.6	(7)	4.5	(7)	5.4	(6)	5.6	(6)	7.5	(6)
GULF OIL CORP	Aaa/AAA	12/78	4.4	(8)	4.2	(8)	5.0	(7)	4.9	(7)	6.5	(8)
BRITISH PETROLEUM CO LTD	Aa /AA	12/78	3.1	(9)	3.0	(10)	1.7	(10)	1.9	(10)	6.1	(9)
TEXACO INC	Aaa/AA+	12/78	3.0	(10)	3.3	(9)	3.3	(9)	3.4	(9)	6.8	(7)
AVERAGE			8.80		8.29		8.45		8.99		12.09	
MEDIAN			4.75		5.38		5.91		5.94		7.72	

LTD/CAPITALIZATION (%)

	RATINGS	FYR END	78		77		76		75		74	
HUDSON'S BAY OIL & GAS CO	A /A	12/78	7.4	(1)	13.2	(1)	19.5	(5)	26.3	(7)	17.8	(6)
IMPERIAL OIL LTD-CL A	NR /AAA	12/78	13.0	(2)	14.5	(2)	16.0	(2)	17.8	(4)	15.5	(3)
BELCO PETROLEUM CORP	Ba /BB*	12/78	15.4	(3)	18.1	(6)	25.0	(7)	29.6	(9)	30.4	(10)
EXXON CORP	Aaa/AAA	12/78	15.6	(4)	16.6	(4)	16.7	(3)	16.9	(2)	16.3	(4)
GULF OIL CORP	Aaa/AAA	12/78	16.1	(5)	15.1	(3)	14.4	(1)	16.7	(1)	18.9	(7)
STANDARD OIL CO (CALIF)	Aaa/AAA	12/78	20.7	(6)	17.0	(5)	18.3	(4)	17.2	(3)	13.6	(1)
TEXACO INC	Aaa/AA+	12/78	27.8	(7)	21.4	(7)	22.3	(6)	20.5	(5)	17.4	(5)
ROYAL DUTCH PETROLEUM CO	NR /NR	12/78	28.9	(8)	26.9	(9)	27.8	(8)	25.1	(6)	21.1	(8)
NATOMAS CO	Baa/BBB	12/78	30.1	(9)	23.2	(8)	41.8	(10)	39.9	(10)	22.7	(9)
BRITISH PETROLEUM CO LTD	Aa /AA	12/78	52.5	M(10)	31.5	(10)	34.6	(9)	28.7	(8)	15.4	(2)
AVERAGE			22.76		19.75		23.64		23.86		18.89	
MEDIAN			18.42		17.55		20.90		22.80		17.58	

LTD/NET PLANT (%)

	RATINGS	FYR END	78		77		76		75		74	
HUDSON'S BAY OIL & GAS CO	A /A	12/78	6.8	(1)	12.2	(1)	17.2	(1)	23.0	(4)	16.5	(1)
IMPERIAL OIL LTD-CL A	NR /AAA	12/78	13.6	(2)	15.9	(3)	18.0	(3)	20.8	(2)	18.0	(2)
BELCO PETROLEUM CORP	Ba /BB*	12/78	15.3	(3)	17.3	(4)	24.4	(5)	28.9	(7)	31.2	(10)
GULF OIL CORP	Aaa/AAA	12/78	16.4	(4)	15.7	(2)	17.6	(2)	20.8	(1)	24.4	(6)
EXXON CORP	Aaa/AAA	12/78	16.4	(5)	18.8	(5)	19.8	(4)	21.4	(3)	20.6	(5)
STANDARD OIL CO (CALIF)	Aaa/AAA	12/78	30.1	(6)	25.3	(7)	26.4	(6)	23.3	(5)	19.0	(3)
ROYAL DUTCH PETROLEUM CO	NR /NR	12/78	32.5	(7)	33.6	(9)	38.9	(8)	36.5	(8)	29.5	(9)
NATOMAS CO	Baa/BBB	12/78	34.0	(8)	24.8	(6)	42.0	(9)	46.3	(10)	28.5	(8)
TEXACO INC	Aaa/AA+	12/78	34.0	(9)	25.9	(8)	27.0	(7)	24.6	(6)	19.8	(4)
BRITISH PETROLEUM CO LTD	Aa /AA	12/78	63.2	M(10)	45.5	(10)	48.0	(10)	44.6	(9)	27.1	(7)
AVERAGE			26.24		23.51		27.94		29.01		23.46	
MEDIAN			23.27		21.85		25.39		23.96		22.47	

TOT LIABILITY/TOT STK EQUITY

	RATINGS	FYR END	78		77		76		75		74	
HUDSON'S BAY OIL & GAS CO	A /A	12/78	76.5	(1)	84.4	(2)	97.8	(5)	113.7	(6)	102.4	(7)
IMPERIAL OIL LTD-CL A	NR /AAA	12/78	86.6	(2)	78.0	(1)	80.8	(1)	86.9	(1)	86.4	(3)
BELCO PETROLEUM CORP	Ba /BB*	12/78	86.8	(3)	102.7	(8)	124.4	(7)	133.8	(8)	142.2	(9)
GULF OIL CORP	Aaa/AAA	12/78	93.8	(4)	93.9	(4)	93.7	(2)	92.4	(2)	97.6	(5)
NATOMAS CO	Baa/BBB	12/78	99.2	(5)	85.7	(3)	169.5	(9)	127.5	(7)	78.2	(1)
STANDARD OIL CO (CALIF)	Aaa/AAA	12/78	103.6	(6)	94.1	(5)	96.5	(3)	98.9	(4)	80.5	(2)
EXXON CORP	Aaa/AAA	12/78	105.3	(7)	97.1	(6)	96.7	(4)	92.9	(3)	99.3	(6)
TEXACO INC	Aaa/AA+	12/78	114.0	(8)	101.5	(7)	102.1	(6)	99.0	(5)	90.8	(4)
ROYAL DUTCH PETROLEUM CO	NR /NR	12/78	160.6	(9)	153.6	(9)	165.0	(8)	142.6	(9)	141.1	(8)
BRITISH PETROLEUM CO LTD	Aa /AA	12/78	245.9	(10)	176.2	(10)	207.0	(10)	169.9	(10)	146.1	(10)
AVERAGE			117.24		106.71		123.35		115.77		106.44	
MEDIAN			101.44		95.56		99.96		106.33		98.41	

Oils Industry (International)

NET TANG ASSETS/LTD (%)

	RATINGS	FYR END	78		77		76		75		74	
HUDSON'S BAY OIL & GAS CO	A /A	12/78	1330.1	(1)	744.5	(1)	504.8	(5)	375.1	(6)	554.7	(6)
IMPERIAL OIL LTD-CL A	NR /AAA	12/78	719.7	(2)	687.0	(2)	619.8	(2)	557.0	(4)	642.3	(3)
BELCO PETROLEUM CORP	Ba /BB*	12/78	618.9	(3)	545.9	(6)	394.2	(7)	328.9	(9)	320.7	(10)
EXXON CORP	Aaa/AAA	12/78	617.6	(4)	578.2	(4)	571.4	(3)	559.5	(3)	595.2	(4)
GULF OIL CORP	Aaa/AAA	12/78	617.5	(5)	657.7	(3)	690.8	(1)	596.7	(1)	528.8	(7)
STANDARD OIL CO (CALIF)	Aaa/AAA	12/78	470.2	(6)	569.8	(5)	529.3	(4)	563.8	(2)	715.6	(1)
TEXACO INC	Aaa/AA+	12/78	358.2	(7)	464.9	(7)	445.2	(6)	487.1	(5)	571.2	(5)
NATOMAS CO	Baa/BBB	12/78	322.9	(8)	415.4	(8)	229.6	(10)	246.7	(10)	433.4	(9)
BRITISH PETROLEUM CO LTD	Aa /AA	12/78	190.5 M(9)		317.1	(10)	289.1	(9)	348.6	(8)	650.6	(2)
ROYAL DUTCH PETROLEUM CO	NR /NR	12/78	NA	(-)	354.8	(9)	340.3	(8)	375.1	(7)	459.9	(8)
AVERAGE			582.83		533.52		461.44		443.85		547.24	
MEDIAN			617.46		557.81		475.00		431.11		562.95	

CASH FLOW/LTD (%)

	RATINGS	FYR END	78		77		76		75		74	
HUDSON'S BAY OIL & GAS CO	A /A	12/78	530.8	(1)	304.7	(1)	171.1	(1)	117.4	(3)	176.0	(2)
BELCO PETROLEUM CORP	Ba /BB*	12/78	176.1	(2)	146.2	(2)	86.5	(8)	64.2	(8)	99.1	(10)
IMPERIAL OIL LTD-CL A	NR /AAA	12/78	146.6	(3)	137.9	(3)	126.8	(3)	120.8	(1)	168.3	(3)
EXXON CORP	Aaa/AAA	12/78	141.1	(4)	116.2	(6)	126.6	(4)	103.6	(4)	167.4	(4)
GULF OIL CORP	Aaa/AAA	12/78	124.0	(5)	121.3	(5)	133.7	(2)	118.9	(2)	122.2	(9)
STANDARD OIL CO (CALIF)	Aaa/AAA	12/78	82.2	(6)	101.9	(7)	91.3	(7)	100.8	(5)	145.8	(5)
ROYAL DUTCH PETROLEUM CO	NR /NR	12/78	71.4	(7)	81.2	(8)	93.4	(5)	83.3	(6)	142.3	(6)
NATOMAS CO	Baa/BBB	12/78	64.9	(8)	135.7	(4)	93.2	(6)	69.5	(7)	219.0	(1)
TEXACO INC	Aaa/AA+	12/78	57.7	(9)	69.6	(10)	58.8	(9)	39.5	(9)	138.9	(7)
BRITISH PETROLEUM CO LTD	Aa /AA	12/78	41.2 U(10)		73.8	(9)	46.0	(10)	33.7	(10)	134.8	(8)
AVERAGE			143.60		128.86		102.74		85.17		151.37	
MEDIAN			103.11		118.75		93.27		92.03		144.04	

NET CASH FL/CAP EXP (%)

	RATINGS	FYR END	78		77		76		75		74	
BRITISH PETROLEUM CO LTD	Aa /AA	12/78	174.4	(1)	161.8	(1)	77.1	(10)	44.1	(9)	116.5	(5)
HUDSON'S BAY OIL & GAS CO	A /A	12/78	131.1	(2)	152.3	(2)	133.0	(3)	57.9	(8)	160.5	(2)
BELCO PETROLEUM CORP	Ba /BB*	12/78	127.6 V(3)		121.7 V(5)		413.3 V(4)		74.7 V(5)		114.5 V(6)	
STANDARD OIL CO (CALIF)	Aaa/AAA	12/78	127.2	(4)	134.4	(4)	134.8	(2)	99.3	(3)	100.8	(9)
TEXACO INC	Aaa/AA+	12/78	116.0	(5)	99.3	(7)	78.9	(9)	24.4	(10)	111.0	(7)
EXXON CORP	Aaa/AAA	12/78	91.2	(6)	87.7	(8)	84.4	(8)	69.0	(6)	137.1	(4)
GULF OIL CORP	Aaa/AAA	12/78	87.9	(7)	59.6	(10)	90.0	(7)	106.8	(2)	106.5	(8)
IMPERIAL OIL LTD-CL A	NR /AAA	12/78	79.9	(8)	107.3	(6)	100.3	(6)	111.9	(1)	100.6	(10)
ROYAL DUTCH PETROLEUM CO	NR /NR	12/78	75.1	(9)	77.0	(9)	102.1	(5)	94.4	(4)	170.8	(1)
NATOMAS CO	Baa/BBB	12/78	66.2	(10)	137.6	(3)	174.8	(1)	63.9	(7)	139.4	(3)
AVERAGE			107.65		113.87		108.87		74.65		125.79	
MEDIAN			103.58		114.48		101.22		71.87		115.50	

AFT TAX RET ON COM EQTY (%)

	RATINGS	FYR END	78		77		76		75		74	
HUDSON'S BAY OIL & GAS CO	A /A	12/78	22.1	(1)	24.3	(1)	23.5	(1)	24.6	(1)	24.5	(3)
BELCO PETROLEUM CORP	Ba /BB*	12/78	19.7	(2)	17.9	(4)	15.7	(4)	12.3	(6)	27.6	(2)
NATOMAS CO	Baa/BBB	12/78	15.3	(3)	18.0	(3)	21.1	(2)	16.4	(3)	30.9	(1)
IMPERIAL OIL LTD-CL A	NR /AAA	12/78	15.1	(4)	15.1	(5)	15.2	(5)	15.8	(4)	20.0	(5)
EXXON CORP	Aaa/AAA	12/78	13.7	(5)	12.4	(7)	14.3	(6)	14.7	(5)	20.0	(6)
ROYAL DUTCH PETROLEUM CO	NR /NR	12/78	13.6	(6)	18.1	(2)	19.8	(3)	16.5	(2)	21.6	(4)
STANDARD OIL CO (CALIF)	Aaa/AAA	12/78	13.4	(7)	13.3	(6)	12.6	(7)	11.9	(7)	15.0	(10)
BRITISH PETROLEUM CO LTD	Aa /AA	12/78	11.9	(8)	11.0	(8)	6.3	(10)	5.4	(10)	18.3	(7)
GULF OIL CORP	Aaa/AAA	12/78	10.2	(9)	10.2	(9)	11.8	(8)	10.8	(8)	16.8	(9)
TEXACO INC	Aaa/AA+	12/78	9.0	(10)	9.9	(10)	9.7	(9)	9.6	(9)	17.6	(8)
AVERAGE			14.40		15.03		14.99		13.80		21.25	
MEDIAN			13.64		14.22		14.77		13.48		20.02	

RET ON TOT ASSETS (%)

	RATINGS	FYR END	78		77		76		75		74	
BELCO PETROLEUM CORP	Ba /BB*	12/78	27.3	(1)	19.0	(6)	17.0	(7)	10.4	(10)	18.4	(8)
HUDSON'S BAY OIL & GAS CO	A /A	12/78	24.2	(2)	26.6	(3)	23.2	(1)	22.4	(5)	21.8	(6)
EXXON CORP	Aaa/AAA	12/78	21.5	(3)	22.1	(4)	22.9	(3)	31.2	(1)	36.2	(2)
BRITISH PETROLEUM CO LTD	Aa /AA	12/78	19.7	(4)	27.0	(2)	22.9	(2)	23.1	(3)	36.2	(3)
ROYAL DUTCH PETROLEUM CO	NR /NR	12/78	15.9	(5)	20.1	(5)	21.4	(4)	23.8	(2)	31.6	(4)
IMPERIAL OIL LTD-CL A	NR /AAA	12/78	15.6	(6)	17.3	(7)	16.2	(8)	17.2	(7)	20.8	(7)
NATOMAS CO	Baa/BBB	12/78	15.5	(7)	32.0	(1)	20.6	(5)	19.1	(6)	36.3	(1)
GULF OIL CORP	Aaa/AAA	12/78	13.7	(8)	16.1	(8)	17.2	(6)	22.7	(4)	31.5	(5)
STANDARD OIL CO (CALIF)	Aaa/AAA	12/78	12.5	(9)	12.7	(9)	11.1	(10)	11.5	(9)	15.6	(10)
TEXACO INC	Aaa/AA+	12/78	10.7	(10)	11.9	(10)	11.3	(9)	11.6	(8)	17.8	(9)
AVERAGE			17.66		20.49		18.38		19.30		26.62	
MEDIAN			15.75		19.55		18.92		20.74		26.66	

Oil Supply and Service Industry

AFT TAX RET ON COM EQTY (%)

	RATINGS	FYR eND	78		77		76		75		74	
HALLIBURTON CO	Aa /AA	12/78	20.1	(1)	21.4	(2)	22.4	(2)	20.2	(4)	16.7	(1)
BAKER INTERNATIONAL CORP	A /A	9/78	19.0	(2)	18.2	(3)	18.5	(3)	21.5	(2)	15.8	(3)
MCDERMOTT (J. RAY) & CO	A /A	3/78	19.0	(3)	27.5	(1)	29.8	(1)	20.8	(3)	11.6	(5)
SMITH INTERNATIONAL INC	A /A	12/78	18.8	(4)	17.0	(5)	18.4	(5)	26.1	(1)	16.3	(2)
DRESSER INDUSTRIES INC	A /A	10/78	16.6	(5)	17.2	(4)	17.0	(6)	18.1	(6)	9.6	(7)
HUGHES TOOL CO	A /A+	12/78	16.5	(6)	12.3	(6)	12.6	(7)	15.8	(7)	9.7	(6)
READING & BATES CORP	Ba /B*	12/78	9.8	(7)	11.2	(7)	18.5	(4)	18.5	(5)	13.8	(4)
AVERAGE			17.14		17.83		19.59		20.14		13.36	
MEDIAN			18.83		17.16		18.47		20.17		13.77	

RET ON TOT ASSETS (%)

	RATINGS	FYR END	78		77		76		75		74	
SMITH INTERNATIONAL INC	A /A	12/78	24.0	(1)	23.2	(1)	23.6	(1)	25.7	(1)	17.0	(3)
HALLIBURTON CO	Aa /AA	12/78	21.6	(2)	22.2	(2)	22.7	(2)	20.6	(4)	18.0	(1)
HUGHES TOOL CO	A /A+	12/78	20.1	(3)	17.6	(5)	18.0	(5)	21.2	(3)	14.6	(4)
DRESSER INDUSTRIES INC	A /A	10/78	18.3	(4)	17.5	(6)	18.0	(6)	18.1	(5)	11.6	(5)
BAKER INTERNATIONAL CORP	A /A	9/78	17.6	(5)	18.4	(4)	19.2	(4)	23.7	(2)	17.1	(2)
READING & BATES CORP	Ba /B*	12/78	9.0	(6)	10.3	(7)	16.5	(7)	14.6	(6)	9.8	(6)
MCDERMOTT (J. RAY) & CO	A /A	3/78	8.4	(7)	20.2	(3)	21.6	(3)	12.5	(7)	9.6	(7)
AVERAGE			17.00		18.48		19.93		19.48		13.97	
MEDIAN			18.30		18.42		19.22		20.60		14.61	

TOT LIABILITY/TOT STK EQUITY

	RATINGS	FYR END	78		77		76		75		74	
SMITH INTERNATIONAL INC	A /A	12/78	53.8	(1)	49.2	(2)	49.4	(2)	98.3	(4)	109.3	(5)
HUGHES TOOL CO	A /A+	12/78	64.4	(2)	47.0	(1)	45.8	(1)	45.4	(1)	30.7	(1)
HALLIBURTON CO	Aa /AA	12/78	71.9	(3)	82.4	(3)	87.0	(4)	89.6	(3)	78.5	(2)
DRESSER INDUSTRIES INC	A /A	10/78	91.9	(4)	101.4	(7)	86.9	(3)	120.4	(5)	118.4	(6)
READING & BATES CORP	Ba /B*	12/78	107.4	(5)	83.5	(4)	93.4	(6)	144.6	(7)	188.3	(7)
BAKER INTERNATIONAL CORP	A /A	9/78	119.5	(6)	92.8	(5)	87.1	(5)	82.0	(2)	103.0	(4)
MCDERMOTT (J. RAY) & CO	A /A	3/78	158.5	(7)	97.9	(6)	117.6	(7)	131.8	(6)	92.4	(3)
AVERAGE			95.35		79.18		81.03		101.74		102.94	
MEDIAN			91.92		83.54		86.96		98.31		103.05	

LTD/NET PLANT (%)

	RATINGS	FYR END	78		77		76		75		74	
HALLIBURTON CO	Aa /AA	12/78	21.6	(1)	29.1	(2)	32.9	(2)	39.0	(2)	33.3	(3)
HUGHES TOOL CO	A /A+	12/78	41.1	(2)	22.4	(1)	28.9	(1)	34.5	(1)	1.7	(1)
SMITH INTERNATIONAL INC	A /A	12/78	41.7	(3)	38.1	(5)	51.8	(5)	93.7	(7)	86.5	(7)
READING & BATES CORP	Ba /B*	12/78	48.2	(4)	35.6	(4)	38.4	(4)	52.7	(5)	63.5	(4)
MCDERMOTT (J. RAY) & CO	A /A	3/78	53.8	(5)	35.6	(3)	36.4	(3)	48.0	(3)	29.2	(2)
DRESSER INDUSTRIES INC	A /A	10/78	68.4	(6)	73.3	(7)	70.9	(7)	82.2	(6)	75.6	(5)
BAKER INTERNATIONAL CORP	A /A	9/78	72.3	(7)	59.4	(6)	60.7	(6)	48.4	(4)	83.0	(6)
AVERAGE			49.59		41.94		45.70		56.93		53.27	
MEDIAN			48.22		35.63		38.36		48.41		63.52	

NET TANG ASSETS/LTD (%)

	RATINGS	FYR END	78		77		76		75		74	
HALLIBURTON CO	Aa /AA	12/78	763.7	(1)	638.0	(2)	527.1	(2)	421.8	(3)	491.9	(2)
SMITH INTERNATIONAL INC	A /A	12/78	521.3	(2)	561.2	(3)	500.2	(3)	273.8	(6)	272.6	(6)
HUGHES TOOL CO	A /A+	12/78	457.6	(3)	809.2	(1)	688.4	(1)	656.5	(1)	12042.5	(1)
DRESSER INDUSTRIES INC	A /A	10/78	389.9	(4)	341.4	(5)	399.6	(4)	307.4	(4)	333.3	(4)
MCDERMOTT (J. RAY) & CO	A /A	3/78	264.8	(5)	514.2	(4)	398.7	(5)	292.3	(5)	456.7	(3)
BAKER INTERNATIONAL CORP	A /A	9/78	243.0	(6)	333.2	(6)	337.9	(6)	435.9	(2)	279.5	(5)
READING & BATES CORP	Ba /B*	12/78	230.1	(7)	299.2	(7)	283.6	(7)	190.6	(7)	174.3	(7)
AVERAGE			410.06		499.49		447.91		368.33		2007.24	
MEDIAN			389.88		514.18		399.55		307.36		333.31	

CASH FLOW/LTD (%)

	RATINGS	FYR END	78		77		76		75		74	
HALLIBURTON CO	Aa /AA	12/78	229.9	(1)	203.4	(1)	172.5	(1)	124.3	(2)	131.2	(2)
HUGHES TOOL CO	A /A+	12/78	109.1	(2)	162.6	(3)	139.4	(2)	141.9	(1)	1931.3	(1)
SMITH INTERNATIONAL INC	A /A	12/78	107.7	(3)	109.6	(4)	102.8	(4)	62.5	(6)	44.6	(6)
DRESSER INDUSTRIES INC	A /A	10/78	80.9	(4)	63.6	(6)	79.7	(5)	64.9	(5)	48.9	(5)
BAKER INTERNATIONAL CORP	A /A	9/78	50.2	(5)	70.6	(5)	72.7	(6)	116.4	(3)	54.9	(4)
MCDERMOTT (J. RAY) & CO	A /A	3/78	47.4	(6)	174.2	(2)	134.9	(3)	65.8	(4)	86.2	(3)
READING & BATES CORP	Ba /B*	12/78	29.4	(7)	50.3	(7)	59.4	(7)	35.5	(7)	23.8	(7)
AVERAGE			93.52		119.19		108.80		87.31		331.57	
MEDIAN			80.87		109.58		102.81		65.75		54.88	

NET CASH FL/CAP EXP (%)

	RATINGS	FYR END	78		77		76		75		74	
MCDERMOTT (J. RAY) & CO	A /A	3/78	234.0	(1)	426.1	(1)	163.4	(1)	75.0	(6)	79.3	(5)
DRESSER INDUSTRIES INC	A /A	10/78	233.3	(2)	182.3	(3)	159.4	(2)	138.1	(2)	111.0	(2)
HALLIBURTON CO	Aa /AA	12/78	144.2	(3)	198.8	(2)	156.0	(3)	110.3	(5)	94.3	(4)
SMITH INTERNATIONAL INC	A /A	12/78	132.5 V	(4)	91.6 V	(6)	154.4 J	(4)	159.3 V	(1)	64.3	(6)
HUGHES TOOL CO	A /A+	12/78	129.5	(5)	111.1	(5)	111.3	(6)	135.9 V	(3)	160.2	(1)
BAKER INTERNATIONAL CORP	A /A	9/78	81.0	(6)	122.7	(4)	126.8	(5)	117.2	(4)	100.7	(3)
READING & BATES CORP	Ba /B*	12/78	38.1	(7)	87.5	(7)	90.1	(7)	46.2	(7)	28.3	(7)
AVERAGE			141.79		174.32		137.35		111.72		91.14	
MEDIAN			132.49		122.71		154.36		117.19		94.28	

PRETAX COVERAGE

	RATINGS	FYR END	78		77		76		75		74	
HALLIBURTON CO	Aa /AA	12/78	22.42P	(1)	21.00P	(1)	19.53P	(1)	15.60P	(2)	19.82P	(2)
SMITH INTERNATIONAL INC	A /A	12/78	17.60H	(2)	20.10H	(2)	13.13	(2)	11.35	(3)	7.59	(4)
HUGHES TOOL CO	A /A+	12/78	9.50P	(3)	9.97P	(4)	9.26	(4)	16.94	(1)	24.58	(1)
MCDERMOTT (J. RAY) & CO	A /A	3/78	9.04	(4)	17.10P	(3)	10.86P	(3)	6.51P	(6)	6.21P	(5)
DRESSER INDUSTRIES INC	A /A	10/78	8.23	(5)	8.47	(6)	8.54	(6)	7.96	(5)	5.72	(6)
BAKER INTERNATIONAL CORP	A /A	9/78	7.42	(6)	9.95	(5)	8.59	(5)	10.95	(4)	8.15	(3)
READING & BATES CORP	Ba /B*	12/78	2.88	(7)	3.83	(7)	3.96	(7)	3.30	(7)	2.94R	(7)
AVERAGE			11.01		12.92		10.55		10.37		10.71	
MEDIAN			9.04		9.97		9.26		10.95		7.59	

Oil Supply and Service Industry

AFTER TAX COVERAGE

	RATINGS	FYR END	78		77		76		75		74	
HALLIBURTON CO	Aa /AA	12/78	12.85P(	1)	11.86P(	2)	11.10P(	1)	8.93P(	2)	11.44P(	2)
SMITH INTERNATIONAL INC	A /A	12/78	9.97H(	2)	10.87H(	3)	7.87 (	2)	6.79 (	3)	4.48 (	5)
MCDERMOTT (J. RAY) & CO	A /A	3/78	6.03 (	3)	12.76P(	1)	7.84P(	3)	5.63P(	5)	4.82P(	3)
HUGHES TOOL CO	A /A+	12/78	5.93P(	4)	6.05P(	5)	5.92 (	4)	10.50 (	1)	14.52 (	1)
DRESSER INDUSTRIES INC	A /A	10/78	4.89 (	5)	5.12 (	6)	5.33 (	6)	4.95 (	6)	3.79 (	6)
BAKER INTERNATIONAL CORP	A /A	9/78	4.67 (	6)	6.10 (	4)	5.42 (	5)	6.47 (	4)	4.71 (	4)
READING & BATES CORP	Ba /B*	12/78	2.36 (	7)	3.23 (	7)	3.10 (	7)	2.71 (	7)	2.52R(	7)
AVERAGE			6.67		8.00		6.65		6.57		6.61	
MEDIAN			5.93		6.10		5.92		6.47		4.71	

AFTER TAX COV (INCL RENTS)

	RATINGS	FYR END	78		77		76		75		74	
SMITH INTERNATIONAL INC	A /A	12/78	4.91H(	1)	4.67H(	1)	4.33 (	1)	4.09 (	2)	3.02 (	2)
HUGHES TOOL CO	A /A+	12/78	4.13P(	2)	4.10P(	2)	4.15 (	2)	6.11 (	1)	6.94 (	1)
HALLIBURTON CO	Aa /AA	12/78	3.51P(	3)	3.46P(	3)	2.67P(	5)	2.15P(	6)	2.17P(	6)
DRESSER INDUSTRIES INC	A /A	10/78	3.08 (	4)	3.26 (	4)	3.31 (	3)	3.17 (	4)	2.59 (	4)
BAKER INTERNATIONAL CORP	A /A	9/78	2.75 (	5)	2.92 (	6)	3.03 (	4)	3.34 (	3)	2.72 (	3)
MCDERMOTT (J. RAY) & CO	A /A	3/78	2.21 (	6)	3.16P(	5)	2.38P(	7)	1.98P(	7)	2.44P(	5)
READING & BATES CORP	Ba /B*	12/78	2.05 (	7)	2.30 (	7)	2.57 (	6)	2.43 (	5)	2.11R(	7)
AVERAGE			3.24		3.41		3.20		3.32		3.14	
MEDIAN			3.08		3.26		3.03		3.17		2.59	

NET INCOME AS % NET SALES

	RATINGS	FYR END	78		77		76		75		74	
MCDERMOTT (J. RAY) & CO	A /A	3/78	12.3 (	1)	15.6 (	1)	13.9 (	2)	10.2 (	4)	8.2 (	3)
READING & BATES CORP	Ba /B*	12/78	12.1 F(	2)	10.8 (	3)	15.2 (	1)	13.8 (	1)	11.0 (	1)
SMITH INTERNATIONAL INC	A /A	12/78	11.1 (	3)	11.1 (	2)	11.8 (	3)	13.6 (	1)	8.1 (	4)
HUGHES TOOL CO	A /A+	12/78	10.6 (	4)	9.6 (	4)	10.4 (	4)	12.5 (	2)	10.7 (	2)
BAKER INTERNATIONAL CORP	A /A	9/78	8.4 (	5)	8.5 (	5)	8.8 (	5)	9.6 (	5)	6.6 (	5)
DRESSER INDUSTRIES INC	A /A	10/78	6.7 (	6)	7.3 (	6)	7.0 (	6)	6.2 (	6)	4.5 (	7)
HALLIBURTON CO	Aa /AA	12/78	6.0 (	7)	6.5 (	7)	6.3 (	7)	5.3 (	7)	4.7 (	6)
AVERAGE			9.65		9.93		10.49		9.90		7.69	
MEDIAN			10.56		9.61		10.35		10.24		8.10	

LTD/CAPITALIZATION (%)

	RATINGS	FYR END	78		77		76		75		74	
HALLIBURTON CO	Aa /AA	12/78	12.6 (	1)	15.2 (	2)	18.6 (	2)	22.4 (	3)	18.7 (	2)
SMITH INTERNATIONAL INC	A /A	12/78	18.8 (	2)	17.4 (	3)	19.6 (	3)	35.7 (	6)	35.3 (	6)
HUGHES TOOL CO	A 7/A+	12/78	20.1 (	3)	11.6 (	1)	13.6 (	1)	14.1 (	1)	0.8 (	1)
DRESSER INDUSTRIES INC	A /A	10/78	24.5 (	4)	27.7 (	5)	24.0 (	4)	30.8 (	4)	28.5 (	4)
MCDERMOTT (J. RAY) & CO	A /A	3/78	28.0 (	5)	19.3 (	4)	24.8 (	5)	33.7 (	5)	21.3 (	3)
BAKER INTERNATIONAL CORP	A /A	9/78	37.4 (	6)	28.6 (	6)	28.7 (	6)	21.9 (	2)	33.5 (	5)
READING & BATES CORP	Ba /B*	12/78	42.7 (	7)	32.9 (	7)	34.5 (	7)	48.2 (	7)	56.6 (	7)
AVERAGE			26.31		21.81		23.40		29.55		27.82	
MEDIAN			24.50		19.28		24.04		30.83		28.53	

PRETAX COVERAGE

	RATINGS	FYR END	78	77	76	75	74
UNION CAMP CORP	Aa /AA	12/78	14.43 (1)	14.62 (1)	17.38 (1)	14.21 (1)	13.92 (1)
DENNISON MFG CO	A /A	12/78	11.26 (2)	9.84 (5)	8.69 (4)	6.44 (6)	7.93 (9)
KIMBERLY-CLARK CORP	Aa /AA	12/78	10.82 (3)	10.31 (2)	10.29 (3)	8.52 (2)	9.30 (7)
GEORGIA-PACIFIC CORP	Aa /AA	12/78	9.28 (4)	9.88 (4)	8.06 (6)	4.38 (13)	4.29 (16)
LOUISIANA PACIFIC	NR /NR	12/78	8.20 (5)	7.44 (7)	5.26 (13)	2.00 (17)	4.80 (15)
GREAT NORTHERN NEKOOSA CORP	A /A+	12/78	7.32 (6)	10.09 (3)	10.93 (2)	7.55 (4)	13.02 (2)
POTLATCH CORP	A /NR#	12/78	6.98 (7)	7.68 (6)	8.22 (5)	7.63 (3)	9.38 (6)
WESTVACO CORP	A /A	10/78	6.46 (8)	7.33 (8)	7.35 (7)	6.26 (7)	9.64 (5)
CHAMPION INTERNATIONAL CORP	A /BBB+	12/78	6.46 (9)	5.22 (13)	4.05 (17)	2.54 (16)	3.86 (17)
BOISE CASCADE CORP	A /A	12/78	6.18 (10)	6.19 (9)	5.40 (12)	5.28 (9)	8.85 (8)
ST REGIS PAPER CO	Baa/BBB*	12/78	5.90 (11)	5.65 (11)	6.09 (8)	6.80 (5)	7.39 (12)
WEYERHAEUSER CO	Aa /AA	12/78	5.78P(12)	5.12P(14)	6.02P(10)	4.59P(11)	7.40P(11)
MEAD CORP	A /A	12/78	5.48 (13)	5.59 (12)	6.08 (9)	3.55 (15)	6.84 (13)
INTL PAPER CO	Aa /AA-	12/78	5.15P(14)	4.57P(15)	5.01P(14)	5.41P(8)	10.80P(4)
HAMMERMILL PAPER CO	Baa/BB*	12/78	4.54 (15)	3.67 (16)	4.40 (16)	4.54 (12)	11.20 (3)
CROWN ZELLERBACH	A /A	12/78	4.39 (16)	5.87 (10)	5.60 (11)	4.65 (10)	7.75 (10)
SCOTT PAPER CO	Aa /A+	12/78	3.81 (17)	3.05 (17)	4.67 (15)	4.01 (14)	5.94 (14)
AVERAGE			7.20	7.18	7.27	5.78	8.37
MEDIAN			6.46	6.19	6.08	5.28	7.93

AFTER TAX COVERAGE

	RATINGS	FYR END	78	77	76	75	74
UNION CAMP CORP	Aa /AA	12/78	9.60 (1)	9.86 (1)	10.64 (1)	8.63 (1)	8.20 (1)
KIMBERLY-CLARK CORP	Aa /AA	12/78	6.60 (2)	6.60 (2)	6.42 (2)	5.34 (3)	5.62 (7)
DENNISON MFG CO	A /A	12/78	6.56 (3)	5.84 (6)	5.23 (6)	3.85 (7)	4.65 (11)
GEORGIA-PACIFIC CORP	Aa /AA	12/78	5.72 (4)	6.14 (4)	5.26 (5)	3.16 (12)	3.05 (16)
LOUISIANA PACIFIC	NR /NR	12/78	5.52 (5)	5.03 (7)	3.70 (11)	1.76 (17)	3.34 (15)
GREAT NORTHERN NEKOOSA CORP	A /A+	12/78	5.13 (6)	6.31 (3)	6.26 (3)	4.79 (4)	7.40 (2)
POTLATCH CORP	A /NR#	12/78	4.97 (7)	5.89 (5)	6.15 (4)	5.85 (2)	6.75 (3)
CHAMPION INTERNATIONAL CORP	A /BBB+	12/78	4.57 (8)	3.74 (12)	2.82 (17)	2.13 (16)	2.92 (17)
WESTVACO CORP	A /A	10/78	4.34 (9)	4.74 (8)	4.63 (8)	4.13 (6)	5.66 (6)
WEYERHAEUSER CO	Aa /AA	12/78	4.18P(10)	3.73P(13)	4.67P(7)	3.23P(10)	5.25P(10)
BOISE CASCADE CORP	A /A	12/78	4.18 (11)	4.07 (10)	3.68 (12)	3.69 (8)	5.48 (8)
ST REGIS PAPER CO	Baa/BBB*	12/78	3.90 (12)	3.82 (11)	4.39 (9)	4.38 (5)	4.64 (12)
INTL PAPER CO	Aa /AA-	12/78	3.55P(13)	3.42P(14)	3.64P(13)	3.57P(9)	6.46P(4)
CROWN ZELLERBACH	A /A	12/78	3.27 (14)	4.31 (9)	4.12 (10)	3.18 (11)	5.28 (9)
HAMMERMILL PAPER CO	Baa/BB*	12/78	3.08 (15)	2.73 (16)	3.25 (15)	3.16 (13)	6.20 (5)
MEAD CORP	A /A	12/78	3.07 (16)	3.13 (15)	3.29 (14)	2.42 (15)	3.63 (14)
SCOTT PAPER CO	Aa /A+	12/78	2.98 (17)	2.41 (17)	3.23 (16)	2.73 (14)	4.05 (13)
AVERAGE			4.78	4.81	4.79	3.88	5.21
MEDIAN			4.34	4.31	4.39	3.57	5.28

AFTER TAX COV (INCL RENTS)

	RATINGS	FYR END	78	77	76	75	74
KIMBERLY-CLARK CORP	Aa /AA	12/78	4.02 (1)	4.20 (1)	3.78 (5)	NA (-)	NA (-)
GREAT NORTHERN NEKOOSA CORP	A /A+	12/78	3.55 (2)	4.02 (3)	4.16 (2)	3.54 (3)	5.17 (2)
CHAMPION INTERNATIONAL CORP	A /BBB+	12/78	3.49 (3)	2.93 (7)	2.32 (13)	1.80 (13)	2.42 (13)
ST REGIS PAPER CO	Baa/BBB*	12/78	3.43 (4)	2.78 (9)	2.88 (8)	2.94 (4)	3.31 (9)
DENNISON MFG CO	A /A	12/78	3.31 (5)	3.20 (4)	3.00 (6)	2.37 (9)	2.67 (12)
BOISE CASCADE CORP	A /A	12/78	3.30 (6)	3.17 (5)	2.77 (10)	2.52 (7)	3.56 (7)
WESTVACO CORP	A /A	10/78	2.86 (7)	2.83 (8)	2.84 (9)	2.45 (8)	3.44 (8)
INTL PAPER CO	Aa /AA-	12/78	2.78P(8)	2.76P(10)	2.95P(7)	2.87P(6)	4.32P(5)
HAMMERMILL PAPER CO	Baa/BB*	12/78	2.63 (9)	2.01 (14)	2.32 (14)	2.19 (11)	3.78 (6)
CROWN ZELLERBACH	A /A	12/78	2.57 (10)	2.75 (11)	2.63 (11)	2.24 (10)	3.21 (10)
SCOTT PAPER CO	Aa /A+	12/78	2.45 (11)	2.07 (13)	2.56 (12)	2.17 (12)	2.91 (11)
MEAD CORP	A /A	12/78	2.32 (12)	2.41 (12)	2.29 (15)	1.75 (14)	2.39 (14)
GEORGIA-PACIFIC CORP	Aa /AA	12/78	NA (-)	NA (-)	NA (-)	NA (-)	NA (-)
LOUISIANA PACIFIC	NR /NR	12/78	NA (-)	NA (-)	NA (-)	NA (-)	NA (-)
POTLATCH CORP	A /NR#	12/78	NA (-)	4.09 (2)	4.01 (4)	3.83 (2)	4.62 (3)
UNION CAMP CORP	Aa /AA	12/78	NA (-)	NA (-)	7.15 (1)	6.11 (1)	5.82 (1)
WEYERHAEUSER CO	Aa /AA	12/78	NA (-)	3.07P(6)	4.07P(3)	2.90P(5)	4.51P(4)
AVERAGE			3.06	3.02	3.31	2.83	3.73
MEDIAN			3.08	2.88	2.88	2.49	3.50

Paper/Forest Products Industry

NET INCOME AS % NET SALES

	RATINGS	FYR END	78		77		76		75		74	
WEYERHAEUSER CO	Aa /AA	12/78	10.9	(1)	9.3	(2)	10.7	(2)	7.9	(2)	10.9	(2)
UNION CAMP CORP	Aa /AA	12/78	10.3	(2)	10.6	(1)	11.8	(1)	10.6	(1)	10.2	(3)
POTLATCH CORP	A /NR#	12/78	8.2	(3)	9.0	(3)	7.6	(4)	7.4	(3)	9.3	(4)
LOUISIANA PACIFIC	NR /NR	12/78	7.8	(4)	7.6	(5)	7.2	(5)	4.3	(12)	12.3	(1)
KIMBERLY-CLARK CORP	Aa /AA	12/78	7.8	(5)	7.6	(4)	7.7	(3)	6.9	(5)	6.6	(12)
GREAT NORTHERN NEKOOSA CORP	A /A+	12/78	6.9	(6)	6.5	(7)	6.9	(8)	6.6	(7)	9.0	(5)
GEORGIA-PACIFIC CORP	Aa /AA	12/78	6.9	(7)	7.1	(6)	7.1	(7)	6.3	(8)	6.8	(11)
CHAMPION INTERNATIONAL CORP	A /BBB+	12/78	5.9	(8)	5.2	(13)	3.5	(16)	2.5	(17)	4.0	(17)
WESTVACO CORP	A /A	10/78	5.8	(9)	6.2	(9)	6.2	(9)	4.9	(10)	7.4	(7)
INTL PAPER CO	Aa /AA-	12/78	5.6	(10)	6.4	(8)	7.2	(6)	7.1	(4)	8.6	(6)
ST REGIS PAPER CO	Baa/BBB#	12/78	5.5	(11)	5.3	(11)	5.6	(10)	6.9	(6)	7.1	(8)
SCOTT PAPER CO	Aa /A+	12/78	5.4	(12)	4.1	(16)	5.3	(12)	5.4	(9)	6.3	(13)
DENNISON MFG CO	A /A	12/78	5.3	(13)	5.2	(12)	5.1	(13)	3.9	(15)	4.3	(16)
BOISE CASCADE CORP	A /A	12/78	5.3	(14)	5.0	(14)	5.0	(14)	4.4	(11)	7.1	(9)
MEAD CORP	A /A	12/78	5.2	(15)	5.4	(10)	5.6	(11)	4.2	(13)	5.4	(15)
CROWN ZELLERBACH	A /A	12/78	4.5	(16)	4.7	(15)	4.6	(15)	4.2	(14)	7.0	(10)
HAMMERMILL PAPER CO	Baa/BB#	12/78	2.9	(17)	2.5	(17)	3.3	(17)	3.1	(16)	5.8	(14)
AVERAGE			6.48		6.33		6.48		5.69		7.53	
MEDIAN			5.79		6.19		6.15		5.44		7.13	

LTD/CAPITALIZATION (%)

	RATINGS	FYR END	78		77		76		75		74	
DENNISON MFG CO	A /A	12/78	19.1	(1)	20.7	(1)	23.6	(2)	23.7	(2)	25.7	(1)
KIMBERLY-CLARK CORP	Aa /AA	12/78	21.4	(2)	23.6	(3)	22.4	(1)	23.5	(1)	26.9	(2)
UNION CAMP CORP	Aa /AA	12/78	21.9	(3)	23.1	(2)	25.7	(4)	31.3	(7)	35.1	(.12)
LOUISIANA PACIFIC	NR /NR	12/78	25.4	(4)	36.2	(13)	41.3	(17)	42.9	(14)	45.9	(15)
BOISE CASCADE CORP	A /A	12/78	28.0	(5)	31.1	(5)	31.7	(9)	27.0	(4)	28.0	(4)
SCOTT PAPER CO	Aa /A+	12/78	28.6	(6)	33.4	(10)	31.1	(7)	34.5	(9)	30.1	(5)
GREAT NORTHERN NEKOOSA CORP	A /A+	12/78	30.5	(7)	24.5	(4)	28.0	(5)	30.5	(5)	31.3	(7)
INTL PAPER CO	Aa /AA-	12/78	30.7	(8)	34.8	(11)	36.6	(14)	43.1	(15)	34.7	(10)
ST REGIS PAPER CO	Baa/BBB#	12/78	31.0	(9)	33.2	(9)	28.3	(6)	30.7	(6)	34.7	(8)
POTLATCH CORP	A /NR#	12/78	31.0	(10)	33.0	(8)	31.3	(8)	25.8	(3)	27.6	(3)
GEORGIA-PACIFIC CORP	Aa /AA	12/78	32.4	(11)	32.4	(6)	24.7	(3)	46.9	(16)	49.3	(17)
WESTVACO CORP	A /A	10/78	32.8	(12)	35.1	(12)	32.2	(10)	35.2	(10)	30.9	(6)
CROWN ZELLERBACH	A /A	12/78	36.8	(13)	32.7	(7)	33.2	(11)	35.2	(11)	34.8	(11)
WEYERHAEUSER CO	Aa /AA	12/78	36.9	(14)	35.7	(14)	35.6	(13)	34.2	(8)	38.0	(14)
CHAMPION INTERNATIONAL CORP	A /BBB+	12/78	38.1	(15)	35.2	(15)	41.0	(16)	47.1	(17)	47.3	(16)
MEAD CORP	A /A	12/78	38.2	(16)	39.9	(16)	35.0	(12)	36.5	(12)	35.4	(13)
HAMMERMILL PAPER CO	Baa/BB#	12/78	40.8	(17)	41.3	(17)	38.8	(15)	36.8	(13)	34.7	(9)
AVERAGE			30.80		32.11		31.80		34.41		34.73	
MEDIAN			30.96		33.21		31.73		34.48		34.68	

TOT LIABILITY/TOT STK EQUITY

	RATINGS	FYR END	78		77		76		75		74	
UNION CAMP CORP	Aa /AA	12/78	56.6	(1)	56.3	(1)	59.0	(1)	72.3	(3)	90.4	(8)
DENNISON MFG CO	A /A	12/78	61.6	(2)	66.5	(3)	68.5	(2)	60.1	(2)	66.5	(2)
SCOTT PAPER CO	Aa /A+	12/78	75.5	(3)	85.0	(6)	83.3	(9)	92.0	(10)	76.5	(3)
GREAT NORTHERN NEKOOSA CORP	A /A+	12/78	76.2	(4)	63.3	(2)	74.9	(5)	83.9	(8)	90.0	(7)
POTLATCH CORP	A /NR#	12/78	77.6	(5)	75.1	(4)	71.5	(3)	60.0	(1)	63.9	(1)
LOUISIANA PACIFIC	NR /NR	12/78	81.8	(6)	89.3	(10)	110.1	(16)	98.3	(12)	111.1	(15)
WESTVACO CORP	A /A	10/78	84.9	(7)	89.3	(11)	82.8	(7)	89.3	(9)	85.1	(5)
KIMBERLY-CLARK CORP	Aa /AA	12/78	86.1	(8)	85.1	(7)	79.0	(6)	78.9	(4)	84.2	(4)
BOISE CASCADE CORP	A /A	12/78	87.3	(9)	87.6	(9)	83.1	(8)	81.2	(6)	91.7	(9)
ST REGIS PAPER CO	Baa/BBB#	12/78	87.3	(10)	84.8	(5)	72.6	(4)	80.4	(5)	88.9	(6)
INTL PAPER CO	Aa /AA-	12/78	91.0	(11)	93.5	(13)	99.3	(13)	122.5	(15)	99.7	(11)
WEYERHAEUSER CO	Aa /AA	12/78	92.6	(12)	91.6	(12)	85.8	(10)	81.5	(7)	93.0	(10)
GEORGIA-PACIFIC CORP	Aa /AA	12/78	93.7	(13)	91.6	(12)	91.1	(11)	133.9	(16)	148.6	(16)
CROWN ZELLERBACH	A /A	12/78	104.0	(14)	93.6	(14)	95.1	(12)	95.8	(11)	105.0	(13)
CHAMPION INTERNATIONAL CORP	A /BBB+	12/78	110.2	(15)	96.0	(15)	132.3	(17)	151.9	(17)	153.2	(17)
HAMMERMILL PAPER CO	Baa/BB#	12/78	120.7	(16)	114.3	(16)	105.2	(14)	101.4	(13)	99.9	(12)
MEAD CORP	A /A	12/78	123.3	(17)	126.0	(17)	106.5	(15)	105.3	(14)	108.6	(14)
AVERAGE			88.85		87.21		88.24		93.45		97.43	
MEDIAN			87.26		87.58		83.26		89.27		91.71	

LTD/NET PLANT (%)

	RATINGS	FYR END	78		77		76		75		74	
KIMBERLY-CLARK CORP	Aa /AA	12/78	25.1	(1)	27.5	(1)	27.8	(2)	32.0	(2)	39.0	(5)
UNION CAMP CORP	Aa /AA	12/78	26.4	(2)	29.3	(2)	38.1	(6)	44.5	(8)	50.7	(11)
LOUISIANA PACIFIC	NR /NR	12/78	31.7	(3)	44.7	(12)	50.5	(14)	60.4	(16)	64.8	(17)
GREAT NORTHERN NEKOOSA CORP	A /A+	12/78	33.4	(4)	29.9	(3)	33.0	(3)	33.5	(3)	34.0	(1)
GEORGIA-PACIFIC CORP	Aa /AA	12/78	34.9	(5)	35.1	(4)	24.5	(1)	54.2	(12)	55.9	(13)
BOISE CASCADE CORP	A /A+	12/78	35.2	(6)	42.7	(8)	48.7	(11)	41.9	(6)	48.8	(8)
SCOTT PAPER CO	Aa /A+	12/78	35.2	(7)	40.6	(6)	36.5	(4)	41.3	(4)	38.5	(4)
POTLATCH CORP	A /NR#	12/78	35.9	(8)	39.7	(5)	37.5	(5)	31.8	(1)	36.4	(2)
INTL PAPER CO	Aa /AA-	12/78	37.6	(9)	42.2	(7)	43.9	(9)	51.5	(11)	49.7	(10)
WESTVACO CORP	A /A	10/78	40.3	(10)	45.8	(13)	41.3	(7)	44.5	(7)	36.5	(3)
DENNISON MFG CO	A /A	12/78	40.7	(11)	43.1	(10)	49.0	(12)	54.6	(14)	55.8	(12)
WEYERHAEUSER CO	Aa /AA	12/78	42.8	(12)	43.0	(9)	43.9	(8)	41.4	(5)	46.2	(7)
CHAMPION INTERNATIONAL CORP	A /BBB+	12/78	47.9	(13)	47.7	(14)	56.2	(16)	61.7	(17)	64.0	(15)
CROWN ZELLERBACH	A /A	12/78	48.6	(14)	44.2	(11)	44.6	(10)	45.3	(9)	43.4	(6)
ST REGIS PAPER CO	Baa/BBB*	12/78	50.8	(15)	54.2	(15)	49.1	(13)	54.3	(13)	64.5	(16)
HAMMERMILL PAPER CO	Baa/BB*	12/78	56.2	(16)	57.7	(16)	52.1	(15)	49.4	(10)	49.0	(9)
MEAD CORP	A /A	12/78	63.8	(17)	63.0	(17)	57.5	(17)	59.2	(15)	56.3	(14)
AVERAGE			40.37		42.96		43.19		47.15		49.02	
MEDIAN			37.56		43.04		43.91		45.28		49.02	

NET TANG ASSETS/LTD (%)

	RATINGS	FYR END	78		77		76		75		74	
DENNISON MFG CO	A /A	12/78	481.4	(1)	458.7	(1)	399.1	(3)	401.0	(2)	368.7	(1)
UNION CAMP CORP	Aa /AA	12/78	451.8	(2)	429.6	(4)	386.4	(4)	317.9	(5)	283.5	(9)
KIMBERLY-CLARK CORP	Aa /AA	12/78	444.7	(3)	399.2	(3)	417.3	(1)	404.2	(1)	348.0	(3)
LOUISIANA PACIFIC	NR /NR	12/78	348.1	(4)	271.0	(14)	238.2	(16)	229.3	(14)	216.2	(15)
SCOTT PAPER CO	Aa /A+	12/78	346.6	(5)	298.2	(8)	319.8	(7)	288.4	(9)	330.3	(4)
BOISE CASCADE CORP	A /A	12/78	342.9	(6)	298.5	(7)	287.8	(11)	298.8	(7)	262.6	(13)
POTLATCH CORP	A /NR#	12/78	318.1	(7)	298.0	(9)	317.4	(8)	384.2	(3)	358.5	(2)
GREAT NORTHERN NEKOOSA CORP	A /A+	12/78	317.5	(8)	394.7	(4)	347.9	(5)	319.1	(4)	308.8	(6)
GEORGIA-PACIFIC CORP	Aa /AA	12/78	305.1	(9)	306.0	(5)	400.7	(2)	208.1	(16)	198.2	(16)
ST REGIS PAPER CO	Baa/BBB*	12/78	303.0	(10)	284.1	(10)	330.2	(6)	307.0	(6)	272.6	(11)
WESTVACO CORP	A /A	10/78	301.4	(11)	281.9	(11)	307.0	(9)	280.1	(11)	317.2	(5)
INTL PAPER CO	Aa /AA-	12/78	300.5	(12)	274.0	(13)	264.3	(14)	225.0	(15)	277.3	(10)
CROWN ZELLERBACH	A /A	12/78	270.1	(13)	303.3	(6)	299.8	(10)	282.1	(10)	285.1	(7)
WEYERHAEUSER CO	Aa /AA	12/78	269.6	(14)	278.4	(12)	279.4	(12)	290.5	(8)	258.9	(14)
CHAMPION INTERNATIONAL CORP	A /BBB+	12/78	250.7	(15)	260.8	(15)	222.6	(17)	195.9	(17)	195.2	(17)
MEAD CORP	A /A	12/78	247.1	(16)	242.1	(16)	275.2	(13)	260.2	(13)	269.3	(12)
HAMMERMILL PAPER CO	Baa/BB*	12/78	241.2	(17)	237.2	(17)	253.0	(15)	265.8	(12)	284.2	(8)
AVERAGE			325.86		312.68		314.47		291.61		284.39	
MEDIAN			305.08		298.03		306.99		288.44		283.50	

CASH FLOW/LTD (%)

	RATINGS	FYR END	78		77		76		75		74	
DENNISON MFG CO	A /A	12/78	105.2	(1)	92.0	(1)	82.8	(2)	66.9	(2)	67.0	(3)
UNION CAMP CORP	Aa /AA	12/78	89.5	(2)	82.0	(2)	75.7	(3)	63.5	(3)	58.6	(6)
LOUISIANA PACIFIC	NR /NR	12/78	82.9	(3)	65.9	(5)	43.1	(13)	27.2	(15)	40.9	(14)
KIMBERLY-CLARK CORP	Aa /AA	12/78	73.9	(4)	69.8	(4)	71.6	(4)	71.3	(1)	61.9	(5)
GEORGIA-PACIFIC CORP	Aa /AA	12/78	65.4	(5)	63.8	(6)	82.8	(1)	31.1	(14)	33.0	(16)
INTL PAPER CO	Aa /AA-	12/78	59.0	(6)	49.0	(9)	48.3	(9)	40.4	(9)	57.1	(7)
POTLATCH CORP	A /NR#	12/78	57.6	(7)	53.6	(7)	51.0	(7)	54.4	(5)	69.8	(2)
BOISE CASCADE CORP	A /A	12/78	56.2	(8)	48.1	(10)	38.9	(14)	39.8	(10)	45.7	(11)
GREAT NORTHERN NEKOOSA CORP	A /A+	12/78	52.4	(9)	72.0	(3)	68.0	(5)	55.1	(4)	65.3	(4)
WEYERHAEUSER CO	Aa /AA	12/78	52.4	(10)	44.7	(12)	44.6	(11)	50.1	(6)	48.5	(9)
ST REGIS PAPER CO	Baa/BBB*	12/78	49.5	(11)	40.6	(14)	46.2	(10)	43.8	(7)	41.4	(13)
WESTVACO CORP	A /A	10/78	49.3	(12)	45.1	(11)	53.9	(6)	43.7	(8)	70.3	(1)
SCOTT PAPER CO	Aa /A+	12/78	46.4	(13)	24.8	(17)	43.5	(12)	33.3	(12)	43.5	(12)
CHAMPION INTERNATIONAL CORP	A /BBB+	12/78	43.7	(14)	43.2	(13)	35.5	(15)	22.7	(17)	29.9	(17)
CROWN ZELLERBACH	A /A	12/78	38.8	(15)	49.7	(8)	48.8	(8)	36.6	(11)	48.4	(10)
MEAD CORP	A /A	12/78	34.1	(16)	33.4	(15)	35.5	(16)	25.6	(16)	36.4	(15)
HAMMERMILL PAPER CO	Baa/BB*	12/78	31.5	(17)	26.7	(16)	31.0	(17)	29.4	(14)	50.6	(8)
AVERAGE			58.11		53.21		53.03		43.23		51.08	
MEDIAN			52.41		49.03		48.32		40.42		48.50	

Paper/Forest Products Industry

NET CASH FL/CAP EXP (%)

	RATINGS	FYR END	78	77	76	75	74
DENNISON MFG CO	A /A	12/78	154.2 V(1)	186.3 V(1)	124.3 V(4)	183.0 V(1)	89.4 V(7)
INTL PAPER CO	Aa /AA-	12/78	133.0 (2)	120.2 (5)	95.9 (10)	80.5 (10)	79.2 (11)
WEYERHAEUSER CO	Aa /AA	12/78	123.9 (3)	73.6 (14)	76.2 (12)	77.0 (11)	65.1 (14)
ST REGIS PAPER CO	Baa/BBB*	12/78	123.5 (4)	164.5 (2)	96.3 (9)	100.3 (6)	122.3 (4)
LOUISIANA PACIFIC	NR /NR	12/78	119.1 J(5)	132.5 V(3)	114.8 V(6)	114.2 (3)	71.7 (12)
HAMMERMILL PAPER CO	Baa/BB*	12/78	118.6 (6)	92.0 (9)	73.3 (13)	59.7 (16)	155.4 (1)
MEAD CORP	A /A	12/78	115.8 (7)	95.8 (7)	112.2 (7)	82.9 (8)	64.7 V(15)
SCOTT PAPER CO	Aa /A+	12/78	105.3 (8)	47.6 (17)	65.1 (14)	44.5 (17)	65.3 (13)
KIMBERLY-CLARK CORP	Aa /AA	12/78	103.2 (9)	63.4 (16)	53.2 (17)	102.1 (5)	105.5 (5)
POTLATCH CORP	A /NR#	12/78	92.8 (10)	88.4 (11)	61.0 (15)	59.7 (15)	102.5 (6)
GEORGIA-PACIFIC CORP	Aa /AA	12/78	90.6 V(11)	84.6 V(12)	103.7 V(8)	95.5 V(7)	80.0 V(10)
UNION CAMP CORP	Aa /AA	12/78	86.2 (12)	67.1 (15)	86.8 (11)	127.2 (2)	151.1 (2)
WESTVACO CORP	A /A	10/78	82.3 (13)	81.9 (13)	138.9 (2)	74.9 (12)	131.5 (3)
BOISE CASCADE CORP	A /A	12/78	73.4 (14)	93.1 (8)	56.3 (16)	61.2 (14)	81.4 (8)
CROWN ZELLERBACH	A /A	12/78	72.3 (15)	110.2 (6)	147.0 (1)	103.0 (4)	46.7 (17)
CHAMPION INTERNATIONAL CORP	A /BBB+	12/78	67.9 (16)	91.3 (10)	132.6 (3)	80.6 (9)	60.6 (16)
GREAT NORTHERN NEKOOSA CORP	A /A+	12/78	41.0 (17)	131.1 (4)	123.3 V(5)	74.7 V(13)	80.9 V(9)
AVERAGE			100.18	101.40	97.71	89.46	91.37
MEDIAN			103.17	92.01	96.32	80.58	80.95

AFT TAX RET ON COM EQTY (%)

	RATINGS	FYR END	78	77	76	75	74
GEORGIA-PACIFIC CORP	Aa /AA	12/78	17.5 (1)	17.1 (1)	15.9 (2)	14.4 (3)	18.3 (6)
MEAD CORP	A /A	12/78	17.4 (2)	16.0 (4)	14.8 (5)	9.3 (13)	16.1 (11)
WEYERHAEUSER CO	Aa /AA	12/78	17.3 (3)	13.5 (8)	14.9 (4)	10.7 (8)	18.5 (5)
UNION CAMP CORP	Aa /AA	12/78	15.4 (4)	15.9 (5)	18.2 (1)	18.5 (1)	22.0 (1)
DENNISON MFG CO	A /A	12/78	15.4 (5)	14.8 (6)	13.6 (8)	9.8 (10)	11.6 (16)
KIMBERLY-CLARK CORP	Aa /AA	12/78	15.2 (6)	14.7 (7)	15.0 (3)	14.1 (4)	14.3 (13)
POTLATCH CORP	A /NR#	12/78	14.9 (7)	16.2 (3)	14.3 (6)	12.7 (5)	17.1 (8)
CHAMPION INTERNATIONAL CORP	A /BBB+	12/78	14.7 (8)	12.5 (10)	10.5 (13)	7.0 (16)	12.8 (14)
LOUISIANA PACIFIC	NR /NR	12/78	14.6 (9)	16.8 (2)	12.9 (11)	6.0 (17)	21.3 (2)
WESTVACO CORP	A /A	10/78	12.9 (10)	13.3 (9)	13.5 (10)	10.3 (9)	17.8 (7)
BOISE CASCADE CORP	A /A	12/78	12.9 (11)	12.1 (13)	10.3 (15)	7.4 (14)	12.7 (15)
GREAT NORTHERN NEKOOSA CORP	A /A+	12/78	12.3 (12)	12.2 (12)	13.5 (9)	11.3 (7)	19.0 (4)
CROWN ZELLERBACH	A /A	12/78	11.7 (13)	12.3 (11)	11.8 (12)	9.7 (12)	17.0 (9)
ST REGIS PAPER CO	Baa/BBB*	12/78	11.2 (14)	10.2 (15)	10.5 (14)	12.3 (6)	15.1 (12)
INTL PAPER CO	Aa /AA-	12/78	10.9 (15)	11.8 (14)	13.9 (7)	14.6 (2)	19.3 (3)
SCOTT PAPER CO	Aa /A+	12/78	10.2 (16)	7.3 (17)	9.3 (17)	9.8 (11)	11.1 (17)
HAMMERMILL PAPER CO	Baa/BB*	12/78	9.7 (17)	7.7 (16)	9.4 (16)	7.3 (15)	16.9 (10)
AVERAGE			13.77	13.19	13.08	10.89	16.52
MEDIAN			14.61	13.28	13.50	10.33	17.02

RET ON TOT ASSETS (%)

	RATINGS	FYR END	78	77	76	75	74
DENNISON MFG CO	A /A	12/78	19.2 (1)	18.4 (1)	17.2 (2)	14.4 (3)	15.5 (11)
GEORGIA-PACIFIC CORP	Aa /AA	12/78	17.8 (2)	17.2 (2)	15.7 (5)	12.5 (7)	15.4 (12)
MEAD CORP	A /A	12/78	16.6 (3)	15.5 (5)	15.9 (4)	9.3 (13)	17.0 (8)
UNION CAMP CORP	Aa /AA	12/78	16.3 (4)	16.7 (3)	20.8 (1)	20.5 (1)	22.6 (1)
WEYERHAEUSER CO	Aa /AA	12/78	15.8 (5)	13.1 (10)	13.4 (9)	12.0 (9)	16.9 (9)
KIMBERLY-CLARK CORP	Aa /AA	12/78	15.5 (6)	14.7 (6)	15.5 (6)	15.1 (2)	15.5 (10)
POTLATCH CORP	A /NR#	12/78	14.8 (7)	14.5 (7)	13.5 (8)	12.7 (6)	17.3 (7)
LOUISIANA PACIFIC	NR /NR	12/78	14.6 (8)	16.3 (4)	11.5 (11)	6.9 (17)	18.7 (4)
WESTVACO CORP	A /A	10/78	13.5 (9)	13.7 (9)	14.9 (7)	10.9 (10)	19.8 (3)
CHAMPION INTERNATIONAL CORP	A /BBB+	12/78	13.0 (10)	12.5 (12)	10.6 (15)	7.2 (16)	11.0 (16)
BOISE CASCADE CORP	A /A	12/78	12.9 (11)	13.0 (11)	10.6 (14)	7.7 (15)	12.5 (15)
GREAT NORTHERN NEKOOSA CORP	A /A+	12/78	12.3 (12)	14.2 (8)	16.1 (3)	12.2 (8)	20.0 (2)
ST REGIS PAPER CO	Baa/BBB*	12/78	12.1 (13)	10.9 (15)	10.8 (13)	12.7 (5)	15.3 (13)
INTL PAPER CO	Aa /AA-	12/78	11.1 (14)	11.2 (14)	13.0 (10)	13.6 (4)	18.4 (5)
CROWN ZELLERBACH	A /A	12/78	10.4 (15)	11.3 (13)	11.1 (12)	10.6 (11)	14.1 (14)
HAMMERMILL PAPER CO	Baa/BB*	12/78	9.9 (16)	7.9 (16)	9.1 (17)	7.9 (14)	18.3 (6)
SCOTT PAPER CO	Aa /A+	12/78	9.4 (17)	7.1 (17)	9.9 (16)	9.7 (12)	10.6 (17)
AVERAGE			13.84	13.43	13.50	11.52	16.40
MEDIAN			13.45	13.71	13.35	11.98	16.86

Retail Stores Industry

PRETAX COVERAGE

	RATINGS	FYR END	79	78	77	76	75
DAYTON-HUDSON CORP	A /A+	1/79	15.00 (1)	10.52 (3)	8.60 (4)	6.84 (5)	3.13 (11)
FEDERATED DEPT STORES INC	Aaa/AAA	1/79	8.77 (2)	14.24 (2)	15.40 (2)	17.06 (3)	10.25 (1)
MERCANTILE STORES CO INC	A /A	1/79	8.70 (3)	10.32 (4)	14.52 (3)	19.92H(2)	10.00H(2)
WALGREEN CO	Baa/BB*	8/78	8.17 (4)	6.91H(5)	6.44H(5)	4.46H(9)	3.93H(7)
ALLIED STORES	Baa/BBB*	1/79	6.06H(5)	6.36 (6)	5.36 (9)	4.56 (8)	2.93 (12)
K MART CORP	A /A*	1/79	5.48 (6)	26.05 (1)	26.75 (1)	22.13 (1)	9.12 (3)
WOOLWORTH (F.W.) CO	A /A	1/79	5.22 (7)	4.24 (12)	4.06 (13)	3.81 (13)	2.61 (15)
MAY DEPARTMENT STORES CO	A /AA	1/79	5.17 (8)	5.19 (9)	5.21 (10)	5.38 (7)	4.45 (5)
MACY (R.H.) & CO	NR /NR	7/78	3.67 (9)	3.68 (14)	3.40 (14)	2.72 (15)	2.76 (13)
ASSD DRY GOODS CORP	A /A+	1/79	3.61 (10)	5.73 (8)	5.61 (7)	7.58 (4)	4.40 (6)
SEARS, ROEBUCK & CO	Aaa/AAA	1/79	3.42H(11)	4.38 (11)	5.07 (11)	4.28 (11)	3.14 (10)
PENNEY (J.C.) CO	A /AA	1/79	3.28H(12)	5.94H(7)	5.53H(8)	4.28H(12)	2.62H(14)
CARTER HAWLEY HALE STORES	A /A	1/79	3.04 (13)	4.52 (10)	4.22 (12)	4.35 (10)	3.15 (9)
ZAYRE CORP	Baa/BB	1/79	2.35 (14)	3.43 (15)	3.34 (15)	2.27 (16)	1.08 (16)
GAMBLE-SKOGMO	NR /NR	1/79	1.49 (15)	1.55 (16)	2.19 (16)	3.07 (14)	3.36 (8)
MURPHY (G.C.) CO	Baa/A	1/79	1.00 (16)	4.21 (13)	6.15 (6)	6.33 (6)	4.68 (4)
AVERAGE			5.28	7.33	7.61	7.44	4.48
MEDIAN			4.42	5.46	5.44	4.51	3.26

AFTER TAX COVERAGE

	RATINGS	FYR END	79	78	77	76	75
DAYTON-HUDSON CORP	A /A+	1/79	7.87 (1)	5.64 (4)	4.66 (4)	3.80 (6)	2.07 (11)
MERCANTILE STORES CO INC	A /A	1/79	5.11 (2)	5.84 (3)	7.91 (3)	10.65H(2)	5.70H(1)
FEDERATED DEPT STORES INC	Aaa/AAA	1/79	5.09 (3)	7.77 (2)	8.43 (2)	9.08 (3)	5.62 (2)
WALGREEN CO	Baa/BB*	8/78	5.01 (4)	4.25H(5)	4.17H(5)	3.28H(7)	2.89H(5)
ALLIED STORES	Baa/BBB*	1/79	3.63H(5)	3.80 (6)	3.24 (10)	2.78 (11)	2.05 (12)
K MART CORP	A /A*	1/79	3.42 (6)	14.08 (1)	14.78 (1)	11.66 (1)	5.36 (3)
WOOLWORTH (F.W.) CO	A /A	1/79	3.18 (7)	2.68 (13)	2.70 (13)	2.57 (13)	1.92 (14)
MAY DEPARTMENT STORES CO	A /AA	1/79	3.11 (8)	3.14 (10)	3.11 (11)	3.17 (8)	2.72 (7)
SEARS, ROEBUCK & CO	Aaa/AAA	1/79	2.76H(9)	3.37 (9)	3.63 (7)	2.88 (9)	2.34 (8)
ASSD DRY GOODS CORP	A /A+	1/79	2.43 (10)	3.46 (8)	3.43 (9)	4.37 (4)	2.74 (6)
MACY (R.H.) & CO	NR /NR	7/78	2.43 (11)	2.43 (14)	2.27 (14)	1.91 (15)	1.96 (13)
PENNEY (J.C.) CO	A /AA	1/79	2.29H(12)	3.66H(7)	3.45H(8)	2.77H(12)	1.89H(15)
CARTER HAWLEY HALE STORES	A /A	1/79	2.11 (13)	2.93 (11)	2.81 (12)	2.81 (10)	2.15 (10)
ZAYRE CORP	Baa/BB	1/79	1.70 (14)	2.22 (15)	2.11 (15)	1.62 (16)	1.05 (16)
GAMBLE-SKOGMO	NR /NR	1/79	1.35 (15)	1.32 (16)	1.64 (16)	2.08 (14)	2.22 (9)
MURPHY (G.C.) CO	Baa/A	1/79	1.03 (16)	2.73 (12)	3.76 (6)	3.84 (5)	2.89 (4)
AVERAGE			3.28	4.33	4.51	4.33	2.85
MEDIAN			2.94	3.42	3.44	3.02	2.28

AFTER TAX COV (INCL RENTS)

	RATINGS	FYR END	79	78	77	76	75
FEDERATED DEPT STORES INC	Aaa/AAA	1/79	3.20 (1)	3.47 (1)	3.44 (1)	3.84 (1)	3.04 (1)
MERCANTILE STORES CO INC	A /A	1/79	3.15 (2)	2.93 (2)	3.29 (2)	3.72H(2)	2.80H(2)
DAYTON-HUDSON CORP	A /A+	1/79	2.69 (3)	2.78 (3)	2.54 (4)	2.25 (5)	1.56 (7)
MAY DEPARTMENT STORES CO	A /AA	1/79	2.56 (4)	2.45 (5)	2.30 (5)	2.39 (3)	2.20 (3)
SEARS, ROEBUCK & CO	Aaa/AAA	1/79	2.38H(5)	2.71 (4)	2.72 (3)	2.28 (4)	2.02 (4)
ALLIED STORES	Baa/BBB*	1/79	2.30H(6)	2.09 (6)	1.91 (7)	1.78 (8)	1.49 (10)
K MART CORP	A /A*	1/79	2.02 (7)	1.92 (7)	1.93 (6)	1.83 (7)	1.50 (9)
MACY (R.H.) & CO	NR /NR	7/78	1.96 (8)	1.89 (9)	1.80 (9)	1.58 (10)	1.61 (6)
ASSD DRY GOODS CORP	A /A+	1/79	1.66 (9)	1.91 (8)	1.85 (8)	2.03 (6)	1.84 (5)
WALGREEN CO	Baa/BB*	8/78	1.60 (10)	1.36H(12)	1.34H(14)	1.25H(15)	1.21H(15)
CARTER HAWLEY HALE STORES	A /A	1/79	1.60 (11)	1.62 (11)	1.57 (11)	1.61 (9)	1.51 (8)
PENNEY (J.C.) CO	A /AA	1/79	1.55H(12)	1.75H(10)	1.63H(10)	1.55H(11)	1.35H(13)
WOOLWORTH (F.W.) CO	A /A	1/79	1.50 (13)	1.32 (13)	1.38 (13)	1.36 (14)	1.25 (14)
ZAYRE CORP	Baa/BB	1/79	1.31 (14)	1.25 (15)	1.24 (16)	1.15 (16)	1.02 (16)
MURPHY (G.C.) CO	Baa/A	1/79	1.01 (15)	1.30 (14)	1.42 (12)	1.43 (12)	1.42 (12)
GAMBLE-SKOGMO	NR /NR	1/79	NA (-)	1.14 (16)	1.28 (15)	1.39 (13)	1.47 (11)
AVERAGE			2.03	1.99	1.98	1.96	1.71
MEDIAN			1.96	1.90	1.82	1.70	1.50

Retail Stores Industry

NET INCOME AS % NET SALES

	RATINGS	FYR END	79	78	77	76	75
SEARS, ROEBUCK & CO	Aaa/AAA	1/79	5.1 (1)	4.9 (1)	4.6 (1)	3.8 (3)	3.9 (1)
MERCANTILE STORES CO INC	A /A	1/79	4.4 C(2)	4.0 C(3)	4.2 C(2)	5.0 C(1)	3.7 C(2)
ALLIED STORES	Baa/BBB*	1/79	4.0 C(3)	3.9 C(4)	3.5 C(4)	3.2 C(6)	2.3 C(8)
FEDERATED DEPT STORES INC	Aaa/AAA	1/79	3.7 C(4)	4.0 C(2)	3.8 C(3)	4.2 C(2)	3.6 C(3)
MAY DEPARTMENT STORES CO	A /AA	1/79	3.6 C(5)	3.6 C(6)	3.3 C(6)	3.3 C(4)	2.8 C(6)
MACY (R.H.) & CO	NR /NR	7/78	3.4 C(6)	3.2 C(8)	2.9 C(9)	2.1 C(12)	2.3 C(7)
DAYTON-HUDSON CORP	A /A+	1/79	3.3 C(7)	3.7 C(5)	3.5 C(5)	3.0 C(8)	1.7 C(13)
CARTER HAWLEY HALE STORES	A /A	1/79	3.0 C(8)	3.3 C(7)	3.1 C(8)	3.3 C(5)	2.9 C(4)
K MART CORP	A /A*	1/79	2.9 (9)	3.0 (10)	3.1 (7)	2.9 (9)	1.9 (9)
PENNEY (J.C.) CO	A /AA	1/79	2.5 (10)	3.1 (9)	2.7 (10)	2.5 (10)	1.8 (11)
WALGREEN CO	Baa/BB*	8/78	2.2 (11)	1.3 (14)	1.3 (14)	0.9 (15)	0.8 (15)
ASSD DRY GOODS CORP	A /A+	1/79	2.1 C(12)	2.9 C(11)	2.6 C(11)	3.1 C(7)	2.9 C(5)
WOOLWORTH (F.W.) CO	A /A	1/79	2.1 C(13)	1.7 C(12)	2.1 C(12)	2.1 C(11)	1.6 C(14)
GAMBLE-SKOGMO	NR /NR	1/79	1.2 (14)	0.6 (16)	1.1 (15)	1.5 (14)	1.7 (12)
ZAYRE CORP	Baa/BB	1/79	1.0 (15)	0.9 (15)	1.0 (16)	0.6 (16)	0.1 (16)
MURPHY (G.C.) CO	Baa/A	1/79	0.0 (16)	1.4 (13)	1.8 (13)	1.8 (13)	1.8 (10)
AVERAGE			2.78	2.84	2.78	2.71	2.23
MEDIAN			2.96	3.16	2.99	2.97	2.07

LTD/CAPITALIZATION (%)

	RATINGS	FYR END	79	78	77	76	75
DAYTON-HUDSON CORP	A /A+	1/79	17.5 (1)	32.3 (10)	33.6 (11)	37.8 (12)	42.6 (13)
FEDERATED DEPT STORES INC	Aaa/AAA	1/79	19.2 (2)	14.7 (1)	13.2 (2)	10.3 (1)	11.6 (1)
SEARS, ROEBUCK & CO	Aaa/AAA	1/79	22.3 (3)	23.4 (6)	20.8 (5)	20.0 (5)	17.3 (4)
ASSD DRY GOODS CORP	A /A+	1/79	25.4 (4)	17.9 (4)	17.5 (4)	20.6 (6)	22.1 (6)
PENNEY (J.C.) CO	A /AA	1/79	26.3 (5)	16.1 (2)	15.6 (3)	17.8 (3)	20.6 (5)
MACY (R.H.) & CO	NR /NR	7/78	26.6 (6)	32.6 (11)	34.4 (12)	35.6 (11)	33.4 (9)
MERCANTILE STORES CO INC	A /A	1/79	31.6 (7)	23.4 (5)	21.2 (6)	18.4 (4)	16.7 (2)
WALGREEN CO	Baa/BB*	8/78	33.0 (8)	33.3 (12)	33.5 (10)	35.3 (10)	34.2 (10)
ALLIED STORES	Baa/BBB*	1/79	38.2 (9)	37.1 (13)	39.3 (13)	46.2 (14)	50.3 (15)
MURPHY (G.C.) CO	Baa/A	1/79	38.3 (10)	26.3 (7)	27.7 (7)	22.0 (7)	23.3 (7)
WOOLWORTH (F.W.) CO	A /A	1/79	39.4 (11)	28.5 (8)	28.5 (8)	32.6 (9)	30.4 (8)
MAY DEPARTMENT STORES CO	A /AA	1/79	42.6 (12)	43.6 (15)	41.6 (14)	40.4 (13)	41.6 (12)
K MART CORP	A /A*	1/79	44.0 (13)	17.7 (3)	12.8 (1)	14.9 (2)	17.2 (3)
CARTER HAWLEY HALE STORES	A /A	1/79	49.0 (14)	29.9 (9)	30.8 (9)	31.8 (8)	35.2 (11)
ZAYRE CORP	Baa/BB	1/79	56.9 (15)	41.9 (14)	45.8 (15)	49.7 (16)	52.7 (16)
GAMBLE-SKOGMO	NR /NR	1/79	65.1 (16)	55.0 (16)	53.0 (16)	48.4 (15)	45.8 (14)
AVERAGE			35.96	29.61	29.33	30.11	30.94
MEDIAN			35.59	29.24	29.63	32.20	31.90

LTD/NET PLANT (%)

	RATINGS	FYR END	79	78	77	76	75
FEDERATED DEPT STORES INC	Aaa/AAA	1/79	26.4 (1)	21.3 (1)	19.0 (1)	15.4 (1)	18.1 (1)
DAYTON-HUDSON CORP	A /A+	1/79	31.5 (2)	47.7 (6)	51.6 (7)	59.2 (9)	66.1 (10)
MACY (R.H.) & CO	NR /NR	7/78	35.3 (3)	43.7 (4)	43.4 (5)	46.7 (7)	44.2 (4)
ASSD DRY GOODS CORP	A /A+	1/79	40.0 (4)	28.7 (2)	30.4 (2)	36.9 (2)	39.8 (3)
PENNEY (J.C.) CO	A /AA	1/79	52.3 (5)	35.7 (3)	35.5 (3)	41.1 (4)	45.6 (5)
MERCANTILE STORES CO INC	A /A	1/79	63.0 (6)	46.5 (5)	43.8 (6)	38.2 (3)	32.6 (2)
MAY DEPARTMENT STORES CO	A /AA	1/79	67.6 (7)	73.1 (12)	69.2 (12)	66.2 (10)	68.7 (11)
MURPHY (G.C.) CO	Baa/A	1/79	71.5 (8)	51.5 (8)	57.0 (8)	43.8 (5)	45.9 (6)
WOOLWORTH (F.W.) CO	A /A	1/79	73.1 (9)	60.3 (10)	61.9 (9)	73.4 (12)	63.6 (9)
ALLIED STORES	Baa/BBB*	1/79	76.0 (10)	76.5 (13)	78.7 (14)	83.3 (14)	87.9 (14)
WALGREEN CO	Baa/BB*	8/78	76.5 (11)	72.5 (11)	73.4 (13)	75.1 (13)	73.3 (12)
K MART CORP	A /A*	1/79	77.4 (12)	48.0 (7)	40.3 (4)	45.6 (6)	50.6 (8)
SEARS, ROEBUCK & CO	Aaa/AAA	1/79	77.9 (13)	78.5 (14)	65.9 (10)	57.1 (8)	49.2 (7)
CARTER HAWLEY HALE STORES	A /A	1/79	79.5 (14)	57.5 (9)	71.1 (11)	71.4 (11)	79.7 (13)
ZAYRE CORP	Baa/BB	1/79	113.8 (15)	118.6 (15)	121.0 (15)	120.4 (15)	119.6 (15)
GAMBLE-SKOGMO	NR /NR	1/79	257.6 (16)	280.4 (16)	283.4 (16)	235.8 (16)	203.4 (16)
AVERAGE			76.22	71.29	71.35	69.36	68.04
MEDIAN			72.29	54.51	59.45	58.16	57.15

TOT LIABILITY/TOT STK EQUITY

	RATINGS	FYR END	79		78		77		76		75	
ASSD DRY GOODS CORP	A /A+	1/79	84.0	(1)	69.2	(1)	64.0	(1)	72.5	(2)	81.1	(3)
MERCANTILE STORES CO INC	A /A	1/79	89.8	(2)	74.9	(2)	71.5	(2)	65.0	(1)	58.3	(1)
FEDERATED DEPT STORES INC	Aaa/AAA	1/79	95.7	(3)	79.8	(3)	77.8	(3)	72.6	(3)	68.3	(2)
DAYTON-HUDSON CORP	A /A+	1/79	102.6	(4)	138.7	(12)	136.4	(11)	138.4	(10)	140.5	(13)
PENNEY (J.C.) CO	A /AA	1/79	105.0	(5)	89.5	(4)	81.8	(4)	89.3	(5)	94.0	(6)
SEARS, ROEBUCK & CO	Aaa/AAA	1/79	115.2	(6)	126.0	(10)	114.1	(9)	118.3	(9)	116.4	(8)
ALLIED STORES	Baa/BBB*	1/79	118.5	(7)	118.0	(9)	123.5	(10)	165.7	(14)	181.5	(14)
WOOLWORTH (F.W.) CO	A /A	1/79	130.1	(8)	96.6	(5)	94.4	(5)	116.2	(8)	119.6	(9)
MACY (R.H.) & CO	NR /NR	7/78	130.1	(9)	139.0	(13)	143.0	(13)	144.4	(12)	132.7	(10)
WALGREEN CO	Baa/BB*	8/78	134.4	(10)	138.6	(11)	138.1	(12)	139.1	(11)	138.3	(11)
K MART CORP	A /A*	1/79	152.5	(11)	103.1	(7)	98.8	(7)	98.5	(7)	86.5	(5)
MURPHY (G.C.) CO	Baa/A	1/79	154.1	(12)	107.4	(8)	99.4	(8)	87.5	(4)	82.0	(4)
MAY DEPARTMENT STORES CO	A /AA	1/79	156.1	(13)	160.0	(14)	149.9	(14)	157.7	(13)	140.3	(12)
CARTER HAWLEY HALE STORES	A /A	1/79	162.7	(14)	99.4	(6)	94.9	(6)	97.7	(6)	105.8	(7)
ZAYRE CORP	Baa/BB	1/79	234.1	(15)	177.5	(15)	182.2	(15)	191.8	(15)	215.4	(16)
GAMBLE-SKOGMO	NR /NR	1/79	329.8	(16)	244.1	(16)	218.7	(16)	197.7	(16)	189.0	(15)
AVERAGE			143.41		122.61		118.02		122.02		121.85	
MEDIAN			130.09		112.69		106.76		117.25		117.99	

NET TANG ASSETS/LTD (%)

	RATINGS	FYR END	79		78		77		76		75	
DAYTON-HUDSON CORP	A /A+	1/79	540.8	(1)	302.3	(10)	291.0	(11)	256.3	(12)	225.7	(13)
FEDERATED DEPT STORES INC	Aaa/AAA	1/79	505.1	(2)	671.8	(1)	748.9	(1)	915.1	(1)	816.0	(1)
SEARS, ROEBUCK & CO	Aaa/AAA	1/79	446.6	(3)	427.2	(6)	479.1	(5)	499.3	(5)	577.2	(3)
ASSD DRY GOODS CORP	A /A+	1/79	389.9	(4)	549.7	(4)	562.5	(4)	479.5	(6)	445.3	(6)
PENNEY (J.C.) CO	A /AA	1/79	376.2	(5)	615.7	(2)	633.6	(3)	557.6	(3)	481.5	(5)
MACY (R.H.) & CO	NR /NR	7/78	363.9	(6)	296.1	(12)	280.5	(12)	272.2	(11)	291.5	(10)
MERCANTILE STORES CO INC	A /A	1/79	316.2	(7)	427.8	(5)	471.4	(6)	543.4	(4)	599.3	(2)
WALGREEN CO	Baa/BB*	8/78	302.6	(8)	300.7	(11)	298.1	(10)	283.6	(10)	292.5	(9)
ALLIED STORES	Baa/BBB*	1/79	258.4	(9)	266.6	(13)	251.3	(13)	213.1	(14)	194.8	(15)
MURPHY (G.C.) CO	Baa/A	1/79	250.4	(10)	362.0	(7)	343.1	(8)	429.1	(7)	404.7	(7)
WOOLWORTH (F.W.) CO	A /A	1/79	249.6	(11)	343.5	(8)	344.0	(7)	301.5	(9)	322.3	(8)
MAY DEPARTMENT STORES CO	A /AA	1/79	227.6	(12)	222.6	(15)	232.7	(14)	239.4	(13)	232.6	(12)
K MART CORP	A /A*	1/79	226.0	(13)	551.2	(3)	762.3	(1)	654.6	(2)	569.0	(4)
CARTER HAWLEY HALE STORES	A /A	1/79	199.6	(14)	326.0	(9)	318.2	(9)	307.3	(8)	280.4	(11)
ZAYRE CORP	Baa/BB	1/79	171.2	(15)	229.7	(14)	210.5	(15)	193.7	(15)	182.9	(16)
GAMBLE-SKOGMO	NR /NR	1/79	137.4	(16)	164.5	(16)	170.0	(16)	187.2	(16)	197.1	(14)
AVERAGE			310.09		378.58		399.82		395.81		382.05	
MEDIAN			280.48		334.74		330.65		304.42		307.41	

CASH FLOW/LTD (%)

	RATINGS	FYR END	79		78		77		76		75	
FEDERATED DEPT STORES INC	Aaa/AAA	1/79	93.0	(1)	128.5	(1)	138.6	(2)	196.2	(1)	151.1	(1)
DAYTON-HUDSON CORP	A /A+	1/79	84.3	(2)	47.7	(7)	44.7	(7)	33.7	(11)	20.9	(13)
MACY (R.H.) & CO	NR /NR	7/78	59.5	(3)	49.3	(6)	43.5	(9)	34.7	(10)	39.6	(8)
WALGREEN CO	Baa/BB*	8/78	48.4	(4)	39.5	(11)	35.7	(12)	NA	(-)	25.8	(12)
PENNEY (J.C.) CO	A /AA	1/79	47.8	(5)	93.0	(3)	91.4	(3)	76.9	(4)	48.7	(7)
MERCANTILE STORES CO INC	A /A	1/79	47.6	(6)	65.9	(5)	75.3	(4)	98.5	(3)	94.6	(2)
ASSD DRY GOODS CORP	A /A+	1/79	42.0	(7)	68.5	(4)	71.3	(5)	60.5	(5)	52.5	(4)
SEARS, ROEBUCK & CO	Aaa/AAA	1/79	39.8	(8)	39.8	(10)	52.1	(6)	53.6	(6)	51.3	(5)
K MART CORP	A /A*	1/79	32.5	(9)	100.8	(2)	155.0	(1)	129.8	(2)	69.6	(3)
MAY DEPARTMENT STORES CO	A /AA	1/79	31.3	(10)	30.5	(13)	28.6	(13)	30.8	(12)	26.1	(11)
ALLIED STORES	Baa/BBB*	1/79	29.7	(11)	30.1	(14)	26.9	(14)	23.4	(13)	16.5	(14)
WOOLWORTH (F.W.) CO	A /A	1/79	26.5	(12)	38.0	(12)	44.3	(8)	35.6	(9)	33.7	(9)
CARTER HAWLEY HALE STORES	A /A	1/79	24.0	(13)	45.3	(8)	39.2	(11)	36.5	(8)	30.3	(10)
MURPHY (G.C.) CO	Baa/A	1/79	18.5	(14)	40.9	(9)	42.0	(10)	53.4	(7)	49.6	(6)
ZAYRE CORP	Baa/BB	1/79	17.5	(15)	24.7	(15)	22.0	(15)	16.3	(14)	11.5	(16)
GAMBLE-SKOGMO	NR /NR	1/79	6.6	(16)	5.0	(16)	8.3	(16)	11.4	(15)	16.4	(15)
AVERAGE			40.55		52.98		57.43		59.40		46.13	
MEDIAN			36.14		43.12		43.94		36.50		36.62	

Retail Stores Industry

NET CASH FL/CAP EXP (%)

	RATINGS	FYR END	79			78			77			76			75		
WALGREEN CO	Baa/BB*	8/78	143.0	J(	1)	119.5	(	7)	143.1	(	6)	NA	(	-)	40.8	(	15)
SEARS, ROEBUCK & CO	Aaa/AAA	1/79	137.1	V(	2)	184.0	V(	2)	255.2	V(	2)	158.2	V(	7)	68.5	V(	13)
ALLIED STORES	Baa/BBB*	1/79	129.0	(	3)	149.3	(	4)	190.5	(	4)	200.8	(	3)	116.4	(	5)
ZAYRE CORP	Baa/BB	1/79	128.6	(	4)	230.4	(	1)	384.4	(	1)	363.7	(	1)	154.1	(	3)
MERCANTILE STORES CO INC	A /A	1/79	118.1	(	5)	108.1	(	9)	108.1	(	8)	171.6	(	5)	124.5	(	4)
MACY (R.H.) & CO	NR /NR	7/78	111.6	(	6)	167.1	(	3)	111.2	(	7)	90.8	(	13)	104.8	(	6)
WOOLWORTH (F.W.) CO	A /A	1/79	107.2	(	7)	116.2	(	8)	146.3	(	5)	160.6	(	6)	103.1	(	7)
FEDERATED DEPT STORES INC	Aaa/AAA	1/79	106.6	(	8)	107.0	(	10)	99.5	(	14)	104.9	(	11)	101.7	(	8)
K MART CORP	A /A*	1/79	98.7	(	9)	97.4	(	12)	234.0	(	3)	218.5	(	2)	100.3	(	9)
PENNEY (J.C.) CO	A /AA	1/79	85.0	(	10)	101.4	(	11)	104.6	(	11)	71.4	(	14)	41.9	(	14)
MAY DEPARTMENT STORES CO	A /AA	1/79	80.8	(	11)	127.4	(	5)	101.3	(	12)	113.8	(	10)	74.9	(	11)
CARTER HAWLEY HALE STORES	A /A	1/79	80.2	(	12)	72.5	(	14)	72.3	(	16)	54.0	(	15)	37.8	(	16)
ASSD DRY GOODS CORP	A /A+	1/79	76.1	V(	13)	70.9	V(	15)	97.4	V(	15)	93.0	V(	12)	70.2	V(	12)
DAYTON-HUDSON CORP	A /A+	1/79	67.6	(	14)	80.5	(	13)	107.8	(	9)	177.3	(	4)	78.3	(	10)
GAMBLE-SKOGMO	NR /NR	1/79	65.2	(	15)	31.4	(	16)	105.0	(	10)	115.0	(	9)	158.7	(	2)
MURPHY (G.C.) CO	Baa/A	1/79	55.2	(	16)	124.4	(	6)	100.8	(	13)	156.5	(	8)	176.7	(	1)
AVERAGE			99.39			117.97			147.58			150.01			97.04		
MEDIAN			102.67			112.12			107.94			156.55			101.02		

AFT TAX RET ON COM EQTY (%)

	RATINGS	FYR END	79			78			77			76			75		
K MART CORP	A /A*	1/79	17.9	(	1)	17.9	(	1)	18.5	(	1)	16.8	(	1)	10.3	(	4)
WALGREEN CO	Baa/BB*	8/78	16.8	(	2)	11.2	(	10)	11.3	(	10)	8.0	(	14)	6.4	(	15)
MERCANTILE STORES CO INC	A /A	1/79	14.2	(	3)	12.5	(	9)	13.0	(	4)	15.8	(	2)	12.2	(	2)
MACY (R.H.) & CO	NR /NR	7/78	13.9	(	4)	13.8	(	4)	12.7	(	5)	8.8	(	13)	9.6	(	7)
MAY DEPARTMENT STORES CO	A /AA	1/79	13.5	(	5)	13.4	(	6)	12.1	(	6)	12.5	(	6)	9.5	(	8)
FEDERATED DEPT STORES INC	Aaa/AAA	1/79	13.1	(	6)	14.0	(	3)	13.2	(	3)	14.8	(	3)	12.4	(	1)
SEARS, ROEBUCK & CO	Aaa/AAA	1/79	13.0	(	7)	12.8	(	7)	11.7	(	9)	9.9	(	8)	9.8	(	6)
ALLIED STORES	Baa/BBB*	1/79	12.7	(	8)	12.6	(	8)	12.0	(	7)	13.5	(	4)	10.0	(	5)
DAYTON-HUDSON CORP	A /A+	1/79	12.0	(	9)	15.8	(	2)	14.6	(	2)	12.9	(	5)	7.0	(	13)
PENNEY (J.C.) CO	A /AA	1/79	11.7	(	10)	13.6	(	5)	11.9	(	8)	11.1	(	7)	8.8	(	11)
CARTER HAWLEY HALE STORES	A /A	1/79	11.5	(	11)	10.3	(	11)	9.2	(	12)	9.6	(	10)	9.0	(	10)
WOOLWORTH (F.W.) CO	A /A	1/79	10.8	(	12)	7.9	(	14)	9.8	(	11)	9.6	(	11)	6.5	(	14)
GAMBLE-SKOGMO	NR /NR	1/79	10.0	(	13)	4.0	(	16)	7.4	(	16)	9.5	(	12)	11.1	(	3)
ZAYRE CORP	Baa/BB	1/79	9.7	(	14)	8.5	(	13)	8.7	(	14)	5.9	(	16)	0.6	(	16)
ASSD DRY GOODS CORP	A /A+	1/79	7.0	(	15)	8.8	(	12)	8.8	(	13)	9.8	(	9)	9.0	(	9)
MURPHY (G.C.) CO	Baa/A	1/79	0.2	(	16)	7.2	(	15)	8.5	(	15)	7.9	(	15)	7.8	(	12)
AVERAGE			11.75			11.52			11.46			11.02			8.75		
MEDIAN			12.35			12.51			11.80			9.84			9.25		

RET ON TOT ASSETS (%)

	RATINGS	FYR END	79			78			77			76			75		
K MART CORP	A /A*	1/79	16.1	(	1)	17.6	(	1)	18.1	(	1)	17.5	(	3)	11.6	(	6)
MERCANTILE STORES CO INC	A /A	1/79	15.8	(	2)	15.2	(	4)	16.0	(	2)	19.7	(	1)	16.3	(	2)
MACY (R.H.) & CO	NR /NR	7/78	15.0	(	3)	14.5	(	6)	13.6	(	6)	10.4	(	11)	11.5	(	7)
WALGREEN CO	Baa/BB*	8/78	14.6	(	4)	10.0	(	13)	9.7	(	13)	6.6	(	16)	5.6	(	15)
PENNEY (J.C.) CO	A /AA	1/79	14.5	(	5)	16.0	(	3)	14.8	(	4)	14.2	(	4)	13.4	(	3)
FEDERATED DEPT STORES INC	Aaa/AAA	1/79	14.4	(	6)	16.4	(	2)	15.3	(	3)	18.1	(	2)	16.3	(	1)
ALLIED STORES	Baa/BBB*	1/79	13.3	(	7)	13.0	(	7)	12.8	(	7)	12.9	(	6)	9.9	(	12)
DAYTON-HUDSON CORP	A /A+	1/79	13.0	(	8)	15.1	(	5)	14.6	(	5)	13.3	(	5)	8.6	(	14)
MAY DEPARTMENT STORES CO	A /AA	1/79	12.7	(	9)	12.3	(	9)	11.8	(	11)	11.9	(	9)	10.0	(	11)
CARTER HAWLEY HALE STORES	A /A	1/79	12.5	(	10)	12.8	(	8)	11.9	(	10)	12.6	(	8)	13.2	(	4)
SEARS, ROEBUCK & CO	Aaa/AAA	1/79	11.7	(	11)	10.5	(	11)	10.5	(	12)	10.3	(	12)	10.6	(	10)
WOOLWORTH (F.W.) CO	A /A	1/79	11.6	(	12)	10.5	(	12)	12.4	(	9)	11.1	(	10)	8.8	(	13)
GAMBLE-SKOGMO	NR /NR	1/79	9.9	(	13)	5.8	(	16)	8.2	(	16)	9.0	(	14)	10.6	(	8)
ZAYRE CORP	Baa/BB	1/79	9.8	(	14)	8.7	(	14)	9.4	(	15)	7.6	(	15)	5.1	(	16)
ASSD DRY GOODS CORP	A /A+	1/79	9.6	(	15)	12.0	(	10)	12.4	(	8)	12.8	(	7)	12.6	(	5)
MURPHY (G.C.) CO	Baa/A	1/79	2.5	(	16)	8.5	(	15)	9.5	(	14)	9.4	(	13)	10.6	(	9)
AVERAGE			12.33			12.43			12.55			12.34			10.91		
MEDIAN			12.88			12.59			12.40			12.25			10.58		

Rubber and Tire Industry

PRETAX COVERAGE

	RATINGS	FYR END	78	77	76	75	74
GENERAL TIRE & RUBBER CO	Ba /BB*	11/78	6.50P(1)	6.95P(1)	5.87P(1)	3.50 (2)	4.13 (2)
DAYCO CORP	Ba /BB*	10/78	3.83 (2)	3.73 (3)	3.48 (2)	2.81 (4)	2.51 (5)
ARMSTRONG RUBBER	Baa/BBB	9/78	3.20 (3)	4.80 (2)	2.94 (5)	1.71 (6)	1.77 (7)
GOODYEAR TIRE & RUBBER CO	A /A-	12/78	3.17 (4)	3.65P(4)	3.14P(4)	3.42P(3)	2.90P(3)
GOODRICH (B.F.) CO	A /BBB	12/78	3.13 (5)	3.46 (5)	1.91 (6)	1.66P(7)	2.81P(4)
UNIROYAL INC	Ba /B*	12/78	1.21P(6)	2.27R(7)	1.85P(7)	1.73P(5)	2.30P(6)
FIRESTONE TIRE & RUBBER CO	A /A-	10/78	-0.74 (7)	3.41 (6)	3.39 (3)	3.98 (1)	5.26 (1)
AVERAGE			2.90	4.04	3.23	2.69	3.10
MEDIAN			3.17	3.65	3.14	2.81	2.81

AFTER TAX COVERAGE

	RATINGS	FYR END	78	77	76	75	74
GENERAL TIRE & RUBBER CO	Ba /BB*	11/78	4.01P(1)	4.09P(1)	3.56P(1)	2.43 (2)	2.89 (2)
DAYCO CORP	Ba /BB*	10/78	2.47 (2)	2.43 (4)	2.36 (2)	2.01 (4)	1.83 (5)
GOODRICH (B.F.) CO	A /BBB	12/78	2.27 (3)	2.46 (3)	1.55 (6)	1.37P(7)	2.05P(3)
GOODYEAR TIRE & RUBBER CO	A /A-	12/78	2.24 (4)	2.38P(5)	1.99P(5)	2.22P(3)	1.97P(4)
ARMSTRONG RUBBER	Baa/BBB	9/78	2.23 (5)	3.05 (2)	2.04 (4)	1.52 (5)	1.53 (7)
UNIROYAL INC	Ba /B*	12/78	1.07P(6)	1.68P(7)	1.45P(7)	1.44P(6)	1.76P(6)
FIRESTONE TIRE & RUBBER CO	A /A-	10/78	-0.47 (7)	2.25 (6)	2.23 (3)	2.75 (1)	3.42 (1)
AVERAGE			1.98	2.62	2.17	1.96	2.21
MEDIAN			2.24	2.43	2.04	2.01	1.97

AFTER TAX COV (INCL RENTS)

	RATINGS	FYR END	78	77	76	75	74
GENERAL TIRE & RUBBER CO	Ba /BB*	11/78	2.76P(1)	2.85P(1)	2.60P(1)	1.95 (2)	2.20 (2)
DAYCO CORP	Ba /BB*	10/78	1.91 (2)	1.84 (4)	1.88 (2)	1.66 (4)	1.55 (5)
GOODRICH (B.F.) CO	A /BBB	12/78	1.85 (3)	1.78 (5)	1.28 (6)	1.21P(7)	1.59P(4)
GOODYEAR TIRE & RUBBER CO	A /A-	12/78	1.81 (4)	1.86P(3)	1.54P(5)	1.71P(3)	1.62P(3)
ARMSTRONG RUBBER	Baa/BBB	9/78	1.73 (5)	2.18 (2)	1.64 (4)	1.36 (5)	1.40 (7)
UNIROYAL INC	Ba /B*	12/78	1.05P(6)	1.36P(7)	1.21P(7)	1.23P(6)	1.42P(6)
FIRESTONE TIRE & RUBBER CO	A /A-	10/78	0.04 (7)	1.77 (6)	1.73 (3)	2.03 (1)	2.36 (1)
AVERAGE			1.59	1.95	1.70	1.59	1.73
MEDIAN			1.81	1.84	1.64	1.66	1.59

NET INCOME AS % NET SALES

	RATINGS	FYR END	78	77	76	75	74
GENERAL TIRE & RUBBER CO	Ba /BB*	11/78	5.3 (1)	5.5 (1)	5.2 (1)	3.6 (2)	4.5 (1)
GOODYEAR TIRE & RUBBER CO	A /A-	12/78	3.0 (2)	3.1 (3)	2.1 (5)	3.0 (3)	3.0 (3)
GOODRICH (B.F.) CO	A /BBB	12/78	2.7 (3)	2.7 (4)	0.8 (7)	1.3 (6)	2.7 (4)
DAYCO CORP	Ba /BB*	10/78	2.7 (4)	2.4 (6)	2.5 (3)	2.2 (4)	1.7 (7)
ARMSTRONG RUBBER	Baa/BBB	9/78	2.5 (5)	4.1 (2)	2.6 (2)	1.6 (5)	1.7 (6)
UNIROYAL INC	Ba /B*	12/78	0.2 (6)	1.3 (7)	0.9 (6)	1.1 (7)	2.1 (5)
FIRESTONE TIRE & RUBBER CO	A /A-	10/78	-3.0 (7)	2.5 (5)	2.4 (4)	3.6 (1)	4.2 (2)
AVERAGE			1.91	3.08	2.36	2.33	2.85
MEDIAN			2.65	2.70	2.44	2.19	2.71

Rubber and Tire Industry

LTD/CAPITALIZATION (%)

	RATINGS	FYR END	78			77			76			75			74		
GENERAL TIRE & RUBBER CO	Ba /BB*	11/78	21.8	(	1)	25.5	(	1)	29.5	(	1)	33.6	(	3)	34.0	(	2)
FIRESTONE TIRE & RUBBER CO	A /A-	10/78	32.7	(	2)	29.9	(	2)	30.2	(	2)	32.0	(	1)	30.3	(	1)
GOODRICH (B.F.) CO	A /BBB	12/78	35.4	(	3)	35.0	(	3)	35.1	(	4)	37.3	(	4)	39.7	(	4)
ARMSTRONG RUBBER	Baa/BBB	9/78	38.8	(	4)	40.1	(	5)	43.4	(	6)	47.6	(	6)	48.4	(	6)
GOODYEAR TIRE & RUBBER CO	A /A-	12/78	40.2	(	5)	36.3	(	4)	33.3	(	3)	32.6	(	2)	34.6	(	3)
UNIROYAL INC	Ba /B*	12/78	46.6	(	6)	42.4	(	6)	42.8	(	5)	42.5	(	5)	43.6	(	5)
DAYCO CORP	Ba /BB*	10/78	56.1	(	7)	61.2	(	7)	63.4	(	7)	65.8	(	7)	67.2	(	7)
AVERAGE			38.80			38.62			39.68			41.65			42.54		
MEDIAN			38.77			36.32			35.13			37.31			39.71		

TOT LIABILITY/TOT STK EQUITY

	RATINGS	FYR END	78			77			76			75			74		
GENERAL TIRE & RUBBER CO	Ba /BB*	11/78	78.1	(	1)	81.8	(	1)	96.5	(	1)	101.3	(	1)	119.3	(	2)
ARMSTRONG RUBBER	Baa/BBB	9/78	109.2	(	2)	135.7	(	4)	137.6	(	5)	150.5	(	5)	171.1	(	6)
GOODRICH (B.F.) CO	A /BBB	12/78	121.6	(	3)	116.5	(	3)	111.7	(	3)	116.7	(	3)	129.4	(	3)
FIRESTONE TIRE & RUBBER CO	A /A-	10/78	147.6	(	4)	109.9	(	2)	108.0	(	2)	108.1	(	2)	106.3	(	1)
GOODYEAR TIRE & RUBBER CO	A /A-	12/78	148.1	(	5)	137.0	(	5)	132.9	(	4)	129.8	(	4)	142.8	(	4)
UNIROYAL INC	Ba /B*	12/78	195.1	(	6)	170.7	(	6)	160.1	(	6)	156.5	(	6)	161.1	(	5)
DAYCO CORP	Ba /BB*	10/78	228.2	(	7)	249.9	(	7)	256.8	(	7)	274.9	(	7)	308.6	(	7)
AVERAGE			146.86			143.08			143.36			148.24			162.67		
MEDIAN			147.65			135.68			132.89			129.82			142.84		

LTD/NET PLANT (%)

	RATINGS	FYR END	78			77			76			75			74		
GENERAL TIRE & RUBBER CO	Ba /BB*	11/78	46.2	(	1)	55.0	(	2)	60.5	(	4)	68.0	(	4)	66.7	(	3)
FIRESTONE TIRE & RUBBER CO	A /A-	10/78	47.3	(	2)	48.5	(	1)	48.9	(	1)	51.7	(	2)	47.0	(	1)
GOODRICH (B.F.) CO	A /BBB	12/78	61.4	(	3)	62.0	(	4)	60.1	(	3)	62.6	(	3)	67.5	(	4)
GOODYEAR TIRE & RUBBER CO	A /A-	12/78	66.0	(	4)	57.4	(	3)	51.6	(	2)	49.6	(	1)	54.8	(	2)
UNIROYAL INC	Ba /B*	12/78	79.5	(	5)	76.2	(	5)	77.9	(	5)	77.4	(	5)	80.1	(	5)
ARMSTRONG RUBBER	Baa/BBB	9/78	88.8	(	6)	89.7	(	6)	92.4	(	6)	96.4	(	6)	93.9	(	6)
DAYCO CORP	Ba /BB*	10/78	129.1	(	7)	149.7	(	7)	168.0	(	7)	183.5	(	7)	199.9	(	7)
AVERAGE			74.05			76.93			79.92			84.16			87.12		
MEDIAN			66.01			61.98			60.48			67.95			67.54		

NET TANG ASSETS/LTD (%)

	RATINGS	FYR END	78			77			76			75			74		
GENERAL TIRE & RUBBER CO	Ba /BB*	11/78	448.3	(	1)	382.4	(	1)	330.6	(	1)	289.5	(	3)	285.7	(	2)
FIRESTONE TIRE & RUBBER CO	A /A-	10/78	300.2	(	2)	328.9	(	2)	323.8	(	2)	306.4	(	1)	314.9	(	1)
GOODRICH (B.F.) CO	A /BBB	12/78	273.6	(	3)	284.3	(	3)	282.8	(	4)	265.6	(	4)	249.7	(	4)
ARMSTRONG RUBBER	Baa/BBB	9/78	253.4	(	4)	244.8	(	5)	228.0	(	5)	207.8	(	6)	204.2	(	6)
GOODYEAR TIRE & RUBBER CO	A /A-	12/78	234.5	(	5)	269.9	(	4)	295.7	(	3)	300.3	(	2)	280.2	(	3)
UNIROYAL INC	Ba /B*	12/78	207.2	(	6)	225.9	(	6)	223.4	(	6)	226.1	(	5)	219.2	(	5)
DAYCO CORP	Ba /BB*	10/78	161.8	(	7)	144.1	(	7)	140.7	(	7)	134.9	(	7)	132.1	(	7)
AVERAGE			268.42			268.62			260.73			247.23			240.84		
MEDIAN			253.35			269.95			282.83			265.60			249.65		

CASH FLOW/LTD (%)

	RATINGS	FYR END	78			77			76			75			74		
GENERAL TIRE & RUBBER CO	Ba /BB#	11/78	72.2	(	1)	60.0	(	1)	50.8	(	1)	34.3	(	3)	36.7	(	3)
GOODRICH (B.F.) CO	A /BBB	12/78	36.3	(	2)	39.4	(	3)	29.7	(	4)	24.6	(	4)	27.5	(	4)
GOODYEAR TIRE & RUBBER CO	A /A-	12/78	31.0	(	3)	37.1	(	4)	34.7	(	3)	40.9	(	1)	38.1	(	2)
ARMSTRONG RUBBER	Baa/BBB	9/78	28.2	(	4)	34.4	(	5)	25.1	(	5)	19.4	(	6)	18.2	(	6)
DAYCO CORP	Ba /BB#	10/78	20.2	(	5)	17.1	(	7)	16.2	(	7)	12.4	(	7)	12.8	(	7)
FIRESTONE TIRE & RUBBER CO	A /A-	10/78	13.7	(	6)	41.4	(	2)	39.7	(	2)	39.6	(	2)	47.6	(	1)
UNIROYAL INC	Ba /B#	12/78	13.2	(	7)	23.4	(	6)	19.8	(	6)	21.8	(	5)	24.5	(	5)
AVERAGE			30.67			36.12			30.87			27.57			29.34		
MEDIAN			28.22			37.14			29.74			24.61			27.51		

NET CASH FL/CAP EXP (%)

	RATINGS	FYR END	78			77			76			75			74		
GENERAL TIRE & RUBBER CO	Ba /BB#	11/78	225.3	(	1)	218.9	(	1)	195.2	(	2)	151.6	(	2)	95.9	(	3)
ARMSTRONG RUBBER	Baa/BBB	9/78	159.2	(	2)	210.6	(	2)	291.6	(	1)	172.9	(	1)	34.5	(	7)
DAYCO CORP	Ba /BB#	10/78	142.9	(	3)	87.4	(	7)	123.8	(	4)	100.8	(	5)	105.5	(	1)
GOODRICH (B.F.) CO	A /BBB	12/78	131.2	(	4)	140.1	(	3)	143.3	(	3)	87.8	(	7)	76.9	(	5)
GOODYEAR TIRE & RUBBER CO	A /A-	12/78	84.2	(	5)	114.6	(	4)	107.6	(	6)	98.7	(	6)	98.8	(	2)
UNIROYAL INC	Ba /B#	12/78	60.4	(	6)	91.4	(	6)	86.2	(	7)	120.1	(	3)	93.7	(	4)
FIRESTONE TIRE & RUBBER CO	A /A-	10/78	13.2	(	7)	108.4	(	5)	121.5	(	5)	111.3	(	4)	73.6	(	6)
AVERAGE			116.61			138.76			152.75			120.46			82.69		
MEDIAN			131.16			114.60			123.79			111.30			93.75		

AFT TAX RET ON COM EQTY (%)

	RATINGS	FYR END	78			77			76			75			74		
DAYCO CORP	Ba /BB#	10/78	14.5	(	1)	14.4	(	1)	15.0	(	1)	11.8	(	1)	10.5	(	3)
GENERAL TIRE & RUBBER CO	Ba /BB#	11/78	12.2	(	2)	13.4	(	2)	13.4	(	2)	8.9	(	3)	11.8	(	1)
GOODYEAR TIRE & RUBBER CO	A /A-	12/78	10.7	(	3)	10.4	(	4)	6.6	(	4)	8.9	(	2)	9.0	(	4)
GOODRICH (B.F.) CO	A /BBB	12/78	8.1	(	4)	7.7	(	5)	1.9	(	7)	3.2	(	7)	7.1	(	6)
ARMSTRONG RUBBER	Baa/BBB	9/78	7.5	(	5)	12.9	(	3)	8.0	(	3)	3.9	(	5)	4.0	(	7)
UNIROYAL INC	Ba /B#	12/78	0.2	(	6)	5.1	(	7)	2.7	(	6)	3.2	(	6)	7.7	(	5)
FIRESTONE TIRE & RUBBER CO	A /A-	10/78	-10.5	(	7)	6.8	(	6)	6.1	(	5)	8.8	(	4)	10.6	(	2)
AVERAGE			6.08			10.10			7.67			6.95			8.68		
MEDIAN			8.06			10.43			6.55			8.78			9.01		

RET ON TOT ASSETS (%)

	RATINGS	FYR END	78			77			76			75			74		
GENERAL TIRE & RUBBER CO	Ba /BB#	11/78	12.5	(	1)	14.4	(	1)	13.7	(	1)	9.4	(	3)	10.5	(	3)
DAYCO CORP	Ba /BB#	10/78	11.8	(	2)	11.1	(	4)	11.2	(	2)	9.2	(	4)	8.3	(	5)
GOODYEAR TIRE & RUBBER CO	A /A-	12/78	11.0	(	3)	.11.4	(	3)	8.8	(	4)	10.7	(	1)	10.7	(	2)
GOODRICH (B.F.) CO	A /BBB	12/78	9.1	(	4)	9.2	(	5)	4.9	(	7)	5.6	(	7)	8.2	(	6)
ARMSTRONG RUBBER	Baa/BBB	9/78	8.9	(	5)	11.8	(	2)	9.0	(	3)	5.9	(	5)	5.3	(	7)
UNIROYAL INC	Ba /B#	12/78	4.8	(	6)	6.5	(	7)	5.1	(	6)	5.7	(	6)	8.8	(	4)
FIRESTONE TIRE & RUBBER CO	A /A-	10/78	-2.1	(	7)	8.9	(	6)	8.1	(	5)	9.6	(	2)	11.2	(	1)
AVERAGE			7.99			10.47			8.68			8.03			9.00		
MEDIAN			9.13			11.10			8.77			9.21			8.76		

Steel Industry

PRETAX COVERAGE

	RATINGS	FYR END	78	77	76	75	74
HARSCO CORP	A /A	12/78	13.33P(1)	13.41P(1)	11.62 (2)	12.26 (2)	9.99 (9)
ARMCO INC	A /A	12/78	6.75 (2)	2.77 (6)	3.17 (8)	5.06 (6)	10.96 (8)
INLAND STEEL CO	Aa /AA-	12/78	5.73P(3)	2.89P(5)	4.95P(5)	4.80P(8)	11.72P(7)
REPUBLIC STEEL CORP	A /A	12/78	5.37 (4)	2.19 (7)	2.39 (10)	5.04 (7)	15.41 (3)
NATIONAL STEEL CORP	Aa /A+	12/78	4.99 (5)	2.00 (8)	2.76 (9)	2.63P(10)	15.64 (2)
COPPERWELD CORP	A /A	12/78	4.82 (6)	6.09 (2)	19.32 (1)	33.22 (1)	38.86 (1)
BETHLEHEM STEEL CORP	A /A	12/78	4.62P(7)	-10.13P(10)	3.42P(7)	5.48P(5)	15.03P(4)
INTERLAKE INC	A /BBB+	12/78	2.50 (8)	4.65 (3)	7.72 (3)	7.69 (4)	12.50 (5)
ALLEGHENY LUDLUM INDS	Baa/BBB	12/78	2.30 (9)	2.95 (4)	3.59 (6)	3.69 (9)	6.00 (10)
U S STEEL CORP	Aa /AA-	12/78	2.22P(10)	1.56P(9)	5.23P(4)	10.69P(3)	12.01P(6)
AVERAGE			5.26	2.84	6.42	9.06	14.81
MEDIAN			4.90	2.83	4.27	5.27	12.25

AFTER TAX COVERAGE

	RATINGS	FYR END	78	77	76	75	74
HARSCO CORP	A /A	12/78	7.11P(1)	7.08P(1)	6.44 (2)	6.78 (3)	5.66 (9)
ARMCO INC	A /A	12/78	4.25 (2)	2.75 (5)	3.25 (7)	3.66 (7)	6.61 (8)
INLAND STEEL CO	Aa /AA-	12/78	4.18P(3)	2.81P(4)	3.70P(5)	3.37P(8)	6.71P(7)
REPUBLIC STEEL CORP	A /A	12/78	4.12 (4)	2.18 (7)	3.29 (6)	4.22 (6)	9.13 (2)
BETHLEHEM STEEL CORP	A /A	12/78	3.63P(5)	-4.52P(10)	3.09PS(8)	4.83P(4)	8.80P(3)
COPPERWELD CORP	A /A	12/78	3.26 (6)	4.60 (2)	11.46 (1)	17.93 (1)	20.33 (1)
NATIONAL STEEL CORP	Aa /A+	12/78	3.23 (7)	1.86 (8)	2.56 (9)	2.44P(10)	8.74 (4)
INTERLAKE INC	A /BBB+	12/78	2.24 (8)	3.02 (3)	5.06 (3)	4.70 (5)	7.11 (6)
U S STEEL CORP	Aa /AA-	12/78	2.18P(9)	1.80P(9)	4.29P(4)	7.51P(2)	7.62P(5)
ALLEGHENY LUDLUM INDS	Baa/BBB	12/78	1.77 (10)	2.39 (6)	2.51 (10)	2.47 (9)	3.56 (10)
AVERAGE			3.60	2.40	4.56	5.79	8.43
MEDIAN			3.45	2.57	3.50	4.46	7.36

AFTER TAX COV (INCL RENTS)

	RATINGS	FYR END	78	77	76	75	74
BETHLEHEM STEEL CORP	A /A	12/78	2.68P(1)	-2.26P(5)	2.36P(5)	3.02P(3)	4.84P(3)
U S STEEL CORP	Aa /AA-	12/78	1.80P(2)	1.50P(4)	2.87P(3)	4.13P(2)	4.15P(5)
ALLEGHENY LUDLUM INDS	Baa/BBB·	12/78	1.50 (3)	1.88 (3)	1.97 (6)	1.95 (6)	2.75 (6)
ARMCO INC	A /A	12/78	NA (-)	2.25 (2)	2.53 (4)	2.74 (5)	4.71 (4)
COPPERWELD CORP	A /A	12/78	NA (-)	NA (-)	9.41 (1)	13.05 (1)	13.82 (1)
HARSCO CORP	A /A	12/78	NA (-)	NA (-)	NA (-)	NA (-)	NA (-)
INLAND STEEL CO	Aa /AA-	12/78	NA (-)	2.44P(1)	3.08P(2)	2.76P(4)	4.91P(2)
INTERLAKE INC	A /BBB+	12/78	NA (-)	NA (-)	NA (-)	NA (-)	NA (-)
NATIONAL STEEL CORP	Aa /A+	12/78	NA (-)	NA (-)	NA (-)	NA (-)	NA (-)
REPUBLIC STEEL CORP	A /A	12/78	NA (-)	NA (-)	NA (-)	NA (-)	NA (-)
AVERAGE			1.99	1.16	3.70	4.61	5.86
MEDIAN			1.80	1.88	2.70	2.89	4.77

NET INCOME AS % NET SALES

	RATINGS	FYR END	78		77		76		75		74	
HARSCO CORP	A /A	12/78	5.7	(1)	6.3	(1)	6.4	(1)	6.8	(2)	5.1	(9)
INLAND STEEL CO	Aa /AA-	12/78	4.9	(2)	3.3	(4)	4.4	(5)	4.0	(6)	6.0	(7)
ARMCO INC	A /A	12/78	4.6	(3)	3.4	(3)	3.8	(6)	3.8	(7)	6.4	(3)
BETHLEHEM STEEL CORP	A /A	12/78	3.6	(4)	-8.3	(10)	3.2	(8)	4.9	(5)	6.4	(4)
REPUBLIC STEEL CORP	A /A	12/78	3.2	(5)	1.4	(9)	2.6	(10)	3.1	(9)	6.2	(6)
NATIONAL STEEL CORP	Aa /A+	12/78	3.0	(6)	1.9	(7)	3.0	(9)	2.6	(10)	6.4	(2)
ALLEGHENY LUDLUM INDS	Baa/BBB	12/78	2.9	(7)	2.5	(5)	3.5	(7)	3.8	(8)	4.6	(10)
COPPERWELD CORP	A /A	12/78	2.7	(8)	4.7	(2)	6.3	(2)	6.5	(3)	5.2	(8)
U S STEEL CORP	Aa /AA-	12/78	2.2	(9)	1.4	(8)	4.8	(4)	6.9	(1)	6.9	(1)
INTERLAKE INC	A /BBB+	12/78	1.1	(10)	2.4	(6)	5.3	(3)	6.2	(4)	6.3	(5)
AVERAGE			3.39		1.91		4.33		4.85		5.95	
MEDIAN			3.09		2.49		4.08		4.41		6.24	

LTD/CAPITALIZATION (%)

	RATINGS	FYR END	78		77		76		75		74	
HARSCO CORP	A /A	12/78	20.8	(1)	23.1	(2)	25.5	(3)	27.9	(6)	14.0	(2)
REPUBLIC STEEL CORP	A /A	12/78	24.1	(2)	25.3	(3)	22.0	(2)	22.1	(2)	17.7	(3)
ARMCO INC	A /A	12/78	28.1	(3)	30.5	(5)	32.2	(8)	30.6	(8)	26.9	(8)
COPPERWELD CORP	A /A	12/78	29.2	(4)	30.3	(4)	29.9	(6)	11.6	(1)	13.9	(1)
U S STEEL CORP	Aa /AA-	12/78	29.4	(5)	30.9	(6)	27.6	(5)	24.1	(3)	22.9	(5)
BETHLEHEM STEEL CORP	A /A	12/78	29.8	(6)	34.6	(7)	27.5	(4)	24.7	(5)	20.7	(4)
INTERLAKE INC	A /BBB+	12/78	30.8	(7)	21.7	(1)	20.7	(1)	24.5	(4)	23.5	(6)
INLAND STEEL CO	Aa /AA-	12/78	34.2	(8)	34.9	(8)	30.3	(7)	34.3	(10)	29.3	(9)
NATIONAL STEEL CORP	Aa /A+	12/78	34.2	(9)	36.1	(9)	37.1	(10)	30.7	(9)	25.3	(7)
ALLEGHENY LUDLUM INDS	Baa/BBB	12/78	45.2	(10)	46.0	(10)	36.2	(9)	30.4	(7)	30.4	(10)
AVERAGE			30.58		31.33		28.90		26.08		22.46	
MEDIAN			29.56		30.72		28.76		26.29		23.18	

TOT LIABILITY/TOT STK EQUITY

	RATINGS	FYR END	78		77		76		75		74	
HARSCO CORP	A /A	12/78	65.6	(1)	61.0	(1)	64.3	(1)	73.4	(4)	75.0	(3)
REPUBLIC STEEL CORP	A /A	12/78	83.4	(2)	80.4	(2)	76.9	(3)	62.0	(1)	65.7	(1)
ARMCO INC	A /A	12/78	96.9	(3)	97.0	(5)	101.5	(8)	95.8	(8)	99.4	(8)
U S STEEL CORP	Aa /AA-	12/78	99.5	(4)	92.8	(4)	78.7	(4)	68.0	(3)	73.3	(2)
INLAND STEEL CO	Aa /AA-	12/78	107.1	(5)	100.8	(6)	87.3	(6)	92.3	(7)	87.3	(6)
BETHLEHEM STEEL CORP	A /A	12/78	109.0	(6)	124.8	(9)	83.4	(5)	75.8	(5)	81.2	(5)
INTERLAKE INC	A /BBB+	12/78	114.9	(7)	81.4	(3)	74.3	(2)	81.8	(6)	105.0	(9)
COPPERWELD CORP	A /A	12/78	117.1	(8)	105.2	(7)	89.6	(7)	64.5	(2)	76.6	(4)
NATIONAL STEEL CORP	Aa /A+	12/78	133.1	(9)	120.7	(8)	121.5	(10)	99.4	(9)	91.9	(7)
ALLEGHENY LUDLUM INDS	Baa/BBB	12/78	149.1	(10)	143.1	(10)	112.9	(9)	99.5	(10)	115.6	(10)
AVERAGE			107.58		100.74		89.05		81.26		87.10	
MEDIAN			108.05		98.91		85.36		78.81		84.27	

LTD/NET PLANT (%)

	RATINGS	FYR END	78		77		76		75		74	
REPUBLIC STEEL CORP	A /A	12/78	30.4	(1)	31.6	(1)	26.4	(1)	27.2	(2)	22.8	(1)
BETHLEHEM STEEL CORP	A /A	12/78	33.4	(2)	38.4	(2)	34.1	(2)	29.4	(3)	25.6	(4)
U S STEEL CORP	Aa /AA-	12/78	36.7	(3)	40.2	(4)	37.1	(4)	33.2	(4)	31.8	(5)
INLAND STEEL CO	Aa /AA-	12/78	39.3	(4)	41.5	(5)	36.2	(3)	45.3	(8)	39.4	(9)
ARMCO INC	A /A	12/78	41.2	(5)	41.6	(6)	43.7	(6)	43.4	(7)	39.1	(8)
COPPERWELD CORP	A /A	12/78	43.1	(6)	46.7	(8)	60.2	(9)	21.7	(1)	25.2	(3)
NATIONAL STEEL CORP	Aa /A+	12/78	43.2	(7)	44.2	(7)	46.0	(7)	36.3	(5)	32.3	(6)
HARSCO CORP	A /A	12/78	46.8	(8)	53.1	(9)	57.1	(8)	64.0	(10)	24.7	(2)
INTERLAKE INC	A /BBB+	12/78	57.3	(9)	39.8	(3)	38.2	(5)	41.1	(6)	37.4	(7)
ALLEGHENY LUDLUM INDS	Baa/BBB	12/78	95.2	(10)	93.5	(10)	72.9	(10)	55.5	(9)	57.1	(10)
AVERAGE			46.67		47.05		45.20		39.70		33.54	
MEDIAN			42.16		41.53		40.94		38.68		32.01	

Steel Industry

NET TANG ASSETS/LTD (%)

	RATINGS	FYR END	78		77		76		75		74	
HARSCO CORP	A /A	12/78	470.4	(1)	423.4	(2)	384.8	(3)	354.3	(6)	706.3	(1)
REPUBLIC STEEL CORP	A /A	12/78	404.1	(2)	385.0	(3)	443.1	(2)	442.6	(2)	552.3	(3)
ARMCO INC	A /A	12/78	347.4	(3)	320.6	(5)	305.4	(8)	320.6	(9)	362.9	(8)
COPPERWELD CORP	A /A	12/78	335.1	(4)	324.1	(4)	327.3	(6)	838.1	(1)	698.7	(2)
BETHLEHEM STEEL CORP	A /A	12/78	327.3	(5)	277.0	(8)	358.9	(4)	398.0	(3)	480.3	(4)
U S STEEL CORP	Aa /AA-	12/78	307.4	(6)	292.7	(6)	332.3	(5)	396.8	(4)	424.5	(5)
INTERLAKE INC	A /BBB+	12/78	298.7	(7)	436.9	(1)	452.5	(1)	383.3	(5)	399.8	(6)
NATIONAL STEEL CORP	Aa /A+	12/78	288.7	(8)	275.2	(9)	268.1	(9)	324.7	(8)	393.4	(7)
INLAND STEEL CO	Aa /AA-	12/78	285.2	(9)	278.7	(7)	319.9	(7)	282.1	(10)	329.6	(9)
ALLEGHENY LUDLUM INDS	Baa/BBB	12/78	213.6	(10)	213.7	(10)	265.1	(10)	325.2	(7)	326.5	(10)
AVERAGE			327.77		322.74		345.74		406.56		467.42	
MEDIAN			317.37		306.67		329.84		368.80		412.15	

CASH FLOW/LTD (%)

	RATINGS	FYR END	78		77		76		75		74	
HARSCO CORP	A /A	12/78	100.6	(1)	90.4	(1)	78.2	(1)	72.1	(2)	164.8	(1)
ARMCO INC	A /A	12/78	66.4	(2)	26.9	(7)	29.5	(10)	38.7	(8)	68.5	(8)
BETHLEHEM STEEL CORP	A /A	12/78	59.3	(3)	6.4	(10)	46.8	(5)	61.2	(5)	87.0	(4)
REPUBLIC STEEL CORP	A /A	12/78	57.8	(4)	37.5	(4)	57.5	(3)	53.8	(6)	101.0	(3)
COPPERWELD CORP	A /A	12/78	50.9	(5)	46.0	(2)	48.8	(4)	174.4	(1)	144.8	(2)
INLAND STEEL CO	Aa /AA-	12/78	48.3	(6)	34.6	(5)	44.1	(6)	37.1	(10)	62.0	(9)
NATIONAL STEEL CORP	Aa /A+	12/78	42.0	(7)	31.4	(6)	34.2	(9)	37.9	(9)	73.9	(6)
INTERLAKE INC	A /BBB+	12/78	38.6	(8)	45.2	(3)	71.9	(2)	65.8	(3)	71.9	(7)
U S STEEL CORP	Aa /AA-	12/78	29.6	(9)	24.2	(8)	42.6	(7)	62.1	(4)	78.7	(5)
ALLEGHENY LUDLUM INDS	Baa/BBB	12/78	25.8	(10)	19.5	(9)	38.8	(8)	44.6	(7)	61.6	(10)
AVERAGE			51.94		36.23		49.24		64.77		91.42	
MEDIAN			49.62		33.01		45.46		57.49		76.27	

NET CASH FL/CAP EXP (%)

	RATINGS	FYR END	78		77		76		75		74	
ARMCO INC	A /A	12/78	312.1	(1)	77.1	(6)	51.4	(9)	70.1	(6)	244.5	(1)
NATIONAL STEEL CORP	Aa /A+	12/78	200.2	(2)	110.5	(3)	76.5	(5)	50.7	(10)	133.0	(8)
BETHLEHEM STEEL CORP	A /A	12/78	137.6	(3)	1.7	(10)	97.8	(4)	59.5	(.D	88.5	(10)
HARSCO CORP	A /A	12/78	134.5	(4)	156.0	(1)	143.7	(2)	131.6	(4)	106.9	(9)
ALLEGHENY LUDLUM INDS	Baa/BBB	12/78	107.2	(5)	125.3	(2)	135.7	(3)	203.7	(1)	239.0	(2)
REPUBLIC STEEL CORP	A /A	12/78	105.5	(6)	84.3	(5)	74.7	(6)	61.2	(7)	178.5	(5)
COPPERWELD CORP	A /A	12/78	98.5	(7)	45.5	(8)	73.5	(7)	156.0	(2)	224.4	(3)
INLAND STEEL CO	Aa /AA-	12/78	80.5	(8)	52.0	(7)	51.4	(10)	57.6	(9)	139.2	(7)
U S STEEL CORP	Aa /AA-	12/78	77.0	(9)	43.3	(9)	69.3	(8)	101.9	(5)	181.4	(4)
INTERLAKE INC	A /BBB+	12/78	52.5	(10)	84.4	(4)	226.2	(1)	134.4	(3)	166.2	(6)
AVERAGE			130.57		78.00		100.01		102.67		170.15	
MEDIAN			106.35		80.69		75.56		86.01		172.35	

AFT TAX RET ON COM EQTY (%)

	RATINGS	FYR END	78		77		76		75		74	
HARSCO CORP	A /A	12/78	16.0	(1)	16.7	(1)	16.4	(1)	17.3	(1)	14.0	(7)
INLAND STEEL CO	Aa /AA-	12/78	12.5	(2)	7.5	(4)	9.2	(4)	8.3	(6)	15.5	(4)
ARMCO INC	A /A	12/78	12.3	(3)	7.8	(3)	8.1	(5)	8.3	(7)	15.6	(3)
BETHLEHEM STEEL CORP	A /A	12/78	9.5	(4)	-20.6	(10)	6.2	(9)	9.3	(5)	13.7	(9)
NATIONAL STEEL CORP	Aa /A+	12/78	8.4	(5)	4.7	(7)	6.8	(8)	4.8	(10)	14.7	(5)
COPPERWELD CORP	A /A	12/78	8.3	(6)	12.5	(2)	15.7	(2)	17.2	(2)	18.7	(1)
REPUBLIC STEEL CORP	A /A	12/78	7.9	(7)	3.1	(8)	5.0	(10)	5.6	(9)	13.9	(8)
ALLEGHENY LUDLUM INDS	Baa/BBB	12/78	6.3	(8)	5.8	(6)	8.0	(7)	7.6	(8)	12.9	(10)
U S STEEL CORP	Aa /AA-	12/78	4.6	(9)	2.7	(9)	8.0	(6)	11.5	(4)	14.3	(6)
INTERLAKE INC	A /BBB+	12/78	3.4	(10)	6.1	(5)	12.6	(3)	15.0	(3)	16.1	(2)
AVERAGE			8.91		4.61		9.59		10.50		14.94	
MEDIAN			8.31		5.92		8.05		8.81		14.50	

RET ON TOT ASSETS (%)

	RATINGS	FYR END	78		77		76		75		74	
HARSCO CORP	A /A	12/78	20.2	(1)	22.1	(1)	21.3	(1)	21.1	(1)	17.1	(2)
ARMCO INC	A /A	12/78	12.9	(2)	6.1	(4)	5.7	(7)	8.1	(7)	15.3	(7)
INLAND STEEL CO	Aa /AA-	12/78	11.0	(3)	6.0	(5)	9.2	(4)	8.4	(6)	16.9	(3)
ALLEGHENY LUDLUM INDS	Baa/BBB	12/78	8.5	(4)	4.8	(6)	8.9	(5)	9.5	(5)	14.7	(8)
NATIONAL STEEL CORP	Aa /A+	12/78	8.3	(5)	4.4	(7)	5.1	(9)	3.9	(10)	15.6	(5)
COPPERWELD CORP	A /A	12/78	8.1	(6)	10.3	(2)	15.3	(2)	20.5	(2)	21.3	(1)
BETHLEHEM STEEL CORP	A /A	12/78	8.0	(7)	-16.9	(10)	5.5	(8)	7.5	(8)	14.6	(10)
REPUBLIC STEEL CORP	A /A	12/78	7.5	(8)	3.1	(8)	2.9	(10)	5.5	(9)	15.6	(4)
U S STEEL CORP	Aa /AA-	12/78	4.2	(9)	2.6	(9)	6.9	(6)	11.1	(4)	14.7	(9)
INTERLAKE INC	A /BBB+	12/78	3.8	(10)	7.4	(3)	13.4	(3)	16.5	(3)	15.5	(6)
AVERAGE			9.26		5.00		9.43		11.23		16.14	
MEDIAN			8.22		5.42		7.92		8.97		15.56	

Textile Industry

PRETAX COVERAGE

	RATINGS	FYR END	78		77		76		75		74	
RIEGEL TEXTILE CORP	Ba /BB*	9/78	10.13 (	1)	13.17 (	2)	19.16 (	2)	6.96 (	2)	6.12 (	5)
REEVES BROTHERS INC	Baa/BBB	6/78	10.07 (	2)	15.64 (	1)	30.28 (	1)	6.72 (	3)	19.14 (	1)
HART SCHAFFNER & MARX CO	Baa/BBB	11/78	7.27 (	3)	6.59 (	3)	7.60 (	3)	3.49 (	4)	4.34 (	7)
WEST POINT-PEPPERELL	Baa/BBB*	8/78	6.10 (	4)	5.37 (	4)	7.51 (	4)	7.23 (	1)	8.70 (	2)
BURLINGTON INDUSTRIES INC	A /A	9/78	4.20 (	5)	5.02 (	5)	7.42 (	5)	3.24 (	5)	6.44 (	4)
STEVENS (J.P.) & CO	Ba /BB*	10/78	3.47 (	6)	4.19 (	6)	5.36 (	6)	3.03 (	6)	4.72 (	6)
LOWENSTEIN (M) CORP	Ba /BB	12/78	3.39H(	7)	-0.50H(	7)	2.46R(	7)	0.10R(	8)	2.42R(	8)
AKZONA	Baa/BBB	12/78	2.78 (	8)	1.41 (	7)	1.21 (	8)	1.69 (	7)	7.61 (	3)
AVERAGE			5.93		6.36		10.13		4.06		7.44	
MEDIAN			5.15		5.19		7.47		3.36		6.28	

AFTER TAX COVERAGE

	RATINGS	FYR END	78		77		76		75		74	
RIEGEL TEXTILE CORP	Ba /BB*	9/78	5.72 (	1)	7.42 (	2)	10.60 (	2)	4.18 (	2)	3.70 (	5)
REEVES BROTHERS INC	Baa/BBB	6/78	5.59 (	2)	8.28 (	1)	15.19 (	1)	4.09 (	3)	10.28 (	1)
HART SCHAFFNER & MARX CO	Baa/BBB	11/78	4.15 (	3)	3.84 (	3)	4.28 (	5)	2.28 (	4)	2.71 (	7)
WEST POINT-PEPPERELL	Baa/BBB*	8/78	3.94 (	4)	3.46 (	5)	4.70 (	3)	4.44 (	1)	5.30 (	2)
BURLINGTON INDUSTRIES INC	A /A	9/78	2.83 (	5)	3.52 (	4)	4.55 (	4)	2.19 (	5)	3.99 (	4)
STEVENS (J.P.) & CO	Ba /BB*	10/78	2.45 (	6)	2.82 (	6)	3.43 (	6)	2.11 (	6)	2.98 (	6)
AKZONA	Baa/BBB	12/78	2.20 (	7)	1.46 (	7)	1.40 (	8)	1.59 (	7)	4.63 (	3)
LOWENSTEIN (M) CORP	Ba /BB	12/78	2.18H(	8)	0.36H(	8)	1.81R(	7)	0.52R(	8)	1.76R(	8)
AVERAGE			3.63		3.90		5.74		2.67		4.42	
MEDIAN			3.38		3.49		4.41		2.24		3.85	

AFTER TAX COV (INCL RENTS)

	RATINGS	FYR END	78		77		76		75		74	
RIEGEL TEXTILE CORP	Ba /BB*	9/78	3.54 (	1)	4.30 (	1)	4.88 (	1)	2.58 (	1)	2.53 (	5)
REEVES BROTHERS INC	Baa/BBB	6/78	3.19 (	2)	3.43 (	2)	4.03 (	2)	1.98 (	3)	3.91 (	1)
WEST POINT-PEPPERELL	Baa/BBB*	8/78	2.91 (	3)	2.62 (	3)	2.72 (	4)	2.45 (	2)	3.09 (	2)
BURLINGTON INDUSTRIES INC	A /A	9/78	2.14 (	4)	2.54 (	4)	3.01 (	3)	1.70 (	4)	2.76 (	4)
STEVENS (J.P.) & CO	Ba /BB*	10/78	1.85 (	5)	1.90 (	5)	2.17 (	5)	1.57 (	5)	2.03 (	6)
HART SCHAFFNER & MARX CO	Baa/BBB	11/78	1.69 (	6)	1.61 (	6)	1.60 (	6)	1.34 (	7)	1.50 (	8)
LOWENSTEIN (M) CORP	Ba /BB	12/78	1.66H(	7)	0.61H(	8)	1.49R(	7)	0.68R(	8)	1.50R(	7)
AKZONA	Baa/BBB	12/78	NA (	-)	1.27 (	7)	1.22 (	8)	1.35 (	6)	2.93 (	3)
AVERAGE			2.43		2.28		2.64		1.71		2.53	
MEDIAN			2.14		2.22		2.44		1.63		2.65	

NET INCOME AS % NET SALES

	RATINGS	FYR END	78		77		76		75		74	
RIEGEL TEXTILE CORP	Ba /BB*	9/78	4.4 (	1)	4.2 (	1)	5.2 (	1)	3.5 (	2)	3.4 (	5)
REEVES BROTHERS INC	Baa/BBB	6/78	3.9 (	2)	3.8 (	2)	4.1 (	3)	1.6 (	6)	4.6 (	1)
WEST POINT-PEPPERELL	Baa/BBB*	8/78	3.7 (	3)	3.3 (	4)	3.8 (	4)	3.8 (	1)	4.3 (	4)
HART SCHAFFNER & MARX CO	Baa/BBB	11/78	3.0 (	4)	2.7 (	5)	2.6 (	6)	1.7 (	5)	2.4 (	7)
BURLINGTON INDUSTRIES INC	A /A	9/78	2.9 (	5)	3.8 (	3)	4.6 (	2)	2.0 (	3)	4.3 (	3)
AKZONA	Baa/BBB	12/78	2.4 (	6)	0.9 (	7)	0.8 (	8)	1.2 (	7)	4.4 (	2)
STEVENS (J.P.) & CO	Ba /BB*	10/78	2.2 (	7)	2.3 (	6)	2.9 (	5)	1.8 (	4)	3.1 (	6)
LOWENSTEIN (M) CORP	Ba /BB	12/78	1.8 (	8)	-1.3 (	8)	1.6 (	7)	-1.3 (	8)	1.9 (	8)
AVERAGE			3.03		2.46		3.19		1.78		3.55	
MEDIAN			2.94		3.01		3.33		1.74		3.83	

LTD/CAPITALIZATION (%)

	RATINGS	FYR END	78		77		76		75		74	
HART SCHAFFNER & MARX CO	Baa/BBB	11/78	21.2	(1)	24.7	(1)	23.4	(3)	26.3	(3)	30.9	(3)
REEVES BROTHERS INC	Baa/BBB	6/78	23.3	(2)	26.7	(3)	10.7	(1)	13.8	(1)	17.4	(2)
RIEGEL TEXTILE CORP	Ba /BB*	9/78	27.8	(3)	26.3	(2)	25.0	(4)	26.4	(4)	34.6	(7)
BURLINGTON INDUSTRIES INC	A /A	9/78	30.1	(4)	30.0	(4)	27.9	(5)	31.2	(5)	32.3	(6)
WEST POINT-PEPPERELL	Baa/BBB*	8/78	30.5	(5)	30.5	(5)	21.3	(2)	16.1	(2)	17.0	(1)
STEVENS (J.P.) & CO	Ba /BB*	10/78	35.4	(6)	35.8	(6)	31.9	(6)	32.0	(6)	31.7	(5)
AKZONA	Baa/BBB	12/78	37.9	(7)	38.1	(7)	37.6	(7)	34.9	(7)	31.3	(4)
LOWENSTEIN (M) CORP	Ba /BB	12/78	39.2	(8)	43.4	(8)	44.4	(8)	46.1	(8)	43.4	(8)
AVERAGE			30.68		31.94		27.77		28.37		29.83	
MEDIAN			30.33		30.25		26.43		28.79		31.52	

TOT LIABILITY/TOT STK EQUITY

	RATINGS	FYR END	78		77		76		75		74	
REEVES BROTHERS INC	Baa/BBB	6/78	66.7	(1)	73.3	(2)	55.8	(1)	48.5	(1)	57.8	(1)
HART SCHAFFNER & MARX CO	Baa/BBB	11/78	69.4	(2)	80.4	(4)	77.3	(3)	68.8	(3)	92.2	(5)
RIEGEL TEXTILE CORP	Ba /BB*	9/78	77.0	(3)	70.6	(1)	80.4	(5)	79.4	(5)	98.0	(7)
BURLINGTON INDUSTRIES INC	A /A	9/78	82.9	(4)	76.1	(3)	78.3	(4)	75.0	(4)	85.5	(3)
WEST POINT-PEPPERELL	Baa/BBB*	8/78	89.4	(5)	82.2	(5)	74.8	(2)	53.7	(2)	59.6	(2)
STEVENS (J.P.) & CO	Ba /BB*	10/78	96.4	(6)	92.7	(6)	86.7	(6)	82.9	(6)	85.9	(4)
AKZONA	Baa/BBB	12/78	128.8	(7)	124.8	(7)	120.2	(7)	108.0	(7)	93.6	(6)
LOWENSTEIN (M) CORP	Ba /BB	12/78	129.1	(8)	140.1	(8)	134.1	(8)	156.4	(8)	138.0	(8)
AVERAGE			92.45		92.51		88.45		84.09		88.83	
MEDIAN			86.14		81.27		79.35		77.22		89.05	

LTD/NET PLANT (%)

	RATINGS	FYR END	78		77		76		75		74	
AKZONA	Baa/BBB	12/78	50.2	(1)	49.3	(1)	48.3	(3)	44.6	(3)	41.0	(2)
BURLINGTON INDUSTRIES INC	A /A	9/78	52.4	(2)	55.3	(3)	53.2	(5)	59.1	(5)	62.0	(4)
RIEGEL TEXTILE CORP	Ba /BB*	9/78	56.7	(3)	54.8	(2)	50.2	(4)	49.9	(4)	69.3	(5)
WEST POINT-PEPPERELL	Baa/BBB*	8/78	64.4	(4)	72.4	(4)	48.2	(2)	35.6	(2)	40.6	(1)
REEVES BROTHERS INC	Baa/BBB	6/78	70.0	(5)	78.8	(5)	27.5	(1)	33.3	(1)	45.3	(3)
STEVENS (J.P.) & CO	Ba /BB*	10/78	93.2	(6)	97.3	(6)	82.7	(6)	85.0	(6)	88.6	(6)
HART SCHAFFNER & MARX CO	Baa/BBB	11/78	97.4	(7)	107.0	(7)	99.2	(7)	114.1	(7)	132.3	(8)
LOWENSTEIN (M) CORP	Ba /BB	12/78	102.6	(8)	112.7	(8)	127.8	(8)	124.8	(8)	100.7	(7)
AVERAGE			73.36		78.46		67.14		68.32		72.48	
MEDIAN			67.21		75.60		51.70		54.54		65.68	

NET TANG ASSETS/LTD (%)

	RATINGS	FYR END	78		77		76		75		74	
HART SCHAFFNER & MARX CO	Baa/BBB	11/78	464.6	(1)	398.8	(1)	419.3	(3)	372.7	(4)	316.8	(3)
REEVES BROTHERS INC	Baa/BBB	6/78	427.0	(2)	372.5	(3)	934.9	(1)	722.2	(1)	572.0	(2)
RIEGEL TEXTILE CORP	Ba /BB*	9/78	358.8	(3)	377.9	(2)	398.8	(4)	377.8	(3)	287.4	(7)
BURLINGTON INDUSTRIES INC	A /A	9/78	330.7	(4)	332.1	(4)	352.2	(5)	318.2	(5)	307.1	(6)
WEST POINT-PEPPERELL	Baa/BBB*	8/78	325.7	(5)	327.8	(5)	469.0	(2)	618.9	(2)	588.8	(1)
STEVENS (J.P.) & CO	Ba /BB*	10/78	278.4	(6)	274.2	(6)	306.5	(6)	303.7	(6)	307.4	(5)
AKZONA	Baa/BBB	12/78	254.7	(7)	257.2	(7)	259.7	(7)	279.2	(7)	314.4	(4)
LOWENSTEIN (M) CORP	Ba /BB	12/78	253.2	(8)	228.2	(8)	223.6	(8)	215.0	(8)	228.2	(8)
AVERAGE			336.63		321.10		420.50		400.98		365.27	
MEDIAN			328.20		329.98		375.49		345.46		310.92	

Textile Industry

CASH FLOW/LTD (%)

	RATINGS	FYR END	78		77		76		75		74	
REEVES BROTHERS INC	Baa/BBB	6/78	60.3	(1)	48.8	(2)	155.4	(1)	70.7	(2)	90.7	(1)
RIEGEL TEXTILE CORP	Ba /BB*	9/78	57.1	(2)	60.2	(1)	81.5	(2)	56.7	(3)	37.9	(6)
HART SCHAFFNER & MARX CO	Baa/BBB	11/78	50.9	(3)	38.4	(5)	39.5	(5)	27.0	(6)	25.8	(7)
BURLINGTON INDUSTRIES INC	A /A	9/78	48.8	(4)	48.0	(3)	57.6	(4)	36.1	(4)	47.4	(3)
WEST POINT-PEPPERELL	Baa/BBB*	8/78	44.9	(5)	40.3	(4)	62.9	(3)	80.2	(1)	84.0	(2)
AKZONA	Baa/BBB	12/78	32.5	(6)	23.9	(7)	24.3	(7)	26.9	(7)	46.8	(4)
STEVENS (J.P.) & CO	Ba /BB*	10/78	32.0	(7)	30.2	(6)	37.5	(6)	29.6	(5)	38.5	(5)
LOWENSTEIN (M) CORP	Ba /BB	12/78	28.4	(8)	0.9	(8)	20.0	(8)	3.6	(8)	20.4	(8)
AVERAGE			44.38		36.34		59.83		41.33		48.95	
MEDIAN			46.88		39.36		48.53		32.86		42.67	

NET CASH FL/CAP EXP (%)

	RATINGS	FYR END	78		77		76		75		74	
HART SCHAFFNER & MARX CO	Baa/BBB	11/78	306.1 V(1)		164.1 V(2)		174.9 V(3)		258.1 V(1)		170.5 V(2)	
LOWENSTEIN (M) CORP	Ba /BB	12/78	196.3	(2)	-1.7	(8)	242.6	(1)	39.2	(8)	93.0	(7)
REEVES BROTHERS INC	Baa/BBB	6/78	161.8	(3)	219.1	(1)	223.6	(2)	80.6	(6)	223.4	(1)
AKZONA	Baa/BBB	12/78	120.4	(4)	86.5	(6)	78.2	(8)	60.3	(7)	91.9	(8)
STEVENS (J.P.) & CO	Ba /BB*	10/78	116.8	(5)	109.0	(5)	162.9	(5)	93.2	(5)	125.0	(3)
RIEGEL TEXTILE CORP	Ba /BB*	9/78	110.6	(6)	121.1	(3)	164.3	(4)	165.0	(2)	125.0	(5)
BURLINGTON INDUSTRIES INC	A /A	9/78	82.5	(7)	81.1	(7)	113.5	(6)	99.5	(3)	111.8	(6)
WEST POINT-PEPPERELL	Baa/BBB*	8/78	81.0	(8)	115.4	(4)	110.6	(7)	94.2	(4)	118.6	(4)
AVERAGE			146.93		111.82		158.82		111.27		131.34	
MEDIAN			118.60		112.18		163.62		93.69		117.58	

AFT TAX RET ON COM EQTY (%)

	RATINGS	FYR END	78		77		76		75		74	
RIEGEL TEXTILE CORP	Ba /BB*	9/78	12.1	(1)	13.7	(1)	16.8	(1)	9.9	(1)	11.5	(2)
REEVES BROTHERS INC	Baa/BBB	6/78	12.0	(2)	11.6	(2)	12.1	(2)	4.2	(6)	12.5	(1)
WEST POINT-PEPPERELL	Baa/BBB*	8/78	11.2	(3)	10.0	(3)	10.7	(· 4)	8.4	(2)	11.1	(4)
HART SCHAFFNER & MARX CO	Baa/BBB	11/78	8.9	(4)	8.1	(5)	7.6	(6)	4.8	(4)	6.9	(7)
LOWENSTEIN (M) CORP	Ba /BB	12/78	7.5	(5)	-5.3	(8)	5.8	(7)	-4.3	(8)	6.8	(8)
STEVENS (J.P.) & CO	Ba /BB*	10/78	7.5	(6)	7.6	(6)	9.3	(5)	4.8	(3)	9.8	(6)
BURLINGTON INDUSTRIES INC	A /A	9/78	6.8	(7)	8.9	(4)	10.8	(3)	4.4	(5)	11.2	(3)
AKZONA	Baa/BBB	12/78	6.8	(8)	2.5	(7)	1.8	(8)	2.5	(7)	10.4	(5)
AVERAGE			9.11		7.15		9.36		4.35		10.00	
MEDIAN			8.23		8.54		10.00		4.60		10.71	

RET ON TOT ASSETS (%)

	RATINGS	FYR END	78		77		76		75		74	
REEVES BROTHERS INC	Baa/BBB	6/78	15.9	(1)	14.3	(2)	16.5	(2)	6.2	(6)	16.3	(1)
RIEGEL TEXTILE CORP	Ba /BB*	9/78	14.6	(2)	16.4	(1)	18.6	(1)	12.1	(1)	13.1	(3)
WEST POINT-PEPPERELL	Baa/BBB*	8/78	12.3	(3)	12.1	(3)	12.4	(4)	11.5	(2)	14.0	(2)
HART SCHAFFNER & MARX CO	Baa/BBB	11/78	12.3	(4)	10.6	(4)	10.2	(6)	7.9	(3)	9.3	(7)
STEVENS (J.P.) & CO	Ba /BB*	10/78	9.1	(5)	9.0	(6)	11.0	(5)	7.2	(4)	12.5	(5)
LOWENSTEIN (M) CORP	Ba /BB	12/78	8.7	(6)	-1.8	(8)	7.5	(7)	0.3	(8)	8.3	(8)
BURLINGTON INDUSTRIES INC	A /A	9/78	8.5	(7)	10.1	(5)	12.7	(3)	6.9	(5)	13.0	(4)
AKZONA	Baa/BBB	12/78	6.9	(8)	3.4	(7)	2.5	(8)	3.5	(7)	11.2	(6)
AVERAGE			11.05		9.29		11.41		6.96		12.22	
MEDIAN			10.71		10.37		11.69		7.05		12.76	

TOT LIABILITY/TOT STK EQUITY

	RATINGS	FYR END	78		77		76		75		74	
REYNOLDS (R.J.) INDS	Aa /AA	12/78	73.7	(1)	81.2	(1)	102.4	(2)	73.4	(2)	84.2	(2)
LIGGETT GROUP	A /A	12/78	97.2	(2)	85.5	(2)	72.8	(1)	70.4	(1)	72.1	(1)
AMERICAN BRANDS INC	Aa /A+	12/78	116.8	(3)	128.3	(3)	109.7	(3)	117.4	(3)	129.8	(3)
PHILIP MORRIS INC	A /A	12/78	165.2	(4)	139.5	(4)	150.5	(4)	155.3	(4)	172.2	(4)
AVERAGE			113.20		108.63		108.83		104.13		114.59	
MEDIAN			106.98		106.89		106.04		95.42		107.03	

LTD/NET PLANT (%)

	RATINGS	FYR END	78		77		76		75		74	
REYNOLDS (R.J.) INDS	Aa /AA	12/78	34.2	(1)	38.1	(1)	33.3	(1)	35.8	(1)	38.5	(1)
AMERICAN BRANDS INC	Aa /A+	12/78	83.0	(2)	123.8	(3)	120.7	(3)	134.2	(4)	115.8	(4)
PHILIP MORRIS INC	A /A	12/78	118.6	(3)	112.2	(2)	118.5	(2)	102.3	(3)	109.6	(2)
LIGGETT GROUP	A /A	12/78	122.4	(4)	130.9	(4)	158.6	(4)	100.7	(2)	111.9	(3)
AVERAGE			89.55		101.24		107.78		93.27		93.94	
MEDIAN			100.81		117.98		119.61		101.50		110.75	

NET TANG ASSETS/LTD (%)

	RATINGS	FYR END	78		77		76		75		74	
REYNOLDS (R.J.) INDS	Aa /AA	12/78	423.5	(1)	380.6	(1)	384.4	(1)	463.0	(1)	388.5	(1)
AMERICAN BRANDS INC	Aa /A+	12/78	311.4	(2)	237.2	(3)	233.0	(3)	211.3	(3)	214.5	(3)
LIGGETT GROUP	A /A	12/78	271.8	(3)	251.3	(2)	249.9	(2)	329.6	(2)	300.0	(2)
PHILIP MORRIS INC	A /A	12/78	164.4	(4)	200.2	(4)	195.6	(4)	208.9	(4)	198.1	(4)
AVERAGE			292.78		267.31		265.74		303.19		275.27	
MEDIAN			291.62		244.21		241.47		270.45		257.25	

CASH FLOW/LTD (%)

	RATINGS	FYR END	78		77		76		75		74	
REYNOLDS (R.J.) INDS	Aa /AA	12/78	102.6	(1)	94.9	(1)	85.4	(1)	112.3	(1)	104.0	(1)
AMERICAN BRANDS INC	Aa /A+	12/78	72.3	(2)	46.8	(2)	37.6	(2)	35.2	(3)	43.6	(2)
LIGGETT GROUP	A /A	12/78	38.0	(3)	26.6	(4)	29.3	(3)	43.6	(2)	35.9	(3)
PHILIP MORRIS INC	A /A	12/78	26.9	(4)	31.1	(3)	27.9	(4)	28.5	(4)	27.4	(4)
AVERAGE			59.92		49.86		45.06		54.88		52.73	
MEDIAN			55.12		38.94		33.47		39.40		39.75	

NET CASH FL/CAP EXP (%)

	RATINGS	FYR END	78		77		76		75		74	
LIGGETT GROUP	A /A	12/78	205.8	(1)	123.1	(3)	180.2	(3)	122.2	(3)	162.3	(2)
AMERICAN BRANDS INC	Aa /A+	12/78	186.4	(2)	225.3	(1)	182.5	(2)	181.5	(2)	159.7	(3)
REYNOLDS (R.J.) INDS	Aa /AA	12/78	151.2	(3)	195.2	(2)	188.8	(1)	198.0	(1)	272.1	(1)
PHILIP MORRIS INC	A /A	12/78	75.1	(4)	118.9	(4)	115.6	(4)	81.9	(4)	71.9	(4)
AVERAGE			154.64		165.62		166.74		145.92		166.51	
MEDIAN			168.82		159.14		181.32		151.86		161.01	

Tobacco Industry

AFT TAX RET ON COM EQTY (%)

	RATINGS	FYR END	78		77		76		75		74	
PHILIP MORRIS INC	A /A	12/78	19.3	(1)	19.8	(1)	18.6	(1)	17.3	(2)	18.1	(2)
REYNOLDS (R.J.) INDS	Aa /AA	12/78	16.6	(2)	17.6	(2)	16.6	(2)	17.7	(1)	18.2	(1)
AMERICAN BRANDS INC	Aa /A+	12/78	15.9	(3)	13.0	(3)	10.6	(3)	13.1	(3)	13.4	(3)
LIGGETT GROUP	A /A	12/78	5.9	(4)	0.3	(4)	9.1	(4)	9.4	(4)	8.5	(4)
AVERAGE			14.42		12.70		13.73		14.37		14.54	
MEDIAN			16.25		15.34		13.59		15.19		15.74	

RET ON TOT ASSETS (%)

	RATINGS	FYR END	78		77		76		75		74	
REYNOLDS (R.J.) INDS	Aa /AA	12/78	20.1	(1)	20.2	(1)	17.8	(1)	26.5	(1)	26.7	(1)
AMERICAN BRANDS INC	Aa /A+	12/78	17.1	(2)	14.4	(3)	14.3	(3)	15.8	(2)	14.5	(3)
PHILIP MORRIS INC	A /A	12/78	16.2	(3)	18.1	(2)	16.2	(2)	14.9	(3)	14.7	(2)
LIGGETT GROUP	A /A	12/78	10.8	(4)	6.4	(4)	12.7	(4)	13.0	(4)	12.0	(4)
AVERAGE			16.04		14.75		15.25		17.54		16.98	
MEDIAN			16.63		16.25		15.27		15.34		14.58	

PRETAX COVERAGE

	RATINGS	FYR END	78		77		76		75		74	
REYNOLDS (R.J.) INDS	Aa /AA	12/78	13.05	(1)	10.55	(1)	11.22	(1)	16.23	(1)	14.81	(1)
AMERICAN BRANDS INC	Aa /A+	12/78	6.77	(2)	6.19	(3)	5.46	(3)	4.98	(3)	4.96	(3)
LIGGETT GROUP	A /A	12/78	5.77	(3)	3.01H	(4)	6.04H	(2)	6.30H	(2)	5.83H	(2)
PHILIP MORRIS INC	A /A	12/78	5.62	(4)	6.75	(2)	5.27	(4)	4.22	(4)	4.01	(4)
AVERAGE			7.80		6.62		7.00		7.93		7.40	
MEDIAN			6.27		6.47		5.75		5.64		5.40	

AFTER TAX COVERAGE

	RATINGS	FYR END	78		77		76		75		74	
REYNOLDS (R.J.) INDS	Aa /AA	12/78	7.28	(1)	6.16	(1)	6.31	(1)	7.44	(1)	6.67	(1)
AMERICAN BRANDS INC	Aa /A+	12/78	3.84	(2)	3.39	(3)	2.95	(4)	2.87	(3)	2.96	(3)
PHILIP MORRIS INC	A /A	12/78	3.56	(3)	4.07	(2)	3.38	(3)	2.83	(4)	2.69	(4)
LIGGETT GROUP	A /A	12/78	2.71	(4)	1.27H	(4)	3.45H	(2)	3.64H	(2)	3.40H	(2)
AVERAGE			4.35		3.72		4.02		4.20		3.93	
MEDIAN			3.70		3.73		3.42		3.26		3.18	

AFTER TAX COV (INCL RENTS)

	RATINGS	FYR END	78		77		76		75		74	
REYNOLDS (R.J.) INDS	Aa /AA	12/78	3.50	(1)	3.38	(2)	3.34	(1)	3.64	(1)	3.22	(1)
AMERICAN BRANDS INC	Aa /A+	12/78	3.27	(2)	2.83	(3)	2.49	(4)	2.50	(4)	2.59	(3)
PHILIP MORRIS INC	A /A	12/78	3.12	(3)	3.50	(1)	3.00	(2)	2.57	(3)	2.45	(4)
LIGGETT GROUP	A /A	12/78	2.14	(4)	1.18H	(4)	3.00H	(3)	3.19H	(2)	2.93H	(2)
AVERAGE			3.01		2.72		2.96		2.97		2.80	
MEDIAN			3.20		3.11		3.00		2.88		2.76	

			NET INCOME AS % NET SALES				
	RATINGS	FYR END	78	77	76	75	74
REYNOLDS (R.J.) INDS	Aa /AA	12/78	8.9 (1)	8.8 (1)	8.2 (2)	9.6 (1)	9.4 (1)
PHILIP MORRIS INC	A /A	12/78	8.2 (2)	8.7 (2)	8.5 (1)	8.3 (2)	8.6 (2)
AMERICAN BRANDS INC	Aa /A+	12/78	6.4 (3)	5.5 (3)	4.6 (4)	5.4 (3)	6.2 (3)
LIGGETT GROUP	A /A	12/78	2.8 (4)	0.3 (4)	5.0 (3)	5.3 (4)	5.1 (4)
AVERAGE			6.58	5.82	6.58	7.15	7.32
MEDIAN			7.32	7.08	6.64	6.85	7.39

			LTD/CAPITALIZATION (%)				
	RATINGS	FYR END	78	77	76	75	74
REYNOLDS (R.J.) INDS	Aa /AA	12/78	21.8 (1)	24.1 (1)	23.4 (1)	18.6 (1)	21.2 (1)
AMERICAN BRANDS INC	Aa /A+	12/78	22.9 (2)	30.2 (2)	30.0 (2)	32.9 (3)	30.3 (3)
LIGGETT GROUP	A /A	12/78	31.1 (3)	32.2 (3)	31.6 (3)	22.8 (2)	24.7 (2)
PHILIP MORRIS INC	A /A	12/78	50.4 (4)	45.8 (4)	46.6 (4)	42.8 (4)	44.1 (4)
AVERAGE			31.53	33.07	32.90	29.29	30.05
MEDIAN			26.98	31.20	30.79	27.87	27.49

RATING ORDER SUPPLEMENT

INTRODUCTION

In this edition of the Ratio Trend Analysis Rating Order Supplement, we have arranged 291 industrial companies by rating categories. This appendix ranks similarly rated companies with the objective of providing an easy-to-use format for determining the relative creditworthiness of industrial companies statistically within their respective rating categories. Ratios calculated are based on the latest annual data available at publication.

The ratings shown were the latest available at publication date. In addition, only companies with published senior debt ratings are used, as those concerns with only subordinated debt ratings would skew the averages and medians. Furthermore, this population includes only those companies rated at least BBB or Baa by Standard & Poor's or Moody's Investors Service, respectively.

This report may be used to:

Determine the relative statistical ranking of a company within its rating category

Compare an industrial concern's ratios with the averages and medians of its rating category and also other rating groups

Identify potential upgrades and downgrades

If you wish the latest rating information, please call the nearest office of Paine, Webber, Jackson & Curtis Incorporated.

TRIPLE A RATED COMPANIES	RATINGS	FYR END	Pretax Coverage	Aft Tax Coverage	Aft Tax Coverage (inc rent)	Ret on Total Assets	Net Inc --------- Net Sales
			x	x	x	%	%
KELLOGG CO	Aaa/AAA	12/77	29.55 (1)	16.03 (1)	NA (-)	32.40 (1)	9.01 (3)
GENERAL MOTORS CORP	Aaa/AAA	12/77	22.48p(2)	12.06p(2)	NA (-)	24.58 (2)	6.07 (10)
GULF OIL CORP	Aaa/AAA	12/77	21.17 (3)	8.13 (11)	3.38 (8)	16.15 (15)	4.22 (18)
IMPERIAL OIL LTD-CL A	NR /AAA	12/77	19.30 (4)	10.44 (4)	NA (-)	17.25 (12)	5.82 (11)
EXXON CORP	Aaa/AAA	12/77	18.81 (5)	6.37 (17)	3.09 (10)	22.12 (6)	4.48 (16)
MERCK & CO	Aaa/AAA	12/77	18.52 (6)	11.78 (3)	NA (-)	23.91 (3)	16.09 (1)
PROCTER & GAMBLE CO	Aaa/AAA	6/77	17.35 (7)	9.70 (5)	NA (-)	20.51 (8)	6.34 (8)
BRISTOL-MYERS CO	Aaa/AAA	12/77	16.12 (8)	9.23 (6)	4.78 (2)	23.01 (5)	7.95 (4)
FORD MOTOR CO	Aaa/AAA	12/77	15.80p(9)	8.92p(7)	NA (-)	16.58 (13)	4.42 (17)
FEDERATED DEPT STORES INC	Aaa/AAA	1/78	15.19h(10)	8.26h(10)	3.53h(7)	16.31h(14)	3.99c(19)
MINNESOTA MINING & MFG CO	Aaa/AAA	12/77	14.99 (11)	8.52 (8)	NA (-)	23.34 (4)	10.37 (2)
STANDARD OIL CO (INDIANA)	Aaa/AAA	12/77	13.85p(12)	6.05p(18)	3.85p(6)	21.22 (7)	7.77 (5)
SHELL OIL CO	Aaa/AAA	12/77	13.61 (13)	8.48 (9)	3.88 (5)	15.06 (18)	7.27 (7)
STANDARD OIL CO (CALIF)	Aaa/AAA	12/77	13.17p(14)	6.67p(14)	2.89p(12)	12.74 (20)	4.86 (14)
BEATRICE FOODS CO	Aaa/AAA	2/78	12.55 (15)	6.87 (13)	3.01 (11)	18.58 (10)	3.51 (20)
WARNER-LAMBERT CO	Aaa/AAA	12/77	12.23 (16)	7.17 (12)	3.90 (4)	17.64 (11)	7.38 (6)
CARNATION CO	Aaa/AAA	12/77	12.21p(17)	6.60p(15)	5.24p(1)	19.44 (9)	4.67 (15)
GENERAL ELECTRIC CO	Aaa/AAA	12/77	10.39 (18)	6.52 (16)	4.10 (3)	15.05 (19)	6.21 (9)
KRAFT INC	Aaa/AAA	12/77	10.01 (19)	5.59 (19)	NA (-)	16.12 (16)	2.94 (21)
DU PONT (E.I.) DE NEMOURS	Aaa/AAA	12/77	6.91p(20)	4.39p(20)	3.24p(9)	15.36 (17)	5.78 (12)
SEARS ROEBUCK & CO	Aaa/AAA	1/78	3.43 (21)	2.43 (21)	2.03 (13)	10.49 (21)	4.87 (13)
AVERAGE			15.13	8.11	3.61	18.95	6.38
MEDIAN			14.99	8.13	3.53	17.64	5.82

FOOTNOTES

a. This year's data reflect a major merger resulting in the formation of a new company.

b. Includes excise tax.

c. Includes sales of leased departments.

d. Combination of a and b.

e. Combination of a and c.

f. Data deleted because of a fiscal year change.

g. Rental expense includes royalties.

h. Interest expense is net of either interest income, interest capitalized or both.

i. Income taxes (total) include other taxes.

j. Capital expenditures are net of current year's retirements and disposals.

k. Current liabilities (other) includes deferred taxes.

m. Long term debt (total) includes current maturities.

p. Adjusted net income excludes all equity earnings of unconsolidated subsidiaries as unremitted earnings were not reported on the source and use of funds statement.

q. Cash flow may include extraordinary items and discontinued operations.

r. Combination of h and p.

s. Combination of h, p and g.

t. Combination of g and h.

u. Combination of m and q.

v. Combination of j and q.

y. The debt components of long term debt include current portion of long term debt.

N.A. Not available.

*Convertible or subordinated debt rating.

#Industrial Revenue Bond or Pollution Control Bond rating.

TRIPLE A RATED COMPANIES	RATINGS	FYR END	LTD --- Cap %	STD --- Cap %	LTD ------ Net Pt. %	NTA --- LTD %	Tot Liab -------- Tot Eqty %
GENERAL MOTORS CORP	Aaa/AAA	12/77	6.35 (1)	4.71 (11)	14.87 (1)	1447.40 (1)	69.08 (7)
BRISTOL-MYERS CO	Aaa/AAA	12/77	9.28 (2)	10.33 (19)	29.69 (13)	968.32 (2)	63.98 (4)
KELLOGG CO	Aaa/AAA	12/77	12.85 (3)	4.38 (10)	19.02 (5)	734.74 (3)	54.06 (1)
FORD MOTOR CO	Aaa/AAA	12/77	13.85 (4)	6.94 (17)	27.19 (11)	591.83 (9)	127.52 (20)
MINNESOTA MINING & MFG CO	Aaa/AAA	12/77	14.32 (5)	3.53 (7)	27.20 (12)	689.98 (4)	55.95 (2)
MERCK & CO	Aaa/AAA	12/77	14.34 (6)	5.70 (12)	25.25 (8)	652.62 (8)	56.01 (3)
IMPERIAL OIL LTD-CL A	NR /AAA	12/77	14.46 (7)	0.62 (1)	15.93 (3)	686.99 (5)	78.02 (11)
FEDERATED DEPT STORES INC	Aaa/AAA	1/78	14.74 (8)	5.78 (14)	21.35 (6)	672.65 (6)	79.76 (12)
GULF OIL CORP	Aaa/AAA	12/77	15.12 (9)	3.05 (6)	15.69 (2)	657.69 (7)	93.88 (16)
EXXON CORP	Aaa/AAA	12/77	16.55 (10)	5.92 (15)	18.84 (-4)	578.16 (10)	97.07 (18)
PROCTER & GAMBLE CO	Aaa/AAA	6/77	16.89 (11)	3.97 (8)	25.92 (10)	575.61 (11)	70.99 (9)
STANDARD OIL CO (CALIF)	Aaa/AAA	12/77	17.03 (12)	0.92 (4)	25.29 (-9)	569.76 (12)	94.05 (17)
WARNER-LAMBERT CO	Aaa/AAA	12/77	17.61 (13)	6.00 (16)	45.62 (18)	502.88 (14)	67.36 (5)
GENERAL ELECTRIC CO	Aaa/AAA	12/77	17.77 (14)	10.68 (20)	35.83 (16)	531.54 (13)	130.47 (21)
BEATRICE FOODS CO	Aaa/AAA	2/78	17.91 (15)	1.21 (5)	39.30 (17)	498.01 (15)	88.34 (13)
CARNATION CO	Aaa/AAA	12/77	20.75 (16)	5.74 (13)	65.60 (20)	457.42 (16)	70.82 (8)
SHELL OIL CO	Aaa/AAA	12/77	22.18 (17)	0.82 (3)	24.38 (7)	448.19 (17)	68.60 (6)
DU PONT (E.I.) DE NEMOURS	Aaa/AAA	12/77	23.01 (18)	4.20 (9)	33.19 (15)	417.05 (19)	72.12 (10)
SEARS ROEBUCK & CO	Aaa/AAA	1/78	23.38 (19)	43.92 (21)	78.52 (21)	427.21 (18)	126.03 (19)
KRAFT INC	Aaa/AAA	12/77	23.72 (20)	6.94 (18)	56.14 (19)	404.67 (20)	88.45 (14)
STANDARD OIL CO (INDIANA)	Aaa/AAA	12/77	26.97 (21)	0.70 (2)	31.05 (14)	364.06 (21)	91.05 (15)
AVERAGE			17.10	6.48	32.18	613.18	83.03
MEDIAN			16.89	4.71	27.19	575.61	78.02

TRIPLE A RATED COMPANIES	RATINGS	FYR END	Cash Flow --------- LTD %	N Cash Fl --------- Cap Exp %	After Tax ROE %	Work Cap -------- LTD %	Current Ratio x
GENERAL MOTORS CORP	Aaa/AAA	12/77	520.50q(1)	192.54q(4)	21.47 (3)	714.31 (1)	1.92 (12)
BRISTOL-MYERS CO	Aaa/AAA	12/77	225.61q(2)	200.83q(3)	18.87 (5)	672.75 (2)	2.39 (7)
KELLOGG CO	Aaa/AAA	12/77	224.41q(3)	124.24v(15)	25.47 (1)	269.49 (8)	2.31 (8)
FORD MOTOR CO	Aaa/AAA	12/77	222.21q(4)	152.63v(8)	19.78 (4)	219.80 (12)	1.38 (19)
MINNESOTA MINING & MFG CO	Aaa/AAA	12/77	174.18q(5)	185.27q(5)	18.25 (7)	357.87 (3)	3.01 (2)
MERCK & CO	Aaa/AAA	12/77	173.68q(6)	143.47q(11)	21.76 (2)	294.40 (6)	2.50 (5)
IMPERIAL OIL LTD-CL A	NR /AAA	12/77	137.94q(7)	107.29q(17)	15.13 (11)	192.78 (13)	2.01 (11)
FEDERATED DEPT STORES INC	Aaa/AAA	1/78	128.52q(8)	106.97q(18)	14.02 (14)	245.90 (9)	1.80 (13)
GULF OIL CORP	Aaa/AAA	12/77	121.27q(9)	59.64q(21)	10.25 (21)	73.07 (19)	1.23 (21)
GENERAL ELECTRIC CO	Aaa/AAA	12/77	120.67q(10)	130.44q(14)	18.31 (6)	190.63 (14)	1.45 (17)
PROCTER & GAMBLE CO	Aaa/AAA	6/77	116.37q(11)	143.44q(12)	17.59 (8)	242.49 (10)	2.23 (9)
EXXON CORP	Aaa/AAA	12/77	116.24q(12)	87.71q(19)	12.42 (20)	119.34 (17)	1.43 (18)
BEATRICE FOODS CO	Aaa/AAA	2/78	110.16q(13)	167.69v(7)	16.34 (9)	288.61 (7)	2.19 (10)
DU PONT (E.I.) DE NEMOURS	Aaa/AAA	12/77	106.51q(14)	143.50q(10)	13.12 (18)	151.13 (16)	2.58 (4)
SHELL OIL CO	Aaa/AAA	12/77	104.80q(15)	73.89q(20)	13.96 (15)	60.69 (21)	1.57 (15)
STANDARD OIL CO (CALIF)	Aaa/AAA	12/77	101.89q(16)	134.40q(13)	13.31 (17)	100.23 (18)	1.34 (20)
WARNER-LAMBERT CO	Aaa/AAA	12/77	89.98q(17)	151.54q(9)	14.90 (13)	320.70 (4)	2.80 (3)
STANDARD OIL CO (INDIANA)	Aaa/AAA	12/77	79.00q(18)	109.26q(16)	15.00 (12)	61.49 (20)	1.51 (16)
CARNATION CO	Aaa/AAA	12/77	78.81q(19)	247.15q(1)	15.35 (10)	315.03 (5)	3.09 (1)
KRAFT INC	Aaa/AAA	12/77	66.19q(20)	211.65q(2)	13.93 (14)	225.53 (11)	2.41 (6)
SEARS ROEBUCK & CO	Aaa/AAA	1/78	39.82q(21)	184.01v(6)	12.84 (19)	180.02 (15)	1.59 (14)
AVERAGE			145.66	145.60	16.29	252.20	2.03
MEDIAN			116.37	143.47	15.13	225.53	2.01

SPLIT Aaa/AA RATED COMPANIES	RATINGS	FYR END	Pretax Coverage x	Aft Tax Coverage x	Aft Tax Coverage (inc rent) x	Ret on Total Assets %	Net Inc -------- Net Sales %
STERLING DRUG INC	Aa /AAA	12/77	16.53 (1)	9.15 (1)	4.36 (1)	18.99 (1)	7.25 (1)
TEXACO INC	Aaa/AA+	12/77	9.79 (2)	4.90 (3)	2.15 (3)	11.86 (3)	3.33 (2)
GENERAL FOODS CORP	Aa /AAA	3/78	9.77 (3)	5.50 (2)	3.55 (2)	15.14 (2)	3.15 (3)
AVERAGE			12.03	6.52	3.35	15.33	4.58
MEDIAN			9.79	5.50	3.55	15.14	3.33

SPLIT Aaa/AA RATED COMPANIES	RATINGS	FYR END	LTD Cap %	STD Cap %	LTD Net Pt. %	NTA LTD %	Tot Liab Tot Eqty %
STERLING DRUG INC	Aa /AAA	12/77	7.67 (1)	9.69 (3)	20.80 (1)	1157.45 (1)	49.68 (1)
GENERAL FOODS CORP	Aa /AAA	3/78	18.12 (2)	9.45 (2)	34.08 (3)	531.38 (2)	107.28 (3)
TEXACO INC	Aaa/AA+	12/77	21.41 (3)	5.33 (1)	25.86 (2)	464.94 (3)	101.54 (2)
AVERAGE			15.74	8.16	26.91	717.92	86.17
MEDIAN			18.12	9.45	25.86	531.38	101.54

SPLIT Aaa/AA RATED COMPANIES	RATINGS	FYR END	Cash Flow LTD %	N Cash Fl Cap Exp %	After Tax ROE %	Work Cap LTD %	Current Ratio x
STERLING DRUG INC	Aa /AAA	12/77	236.43q(1)	191.91q(1)	14.03 (2)	734.68 (1)	2.67 (1)
GENERAL FOODS CORP	Aa /AAA	3/78	88.51q(2)	117.87q(2)	14.44 (1)	291.78 (2)	1.88 (2)
TEXACO INC	Aaa/AA+	12/77	69.62q(3)	99.26q(3)	9.91 (3)	83.19 (3)	1.42 (3)
AVERAGE			131.52	136.35	12.79	369.88	1.99
MEDIAN			88.51	117.87	14.03	291.78	1.88

DOUBLE A RATED COMPANIES	RATINGS	FYR END	Pretax Coverage x	Aft Tax Coverage x	Aft Tax Coverage (inc rent) x	Ret on Total Assets %	Net Inc Net Sales %
TIMES MIRROR CO	Aa /AA	12/77	75.08 (1)	40.77 (1)	8.37 (1)	21.52 (8)	8.51 (10)
CBS INC	Aa /AA	12/77	43.15 (2)	21.77 (2)	5.19 (4)	24.38 (3)	6.56 (23)
CHAMPION SPARK PLUG	Aa /AA	12/77	27.84 (3)	14.40 (3)	6.57 (2)	21.63 (7)	8.72 (8)
TEXAS INSTRUMENTS INC	Aa /AA	12/77	23.98 (4)	13.71 (4)	3.44 (19)	17.54 (18)	5.70 (31)
HALLIBURTON CO	Aa /AA	12/77	21.00p(5)	11.86p(5)	3.46p(17)	22.24 (5)	6.55 (24)
MCGRAW-EDISON CO	Aa /AA	12/77	20.94 (6)	11.26 (6)	NA (-)	18.97 (14)	5.49 (35)
AMP INC	Aa /AA	12/77	17.87 (7)	10.06 (7)	5.47 (3)	26.72 (2)	12.00 (1)
TIME INC	Aa /AA	12/77	16.22 (8)	9.37 (10)	4.15 (8)	16.36 (26)	7.24 (18)
DIAMOND INTERNATIONAL CORP	Aa /AA	12/77	16.00 (9)	9.77 (9)	NA (-)	13.45 (41)	4.79 (43)
PHILLIPS PETROLEUM CO	Aa /AA	12/77	14.99p(10)	6.82p(13)	4.80p(5)	21.74 (6)	8.23 (12)
GENERAL SIGNAL CORP	Aa /AA	12/77	14.94p(11)	7.82p(11)	NA (-)	17.24 (22)	5.48 (36)
UNION CAMP CORP	Aa /AA	12/77	14.62 (12)	9.86 (8)	NA (-)	16.70 (24)	10.60 (3)
MOBIL CORP	Aa /AA	12/77	12.72 (13)	3.35 (50)	2.04 (43)	23.23 (4)	3.13 (51)
CONTINENTAL OIL CO	Aa /AA	12/77	12.15p(14)	4.32p(43)	3.13p(30)	21.46 (9)	4.37 (46)
CONSOLIDATED FOODS CORP	Aa /AA	6/77	12.14p(15)	6.55p(15)	2.45p(41)	16.12 (27)	3.05 (52)
SUN CO	Aa /AA	12/77	12.02p(16)	6.25p(18)	3.44p(20)	15.60 (30)	5.64 (32)
U S GYPSUM CO	Aa /AA	12/77	11.31 (17)	6.51 (16)	NA (-)	14.04 (38)	5.08 (40)
AMERICAN HOSPITAL SUPPLY	Aa /AA	12/77	11.08 (18)	6.85 (12)	3.38 (24)	14.12 (37)	5.24 (39)
UNITED TECHNOLOGIES CORP	Aa /AA	12/77	10.74 (19)	6.13 (21)	3.21 (29)	14.95 (33)	3.53 (49)
REYNOLDS (R.J.) INDS	Aa /AA	12/77	10.55 (20)	6.16 (19)	3.38 (23)	20.16 (11)	8.79 (7)
JOHNS-MANVILLE CORP	Aa /AA	12/77	10.39p(21)	5.97p(22)	3.60p(15)	15.87 (29)	7.02 (21)
RICHARDSON-MERRELL INC	Aa /AA	6/77	10.37 (22)	5.91 (23)	3.65 (14)	18.10 (16)	6.84 (22)
KIMBERLY-CLARK CORP	Aa /AA	12/77	10.31 (23)	6.60 (14)	4.20 (7)	14.65 (35)	7.57 (17)
BURROUGHS CORP	Aa /AA	12/77	9.97 (24)	5.90 (24)	3.77 (12)	16.43 (25)	10.29 (4)
GEORGIA-PACIFIC CORP	Aa /AA	12/77	9.88 (25)	6.14 (20)	NA (-)	17.21 (23)	7.13 (19)
BRITISH PETROLEUM CO LTD	Aa /AA	12/77	9.87 (26)	2.46 (53)	NA (-)	27.02 (1)	2.99 (53)
XEROX CORP	Aa /AA	12/77	9.72p(27)	5.51p(29)	2.92p(33)	19.42 (13)	8.01 (15)
NABISCO INC	Aa /AA	12/77	9.66 (28)	6.41 (17)	3.78 (11)	17.44 (19)	5.01 (41)
ELTRA CORP	Aa /AA	9/77	9.31 (29)	5.61 (27)	3.46 (18)	12.67 (48)	4.61 (45)
MOTOROLA INC	Aa /AA	12/77	9.28r(30)	5.60r(28)	3.31r(25)	15.06h(32)	5.75 (30)

IV-4

DOUBLE A RATED COMPANIES	RATINGS	FYR END	Pretax Coverage	Aft Tax Coverage	Aft Tax Coverage (inc rent)	Ret on Total Assets %	Net Inc Net Sales %
			x	x	x	%	%
CATERPILLAR TRACTOR CO	Aa /AA	12/77	9.19 (31)	5.69 (26)	NA (-)	20.13 (12)	7.61 (16)
PEPSICO INC	Aa /AA	12/77	9.01 (32)	5.45 (31)	3.93 (10)	18.53 (15)	5.28 (38)
UNION OIL CO OF CALIFORNIA	Aa /AA	12/77	8.45p(33)	4.97p(34)	2.60p(39)	14.48 (36)	5.90 (28)
NORTON SIMON INC	Aa /AA	6/77	8.41 (34)	5.48 (30)	3.28 (26)	13.20 (45)	5.63 (33)
KERR-MCGEE CORP	Aa /AA	12/77	8.25 (35)	5.16 (33)	4.20 (6)	12.88 (47)	5.50 (34)
RALSTON PURINA CO	Aa /AA	9/77	8.21 (36)	4.82 (36)	3.48 (16)	17.39 (20)	3.80 (47)
CORNING GLASS WORKS	Aa /AA	12/77	8.12 (37)	5.24 (32)	3.40 (21)	15.14 (31)	8.22 (13)
SMITHKLINE CORP	Aa /AA	12/77	8.07 (38)	5.70 (25)	3.94 (8)	20.48 (10)	11.44 (2)
DEERE & CO	Aa /AA-	10/77	7.43 (39)	4.56 (39)	3.39 (22)	14.88 (34)	7.09 (20)
ARMSTRONG CORK CO	Aa /AA	12/77	7.39 (40)	3.72 (47)	NA (-)	13.42 (43)	3.71 (48)
ANHEUSER-BUSCH INC	Aa /AA	12/77	7.36 (41)	4.44 (40)	NA (-)	14.01 (40)	5.00 (42)
MONSANTO CO	Aa /AA	12/77	7.23p(42)	4.35p(42)	3.24p(28)	14.02 (39)	6.00 (27)
CPC INTL INC	Aa /AA	12/77	7.09 (43)	4.36 (41)	3.01 (32)	17.61 (17)	4.63 (44)
UPJOHN CO	Aa /AA	12/77	7.08 (44)	4.86 (35)	3.28 (27)	15.99 (28)	8.07 (14)
ABBOTT LABORATORIES	Aa /AA	12/77	6.82 (45)	4.74 (37)	3.72 (13)	17.29 (21)	9.47 (5)
SQUIBB CORP	Aa /AA	12/77	6.44p(46)	4.73p(38)	2.77p(37)	13.43 (42)	8.39 (11)
AMERICAN CYANAMID CO	Aa /AA	12/77	5.71 (47)	3.93 (44)	2.80 (35)	12.18 (49)	5.78 (29)
WEYERHAEUSER CO	Aa /AA	12/77	5.12p(48)	3.73p(46)	3.07p(31)	13.10 (46)	9.26 (6)
UNION CARBIDE CORP	Aa /AA-	12/77	4.99p(49)	3.79p(45)	2.78p(36)	9.61 (52)	5.47 (37)
PFIZER INC	Aa /AA	12/77	4.71 (50)	3.56 (48)	2.86 (34)	13.21 (44)	8.63 (9)
INTL PAPER CO	Aa /AA-	12/77	4.57p(51)	3.42p(49)	2.76p(38)	11.22 (51)	6.37 (26)
ATLANTIC RICHFIELD CO	Aa /AA-	12/77	4.19p(52)	3.29p(51)	2.54p(40)	11.38 (50)	6.40 (25)
INLAND STEEL CO	Aa /AA-	12/77	2.89p(53)	2.81p(52)	2.44p(42)	6.04 (53)	3.27 (50)
U S STEEL CORP	Aa /AA-	12/77	1.56p(54)	1.80p(54)	1.50p(44)	2.59 (54)	1.43 (54)
AVERAGE			12.16	6.93	3.55	16.37	6.41
MEDIAN			9.69	5.61	3.39	16.06	5.95

DOUBLE A RATED COMPANIES	RATINGS	FYR END	LTD Cap %	STD Cap %	LTD Net Pt. %	NTA LTD %	Tot Liab Tot Eqty %
TEXAS INSTRUMENTS INC	Aa /AA	12/77	3.83 (1)	6.35 (40)	7.53 (1)	2454.37 (1)	68.55 (11)
CHAMPION SPARK PLUG	Aa /AA	12/77	5.60 (2)	5.57 (37)	16.00 (3)	1698.33 (2)	39.34 (1)
TIMES MIRROR CO	Aa /AA	12/77	6.25 (3)	1.07 (7)	10.65 (2)	1399.52 (3)	54.04 (4)
BURROUGHS CORP	Aa /AA	12/77	9.45 (4)	11.12 (51)	18.43 (5)	1035.01 (4)	57.28 (6)
CBS INC	Aa /AA	12/77	10.70 (5)	0.44 (3)	37.27 (23)	787.33 (9)	87.61 (30)
GENERAL SIGNAL CORP	Aa /AA	12/77	10.84 (6)	8.73 (48)	32.25 (16)	878.35 (5)	72.43 (12)
DIAMOND INTERNATIONAL CORP	Aa /AA	12/77	11.90 (7)	3.20 (24)	17.61 (4)	819.50 (6)	50.97 (3)
MCGRAW-EDISON CO	Aa /AA	12/77	12.06 (8)	1.78 (11)	54.40 (46)	805.32 (8)	41.33 (2)
AMP INC	Aa /AA	12/77	12.27 (9)	7.91 (47)	28.05 (11)	811.80 (7)	67.33 (10)
HALLIBURTON CO	Aa /AA	12/77	15.25 (10)	0.57 (4)	29.08 (12)	638.05 (10)	82.44 (22)
UNITED TECHNOLOGIES CORP	Aa /AA	12/77	15.56 (11)	2.12 (17)	37.20 (22)	634.31 (11)	104.51 (44)
RICHARDSON-MERRELL INC	Aa /AA	6/77	15.95 (12)	5.47 (35)	45.72 (38)	485.47 (15)	59.79 (7)
CPC INTL INC	Aa /AA	12/77	17.63 (13)	9.42 (49)	24.46 (6)	535.05 (12)	99.39 (41)
TIME INC	Aa /AA	12/77	18.80 (14)	1.44 (9)	37.99 (24)	463.94 (17)	91.01 (35)
CORNING GLASS WORKS	Aa /AA	12/77	19.24 (15)	2.48 (19)	44.02 (36)	509.06 (13)	62.24 (9)
CONSOLIDATED FOODS CORP	Aa /AA	6/77	19.81 (16)	1.26 (8)	48.70 (40)	439.74 (22)	78.10 (15)
SMITHKLINE CORP	Aa /AA	12/77	19.96 (17)	12.32 (53)	59.51 (47)	440.39 (21)	77.20 (14)
MOTOROLA INC	Aa /AA	9/77	20.25 (18)	7.87 (45)	45.57 (37)	480.66 (16)	80.12 (17)
ELTRA CORP	Aa /AA	12/77	20.57 (19)	3.92 (30)	67.87 (51)	486.18 (14)	86.09 (27)
SUN CO	Aa /AA	12/77	21.09 (20)	2.45 (18)	24.60 (7)	442.24 (20)	87.68 (31)
JOHNS-MANVILLE CORP	Aa /AA	12/77	21.49 (21)	1.95 (14)	32.09 (15)	445.94 (19)	79.66 (16)
ABBOTT LABORATORIES	Aa /AA	12/77	21.66 (22)	10.80 (50)	50.20 (41)	446.27 (18)	87.35 (29)
U S GYPSUM CO	Aa /AA	12/77	22.35 (23)	2.48 (20)	30.74 (14)	433.41 (23)	76.52 (13)
KERR-MCGEE CORP	Aa /AA	12/77	22.99 (24)	2.72 (22)	24.76 (8)	414.24 (27)	82.82 (23)
PHILLIPS PETROLEUM CO	Aa /AA	12/77	23.02 (25)	1.97 (15)	25.92 (9)	417.17 (26)	80.08 (32)
UNION CAMP CORP	Aa /AA	12/77	23.14 (26)	2.03 (16)	29.31 (13)	428.92 (24)	56.31 (5)
ARMSTRONG CORK CO	Aa /AA	12/77	23.34 (27)	3.98 (31)	38.34 (27)	419.93 (25)	60.66 (8)
KIMBERLY-CLARK CORP	Aa /AA	12/77	23.60 (28)	5.54 (36)	27.51 (10)	399.21 (28)	85.13 (24)
REYNOLDS (R.J.) INDS	Aa /AA	12/77	24.13 (29)	7.91 (46)	38.08 (26)	380.63 (31)	81.21 (21)
DEERE & CO	Aa /AA-	10/77	24.43 (30)	11.65 (52)	70.81 (53)	399.04 (29)	114.28 (47)

DOUBLE A RATED COMPANIES	RATINGS	FYR END	LTD --- Cap %	STD --- Cap %	LTD ------ Net Pt. %	NTA --- LTD %	Tot Liab -------- Tot Eqty %
NORTON SIMON INC	Aa /AA	6/77	25.37 (31)	1.92 (13)	91.94 (54)	382.86 (30)	80.82 (19)
XEROX CORP	Aa /AA	12/77	26.43 (32)	4.29 (32)	38.72 (28)	358.62 (32)	98.43 (40)
MOBIL CORP	Aa /AA	12/77	27.17 (33)	5.87 (39)	34.03 (17)	355.81 (33)	149.43 (53)
AMERICAN CYANAMID CO	Aa /AA	12/77	27.46 (34)	5.59 (38)	40.89 (30)	352.72 (34)	90.12 (33)
AMERICAN HOSPITAL SUPPLY	Aa /AA	12/77	27.57 (35)	3.28 (25)	70.07 (52)	351.13 (35)	80.53 (18)
SQUIBB CORP	Aa /AA	12/77	28.97 (36)	7.74 (43)	64.93 (48)	326.81 (40)	86.68 (28)
PFIZER INC	Aa /AA	12/77	29.17 (37)	21.07 (54)	67.85 (50)	311.78 (41)	118.17 (49)
UPJOHN CO	Aa /AA	12/77	29.18 (38)	3.51 (28)	52.68 (45)	334.95 (36)	90.93 (34)
UNION OIL CO OF CALIFORNIA	Aa /AA	12/77	29.59 (39)	1.64 (10)	34.53 (18)	334.38 (37)	93.83 (39)
MONSANTO CO	Aa /AA	12/77	30.03 (40)	3.90 (29)	42.79 (34)	327.17 (39)	81.19 (20)
CATERPILLAR TRACTOR CO	Aa /AA	12/77	30.14 (41)	2.98 (23)	50.57 (42)	329.58 (38)	85.49 (26)
NABISCO INC	Aa /AA	12/77	30.18 (42)	1.78 (12)	50.62 (43)	289.42 (48)	118.49 (50)
PEPSICO INC	Aa /AA	12/77	30.57 (43)	3.36 (27)	50.93 (44)	286.11 (49)	110.66 (46)
U S STEEL CORP	Aa /AA-	12/77	30.91 (44)	3.36 (26)	40.18 (29)	305.94 (43)	92.82 (37)
UNION CARBIDE CORP	Aa /AA-	12/77	31.97 (45)	6.69 (41)	41.68 (32)	301.50 (44)	117.88 (48)
RALSTON PURINA CO	Aa /AA	9/77	32.06 (46)	7.87 (44)	47.56 (39)	295.00 (47)	103.44 (43)
CONTINENTAL OIL CO	Aa /AA	12/77	32.13 (47)	4.59 (33)	35.96 (21)	300.76 (45)	132.50 (52)
GEORGIA-PACIFIC CORP	Aa /AA	12/77	32.38 (48)	2.61 (21)	35.14 (19)	306.01 (42)	91.56 (36)
ANHEUSER-BUSCH INC	Aa /AA	12/77	33.16 (49)	0.00 (2)	35.45 (20)	299.12 (46)	106.32 (45)
INTL PAPER CO	Aa /AA-	12/77	34.85 (50)	4.82 (34)	42.16 (33)	273.95 (52)	93.53 (38)
INLAND STEEL CO	Aa /AA-	12/77	34.87 (51)	0.75 (5)	41.50 (31)	278.68 (50)	100.78 (42)
WEYERHAEUSER CO	Aa /AA	12/77	35.73 (52)	0.77 (6)	43.04 (35)	278.38 (51)	85.27 (25)
ATLANTIC RICHFIELD CO	Aa /AA	12/77	36.22 (53)	7.54 (42)	38.14 (26)	269.87 (53)	124.54 (51)
BRITISH PETROLEUM CO LTD	Aa /AA	12/77	39.89m(54)	0.00m(1)	65.57m(49)	250.70m(54)	176.19 (54)
AVERAGE			23.39	4.67	40.96	517.23	88.33
MEDIAN			23.47	3.44	38.53	406.72	86.38

DOUBLE A RATED COMPANIES	RATINGS	FYR END	Cash Flow ---------- LTD %	N Cash Fl ---------- Cap Exp %	After Tax ROE %	Work Cap -------- LTD %	Current Ratio x
TEXAS INSTRUMENTS INC	Aa /AA	12/77	757.31q(1)	96.60v(37)	15.66 (20)	1173.96 (1)	1.75 (46)
TIMES MIRROR CO	Aa /AA	12/77	381.69q(2)	150.16q(23)	17.55 (10)	679.19 (3)	2.38 (19)
CHAMPION SPARK PLUG	Aa /AA	12/77	317.21q(3)	199.20v(9)	14.50 (25)	1128.47 (2)	3.30 (2)
BURROUGHS CORP	Aa /AA	12/77	250.14q(4)	151.74q(22)	12.70 (38)	370.18 (9)	1.91 (38)
AMP INC	Aa /AA	12/77	236.07q(5)	207.99q(7)	22.68 (1)	525.74 (7)	2.69 (11)
CBS INC	Aa /AA	12/77	213.86q(6)	232.22q(2)	22.46 (2)	586.37 (6)	2.10 (29)
HALLIBURTON CO	Aa /AA	12/77	203.42q(7)	198.78q(10)	21.38 (3)	306.40 (11)	2.04 (31)
DIAMOND INTERNATIONAL CORP	Aa /AA	12/77	148.28q(8)	109.73q(32)	11.14 (50)	289.36 (13)	2.28 (23)
GENERAL SIGNAL CORP	Aa /AA	12/77	148.12q(9)	222.87q(3)	13.76 (28)	609.83 (5)	2.34 (21)
CPC INTL INC	Aa /AA	12/77	125.85q(10)	123.78q(28)	16.68 (13)	208.09 (21)	1.77 (44)
XEROX CORP	Aa /AA	12/77	124.45q(11)	137.02q(25)	16.45 (16)	123.80 (32)	1.94 (35)
MCGRAW-EDISON CO	Aa /AA	12/77	124.44q(12)	161.35q(16)	13.13 (37)	621.51 (4)	4.09 (1)
UNITED TECHNOLOGIES CORP	Aa /AA	12/77	116.11q(13)	158.89q(17)	14.81 (22)	384.16 (8)	1.93 (37)
PHILLIPS PETROLEUM CO	Aa /AA	12/77	106.34q(14)	76.22q(48)	16.75 (12)	42.59 (53)	1.32 (53)
TIME INC	Aa /AA	12/77	101.44q(15)	209.50q(6)	16.45 (15)	260.80 (16)	2.71 (10)
SMITHKLINE CORP	Aa /AA	12/77	97.67q(16)	156.31q(20)	21.14 (5)	274.96 (15)	2.44 (16)
CORNING GLASS WORKS	Aa /AA	12/77	97.39q(17)	182.47q(12)	13.82 (27)	215.65 (20)	2.74 (9)
RICHARDSON-MERRELL INC	Aa /AA	6/77	95.23q(18)	214.71q(4)	13.70 (29)	293.18 (12)	2.55 (14)
REYNOLDS (R.J.) INDS	Aa /AA	12/77	94.94q(19)	195.15q(11)	17.63 (9)	155.09 (27)	2.40 (17)
SUN CO	Aa /AA	12/77	93.45q(20)	125.45q(27)	12.25 (40)	59.55 (45)	1.39 (52)
MOTOROLA INC	Aa /AA	12/77	89.87q(21)	113.36q(30)	13.51 (33)	283.31 (14)	2.47 (15)
UNION OIL CO OF CALIFORNIA	Aa /AA	12/77	86.94q(22)	97.58q(36)	13.60 (30)	54.80 (48)	1.67 (48)
KERR-MCGEE CORP	Aa /AA	12/77	86.40q(23)	84.08q(47)	11.88 (45)	82.30 (41)	1.78 (42)
CONSOLIDATED FOODS CORP	Aa /AA	6/77	85.36q(24)	156.94q(19)	12.48 (39)	256.97 (17)	2.38 (18)
JOHNS-MANVILLE CORP	Aa /AA	12/77	84.60q(25)	138.48q(24)	13.82 (26)	180.16 (23)	2.56 (13)
UNION CAMP CORP	Aa /AA	12/77	81.98q(26)	67.11q(51)	15.86 (19)	93.53 (40)	2.80 (7)
ABBOTT LABORATORIES	Aa /AA	12/77	80.93q(27)	178.71q(13)	17.72 (8)	138.61 (28)	1.76 (45)
NABISCO INC	Aa /AA	12/77	75.03 (28)	212.95 (5)	21.35 (4)	136.62 (30)	2.06 (30)
ELTRA CORP	Aa /AA	9/77	72.11q(29)	155.78q(21)	11.95 (42)	329.21 (10)	2.87 (6)
U S GYPSUM CO	Aa /AA	12/77	70.13q(30)	95.73q(38)	11.23 (49)	138.15 (29)	2.22 (24)

IV-6

DOUBLE A RATED COMPANIES

DOUBLE A RATED COMPANIES	RATINGS	FYR END	Cash Flow LTD %	N Cash Fl Cap Exp %	After Tax ROE %	Work Cap LTD %	Current Ratio x
KIMBERLY-CLARK CORP	Aa /AA	12/77	69.84q(31)	63.36q(52)	14.65 (23)	68.83 (42)	1.62 (50)
PEPSICO INC	Aa /AA	12/77	68.68q(32)	86.57q(44)	19.28 (6)	97.21 (39)	1.74 (47)
CATERPILLAR TRACTOR CO	Aa /AA	12/77	67.53q(33)	105.91q(34)	19.00 (7)	128.24 (31)	2.36 (20)
CONTINENTAL OIL CO	Aa /AA	12/77	65.98q(34)	88.97q(42)	13.34 (36)	68.22 (43)	1.58 (51)
AMERICAN HOSPITAL SUPPLY	Aa /AA	12/77	65.69q(35)	165.61v(14)	13.47 (34)	207.10 (22)	3.06 (5)
GEORGIA-PACIFIC CORP	Aa /AA	12/77	63.80q(36)	84.60v(46)	17.14 (11)	61.07 (44)	2.18 (25)
MONSANTO CO	Aa /AA	12/77	63.53q(37)	89.49q(41)	11.44 (47)	104.79 (35)	2.65 (12)
DEERE & CO	Aa /AA-	10/77	62.44q(38)	106.35v(33)	16.27 (18)	224.55 (19)	1.94 (36)
AMERICAN CYANAMID CO	Aa /AA	12/77	60.79q(39)	86.05v(45)	11.93 (43)	114.02 (34)	1.99 (32)
MOBIL CORP	Aa /AA	12/77	60.34q(40)	112.32q(31)	12.18 (41)	52.54 (51)	1.21 (54)
UPJOHN CO	Aa /AA	12/77	59.13q(41)	239.09q(1)	16.67 (14)	162.72 (25)	2.79 (8)
ARMSTRONG CORK CO	Aa /AA	12/77	59.08q(42)	129.94q(26)	7.99 (52)	171.02 (24)	3.21 (4)
ANHEUSER-BUSCH INC	Aa /AA	12/77	56.00q(43)	100.14q(35)	13.51 (32)	55.73 (47)	1.89 (40)
UNION CARBIDE CORP	Aa /AA-	12/77	54.78q(44)	88.74q(43)	11.30 (48)	102.77 (36)	2.16 (26)
PFIZER INC	Aa /AA	12/77	54.73q(45)	201.33q(8)	15.63 (21)	160.73 (26)	1.97 (34)
RALSTON PURINA CO	Aa /AA	9/77	52.48q(46)	93.99q(39)	16.44 (17)	100.73 (37)	1.98 (33)
BRITISH PETROLEUM CO LTD	Aa /AA	12/77	51.25m(47)	161.78 (15)	11.02 (51)	100.19m(38)	1.88 (41)
ATLANTIC RICHFIELD CO	Aa /AA	12/77	50.67q(48)	71.35q(50)	13.54 (31)	41.23 (54)	1.63 (49)
NORTON SIMON INC	Aa /AA	6/77	50.47q(49)	157.78q(18)	11.91 (44)	247.75 (18)	3.29 (3)
INTL PAPER CO	Aa /AA-	12/77	49.03q(50)	120.21q(29)	11.80 (46)	54.14 (49)	2.15 (27)
SQUIBB CORP	Aa /AA	12/77	46.05q(51)	93.26q(40)	14.53 (24)	123.33 (33)	2.31 (22)
WEYERHAEUSER CO	Aa /AA	12/77	44.67q(52)	73.61q(49)	13.45 (35)	43.76 (52)	2.11 (28)
INLAND STEEL CO	Áa /AA-	12/77	34.61q(53)	52.04q(53)	7.49 (53)	53.21 (50)	1.90 (39)
U S STEEL CORP	Aa /AA-	12/77	24.22q(54)	43.32q(54)	2.68 (54)	57.73 (46)	1.78 (43)
AVERAGE			110.79	133.79	14.53	233.41	2.22
MEDIAN			77.98	124.61	13.79	146.85	2.13

SPLIT Aa/A RATED COMPANIES

SPLIT Aa/A RATED COMPANIES	RATINGS	FYR END	Pretax Coverage x	Aft Tax Coverage x	Aft Tax Coverage (inc rent) x	Ret on Total Assets %	Net Inc Net Sales %
HERSHEY FOODS CORP	Aa /A+	12/77	30.47 (1)	15.88 (1)	NA (-)	18.63 (2)	5.37 (8)
SUPERIOR OIL CO	A /AA	12/77	23.28 (2)	13.54 (2)	NA (-)	12.88 (14)	11.47 (1)
CROWN CORK & SEAL CO INC	A /AA	12/77	19.32p(3)	10.55p(3)	NA (-)	17.13 (4)	5.13 (10)
DIGITAL EQUIPMENT	Aa /A	6/77	16.06 (4)	10.26 (4)	4.27 (1)	17.57 (3)	10.25 (2)
DANA CORP	A /AA	8/77	13.16 (5)	7.22 (5)	NA (-)	20.68 (1)	6.01 (5)
HEINZ (H.J.) CO	Aa /A	4/77	10.68 (6)	6.33 (6)	3.50 (2)	13.43 (12)	4.48 (14)
WESTINGHOUSE ELECTRIC CORP	A /AA-	12/77	9.52 (7)	6.25 (7)	3.16 (5)	8.47 (20)	4.42 (15)
ANCHOR HOCKING CORP	A /AA	12/77	7.99 (8)	5.14 (8)	3.26 (4)	13.75 (11)	4.69 (13)
BLACK & DECKER MFG CO	A /AA	9/77	7.95 (9)	4.45 (11)	3.07 (6)	16.94 (5)	6.36 (4)
BORDEN INC	Aa /A	12/77	7.55 (10)	4.78 (9)	2.79 (8)	13.35 (13)	3.64 (19)
BORG-WARNER CORP	A /AA-	12/77	7.48 (11)	4.71 (10)	3.43 (3)	13.87 (10)	5.12 (11)
AMERICAN BRANDS INC	Aa /A+	12/77	6.19 (12)	3.39 (14)	2.83 (7)	14.36 (9)	5.46 (7)
CONTINENTAL GROUP	A /AA	12/77	6.13 (13)	4.18 (12)	2.31 (13)	9.19 (18)	3.93 (17)
PENNEY (J.C.) CO	A /AA	1/78	5.94h(14)	3.66h(13)	1.75h(16)	16.05h(6)	3.15 (21)
PPG INDUSTRIES INC	Aa /A	12/77	5.64 (15)	3.36 (15)	2.56 (10)	11.44 (17)	3.66 (18)
MAY DEPARTMENT STORES CO	A /AA	1/78	5.14 (16)	3.09 (17)	2.42 (12)	12.33 (15)	3.56 (20)
INGERSOLL-RAND CO	A /AA	12/77	5.09p(17)	3.16p(16)	2.59p(9)	15.22 (8)	5.57 (6)
DOW CHEMICAL	Aa /A	12/77	4.59 (18)	3.04 (18)	2.43 (11)	15.23 (7)	8.91 (3)
SEARLE (G.D.) & CO	Aa /A+	12/77	3.52 (19)	2.10 (20)	1.76 (15)	11.82 (16)	4.73 (12)
SCOTT PAPER CO	Aa /A+	12/77	3.05 (20)	2.41 (19)	2.07 (14)	7.13 (21)	4.09 (16)
NATIONAL STEEL CORP	Aa /A+	12/77	2.00 (21)	1.86 (21)	NA (-)	4.40 (22)	1.92 (22)
STANDARD OIL CO (OHIO)	A /AA-	12/77	1.55p(22)	1.40p(22)	1.31p(17)	8.78 (19)	5.16 (9)
AVERAGE			9.20	5.49	2.68	13.30	5.32
MEDIAN			6.84	4.32	2.59	13.59	4.92

SPLIT Aa/A RATED COMPANIES	RATINGS	FYR END	LTD Cap %	STD Cap %	LTD Net Pt. %	NTA LTD %	Tot Liab Tot Eqty %
CROWN CORK & SEAL CO INC	A /AA	12/77	3.41 (1)	12.14 (20)	4.67 (1)	2835.11 (1)	74.45 (5)
HERSHEY FOODS CORP	Aa /A+	12/77	10.18 (2)	0.00 (1)	20.56 (3)	901.57 (3)	52.56 (2)
DIGITAL EQUIPMENT	Aa /A	6/77	10.96 (3)	3.47 (15)	34.12 (6)	912.16 (2)	45.55 (1)
SUPERIOR OIL CO	A /AA	12/77	11.68 (4)	3.13 (14)	12.43 (2)	843.27 (4)	72.19 (4)
BORG-WARNER CORP	A /AA-	12/77	14.48 (5)	1.70 (9)	33.26 (5)	681.15 (5)	66.42 (3)
WESTINGHOUSE ELECTRIC CORP	A /AA-	12/77	15.12 (6)	2.76 (13)	30.19 (4)	614.17 (7)	140.97 (18)
PENNEY (J.C.) CO	A /AA	1/78	16.07 (7)	0.00 (2)	35.65 (7)	615.66 (6)	89.48 (11)
HEINZ (H.J.) CO	Aa /A	4/77	17.61 (8)	10.14 (17)	39.30 (8)	550.99 (8)	94.48 (13)
BLACK & DECKER MFG CO	A /AA	9/77	18.19 (9)	10.47 (19)	43.80 (11)	511.92 (9)	74.49 (6)
INGERSOLL-RAND CO	A /AA	12/77	23.38 (10)	19.68 (21)	62.60 (18)	424.03 (10)	92.78 (12)
DANA CORP	A /AA	8/77	25.06 (11)	0.50 (3)	62.45 (17)	386.51 (11)	82.69 (8)
BORDEN INC	Aa /A	12/77	25.65 (12)	1.19 (7)	48.11 (15)	344.72 (13)	85.53 (10)
ANCHOR HOCKING CORP	A /AA	12/77	27.40 (13)	2.23 (12)	43.67 (10)	354.87 (12)	82.21 (7)
CONTINENTAL GROUP	A /AA	12/77	28.63 (14)	1.23 (8)	44.67 (13)	327.60 (14)	112.66 (15)
AMERICAN BRANDS INC	Aa /A+	12/77	30.23 (15)	23.69 (22)	123.81 (21)	237.16 (18)	128.31 (17)
PPG INDUSTRIES INC	Aa /A	12/77	32.18 (16)	1.86 (11)	45.75 (14)	302.12 (15)	99.05 (14)
SCOTT PAPER CO	Aa /A+	12/77	33.37 (17)	0.78 (5)	40.61 (9)	298.15 (16)	85.02 (9)
NATIONAL STEEL CORP	Aa /A+	12/77	36.05 (18)	0.97 (6)	44.15 (12)	275.25 (17)	120.73 (16)
DOW CHEMICAL	Aa /A+	12/77	43.16 (19)	10.40 (18)	55.82 (16)	224.56 (19)	146.23 (19)
MAY DEPARTMENT STORES CO	A /AA	1/78	43.57 (20)	1.77 (10)	73.11 (19)	222.62 (20)	159.96 (21)
SEARLE (G.D.) & CO	Aa /A+	12/77	47.43 (21)	7.12 (16)	205.28 (22)	198.16 (21)	151.69 (20)
STANDARD OIL CO (OHIO)	A /AA-	12/77	73.62 (22)	0.73 (4)	81.43 (20)	129.30 (22)	363.06 (22)
AVERAGE			26.70	5.27	53.88	554.23	110.02
MEDIAN			25.35	2.05	43.98	370.69	91.13

SPLIT Aa/A RATED COMPANIES	RATINGS	FYR END	Cash Flow LTD %	N Cash Fl Cap Exp %	After Tax ROE %	Work Cap LTD %	Current Ratio x
CROWN CORK & SEAL CO INC	A /AA	12/77	713.02q(1)	154.94q(8)	14.87 (3)	1056.74 (1)	1.66 (16)
HERSHEY FOODS CORP	Aa /A+	12/77	165.93 (2)	122.03 (12)	13.88 (5)	468.93 (3)	2.66 (4)
DIGITAL EQUIPMENT	Aa /A	6/77	164.39q(3)	103.98q(14)	14.75 (4)	634.05 (2)	3.49 (1)
SUPERIOR OIL CO	A /AA	12/77	158.77q(4)	83.38q(18)	9.73 (18)	93.07 (16)	1.40 (21)
BORG-WARNER CORP	A /AA-	12/77	109.76q(5)	165.45q(7)	11.81 (16)	225.90 (8)	2.06 (12)
WESTINGHOUSE ELECTRIC CORP	A /AA-	12/77	101.90 (6)	144.33 (9)	11.88 (14)	189.82 (10)	1.30 (22)
BLACK & DECKER MFG CO	A /AA	9/77	93.63q(7)	224.03q(4)	12.83 (10)	308.11 (5)	2.52 (5)
PENNEY (J.C.) CO	A /AA	1/78	93.01q(8)	101.40q(15)	13.61 (6)	255.18 (7)	1.75 (15)
HEINZ (H.J.) CO	Aa /A	4/77	92.78q(9)	190.99q(6)	12.70 (11)	337.14 (4)	2.25.(9)
DANA CORP	A /AA	8/77	75.31q(10)	192.70q(5)	17.87 (1)	209.21 (9)	2.78 (3)
INGERSOLL-RAND CO	A /AA	12/77	65.78q(11)	248.85q(2)	11.88 (15)	263.01 (6)	2.37 (8)
PPG INDUSTRIES INC	Aa /A	12/77	60.32q(12)	125.90q(11)	8.63 (20)	115.35 (14)	2.80 (2)
ANCHOR HOCKING CORP	A /AA	12/77	58.19q(13)	74.90q(19)	12.98 (9)	146.83 (12)	2.52 (6)
BORDEN INC	Aa /A	12/77	58.11q(14)	101.34q(16)	12.37 (12)	148.28 (11)	2.21 (10)
CONTINENTAL GROUP	A /AA	12/77	56.69q(15)	87.27q(17)	12.36 (13)	62.64 (18)	1.53 (18)
AMERICAN BRANDS INC	Aa /A+	12/77	46.76q(16)	225.28q(3)	13.05 (8)	146.12 (13)	1.84 (13)
DOW CHEMICAL	Aa /A+	12/77	42.54q(17)	68.37q(20)	17.83 (2)	37.31 (20)	1.50 (19)
SEARLE (G.D.) & CO	Aa /A+	12/77	41.51 (18)	263.44 (1)	9.29 (19)	79.40 (17)	2.38 (7)
NATIONAL STEEL CORP	Aa /A+	12/77	31.41q(19)	110.47q(13)	4.69 (22)	60.17 (19)	1.78 (14)
MAY DEPARTMENT STORES CO	A /AA	1/78	30.53q(20)	127.41q(10)	13.37 (7)	102.90 (15)	2.17 (11)
SCOTT PAPER CO	Aa /A+	12/77	24.84 (21)	47.61 (21)	7.26 (21)	25.70 (21)	1.49 (20)
STANDARD OIL CO (OHIO)	A /AA-	12/77	8.72q(22)	32.57q(22)	10.82 (17)	11.96 (22)	1.56 (17)
AVERAGE			104.27	136.21	12.20	226.26	2.09
MEDIAN			63.05	123.96	12.54	147.56	2.11

SINGLE A COMPANIES	RATINGS	FYR END	Pretax Coverage x	Aft Tax Coverage x	Aft Tax Coverage (inc rent) x	Ret on Total Assets %	Net Inc / Net Sales %
HUDSON'S BAY OIL & GAS CO	A /A	12/77	62.47 (1)	31.87 (1)	9.79 (1)	26.65 (2)	27.35 (1)
PACCAR INC	A /A	12/77	48.28 (2)	24.84 (2)	NA (-)	27.34 (1)	5.32 (48)
WHIRLPOOL CORP	A /A	12/77	24.95 (3)	12.99 (5)	NA (-)	24.14 (7)	5.67 (45)
CONSOLIDATED FREIGHTWAYS INC	A /A	12/77	24.50 (4)	13.54 (4)	5.42 (2)	20.13 (13)	4.76 (62)
HOOVER UNIVERSAL INC	A /A	7/77	21.74 (5)	11.94 (7)	NA (-)	24.76 (5)	6.24 (32)
HANNA MINING CO	A /A	12/77	19.78 (6)	14.65 (3)	NA (-)	12.34 (85)	13.73 (4)
TEKTRONIX INC	A /A	5/77	18.92 (7)	11.23 (8)	5.38 (3)	19.23 (17)	9.66 (9)
MAYER (OSCAR) & CO	A /A+	10/77	18.16 (8)	10.73 (9)	NA (-)	17.50 (29)	2.95 (103)
MCDERMOTT (J. RAY) & CO	A /A	3/77	17.10p(9)	12.76p(6)	3.16p(27)	20.19 (12)	15.65 (2)
OWENS-CORNING FIBERGLAS CORP	A /A	12/77	16.71 (10)	9.51 (10)	4.66 (5)	21.39 (10)	7.60 (21)
HORMEL (GEO.A.) & CO	A /A	10/77	16.41 (11)	8.99 (11)	NA (-)	17.44 (31)	1.98 (111)
AMERICAN BROADCASTING	A /A	12/77	15.43 (12)	7.84 (13)	3.36 (21)	25.72 (4)	6.83 (26)
SCOTT & FETZER CO	A /A	11/77	15.17 (13)	7.77 (15)	4.80 (4)	26.65 (3)	7.63 (20)
RAYTHEON CO	A /A	12/77	14.93 (14)	8.82 (12)	3.36 (20)	11.93 (88)	4.02 (82)
RELIANCE ELECTRIC CC	A /A	10/77	14.23 (15)	7.82 (14)	3.37 (19)	21.00 (11)	6.45 (30)
HARSCO CORP	A /A	12/77	13.80 (16)	7.46 (18)	NA (-)	22.09 (9)	6.33 (31)
JOY MFG CO	A /A	9/77	13.51 (17)	7.48 (17)	3.97 (9)	18.24 (20)	7.11 (23)
HARRIS CORP	A /A	6/77	13.13 (18)	7.61 (16)	3.48 (16)	13.74 (67)	6.20 (33)
COMBUSTION ENGINEERING INC	A /A	12/77	12.39 (19)	6.70 (22)	2.60 (52)	8.74 (109)	3.29 (97)
LUCKY STORES INC	A /A	1/78	12.29 (20)	6.85 (20)	1.88 (89)	17.13 (32)	1.57 (115)
CUMMINS ENGINE	A /A-	12/77	11.98 (21)	6.78 (21)	3.97 (8)	17.09 (33)	5.30 (49)
MARTIN MARIETTA CORP	A /A	12/77	11.68 (22)	6.69 (24)	3.85 (10)	15.12 (50)	7.09 (24)
BUCYRUS-ERIE CO	A /A	12/77	11.11 (23)	6.69 (25)	NA (-)	15.91 (40)	9.58 (12)
TEXTRON INC	A /A	12/77	11.09 (24)	6.13 (31)	3.53 (13)	16.47 (35)	4.88 (58)
DART INDUSTRIES	A /A	12/77	11.07 (25)	6.61 (26)	3.08 (29)	15.36 (47)	6.82 (27)
BAKER INTERNATIONAL CORP	A /A	9/77	11.01h(26)	6.70h(23)	3.00h(32)	18.22h(21)	8.52 (17)
IDEAL BASIC INDUSTRIES INC	A /A	12/77	10.83 (27)	7.37 (19)	NA (-)	14.37 (59)	10.00 (7)
DAYTON-HUDSON CORP	A /A	1/78	10.58 (28)	5.70 (36)	2.80 (42)	15.06 (53)	3.73c(89)
HUGHES TOOL CO	A /A	12/77	10.36 (29)	6.44 (28)	4.34 (6)	17.57 (27)	9.61 (10)
MERCANTILE STORES CO INC	A /A	1/78	10.32 (30)	5.84 (34)	2.93 (36)	15.18 (48)	3.96c(85)

SINGLE A COMPANIES	RATINGS	FYR END	Pretax Coverage x	Aft Tax Coverage x	Aft Tax Coverage (inc rent) x	Ret on Total Assets %	Net Inc / Net Sales %
MASCO CORP	A /A	12/77	10.28 (31)	6.04 (32)	NA (-)	22.98 (8)	11.02 (5)
FEDERAL-MOGUL CORP	A /A	12/77	10.22 (32)	5.86 (33)	3.58 (11)	19.85 (14)	6.49 (29)
GREAT NORTHERN NEKOOSA CORP	A /A+	12/77	10.09 (33)	6.31 (29)	4.02 (7)	18.40 (19)	5.23 (50)
DENNISON MFG CO	A /A	12/77	9.84 (34)	5.81 (35)	3.20 (25)	19.85 (15)	8.55 (16)
REVLON INC	A /A+	12/77	9.74 (35)	5.63 (37)	3.39 (17)	24.63 (6)	4.63 (71)
MARATHON OIL CO	A /A+	12/77	9.69 (36)	3.25 (86)	NA (-)	17.68 (24)	4.02 (81)
GENERAL MILLS INC	A /A	5/77	9.55p(37)	5.36p(41)	3.39p(18)	10.53 (97)	1.04 (119)
COLONIAL STORES INC	A /A	12/77	9.55 (38)	6.23 (30)	1.61 (95)	18.87 (18)	5.93 (38)
REXNORD INC	A /A	10/77	9.50p(39)	5.48p(40)	NA (-)	18.87 (18)	6.77 (28)
NATIONAL DISTILLERS &CHEMICL	A /A	12/77	9.29 (40)	5.55 (39)	3.57 (12)	12.98 (76)	3.90 (86)
WITCO CHEMICAL CORP	A /A	12/77	9.11 (41)	5.61 (38)	3.32 (23)	13.87 (64)	5.14 (53)
STANLEY WORKS	A /A	12/77	8.73 (42)	4.80 (48)	2.90 (37)	17.65 (26)	14.43 (3)
BIG THREE INDUSTRIES	A /A	12/77	8.64 (43)	6.48 (27)	NA (-)	15.06 (52)	4.36 (75)
QUAKER OATS CO	A /A+	6/77	8.64 (44)	4.96 (44)	3.07 (30)	16.61 (34)	6.03 (36)
PITNEY-BOWES INC	A /A	12/77	8.55 (45)	4.90 (45)	2.61 (51)	15.59 (42)	7.29 (22)
DRESSER INDUSTRIES INC	A /A	10/77	8.47 (46)	5.12 (43)	3.26 (24)	17.51 (28)	3.20 (99)
NORTH AMERICAN PHILIPS CORP	A /A	12/77	8.20p(47)	4.63p(47)	2.60p(53)	13.15 (72)	2.96 (102)
BROWN GROUP INC	A /A	10/77	8.10 (48)	4.57 (52)	1.53 (96)	14.98 (54)	3.16 (100)
AMERICAN CAN CO	A /A	12/77	8.05 (49)	4.74 (49)	2.63 (50)	10.90 (93)	4.72 (64)
TRW INC	A /A	12/77	8.00 (50)	4.86 (46)	2.87 (38)	16.36 (37)	7.77 (19)
VULCAN MATERIALS CO	A /A	12/77	7.86 (51)	5.18 (42)	3.52 (14)	17.48 (30)	6.03 (37)
QUAKER STATE OIL REFINING	A /A	12/77	7.78 (52)	4.52 (54)	NA (-)	15.55 (43)	2.54 (105)
PET INC	A /A	3/77	7.70 (53)	4.47 (55)	2.52 (57)	12.64 (83)	1.88 (112)
SOUTHLAND CORP	A /A	12/77	7.36p(54)	4.17p(60)	1.65p(93)	13.78 (66)	6.19 (34)
WESTVACO CORP	A /A	10/77	7.33 (55)	4.74 (50)	2.83 (40)	13.71 (68)	3.43 (92)
ASHLAND OIL INC	A /A	9/77	7.23 (56)	4.35 (58)	2.04 (60)	13.41 (70)	4.64 (70)
CUTLER-HAMMER INC	A /A	12/77	7.14 (57)	4.14 (61)	2.70 (43)	16.26 (38)	5.78 (40)
GOULD INC	A /A	12/77	6.82 (58)	4.40 (56)	2.65 (47)	15.73 (41)	8.70 (15)
PHILIP MORRIS INC	A /A	12/77	6.75 (59)	4.07 (63)	3.50 (15)	18.14 (22)	10.59 (6)
DIAMOND SHAMROCK CORP	A /A	12/77	6.64 (60)	4.57 (53)	3.33 (22)	16.44 (36)	10.59 (6)

SINGLE A COMPANIES	RATINGS	FYR END	Pretax Coverage x	Aft Tax Coverage x	Aft Tax Coverage (inc rent) x	Ret on Total Assets %	Net Inc / Net Sales %
STAUFFER CHEMICAL CO	A /A	12/77	6.58p(61)	4.36p(57)	3.16p(28)	46.03 (39)	9.41 (13)
MARYLAND CUP CORP	A /A	9/77	6.45 (62)	3.96 (64)	NA (-)	15.17 (49)	4.68 (68)
COPPERWELD CORP	A /A	12/77	6.09 (63)	4.60 (51)	NA (-)	10.30 (103)	4.70 (67)
CITIES SERVICE CO	A /A	12/77	6.08p(64)	3.71p(70)	2.25p(72)	12.14 (66)	4.79 (61)
BROCKWAY GLASS CO	A /A	12/77	6.04 (65)	3.87 (66)	NA (-)	12.96 (78)	4.00 (83)
RCA CORP	A /A	12/77	5.93 (66)	3.62 (73)	2.44 (62)	13.03 (75)	4.20 (78)
BOISE CASCADE CORP	A /A	12/77	5.90 (67)	3.78 (67)	2.96 (34)	13.04 (74)	4.99 (57)
BENDIX CORP	A /A	9/77	5.89 (68)	3.72 (68)	2.66 (46)	14.23 (60)	3.60 (91)
HARRAH'S	NR /A	6/77	5.85 (69)	3.62 (72)	2.96 (33)	17.66 (25)	9.06 (14)
PENNWALT CORP	A /A	12/77	5.80 (70)	3.40 (80)	2.44 (63)	15.09 (51)	5.00 (56)
CROWN ZELLERBACH	A /A	12/77	5.80 (71)	4.24 (59)	3.00 (31)	11.33 (92)	4.71 (65)
STANDARD BRANDS INC	A /A	12/77	5.79 (72)	3.71 (69)	2.81 (41)	12.83 (80)	3.23 (98)
ASSD DRY GOODS CORP	A /A+	1/78	5.73 (73)	3.46 (78)	1.91 (86)	12.03 (87)	2.87c(104)
INTL MINERALS & CHEMICAL	A /A	6/77	5.72 (74)	4.12 (62)	3.17 (26)	14.54 (58)	8.45 (18)
CARRIER CORP	A /A-	10/77	5.71p(75)	3.39p(81)	2.36p(67)	14.74 (55)	4.36 (74)
FMC CORP	A /A	12/77	5.70 (76)	3.89 (65)	2.84 (39)	11.49 (90)	5.55 (46)
SYBRON CORP	A /A	12/77	5.66 (77)	3.58 (75)	2.55 (54)	13.82 (65)	4.67 (69)
NORTON CO	A /A	12/77	5.66 (78)	3.52 (76)	2.54 (56)	14.61 (56)	4.88 (59)
ROCKWELL INTL CORP	A /A	9/77	5.65 (79)	3.30 (85)	2.14 (76)	10.42 (99)	2.46 (107)
MORTON-NORWICH PRODUCTS	A /A	6/77	5.61p(80)	3.67p(71)	2.65p(48)	14.18 (61)	5.20 (51)
MEAD CORP	A /A	12/77	5.59 (81)	3.13 (92)	2.41 (65)	15.50 (44)	5.38 (47)
MCDONALD'S CORP	A /A	12/77	5.49 (82)	3.30 (84)	2.41 (64)	19.83 (16)	9.88 (8)
ALLIED CHEMICAL CORP	A /A	12/77	5.49 (83)	3.61 (74)	2.69 (44)	10.36 (101)	4.73 (63)
GARDNER-DENVER CO	A /A+	12/77	5.48 (84)	3.24 (87)	2.94 (35)	12.98 (77)	4.70 (66)
NCR CORP	A /A	12/77	5.47 (85)	3.46 (79)	2.50 (59)	13.69 (69)	5.70 (43)
PILLSBURY CO	A /A	5/77	5.45 (86)	3.23 (88)	2.27 (68)	12.73 (82)	3.96 (84)
EATON CORP	A /A	12/77	5.37 (87)	3.07 (94)	2.48 (60)	17.77 (23)	5.04 (55)
SUNBEAM CORP	A /A	3/78	5.23 (88)	3.13 (91)	2.51 (58)	14.60 (57)	3.79 (87)
HONEYWELL INC	A /A	12/77	5.22 (89)	3.30 (83)	2.26 (69)	11.87 (89)	4.61 (72)
HUDSON BAY MINING & SMELT-A	A /A	12/77	5.20 (90)	2.98 (95)	2.45g(.61)	6.97 (114)	1.27 (118)
BURLINGTON INDUSTRIES INC	A /A	9/77	5.02 (91)	3.52 (77)	2.54 (55)	10.10 (104)	3.77 (88)
CLARK EQUIPMENT CO	A /A	12/77	4.94 (92)	2.91 (97)	2.38 (66)	15.49 (45)	4.61 (73)
NL INDUSTRIES	A /A	12/77	4.79 (93)	3.17 (90)	2.26 (70)	10.61 (94)	4.19 (79)

SINGLE A COMPANIES	RATINGS	FYR END	Pretax Coverage x	Aft Tax Coverage x	Aft Tax Coverage (inc rent) x	Ret on Total Assets %	Net Inc / Net Sales %
SPERRY RAND CORP	A /A	3/78	4.57 (94)	2.76 (99)	2.13 (77)	13.30 (71)	4.84 (60)
WARNER COMMUNICATIONS INC	A /A	12/77	4.55 (95)	3.31 (82)	2.67 (45)	13.13 (73)	5.85 (39)
GREYHOUND CORP	A /A	12/77	4.55 (96)	3.21 (89)	1.93 (85)	10.35 (102)	2.15 (109)
CARTER HAWLEY HALE STORES	A /A	1/78	4.52 (97)	2.94 (96)	1.62 (94)	12.83 (79)	3.33c(95)
AVERY INTERNATIONAL	A /A	11/77	4.41 (98)	2.74 (101)	2.14 (75)	13.97 (63)	3.62 (90)
HEUBLEIN INC	A /A	6/77	4.20 (99)	2.59 (103)	1.91 (87)	15.36 (46)	4.24 (77)
ALUMINUM CO OF AMERICA	A /A	12/77	4.17 (100)	3.09 (93)	2.65 (49)	10.06 (105)	5.71 (42)
WOOLWORTH (F.W.) CO	A /A	1/78	4.13 (101)	2.57 (105)	1.30 (99)	10.47 (98)	1.66c(114)
HERCULES INC	A /A	12/77	4.02 (102)	2.53 (107)	1.94 (84)	9.36 (107)	3.41 (93)
TENNECO INC	A /A	12/77	4.02 (103)	2.56 (106)	2.23 (74)	12.81 (81)	5.74 (41)
OWENS-ILLINOIS INC	A /A	12/77	3.83p(104)	2.87p(98)	2.09p(79)	7.55 (112)	3.30 (96)
GOODYEAR TIRE & RUBBER CO	A /A	12/77	3.65p(105)	2.38p(110)	1.86p(90)	11.38 (91)	3.10 (101)
SAFEWAY STORES INC	A /A	12/77	3.63 (106)	2.46 (108)	1.65 (92)	9.93 (106)	0.91 (120)
FIRESTONE TIRE & RUBBER CO	A /A+	10/77	3.41 (107)	2.25 (114)	1.77 (91)	8.88 (108)	2.49 (106)
SEAGRAM CO LTD	A /A	7/77	3.29 (108)	2.32 (111)	NA (-)	10.58 (96)	7.03 (25)
TEXASGULF INC	A /A+	12/77	3.25 (109)	2.56 (104)	2.13 (78)	6.18 (118)	9.59 (11)
INTL TELEPHONE & TELEGRAPH	A /A	12/77	3.21 (110)	2.31 (113)	1.89 (88)	10.36 (100)	4.28 (76)
ESMARK INC	A /A	10/77	3.14p(111)	2.40p(109)	1.95p(82)	8.26 (110)	1.28 (117)
SCHLITZ (JOSEPH) BREWING	A /A	12/77	3.09 (112)	2.18 (115)	NA (-)	2.11 (110)	2.11 (110)
HOSPITAL CORP OF AMERICA	NR /A	12/77	3.07 (113)	2.17 (117)	2.01 (81)	12.53 (84)	6.12 (35)
ROHM & HAAS CO	A /A	12/77	3.04 (114)	2.32 (112)	1.95 (83)	10.60 (95)	4.06 (80)
LIGGETT GROUP	A /A	12/77	3.01h(115)	1.27h(122)	1.18h(100)	6.35h(117)	0.32 (122)
ARMCO STEEL CORP	A /A	12/77	2.77 (116)	2.75 (100)	2.25 (71)	6.15 (119)	3.38 (94)
INCO LTD	A /A	12/77	2.62i(117)	1.92 (118)	NA (-)	6.94i(115)	5.11 (54)
CENTRAL SOYA CO	A /A	8/77	2.38 (118)	1.79 (119)	NA (-)	7.99 (111)	0.57 (121)
STALEY (A.E.) MFG CO	A /A	9/77	2.36 (119)	2.64 (102)	2.24 (73)	6.60 (116)	2.19 (108)
REPUBLIC STEEL CORP	A /A	12/77	2.19 (120)	2.18 (116)	NA (-)	3.13 (122)	1.41 (116)
PHELPS DODGE CORP	A /A-	12/77	1.60 (121)	1.47 (121)	1.41 (97)	3.79 (121)	1.67 (113)
AMAX INC	A /A+	12/77	1.51 (122)	1.48 (120)	1.36 (98)	5.53 (120)	5.16 (52)
ASARCO INC	A /A-	12/77	-0.17 (123)	-0.32 (123)	NA (-)	0.65 (123)	-2.82 (123)
BETHLEHEM STEEL CORP	A /A	12/77	-10.13p(124)	-4.52p(124)	-2.26p(101)	-16.92 (124)	-8.35 (124)

AVERAGE			8.49	5.08	2.73	14.02	5.22
MEDIAN			6.27	4.10	2.61	14.06	4.75

			LTD	STD	LTD	NTA	Tot Liab
			---	---	------	---	--------
			Cap	Cap	Net Pt.	LTD	Tot Eqty
SINGLE A COMPANIES	RATINGS	FYR END	%	%	%	%	%
PACCAR INC	A /A	12/77	5.71 (1)	4.28 (80)	23.63 (6)	1734.16 (1)	67.43 (12)
HANNA MINING CO	A /A	12/77	9.63 (2)	0.00 (4)	77.96 (108)	1015.97 (2)	34.54 (1)
RAYTHEON CO	A /A	12/77	11.47 (3)	2.33 (54)	26.34 (7)	810.68 (4)	190.80 (119)
HUGHES TOOL CO	A /A	12/77	11.62 (4)	2.47 (55)	22.42 (4)	809.21 (5)	47.02 (2)
MAYER (OSCAR) & CO	A /A+	10/77	12.18 (5)	0.00 (2)	15.83 (2)	813.48 (3)	56.29 (5)
TEKTRONIX INC	A /A	5/77	12.67 (6)	1.71 (39)	41.71 (32)	787.15 (6)	51.51 (3)
HUDSON'S BAY OIL & GAS CO	A /A	12/77	13.20 (7)	3.79 (75)	12.22 (1)	744.48 (7)	84.36 (33)
WHIRLPOOL CORP	A /A	12/77	13.53 (8)	3.23 (68)	38.33 (28)	723.54 (8)	65.22 (10)
JOY MFG CO	A /A	9/77	14.60 (9)	6.42 (96)	44.73 (42)	672.49 (9)	59.16 (6)
HORMEL (GEO.A.) & CO	A /A	10/77	15.54 (10)	0.53 (11)	26.25 (9)	632.30 (10)	68.41* (13)
CONSOLIDATED FREIGHTWAYS INC	A /A	12/77	16.04 (11)	1.66 (37)	19.92 (3)	559.08 (11)	113.58 (83)
HONEYWELL INC	A /A	12/77	17.32 (12)	8.23 (111)	30.81 (13)	556.22 (12)	100.98 (69)
ASSD DRY GOODS CORP	A /A+	1/78	17.92 (13)	1.25 (30)	28.72 (10)	549.67 (13)	69.20 (15)
MCDERMOTT (J. RAY) & CO	A /A	3/77	19.28 (14)	0.27 (9)	35.63 (21)	514.18 (14)	97.86 (65)
IDEAL BASIC INDUSTRIES INC	A /A	12/77	19.60 (15)	0.00 (1)	23.52 (5)	506.04 (15)	54.76 (4)
COLONIAL STORES INC	A /A	12/77	19.62 (16)	0.11 (7)	31.97 (15)	482.21 (18)	79.71 (30)
FEDERAL-MOGUL CORP	A /A	12/77	19.74 (17)	6.66 (101)	40.67 (30)	494.51 (16)	74.78 (20)
NORTON CO	A /A	12/77	20.10 (18)	11.22 (121)	46.25 (47)	482.53 (17)	77.27 (25)
DENNISON MFG CO	A /A	12/77	20.69 (19)	5.39 (89)	43.11 (40)	458.66 (19)	66.53 (11)
OWENS-CORNING FIBERGLAS CORP	A /A	12/77	21.17 (20)	2.58 (58)	30.51 (12)	453.69 (20)	81.82 (32)
REXNORD INC	A /A	10/77	22.54 (21)	5.17 (88)	46.65 (49)	429.77 (21)	78.23 (28)
HOOVER UNIVERSAL INC	A /A	7/77	22.57 (22)	0.70 (15)	42.56 (36)	420.49 (24)	95.55 (56)
DART INDUSTRIES	A /A	12/77	22.92 (23)	2.09 (50)	49.86 (58)	380.39 (38)	70.24 (16)
BENDIX CORP	A /A	9/77	22.97 (24)	7.71 (108)	47.08 (51)	397.56 (27)	115.86 (85)
HARSCO CORP	A /A	12/77	23.05 (25)	0.30 (10)	53.12 (65)	423.40 (23)	61.05 (7)
MARTIN MARIETTA CORP	A /A	12/77	23.17 (26)	1.73 (40)	35.42 (20)	394.70 (29)	89.73 (43)
MERCANTILE STORES CO INC	A /A	1/78	23.37 (27)	1.39 (32)	46.49 (48)	427.85 (22)	74.95 (22)
SCOTT & FETZER CO	A /A	11/77	23.88 (28)	0.70 (16)	83.38 (110)	409.81 (25)	69.02 (14)
STANLEY WORKS	A /A	12/77	23.89 (29)	3.29 (70)	60.08 (86)	405.58 (26)	75.38 (23)
QUAKER OATS CO	A /A+	6/77	24.36 (30)	10.35 (118)	37.32 (26)	361.54 (37)	96.09 (58)

			LTD	STD	LTD	NTA	Tot Liab
			---	---	------	---	--------
			Cap	Cap	Net Pt.	LTD	Tot Eqty
SINGLE A COMPANIES	RATINGS	FYR END	%	%	%	%	%
TEXTRON INC	A /A	12/77	24.49 (31)	2.31 (53)	96.23 (113)	387.87 (33)	88.60 (40)
GREAT NORTHERN NEKOOSA CORP	A /A+	12/77	24.52 (32)	1.16 (28)	29.94 (11)	394.69 (30)	63.29 (8)
NATIONAL DISTILLERS &CHEMICL	A /A	12/77	24.70 (33)	2.80 (61)	60.93 (88)	395.17 (28)	78.66 (29)
COMBUSTION ENGINEERING INC	A /A	12/77	25.01 (34)	2.54 (57)	33.69 (16)	332.16 (53)	274.63 (124)
NORTH AMERICAN PHILIPS CORP	A /A	12/77	25.06 (35)	0.71 (17)	66.96 (99)	389.75 (32)	130.06 (98)
GARDNER-DENVER CO	A /A+	12/77	25.16 (36)	6.62 (99)	118.68 (122)	371.57 (40)	71.87 (17)
RELIANCE ELECTRIC CO	A /A	10/77	25.22 (37)	0.99 (21)	65.96 (96)	372.27 (39)	92.48 (47)
BIG THREE INDUSTRIES	A /A	12/77	25.25 (38)	2.19 (52)	27.11 (8)	391.76 (31)	64.36 (9)
REPUBLIC STEEL CORP	A /A	12/77	25.32 (39)	1.00 (22)	31.59 (14)	385.05 (34)	80.38 (31)
REVLON INC	A /A+	12/77	25.39 (40)	9.38 (114)	93.50 (111)	331.53 (56)	94.18 (53)
PET INC	A /A	3/77	25.65 (41)	1.02 (25)	55.51 (73)	348.08 (45)	72.06 (18)
CLARK EQUIPMENT CO	A /A	12/77	26.03 (42)	7.21 (106)	56.30 (76)	384.12 (35)	87.29 (35)
BUCYRUS-ERIE CO	A /A	12/77	26.07 (43)	0.00 (3)	66.81 (98)	382.05 (36)	119.19 (87)
BROWN GROUP INC	A /A	10/77	26.20 (44)	2.05 (48)	96.28 (114)	371.10 (41)	77.90 (26)
NL INDUSTRIES	A /A	12/77	26.40 (45)	6.95 (104)	48.64 (55)	363.17 (43)	88.35 (39)
SPERRY RAND CORP	A /A	3/78	26.77 (46)	15.14 (123)	107.36 (119)	370.46 (42)	129.15 (95)
GOULD INC	A /A	12/77	26.82 (47)	3.61 (72)	65.72 (95)	320.85 (60)	91.06 (45)
CUMMINS ENGINE	A /A-	12/77	27.30 (48)	0.94 (19)	48.06 (53)	356.08 (44)	114.77 (84)
GENERAL MILLS INC	A /A	5/77	27.59 (49)	3.11 (66)	51.13 (61)	296.34 (79)	99.66 (67)
DRESSER INDUSTRIES INC	A /A	10/77	27.73 (50)	4.05 (79)	73.33 (104)	341.38 (47)	101.44 (70)
AMERICAN CAN CO	A /A	12/77	27.80 (51)	4.78 (84)	42.61 (37)	332.05 (55)	132.47 (100)
WITCO CHEMICAL CORP	A /A	12/77	27.81 (52)	2.04 (47)	51.27 (62)	333.51 (51)	96.30 (59)
AMERICAN BROADCASTING	A /A	12/77	28.34 (53)	1.01 (23)	98.24 (116)	297.74 (77)	91.10 (46)
WOOLWORTH (F.W.) CO	A /A	1/78	28.53 (54)	1.76 (42)	60.27 (87)	343.45 (46)	96.59 (61)
BAKER INTERNATIONAL CORP	A /A	9/77	28.56 (55)	4.45 (83)	59.38 (65)	333.18 (52)	92.76 (48)
SYBRON CORP	A /A	12/77	28.67 (56)	2.52 (56)	98.03 (115)	307.13 (68)	90.50 (44)
SUNBEAM CORP	A /A	3/78	28.67 (57)	16.49 (124)	100.34 (117)	317.48 (65)	119.52 (88)
VULCAN MATERIALS CO	A /A	12/77	28.93 (58)	2.02 (46)	35.09 (19)	339.19 (49)	88.17 (38)
AMAX INC	A /A+	12/77	29.17 (59)	1.75 (41)	34.97 (18)	339.90 (48)	74.83 (21)
ROCKWELL INTL CORP	A /A	9/77	29.42 (60)	6.91 (103)	61.28 (89)	319.53 (62)	170.92 (116)

IV-11

SINGLE A COMPANIES	RATINGS	FYR END	LTD --- Cap %	STD --- Cap %	LTD ------ Net Pt. %	NTA ------ LTD %	Tot Liab -------- Tot Eqty %
BROCKWAY GLASS CO	A /A	12/77	29.65 (61)	0.06 (5)	38.23 (27)	334.89 (50)	78.10 (27)
FIRESTONE TIRE & RUBBER CO	A /A+	10/77	29.90 (62)	10.51 (120)	48.53 (54)	328.86 (57)	109.86 (76)
CARTER HAWLEY HALE STORES	A /A	1/78	29.95 (63)	0.60 (.14)	57.51 (81)	326.03 (58)	99.42 (66)
BURLINGTON INDUSTRIES INC	A /A	9/77	30.00 (64)	2.76 (60)	55.32 (72)	332.12 (54)	76.10 (24)
TRW INC	A /A	12/77	30.24 (65)	4.86 (85)	66.31 (97)	263.65 (101)	122.37 (89)
COPPERWELD CORP	A /A	12/77	30.26 (66)	6.85 (102)	46.72 (50)	324.09 (59)	105.21 (74)
HARRIS CORP	A /A	6/77	30.30 (67)	2.07 (49)	94.27 (112)	318.12 (64)	151.64 (110)
HERCULES INC	A /A	12/77	30.31 (68)	6.63 (100)	45.67 (44)	312.20 (67)	95.04 (55)
HUDSON BAY MINING & SMELT-A	A /A	12/77	30.35 (69)	1.07 (26)	42.86 (39)	312.22 (66)	142.88 (108)
ARMCO STEEL CORP	A /A	12/77	30.53 (70)	5.90 (94)	41.56 (31)	320.61 (61)	97.04 (63)
CARRIER CORP	A /A-	10/77	30.72 (71)	9.12 (113)	68.74 (100)	319.33 (63)	134.02 (101)
BOISE CASCADE CORP	A /A	12/77	31.06 (72)	3.07 (65)	42.70 (38)	298.49 (76)	87.58 (36)
INTL TELEPHONE & TELEGRAPH	A /A	12/77	31.38 (73)	3.15 (122)	93.82 (68)	297.09 (78)	138.99 (104)
CENTRAL SOYA CO	A	8/77	31.60 (74)	7.58 (107)	75.19 (106)	301.33 (73)	97.20 (64)
QUAKER STATE OIL REFINING	A /A	12/77	31.70 (75)	4.04 (78)	36.92 (24)	301.55 (72)	94.04 (52)
LIGGETT GROUP	A /A	12/77	32.16 (76)	3.01 (63)	130.92 (123)	251.27 (106)	85.46 (34)
MASCO CORP	A /A	12/77	32.25 (77)	2.95 (62)	106.95 (118)	284.99 (86)	72.93 (19)
DAYTON-HUDSON CORP	A /A	1/78	32.35 (78)	1.16 (27)	47.74 (52)	302.35 (71)	138.73 (103)
STANDARD BRANDS INC	A /A	12/77	32.39 (79)	6.98 (105)	55.72 (75)	271.90 (94)	129.34 (96)
EATON CORP	A /A	12/77	32.44 (80)	8.31 (112)	71.49 (102)	299.01 (75)	108.58 (75)
LUCKY STORES INC	A /A	1/78	32.49 (81)	0.95 (20)	54.22 (71)	289.98 (83)	164.51 (113)
CITIES SERVICE CO	A /A	12/77	32.61 (82)	1.67 (38)	36.96 (25)	304.36 (69)	93.01 (49)
ASARCO INC	A /A-	12/77	32.71 (83)	1.23 (29)	56.63 (78)	300.05 (74)	89.06 (41)
CROWN ZELLERBACH	A /A	12/77	32.73 (84)	1.80 (43)	44.20 (41)	303.31 (70)	93.56 (51)
TEXASGULF INC	A /A+	12/77	32.77 (85)	3.77 (73)	36.75 (23)	287.62 (84)	96.49 (60)
FMC CORP	A /A	12/77	32.91 (86)	2.75 (59)	56.43 (77)	291.10 (80)	125.01 (91)
NCR CORP	A /A	12/77	33.44 (87)	5.58 (90)	78.28 (109)	275.56 (92)	128.75 (94)
SEAGRAM CO LTD	A /A	7/77	33.51 (88)	6.02 (95)	76.55 (107)	290.62 (81)	100.16 (68)
MORTON-NORWICH PRODUCTS	A	6/77	33.53 (89)	1.88 (44)	64.47 (94)	279.65 (90)	94.93 (54)
HEUBLEIN INC	A	6/77	33.79 (90)	5.87 (92)	74.82 (105)	252.15 (104)	110.81 (80)
MARYLAND CUP CORP	A /A	9/77	34.20 (91)	1.34 (31)	53.10 (64)	290.51 (82)	87.73 (37)
AVERY INTERNATIONAL	A	11/77	34.40 (92)	8.01 (110)	72.40 (103)	281.68 (89)	110.21 (77)
ROHM & HAAS CO	A /A	12/77	34.41 (93)	5.89 (93)	57.17 (79)	274.70 (93)	93.36 (50)

SINGLE A COMPANIES	RATINGS	FYR END	LTD --- Cap %	STD --- Cap %	LTD ------ Net Pt. %	NTA --- LTD %	Tot Liab -------- Tot Eqty %
PITNEY-BOWES INC	A /A	12/77	34.56 (94)	1.95 (45)	53.57 (67)	286.82 (85)	151.90 (111)
BETHLEHEM STEEL CORP	A /A	12/77	34.64 (95)	0.10 (6)	38.36 (29)	276.98 (91)	124.83 (90)
GREYHOUND CORP	A /A	12/77	34.67 (96)	3.05 (64)	53.98 (69)	217.18 (118)	130.58 (99)
INCO LTD	A /A	12/77	34.75 (97)	10.08 (117)	41.85 (33)	283.12 (87)	112.85 (82)
OWENS-ILLINOIS INC	A /A	12/77	34.86 (98)	3.27 (69)	45.50 (43)	262.77 (102)	115.97 (86)
WESTVACO CORP	A /A	10/77	35.06 (99)	2.16 (51)	45.76 (45)	281.93 (88)	89.33 (42)
CUTLER-HAMMER INC	A /A	12/77	35.24 (100)	4.88 (86)	112.23 (121)	269.30 (98)	110.55 (78)
PENNWALT CORP	A /A	12/77	35.42 (101)	3.83 (76)	70.01 (101)	269.53 (97)	103.79 (72)
SCHLITZ (JOSEPH) BREWING	A /A	12/77	35.52 (102)	0.14 (8)	34.80 (17)	267.38 (100)	103.74 (71)
GOODYEAR TIRE & RUBBER CO	A /A	12/77	36.32 (103)	9.82 (116)	57.40 (80)	269.95 (96)	136.99 (102)
PHELPS DODGE CORP	A /A-	12/77	36.67 (104)	6.59 (97)	42.47 (35)	271.46 (95)	95.75 (57)
STALEY (A.E.) MFG CO	A /A	9/77	36.85 (105)	9.56 (115)	36.48 (22)	267.42 (99)	148.08 (109)
INTL MINERALS & CHEMICAL	A /A	6/77	37.34 (106)	5.15 (87)	49.70 (56)	260.00 (103)	110.78 (79)
ESMARK INC	A /A	10/77	37.37 (107)	6.61 (98)	58.44 (84)	243.81 (109)	141.84 (107)
STAUFFER CHEMICAL CO	A /A	12/77	38.07 (108)	3.15 (67)	53.19 (66)	248.84 (107)	111.27 (81)
ALUMINUM CO OF AMERICA	A /A	12/77	38.62 (109)	0.54 (13)	57.53 (82)	251.85 (105)	105.17 (73)
MEAD CORP	A /A	12/77	39.87 (110)	1.49 (34)	62.96 (93)	242.07 (110)	125.99 (92)
SOUTHLAND CORP	A /A	12/77	39.89 (111)	1.02 (24)	54.10 (70)	248.22 (108)	129.70 (97)
PILLSBURY CO	A /A	5/77	40.00 (112)	3.97 (77)	62.27 (92)	235.08 (111)	184.97 (118)
ALLIED CHEMICAL CORP	A /A	12/77	40.93 (113)	1.64 (36)	45.65 (46)	231.52 (113)	139.88 (106)
ASHLAND OIL INC	A /A	9/77	41.56 (114)	1.53 (35)	49.79 (57)	233.37 (112)	171.14 (117)
DIAMOND SHAMROCK CORP	A /A	12/77	42.34 (115)	1.39 (33)	51.03 (60)	218.44 (117)	126.34 (93)
RCA CORP	A /A	12/77	42.94 (116)	7.74 (109)	61.36 (90)	223.23 (115)	204.25 (121)
HARRAH'S	NR /A	6/77	43.58 (117)	0.54 (12)	58.01 (83)	189.63 (121)	96.78 (62)
TENNECO INC	A /A	12/77	43.71 (118)	10.48 (119)	49.99 (59)	223.23 (116)	168.82 (115)
MARATHON OIL CO	A- /A+	12/77	43.93 (119)	4.44 (82)	42.34 (34)	224.29 (114)	167.76 (114)
WARNER COMMUNICATIONS INC	A /A	12/77	44.70 (120)	0.83 (18)	132.35 (124)	169.35 (123)	214.05 (122)
PHILIP MORRIS INC	A /A	12/77	45.77 (121)	4.39 (81)	112.15 (120)	200.19 (119)	139.52 (105)
SAFEWAY STORES INC	A /A	12/77	49.65 (122)	5.73 (91)	55.67 (74)	197.62 (120)	201.89 (120)
MCDONALD'S CORP	A /A	12/77	51.68 (123)	3.78 (74)	51.57 (63)	184.37 (122)	155.81 (112)
HOSPITAL CORP OF AMERICA	NR /A	12/77	61.24 (124)	3.41 (71)	61.80 (91)	159.90 (124)	225.08 (123)

AVERAGE			29.42	3.90	55.58	368.15	107.58
MEDIAN			29.93	2.98	51.42	319.43	96.91

IV-12

SINGLE A COMPANIES	RATINGS	FYR END	Cash Flow LTD %	N Cash Fl Cap Exp %	After Tax ROE %	Work Cap LTD %	Current Ratio x
PACCAR INC	A /A	12/77	418.37q(1)	467.66v(1)	22.95 (4)	1044.81 (1)	2.08 (69)
HUDSON'S BAY OIL & GAS·CO	A /A	12/77	304.68q(2)	152.26q(36)	24.28 (3)	125.83 (69)	1.50 (110)
RAYTHEON CO	A /A	12/77	224.47q(3)	123.93q(54)	18.17 (21)	381.51 (6)	1.28 (117)
CONSOLIDATED FREIGHTWAYS INC	A /A	12/77	179.11q(4)	106.10q(76)	22.13 (5)	103.93 (82)	1.25 (120)
MCDERMOTT (J. RAY) & CO	A /A	3/77	174.20 (5)	426.14 (2)	27.54 (1)	278.75 (12)	2.09 (68)
MAYER (OSCAR) & CO	A /A+	10/77	171.98q(6)	142.68q(38)	14.49 (50)	206.88 (31)	1.92 (84)
WHIRLPOOL CORP	A /A	12/77	169.18q(7)	197.82q(13)	19.85 (13)	414.34 (4)	2.47 (43)
HUGHES TOOL CO	A /A	12/77	162.64q(8)	111.09q(69)	12.35 (75)	405.96 (5)	3.07 (19)
HONEYWELL INC	A /A	12/77	149.45 (9)	94.02 (83)	11.11 (92)	232.88 (21)	1.92 (85)
TEKTRONIX INC	A /A	5/77	146.64q(10)	245.18q(5)	16.04 (32)	568.00 (2)	3.68 (7)
HORMEL (GEO.A.) & CO	A /A	10/77	120.33q(11)	205.84q(11)	14.31 (51)	280.78 (11)	2.04 (72)
OWENS-CORNING FIBERGLAS CORP	A /A	12/77	119.69q(12)	162.81q(28)	20.28 (10)	148.55 (59)	1.96 (82)
HOOVER UNIVERSAL INC	A /A	7/77	118.70 (13)	131.22 (43)	24.37 (2)	207.05 (29)	2.00 (76)
HANNA MINING CO	A /A	12/77	111.12q(14)	229.89q(7)	12.80 (70)	176.40 (44)	1.99 (79)
JOY MFG CO	A /A	9/77	107.41q(15)	126.99q(50)	13.92 (58)	474.56 (3)	3.23 (14)
FEDERAL-MOGUL CORP	A /A	12/77	106.16q(16)	152.84q(34)	15.78 (35)	305.96 (9)	3.08 (17)
COLONIAL STORES INC	A /A	12/77	92.36q(17)	90.19q(86)	10.42 (99)	214.86 (26)	2.26 (56)
DENNISON MFG CO	A /A	12/77	91.99q(18)	186.28v(15)	14.81 (49)	244.30 (18)	2.78 (24)
HARSCO CORP	A /A	12/77	90.37q(19)	155.99q(33)	16.67 (30)	244.61 (17)	3.91 (3)
IDEAL BASIC INDUSTRIES INC	A /A	12/77	86.88q(20)	107.22q(73)	13.14 (66)	134.69 (66)	3.28 (11)
VULCAN MATERIALS CO	A /A	12/77	81.86q(21)	128.00q(49)	17.77 (22)	98.35 (87)	2.41 (45)
SCOTT & FETZER CO	A /A	11/77	80.39 (22)	273.63 (3)	20.10 (11)	299.22 (10)	3.70 (6)
NCR CORP	A /A	12/77	79.73q(23)	198.38q(12)	14.02 (55)	168.24 (47)	2.24 (57)
MARTIN MARIETTA CORP	A /A	12/77	78.38q(24)	150.69q(37)	14.07 (54)	129.52 (67)	1.88 (88)
RELIANCE ELECTRIC CO	A /A	10/77	77.62q(25)	166.26q(24)	18.64 (16)	235.05 (19)	2.50 (40)
NORTON CO	A /A	12/77	77.41q(26)	115.97q(62)	11.90 (84)	272.06 (14)	2.48 (41)
REXNORD INC	A /A	10/77	76.98q(27)	179.21q(20)	15.55 (39)	234.16 (20)	2.67 (34)
COMBUSTION ENGINEERING INC	A /A	12/77	76.90q(28)	165.19q(25)	15.12 (43)	62.47 (104)	1.09 (122)
BIG THREE INDUSTRIES	A /A	12/77	76.80q(29)	58.97v(112)	15.69 (36)	64.42 (102)	2.31 (51)
CUMMINS ENGINE	A /A-	12/77	75.70q(30)	142.47q(39)	17.35 (25)	167.71 (48)	1.99 (78)

SINGLE A COMPANIES	RATINGS	FYR END	Cash Flow LTD %	N Cash Fl Cap Exp %	After Tax ROE %	Work Cap LTD %	Current Ratio x
QUAKER OATS CO	A /A+	6/77	75.35q(31)	125.07q(52)	14.82 (48)	153.58 (54)	2.03 (73)
BENDIX CORP	A /A	9/77	73.65q(32)	106.45q(75)	13.97 (57)	201.96 (34)	1.77 (97)
GREAT NORTHERN NEKOOSA CORP	A /A+	12/77	72.03q(33)	131.10q(45)	12.17 (80)	104.00 (80)	3.02 (21)
BAKER INTERNATIONAL CORP	A /A	9/77	70.57q(34)	122.71q(56)	18.18 (20)	190.16 (38)	2.83 (27)
LUCKY STORES INC	A /A	1/78	69.62q(35)	113.06q(67)	21.79 (6)	121.49 (73)	1.54 (107)
DART INDUSTRIES	A /A	12/77	68.72q(36)	152.51q(35)	12.43 (74)	206.89 (30)	2.90 (22)
ASSD DRY GOODS CORP	A /A+	1/78	68.49q(37)	70.92v(107)	8.76 (106)	202.97 (33)	2.10 (66)
NORTH AMERICAN PHILIPS CORP	A /A	12/77	67.59 (38)	136.64 (41)	13.33 (63)	334.94 (7)	2.86 (26)
PITNEY-BOWES INC	A /A	12/77	67.32q(39)	113.22v(66)	18.38 (18)	113.46 (75)	1.66 (103)
QUAKER STATE OIL REFINING	A /A	12/77	66.96q(40)	76.64q(104)	13.66 (60)	77.19 (95)	2.38 (46)
STANLEY WORKS	A /A	12/77	66.74q(41)	176.91q(22)	13.49 (62)	247.47 (15)	3.04 (20)
SPERRY RAND CORP	A /A	3/78	66.11q(42)	135.37q(42)	12.31 (77)	151.71 (56)	1.71 (99)
MERCANTILE STORES CC INC	A /A	1/78	65.93q(43)	108.08q(72)	12.46 (73)	219.41 (24)	2.70 (33)
WITCO CHEMICAL CORP	A /A	12/77	64.12q(44)	121.26q(59)	13.52 (61)	167.52 (49)	2.50 (39)
BUCYRUS-ERIE CO	A /A+	12/77	64.01q(45)	213.85q(10)	18.48 (17)	201.87 (35)	1.90 (87)
REVLON INC	A /A+	12/77	63.74q(46)	262.24q(4)	18.31 (19)	227.07 (23)	2.30 (54)
AMERICAN BROADCASTING	A /A	12/77	63.64q(47)	176.96q(21)	21.79 (7)	208.45 (28)	2.77 (29)
DRESSER INDUSTRIES INC	A /A	10/77	63.62q(48)	182.35q(18)	17.16 (26)	198.70 (36)	2.31 (52)
TRW INC	A /A	12/77	63.12q(49)	161.67q(29)	15.03 (45)	139.29 (68)	1.78 (96)
GENERAL MILLS INC	A /A	5/77	63.09q(50)	115.41q(64)	16.15 (31)	107.99 (78)	1.72 (98)
TEXTRON INC	A /A	12/77	62.48q(51)	190.36q(14)	15.57 (37)	245.54 (16)	2.50 (38)
HARRIS CORP	A /A	6/77	59.91q(52)	115.90v(63)	17.40 (24)	204.84 (32)	1.82 (91)
HUDSON BAY MINING & SMELT-A	A /A	12/77	59.46q(53)	92.53q(85)	1.73 (120)	194.19 (37)	3.62 (9)
GOULD INC	A /A	12/77	59.28q(54)	171.47v(23)	15.17 (42)	164.45 (50)	2.33 (50)
RCA CORP	A /A	12/77	58.91q(55)	100.07q(78)	17.04 (28)	90.71 (88)	1.70 (101)
GARDNER-DENVER CO	.A /A+	12/77	58.61q(56)	230.23q(6)	9.11 (103)	308.05 (8)	4.31 (2)
BROCKWAY GLASS CC	A /A	12/77	57.41q(57)	125.35q(51)	10.97 (95)	85.70 (90)	2.33 (49)
AMERICAN CAN CO	A /A	12/77	56.24 (58)	130.42 (46)	11.82 (86)	170.12 (46)	1.99 (77)
MASCO CORP	A /A	12/77	55.63q(59)	219.64q(9)	19.11 (15)	161.43 (51)	4.34 (1)
CITIES SERVICE CO	A /A	12/77	55.60q(60)	87.73q(88)	10.85 (96)	48.99 (110)	1.82 (92)

SINGLE A COMPANIES	RATINGS	FYR END	Cash Flow LTD %	N Cash Fl Cap Exp %	After Tax ROE %	Work Cap LTD %	Current Ratio x
ROCKWELL INTL CORP	A /A	9/77	52.20q(61)	99.49q(79)	10.97 (94)	144.29 (61)	1.49 (112)
CARRIER CORP	A /A-	10/77	51.69q(62)	158.33q(31)	14.88 (47)	178.80 (42)	2.05 (71)
EATON CORP	A /A	12/77	51.51q(63)	181.43q(19)	14.15 (53)	174.45 (45)	2.76 (30)
HERCULES INC	A /A	12/77	51.09q(64)	98.79q(80)	7.65 (112)	99.42 (85)	2.20 (60)
SUNBEAM CORP	A /A	3/78	50.88q(65)	124.16q(53)	13.05 (69)	228.82 (22)	2.23 (58)
STAUFFER CHEMICAL CO	A /A	12/77	50.51q(66)	89.32q(87)	17.14 (27)	84.67 (91)	2.73 (32)
CROWN ZELLERBACH	A /A	12/77	49.74q(67)	110.25q(70)	12.28 (78)	84.10 (92)	2.31 (53)
CLARK EQUIPMENT CO	A /A	12/77	49.18q(68)	92.74q(84)	12.21 (79)	148.55 (60)	2.17 (65)
NL INDUSTRIES	A /A	12/77	49.01q(69)	77.99q(101)	10.05 (101)	135.42 (65)	2.20 (61)
INTL MINERALS & CHEMICAL	A /A	6/77	48.91q(70)	83.12q(94)	16.80 (29)	65.87 (100)	1.99 (81)
NATIONAL DISTILLERS &CHEMICL	A /A	12/77	48.48q(71)	83.69q(93)	11.89 (85)	209.34 (27)	2.88 (25)
ASHLAND OIL INC	A /A	9/77	48.41q(72)	53.58q(116)	17.62 (23)	55.75 (108)	1.55 (106)
MARYLAND CUP CORP	A /A	9/77	48.23q(73)	111.50q(68)	13.10 (67)	124.82 (71)	3.75 (4)
BROWN GROUP INC	A /A	10/77	48.07.(74)	225.54 (8)	11.75 (87)	272.13 (13)	3.38 (10)
BURLINGTON INDUSTRIES INC	A /A	9/77	48.00q(75)	81.10q(97)	8.95 (105)	156.11 (53)	3.27 (12)
DAYTON-HUDSON CORP	A /A	1/78	47.65q(76)	80.47q(98)	15.81 (34)	101.50 (83)	1.56 (104)
PET INC	A /A	3/77	47.00q(77)	163.92q(26)	9.50 (102)	187.10 (39)	3.08 (18)
STALEY (A.E.) MFG CO	A /A	9/77	46.85q(78)	46.74q(117)	11.36 (90)	29.03 (116)	1.26 (119)
FMC CORP	A /A	12/77	46.12 (79)	102.78 (77)	13.08 (68)	113.30 (76)	1.80 (94)
COPPERWELD CORP	A /A	12/77	46.02q(80)	45.46q(120)	12.48 (72)	137.29 (64)	2.21 (59)
BOISE CASCADE CORP	A /A	12/77	45.48q(81)	87.21q(89)	12.10 (81)	63.66 (103)	1.80 (93)
DIAMOND SHAMROCK CORP	A /A	12/77	45.37q(82)	58.98q(111)	20.02 (12)	43.33 (114)	1.99 (80)
MARATHON OIL CO	A /A+	12/77	45.36q(83)	81.27q(96)	15.31 (41)	7.02 (123)	1.08 (123)
CARTER HAWLEY HALE STORES	A .	1/78	45.30q(84)	72.53q(105)	10.32 (100)	150.74 (58)	2.35 (47)
WESTVACO CORP	A /A	10/77	45.12q(85)	81.93q(95)	13.28 (64)	89.35 (89)	3.26 (13)
SCHLITZ (JOSEPH) BREWING	A /A	12/77	43.47q(86)	184.06q(17)	5.54 (116)	24.27 (119)	1.55 (105)
SYBRON CORP	A /A	12/77	42.77q(87)	142.18q(40)	11.14 (91)	217.00 (25)	3.17 (15)
STANDARD BRANDS INC	A /A	12/77	42.43q(88)	131.21q(44)	14.01 (56)	122.86 (72)	1.91 (86)
ROHM & HAAS CO	A /A	12/77	42.27q(89)	129.64q(47)	8.64 (107)	103.93 (81)	2.60 (37)
SOUTHLAND CCRP	A /A	12/77	41.55q(90)	59.07q(110)	13.73 (59)	64.97 (101)	1.79 (95)
GREYHOUND CORP	A /A	12/77	41.51q(91)	58.74q(113)	12.00 (83)	47.03 (111)	1.47 (115)
FIRESTONE TIRE & RUBBER CO	A /A+	10/77	41.36q(92)	108.44q(71)	6.81 (113)	138.30 (63)	2.02 (74)
MORTON-NORWICH PRODUCTS	A /A	6/77	40.84q(93)	128.33q(48)	13.18 (65)	138.45 (62)	3.16 (16)

	RATINGS	FYR END	Cash Flow LTD %	N Cash Fl Cap Exp %	After Tax ROE %	Work Cap LTD %	Current Ratio x
PILLSBURY CO	A /A	5/77	40.75q(94)	77.21q(102)	14.92 (46)	77.84 (94)	1.50 (111)
ESMARK INC	A /A	10/77	40.66q(95)	122.60q(57)	8.96 (104)	105.57 (79)	2.08 (70)
CUTLER-HAMMER INC	A /A	12/77	40.64q(96)	185.00q(16)	15.09 (44)	153.04 (55)	2.67 (35)
INTL TELEPHONE & TELEGRAPH	A /A	12/77	40.19q(97)	84.87q(91)	11.05 (93)	74.08 (97)	1.48 (113)
PENNWALT CORP	A /A	12/77	40.00q(98)	107.12q(74)	12.32 (76)	125.59 (70)	2.66 (36)
AVERY INTERNATIONAL	A /A	11/77	39.93q(99)	158.11q(32)	11.55 (89)	150.97 (57)	2.47 (44)
OWENS-ILLINOIS INC	A /A	12/77	39.63q(100)	87.18q(90)	8.41 (109)	68.95 (98)	2.01 (75)
SEAGRAM CO LTD	A /A	7/77	39.41q(101)	163.55q(27)	8.51 (108)	176.72 (43)	3.64 (8)
ALLIED CHEMICAL CORP	A /A	12/77	38.69q(102)	57.90q(115)	11.56 (88)	40.17 (115)	1.69 (102)
WOOLWORTH (F.W.) CO	A /A	1/78	38.03q(103)	116.16q(61)	7.88 (110)	156.42 (52)	2.29 (55)
REPUBLIC STEEL CORP	A /A	12/77	37.50q(104)	84.31q(92)	3.08 (119)	99.57 (84)	2.17 (64)
TENNECO INC	A /A	12/77	37.24q(105)	97.09q(81)	14.29 (52)	23.74 (120)	1.27 (118)
GOODYEAR TIRE & RUBBER CO	A /A	12/77	37.14q(106)	114.60q(65)	10.43 (98)	110.17 (77)	1.96 (83)
HEUBLEIN INC	A /A	6/77	36.32 (107)	80.04 (99)	12.60 (71)	18.70 (74)	2.09 (67)
WARNER COMMUNICATIONS INC	A /A	12/77	33.64q(108)	58.57q(30)	20.30 (9)	58.68 (106)	1.47 (114)
ALUMINUM CO OF AMERICA	A /A	12/77	33.52q(109)	21.55q(58)	10.78 (97)	57.21 (107)	2.19 (63)
MEAD CORP	A /A	12/77	33.39q(110)	95.80q(82)	16.02 (33)	51.23 (109)	1.71 (100)
AMAX INC	A /A+	12/77	33.08q(111)	46.53q(118)	3.36 (118)	60.53 (105)	2.48 (42)
PHILIP MORRIS INC	A /A	12/77	31.11q(112)	118.93q(60)	19.84 (14)	99.25 (86)	2.76 (31)
HARRAH'S	NR /A	6/77	30.91q(113)	79.46q(100)	15.56 (36)	24.28 (118)	2.33 (48)
MCDONALD'S CORP	A /A	12/77	30.84q(114)	68.32q(108)	21.26 (8)	-0.98 (124)	0.97 (124)
SAFEWAY STORES INC	A /A	12/77	30.53q(115)	63.03q(109)	12.06 (82)	20.49 (121)	1.20 (121)
ARMCO STEEL CORP	A /A	12/77	26.95q(116)	77.07q(103)	7.78 (111)	74.10 (96)	1.83 (90)
LIGGETT GROUP	A /A	12/77	26.62q(117)	123.13q(55)	0.30 (122)	186.59 (40)	3.72 (5)
CENTRAL SOYA CO	A /A	8/77	25.10q(118)	58.06q(114)	5.21 (117)	182.25 (41)	2.89 (24)
TEXASGULF INC	A /A+	12/77	24.23q(119)	29.40q(122)	6.16 (114)	68.15 (99)	2.90 (23)
INCO LTD	A /A	12/77	22.86q(120)	30.56q(121)	5.91 (115)	81.03 (93)	2.19 (62)
HOSPITAL CORP OF AMERICA	NR /A	12/77	22.49q(121)	71.59q(106)	15.50 (40)	10.75 (122)	1.41 (116)
PHELPS DODGE CORP	A /A-	12/77	16.47 (122)	46.16 (119)	1.39 (121)	24.65 (117)	1.53 (109)
ASARCO INC	A /A-	12/77	11.24q(123)	26.60q(123)	-3.65 (123)	43.91 (113)	1.87 (89)
BETHLEHEM STEEL CORP	A /A	12/77	6.43q(124)	1.65q(124)	-20.57 (124)	44.79 (112)	1.53 (108)

			Cash Flow LTD	N Cash Fl Cap Exp	After Tax ROE	Work Cap LTD	Current Ratio
AVERAGE			67.61	126.19	13.22	158.68	2.29
MEDIAN			51.60	115.94	13.41	138.38	2.19

			Pretax Coverage	Aft Tax Coverage	Aft Tax Coverage (inc rent)	Ret on Total Assets	Net Inc ---------- Net Sales
SPLIT A/BBB RATED COMPANIES	RATINGS	FYR END	x	x	x	%	%
ALLIS-CHALMERS CORP	Baa/A-	12/77	9.91 (1)	5.87 (1)	NA (-)	11.47 (10)	4.36 (7)
FERRO CORP	Baa/A	12/77	9.17 (2)	5.41 (2)	NA (-)	16.87 (2)	4.98 (3)
OCCIDENTAL PETROLEUM CORP	A /BBB	12/77	8.551(3)	2.86p(14)	2.17p(6)	24.541(1)	3.62 (10)
UMC INDUSTRIES	A /BBB	12/77	7.76 (4)	4.41 (4)	2.73 (2)	15.78 (3)	4.42 (6)
MALLORY (G.C.) & CO	Baa/A	12/77	7.60 (5)	4.54 (3)	2.43 (5)	13.01 (7)	3.97 (8)
U S SHOE CORP	Baa/A	7/77	6.87 (6)	4.00 (6)	1.72 (13)	14.12 (4)	3.16 (13)
OUTBOARD MARINE CORP	A /BBB	9/77	6.46 (7)	4.03 (5)	2.71 (4)	13.83 (6)	4.73 (4)
COLT INDUSTRIES INC	Baa/A	12/77	6.27 (8)	3.91 (7)	2.73 (3)	13.90 (5)	4.55 (5)
AMERICAN STORES CO	A /BBB+	3/77	6.15 (9)	3.72 (10)	1.49 (14)	9.90 (13)	0.75 (21)
KROGER CO	A /BBB	12/77	6.06 (10)	3.83 (8)	1.48 (15)	9.06 (16)	0.90 (20)
MACMILLAN INC	Baa/A-	12/77	5.28 (11)	3.19 (11)	1.77 (12)	9.04 (17)	3.78 (. 9)
CHAMPION INTL CORP	A /BBB+	12/77	5.22 (12)	3.74 (9)	2.93 (1)	2.45 (9)	5.17 (2)
NATIONAL CAN CORP	Baa/A-	12/77	4.91p(13)	3.08p(12)	2.07p(7)	1.34 (12)	2.59 (15)
INTERLAKE INC	A /BBB+	12/77	4.65 (14)	3.02 (13)	NA (-)	7.39 (20)	2.44 (17)
MURPHY (G.C.) CO	Baa/A	1/78	4.21 (15)	2.73 (16)	1.30 (16)	8.47 (18)	1.42 (19)
MISSOURI PACIFIC CORP	Baa/A-	12/77	3.71 (16)	2.78 (15)	1.86 (10)	13.00 (8)	7.61 (1)
GOODRICH (B.F.) CO	A /BBB	12/77	3.46 (17)	2.46 (18)	1.78 (11)	9.18 (14)	2.70 (14)
LONE STAR INDUSTRIES	Baa/A	12/77	3.17p(18)	2.56p(17)	2.04p(8)	9.07 (15)	3.45 (11)
INTL HARVESTER CO	A /BBB	10/77	3.14 (19)	2.12 (21)	NA (-)	11.43 (11)	3.37 (12)
STOKELY-VAN CAMP INC	A /BBB	5/77	2.98 (20)	2.16 (20)	NA (-)	8.08 (19)	1.56 (18)
ALLEGHENY LUDLUM INDS	A /BBB	12/77	2.95 (21)	2.39 (19)	1.88 (9)	4.79 (21)	2.54 (16)
KENNECOTT COPPER CORP	A /BBB	12/77	0.74 (22)	1.01 (22)	1.01 (17)	1.27 (22)	0.03 (22)
AVERAGE			5.42	3.35	2.01	11.27	3.28
MEDIAN			5.25	3.13	1.88	11.38	3.41

			LTD --- Cap	STD --- Cap	LTD ------ Net Pt.	NTA --- LTD	Tot Liab ---------- Tot Eqty
SPLIT A/BBB RATED COMPANIES	RATINGS	FYR END	%	%	%	%	%
FERRO CORP	Baa/A	12/77	11.03 (1)	3.84 (12)	27.33 (1)	885.52 (1)	60.76 (1)
ALLIS-CHALMERS CORP	Baa/A-	12/77	21.28 (2)	5.81 (16)	48.44 (8)	456.81 (2)	120.09 (14)
INTERLAKE INC	A /BBB+	12/77	21.65 (3)	3.11 (9)	39.78 (4)	436.88 (3)	81.44 (4)
MALLORY (P.R.) & CO	Baa/A	12/77	22.17 (4)	13.64 (22)	56.53 (11)	396.87 (4)	94.21 (7)
OUTBOARD MARINE CORP	A /BBB	9/77	25.22 (5)	5.13 (15)	57.88 (12)	354.48 (7)	78.69 (3)
MURPHY (G.C.) CO	Baa/A	1/78	26.28 (6)	0.35 (2)	51.51 (10)	362.01 (6)	107.39 (11)
UMC INDUSTRIES	A /BBB	12/77	26.32 (7)	3.14 (10)	108.52 (19)	372.58 (5)	77.26 (2)
KENNECOTT COPPER CORP	A /BBB	12/77	26.98 (8)	9.51 (20)	39.10 (3)	350.58 (8)	91.71 (6)
MACMILLAN INC	Baa/A-	12/77	28.22 (9)	3.39 (11)	170.41 (22)	246.60 (20)	96.32 (9)
AMERICAN STORES CO	A /BBB+	3/77	29.07 (10)	2.55 (7)	51.33 (9)	342.25 (9)	131.87 (17)
KROGER CO	A /BBB	12/77	30.74 (11)	0.82 (3)	48.29 (7)	316.44 (10)	186.73 (21)
OCCIDENTAL PETROLEUM CORP	A /BBB	12/77	31.33 (12)	3.86 (13)	27.40 (2)	306.56 (11)	150.92 (20)
STOKELY-VAN CAMP INC	A /BBB	5/77	32.61 (13)	0.02 (1)	103.38 (18)	296.95 (12)	85.08 (5)
U S SHOE CORP	Baa/A	7/77	33.67 (14)	7.62 (18)	129.41 (21)	282.64 (15)	106.82 (10)
INTL HARVESTER CO	A /BBB	10/77	34.82 (15)	10.99 (21)	120.11 (20)	284.35 (13)	118.49 (13)
GOODRICH (B.F.) CO	A /BBB	12/77	34.97 (16)	2.34 (6)	61.98 (14)	284.34 (14)	116.51 (12)
CHAMPION INTL CORP	A /BBB+	12/77	35.22 (17)	2.95 (8)	47.66 (6)	260.81 (16)	96.03 (8)
LONE STAR INDUSTRIES	Baa/A	12/77	37.07 (18)	1.32 (4)	46.09 (5)	255.08 (18)	124.61 (16)
COLT INDUSTRIES INC	Baa/A	12/77	37.44 (19)	4.61 (14)	85.57 (16)	250.14 (19)	120.86 (15)
NATIONAL CAN CORP	Baa/A-	12/77	37.69 (20)	9.41 (19)	71.23 (15)	257.24 (17)	146.25 (19)
ALLEGHENY LUDLUM INDS	A /BBB	12/77	46.02 (21)	2.24 (5)	93.53 (17)	213.75 (21)	143.13 (18)
MISSOURI PACIFIC CORP	Baa/A-	12/77	62.14 (22)	5.90 (17)	60.29 (13)	155.66 (22)	275.48 (22)
AVERAGE			31.45	4.66	70.26	334.93	118.67
MEDIAN			31.03	3.61		301.75	111.95

SPLIT A/BBB RATED COMPANIES	RATINGS	FYR END	Cash Flow LTD %	N Cash Fl Cap Exp %	After Tax ROE %	Work Cap LTD %	Current Ratio x
FERRO CORP	Baa/A	12/77	152.80q(1)	118.24q(10)	13.19 (2)	542.65 (1)	2.58 (9)
OCCIDENTAL PETROLEUM CORP	A /BBB	12/77	81.29q(2)	80.89q(19)	11.62 (11)	46.98 (21)	1.44 (21)
ALLIS-CHALMERS CORP	Baa/A-	12/77	68.28q(3)	115.30q(13)	12.77 (4)	157.88 (11)	1.51 (20)
OUTBOARD MARINE CORP	A /BBB	9/77	67.43 (4)	153.35 (4)	11.58 (12)	213.98.(4)	3.12 (3)
MALLORY (P.R.) & CO	Baa/A	12/77	65.57 (5)	79.25 (20)	11.42 (13)	206.24 (5)	1.92 (16)
AMERICAN STORES CO	A /BBB+	3/77	58.84q(6)	136.37q(6)	10.14 (14)	164.67 (10)	1.82 (18)
KROGER CO	A /BBB	12/77	57.54q(7)	109.33q(14)	12.30 (8)	136.35 (14)	1.53 (19)
UMC INDUSTRIES	A /BBB	12/77	47.33q(8)	205.01q(2)	12.31 (7)	279.03 (2)	3.52 (2)
INTERLAKE INC	A /BBB+	12/77	45.22q(9)	84.43q(18)	6.07 (19)	165.06 (9)	2.03 (14)
CHAMPION INTL CORP	A /BBB+	12/77	43.21 (10)	91.33 (17)	12.52 (6)	65.02 (20)	2.25 (11)
MURPHY (G.C.) CO	Baa/A	1/78	40.93 (11)	124.40 (8)	7.22 (18,	204.26 (6)	2.24 (12)
GOODRICH (B.F.) CO	A /BBB	12/77	39.43q(12)	140.05q(5)	7.65 (16)	134.09 (15)	2.54 (10)
COLT INDUSTRIES INC	Baa/A	12/77	37.98q(13)	195.60q(3)	12.98 (3)	157.01 (12)	3.01 (4)
U S SHOE CORP	Baa/A	7/77	35.44q(14)	117.94q(11)	12.75 (5)	203.39 (7)	3.01 (5)
MACMILLAN INC	Baa/A-	12/77	35.32q(15)	409.20q(1)	7.41 (17)	197.75 (8)	2.59 (8)
NATIONAL CAN CORP	Baa/A-	12/77	35.19 (16)	116.40 (12)	12.18 (9)	111.77 (16)	1.98 (15)
LONE STAR INDUSTRIES	Baa/A	12/77	34.61q(17)	46.06q(21)	9.95 (15)	89.71 (18)	2.60 (7)
MISSOURI PACIFIC CORP	Baa/A-	12/77	25.55q(18)	96.52q(16)	23.38 (1)	10.96 (22)	1.26 (22)
INTL HARVESTER CO	A /BBB	10/77	25.18 (19)	106.80 (15)	11.66 (10)	137.77 (13)	2.22 (13)
STOKELY-VAN CAMP INC	A /BBB	5/77	23.77q(20)	118.35q(9)	5.53 (21)	216.50 (3)	4.64 (1)
ALLEGHENY LUDLUM INDS	A /BBB	12/77	19.54q(21)	125.27q(7)	5.76 (20)	92.14 (17)	2.64 (6)
KENNECOTT COPPER CORP	A /BBB	12/77	5.81 (22)	7.12 (22)	0.02 (22)	84.91 (19)	1.84 (17)
AVERAGE			47.56	126.24	10.47	164.46	2.38
MEDIAN			40.18	117.17	11.60	157.45	2.25

Baa/BBB COMPANIES	RATINGS	FYR END	Pretax Coverage x	Aft Tax Coverage x	Aft Tax Coverage (inc rent) x	Ret on Total Assets %	Net Inc Net Sales %
DATA GENERAL CORP	Baa/BBB	9/77	240.65 (1)	125.80 (1)	9.14 (1)	20.16 (5)	11.22 (3)
TELEDYNE INC	Baa/BBB	12/77	19.96 (2)	10.56 (2)	NA (-)	26.12 (2)	8.78 (6)
NATOMAS CO	Baa/BBB	12/77	18.84h(3)	6.62h(5)	4.85h(2)	32.03h(1)	12.84 (1)
REEVES BROTHERS INC	Baa/BBB	6/77	15.64 (4)	8.28 (3)	3.43 (4)	14.34 (9)	3.80 (19)
IOWA BEEF PROCESSORS	Baa/BBB	10/77	13.28 (5)	7.71 (4)	NA (-)	21.38 (4)	1.48 (35)
ARVIN INDUSTRIES INC	Baa/BBB	12/77	8.28 (6)	4.78 (6)	NA (-)	24.75 (3)	6.30 (8)
HILTON HOTELS CORP	NR /BBB	12/77	7.07 (7)	4.71 (7)	3.52 (3)	14.37 (8)	10.78 (4)
HART SCHAFFNER & MARX CO	Baa/BBB	11/77	6.59 (8)	3.84 (9)	3.84 (9)	10.65 (25)	2.73 (28)
U S INDUSTRIES	Baa/BBB	12/77	6.02p(9)	3.22p(17)	1.91p(21)	12.80 (13)	3.22 (26)
INTL MULTIFOODS CORP	Baa/BBB	2/78	5.98p(10)	3.82p(10)	2.02p(17)	14.00 (10)	2.73 (29)
KIDDE (WALTER) & CO	Baa/BBB	12/77	5.95 (11)	3.67 (13)	2.41 (10)	11.90 (18)	3.85 (18)
UV INDUSTRIES INC	Baa/BBB	12/77	5.93 (12)	3.59 (15)	2.87 (6)	15.32 (6)	6.51 (7)
BEMIS CO	Baa/BBB	12/77	5.29 (13)	3.59 (14)	2.80 (7)	10.08 (26)	2.64 (31)
METRO-GOLDWYN-MAYER INC	Baa/BBB	8/77	5.06h(14)	3.68h(12)	3.36h(5)	14.67h(7)	11.50 (2)
AMF INC	Baa/BBB	12/77	4.87 (15)	3.05 (19)	2.06 (16)	12.28 (14)	3.48 (23)
ARMSTRONG RUBBER	Baa/BBB	9/77	4.80 (16)	3.05 (18)	2.18 (15)	11.81 (19)	4.06 (16)
BROWNING-FERRIS INDS	Baa/BBB+	9/77	4.74 (17)	2.99 (21)	2.33 (11)	13.94 (11)	5.60 (10)
GENERAL PORTLAND INC	Baa/BBB	12/77	4.72 (18)	3.33 (16)	2.20 (13)	8.21 (31)	4.03 (17)
HOLIDAY INNS INC	NR /BBB	12/77	4.39 (19)	2.96 (22)	1.81 (25)	11.31 (23)	5.12 (13)
AMERICAN AIRLINES INC	Baa/BBB	12/77	4.39 (20)	4.39 (8)	1.42 (32)	5.14 (36)	3.59 (20)
FLINTKOTE CO	Baa/BBB	12/77	4.38p(21)	2.99p(20)	1.84p(23)	9.55 (27)	3.54 (21)
CRANE CO	Baa/BBB	12/77	4.35 (22)	3.81 (11)	2.58 (8)	12.23 (15)	5.84 (9)
SCM CORP	Baa/BBB	6/77	4.26 (23)	2.76 (25)	1.76 (27)	11.80 (20)	2.72 (30)
CASTLE & COOKE INC	Baa/BBB	12/77	4.07 (24)	2.92 (23)	1.82 (24)	11.92 (17)	4.54 (14)
SIGNAL COS	Baa/BBB	12/77	4.02 (25)	2.59 (27)	2.19 (14)	11.08 (24)	3.42 (24)
WICKES CORP	Baa/BBB	1/78	3.89 (26)	2.51 (30)	1.70 (28)	11.65 (22)	1.85 (33)
PENNZOIL CO	Baa/BBB	12/77	3.74h(27)	2.83h(24)	2.42h(9)	11.79h(21)	9.26 (5)
WALTER (JIM) CORP	Baa/BBB	8/77	3.64 (28)	2.47 (32)	2.28 (12)	12.08 (16)	5.58 (11)
FEDERAL PAPER BOARD CO	Baa/BBB	12/77	3.63 (29)	2.73 (26)	1.97 (19)	9.10 (29)	3.48 (22)
GAF CORP	Baa/BBB	12/77	3.59 (30)	2.49 (31)	1.87 (22)	9.14 (28)	2.83 (27)

		Pretax Coverage	Aft Tax Coverage	Aft Tax Coverage (inc rent)	Ret on Total Assets	Net Inc / Net Sales
Baa/BBB COMPANIES	RATINGS FYR END	x	x	x	%	%
PULLMAN INC	Baa/BBB 12/77	3.58 (31)	2.58 (28)	1.53 (31)	5.99 (34)	1.64 (34)
REICHHOLD CHEMICALS INC	Baa/BBB+ 12/77	3.56p(32)	2.56p(29)	1.93p(20)	7.77 (33)	2.03 (32)
FRUEHAUF CORP	Baa/BBB 12/77	3.23 (33)	2.14 (33)	1.99 (18)	13.12 (12)	3.39 (25)
WILLIAMS COS	Baa/BBB 12/77	2.67p(34)	2.12p(34)	1.77p(26)	8.50 (30)	5.27 (12)
GULF & WESTERN INDS INC	Baa/BBB 7/77	2.47 (35)	2.04 (35)	1.69 (29)	8.08 (32)	4.13 (15)
CHRYSLER CORP	Baa/BBB- 12/77	1.90 (36)	1.44 (37)	NA (-)	5.48 (35)	0.75 (38)
AKZONA	Baa/BBB 12/77	1.41 (37)	1.46 (36)	1.27 (33)	3.45 (37)	0.93 (37)
CYPRUS MINES CORP	Baa/BBB 12/77	0.89 (38)	1.04 (38)	NA (-)	3.27 (38)	1.48 (36)
SHERWIN-WILLIAMS CO	Baa/BBB- 12/77	0.40 (39)	0.60 (39)	0.86 (34)	0.99 (39)	-0.79 (39)
AVERAGE		11.59	6.61	2.39	12.11	4.52
MEDIAN		4.39	2.99	2.00	11.80	3.59

		LTD / Cap	STD / Cap	LTD / Net Pt.	NTA / LTD	Tot Liab / Tot Eqty
Baa/BBB COMPANIES	RATINGS FYR END	%	%	%	%	%
U S INDUSTRIES	Baa/BBB 12/77	17.15 (1)	1.74 (13)	60.00 (15)	471.73 (1)	64.37 (2)
PULLMAN INC	Baa/BBB 12/77	22.35 (2)	7.99 (34)	59.51 (14)	441.63 (2)	173.88 (35)
NATOMAS CO	Baa/BBB 12/77	23.16 (3)	4.94 (24)	24.85 (1)	415.36 (3)	85.66 (6)
GENERAL PORTLAND INC	Baa/BBB 12/77	24.16 (4)	0.93 (6)	43.68 (3)	339.60 (4)	57.34 (1)
HART SCHAFFNER & MARX CO	Baa/BBB 11/77	24.66 (5)	5.02 (25)	107.03 (33)	398.81 (4)	80.39 (5)
REEVES BROTHERS INC	Baa/BBB 6/77	26.71 (6)	0.63 (5)	78.82 (24)	372.48 (5)	73.32 (4)
IOWA BEEF PROCESSORS	Baa/BBB 10/77	26.72 (7)	2.71 (15)	47.84 (10)	366.65 (6)	70.65 (3)
BEMIS CO	Baa/BBB 12/77	27.71 (8)	1.68 (11)	43.90 (4)	336.28 (9)	92.67 (9)
DATA GENERAL CORP	Baa/BBB 9/77	28.96 (9)	0.00 (1)	161.19 (38)	345.30 (7)	87.10 (7)
REICHHOLD CHEMICALS INC	Baa/BBB+ 12/77	29.08 (10)	6.03 (28)	45.26 (5)	334.83 (10)	102.87 (13)
INTL MULTIFOODS CORP	Baa/BBB 2/78	29.18 (11)	5.19 (26)	77.74 (23)	309.50 (11)	97.82 (12)
CHRYSLER CORP	Baa/BBB- 12/77	29.99 (12)	8.22 (35)	71.41 (18)	270.68 (15)	162.20 (31)
FLINTKOTE CO	Baa/BBB 12/77	31.01 (13)	1.67 (10)	45.67 (7)	305.56 (13)	94.58 (11)
TELEDYNE INC	Baa/BBB 12/77	31.44 (14)	0.52 (3)	128.61 (37)	305.98 (12)	107.87 (15)
SIGNAL COS	Baa/BBB 12/77	33.06 (15)	3.88 (22)	100.87 (31)	293.41 (14)	146.27 (28)
GAF CORP	Baa/BBB 12/77	36.79 (16)	7.56 (32)	72.97 (21)	253.41 (21)	131.27 (22)
AMF INC	Baa/BBB 12/77	36.83 (17)	8.33 (36)	80.26 (26)	250.71 (22)	142.32 (27)
SCM CORP	Baa/BBB 6/77	36.92 (18)	6.22 (29)	71.47 (19)	268.35 (16)	123.46 (18)
FEDERAL PAPER BOARD CO	Baa/BBB 12/77	37.33 (19)	0.55 (4)	46.38 (8)	266.89 (17)	93.74 (10)
AMERICAN AIRLINES INC	Baa/BBB 12/77	37.39 (20)	2.28 (14)	45.66 (6)	256.19 (19)	157.99 (30)
HOLIDAY INNS INC	NR /BBB 12/77	38.06 (21)	3.59 (19)	42.43 (2)	255.91 (20)	105.94 (14)
AKZONA	Baa/BBB 12/77	38.09 (22)	6.40 (31)	49.35 (12)	257.22 (18)	124.76 (19)
KIDDE (WALTER) & CO	Baa/BBB 12/77	38.23 (23)	2.85 (16)	172.17 (39)	235.00 (26)	114.90 (17)
ARVIN INDUSTRIES INC	Baa/BBB 12/77	39.06 (24)	1.57 (9)	102.38 (32)	247.84 (23)	90.25 (8)
CASTLE & COOKE INC	Baa/BBB 12/77	39.14 (25)	11.36 (38)	80.04 (25)	240.57 (25)	129.74 (21)
BROWNING-FERRIS INDS	Baa/BBB+ 9/77	39.21 (26)	3.10 (18)	47.49 (9)	222.74 (30)	111.34 (16)
ARMSTRONG RUBBER	Baa/BBB 9/77	40.08 (27)	1.72 (12)	89.66 (28)	244.75 (24)	135.68 (24)
SHERWIN-WILLIAMS CO	Baa/BBB- 12/77	42.09 (28)	6.39 (30)	97.77 (30)	230.62 (27)	126.74 (20)
CYPRUS MINES CORP	Baa/BBB 12/77	43.30 (29)	3.82 (20)	47.77 (11)	224.21 (28)	138.97 (25)
WICKES CORP	Baa/BBB 1/78	43.42 (30)	9.68 (37)	113.23 (34)	224.07 (29)	179.78 (36)

		LTD / Cap	STD / Cap	LTD / Net Pt.	NTA / LTD	Tot Liab / Tot Eqty
Baa/BBB COMPANIES	RATINGS FYR END	%	%	%	%	%
FRUEHAUF CORP	Baa/BBB 12/77	44.46 (31)	4.61 (23)	67.15 (17)	214.90 (32)	181.49 (37)
CRANE CO	Baa/BBB 12/77	45.59 (32)	5.19 (27)	81.57 (27)	215.50 (31)	154.74 (29)
UV INDUSTRIES INC	Baa/BBB 12/77	47.40 (33)	1.48 (8)	123.67 (36)	187.59 (36)	141.87 (26)
HILTON HOTELS CORP	NR /BBB 12/77	48.09 (34)	1.42 (7)	72.09 (20)	205.39 (33)	133.70 (23)
WALTER (JIM) CORP	Baa/BBB 8/77	49.20 (35)	6.07 (29)	94.71 (29)	202.19 (34)	196.60 (38)
METRO-GOLDWYN-MAYER INC	Baa/BBB 8/77	49.95 (36)	0.26 (2)	73.93 (22)	159.03 (39)	170.35 (34)
WILLIAMS COS	Baa/BBB 12/77	50.22 (37)	3.86 (21)	62.64 (16)	189.82 (35)	162.72 (32)
PENNZOIL CO	Baa/BBB 12/77	51.95 (38)	2.93 (17)	56.38 (13)	184.18 (37)	169.51 (33)
GULF & WESTERN INDS INC	Baa/BBB 7/77	57.35 (39)	7.90 (33)	122.84 (35)	165.26 (38)	237.60 (39)
AVERAGE		36.81	4.37	77.19	274.62	126.99
MEDIAN		37.39	3.82	72.09	255.91	126.74

Baa/BBB COMPANIES	RATINGS	FYR END	Cash Flow LTD %	N Cash Fl Cap Exp %	After Tax ROE %	Work Cap LTD %	Current Ratio x
NATOMAS CO	Baa/BBB	12/77	135.67q(1)	137.65q(14)	17.98 (8)	36.65 (33)	1.37 (36)
IOWA BEEF PROCESSORS	Baa/BBB	10/77	71.10q(2)	202.97q(9)	18.43 (6)	181.32 (6)	3.59 (5)
TELEDYNE INC	Baa/BBB	12/77	65.54q(3)	337.13q(1)	28.17 (1)	112.03 (21)	1.99 (28)
U S INDUSTRIES	Baa/BBB	12/77	61.34q(4)	142.24q(13)	7.72 (31)	237.06 (4)	2.35 (19)
DATA GENERAL CORP	Baa/BBB	9/77	57.38q(5)	223.78q(4)	19.56 (5)	283.26 (2)	3.49 (6)
BEMIS CO	Baa/BBB	12/77	53.04q(6)	62.42q(35)	9.73 (26)	124.28 (18)	2.10 (26)
BROWNING-FERRIS INDS	Baa/BBB+	9/77	51.87q(7)	85.66q(27)	12.34 (18)	28.92 (36)	1.65 (32)
GENERAL PORTLAND INC	Baa/BBB	12/77	50.10q(8)	192.01q(10)	6.37 (35)	116.64 (20)	4.05 (3)
REEVES BROTHERS INC	Baa/BBB	6/77	48.78q(9)	219.06q(7)	11.57 (20)	257.22 (3)	3.87 (4)
INTL MULTIFOODS CORP	Baa/BBB	2/78	47.55q(10)	135.08q(15)	13.73 (13)	190.21 (5)	2.61 (12)
ARVIN INDUSTRIES INC	Baa/BBB	12/77	46.87q(11)	222.26q(5)	22.75 (2)	155.93 (9)	5.45 (1)
METRO-GOLDWYN-MAYER INC	Baa/BBB	8/77	44.87q(12)	76.07q(31)	21.03 (3)	26.65 (37)	1.55 (34)
AMF INC	Baa/BBB	12/77	43.99q(13)	126.48q(16)	12.55 (17)	139.22 (14)	2.06 (27)
REICHHOLD CHEMICALS INC	Baa/BBB+	12/77	43.10q(14)	80.32q(28)	7.51 (32)	131.20 (17)	2.11 (25)
AMERICAN AIRLINES INC	Baa/BBB	12/77	42.24q(15)	65.69q(34)	10.41 (25)	57.64 (31)	1.46 (35)
PULLMAN INC	Baa/BBB	12/77	41.73q(16)	77.23q(29)	9.24 (27)	142.58 (11)	1.29 (38)
HOLIDAY INNS INC	NR /BBB	12/77	40.19q(17)	97.85q(22)	10.43 (24)	13.59 (39)	1.25 (39)
CRANE CO	Baa/BBB	12/77	38.97q(18)	96.15q(23)	20.26 (4)	87.47 (26)	2.40 (18)
CHRYSLER CORP	Baa/BBB-	12/77	38.72 (19)	111.52 (17)	4.27 (36)	84.84 (27)	1.34 (37)
HART SCHAFFNER & MARX CO	Baa/BBB	11/77	38.44q(20)	164.15v(11)	8.13 (30)	305.37 (1)	3.10 (9)
FLINTKOTE CO	Baa/BBB	12/77	38.01q(21)	104.54q(18)	8.48 (29)	95.22 (25)	2.41 (16)
FRUEHAUF CORP	Baa/BBB	12/77	37.46q(22)	98.98v(19)	14.81 (10)	73.67 (28)	1.84 (31)
SCM CORP	Baa/BBB	6/77	36.25q(23)	98.49q(20)	10.89 (22)	141.41 (12)	2.53 (13)
ARMSTRONG RUBBER	Baa/BBB	9/77	34.40q(24)	210.57q(8)	12.89 (16)	132.90 (16)	2.46 (15)
SIGNAL COS	Baa/BBB	12/77	33.81q(25)	273.32q(2)	11.56 (21)	179.20 (7)	2.29 (21)
CASTLE & COOKE INC	Baa/BBB	12/77	33.19 (26)	93.40 (24)	13.00 (15)	103.47 (23)	2.26 (22)
FEDERAL PAPER BOARD CO	Baa/BBB	12/77	32.84q(27)	76.13q(30)	6.93 (34)	68.80 (29)	2.73 (10)
GAF CORP	Baa/BBB	12/77	32.79 (28)	98.49 (21)	7.08 (33)	144.79 (10)	2.49 (14)
WICKES CORP	Baa/BBB	1/78	29.16q(29)	142.72q(12)	13.20 (14)	138.66 (15)	2.13 (24)
HILTON HOTELS CORP	NR /BBB	12/77	27.82q(30)	52.84q(37)	18.31 (7)	21.62 (38)	1.60 (33)

Baa/BBB COMPANIES	RATINGS	FYR END	Cash Flow LTD %	N Cash Fl Cap Exp %	After Tax ROE %	Work Cap LTD %	Current Ratio x
UV INDUSTRIES INC	Baa/BBB	12/77	26.99q(31)	249.46q(3)	15.89 (9)	117.65 (19)	4.56 (2)
KIDDE (WALTER) & CO	Baa/BBB	12/77	26.13q(32)	220.71q(6)	10.88 (23)	157.32 (8)	3.13 (8)
PENNZOIL CO	Baa/BBB	12/77	25.61q(33)	72.25q(33)	14.44 (11)	29.93 (35)	1.98 (29)
AKZONA	Baa/BBB	12/77	23.90q(34)	86.50q(26)	2.51 (37)	98.02 (24)	2.65 (11)
CYPRUS MINES CORP	Baa/BBB	12/77	23.78q(35)	29.46q(38)	1.28 (38)	14.14 (32)	2.40 (17)
WILLIAMS COS	Baa/BBB	12/77	23.31q(36)	87.56q(25)	9.11 (28)	30.05 (34)	1.90 (30)
WALTER (JIM) CORP	Baa/BBB	8/77	15.81q(37)	61.21v(36)	14.06 (12)	109.33 (22)	2.31 (20)
GULF & WESTERN INDS INC	Baa/BBB	7/77	13.51q(38)	75.53q(32)	11.75 (19)	61.77 (30)	2.17 (23)
SHERWIN-WILLIAMS CO	Baa/BBB-	12/77	5.65q(39)	2.73v(39)	-3.55 (39)	141.01 (13)	3.29 (7)
AVERAGE			40.56	127.96	11.94	117.98	2.47
MEDIAN			38.44	98.49	11.57	116.64	2.31

SPLIT Baa/BB RATED COMPANIES	RATINGS	FYR END	Pretax Coverage x	Aft Tax Coverage x	Aft Tax Coverage (inc rent) x	Ret on Total Assets %	Net Inc Net Sales %
ZAYRE CORP	Baa/BB	1/78	3.44 (1)	2.23 (2)	1.26 (5)	8.68 (4)	0.93 (5)
TALLEY INDUSTRIES INC	Baa/BB	3/78	3.34 (2)	2.46 (1)	2.00 (1)	11.92 (2)	3.15 (3)
SINGER CO	Baa/BB	12/77	3.25 (3)	2.22 (3)	1.63 (3)	13.21 (1)	3.26 (2)
A-T-O INC	Baa/BB	12/77	2.89 (4)	2.06 (4)	1.77 (2)	9.10 (3)	2.03 (4)
CONTROL DATA CORP	Baa/BB	12/77	2.34 (5)	1.78 (5)	1.38 (4)	7.34 (5)	4.18 (1)
ADDRESSOGRAPH-MULTIGRAPH	Baa/BB	7/77	0.06p(6)	-0.25p(6)	0.45p(6)	0.25 (6)	-2.35 (6)
AVERAGE			2.55	1.75	1.41	8.42	1.87
MEDIAN			3.07	2.14	1.50	8.89	2.59

SPLIT Baa/BB RATED COMPANIES	RATINGS	FYR END	LTD --- Cap %	STD --- Cap %	LTD ------ Net Pt. %	NTA --- LTD %	Tot Liab -------- Tot Eqty %
CONTROL DATA CORP	Baa/BB	12/77	23.92 (1)	12.94 (4)	88.77 (2)	404.27 (1)	90.19 (1)
ADDRESSOGRAPH-MULTIGRAPH	Baa/EB	7/77	31.07 (2)	10.33 (3)	79.44 (1)	304.76 (2)	137.09 (2)
ZAYRE CORP	Baa/BB	1/78	41.86 (3)	4.23 (1)	118.63 (3)	229.66 (3)	177.53 (4)
SINGER CO	Baa/BB	12/77	43.33 (4)	18.46 (6)	125.61 (4)	210.12 (4)	219.61 (6)
TALLEY INDUSTRIES INC	Baa/BB	3/78	46.64 (5)	9.36 (2)	160.80 (6)	203.41 (5)	169.19 (3)
A-T-O INC	Baa/BB	12/77	48.01 (6)	14.34 (5)	129.51 (5)	191.97 (6)	197.58 (5)
AVERAGE			39.14	11.61	117.13	257.36	165.20
MEDIAN			42.59	11.64	122.12	219.89	173.36

SPLIT Baa/BB RATED COMPANIES	RATINGS	FYR END	Cash Flow --------- LTD %	N Cash Fl --------- Cap Exp %	After Tax ROE %	Work Cap -------- LTD %	Current Ratio x
CONTROL DATA CORP	Baa/BB	12/77	52.78q(1)	123.41v(4)	6.51 (5)	96.09 (6)	1.63 (6)
SINGER CO	Baa/BB	12/77	36.03 (2)	210.11 (2)	16.00 (1)	109.67 (5)	T.64 (5)
TALLEY INDUSTRIES INC	Baa/BB	3/78	28.67 (3)	160.63 (3)	10.59 (2)	142.63 (3)	2.77 (1)
ZAYRE CORP	Baa/BB	1/78	24.72q(4)	230.43q(1)	8.46 (4)	155.72 (2)	2.14 (3)
A-T-O INC	Baa/BB	12/77	21.16q(5)	73.61v(5)	8.77 (3)	126.51 (4)	2.36 (2)
ADDRESSOGRAPH-MULTIGRAPH	Baa/BB	7/77	13.37 (6)	36.45 (6)	-7.06 (6)	167.87 (1)	1.82 (4)
AVERAGE			29.46	139.11	7.21	133.08	2.06
MEDIAN			26.70	142.02	8.61	134.57	1.98

INDEX

1

INDEX

INDEX

INDEX

4

INDEX

5

INDEX

INDEX